GEORGE CARDINAL PELL

George Cardinal Pell's coat of arms when he was the archbishop of Sydney from 2001 to 2014. On the left side is the Southern Cross constellation signifying the See of Sydney. On the right side is the pelican, a symbol of Christ nourishing us with his Body and Blood in the Eucharist and an emblem of the Pell family; the sun representing Saint Thomas Aquinas; and the monogram *MR*, which stands for *Maria Regina* (Mary, the Queen). The motto "Be not afraid" is taken from Christ's encouraging words to his disciples in the Gospels and refers to John Paul II's first homily as pope on November 2, 1978.

TESS LIVINGSTONE

George Cardinal Pell

Pax Invictis

A Biography

With a foreword by George Weigel

Second Edition of
George Pell
Defender of the Faith Down Under

IGNATIUS PRESS   SAN FRANCISCO

Original edition published in 2002 by Duffy & Snellgrove
Potts Point, New South Wales, Australia
© 2002 by Tess Livingstone
First American edition © 2004 by Ignatius Press, San Francisco

Quotations from official Church documents are taken
from the website of the Holy See: www.vatican.va

*Ignatius Press gratefully acknowledges the generous gift of Teresa DeMaria,
which made the publication of this book possible.*

Cover photo by Andrew Quilty
Used with permission of the Archdiocese of Sydney

Cover design by Enrique J. Aguilar

Second Edition © 2024 by Ignatius Press, San Francisco
Foreword to Second Edition © 2024 by George Weigel
All rights reserved
ISBN 978-1-62164-657-0 (HB)
ISBN 978-1-64229-286-2 (eBook)
Library of Congress Control Number 2024931052
Printed in the United States of America ∞

To the memory of George Cardinal Pell, whose faith in Christ and legacy will continue to light the way for many. And for Jacinta, with much love, always.

CONTENTS

FOREWORD

Shortly after Cardinal George Pell's 2014 appointment as the first prefect of the Vatican's new Secretariat for the Economy, I was in Rome and Pell invited me to come to Domus Australia—the pilgrimage center and boutique hotel he had created while Archbishop of Sydney—for a chat. We had been friends for almost half a century, so the conversation was candid, uninhibited, and bracing, like Pell himself. The cardinal told me, for example, that he was going to bring Danny Casey, his business manager at the Archdiocese of Sydney, to work with him at the secretariat; when I asked whether Danny spoke Italian, Pell replied, "No, and that's good, because he won't have to listen to the lies."

The cardinal then said that he'd been getting conflicting advice about where he should live. Some were arguing for Domus Australia, where Pell had an apartment; others said he should live in the Vatican like other heads of major Vatican offices. What did I think? I pondered the question for a moment and then said, "You'd be living with a friendlier class of people here, but on balance, I think you'd better insist on a Vatican apartment. They're very turf-conscious over there, and it's important for you to put down a marker—this new office is real. But George, promise me something. Whether you live here or in the Vatican, promise me that if you get a car, you'll get one with a remote starter."

My old friend simply stared at me, as if I had slipped a gear.

"I'm not being melodramatic," I continued. "You're going to be dealing with hundreds of millions, maybe billions, of euros of dodgy money. The people involved don't play well with other children. And I don't want to be sending your sister an email saying, 'Dear Marg, I've picked up the pieces of George in the Piazza della Città Leonina, and I'll be forwarding them in a Ziploc bag.'"

As things turned out, the people who didn't play well with other children, whose name was Legion and who could be found all over the world, tried to do in George Pell non-kinetically, through the instrument of vicious criminal charges (which in fact were so preposterous that they never should have been brought to trial). The cardinal eventually defeated them, in the last great triumph of his life. But the cost was enormous: to Pell personally, to the reputations of the Australian media and the criminal justice system of the State of Victoria, and to the financial reform of the Vatican. So, I wasn't being melodramatic that Roman evening. In reality, the drama would be greater than either my friend or I could imagine.

But however painful, that last drama was of a piece with a very dramatic life, as Tess Livingstone's biography demonstrates. Dramatic lives lived against the grain of the conventional wisdom of the day always draw violent criticism. George Pell's dramatic life certainly did, and his friends often had occasion to think that he deserved a better class of enemies.

Sixteen months before then-Archbishop Pell's March 2002 translation from the Archdiocese of Melbourne to his new post as archbishop of Sydney, I had been on a book tour Down Under and thought I knew something about the robust give-and-take of Aussie journalism. But it was difficult to recognize the man I had known for decades in many of the reports I read on his appointment as metropolitan archbishop of Australia's largest city.

According to one feature story, a "key" to understanding Pell is his "love of Church trappings.... Back home in Melbourne, it is said, his vestments line his hall: gorgeous and theatrical." I do not know who was "saying" these things, but they obviously had not stayed in Archbishop Pell's home in Melbourne, as I had just done. There was nary a vestment on display in the halls, or anywhere else for that matter.

What I did see were books—books in profusion. The hallways were filled with packed bookcases. The floor behind the desk in Archbishop Pell's study was piled high with new titles in history, philosophy, theology, political theory, social and medical ethics. His sitting room held a year's worth of the back issues of the major opinion journals in the Anglosphere.

There were very few Catholic bishops anywhere who were, in fact, less interested in "Church trappings" than Cardinal George Pell, whose sartorial style bespoke "Salvation Army Thrift Shop" far more than "Brooks Brothers", and whose manner of wearing ecclesiastical rig gave his more fastidious secretaries heartburn. By the same token, there were few senior churchmen who were so intellectually engaged or who read as widely. Inside and outside the Catholic Church of the twenty-first century, bishops are usually thought of as managers. Throughout his thirty-seven years as a diocesan bishop, George Pell lived an earlier model of episcopacy: the bishop as intellectual leader and champion of culture, the model pioneered by such giant figures of Western civilization as Ambrose and Augustine.

The press accounts of Pell's Sydney appointment were also replete with claims that Pell was an authoritarian who enjoyed imposing his judgments on others, charges that continued after Pell's appointment to Rome in 2014. It was an indictment that missed both the nature of episcopal leadership in the Catholic Church and the character of George Pell, son of a provincial publican.

The Catholic Church is not simply a voluntary association dedicated to humanitarian causes. It is a community of disciples who measure their fidelity according to an authoritative tradition, not according to their personal opinions. And that authoritative tradition, Catholics believe, binds and frees at the same time.

This is, admittedly, a difficult notion to grasp in cultures in which freedom has become synonymous with liberation from any "external" authority—which describes a lot of the Western world. The Catholic Church, however, has a different understanding of freedom. The Catholic Church teaches that a truly human freedom is one in which we freely choose to do what is right—which we can know by both reason and revelation—and do so as a matter of habit (in Latin, *habitus*, another word for "virtue"). Freedom is not doing things "my way". Freedom is doing the right thing in the right way for the right reason, and as a matter of self-mastery.

A Catholic bishop, teaching authoritatively, is speaking for the binding-and-liberating tradition of the Church. He is not imposing his personal opinions on the Catholic community or on the world. When Pope John Paul II taught that using the natural cycles of fertility is the method of regulating births most consistent with human dignity, he was not teaching the personal moral opinions of Karol Wojtyła; he was proposing the settled teaching of the Catholic Church. Similarly, when Cardinal Pell taught that homosexual

acts are sinful, he was not imposing on others the personal crotch-
ets of George Pell of Ballarat; he was teaching the moral truth that
the Catholic Church has taught for two millennia, and that Judaism,
Christianity's parent, taught for millennia before that. Bishops are
servants, not masters, of the truth the Church bears in the world and
proposes to the world. And bishops, if they are true to the oath they
swear before their episcopal ordination, must be faithful and courageous servants of the truth, even if such fidelity involves personal risk.
Throughout his Australian episcopates, George Pell had ample reason
to know about those risks as he was subjected to unprecedented campaigns of calumny, some of them engineered by the taxpayer-funded
Australian Broadcasting Corporation.

In understanding the Church's authoritative tradition, of course,
the bishop ought to consult broadly with knowledgeable people.
Similarly, bishops in a media age ought to take counsel with experienced men and women who can help bishops propose Catholic
teaching so that it can be "heard" by others. And that brings us back
to George Pell as a man of ideas and culture.

During his years as archbishop of Melbourne, Pell hosted a quarterly dinner seminar of local intellectuals and activists to exchange
ideas in an informal but robust setting. I was fortunate enough to
address one of these sessions in October 2000 and was struck by the
diversity of the community of conversation in which George Pell
lived. This was clearly not a man who liked his ideas or his intellectuals in one flavor. I was also impressed by the utter frankness of
the debate, which Pell obviously relished. An archbishop who took
copious notes of what others were saying (as I watched Pell do that
night) was a man who understood that teachers must study and learn
before they teach.

When I first met George Pell in 1967, I was struck by the unaffected
freshness of his personality and by his utter lack of clerical pretense.
Those same qualities were on display throughout his life. He combined the rugged good humor (and vocabulary) of a star athlete with
the intellectual edge of an Oxford-trained historian and the piety of
a convinced Christian disciple. He was at home with lay people and
children in an easygoing way that few other senior Catholic prelates
could match. He attracted deep loyalties, not because he demanded

obeisance, but because he was a lovable man and a magnet for friend-ships that he worked hard to keep green.

That Cardinal Pell was a sign of contradiction in an Australian society lurching steadily leftward toward the Promised Land of Woke, in the Catholic Church in Australia, and indeed throughout the Catholic world, was obvious. (As he said on one memorable occasion just prior to the synod of 2015, "I'm supposed to be the bull who carries his own china shop around with him.") But why was he a sign of contradiction? Pell became a lightning rod for controversy and polemics, not because he was the conniving, authoritarian heavy portrayed by his clerical and media enemies, but because he had ideas—ideas that challenged the dominant consensus among Western intellectual and cultural tastemakers; ideas that also challenged the doctrinal and moral mushiness of Catholic Lite. And that, I suggest, is why the attacks on him over the decades had a particularly venomous personal character: as any veteran debater knows, *ad hominem* attacks are the last refuge of people who have the sneaking, nerve-racking suspicion that they are about to lose an argument on the merits.

As a matter of both faith and reason, George Pell believed that there are truths embedded in the world and in us. He was convinced that, in knowing those truths, we incur certain moral obligations. He believed that living according to those obligations is liberating, in the deepest sense of human freedom. These were all profoundly coun-tercultural claims in the last half-century of Pell's life. Yet the idea that truths are built into the world and into us is one of the building blocks on which democracy was slowly constructed by the English-speaking peoples from Magna Carta on. The same idea undergirds the Universal Declaration of Human Rights. Thus Pell, although his political enemies would never concede the point, was the defender of the moral foundations of the liberal political order they claimed he was dismantling.

There are, indeed, many ironies in the fire.

The Vatican bureaucracy was beset by scandals of various sorts in the last years of Pope Benedict XVI. Thus in the conclave of March 2013, the candidacy of Cardinal Jorge Mario Bergoglio, S.J., was promoted by advocates who claimed that the archbishop of Buenos Aires was a tough-minded, no-nonsense reformer, who would take a fire hose to the detritus of corruption in the Roman Curia while advancing the doctrinal and pastoral project of John Paul II and Benedict XVI—dynamic orthodoxy in the service of evangelization. Going into that conclave, it seemed to many that no Italian cardinal was *papabile*, Italian curialists having made a thoroughgoing mess of the last years of Benedict's pontificate. Cardinal Pell was on a different page, however. He firmly—some would say, obstinately—insisted that Benedict's successor had to be Cardinal Angelo Scola, the archbishop of Milan, and no amount of argument could dissuade him.

It may be assumed that, when the Bergoglio tide in the conclave became irreversible, Pell, for the sake of unity, joined the consensus in favor of the Argentine cardinal. But his concerns about what the conclave had wrought were evident in the expression on his face at one of the windows near the central loggia of Saint Peter's, as the new pope was presented to the throng gathered in the Piazza San Pietro. In that moment, a photographer took a telling picture of Cardinal Pell standing beside his friend Cardinal Francis George of Chicago (a sceptic about Bergoglio going into the conclave). In a virtually identical photo from 2005, both men had looked jubilant. Now, they both looked very pensive.

When he accepted Pope Francis's invitation to spearhead Vatican financial reform as the prefect of a new curial dicastery, the Secretariat for the Economy, George Pell, never a fool or a naif, understood that he was walking into a minefield; he knew full well that, as he put it, "the people who destroyed the pontificate of Benedict XVI" were the chief opponents of the new secretariat. Given that fact of curial life, Pell had a choice between two strategies. He could go slowly and try to get "buy-in" from the curial recalcitrants, largely Italian. Or he could put the pedal to the floorboard, on the theory that Francis' would be a short pontificate and that the window of opportunity for deep reform could close precipitously. He chose the latter strategy, alienating many, but getting some good work done.

The all-in strategy also assumed that Francis was serious about financial reform and would back Pell to the hilt. Events would eventually call that assumption into question, as the pope sided with the recalcitrants on more than one occasion. Why? one wondered. Did the pope resent Pell's decisive role in reversing the course of the 2014 Synod on Marriage and the Family? Francis was certainly angered by the letter sent to him by thirteen cardinals (including Pell) at the beginning of second Synod on Marriage and the Family in October 2015, protesting what they regarded as defective synodal procedures. But what did such matters have to do with standing firm for fiscal probity in the Holy See?

For his part, Pell found the pope, whose declaratory reform agenda he supported and in service to which he had uprooted his life, a continuous puzzle. Shortly after his appointment to Rome, the cardinal described Pope Francis as "utterly formidable", "very, very cunning", and "absolutely a Jesuit—there's just one bloke running the show." A few years later, Pell would muse, almost wistfully, "I think he likes me more than I like him"—to which a friend replied, "Perhaps that's because he's a bit afraid of you and you're not afraid of him."

What Pell perceived originally as the pope's cunning seemed over time to be less a clever strategy than a matter of an autocrat playing curial factions off against each other in order to concentrate power in his own hands. But whatever his thinking about that, George Pell remained loyal to Francis throughout his service as prefect of the Secretariat for the Economy—even though he had ample reason to think that the papal support on which he had relied to execute his get-it-done-*now* strategy was less than whole-hearted, not least because of the pope's failure to stop the curial recalcitrants from trying to gut the statutes for the new secretariat when they were being vetted by the Pontifical Council for Legislative Texts for their conformity to canon law.

George Pell's valiant efforts to cleanse the Augean stables of Vatican finance ended when his enemies took him out of play through an intellectually and morally corrupt legal process that led him to spend 404 days in solitary confinement before he was exonerated by Australia's High Court. During that time, in a needless cruelty, Pell was prevented from celebrating Holy Mass and had to draw on the treasury of spiritual capital he had accumulated over a lifetime. Because that treasury was a substantial one, calumny and injustice never defeated him, and he put his time as (in his words) "a guest of Her Majesty" to good use by writing his three-volume *Prison Journal*, which is now regarded as a modern spiritual classic. He continued to be an influential figure in world Catholic circles after his release from prison, as those seeking courage during the turbulence of Francis' pontificate often found themselves in Pell's Vatican apartment, drawing strength from a strong man who, as the epitaph on his grave reads, "loved Christ and the Church vehemently". It was that love, not any personal animus, that prompted his public criticisms of the pontificate, which were published shortly after his untimely death.

It was said when he died that the Church and the world wouldn't see the like of George Pell again. Perhaps that's true. I hope it isn't. But if it is, the Church and the world will be the poorer for it.

George Weigel
April 23, 2024
Commemoration of Saint George, Martyr

PROLOGUE

George Pell was not the first cardinal of the Catholic Church wrongly imprisoned. There is an illustrious group of others that includes Saint John Fisher, chancellor of the University of Cambridge, who was tortured in the Tower of London and beheaded in 1535, during the reign of Henry VIII. As Pell once wrote of Fisher, he continues to be venerated while his fellow bishops who acquiesced to the Tudor tyrant are largely forgotten. Pell also endorsed Fisher's prayer, that God might "set in Thy church strong and mighty pillars that may suffer and endure".

In the mid-twentieth century, Aloysius Stepinac, the archbishop of Zagreb, a staunch opponent of Nazism and Communism, served five years in jail after being convicted of treason by the Yugoslav government. Pope Pius XII promoted Stepinac to the College of Cardinals while he was under house arrest in 1953. On June 21, 1999, the feast of Saint Aloysius, Pell, as archbishop of Melbourne, made a pilgrimage to the church presbytery in Stepinac's home village of Krasic in Croatia, where Stepinac served as a curate during the final years of his life, despite being a Prince of the Church. Another of Pell's teenage heroes was Cardinal Joseph Mindszenty, who was arrested by the Hungarian secret police in 1948, tortured, and forced to confess to crimes he did not commit and for which he was sentenced to life in prison. He was released during the 1956 uprising and granted asylum in the U.S. Embassy in Budapest, where he spent another fifteen years before being exiled to Vienna. There, he lived in a college for Hungarian seminarians who were studying at the nearby university.

More recently, the bishop of Shanghai, Ignatius Kung Pin-mei, a champion of the Chinese Underground Church, spent thirty years in prison for opposing Communist Party control over Catholicism in China. Pope John Paul II named Kung a cardinal *in pectore* in 1979. In 1975, Francis-Xavier Nguyễn Văn Thuận, the coadjutor archbishop of Saigon, was arrested by Communist authorities in Vietnam. He spent thirteen years in a "reeducation camp", mostly in solitary confinement. Pell admired him so much that he included his portrait in the chapel of Domus Australia, the guest house/retreat center Pell had built in Rome.

Unlike the others in that select band of cardinals, state power was stacked against Pell, not by a ruthless monarch or an authoritarian dictatorship, but by the second largest state, in terms of population, in modern Australia—a nation in which stability, robust democracy, the rule of law, and the principle of a "fair go" have traditionally been prized. Pell's treatment raised hard questions that Australia's legal and political system, especially in the state of Victoria, still needs to face. One of the hardest aspects of his punishment to bear was that he was forbidden from offering Mass, something even Nguyễn Văn Thuận managed in a Vietnamese jail, lying on the wooden plank he was given as a bed, and using a few drops of altar wine smuggled in as medicine and particles of bread.

A year after Pell's death in Rome, from a cardiac arrest after a hip replacement, questions about the legal processes that saw him charged, convicted, and jailed remain unanswered. Those questions centre on the circumstances surrounding his arrest including Operation Tethering, a "get Pell" operation launched by Victoria police in 2013, when no complaint about him had been made. The questions also relate to his prosecution and conviction for serious crimes of child sexual abuse, including rape, which it would have been logistically impossible for him to commit in Saint Patrick's Cathedral, Melbourne, immediately after Sunday Mass—while still vested. The grave injustice cost him more than four hundred days in jail, largely in solitary confinement. In a split decision, 2-1, the Victorian Court of Appeal turned down his initial appeal, but the convictions were subsequently quashed by the unanimous seven-to-zero decision of Australia's most senior court, the High Court, based in Canberra.

Offering Mass for Pell on January 10, 2024, the first anniversary of his death, Pell's successor as the archbishop of Sydney, Anthony Fisher, a qualified lawyer before he became a Dominican priest, declared that the late cardinal's wrongful conviction and imprisonment were the result of "the corrupt Victorian legal system" following a media, political, and police witch-hunt. "Perhaps worst of all, there seems to be no mood in Victoria for a serious inquiry into the justice system", Fisher said. Pell himself spoke of the need for such an inquiry. In April 2024, Fisher's criticisms were backed by a definitive source, Gavin Silbert, an experienced barrister who was Victoria's chief crown prosecutor from 2008 to 2018.

Like Saint John Fisher, Stepinac, and the other cardinals wrongly imprisoned, Pell will not be forgotten. His life was a heady mix of achievement—in Australia, the Vatican, and the worldwide Church—and of controversies that drew international attention. Those who knew him appreciated his candour, dry wit, and intelligent observations on a vast range of subjects—from theology to news, history to sport—as well as his favourite homey sayings such as, "What's there in the cat comes out in the kitten", delivered in a sage tone to friends whose children were excelling at something or, on the other hand, leading their parents in a merry dance.

In his own words, Pell "enjoyed the one hundredfold in this life" and drew satisfaction, however long his days (7 A.M. to around midnight was usual when he led the Archdioceses of Melbourne and Sydney), from work he believed had "ultimate significance". Living and working in Rome suited him, as did leading the reform of the Vatican's corrupt, sclerotic financial system—a task that was as rewarding as it was frustrating. When he left Australia in 2014 to take on that challenge, his golden career was approaching its pinnacle. The next and last nine years of his life, however, were harder than he could ever have imagined when he was featured as one of the fifty most influential Australians in *The Australian*'s fiftieth anniversary magazine in 2014. But his handling of adversity will shape how he is remembered and esteemed for generations to come.

On a personal level, Pell delighted in his close, supportive family. He had great talent for friendship; he loved sport and excelled at it as a young man. Music, collecting art, gardening, reading, and writing brought him real happiness, and his legacy of books, speeches, sermons, and articles, all penned by hand, is formidable. Some of those works, including his three-volume *Prison Journal*, will be studied for a long time. Perhaps longer than many of his contemporaries realise.

At Domus Australia on January 9, 2024, on the eve of the first anniversary of Pell's death, his old friend Cardinal Gerhard Müller likened Pell's *Prison Journal*, handwritten in notebooks from his prison cell, to *On the Consolation of Philosophy*, the last work of Roman senator, philosopher, and historian Anicius Boethius (480–524). It, too, was written in jail, fifteen hundred years ago, as Boethius awaited execution. It was one of the most influential works of the early Middle Ages and remains an important philosophy text, rich in ideas, many of which were broadly simpatico with Pell's outlook. If Pell's work proves as enduring as that of Boethius, readers centuries from now might find that the achievements, high points, and slings and arrows of Pell's big life, captured in these pages, put the man and his world in context.

Now Let Your Servant Go in Peace

The memories flowed thick and fast. Through shock and feelings of disbelief, it was hard to breathe. The numbness made it bearable, just. Pink blooms from the roses George Pell had planted years earlier on his balcony were flourishing, visible from the ground as the forlorn group of family and friends, united in grief, followed his hearse from the presbytery to Saint Mary's Cathedral, Sydney, where his body would lie in state. With wry smiles, a few friends thought the cardinal would be pleased his coffin would be closed. He had said after a royal lying-in-state a few years before, "I don't think I'd like that ... people filing past, looking up me nose." On serious or sad occasions, to lighten a mood, he would sometimes revert to the idiom he had heard in the pub owned by his family when he was young.

The sprawling, shady old jacaranda, and the new one he had planted to be there when the old one died, looked healthy. Another consoling sign of continuity was the presence of Pell's well-chosen successor and protégé, Archbishop Anthony Fisher.

Wednesday, February 1, 2023, was a sultry summer day on which Pell would have thought about a swim after work. After his body's last night in the presbytery, in a coffin in the downstairs reception room, his final secretary in Rome, Irish-born Father Joseph Hamilton, had read in Latin and English a summary of the cardinal's eventful life, from a scroll. It had then been rolled up and placed in the cardinal's coffin before his final journey to the cathedral. His funeral was set for the next day, Candlemas—an appropriate feast on which to farewell a man who appreciated Simeon's words at the Presentation of the Baby Jesus in the Temple: "Lord, now let your servant depart in peace ..."

Those following Pell's coffin into the cathedral were pleased to be part of the tribute; but our silent longing was that all this might be taking place in a decade's time, or later. We were not ready for life without him. Some of the young priests walking in the group were appalled when a few protestors shrieked vulgar expletives in their direction. Over many years, Pell had learned to take such abuse in his stride. Never one to wear his heart on his sleeve or to voice personal anxieties, he kept his equilibrium, or did a good job of appearing to, under duress.

Walking behind the casket, a friend from Sydney who had been in Rome recently mentioned that the cardinal had been a little concerned, given his cardiac history, about the hip operation after which he had died on January 10 at Salvator Mundi International Hospital in the Eternal City. Before entering the hospital, he had been to confession. He had also called family and friends, saying little, if anything, about any anxieties. Chatting to the anesthetist in Italian before being put under for the operation, Pell had said: "I know I'm a high-risk patient, but I welcome His [the Lord's] will for me." His death was a shock.

Speaking at an Aid to the Church in Need charity lunch in Melbourne sometime after Pell's death, David, his brother, revealed that Father Andrew Kwiatowski, a young Melbourne priest studying in Rome, had been assigned to look after the cardinal during his convalescence. Father Andrew messaged David at 3:40 A.M. to let him know that his brother "was well and that the doctors were pleased with the surgery". He was in good spirits and seemed fine. That was around 6:00 P.M. Central European Time (CET). David received another call around 9:40 P.M. CET. "Apparently, George had made a couple of calls, had something to eat, and had done a couple of leg exercises", he said, "certainly, no indication of what was to happen." David had two missed messages from his brother's phone at 7:23 A.M., Australian Eastern Standard Time. "It took me twenty minutes and four goes to get a pickup", he said about his attempts to call him back. "It was an Italian nurse, I presume, who answered. She was speaking at a hundred miles per hour, and I gathered that he may have died. It was not until I said, 'Mio fratello cardinale', that she realised who I was and said, 'I sorry but he dead.'"

Thirteen years earlier, working on the reform of the English translation of the Mass as president of the Vox Clara Committee, Pell had collapsed in Rome, at the home of American Cardinal James Francis Stafford in Trastevere, after a long flight from Australia. On that occasion he was rushed to the Gemelli Clinic, where a pacemaker was fitted. A few days later, he was back at the North American College, pen in hand, working through texts as he chaired Vox Clara.

Few people were indifferent about Pell, the most memorable character ever to have risen through the ranks of the Church in Australia. As his family and friends following the hearse on February 1 turned into College Street from Saint Mary's Road, police were keeping bellowing protesters in check. "George Pell, go to hell," the mainly scruffy crowd snarled through megaphones. In his eulogy at Pell's funeral Mass the following day, former Australian prime minister Tony Abbott said that as he heard the chant he thought, "Ah ha! At least they now believe in the afterlife! Perhaps this is Saint George Pell's first miracle!"

As Cardinal Pell's coffin was carried into Saint Mary's, the sanctuary looked mostly as it had for his farewell Mass when he left for Rome in 2014 to become the inaugural prefect of the newly formed Secretariat for the Economy. A portrait of the cardinal to the left of the altar, directly across from the pulpit where he had preached most Sundays for thirteen years, was all that was different. The *Risen Christ* and *Mary Magdalene*, statues by English sculptor Nigel Boonham, commissioned by the cardinal, still formed a triptych with the main altar (blessed by Benedict XVI during World Youth Day in 2008). The altar depicts the entombed Christ after His crucifixion. Rarely given to hyperbole, Pell once lauded Boonham's sculptures as being "worthy of the great seventeenth-century Roman sculptor and architect Giovanni Lorenzo Bernini". He had wanted them to focus worshippers' attention on the mystery of the Redemption.

Twenty-two years earlier, when Pell, then fifty-nine, was installed as archbishop of Sydney on the evening of May 10, 2001, protestors had also been out in force, shrieking the same mantra: "George Pell, go to hell." That historic, unprecedented appointment was made by Saint John Paul II, who had tapped the piece of paper put in front of him, rejecting the three other bishops' names listed, and insisting, "I want Pell." At the time, Pell, born and raised in Victoria, had served for an eventful five years as archbishop of Melbourne, a city with a culture and a personality as different from Sydney's as that of

Cambridge, Massachusetts, is from Rodeo Drive in Beverly Hills. No Church leader, not even Irish-born Archbishop Daniel Mannix, one of Pell's heroes, who reigned over the Melbourne Archdiocese from 1917 to 1963, had made the same transition.

At one point during Pell's funeral Mass, the noise of the baying mob outside broke through the cathedral's thick walls in what sounded, briefly, like a dull but menacing roar. The venom was a sign of deeply entrenched hatred among a small, sometimes vocal section of the Australian population that had been percolating below the surface of what, until recent times, was a peaceful, even laconic culture. The fact that the Mass was being offered for a man who had been wrongfully imprisoned for more than a year, for offenses it would have been impossible, logistically, for him to commit, cut no ice with the seething demonstrators. If they understood that in Victoria the power of the state had been misused in an effort to destroy Pell unjustly, it did not worry them.

Almost a year after Pell's death, *The Australian*'s columnist Henry Ergas noted that 2023 "will be remembered as the year of living angrily. As storm followed storm, the debate, if one can call it that, was almost always vituperative, rarely civil, and never friendly."[1] The persecution and near judicial execution of Pell, he reflected, was a crucial step in the degeneration towards limitless conflict.

> More clearly than in any previous case that maelstrom involved the convergence of virtual lynch mobs on Twitter, unabashedly one-sided reporting by the ABC [the taxpayer-funded Australian Broadcasting Corporation] and SBS [the Special Broadcasting Service, which is partly taxpayer-funded] and a political chorus led by the Greens but which included substantial parts of the ALP [Australian Labor Party].
>
> As well as paying for the sins of the church, Pell stood for everything his assailants detested: attachment to tradition; a scholar's love of the Western canon; and an adamant rejection of the belief that personal identity and sexual preference are mere consumer items, to be adopted and discarded as readily as a snake sheds its skin. Expressed by a Muslim cleric ... conservative Islamic values would have been entirely acceptable. Expressed by a Christian prelate from Ballarat, conservative Western values were not.

[1] Henry Ergas, "Goodbye, 2023: The Year of Living Angrily", *The Australian*, December 29, 2023.

Viewed in the longer term, that episode's legacy to our political culture was three-fold: the cult of the victim, whose allegations had to be taken at face value; the entrenchment of self-loathing, in which Western values were necessarily despicable; and a vision of the world dichotomised into saints and devils, along with a scarcely concealed command to extirpate the latter.

That Manichean vision, Ergas noted, is reflected in climate change activism. Pell, a staunch opponent of climate alarmism, including within the Catholic Church, would have agreed wholeheartedly and had said similar things to his friends.

During his final years in Rome, Sydney and Melbourne and their Catholic communities had remained close to Pell's heart. "Every day in his chapel during Mass, he named his successors to the Sees of Sydney and Melbourne in the Roman Canon, alongside that of the Holy Father", Father Hamilton revealed, preaching at the memorial Vespers for Pell in the cathedral the evening before the funeral. "The more rubrically minded among us may have rolled our eyes, but we appreciated his big-hearted intentions. Both his courage and generosity of spirit were well known throughout the Eternal City, and acknowledged even by those who disagreed with him."[2]

The Vespers service began with the *Dies Irae*, which, Hamilton pointed out, commanded us to

recall the four last things: death, judgement, heaven, and hell. Our cardinal did not view these as negative spiritual relics inherited from the medieval period to be feared and supressed, but rather as timely and timeless realities of the Christian faith.... Now he too stands before the dread throne, before the *Rex Tremendae Maiestatis*, but he does so robed in the mantle of a confessor. The inclusion this evening of the *Dies Irae*, one of the great masterpieces of the Church's treasury of sacred music, is made even more appropriate by the fact that our cardinal loved, cultivated, and protected the magnificent musical patrimony of this cathedral.

In a sermon rich in historical context, which Pell would have appreciated, Hamilton said:

[2] Joseph Hamilton, "George Pell, Lion of the Church", *First Things*, February 2, 2023, https://www.firstthings.com/web-exclusives/2023/02/george-pell-lion-of-the-church.

Both Franciscans and Dominicans claim authorship of the *Dies Irae*. But this evening's office calls us further back in time than the frivolous squabbling of medieval mendicants.... Braulio of Saragossa [d. 651], another confessor bishop, whom we heard from in the second reading this evening, applies a pastoral touch to the Scriptures that for centuries have formed the core of the Roman requiem liturgy. Braulio acknowledges the raw psychological reality of bereavement. Our cardinal is dead. We are grieving. We are going to miss him. His passing is a loss for us, for the Church, for his brother cardinals, for the Holy Father, for the global Catholic community. This evening's liturgy acknowledges all this. However, Braulio consoles us by reminding us that the grieving process is natural. But for Christians, the blackness of grief is shot through with the power of the Holy Spirit—like the black and silver vestments of old—to bring us the shining hope and consolation that is the Resurrection. Not all tears are evil. The tears we shed for our cardinal can be tears of gratitude and healing, as well as loss.

Braulio and his mentor, St. Isidore of Seville, lived and battled through a profound moment of crisis in the life of the Christian Church in Spain at the turn of the seventh century. With the collapse of Rome and the withdrawal of her legions, the country had been overrun by the barbarian Visigoths, who held Trinitarian Christianity and classical learning equally in contempt. Isidore perceived that the roots of classical culture needed to be preserved in order for the Church to survive. He worked tirelessly to do so and laid the foundations for Catholicism to not only survive but flourish despite the Arab conquest of the eighth century.

In Sydney, as we look down to the campus of Notre Dame at Broadway, and over to Campion College, we might observe that our cardinal did exactly the same, although the barbarians he faced were definitively more woke than their more original Visigoth forebears.

Hamilton, originally from the Golden Vale of County Limerick, Ireland, was part of the extensive, eclectic group of characters who were close to George Pell. The young man had come to Sydney as a layman working in international finance, and on his first visit to Saint Mary's, the daily Mass-goer told a friend, "I'm going to be ordained a priest here." He was ordained, by Archbishop Fisher on the Feast of the Sacred Heart in 2016, after studies at the Good Shepherd Seminary in Homebush and the North American College in

Rome, during which he mastered a good imitation of Pell telling him that his Porsche would have to go.

"As evening falls, and the sun makes its way towards the Western rim of the Australian continent, the great South Land of the Holy Spirit—the Church in Sydney—gathers with us to pray for her bishop as Christians have done since time immemorial", Hamilton began his sermon.

> But for us the office of Vespers today is a little different than usual. For 22 days now we have been inundated by plaudits, protests, and pundits surrounding the passing of our cardinal. Though locally this may seem like a tsunami of hatred, it fades to less than a ripple when viewed from the perspective of the global Church. For the vast majority of the worldwide Catholic family, Cardinal George Pell was another Clemens August Graf von Galen, a lion of the Church, a magnet for vocations, a confessor bishop, a true cardinal priest. And now, at the hour of Vespers, we gather to do for him what Christians have done since the first centuries: to chant the psalms, to listen to the Scriptures, to hear the testimonies of the Church Fathers, and to pray for the repose of his soul.

In the months leading up to his death, Pell had needed his second hip replacement—the first had been in Australia fifteen years earlier. Ignoring the advice of several friends, including other cardinals, who urged him not to have the surgery at Salvator Mundi, Pell resisted the idea of returning to Australia for the operation. It was a tumultuous time in the Vatican, and he did not want to leave the Eternal City. Tensions were running high as the trial over alleged financial crimes in the Vatican, involving billions of euros, continued into its second year, and Pell hoped to be called as a witness. Members of the hierarchy in Germany had embraced once-unthinkable theological notions under the banner of "synodality", and under the leadership of Pope Francis the universal Church seemed to be moving in ever more unpredictable directions. Pell, convinced that Francis was desperately ill, thought that the pope could die soon, and he did not want to "be trapped on the wrong side of the world as the cardinals gathered for the conclave", his close friend Terry Tobin said. While too old, at eighty-one, to vote in another conclave, he was determined to have his say when all the cardinals gathered for several days of pre-conclave discussions. "He was insistent that the two qualifications for the next pope were, first, faithfulness to the tradition as handed down from apostolic times and, [second], respect for the rule of law", Tobin recalled. The first qualification echoed Irenaeus, he added; the second referred to the ongoing Vatican finance trials and certain papal decisions.

Pell had been in a lot of pain; walking, his main form of exercise, which he normally enjoyed, was very difficult. He had slowed down a little, offering his morning Mass in his chapel at 7:30 rather than 7 A.M. and going to bed by about 11 rather than reading until 12:30 A.M. or later, as he had done for years. And he no longer walked to the Santi Celso e Giuliano, a minor basilica operated by the Institute of Christ the King, for daily Vespers.

In his final years in Rome, Pell was close to the Institute of Christ the King community, which exclusively celebrates the sacraments in the Extraordinary Form. He was fond of their large dog (and large dogs in general) and took a keen interest in its welfare. In his own words, Pell was "not an Extraordinary Form man", but he was pastorally sensitive to those who preferred to worship in the older rite and was happy on occasion to celebrate the sacraments for them. During a visit to Belgium, he confirmed teenagers at an Institute of Christ the King parish. He ordained two monks at the Benedictine monastery near Norcia, Italy, in September 2021. In June 2022, during a visit to Chavagnes International College in France, he made a point of being driven some three hours away to visit the seminary for the Institute of the Good Shepherd, where he delivered an encouraging address to the community. Pell had hoped to be well enough to offer Mass in the Extraordinary Form after the Paris to Chartres pilgrimage in June 2023.

Pope Francis and the Congregation for Divine Worship (led by the English prefect Cardinal Arthur Roche) had cracked down on the celebration of the Extraordinary Form; so the cardinal's acceptance of the invitation from Chartres was telling. He would have been deeply hurt had he seen the letter from a hostile, junior French bishop that arrived after he went to the hospital. It suggested that he back out of the Chartres Mass in view of his jailing for child abuse in Australia (despite his victory in the High Court, which overturned the original verdict with a seven-to-zero ruling).

In private, Pell had parodied the title of Francis' apostolic letter limiting the celebration of the Extraordinary Form of the Mass, *Traditionis Custodes*, as "jailers of tradition". He was convinced the document would not last beyond Francis' pontificate. While making it clear that he personally celebrated Mass in the Ordinary Form, Pell was magnanimous about the place of the older rite. "For those people whose piety is helped by the Mass in this form, well, God bless them", he told the *Catholic Herald*.[3]

After celebrating Christmas 2022 with friends in Rome, Pell had been in good spirits in January, giving numerous interviews to Catholic and secular media after Pope Benedict XVI died on December 31, 2022. He had known the former pope well for decades and liked and respected him. Pell had been unhappy with Benedict's funeral, believing he deserved a more solemn ceremony. While the death of the pope emeritus was not unexpected (Benedict was ninety-five and had been frail for a long time), Pell said he was surprisingly saddened by the loss. "I'd known him well enough. I admired what he was about. I thought he was very good for the Church, and so it was sad to see another wonderful stage in Church history ending", he told EWTN's Colm Flynn.[4]

Pell was pleased that Benedict was buried in the chasuble he wore at World Youth Day in Sydney in July 2008, he said. His abiding memory of that extraordinary week was Benedict's insistence on reverence and quiet at the liturgical celebrations, including the final Mass, which attracted four hundred thousand worshippers to Randwick Racecourse. "After Communion I could hear the birds singing . . . a wonderful moment of recollection and adoration and prayer." Benedict will be remembered for his contribution to the liturgy, Pell said, which should be beautiful. "We Catholics are not innovators in liturgy", he added. "We're people of tradition. The rites go back to the time of Christ. The Roman rite is remarkably similar for 1,500 years; 80 percent of the prayers in the Roman Missal are over 1,000 years old. [Benedict] understood that—in making

[3] William Cash, "The Ordeal of Cardinal Pell", *Catholic Herald*, November 29, 2021, https://catholicherald.co.uk/the-ordeal-of-cardinal-pell/.

[4] "Cardinal George Pell Remembers Pope Benedict XVI" (interview with Colm Flynn), EWTN, January 2, 2023, https://www.youtube.com/watch?v=Qqjda3FT5vo.

the old rite more available, and in another direction opening it up so that those who were [formerly] Anglicans and came [into full communion with Rome] could continue to worship in a way that was constant with the beautiful English language tradition that they had developed."

Benedict, Pell told EWTN, was the "complete opposite of the caricatures" his enemies had contrived. Names such as God's Rottweiler and the Panzer Cardinal were "absurd", he said. There was "nothing Prussian about him. He was a Bavarian. He was a quiet, gentle, pious man—absolute gentleman." As pope his was a scriptural role, as the rock foundation of the Church, the guarantor that the people in the pews are receiving the same teachings that Christ and the apostles gave. In these terms, Pell said, Benedict was a magnificent success. "He realised that the secrets of our vitality are in the redemptive activity and teaching of Jesus Christ ... He wasn't the greatest administrator, greatest executive, not a natural politician, not a backslapper in the Irish-American tradition", the cardinal added. "But he did what he was supposed to, and that is, to strengthen the faith of his brothers." Like Pell, Benedict enjoyed a vast range of reading material. In his last weeks, the former pope had been reading the first volume of Pell's *Prison Journal.*

On the Monday night before Pell went to Salvator Mundi for his hip surgery, he told me on the phone how annoyed he was that a significant number of priests, including some who had come from overseas, had found themselves blocked from concelebrating the late pope's Requiem Mass. Bureaucratic obstacles had been put in their way, Pell explained to Terry Tobin on the eve of his surgery. He was also indignant that during the Mass nearby shops had remained open and the Roman Canon had not been said but rather the Third Eucharistic Prayer.

For Pell, one of the highlights of the week had been the attendance of ninety-one-year-old Cardinal Joseph Zen, the retired bishop of Hong Kong. Chinese authorities had released Zen's passport for five days to allow him to travel for Benedict's funeral. On the night of the funeral, Pell had hosted a small dinner at his apartment, almost beside Saint Peter's Square, and Zen had been the guest of honour and the star of the evening. Pell regarded the courageous old cardinal (born in Shanghai in 1932), who had endured the wrath of Chinese

Communist Party (CCP) authorities, as a "prophet". Like Pell, but for a different reason, he is one of the "white martyrs" of the College of Cardinals.

Professor Tracey Rowland, who holds the Saint John Paul II Chair of Theology at the University of Notre Dame in Australia and is one of the world's leading scholars on the theology of Benedict, attended the dinner. "The dominant thought in my mind at the event was that I was in the presence of two men, two princes of the Church, who had both been in prison just because they are confessors of the faith", Rowland said. "The cultural Marxists who run the state of Victoria hated Cardinal Pell because he defended the sanctity of human life and believed in a natural human ecology, a natural moral law, in other words; and the Chinese Communists know that Cardinal Zen is the great defender of the faithful Chinese Catholics who don't want to be governed by bishops who are in bed with the Communists."

"I was in the presence of two irrepressible alpha males whose faith ran deeper than any tribal ideology", she added. "Both had the hearts of lions, though Cardinal Pell always looked a bit ursine and Cardinal Zen looks more like a very clever fox."

Cardinal Zen had fled Shanghai for Hong Kong when the Communist Party seized power over mainland China seventy years earlier. Hong Kong's reverting to Chinese control was problematic for him, and he was arrested in May 2022 on suspicion of colluding with foreign forces, in violation of the new Beijing-imposed National Security Law. He was detained, before being released and later fined.

The conversation during the evening was light-hearted and upbeat, Rowland said. Neither cardinal complained about what he had been through, though their mutual respect was clear. "Cardinal Zen was an absolutely awesome raconteur", Rowland recalled. "He had a whole room full of people laughing along with his stories about this or that battle with the Communists." The anecdotes included instances of the CCP's dismay at his converting fellow inmates while being held in detention.

Zen had fought a legal battle just to be allowed to board a plane in order to attend Pope Benedict's funeral; he respected Benedict so much that he made the effort, Rowland recalled. "Although he had to fly to Europe from Asia after a legal battle, he showed no signs of jet lag, which is quite something for someone who is ninety-one. I can remember saying to one of the other guests as we left the event, 'I want Zen for the next pope, and I don't care if he is almost a hundred.' It was a huge honour just to be in the same room as these two battle-scarred lions."

Pell had been close to Benedict and had penned a masterful obituary about the late pontiff several years earlier for *The Australian* newspaper. It was posted online as soon as Benedict's death was announced and displayed across two broadsheet pages of the paper's print edition on January 1, 2023. Pell's own obituary (written by me at the same time he was writing Benedict's, although I never had the heart to tell him) also covered two pages, with news stories on his sudden death taking up most of the front page. The fact it appeared less than a fortnight after his tribute to Benedict felt incomprehensible.

The extent of the coverage reflected Pell's profile in Australia. His life, which was so often newsworthy, had echoes of the observation made in 2010 by his old friend Cardinal Francis George of Chicago: "I expect to die in bed, my successor will die in prison and his successor will die a martyr in the public square. His successor will pick up the shards of a ruined society and slowly help rebuild civilization, as the church has done so often in human history."[5] It was that rebuilding, of Church and civil society, in which Pell was heavily engaged for a long time.

Through tears, inspiring music, gentle humour, and spontaneous outbreaks of applause, some in the vast congregation in Saint Mary's Cathedral at his funeral Mass came to know George Pell as never before. The stories—in the homily by Archbishop Anthony Fisher and the tributes by the cardinal's brother, David Pell, and former Australian prime minister Tony Abbott—were telling. They ranged from Pell's efforts to ensure Indigenous Youth were included in World Youth Day 2008 and his making friends at David's Place, a centre for the homeless in Sydney's suburb of Rushcutters Bay, to his washing his socks in the shower, putting his jumpsuit on backwards, and sweeping the area outside his cell so that he could hear the birds sing during his 407 days in jail.

[5] Francis George, "The Wrong Side of History", *Chicago Catholic*, October 20, 2012, https://www.chicagocatholic.com/cardinal-george/-/article/2012/10/21/the-wrong-side -of-history.

David Pell's tribute showed the family's generosity of spirit, in accepting that George would want to return to Rome, at least for a while, after his release from jail: "In the period just before he was acquitted of all charges, he asked me what he should do. I explained to him that the family was happy for him to return to Rome. He rang back the next day and asked me if I was sure. I replied, 'Of course, you owe Australia nothing. Put on your red zucchetto, red soutane, and get back to Saint Peter's.' Your Grace, I think it was probably the first time he ever did as he was told!"[6]

Recalling his brother's installation as archbishop of Melbourne in 1996, David remembered that the "excitement and the joy that surrounded his acceptance as a shepherd to the flock, and a defender of the faith, was overwhelming." This was a new beginning. He did not realise then that he would be so unjustly persecuted for the failings of his immediate predecessor, Archbishop Frank Little, and other bishops. "Similarly here in Sydney his reception as archbishop was spectacular. He was at home here. He loved Sydney, and gauging by the outpouring of love as he [lay] in state and today, Sydney loved him."

Tony Abbott, in one of the most memorable speeches of his long career in public life, paid tribute to "one of our country's greatest sons". Pell, he said, was a priest, a bishop, and the prefect of a Vatican secretariat,

> but he was never a mere functionary; in each of these roles—a thinker, a leader, a Christian warrior, and a proud Australian who wanted our country and our civilisation, to succeed. In the pulpit, from the lectern, on TV, in the opinion pages, across the dinner table, after Mass or in confession, as everyone here would know.
>
> He was always thoughtful, often charismatic, occasionally imperious, constantly concerned for the wellbeing of others, and a pastoral priest who could find an echo of Christ, even in the worst sinner.[7]

Far from being an apologist for, or a dissembler about, the sins of the Church—personal, financial, or intellectual—he was their

---

[6] Staff writers, "David Pell's Eulogy for Cardinal Pell: A Good and Holy Man, and a Proud Australian", *Catholic Weekly*, February 2, 2023, https://www.catholicweekly.com.au/david-pells-eulogy-for-cardinal-pell-a-good-and-holy-man-and-a-proud-australian/.

[7] With Megan Gorrey, "Pell a Saint for Our Times, Abbott Says", *Sydney Morning Herald*, February 2, 2023.

hammer. "As he knew—*Eccelesia semper reformanda*—the Church is always in need of reform", Abbott said.

"Here in Australia," he continued,

> he was the first archbishop to sack misbehaving clergy and report them to the police, rather than hide them in another parish. In Rome, he tried to ensure that the collections from the faithful were used for the glory of God, rather than the indulgence of the higher clergy. And most recently, he called a draft Vatican document, further eroding the apostolic tradition, a 'toxic nightmare'. He was never one to mince his words. To the smug, to the venal, to the lazy, to the wayward, and to the intellectually sloppy, he was an existential reproach. And because that's all of us, in some way, it's hardly surprising that he became a target. For all his presence and his natural authority, he was personally humble.
>
> And never fell for the modern conceit that he was bigger than that which had shaped him, faith, church and country.

In a celebrated 1998 eulogy for another Catholic hero, B. A. Santamaria, Abbott recalled, Pell declared that it was "the mark of the false prophet, that all men speak well of him" before observing that Bob [Santamaria] had "triumphantly avoided this fate". "And so it was, even more, with the cardinal himself", Abbott said.

> His recent observation, that the climate change movement, quote, "had some of the characteristics of a low-level, not too demanding pseudo-religion" was the kind of comment that enraged its adherents, precisely because it was true.
>
> And throughout history, that's what people have been martyred for—for telling the unpopular, unpalatable truth.
>
> And it's not possible to honour the Cardinal without some reference to his persecution. He was made a scapegoat for the church itself. He should never have been investigated in the absence of a complaint.
>
> He should never have been charged in the absence of corroborating evidence, and he should never have been convicted in the absence of a plausible case, as the High Court so resoundingly made plain.

Pell was instrumental, Abbott noted, in the foundation of three centres of higher learning: Australian Catholic University; University of Notre Dame in Australia (which encompassed the nation's first Catholic medical and law schools), and Campion College—perhaps his favourite—named for the Jesuit martyr (at whose name-sake college Pell studied in Oxford). Campion, Abbott said, was "our first liberal arts school, dedicated to giving students a good grounding in the great books and the great debates, that have shaped our civilisation and made it man's finest social and cultural achievement so far".

The former prime minister was undoubtedly prescient when he said that, over time, there should and will be "Pell study courses, Pell spirituality courses, Pell lectures, Pell high schools, and Pell university colleges. Just as there are, for the other saints. If we can direct our prayers to Mother Teresa, Thomas Becket, and St Augustine, why not the late Cardinal too, who has been just as pleasing to God, I'm sure, and has the added virtue of being the very best of us?" Should that day arise in future, one of Pell's far-sighted priest friends has sent a few relics to a *custos* (guardian of relics) in the United States.

The fact that the funeral was held on Candlemas Day was poignant. Before heading to Rome in 2014, Pell had devoted one of his final weekly *Sunday Telegraph* columns to the feast, regretting that it had slipped beneath the radar. In the Christian calendar, he wrote, it commemorates the presentation of baby Jesus in the Temple of Jerusalem by His mother, Mary, and His foster father, Joseph, forty days after Christmas. In his column, he referred to Simeon's words on seeing the child in Saint Luke's Gospel: "Lord, now let your servant depart in peace, / according to your word; / for my eyes have seen your salvation / which you have prepared in presence of all the peoples / a light for revelation to the Gentiles" (Lk 2:29–32, RSV second Catholic edition). They are a fine epitaph for a man of faith. While Simeon blessed Mary, he warned that her child would be "a sign of contradiction"—a description that in a far smaller way applied to Pell himself. Simeon was prophesying both the universal salvation that would be proclaimed by Jesus and the necessity of his suffering.

Pell recounted that Simeon, a deeply religious man who was a regular at the Temple, had been told by God that he would meet the Messiah before his death. "So he prayed in thanks to God because he believed he had seen salvation, the light for the pagans, embodied

in this helpless baby child."[8] Mary and Joseph, who were poor, had
offered a couple of doves for sacrifice at the presentation. "We should
never forget Jesus was a Jew, who was inserted into this tradition by
his parents", the cardinal told readers.

> He regularly preached in local synagogues and loved the Great Tem-
> ple enough to weep over the prospect of its destruction.
> All Christian denominations have Jewish roots.
> Jewish history and scriptures, which Christians know as the Old
> Testament, are the essential foundation for all Christianity.

Simeon, the cardinal wrote, told the young mother that her first-
born would cause division, and was

> destined for the rise and fall of many as all would be forced to declare
> where they stood, and that a sword would pierce her soul too.
> The word Simeon used is not a dagger or a small sword, but the
> type of mighty weapon used by Goliath, by the angel at the gates of
> Paradise.
> The piercing mentioned was not a smaller nick but a wound that
> would pass clean through Mary's heart or soul. She was to suffer be-
> cause of her Son. Why such harsh words? What might it mean for us?
> The coming of Christ means that every person has to choose good
> or evil, search for faith rather than wallow in disbelief or doubt.
> Earnest searching is a minimum requirement. None of us, good,
> bad, or indifferent, can avoid this challenge.

Nor could the cardinal, as his three-volume *Prison Journal* attests.
It will stand the test of time, as a classic work of grace and religious
insights. Pell was a born writer and the *Prison Journal*, written under
extraordinary duress, reflected his talent. Throughout his working
life he put that talent to good use, in sermons, speeches, books,
and for thirteen years, writing his 450-word weekly column for
the *Sunday Telegraph*, Australia's largest-selling newspaper with millions of readers. His columns, always written in longhand, always to
length, and always on time, were often penned after the working

[8] George Pell, "Christ's Visit to Temple Has Great Meaning", *Sunday Telegraph*, February 8, 2014, https://www.dailytelegraph.com.au/news/opinion/christs-visit-to-temple-has
-deep-meaning/news-story/b3c97eb445915b3e53595c47534e75b2.

day, at 11 P.M. or later. He was a model contributor, ranging over topics from Harry Potter to Anzac Day,[9] providing fresh insights and a dash of humour.

In his funeral homily for Pell, Archbishop Fisher drew parallels between the cardinal and his name saint, the "rather martial" Saint George, and the man who popularised him as Patron of England, King Richard I, who ruled over England at the end of the twelfth century and who wore the cross of Saint George on his chest. Richard was six feet, five inches tall (slightly taller than Pell), like him a striking, athletic man who dominated every room he entered. "He was a far from perfect prince, but the calumnies of his enemies were baseless and his imprisonment wrongful, and he is remembered by history as Cœur de Lion—The Lionheart—because of his courage", Fisher said. "George Pell was also a giant of a man with a big vision, who looms large in the history of the Church in Australia and amongst churchmen internationally. He had a big heart, too, strong enough to fight for the faith and endure persecution, but soft enough to care for priests, youth, the homeless, prisoners, and imperfect Christians."[10]

That heart, as Fisher said, ultimately gave out "but only after more than eighty years of being gradually conformed to the Sacred Heart of Jesus." In 2023, "the lion's roar was unexpectedly silenced. But George the Lionheart was dressed with the cross on his chest and ready, awaiting His Master's return. His influence has been far-reaching, and we can be confident it will long continue."

Like the small jacaranda tree growing outside the cathedral, planted by Pell looking to the future, the story of the Church in Sydney goes on. Only the day before, Fisher told the congregation, he had celebrated Mass to welcome seventeen new admissions to Sydney's Seminary of the Good Shepherd—the largest intake in its history. "You have to go back thirty-seven years to 1986 since that many entered its predecessor seminary of St Patrick's Manly", Fisher said. "For our

---

[9] Anzac Day, commemorated in Australia and New Zealand every year, marks the landing of the Australian and New Zealand Army Corps (Anzacs) at Gallipoli in the Dardenelles on April 25, 1915, during World War I. Over the years it has acquired a deep symbolism and reverence in Australia and is a day when all those who perished in war are remembered and prayed for at dawn services, Masses, and memorial ceremonies around the nation.

[10] Anthony Fisher, "Homily for the Solemn Pontifical Funeral Mass of George Cardinal Pell AC", Catholic Archdiocese of Sydney, February 3, 2023, https://www.sydneycatholic.org /homilies/2023/homily-for-the-solemn-pontifical-funeral-mass-of-george-cardinal-pell-ac/.

family to receive seventeen newcomers as it loses one leonine old-timer is a great grace!" That news drew thunderous applause. "I know that Cardinal Pell, such a great friend of seminarians and young priests, and such a believer in the good that priests do, was interceding for this.... God grant an eternal reward to this man of ἀναίδεια [Greek for persistence and shameless determination], who loved his Lord and served his Church shamelessly, vehemently, courageously to the end." A few weeks after offering Pell's Requiem, Anthony Fisher, leading the Easter ceremonies, said he felt his predecessor's spirit "below me, above me, and beside me".

The absence of several prominent political figures at the funeral raised eyebrows, including that of the Prime Minister Anthony Albanese (who had attended Saint Mary's Cathedral School). The absence of the New South Wales premier Dominic Perrottet, a graduate of Opus Dei's Redfield College in Sydney, drew even more comment. The state opposition leader Chris Minns, also a Catholic, who beat Perrottet a few weeks later in the state election, did not attend either. Pell had expressed a liking for all three men. As Australian political journalist Paul Kelly wrote: "The church's celebration of Pell's life was a magnificent event yet evidence of a diminished nation, its culture fragmented and its current secular leaders hiding in fear, unable to pay respects to the life of George Pell, who attained the most senior position in the Catholic hierarchy of any Australian."[11] Opposition leader Peter Dutton attended, as did former Prime Minister John Howard, the nation's second-longest-serving prime minister and most respected political leader.

The music chosen for the Requiem Mass accorded with Pell's tastes—pieces by Mendelssohn, Bach, and Victoria. Edward Elgar's *The Dream of Gerontius*, which uses the words from Saint John Henry Newman's poem of the same name, and an offertory motet written for the occasion by Scottish composer Sir James MacMillan, were also played and sung.[12]

After the Mass, Pell was buried in the cathedral crypt, near his predecessors and other prominent churchmen, including Irishman Father John Therry, who in 1821 was granted the land on which Saint

---

[11] Paul Kelly, "Pell Funeral Marks Fracture of Church and State Relations", *The Australian*, February 8, 2023.

[12] A recording of the Mass is available at https://www.youtube.com/watch?v=fgL7QnnxN10&t=1527s

Mary's Cathedral was built. Some of those who offer and attend Mass in Saint Mary's, or enter the cathedral for some quiet reflection, gain a sense of the great and colourful characters of the past by looking around the crypt. Buried there are English Benedictine Archbishop John Bede Polding, who became Sydney's first Catholic archbishop in 1843, and Irish-born Cardinal Patrick Francis Moran, who was named Australia's first cardinal in 1885.

In the southwestern corner of the cathedral is the bronze sculpture of a fallen soldier, a memorial originally dedicated to the Australians who lost their lives in World War I. It was first blessed in 1931 by Archbishop Michael Kelly, the fourth archbishop of Sydney, moved to the crypt in 1937, and brought upstairs into the body of the cathedral in 2004 by Pell, who rededicated it to the more than a hundred thousand Australians who have died in service to the nation since 1885. Pell added an extra inscription, *Pax Invictis* (Peace to the Unconquered). His idea for the inscription came from a war memorial he had long admired near Saint Patrick's Cathedral in Melbourne: *The Cross of Sacrifice* outside Saint Peter's Eastern Hill, an Anglican parish. The monument, where Pell often stopped, had been unveiled in 1924, in memory of the 366 young men and women from that small community who had served in World War I.

2

Farewell at the Altar of the Chair

Pell's funeral Mass at his cathedral in Sydney, on the morning of February 2, 2023, was his second. The first was offered in Saint Peter's Basilica in Rome, at the Altar of the Chair, where he had been ordained in 1966. It was one of the best-attended funerals of any Roman cardinal for years, filling a vast section of the basilica, with mourners from Rome, various European countries, Britain, Ireland, and the United States, as well as family and friends from Australia. George Weigel, Pell's great friend for more than half a century, later wrote:

> After a day of visitation in the little Church of St. Stephen of the Abyssinians behind St. Peter's, where friends could come and pray by his casket and sprinkle it with holy water (a lovely Italian custom), Cardinal Pell's Requiem Mass was celebrated on January 14 in the apse of the Vatican Basilica, beneath Gianlorenzo Bernini's colossal bronze masterpiece, the *Altar of the Chair*. Non-papal liturgies, including cardinals' requiems, are always celebrated in that large space. But veterans of such events said that the congregation that assembled to bid farewell to George Pell, and to beg the Father of Mercies to take his servant into the embrace of the Trinity, was the largest they had ever seen—larger even than congregations for the diaconate ordinations celebrated there by the Pontifical North American College. Shortly before the Mass began, the *Sanpietrini*, the basilica work force, were frantically setting up chairs behind the pews in the vast apse, the pews having long since overflowed. And thus, the congregation filled the entire area between the *Altar of the Chair* and another Bernini triumph, the baldacchino over the papal high altar beneath the basilica's great dome. As one of the cardinal's longtime collaborators

said, "When people fly in from all over the world on short notice, something is being said."[1]

A few of those attending recalled a memorable sermon Pell had delivered at the same altar, in April 2008, during a Vatican meeting on strengthening the family. "Catholic comes from the Greek word for universal, which means that following Christ is open to people of every nation, class, and tribe", he told delegates from around the world. "It also means that within the Catholic Church community and therefore linked to God's love, we have people of nearly every level of understanding and many levels of moral goodness. As I have often explained, sinfulness is one regular characteristic of Catholic communities. So are imperfect families. Not all Catholics are saints." Over the centuries, he said,

> Catholic leaders have worked hard to develop a Catholic culture, a way of worshipping, interacting, and relating to the society around them. *I am not just talking about the world of high culture exemplified by Dante, Michelangelo, or Palestrina but about what the Anglo-American writer T. S. Eliot called 'the total harvest of thinking and feeling', which is also expressed in a thousand ordinary ways in laws, rituals, folk stories, and habits of daily living.* This prevents us from being submerged by hostile forces and helps us pass on our treasures to the youngsters in our midst and to outsiders who are looking for meaning and healing.[2]

Pell's long-standing friend Father Alexander Sherbrooke, the parish priest of Saint Patrick's Church in Soho Square, London, where Pell, like Fulton Sheen fifty years earlier, had often stayed, wrote about the funeral for *The Priest*, the magazine of the Australian Confraternity of Catholic Clergy. He recalled: "The most abiding memory of those precious few hours for many was in the Church of Saint Stephen of the Abyssinians, where his body lay. A family of parents and some eight children came in to surround his body, prayed, and sang. He was truly a father, a lover of family and

[1] George Weigel, "Letters from Rome: #5; On the Death and Requiem of Cardinal George Pell", *First Things*, January 16, 2023, https://www.firstthings.com/web-exclusives/2023/01/letters-from-rome-5.

[2] George Pell, *Test Everything: Hold Fast to What Is Good* (San Francisco: Ignatius Press, 2015), p. 239, italics in the original.

the sacrament of marriage and the most resolute defender of Catholic orthodoxy."

The principal celebrant and preacher of Pell's Requiem, Cardinal Giovanni Battista Re, dean of the College of Cardinals, noted that Pell's final years had been "marked by an unjust and painful conviction". His thirteen months in jail, mainly in solitary confinement, for a crime of child abuse it was logistically impossible for him to have committed, was "an experience of great suffering sustained with faith in the judgment of God".[3]

As is customary at the funeral of a cardinal at the Vatican, Pope Francis offered the commendation and farewell. "May God unite his soul with those of all the saints and faithful departed", the pope prayed. "May he be given a merciful judgement so that, redeemed from death, freed from punishment, reconciled to the Father, carried in the arms of the Good Shepherd, he may deserve to enter fully into everlasting happiness in the company of the eternal King together with all the saints."[4]

That morning Francis had visited the staff and students at the North American College, many of whom had been close to Pell and attended the funeral. He also comforted Pell's family. When Pell's brother, David, told Francis that George had been his friend, the pope patted him on the shoulder. David's grief was compounded by the recent loss of his sister, Margaret, who had died thirteen months earlier.

The cardinal's official funeral notice told a story of family love:

PELL, His Eminence George Cardinal AC[5]
   Loved son of George Arthur and Margaret Lilian (née Burke; both deceased). Beloved nephew of Mollie (Mary) Burke (deceased). Loved brother of Margaret (deceased) and David and brother-in-law

---

[3] Frances D'Emilio, "Vatican Holds Funeral for Cardinal Who Decried Francis' Rule", Associated Press, abc27 News, January 14, 2023, https://www.abc27.com/news/top-stories/ap-top-headlines/ap-vatican-holds-funeral-for-cardinal-who-decried-francis-rule/.

[4] Catholic News Agency, "'A Man of the Church': Cardinal George Pell's Funeral Celebrated at Vatican", Catholic Times, January 14, 2023, https://catholictimescolumbus.org/news/catholic-news-agency-55006adc-4a64-42da-9f08-ecbfff84f775/a-man-of-the-church-cardinal-george-pell-s-funeral-celebrated-at-vatican.

[5] AC stands for Commander in the Order of Australia, the highest civil honor given to Australian citizens who have distinguished themselves in the service of their country or their fellowmen.

of Judith. Dearly loved uncle of Sarah Jane, Nicholas, Rebecca and Georgina. Very much loved great uncle of Sonny and Billie.[6]

Pell was close to his family. Over many years, he phoned them every few days from wherever he was in the world. His best friend had been his sister, Margaret, a talented, professional violinist and a "good scout", as he said at her funeral in Bendigo in December 2021. When he called his niece Georgina before his operation, her daughter, Billie, then about twenty months old, roared in excitement, "George, George, George!" The previous year, with his grandnephew, Sonny, he kicked a football for the first time in forty years.

In his eulogy for Pell at Sydney's Saint Mary's Cathedral on February 2, David said his older brother was a prince of the Church, a good and holy man, and a proud Australian. He enjoyed a bet on the Melbourne Cup, Australia's biggest horse race, which stops the nation every year on the first Tuesday in November, and he was a passionate fan of Aussie Rules football, a sport he had played as a young man. "He believed in the rule of law and a fair go to all, and in Aussie Rules parlance, he played the ball and not the man."[7] As a member of Pope Francis' nine-member Council of Cardinals, he was the pope's friend as well as his "best theological adviser", said David Pell, quoting Cardinal Gerhard Müller, the former prefect of the Congregation for the Doctrine of the Faith. Cardinal Pell loved his family, writing to his niece during his imprisonment: "Family means a lot when they stick, and stand fast in times of trouble." The cardinal wrote that he had to "keep battling on", David added, but he did not want the younger members of the family to "get into a stew" about his predicament.

Despite that predicament, George Pell believed his life to be a fortunate one. "If I have encountered more than a usual share of adversity, my life has been showered with blessings: a good family and education, many true friends, enjoyable and worthwhile work in three countries, and with three popes", he wrote in *Prison Journal*.

---

[6] "George Pell", *Sydney Morning Herald*, January 25, 2023, https://tributes.smh.com.au /obituaries/469921/george-pell/?r=https://tributes.smh.com.au/obituaries/smh-au/.

[7] Staff writers, "David Pell's Eulogy for Cardinal Pell: A Good and Holy Man, and a Proud Australian", *Catholic Weekly*, February 2, 2023, https://www.catholicweekly.com.au /david-pells-eulogy-for-cardinal-pell-a-good-and-holy-man-and-a-proud-australian/.

"A strong, good father and a loving mother with faith and her sister, Molly, who lived with us, laid the foundation for all this. I cannot pretend my years have been dominated by adversity. By any standards, I have enjoyed the one hundredfold in this life."[8] Early on, Pell took to heart the Lord's teaching on the talents, that more was expected of those who had received more. "So, I decided to strive to do what I was asked, not just by my superiors but by those around me who asked for help. This was to be my principal form of penance, as I wasn't someone who fasted much, and I abstained mainly at Lent—from alcohol."

The cardinal joked to friends that his time as a "guest of Her Majesty" in prison was "a long retreat". The 407 days he spent behind bars would equal about ten Lents in succession, "which he hoped would make up in some way for Lents not well observed". So said his former student and master of ceremonies, Monsignor Charles Portelli, at a memorial Mass for Pell. It was concelebrated by forty priests at Portelli's Melbourne parish, Saint Mary MacKillop, on January 23, 2023. "Shortly before his sentencing we were able to meet for the first time in three years," Portelli said in his homily. "He showed me letters he had received from both Francis and Benedict. Both encouraged him to carry the cross which had come his way. The cardinal said to me that he accepted the ordeal ahead as God's will for him. He said this without any trace of recrimination or bitterness. He remained the same, maybe even more so after the spectacular decision of the High Court."

Those attitudes revealed much about Pell's nature, Portelli said. He normally saw a "glass half full" rather than "a glass half empty". He counted his blessings, appreciated his talents, and understood his place in the order of the world. He was also patient in providing help to those he encountered as a priest and in everyday life. Portelli's observation struck a chord. The first time Archbishop Pell visited my home, the cleaning lady turned up unexpectedly; she was in tears and distraught that her son was in custody for throwing another young man through the window of a pizza shop. She poured out her heart to "Father Pell", whose kindness and understanding

<hr>

[8] George Pell, *Prison Journal*, vol. 3, *The High Court Frees an Innocent Man* (San Francisco: Ignatius Press, 2021), p. 30.

consoled her. Portelli also described Pell's rare capacity for befriend-
ing countless characters—from a former speaker of the U.S. Congress to the homeless beggar on the corner near his apartment in
Rome, to whom he would give "a few shillings" when they met
in the street.

Few people were aware of the cardinal's empathy and concern
for those who were in trouble or in need. "These encounters were
never recorded or the subject of commentary. Like most men of his
background and generation, he did not wear his heart on his sleeve",
Portelli said.

> I remember being with him when he visited a facility for severely
> disabled children. A suitable speech had been prepared for the occa-
> sion, but when he saw his congregation he put the speech aside and
> spoke very tenderly to the children and their families about the Good
> Shepherd. He was genuinely and deeply moved not because of the
> appalling disabilities they endured but because he could see in their
> faces a profound joy which suffering could not destroy.

Pell's best "street friend" in Rome, a man named Michel, who was
often outside the cardinal's apartment beside the Vatican, has since been
the beneficiary of the generosity of one of the cardinal's best friends in
Rome, Australian-born Columban priest Father Robert McCulloch,
S.S.C., his order's procurator general, who was also impressed by Pell's
kindness to Michel and others. Pell and McCulloch became friends
in the 1970s, when Pell was working in Ballarat after returning from
Oxford and McCulloch, who was ordained in 1970, was visiting his
parents in the city while on leave from his missionary and charitable
work in the Philippines and Pakistan. McCulloch worked in Pakistan for thirty-four years, establishing one of the nation's best hospitals,
Saint Elizabeth's in Hyderabad. He also set up Pakistan's first home-
based palliative care units, initiatives that Pell followed closely.

In an interview in August 2023, when he was visiting Australia,
McCulloch evoked a striking image of Saint Peter's Square and its
surrounds, saying it reflected major strands of the cardinal's spiritual
life. These were Saint Peter's and the papacy, to which Pell had great
fidelity; the twelfth-century Basilica of Santo Spirito in Sassia, to
which Pell, in his later years in Rome, would walk every day to pray

before the Blessed Sacrament; and his apartment, in a street just to the right of the square, where he supported people in need.

Pell was generous by nature. He was excellent at keeping in touch with friends—priests, artists, writers, accountants, teachers, business people, lawyers, medicos, academics, and journalists. When he was archbishop of Sydney, the best time to chat was often 11 P.M. local time, after the day's work and the evening's functions were done, and before he settled down to write a newspaper column, a sermon, a scholarly article for a journal, or a keynote speech. He had the knack of instilling confidence in his friends rather than giving advice, which was always adroit. His episcopal motto, "Be not afraid" crops up frequently in the Bible. It suited his temperament and philosophy, and it spilled over to countless others.

One of life's unaffected sophisticates, Pell knew plenty about art, literature, opera, music, and history, as well as sport. He and Margaret and their guests liked to share a bottle of Penfolds Grange, one of Australia's finest wines, to see in the New Year, but simple pleasures were a treat for him—card games, singalongs, home-cooked steak-and-onions. He normally had a theology book and a serious nonfiction book, as well as a thriller, on the go. It was wonderful, he said, to hit the jackpot when he found that a thriller given to him as a gift was "trashy" but kept him up until 2 A.M., "impossible to put down".

Pell's Roman friends, such as Cardinal Raymond Burke, whose apartment is a three-minute walk from Pell's old apartment, miss him enormously. The two first met in Rome in 2007, when both were visiting the city—Burke from his Archdiocese of Saint Louis in the United States, and Pell from Sydney. Burke was impressed by Pell's wit and presence as he explained why Catholics from Europe and the United States should make the long trip Down Under for World Youth Day the following year, reversing the process of long-haul travel undertaken by so many Australians. They grew closer through the years, especially after they were both appointed to the Roman Curia. After Pell's return to Rome after being exonerated by the High Court, Burke found him "full of energy to assist so many today who suffer from the pervasive confusion and division in the Church and, as a result, are profoundly discouraged and even feel abandoned by those ordained to be their spiritual fathers." Pell had "an unusually fruitful life in service of Christ and His Bride, the Church", Burke said. He was always a proud son of Australia and happily spoke about his homeland, but "his heart was Roman" and "belonged to the Heart of Christ".[9]

[9]Raymond Burke, "Death of Cardinal George Pell" (statement), Cardinal Raymond Burke (website), January 11, 2023, https://www.cardinalburke.com/presentations/cardinal-pell-death.

3

The State of Play When He Left the Field

No slouch at ecclesial politics and determined to exert an influence on the next conclave, which he believed, mistakenly, would occur sooner rather than later, Pell knew the state of play was delicately poised. That point was not lost on most of his friends praying for his soul at his funeral Masses in Rome and Sydney.

Two days before the Sydney funeral, Sandro Magister, a prominent Vaticanista (who had been "frozen out" by the Vatican press office for six months in 2015 for publishing a leaked draft of Pope Francis' environment encyclical *Laudato Si'* in the Italian newspaper *L'Espresso*, three days before its official release), had stated that Pell was Demos, the author of the excoriating analysis of the Francis pontificate that centred on problems within the hierarchy and challenges awaiting the next pontiff. Amid great intrigue, the Demos memo, addressed to all cardinals, began circulating among them at the beginning of Lent 2022. It was first published by Magister on his blog, *Settimo Cielo*, with an interesting aside: "Its author, who goes by the name of Demos, 'people' in Greek, is unknown but shows himself a thorough master of the subject. It cannot be ruled out that he himself is a cardinal."[1]

In the first edition of this biography, published in 2002, Pell recalled his uncle Harry Burke, with great affection, as "a real mentor" and a man "deeply interested in politics", who used to write to the *Ballarat Courier* (Pell's hometown newspaper) under the pseudonym of Demos. Some people therefore supposed that Pell might be the Demos who wrote the memo or that he had a significant hand in it. Those familiar with Pell's prose style recognized it throughout

[1] Demos, *Memorandum*, posted by Sandro Magister, *Settimo Cielo* (blog), March 15, 2022.

much, but not all, of the analysis. The memo, in fact, was a combined effort by several authors, including other cardinals, with Pell contributing his parts and the name Demos, which appropriately is a collective noun. After Pell's death, one of his close associates, in collaboration with two others, wrote to Francis making it clear that the memo was not Pell's alone.

The memo had one overarching theme in anticipating the next conclave: "The first tasks of the new pope will be to restore normality, restore doctrinal clarity in faith and morals, restore a proper respect for the law and ensure that the first criterion for the nomination of bishops is acceptance of the apostolic tradition." It also stated that "the new pope must understand that the secret of Christian and Catholic vitality comes from fidelity to the teachings of Christ and Catholic practices. It does not come from adapting to the world or from money."

After reiterating one of Pell's favourite teaching themes, that the "Successor of St. Peter is the rock on which the Church is built, a major source and cause of worldwide unity", the memo noted some serious concerns, including:

(A) The German synod speaks on homosexuality, women priests, and communion for the divorced. The papacy is silent.

(B) Cardinal [Jean-Claude] Hollerich [the archbishop of Luxemburg] rejects Christian teaching on sexuality. The papacy is silent.... The Congregation for the Doctrine of the Faith must act and speak.

(C) The silence is emphasised when contrasted with the active persecution of the Traditionalists and the contemplative convents.

2. The Christo-centricity of teaching is being weakened; Christ is being moved from the centre. Sometimes Rome even seems to be confused about the importance of a strict monotheism, hinting at some wider concept of divinity; not quite pantheism, but like a Hindu panentheism variant.

(A) Pachamama [the pagan image prominent at the Synod on the Amazon in 2019] is idolatrous; perhaps it was not intended as such initially....

(C) The Christo-centric legacy of St. John Paul II in faith and morals is under systematic attack. Many of the staff of the Roman Institute for the Family have been dismissed; most students have left. The Academy for Life is gravely damaged, e.g., some members recently supported assisted suicide. The Pontifical Academies have members and visiting speakers who support abortion....

(E) Many staff, often priests, have been summarily dismissed from the Vatican Curia, often without good reason.

(F) Phone tapping is regularly practiced....

4. (A) The financial situation of the Vatican is grave. For the past ten years (at least), there have nearly always been financial deficits. Before COVID, these deficits ranged around €20 million annually. For the last three years, they have been around €30–35 million annually. The problems predate both Pope Francis and Pope Benedict.

(B) The Vatican is facing a large deficit in the Pensions Fund. Around 2014 experts ... estimated the deficit would be around €800 million in 2030. This was before COVID.

(C) .... In the 1980s, the Vatican was forced to pay out $230 million after the Banco Ambrosiano scandal. Through inefficiency and corruption during the past 25–30 years, the Vatican has lost at least another €100 million....

5. The political influence of Pope Francis and the Vatican is negligible. Intellectually, papal writings demonstrate a decline from the standard of St. John Paul II and Benedict. Decisions and policies are often "politically correct", but there have been grave failures to support human rights in Venezuela, Hong Kong, mainland China, and now in the Russian invasion.

There has been no public support for the loyal Catholics in China who have been intermittently persecuted for their loyalty to the papacy for more than 70 years. No public Vatican support for the Catholic community in Ukraine, especially the Greek Catholics.

6. At a different, lower level, the situation of Tridentine traditionalists (Catholic) should be regularised.

At a further and lower level, the celebration of "individual" and small group Masses in the mornings in St. Peter's Basilica should be permitted once again. At the moment, this great basilica is like a desert in the early morning.

As the next conclave draws nearer, the second half of the memo will become more pertinent. Its first point was that "the College of

Cardinals has been weakened by eccentric nominations and has not been reconvened after the rejection of Cardinal Kasper's views in the 2014 consistory." Pell, along with a number of other senior cardinals, had expressed concern that many members of the college had hardly met during Francis' papacy and were unknown to each other. Pell had also been dismayed that the archbishops of major dioceses, such as Venice (which produced three twentieth-century popes: Pius X, John XXIII, and John Paul I), Los Angeles (with five million Catholics), and Paris, were regularly overlooked when new members were promoted to the college, while bishops from Mongolia and Papua New Guinea, with relative handfuls of Catholics (about 2,000 in Mongolia), were elevated. He was also keen to see Archbishop Sviatoslav Shevchuk, the archbishop of Kyiv and primate of the Ukrainian Greek Catholic Church, promoted. After the Russian invasion of Ukraine, Pell said that Shevchuk, still in his early fifties, had the makings of a future pope. He would have been saddened, but not surprised, that in the first consistory after his death, Australia was left with no cardinal; it has not had a voting cardinal since Pell turned eighty in 2021. Thirteen months after Pell's death, an updated version of the Demos memo was circulated among cardinals in Rome, signed Demos II.

For decades, in and out of season, addressing groups ranging from the most sophisticated theologians to primary school children, Pell had preached the primacy of the papacy and Peter's role as the "rock man" of the Church. Disloyalty to any pope ran deeply against his grain. And in the early days of Francis' pontificate, Pell was inclined to rebuke gently his friends, especially priests, who criticized Francis. Error, however, even when promulgated by popes, has no rights. Exasperation and a sense of desperation moved Pell and others to challenge Francis' agenda publicly. As Pell's friend Father Robert McCulloch, S.S.C., explained, the cardinal remained loyal to the Holy Father but was annoyed by Bergoglio.

Pell was not the only Roman-based cardinal who found Francis trying. In recent years, one of Pell's brother cardinals, who had been in the college longer than Pell and who was regarded as an ally of Francis, made the mistake of using his best silverware when he hosted the pope to dinner. Francis was angered by the silverware because he thought it looked too expensive. The pontiff complained and the Vatican gendarmerie appeared at the cardinal's flat the next day to

remove the offending cutlery. Pell took mischievous delight in buying his colleague a grand set to replace it.

Anonymous subterfuge in attacking those with whom he disagreed
was not Pell's style. Much more typical of his approach was the well-
targeted, incisive critique written by Pell alone and published posthumously under his name in *The Spectator* the day before his Vatican
funeral. It was aimed at what the Catholic Synod of Bishops called
"God's dream" of synodality in a document prepared for their meetings with the pope in October 2023. "Unfortunately this divine dream
has developed into a toxic nightmare despite the bishops' professed
good intentions", Pell wrote. The bishops' document, entitled *Enlarge
the Space of Your Tent*, says "the people of God need new strategies;
not quarrels and clashes but dialogue, where the distinction between
believers and unbelievers is rejected." Pell continued:

> Because of differences of opinion on abortion, contraception, the ordi-
> nation of women to the priesthood and homosexual activity, some felt
> that no definitive positions on these issues can be established or pro-
> posed. This is also true of polygamy, and divorce and remarriage....
>   What is one to make of this potpourri, this outpouring of New
> Age good will? It is not a summary of Catholic faith or New Tes-
> tament teaching. It is incomplete, hostile in significant ways to the
> apostolic tradition and nowhere acknowledges the New Testament
> as the Word of God, normative for all teaching on faith and morals.[2]

In putting his name to the article, which he had pushed unusually hard to have published as soon as possible, Pell was willing to
face the wrath of Francis and any others who might object to his
words, recalled his friend Father Alexander Sherbrooke. Had they
confronted him publicly, he said, Pell would not have backed away
from a showdown. He always picked his battles carefully. And he had
acquired plenty of experience in standing his ground, especially from
2014 to 2017.

Aside from his role as prefect of the Secretariat for the Economy,
Pell retained his intense interest in moral theology while working

---

[2] George Pell, "The Catholic Church Must Free Itself from This 'Toxic Nightmare'",
The Spectator, January 11, 2023, https://www.spectator.co.uk/article/the-catholic-church
-must-free-itself-from-this-toxic-nightmare/.

at the heart of the Church. When conflict erupted in the Vatican in October 2015 during the three-week Synod on the Family, he was a central player. Pell was one of thirteen cardinals who warned Francis in a letter that the Church was in danger of collapsing like most liberal Protestant churches in the modern era. In their joint letter, the cardinals wrote that the threat of collapse has been accelerated by the abandonment of "key elements of Christian belief and practice in the name of pastoral adaptation".[3] The letter also complained that the synod process seemed "designed to facilitate pre-determined results on important disputed questions".[4]

Pell handed the letter to Francis personally at a meeting of the synod. It was reportedly signed by thirteen cardinals. Among them were the archbishops of Bologna, Toronto, New York, Galveston-Houston, Nairobi, Mexico City, Utrecht, Durban, and Caracas, and several important Vatican officials: Pell; German Cardinal Gerhard Müller, prefect of the Congregation for the Doctrine of the Faith; and Guinean Cardinal Robert Sarah, prefect of the Congregation for Divine Worship. Cardinal Elio Sgreccia, president emeritus of the Pontifical Council for Life, was also a signatory. While the pope had ostensibly encouraged free debate at the synod, the authors of the letter were courageous. Some believed they had put their careers on the line by defending Church teaching about the indissolubility of marriage and the Eucharist.

The Synod on the Family was attended by about three hundred delegates, mainly bishops, from around the world. One participant told the synod that "a little bit of smog or fog has entered the *aula* (auditorium)", a reference to Pope Paul VI's statement fifty years ago that "the smoke of Satan" had entered the Church.[5] Under discussion was whether long-established Church teaching should be changed to allow Catholics who had been married in the Church and were now divorced and civilly remarried to receive Holy Communion. Such a

---

[3] David Gibson, "Cardinals' Secret Letter to Francis Warns of Plot to Rig Reforms", *Washington Post*, October 12, 2015, https://www.washingtonpost.com/national/religion/cardinals-secret-letter-to-francis-warns-of-plot-to-rig-reforms/2015/10/12/d763e01e-7122-11e5-ba14-318f8e87a2fc_story.html.

[4] Nicole Winfield, "Vatican Family Synod Takes New Twist with Disputed Letter", Associated Press, October 12, 2015, https://apnews.com/article/5b1d0b6847ce4d34834075f5df005021.

[5] Told by Pell in conversation.

change was being pushed by a group of German bishops led by Cardinal Walter Kasper, then eighty-two.

In a statement released after the leaking of the letter by the cardinals, a spokesman for Cardinal Pell said: "There is strong agreement in the synod on most points but obviously there is some disagreement because minority elements want to change the Church's teachings on the proper dispositions necessary for the reception of Communion. Obviously there is no possibility of change on this doctrine."[6] Much of the synod discussion was kept under wraps, but the day after receiving the letter, the pope made an unscheduled intervention, reportedly urging the synod fathers not to indulge in a mentality that saw plots and conspiracy theories, which he said were "sociologically weak and spiritually unhelpful".[7]

Critics of the synod process, including Pell, feared a subtle undermining of doctrine, leaving the bishops' conferences of individual nations or regions to set their own rules on Communion for the divorced and remarried whose first marriages have not been annulled. Such an approach, Pell told *The Australian*, would draw the Catholic Church closer to liberal Protestantism, under which different rules apply in different places.[8]

Tensions over the synod had been building for weeks before it began after the pope had invited retired Belgian Cardinal Godfried Danneels, then eighty-two, to be one of his forty-five personal appointees to the meetings. A fortnight earlier, Edward Pentin had reported in the *National Catholic Register* that at the launch of his biography in Brussels, Danneels had boasted about his membership in a group of cardinals and bishops who secretly met in or near Saint Gallen, Switzerland, from about 1996 to 2006, to discuss Church-related topics, including issues surrounding Catholic sexual morality. The group, which included Cardinal Walter Kasper, had no formal

---

[6] Edward Pentin, "Cardinal Pell: Many Synod Fathers Still Concerned about Drafting Committee Composition", *National Catholic Register*, October 12, 2015, https://www.ncregister.com/blog/cardinal-pell-many-synod-fathers-still-concerned-about-drafting-committee-composition.

[7] Gibson, "Secret Letter".

[8] Tess Livingstone, "George Pell and Cardinals Warn Pope of Catholic Church Collapse", *The Australian*, October 14, 2015, https://www.theaustralian.com.au/news/nation/george-pell-and-cardinals-warn-pope-of-catholic-church-collapse/news-story/bd5ef699ea8b384fd3d3dae7b0b933bc.

name, but Danneels said jokingly that they had referred to themselves as a "mafia", a name that has stuck, especially among their critics.[9] At the death of John Paul II, members of the group favoured Cardinal Jorge Bergoglio, S.J., over Cardinal Joseph Ratzinger to lead the Church, but Ratzinger was elected pope in the 2005 papal conclave. After Benedict XVI retired in 2013, Bergoglio (now Pope Francis) was chosen.

In London, in November 2021, Pell pursued themes related to those discussed at the synod with a writer for the *Catholic Herald*. He described himself as an "up and down the wicket" sort of Catholic. "I don't invent any teachings", he said. "I follow the doctrines of the church and try very hard not to push the more difficult ones away."[10] His commitment as a "baptised Catholic, priest, bishop, or cardinal" was to be true to what the Church has always taught. He was unimpressed by reports that the bishops of New Zealand would allow priests to give the last rites to those choosing to die by assisted suicide, which had recently become legal there. "We can't have one set of commandments in New Zealand and everybody else singing to a different sheet."

[9] Edward Pentin, "Cardinal Danneels Admits to Being Part of 'Mafia' Club Opposed to Benedict XVI", *National Catholic Register*, September 24, 2015, https://www.ncregister.com /blog/cardinal-danneels-admits-to-being-part-of-mafia-club-opposed-to-benedict-xvi. The book launch was recorded and can be found on YouTube at https://www.youtube.com /watch?v=DxVVrdXaJoA.

[10] William Cash, "The Ordeal of Cardinal Pell: An Interview", *Catholic Herald*, January 11, 2023 (first published in December 2021), https://catholicherald.co.uk/the-ordeal-of -cardinal-pell-an-interview/.

4

The Money Trail

The icon of the Blessed Virgin Mary was exquisite, the two staffers from the Secretariat for the Economy agreed, glancing up occasionally as they labouriously counted out €200,000 in cash. It was 2015, and they were in the office of a cardinal, the head of a Vatican department. One of his staff members had been hurrying out the door with the money in plastic bags when he was intercepted by Secretariat of the Economy officials. They had been sent on a spot inspection by Cardinal Pell, whom Pope Francis had appointed as prefect of the new secretariat in April 2014.

When his appointment was announced, Pell, his senior staff (including accountant Danny Casey, whose job was to lead the practical implementation of the reforms), and several of Pell's priest friends understood that the new secretariat would rank alongside the Secretariat of State, a point reported in the Australian media. The motu proprio establishing the agency, *Fidelis Dispensator et Prudens*, specifies that the Secretariat for the Economy be presided over by a cardinal prefect, "who acts in collaboration with the Secretary of State".[1] As the Associated Press noted, "The changes appear to significantly diminish the scope of the Secretariat of State, which previously had administrative control over the Holy See while also handling diplomatic relations. The new Secretariat for the Economy's name suggests some sort of parity with the Secretariat of State."[2] Years later, Pell confirmed that he had understood that parity between the two

[1] Francis, Apostolic Letter Issued Motu Proprio *Fidelis Dispensator et Prudens* (February 24, 2014), no. 6.
[2] Nicole Winfield, "Pope Makes First Overhaul of Vatican in 25 Years", Associated Press, February 24, 2014, https://news.yahoo.com/pope-makes-first-overhaul-vatican-25-years-134346476.html.

secretariats had been part of the original blueprint approved by Francis, and Casey said that he and Pell had believed such parity would have provided a once-in-five-hundred-years opportunity to address the problems at the heart of the Vatican's finances.

But Father Mark Withoos, Pell's secretary in Rome at the time, said that while the Secretariat for the Economy was supposed to have equal billing with the Secretariat of State, he had been doubtful from the start that would turn out to be the case in practice. His doubts proved correct. Shortly after taking up his role, Pell realised that senior figures in the Secretariat of State and elsewhere in the Vatican refused to accept and to cooperate with the reform process, and that Francis was reluctant to force them to do so. Some in the Vatican were also eager to drive a wedge between Pell's secretariat and the Council for the Economy—creating tensions akin to those caused when a chief executive is at odds with the board of his corporation.

In the face of mounting obstacles to reform, Pell and his staff opted for direct measures, hence the stakeout. It yielded results, although the cardinal whose staff attempted to hide plastic bags full of euros held on to his position, at the behest of Francis, after Pell reported the matter. For Pell, there was an irritating but amusing side to the situation. In one of his 2004 weekly columns in the *Sunday Telegraph*, Pell had dismissed Dan Brown's best-selling novel *The Da Vinci Code* as a "ragbag of a book". He particularly took exception to the plot involving an Italian bishop "running around Europe" with a briefcase full of Vatican banknotes. Truth, Pell found, was sometimes stranger than fiction.

Pell had his eye on a number of recalcitrant cardinals, and he knew that tensions were running high. A monsignor in the Administration of the Patrimony of the Holy See (APSA),[3] who supported the reform process, told Pell that when he had asked a curial cardinal some awkward financial questions, the man gave him a thinly veiled threat. They were standing beside a window overlooking the Vatican grounds when the cardinal remarked that it would "only take one push". Another monsignor said a cardinal took him shooting to show off his gun collection and his prowess at using firearms. This

---

[3] The Administration of the Patrimony of the Holy See (APSA) controls the vast majority of the Vatican's investments and assets, the income of which helps to pay for the Vatican's expenses.

monsignor also interpreted the behaviour of the cardinal as a warning against digging into Vatican finances.

In an effort to apply international accounting standards to Vatican finances, Pell requested an audit of all the assets held by the various departments in the Vatican. While that would be considered normal operating procedure for businesses and organizations that are held accountable by their shareholders and board members, it was resisted by curial officials accustomed to running their departments like personal fiefdoms and to controlling discretionary funds "off the books", sometimes even holding large amounts of cash in their offices without proper records of where it came from or how it was spent. When the audit began, it was not unusual for those cardinals, some of whom were good friends of Pell, to call him and say something along the lines of "I've got a reserve of €100,000. I don't need to declare it, do I?" Most of these cardinals, if not all, Pell believed, were acting out of a desire to maintain control and autonomy, not to feather their nests personally. Regardless, some resisted the need for transparency and met with harsh consequences.

Pell's friend Cardinal Gerhard Müller, while he was the head of the Congregation for the Doctrine of the Faith (renamed the Dicastery for the Doctrine of the Faith, DDF, in 2022), was investigated in 2015 after his staff was found trying to conceal large amounts of cash. The investigation by the auditor general discovered that "hundreds of thousands of euros at the DDF were either misappropriated, improperly documented, or otherwise unaccounted for". Some of the funds had been deposited in Müller's personal bank account.[4] Pope Francis ordered Müller to repay hundreds of thousands of euros to the DDF, and he did not renew his term as its prefect in 2017. The latter decision was widely interpreted at the time as having something to do with Müller's theological differences with the pope.

After The Pillar broke this story in July 2024, Cardinal Müller issued a statement accusing its authors of "typical intrigue" and using "reputational damage as a means of their Church politics".[5] He acknowledged that his department kept "unusually large" amounts of cash in

[4] "Card. Müller's Non-Renewal at DDF Followed Financial Investigation", The Pillar, July 31, 2024, https://www.pillarcatholic.com/p/card-mullers-non-renewal-at-ddf-followed.
[5] "'Typical Intrigue': Card. Müller Responds to Pillar Report", The Pillar, August 2, 2024, https://www.pillarcatholic.com/p/typical-intrigue-card-muller-responds.

the office, but he did not address the other improprieties discovered by the auditor general. He had "not lost a single penny" of the Vatican's money, he said, and he claimed that his assertion had been validated by Cardinal Pell's Secretariat for the Economy.

There is no evidence that Müller had attempted to enrich himself with curial funds, and no criminal charges were brought against him. He and Cardinal Pell remained friends as the old ways of doing things in the Vatican were replaced by improved accounting practices, which this episode shows were pursued by Pell, for the good of the Church, without fear or favour.

Pell and his team uncovered many other instances of financial mismanagement, large and petty. They found that there was no inventory of the Vatican's near-priceless art collections, pieces of which adorned many departments and chapels around the city-state. Nor was there a complete list of Vatican-owned properties, and what they were earning, available. In December 2017, in the whistleblowing book *The Dictator Pope*, published under the pseudonym Marcantonio Colonna (the name of the commander of the papal flagship in the Battle of Lepanto in 1571), English historian Henry Sire detailed how eighty valuable properties in and around Rome, owned by the Canons of Saint Peter, a group of retired priests who assist at Masses and other services at Saint Peter's Basilica, "fell off the list" and were unaccounted for. Despite owning three hundred properties that should have been earning considerable rent, the canons were €700,000 in the red.[6] Pell confirmed the veracity of Sire's revelations. In August 2021, Pope Francis moved the financial management of the group to the Fabric of Saint Peter, which oversees Saint Peter's Basilica.[7] When Sire's book appeared, Pell said to an Australian priest, "Get it! Read it! Read it all. It's all true—and worse than he says."

Pell and his team also discovered that the cards allowing Vatican staff members to make purchases within the city-state—from petrol to luxury goods—without paying duties, sales tax, or Italy's hefty 22 percent value-added tax (VAT) far exceeded the number of eligible

[6] Marcantonio Colonna, *The Dictator Pope: The Inside Story of the Francis Papacy* (Washington, D.C.: Regnery, 2018), chap. 3.

[7] Hannah Brockhaus, "Pope Francis Makes Changes to the Vatican's Chapter of St. Peter", *Catholic News Agency*, August 28, 2021, https://www.catholicnewsagency.com/news/248806/pope-francis-makes-changes-to-the-vaticans-chapter-of-st-peter.

employees and their immediate family members. "George found there were fifty thousand cards for the three thousand staff", one of his Roman friends said. Pell closed more than four thousand Vatican Bank accounts held by people not entitled to them. And he reported two hundred of the owners to authorities, mainly on suspicion of money laundering. That swoop earned Pell dozens of enemies, inside and outside the Church. "George signed his ticket out of Rome when he started looking at those accounts and even murkier matters", a former colleague told me.

Financial corruption has dogged the Church for centuries. In more recent times, two notorious cases stand out. In 1974, the Holy See lost millions of dollars after the collapse of Franklin National Bank in New York. The controlling interest in Franklin was owned by Michele Sindona, who had been involved with the Vatican Bank since 1969. Tried and convicted for committing financial crimes and instigating murder, Sindona went to prison, where he died after drinking poisoned coffee. During the papacy of John Paul II, in 1981, Roberto Calvi was found guilty of illegally transferring millions of dollars to foreign countries while he was chairman of Banco Ambrosiano. Much of the money had been transferred through the Vatican Bank, one of Ambrosiano's largest shareholders. A year later, Ambrosiano collapsed, and Calvi's dead body was found hanging from Blackfriars Bridge in London. Without admitting to any wrongdoing, the Vatican Bank paid more than US$200 million in settlement fees to Ambrosiano's foreign creditors.

Early in his pontificate, Benedict XVI appointed Pell to the quaintly but aptly named Council of Cardinals for the Study of the Organizational and Economic Problems of the Holy See. In that role, Pell had access to many of the Vatican's financial reports and learned a great deal about its money problems. When he arrived in Rome to take the helm of the Secretariat for the Economy, he already had a fair idea of the challenges he would be facing.

And he already had seen how ugly staff conflicts could be. In 2012, after Benedict's butler Paolo Gabriele leaked some of his private papers to the press, Pell was one of a small group of cardinals who discussed the matter with the pope. The butler was jailed, then later released after being pardoned by Benedict, but great damage had been done to the reputation of the pope and the Church. The documents, splashed in the Italian newspapers, revealed many Vatican secrets, including tax problems, funding challenges, and sex-abuse scandals, as well as negotiations with some hard-line traditionalist rebels such as British-born Bishop Richard Williamson, a former member of the Society of Saint Pius X (SSPX) who deeply embarrassed the Vatican by denying the Holocaust shortly before he was brought back into communion with the pope. The secret papers lifted the lid on some serious issues and divisions inside the Church, not to mention the untrust-worthiness of some Vatican employees. Years earlier, a small group of cardinals, including Pell and Benedict's friend Joachim Meisner of Cologne, approached the pope to urge him to sack a top official (a senior cardinal) they did not trust. Benedict refused to hear their arguments and cut them short. Much as Pell had admired Benedict's scholarship and intellect, the cardinal had reservations about his judgement of personnel. Some of Pell's friends, ironically, worried that his own tendency to see the best in people sometimes clouded his judgement in appointing and promoting individuals who occasionally let him down, badly.

When Pell arrived in Rome to take charge of the Vatican's finances on March 31, 2014, he expected to meet resistance. He was intensely annoyed, but not very surprised, when his office was broken into during his first week on the job. His office was in Torre de San Giovanni, a tower built around 800 on a small hilltop at the back of the Vatican Gardens. Despite its age, the tower, used by Pope John XXIII as a retreat in the early 1960s, was decked out in 1960s décor. The building was also surrounded by security cameras. Regular checks revealed listening devices in Pell's office, on his telephones and those of his staff. (Bugs were also discovered on his home telephone at Domus Australia.) Later in 2014, when Pell and accountant Danny Casey, his former business manager from the Archdiocese of Sydney who led the project management office in the Secretariat for the Economy, began investigating a €50 million transaction involving two Vatican-owned hospitals and APSA, a car was fire-bombed outside the door of Casey's flat at 3:30 A.M. Casey and Pell suspected that a message for them had been intended by the arson, but they resolved to carry on.

Hospital finances were to be a major challenge for Pell and Casey throughout their time in Rome. In October 2017, a Vatican court found Giuseppe Profiti, the former president of Bambino Gesu, the

Vatican-owned children's hospital, guilty of abuse of office for using
€422,000 from the hospital's foundation to renovate the Vatican-
owned apartment of Cardinal Tarcisio Bertone, Benedict XVI's former secretary of state. In July 2023, *The Wall Street Journal* reported
that "over the past decade, senior Vatican officials became embroiled
in scandal over a €50m ($81m) loan used to purchase a bankrupt
Roman hospital run into the ground by fraudsters and embezzlers."[8]

Another attempt at intimidating Pell's staff was felt by an Italian
staffer. In late 2014, he was asked by a cardinal how many children
he had. Was it three? No, the man said, he had four children. The
cardinal then reminded the staffer that he and other cardinals would
still be around long after Pell and Casey had returned to Australia. The
staffer was unnerved. Few Vatican employees have forgotten the story
of fifteen-year-old Emanuela Orlandi, who disappeared in June 1983,
when her father was working for the Holy See and the family lived in
a Vatican apartment. The girl set out for a flute lesson and was never
seen again. Her unsolved disappearance, which has been blamed var-
iously on the mafia, international terrorists, and high-ranking Church
officials, was dramatized in the 2022 Netflix documentary *Vatican Girl*.

Despite efforts to stop Pell, his leadership skills came to the fore,
attracting several senior people from other departments who wanted
to work for him. They sensed that, at last, reform was in the offing
and that Pell would not be deterred by whatever obstacles were put
in his path. As Pell and his team began working with the different
dicasteries, the cardinal brought several English-speaking business and
financial experts from top international firms on board. He made
sure that language was not a barrier to communication; when non-
English speakers met with Pell's people, the cardinal ran the meetings
in Italian, drawing on the language skills he had acquired as a student at Propaganda Fide in the 1960s and which had improved over
the years during his service with the Congregation for the Doctrine
of the Faith, under the then-Cardinal Ratzinger in the 1980s, and
other congregations. Quarterly newsletters, in Italian and English,
kept Vatican staff abreast of progress in establishing better budgeting,
accounting, and reporting processes throughout the Holy See.

---

[8] Tim Busch, "The Vatican Can Clean Up Its Financial Act", *Wall Street Journal*,
July 25, 2023, https://www.wsj.com/articles/the-vatican-can-clean-up-its-financial-act-pope
-francis-becciu-pell-literacy-870133b5.

The July 2014 newsletter shows that in his first few weeks as prefect, Pell met with ten cardinals in charge of different Vatican departments: Cardinals Mauro Piacenza (Apostolic Penitentiary), Raymond Burke (Apostolic Signatura), Gerhard Müller (Congregation for the Doctrine of the Faith), João Braz de Aviz (Consecrated Life), Leonardo Sandri (Eastern Churches), Beniamino Stella (Clergy), Kurt Koch (Christian Unity), Raffaele Farina (Vatican Archivist), Francesco Coccopalmerio (Legislative Texts), Peter Turkson (Justice and Peace), and Antonio Maria Veglio (Migrants and Itinerant Peoples). They would be consulted about the 2015 budget, the newsletter said, but once it was finalized, they would not be authorized to exceed it, although alternative forms of supplementary income should be considered.

A major part of Pell's job was straightforward (or should have been straightforward)—quantifying the Vatican's assets, liabilities, revenues, and expenses. Eight months into the job, the cardinal was asked by *The Catholic Herald* in London to write about his findings, and the essay drew widespread comment in the international financial press. The good news, he revealed, was that the Vatican's financial position was "much healthier than it seemed, because some hundreds of millions of euros were tucked away in particular sectional accounts and did not appear on the balance sheet." The funds discovered "off the books" amounted to about €1 billion.[9]

Not everyone concerned seemed happy for the information to emerge. A few days later, in his Christmas address to Vatican cardinals, Pope Francis listed what he regarded as the fifteen "ailments of the Curia". In what could have been a slap at Pell's public revelation about the billion euros, Francis complained about defaming or discrediting others "even in newspapers or magazines, to show themselves as more capable ... in the name of justice and transparency".[10] The Vatican later insisted that the money referred to by Pell had not been hidden, but had been kept by the Secretariat of State for "special projects" without appearing on the Vatican's books. Some

---

[9] Cardinal George Pell, *Catholic Herald* magazine, December 5, 2014, quoted in "We've Discovered Hundreds of Millions of Euros Off the Vatican's Balance Sheet, Says Cardinal", *Catholic Herald*, December 3, 2014, https://catholicherald.co.uk/weve-discovered-hundreds -of-millions-of-euros-off-the-vaticans-balance-sheet-says-cardinal/.

[10] Nicole Winfield, Associated Press, "Pope Francis: Merry Christmas, Power-Hungry Hypocrites", *Detroit Free Press*, December 22, 2014, https://www.freep.com/story/news /world/2014/12/22/pope-francis-vatican-holy-see/20759447/.

believe the discovery had adverse consequences for Pell. "By the time George and his team found the 1.2 billion Euro that was not properly accounted for, his fate was sealed", David Pell said in his eulogy at his brother's funeral in Sydney.[11]

The relationship between Pope Francis and Pell was complicated by the fact that they were on different pages regarding the approach to take with contested Church teachings. Vatican insiders say that another unhelpful fact was that, as an Argentinian, Francis has an instinctive suspicion of "Anglos", which included Australians. This suspicion has been shaped by centuries of not-always-friendly relations between Spanish-speaking and English-speaking countries. A recent example of this was the 1982 war over the Falkland Islands, a U.K. territory three hundred miles off the coast of Argentina. At a memorial Mass in Buenos Aires marking the thirtieth anniversary of the Falklands conflict, Cardinal Jorge Bergoglio told the congregation that they had come together to "pray for those who have fallen, the sons of our homeland who went out to defend their mother country, to reclaim what is theirs of the homeland, that which was usurped from them."[12]

In the Italian-dominated Vatican City, Pell was seen as an outsider from the moment he arrived. His friend Bishop Peter Elliott from Melbourne visited Rome around the time that Pell took charge at the Secretariat for the Economy, and he encountered an attitude that Pell would soon know very well. During lunch with a monsignor, when Elliott mentioned Pell, the man's previously affable demeanour changed to outright hostility. "We have our own way of doing things", he said. "We don't need foreigners."

The pope met regularly with Pell, and the two conversed in Italian, but sometimes cultural differences proved a barrier. On one occasion, Pell told Francis that a particular financial outrage "*prenda la torta*" (takes the cake). "*Che torta?*" (What cake?) Francis replied in confusion. Pell was annoyed by the chair provided for him when he first met with Francis. It was so low that Pell struggled to stand up. "Me bottom was

[11] Staff writers, "David Pell's Eulogy for Cardinal Pell: A Good and Holy Man, and a Proud Australian", *Catholic Weekly*, February 2, 2023, https://www.catholicweekly.com.au /david-pells-eulogy-for-cardinal-pell-a-good-and-holy-man-and-a-proud-australian/.

[12] Sorcha Pollak, "Pope Francis Criticized Britain over Falkland Islands", *Time*, March 14, 2013, https://world.time.com/2013/03/14/pope-francis-criticized-britain-over-falkland-islands.

almost on the floor", he told a friend in exasperation. He complained to the pope, and a proper chair was ready for their next meeting.

Although cultural differences were real, according to Pell's prison writings the Anglo-Latin divide was used as an excuse to prevent the implementation of international accounting principles inside the Vatican. When the Secretariat of State cancelled an audit of Vatican finances by PricewaterhouseCoopers in 2016, they said there had been a "clash of mentalities" between those defending the sovereignty of the Holy See and those who took a "company-like" position, Pell wrote. "An antipathy to 'Anglo' methods, toward those who would 'turn the Church into a business', also played well." But, Pell, said, "the real and underlying issue was fear of the truth, of the revelation of the mess that had been concealed.... The fact that many, if not most, Western governments were using standards similar to those we proposed (we had drawn on Singapore's models) cut no ice at all."[13]

A layman who has worked in Vatican finances for years said the biggest problem facing Pell was obstruction by those who resisted financial reform.

Cardinal Pell was surrounded by individuals who were playing both sides from the middle as well as two-faced traitors at various levels. Numerous of his dicastery's staffers came from APSA, the structure to which they remained loyal, although they were on the Secretariat for the Economy payroll. These individuals, including people Cardinal Pell thought he could trust, were basically loyal to the "old guard", which they believed would sooner or later win back control of the Vatican and expel the reformist army, which did indeed ultimately happen. Various of these people covertly strove to hamstring [Pell's] programs while keeping his adversaries informed of his moves.

Pope Francis should have removed and replaced the people blocking the reforms he asked Pell to make, the official said. Instead, he

signed one deleterious executive order (motu proprio) after another, including granting to APSA the authority to "restructure itself" in 2014, effectively empowering them to exclude the prefect of the

[13] George Pell, *Prison Journal*, vol. 2, *The State Court Rejects the Appeal* (San Francisco: Ignatius Press, 2021), p. 297.

Secretariat for the Economy, Cardinal Pell, and entrusting the restructuring project to the exact same people that got the Vatican into trouble to start with, people who should have been fired on the spot for all their wrongdoing, perhaps even arrested. This allowed APSA to erect even taller barriers to keep out those charged with its control and shield the identity of numerous ciphered accounts held in Switzerland for Vatican officials and friends. The pope's ill-advised actions, and his inaction where action was needed, effectively fostered the re-emergence of the old guard and its return to power.

A proposal by Pell that Francis did approve was the June 2015 appointment of Libero Milone as the Vatican's first internal auditor general, on a five-year contract. The Dutch-born, English-educated former CEO of Deloitte in Italy speaks English and Italian. A member of the Institute of Chartered Accountants in England and Wales, Milone had been part of the global Deloitte management team based in New York for five years. Pell chose well. He knew he was hiring a very qualified individual with enough experience in global auditing to avoid being manipulated or having the wool pulled over his eyes by Vatican insiders resisting reform.

After the Secretariat of State suspended the audit by PricewaterhouseCoopers (PwC) in 2016, Milone's work became even more crucial. A statement from Pell's office at the time of the PwC suspension said the cardinal was "surprised" that the audit had been stopped and anticipated that it would resume "after discussions and clarification of some issues".[14] It was a reasonable assumption given that an independent, external audit in accordance with international accounting standards had been one of the clear demands of Pope Francis. It had also been a public item of Vatican policy for three years and explicitly approved by the Council for the Economy. It did not work out the way Pell envisaged, however. The audit was not resumed. As Pell wrote in a memo the following year, the suspension of the PwC external audit "projected negative publicity everywhere in the financial world, damaged the reputation of the Vatican, and planted seeds of doubt about the Holy Father's commitment to the reforms. It was seen by the world for what it was, and it paints a grim

[14] "Vatican Suspends PwC Audit", *Reuters*, April 21, 2016, https://www.reuters.com/article/idUSKCN0XI2G7/.

prospect when placed together with the present harassment of the Auditor General."

Even with Milone in place as an ally, Pell found that the lack of collaboration and cooperation between the Secretariat of State and the Secretariat for the Economy was a fundamental flaw in the reform process. At one stage, the relationship became so fraught that the Secretariat of State refused to allocate funds to the Office of the Auditor General and to the Secretariat for the Economy. As Pell complained in an internal memo to colleagues in April 2017, the lack of funds meant that they were unable to pay their own bills autonomously and had to depend on APSA, one of the agencies they were charged with overseeing, for funds. The financial independence of the Secretariat for the economy and the auditor general would have helped the Vatican comply with international "best practices", Pell noted in the same memo. The Secretariat of State's refusal to follow international best accounting practices was problematic. "The Holy Father's choice to charge the Office of the Auditor General with the task of the audit of the single financial statements of Vatican Entities and of the consolidated financial statement of the Holy See, should now be supported, entrusting the Office of the Auditor General (OAG) with all necessary powers to assure the desired result within the timeframe illustrated by Cardinal Marx", Pell wrote.

Further delays in implementing accounting reforms would be catastrophic, Pell warned. As his investigations proceeded, he told friends that the money trail was increasingly leading him to "look north" (to Switzerland). The key problem, one curial official said, was that the pope "essentially denied the secretariat the needed independence from other Vatican structures still controlled by corrupt leadership".

Francis and Pell met regularly, the official said, but Francis also met, and dined with, those who opposed the financial reforms and listened to their complaints about the way Pell was going about things. In staff debriefings following his meetings with the pope, Pell often appeared perplexed by his enigmatic conduct. Newcomers to the Vatican were shocked and dismayed; those with experience of the place, less so.

"It seemed increasingly evident that the pope was not fully levelling with His Eminence", a long-serving official said. In 2014, at Pell's request, the official met with the pope. "I personally told him to his face that the document that he signed for APSA was a

screw-up, that he mustn't sign any more of these documents orig-
inating from old guard circles. He understood, but I had this eerie
feeling in my stomach that the old guard bastards somehow had him
on strings. Time told me that I was right." Pell was amazed that the
pope talked with the man for an hour when he tended to dismiss
many visitors after five minutes, the official said, adding, "I think
that [the pope] was genuinely interested in knowing more about the
murky waters in which he had launched his boat, and since I had
been there for years my intel helped him. What his final objective
was remains a mystery."

"The Vatican is like a small village, nothing that happens is missed,
and word gets around fast", a long-time staffer told me. Francis'
choice of dining companions and the decisions he made after listening
to their advice caused him and other Vatican staff members to wonder "if we were finally witnessing the end of the 'bad old days' as the
cardinal referred to them, or whether the old guard would re-emerge
victorious and toss the reformists back into the sea." Some predicted
the latter and understandably tried to remain on good terms with the
men they expected to stay in power. One staffer who grew fond of
Pell said that the cardinal "did not fool himself into thinking that he
was parachuting into a picnic grounds; he was prepared for a jungle,
but not a cesspool! I'll never forget him; he was so good to me."

It didn't take Pell long to figure out that when it came to some
Vatican dealings, "cesspool" was not an exaggeration. When his
brother, David, an experienced accountant, visited him in Rome,
Pell told him he detected many allegedly serious fraud issues. "I suggested that laypeople were involved", David recalled. "But he said
no, but clergy were. I expressed disbelief, and he added that it went
as far up as the red hat!"

Establishing internationally accepted standards of accountability
and transparency was Pell and Casey's priority. What they wanted
to avoid was any repeat of an incident that occurred in late 2014
when an official from one Vatican department arrived with the "sign
page" for a major transaction, without the accompanying 650-page
contract. Both Pell and Casey refused to sign it. They were even less
inclined to do so after two staff members, both qualified accountants,
had divvied up the pages and perused them overnight, concluding
that the contract was a bad deal for the Church.

The now infamous Sloane Avenue property in London was another bad deal. The purchase of the building got past Pell and Casey without their knowledge due to accounting and finance methods that shielded the transaction from view. It was bought in stages from 2014 to 2018 for €200 million, but payments to brokers and creditors raised the total investment to €350 million, which prompted a financial investigation. The Vatican lost more than €200 million when it sold the property in 2022, according to the Demos memo.

Early on in his time in Rome, Pell put a proposition to Francis—that the proportion of the Peter's Pence collection diverted to administration costs be reduced over three years, to 75, 50, and then 25 percent. Apart from delivering more funds to the poor, such a step would have forced the issue on reform and strengthened the need to know where investments were and how they were being managed. Pell believed that using Peter's Pence to keep the Holy See afloat was masking systemic corruption and financial mismanagement in the Vatican.

The Secretariat of State, with the support of three cardinals, objected to Pell's plan. They won the day with the Holy Father, despite the very public position he had taken about the need for the Church to focus on the poor. For Pell, it was hard to reconcile. Without losing his temper, he made his disgust plain to Francis, who nevertheless refused to give away more of the alms collected by the Holy See. Why he did so is impossible to know, but the reason was not likely to have been mistrust of Pell. When an Australian bishop discussed George Pell with Francis, the pope poked him in the chest and said, "He's an honest man", said David Pell in his eulogy at his brother's funeral.[15]

On June 8, 2016, Pell turned seventy-five, the age at which all bishops submit their resignations to the Holy Father. Francis indicated that he wanted Pell to stay on until 2019. He was making progress, and Francis knew it. He also needed Pell's highly respected standing in international financial circles if the Vatican's lost credibility was to be restored. Persisting was difficult, however. Danny Casey said that, whenever he returned to Rome from a break, he felt as though he were "re-entering a war zone".

A year later, in June 2017, just days before Cardinal Pell returned to Australia to face sex-abuse charges, Milone was forced to resign

[15] "David Pell's Eulogy".

after an extraordinary raid on his office by Vatican police and firemen, despite the office being on Italian, not Vatican, territory. The men burst in unexpectedly, confiscating electronic equipment and forcing open the safe with axes, crowbars, sledgehammers, chisels, and power-drills. Milone was threatened with prosecution for criminal activity if he did not leave his position.

Speaking to media organisations in September that year, Milone said the raid and his forced resignation were intended to slow down Pope Francis' efforts at financial reform.[16] But the Holy See's then-deputy secretary of state, Archbishop Giovanni Angelo Becciu, said Milone's claims were "false and unjustified". "He went against all the rules and was spying on the private lives of his superiors and staff, including me", Becciu said. "If he had not agreed to resign, we would have prosecuted him." Domenico Giani, the Vatican's police chief (who resigned in October 2019), said there had been "overwhelming evidence" against Milone that had justified the raid. Despite many requests from Milone's lawyers, it was not produced. In conversation, Pell told friends that the "spying" was merely the normal investigations of an auditor.

In November 2022, Milone and his former deputy at the Vatican, Ferruccio Panicco, filed a lawsuit against the Holy See for breach of contract, loss of earnings, damage to reputation, and moral damage to them and their families caused by their being unlawfully accused of crimes and threatened with prosecution if they did not resign in 2017. In an interview with *The Australian* Milone said he would not be intimidated or silenced by powers in the Vatican who he thinks behave like the "mafia and use every method including blackmail and dirty dossiers" to impede financial reform.[17] The suit sought €9 million in compensation. In addition to the damages listed in the suit, Panicco accused the Vatican of delaying his cancer treatments. He had been monitored regularly and treated by Vatican medical teams, but this stopped abruptly after his forced resignation. That was because his personal medical records, which he had kept in his office, were taken in the raid. Panicco died of cancer in June 2023.

---

[16] Philip Pullella, "Auditor Says He Was Forced to Quit Vatican after Finding Irregularities", *Reuters*, September 23, 2017, https://www.reuters.com/article/idUSKCN1BZ03Q/.

[17] Paola Totaro, "Church Sins, Secrets Exposed in Battle with Vatican 'Mafia'", *The Australian*, November 10, 2022.

On January 24, 2024, a Vatican tribunal rejected Milone's lawsuit and ordered him to pay almost €50,000 in legal fees, of which €24,668.00 should be paid "to the Secretariat of State of the Holy See and €24,668 to the Office of the Auditor General". Panicco's estate was ordered to repay €64,140 with €32,070 earmarked for the Secretariat of State and €32,070 to the Office of the Auditor General. The judgement stated that after "careful examination" any suggestion that the Secretariat of State was involved in Milone's dismissal "must be excluded". Milone has appealed the decision.

Milone has suggested that the timing of the raid and the sexual assault charges against Pell was no mere coincidence. "Maybe there is a connection between getting me out and his return to Australia [to face charges].... Our dates of exit were basically the same", he said. Pell, he added, was "the victim of a real, villainous, and infamous conspiracy" to derail the financial reform that was underway.[18]

Milone also mentioned a financial irregularity Pell and his team had discovered, this one concerning a property on High Street in Kensington, London. "In the Kensington transaction almost €100 million was transferred out of an APSA Swiss bank account that ended up in a Jersey, Channel Islands, bank account. Despite his persistent efforts, well within his right to know, to his dying day Pell never knew the identity of the final beneficiary of this sale", Milone said, which was a violation of an international accounting rule intended to prevent money laundering. His efforts to bring Vatican bookkeeping into the light were "blocked in every way", he said. "In modern countries, if audits and financial investigations are blocked, it is deemed a crime and, if proven, those responsible go to jail."

The person who went to jail, however, was Cardinal Pell.

[18] Paola Totaro, "George Pell Was Trapped in a 'Vatican conspiracy'", *The Australian*, November 10, 2022.

5

Child of the Trinity

George Pell was born in Ballarat, Victoria, on Trinity Sunday, June 8, 1941. The baby's father, George Arthur Pell, manager of the Gordon Gold Mine outside Ballarat, was thirty-four; his mother, Margaret Lillian Burke, was thirty-seven. They had met in Ballarat in 1938 and were married in April 1939, in Saint Alipius Church, Ballarat East. George Arthur was a nonattending, nominal member of the Church of England and a fee-paying, nonattending Mason. Margaret was a devoted Catholic. In those pre-ecumenical days, mixed marriages were not contracted in front of the altar, but in the sacristy. Margaret and George Arthur were strong, interesting characters. Like most of their contemporaries, neither had the chance to finish secondary school. From all accounts, they were very well suited.

The Pell ancestors were from Leicestershire in England. George Arthur was one of six children and grew up in Western Australia. He worked in Kalgoorlie's gold mines and came east with a cousin in 1936 for the Melbourne Cup, Australia's biggest annual horse race, and stayed. His cousin was a Temby, a famous West Australian racing family. George Arthur was an excellent athlete—captain of Perth City Surf Life Saving Club, Western Australian heavyweight boxing champion, and at one stage a leading contender for the heavyweight boxing championship of the British Empire. He boxed under the name "Bell" because his mother did not approve. Whether she eventually found out was a matter of family conjecture. His youngest son, David Pell, who has the newspaper cuttings, said one article described George Arthur's last fight as "the most gruesome and bloodiest fight seen in the West Perth Stadium"—he won by a knockout in the twelfth round. His photo appeared in the American *Ring* magazine—as a "great white hope"!

Margaret Lillian, known as Lil, was of Irish descent and the fifth of twelve children of Paddy and Catherine Burke. Within the family, she was regarded as a born leader. Staunch piety was a Burke family trait. One of the cardinal's aunts was baptised with the second name of "Mannix" in honour of the long-serving Melbourne archbishop, Doctor Daniel Mannix, whose portrait hung on the wall of the Pell home. Pell later recalled some of the family's Lenten observances: "One of my great-grandmothers, a strong Irish Australian Catholic, used to fast on black tea with bread and dripping on every Friday in Lent." The less heroic, he admitted, might only give up chocolates. "I can remember sitting poised, with a box of chocolates on my knees, waiting for the fast to end at midday on Holy Saturday."

Baby George was not his parents' first child. Twins, a boy and a girl, had been born and died the year before, in 1940, so it was hardly surprising that George received considerable affection. He was graced with only one Christian name because his mother thought one so very English name was quite enough. The second or third name he would have been given—Berkeley—was also quintessentially English, after his paternal great-great-grandmother, formerly Miss Elizabeth Berkeley. Miss Berkeley, the daughter of a Protestant doctor, Thomas Berkeley, from Skibbereen in Ireland, married Joseph Thompson in Saint James' Anglican Church, Sydney, in November 1840. "My paternal grandmother was pressuring my mother that I should be George Something Berkeley Pell, and Mother felt that George was enough for that tradition, so they couldn't agree on other names, so they just left it at George."

When George was born, Irish-born Doctor Daniel Mannix was twenty-four years into his reign as archbishop of Melbourne, which extended from 1917 to his death in 1963 at the age of ninety-nine. Across the world, Karol Wojtyła, twenty-one, was a forced labourer shoveling limestone in a quarry in Nazi-occupied Poland. In Germany, fourteen-year-old Joseph Ratzinger, against his will, was conscripted into the Hitler Youth. The ascetic Eugenio Pacelli was in his second year as Pope Pius XII.

The country town of Ballarat, seventy-one miles northwest of Melbourne, then had a population of fewer than fifty thousand. The Pell family home at 66 Rowe Street was a solid, weatherboard house with an iron roof and attractive, intricate iron lace decorating the front. Paddy Burke, the cardinal's grandfather, who worked in the local railways, had built the house, adding some rooms on in stages. He called it Innisfail, an affectionate name the Irish sometimes use for their homeland. The Pells shared the home with Margaret's sister, Molly Burke. It stands on a large corner block, then as now an average home in an average part of town, neither poor nor palatial.

During the war, George Arthur was in the Construction Corps of the Australian Defence Force, using his expertise with explosives and mining. When his daughter, Margaret, was born in 1944, he was underwater in Williamstown, Melbourne, blowing up a sunken steamship, the SS *Kakarriki*. From all accounts, David Pell relates, his father had an interesting life:

> He was one of the last to evacuate off Misima Island, in the Milne Bay Province of Papua New Guinea, during the Second World War. He was not military. The locals would come and tell them that the Japs had been there during the night, so he was going—boat ticket or not. No one dared to argue with him or tried to stop him getting on; he sat up on deck for a couple of nights with Philip Strong, the then Anglican bishop of New Guinea and later archbishop of Brisbane. When they pulled into the Port of Townsville, no one was to be seen. Then Dad saw a head pop around the corner of the shed, and he yelled out, "We are bloody Aussies", and they came out from everywhere. They thought it was the Japanese. Mum did a fine job of curbing the adventure boy!

Margaret and her children were always Sunday Mass-goers and said the Rosary at home every day. They attended the Novena to Our Lady of Perpetual Help every Wednesday night at the cathedral in Ballarat, which would often be packed. On Saturday afternoons, at least once a month when they were old enough, the Pell children would ride their bikes to the local church for confession. They also attended First Friday and First Saturday Masses with their mother.

At one side of the house at Rowe Street, a small opening led down to a cool area that the Pells called "the cellar". On hot summer Sundays, after Mass, the Pells would gather here with friends and relatives for a "Catholic" hour. This was nothing to do with religion. It meant hot scones and butter, with beer for the adults, and lots of lively conversation before the traditional Sunday roast lunch.

The Pell and Burke families were close. In the days before professional spin doctors, Pell's Uncle Harry Burke was part of Liberal Premier Tom Holloway's campaign team and wrote many of his speeches. He also wrote to newspapers under the Demos pseudonym that his nephew made famous more than sixty years later in Rome. "He was a most lovely man", Pell recalled in 2001. "For years and years, I used to go up and talk politics with him and listen to him."

Pell's birth date, June 8, 1941, was Trinity Sunday that year. June 8 in the Catholic calendar is also the feast of Saint Medard (d. 560), a French bishop whose story bears a passing resemblance to Pell's. From all accounts, Medard was a pious youth and an excellent scholar, and after he became a priest he encouraged young people of that time to study and take an interest in spiritual matters. He is also the patron saint for, among other things, toothaches and brewers. George Pell, a publican's son who missed a lot of school when very young due to a growth under his chin, possibly caused by the filling of a baby tooth, also showed early signs of being a good scholar as well as a sportsman. While he had no interest in being a priest until his final year at school, one of his former teachers remembered he was prayerful and involved in sodalities (prayer groups) at school.

The cardinal's father was a supporter of the Liberal Party, which had been founded by Robert Menzies in 1944 as an anti-socialist, pro–private enterprise party. His mother leaned to the old Labor Party, initially, but like many Catholics of the time, she sided strongly with the Democratic Labor Party when it formed in the mid-1950s under the leadership of the brilliant Melbourne Catholic lawyer B. A. Santamaria.

Santamaria and his supporters, who formed what was known as "The Movement", precipitated a major split in the Australian Labor Party over concerns about rising Communist influence in the trade unions and, through them, the party. The split, which shaped Australian politics for decades, led to the formation of the Democratic Labor Party (DLP), a small influential party in several Australian states that backed the Liberal government in the Senate, Australia's upper house. By siphoning votes away from the Labor Party, the DLP kept them out of office nationally until 1972. The DLP also used its leverage in the Senate to lobby successfully for government assistance for

Catholic schools. George Pell's parents thought Santamaria "had style and wit"; they regarded him as "somebody to be admired". Like many "mixed marriage" couples, the Pells found that the Labor split brought them closer together politically.

By today's standards, children in country Australia in the 1940s and 1950s lived carefree lives. In Ballarat, George and sister Margaret and their friends rolled down Black Hill behind their home in a billy cart, paddled in Yarrawee Creek, rode their bikes around town, and explored far and wide. They played games with their cousins, their neighbours, and their schoolmates, with Paddy, the family's collie/ heeler tagging along. Television did not arrive until George was fifteen. For entertainment, his mother, who had an excellent singing voice, used to lead sing-alongs around the piano.

George's first school was Loreto Convent, Ballarat, where he made his First Communion in 1948. Unlike most future priests of his generation, he was never an altar boy because of a childhood illness that at one point became so severe his parents feared for his life. He had an abscess or growth in his throat and was ill for several years. His sister, Margaret, remembered that over the space of several years he underwent the ordeal of twenty-four operations—several of them major ones—to remove the growth, which kept recurring. The boy was taken to every available specialist. All the while, his mother prayed to Saint Blaise, the patron saint of sore throats. "When he was seven, eight, and nine, he had to wear a poultice tied around his head so it was pressed up against his throat", Margaret said. "I would fight his battles for him when kids would sling off and laugh at him." (Perhaps this was where his hide, which friends and foes claimed was "several rhinoceroses thick", developed.) "Finally, a Dr. Greening did the last operation and took out what looked like a little plant with roots", Margaret added, "and he recovered and never had any problems again." Doctors attributed the problematic growth to the filling in a rotten baby tooth that should have been left alone. Something poisonous from the filling had seeped down into the gum and throat. Despite missing a lot of school, George had no problem keeping up with his classmates. During his illness, he became an avid reader and read voraciously for the rest of his life.

Shortly after George recovered, his brother, David, was born in 1951. A major crash in the value of mining company shares in 1949/1950 had compelled George Arthur to leave the mining industry and venture into the hotel business. The family left Rowe Street and moved to the Cattle Yards Inn. Running the place was a baptism of fire, especially for the parents, as they hosted large numbers of customers and guests during regular cattle and sheep sale days. During these busy times, George and Margaret babysat their little brother. When David was two or three years old, his older siblings decided that it was safe for the three of them to walk along the top on the six-foot-high railings surrounding the sale yards, which were across the road from the hotel. "George dropped down, and I followed, [landing] on my head!" David recalled.

The family moved to the Royal Oak Hotel, which was a step up from the Cattle Yards Inn but still very hard work. George Arthur and Lil, both straight shooters, were able to develop a "congregation" of regular customers. The hotel was home to the family for twenty-three years, and the children grew up with an appreciation that it was the customers who allowed them to pay the bills. The children also owed a great debt to Auntie Molly. The pub could not have survived without her helping with the kids and filling in at the pub during George Arthur's lunchtimes.

By that stage, George was embarking on a vital stage of his life, as a student at the school that has produced more Catholic priests than any other in Australia, Saint Patrick's Christian Brothers College, Ballarat. One of the classmates who started with him in grade five was Michael Mason, who became Father Michael Mason, C.S.s.R., a Redemptorist priest who later achieved a Ph.D. in sociology. Mason remembered the ten-year-old George as big for his age, a good scholar, and prominent because of his prowess at running and football. They were playmates. George was a responsible kind of boy and, unlike many of his friends, not a troublemaker. "Neither parent would have been very tolerant of mischief" was Mason's impression.

In the Pell family, it was taken for granted that Margaret would have the same educational opportunities as her brothers. Their mother was keen for her children to learn music. George studied piano and sang in competitions. As an adult he enjoyed many concerts and operas at the Sydney Opera House and occasionally lamented how wonderful it would have been to be born with the singing voice of Luciano Pavarotti. Margaret learned piano and violin as a child, with a talent that took her, at a very young age, to the top of her field in the first violin section of the Melbourne Symphony Orchestra, where she stayed for thirty years.

When Michael Mason first knew George, the family was running the Cattleyards Inn, opposite the Ballarat saleyards: "They were very hard-working, really, that's what struck you. I never encountered the Pells sitting around. It was the nature of the work; it was from morning to late at night. They were always bustling; there were always a lot of things to do around the place." He remembers the primary-school-aged George helping out in the bar on Saturdays. "I remember going in there, and he'd be serving people, and I remember thinking, 'Crikey, this would be a pretty scary place to work.' The Cattleyards was a very old pub, right opposite the saleyards. There'd be farmers and people like that."

Later, the Royal Oak in Raglin Street South was close to an area where most people worked in the nearby woolen mills. "It was definitely very working class", Mason recalls. "George was obviously very well accepted, and later when Marg was a bit older they used to help out many times. I'd go down there to play chess. He'd be allowed to come out, and we'd go out on our bikes and muck around." For the children, part of pub life was knowing who drank what, who had had too much and would not be served, and what to do about it. Such experiences gave Pell an ease at mixing with people.

George's secondary school, Saint Patrick's, is set in extensive, leafy grounds on Sturt Street at the western edge of Ballarat. Since its opening in 1893, more than 310 graduates of the college have been ordained priests. It is the alma mater of five bishops—Pell; his predecessor as archbishop of Melbourne, Sir Frank Little; retired Brisbane bishops Brian Finnigan and Joseph Oudeman; and Sandhurst bishop Shane Mackinlay. Little was dux, the best academic student in the school, in 1942; Mackinlay was dux in 1982. While Saint Patrick's was always a sports-oriented school, the yearbooks from the 1950s show that the principal of the time, Brother John Lynch, also put strong emphasis on academic laurels, public speaking, cultural events, and music appreciation. Gilbert and Sullivan operettas were favourites. The 1958 Saint Patrick's production of *The Mikado* featured George Pell as Pooh-Bah.

While the vigorous masculinity of Saint Patrick's might have crushed more timid or indifferent students, it suited Pell perfectly, as the honour boards around the school demonstrate: College Captain 1959, Rev. Br. D. G. Purton Oratory Award 1958 & 1959, Cadet

Corps Under Officer.... In a highly competitive school, Pell was sprint champion from his under-twelve year through to under-sixteen, when pulled muscles took their toll. He made the athletics team every year and was a good long-jumper and shot-putter. He also played cricket and rowed, but he felt a bit awkward as an oarsman. Later, he became a good tennis player and swimmer.

But the only real game in Sturt Street and in George's schoolboy heart was football, of the Australian Rules variety, a fast-paced game with eighteen players a side in which points are scored for kicking goals rather than for scoring tries as in rugby. An outsider can perhaps begin to understand what the sport meant at Saint Pat's from Gerard Ryan's book *Ecka Dora*, the history of the 1st XVIII football team at the school. The book talks about "the aura" of the 1st XVIII as small boys stood at the front of the assembly watching the senior students being presented with their team jumpers (sweaters) and listening to the headmaster speak about "the responsibility these young men have in upholding the tradition of the College". No student, Ryan contended, could have gone through Saint Patrick's without being "imbued with some of the spirit" of the team.[1] In 1956, when he was in year 10, George joined the 1st XVIII. In photos on the college walls, he stands in the centre of the back row of the team photograph from that year—as tall and strong as the older boys, but with a younger face than theirs. In a legendary football school at a legendary time, George Pell played as ruckman for four years, from 1956 to 1959. Part of his role in the game was to punch the ball out. Another former fellow pupil, Paul Bongiorno, Network Ten's former political editor, remembered that George could punch the ball out "as far as some people could kick it". Brother William Theodore O'Malley coached the team for twenty years, including the time George was on it. In a newspaper tribute to O'Malley in 2000, Pell wrote:

> His teams were full of confidence, fight and spirit, and he was capable of eloquent flights of oratory in tight matches, which frequently called on the memories of past victories and the need for heroism and sacrifice. In retrospect, many of us took it a bit too seriously, but it

[1] Gerard Ryan, *"Ecka Dora": St Patrick's College 1st XVIII: 1893–1993* (Ballarat: Board of St Patrick's College Ballarat, n.d.), p. 3.

was a marvellous experience. We learnt to win, believe in ourselves and in the romance of tradition. I would not have missed it. Barry Richardson, the Richmond champion of the 1960s and 1970s, found the spirit at Richmond an anti-climax, something less, after St Pat's College football.[2]

Old Bill, as O'Malley was known out of earshot, kept a firm hand on his players. Catching the ball with one hand was strictly forbidden—which is exactly what George Pell did one day at practice. Old Bill angrily marched him off the field for the rest of the session, lecturing him all the way to the sidelines. "I think old Bill thought George was being a bit of a lair, showing off a bit, but the catch was freakish", one onlooker remembered. Up to 1954, when it lost in the finals to neighbouring Ballarat College, Saint Patrick's had not lost even a game in the Ballarat public schools premiership competition for forty-nine years. The team was back on top the following year and remained there during George Pell's playing days. George later played Aussie Rules at the seminary at Werribee, as a student and subsequently as the rector. As rector, his students and colleagues (both supporters and detractors) were struck by how fast and strongly he played.

A large glass cabinet packed with football memorabilia has long had pride of place in Saint Patrick's foyer. It contains a football or two, mementos of vital games through the years, and a large photograph of Brother O'Malley and his list of the "best twenty players" from his time as football master, 1928 to 1959. Along with names of subsequent professionals such as Frank Hickey (Fitzroy), John James (Carlton), Frank Drum (Richmond), Less Mogg (North Melbourne), Kevin Hogan (Richmond), Brian Molony (Saint Kilda), Bill Drake (Footscray), Brian Gleeson (Saint Kilda), and Jack Cunningham (Hawthorn) are several who became priests, including George Pell. "Some say being named in such a team was a boost to my priesthood. Others, more unkindly, said being a priest helped my chance of being named in the team", Pell once said. Two of the players listed—John James and Brian Gleeson from the class of 1952—later won Brownlow Medals (for being the fairest and best player in the Australian Football League).

---

[2] George Pell, *The Age*, December 29, 2000.

In 1959, George Pell was offered a professional contract by Richmond, which he signed. Not surprisingly, his father was ecstatic. At that point, George was completing year twelve for the second time, this time living at the school as a boarder. The first time around, excellent academic results, especially in French, Latin, history, and English, meant he had been offered a scholarship to study law at Melbourne University. But he decided to repeat year twelve and do physics and chemistry with a view to becoming a doctor. Repeating year twelve was not unusual at that time, when as many as a quarter of the students, uncertain of what tertiary courses to pursue, did the same thing. Under the public exam system, different books were set for English each year, and George, being attached to school and sport, found "doing a second year of school quite convenient". But he did not enjoy studying science.

The school's yearbooks from the late 1950s show that scholastic results in public exams "were the best for some time". One of Saint Patrick's Latin teachers, Brother Lou Williams, nicknamed "Chesty", was regarded as a genius by his students for the way he encouraged students to piece together their own translations of the set Latin texts rather than learning off translations written by others. By the time the exam came around, students were proficient and excelled in the subject. This was to stand Pell in good stead a few years later in Rome, grappling with textbooks and lectures in Latin.

In George's day, Saint Patrick's had few academic failures. Brother O'Malley, for example, taught year ten Intermediate A, comprising students taking Latin and French, and he prided himself on his class' success in the government-supervised external exams. Pell's recollections of O'Malley were an insight into his schooldays:

Classes began about 8:15 or 8:30 A.M., with an oral test in the section of a Latin author to be learnt overnight. Julius Caesar's Gallic Wars was one such. One miss and you were sent to the line, and a second miss meant one cut with the strap [something Pell admits he, like all his classmates, received "many times"]. Although Brother Bill mellowed with the years, he remained in charge until his last year of teaching, as (former Victorian Labor Premier) Steve Bracks reminded me a little ruefully. (He was in Inter A in that year.)

Old Bill was nearly always just, although he could be fierce when provoked to righteous indignation. Ronald Conway, writer and psychologist, claimed that fifteen-year-old boys are half angel and half orangutan. This underestimated our animality, but we knew where we stood, we knew that he liked us, wanted what was good for us, and we had no problem with discipline justly enforced. There were no drugs then to distort perceptions, less family breakdown, little psychologising, and students, like the teachers, did not wear their hearts on their sleeves. There were many worse ways of producing men.

There was an examination in all subjects once a month, and the class was graded into places on the results. The front row was the prime minister and cabinet [George's classmates recall he usually made it into the cabinet, if not into the prime minister's seat] from the dux in descending order to those in the back bench on the last row. I never heard anyone in the last row complaining of damage to their self-esteem, probably because they were confident in Brother Bill's ability to get them a pass. And, for better or for worse, we thought it was something of an honour even to be in Inter A. Competition within the rules was taken for granted, and we were taught that there was honour in victory or defeat, provided these were accepted graciously after we had given our best efforts. We were punished for cheating or whingeing.[3]

Years later, Pell arranged for Brother Bill's image to be immortalized in the chapel of Domus Australia in Rome. It is amazing where little pieces of Ballarat can be discovered across the world. As College Archivist Carolyn Banks told the school in 2015:

Almost two years ago I was contacted by renowned Australian portrait artist Paul Newton for images of Brother O'Malley. Paul had been commissioned by Cardinal George Pell (SPC 1949–959) to paint a portrait of the man who had such a dramatic impact on him as a young school boy in Ballarat so many years ago. Several images of Brother Bill were sent to Paul, and in due course, the portrait was completed and transported to Rome, where it hangs in the beautifully renovated Chapel of Saint Peter Chanel.

In 1959, as he approached the end of year twelve, with a football contract in the bag, the young George's future was full of promise. Decisions, decisions—law, medicine, or professional sport: choices

[3] Ibid.

most young men would dream about. Staying at school gave him time to think.

Life in Ballarat was good, and he and his Saint Patrick's friends went to school dances and enjoyed mixing with the girls from the city's Catholic secondary colleges, Loreto Convent and Sacred Heart. One Brother even instituted dancing classes and encouraged the boys to organize socials with the girls. These, the headmaster wrote in one of his annual reports, were "smart without sophistication, elegant without ostentation, decorous without stiffness, carefree and friendly without boisterousness". The young ladies' grace and charm, he said, brightened "so considerably, if only temporarily, the somewhat severe masculine atmosphere of Saint Patrick's". For many, it was an age of innocence, happiness, and growing prosperity. Like his classmates, George enjoyed the girls' company, but there were no serious romances. In fact, he was feeling dissatisfied and unsettled, despite all that was happening. The time had come to deal with what he described later as "a small cloud" that had been "on the horizon for some time".

"I was waiting for you to come along. I thought you might have come along earlier", said Father John Molony, part-time chaplain at Saint Patrick's College in 1959. George had come, reluctantly, to ask him whether, perhaps, he should try to become a priest. Michael Mason had already begun his first year as a Redemptorist seminarian in Wendouree near Ballarat, and while that had some significance as George pondered his own future, he was far from sure. "I think I would have been quite relieved if Father Molony had said, 'No, you're not suited.' It wasn't as though I was brim full of enthusiasm to become a priest", he recalled.

He later said, "To put it crudely, I feared and suspected and eventually became convinced that God wanted me to do His work, and I was never able to successfully escape that conviction. I fought against it for a long time and made the decision to be a priest in my final year of schooling. I still marvel that I made that leap of being interested in it and thinking about it to saying 'I'll have a go.'"[4]

Molony had been educated at the Pontifical Urban University in Rome. Later, he was to leave the priesthood, marry, and become

[4] Interview with Bryan Patterson, September 21, 1997.

Manning Clark Professor of History at the Australian National University and a professor at the Australian Studies Centre in Dublin.

In 2001, he had clear memories of the eighteen-year-old George Pell coming to him—a highly gifted student academically and at sport, active in the school sodalities. "Most of all, I remember his determination. As a young man, once he knew the direction he wanted his life to take, he followed that direction with real determination."

Pell recalled, "He was a very good friend and a powerful influence on me. He used to lecture us for an hour or so a week, and that was probably the first time that I had been introduced to anything like theology or to an intellectually stimulating presentation of debate, and I found him a most interesting teacher."

Michael Mason agreed.

John had a heck of an impact on us. He came in our last year. The thing about him was that he was a great scholar, a real intellectual. He'd read stuff and studied stuff, and it was all right to ask him questions, and this was kind of new. It was wonderful to actually say: "Well, what's wrong with Communism actually?" and "What is dialectical materialism?"

I can remember the enthusiasm he generated. For the first time we could let loose our curiosity and our intellectual rationality. There had to be reasons for things, and we were bursting to know all that. This door opened which showed there was a lot of thinking about these things that we hadn't been exposed to.

The intellectual, emotional, and spiritual factors behind any man's vocation to the priesthood are complex. Essentially, it requires a sense of the transcendent and a willingness to continue the saving work of Jesus Christ. Accepting the mission of Christ is often difficult, for it means struggling with faith and trusting in the unseen and unfathomable God. As Saint Paul says, we "see these things darkly". Even Pell, after thirty-five years of priesthood, admitted he had experienced "moments of difficulty" but "not serious doubt, no".

The loss of loved ones often sparks an interest in the final things—death, judgement, heaven, and hell—especially in the young, and George Pell was no exception. In his last year at school, there were three deaths in his immediate circle within a few months. His English literature teacher, Brother J.B. Ulmer, a man whom he had admired and who had helped instill a deep love of the subject in George, died suddenly of a heart attack. Two of his uncles, to whom he had also been close, also died of sudden heart attacks. The young man's outlook turned more serious, his thoughts wandering occasionally to the mysteries of the next life. The foundations for responding to Christ's call to the priesthood were there—strong faith from his mother and a thorough grounding in the Catholic faith at school, to which Brother O'Malley contributed. "My greatest debt to Brother Bill is a religious one", Pell said. "Fifteen-year-old boys are often looking for a cause to follow or leader to admire. In him, many of us found an admirable man of faith and integrity, who prayed without embarrassment and urged us to pray outside formal prayer times, to repeat often what he called aspirations and what we might now call mantras." O'Malley's favourite was "Lord, I believe; help my unbelief."

O'Malley's exhortations did not go unheeded. The college chapel was the centre of life at Saint Patrick's, with students frequently attending Mass and Benediction and dropping in for a few minutes of private prayer. In 1949, George Pell's first year, the college newspaper highlighted the tradition: "Big and small drop in for a few moments to converse with the Prisoner of Love in the Tabernacle. This beautiful custom has existed in the College for many years. Our fathers did as we do in the matter. College boys have their God very near them."

In Victoria in those days, the Christian Brothers and their old boys and students and their families were the core of Archbishop Mannix' support. As a senior student in 1959, Pell attended the opening of the Christian Brothers teacher training college. The archbishop of Melbourne, then ninety-five, gave what Pell recalled as "the finest speech of the day", receiving "a tumultuous reception".

As the decision about his own future crystallized in his mind, George had to tell his family. He knew his mother would be overjoyed, but he dreaded telling his father he wanted to be a priest, so he dithered and put it off. The priest in charge of the cathedral, Monsignor Leo Fiscalini, a great friend of Pell's mother, said that if Pell was going to go ahead he should tell his father quickly, so he did.

George Arthur thought it was a waste of time. He had high ambitions for his son both sports-wise and intellectually, and he was disappointed. His father lamented to Sister Ann Forbes, a good friend of the family, that as George was joining the Church he might as well have been "a bloody dill.[5] But you probably don't want dills, do you?"

However, George Arthur told his son that when he was young he had followed his own path, and, Pell remembered, "he would let me follow mine. I suppose it was only many years later that I realised just how broad-minded, how magnanimous, that was."

By the time Pell was aware of his calling to the priesthood, his reputation as a leader was well established. He was school captain, had played in the 1st XVIII for four years, was active in the Australian Army Cadets, and a was leading debater. At Corpus Christi Seminary, those leadership qualities impressed the Jesuit Fathers sufficiently for them to place him in charge of the first-year students as prefect when he was just three years older. As Pell was to find throughout his extraordinary career, leadership had its costs.

David, ten years younger than George, remembered his older brother playing for Saint Patrick's College, where David started in grade three. For home games of football, the entire college student body assembled to watch the whole game; no one could leave early.

> We had to actively participate in the college war cries and encouragement for the 1st XVIII team. After each Wednesday game, there was always a summary of the game published up on the school noticeboard. I can recall after one game, there was a drawing of George with the football on a string—he had played well and kicked a few goals. In those years, there was a fierce rivalry between SPC and Bendigo High School. I reckon High School had beaten Saint Pat's for the first time, and at the repeat match at Saint Pat's, it was on. George got chopped in the throat at the first bounce, and it was on for one and all! He wacked everyone and anyone who dared to get near him. He played well, kicked a few goals. Our pub roof was bricked that night. He reckoned that he had a temper but controlled it—I never saw any evidence of him losing his cool. But, I can say that he was very competitive.

When Pell was at school, his father would always turn up to watch him play Australian football on Wednesday afternoons. David Pell

---

[5] Dill is Australian slang for a person who is not especially bright or clever.

recalled, in a fundraising speech for Aid to the Church in Need a few
months after his brother's death, his father would

> sit on the other side of the oval in his Ford Pilot. He was there when
> the Richmond Footy Club officials said, "That's the one we want",
> when the team first jogged out on the ground around to the other side
> of the ground and then sprinted off together—George after twenty-
> five meters was five meters ahead of the rest of the players. I can
> remember when the sign-up team came home one Sunday to talk
> to Mum and Dad and to get George's signature—they all were big
> broad-shouldered men in gabardine overcoats—as was the fashion
> of the day. Much excitement. Then the letdown, as Mum told me
> that George was becoming a priest. I believe that Dad said, "What a
> bloody waste." This certainly changed over the years, as Dad, along
> with Mum, were his number one supporters. In a small way, we were
> pleased that Mum and Dad were not alive when George's hell was
> unfolding here in Melbourne.

6

Corpus Christi

George Pell first met Denis Hart and Gerry Diamond on March 1, 1960, the day the three of them entered Corpus Christi Seminary, Werribee, in outer suburban Melbourne. Corpus Christi was the seminary for Melbourne, rural Victoria, and Tasmania. The three students were part of a class of thirty-two newcomers. Denis and Gerry were students for the Archdiocese of Melbourne under Archbishop Daniel Mannix, while George belonged to the Diocese of Ballarat, under Bishop Sir James Patrick O'Collins. George's cousin Henry Nolan, who later became vicar-general of the Diocese of Ballarat and decades later accompanied George to receive his cardinal's biretta from Pope John Paul II in Saint Peter's Square, went with him to Werribee.

Denis Hart, from Hawthorn, went to Xavier College, then one of Melbourne's best schools, run by the Jesuits, before entering the seminary. He was eventually appointed auxiliary bishop of Melbourne under Pell and followed him as archbishop. He recalled that, as a seminarian, Pell was "a very complete kind of leader, not only academic but sporty. He was well-read, he had a great intellectual curiosity, even at a young age, and a great interest in literature. In a way he was probably the most well-rounded member of our year." Diamond was struck by Pell's height and by his awesome football reputation "from the wilds of Ballarat". Before long, he was also impressed by the young man's interest in writers such as G. K. Chesterton and Hilaire Belloc and by his skill with words, a talent honed by years of copious reading and school debating.

Diamond regularly topped the class in nearly everything, with Pell outshining him in English and coming close to the top in other subjects. It was no two-horse race, however. Four of those in the class who were not ordained excelled elsewhere—one as an international

maritime engineer, two as senior Melbourne academics in philosophy, while another became Victoria's state architect.

Aside from the fact that two future archbishops joined the seminary, March 1, 1960, was notable for another reason. Until that year,
students for the priesthood had completed all eight years of their
training at Werribee, but by the beginning of the 1960s the number
of students was so large that overcrowding was a major problem. A
second seminary, at Glen Waverley, was built for students completing the second half of their training, four years of theology. Werribee was to cater for the first-year class and the second-, third-, and
fourth-year students, who formed first, second, and third philosophy.

The seminary in Werribee Park looked like a gracious sandstone
country manor. It was set in extensive grounds, conducive to study,
prayer, and contemplation. While founded to train secular priests, it
was staffed by Jesuits, renowned for their rigorous academic standards
and for encouraging young men to study and learn independently.
From 1923 to 1973, when it was closed and the students were transferred to a modern but rather soulless centre at Clayton near Monash
University, Werribee turned out more than 760 priests.

The routine of the seminary, like most seminaries around the world
at the time, was designed to foster growth in faith and in moral virtue. It included daily Mass, meditation, spiritual reading, and examination of conscience, as well as weekly confession and Benediction.
Seminarians were expected to continue their daily spiritual life over
the holidays.

Sceptics sometimes claim that men entering seminaries do so to
shy away from the real world, from relationships with women, or
from earning a living and climbing the career ladder. But to meet
some of the group who started at Werribee in 1960 (and many other
impressive priests) was to realise they would have excelled in life
outside the Church.

For many people, it is not easy to understand why such men
would opt for the priesthood, putting the spiritual side of life ahead
of professional or business careers and love and marriage. Being religious cranks or fanatics has nothing to do with it. In fact, anybody
so inclined inevitably fails in a vocation. Rather, those called to the
priesthood and who succeed at it tend to be normal men, grounded
in the faith of the universal Church, with a strong desire to help

others come to the knowledge and love of God. The commitment needs far more depth than wanting to be some kind of social worker with a touch of religion thrown in. Good priests understand and appreciate how much the faith has to offer the world. If what the Church teaches is true, it is hardly surprising that the Lord would call people of talent (including men of the caliber of John Henry Newman, Fulton Sheen, and Karol Wojtyła) to the priesthood.

The Werribee group who came together in 1960 bonded with a greater sense of "year consciousness" than many classes. Each year the students traditionally put on a play, an event they referred to as the Werribee Wintergarden. In 1960, the first years performed the light comedy *Arsenic and Old Lace*, with George Pell playing the lead, Mortimer Brewster.

After 1960, a few other students from interstate and overseas joined the class, taking the total to thirty-eight. In second year, when the class was in first philosophy, they made their mark by fielding not one but two football teams in the seminary competition. They managed this by having the nineteenth and twentieth men from the firsts (Denis Hart and Ted Teal) play for the seconds. Not surprisingly, George Pell, who could have been wearing black and gold for Richmond at the Melbourne Cricket Ground, was a key man in the firsts. "The couple of years ahead of us were football mad, and here were these upstarts in first philosophy, second years, taking on the rest of the house, actually the best of the rest of the house, and winning", Gerry Diamond recalled. The team's motif was "play the man", a mischievous twist of the "play the ball, not the man" motto.

Not everybody, however, was amused, either by George Pell's dominance on the field, by the way he went about his duties as a prefect in his later years at Werribee, or by his high spirits. The Jesuit method of running the seminary trained the students in authority and responsibility. Teachers were scarcely seen outside of classes, so seminary life was organized by the students themselves.

A head prefect from the senior class coordinated the whole place, and another prefect was in charge of the first years. There was a music prefect (Denis Hart held that job in his time), a kitchen prefect (who liaised with the nuns over meals and who organized the provisions for days off), a press prefect (in charge of stationery), and others. In his second year, George Pell was the class prefect during the class' spiritual semester, a six-month intensive period of prayer, a role he carried out with no fuss.

In the second half of his third year at Werribee, Pell was appointed first-year prefect. It was an important job. There was a priest who was dean of discipline, who worked from something of a remove, but for those in the first year, the prefect was responsible for the implementation of discipline. Pell found the role straightforward and had no trouble exercising authority when appropriate. He continued in the job in the first half of his fourth year. And in the atmosphere of intellectual upheaval and social experimentation that began permeating the Church during the Second Vatican Council, some of those in the first year did not like his style.

Melbourne priest Father Martin Dixon was in that first-year class. In 2001, his assessment of his old prefect was that "George has always been a big bully on and off the field; he's a tall strongman, and he loves a fight and will do anything to get his own way." Dixon said Pell came as something of a shock after his more reticent, gentle predecessor in the role. "George was supposed to be looking after and guiding the first-year class, helping us settle in, but he was quite authoritarian." Others from that first-year class backed up Dixon's assessment but were not as brave in saying so publicly.

Another member of the rhetoric class, Paul Bongiorno, had no problems with his old schoolmate's style and got on well with him. "He was dominant but very fair, and I guess I was pretty compliant", he said. "George thought men had to be men and that pansies belonged in the garden, and no matter whether individuals wanted to play football or basketball, at the prescribed times he'd push them out. But that was his job."

Pell, Gerry Diamond insisted, was merely bringing those in the first year into line with the standards prevailing at the time, insisting that they kept silent at the prescribed times, turned up for prayer dressed correctly, and kept the rules generally. A generational change was taking place, influenced by the inferences drawn from the Second Vatican Council and the rebellions of the swinging 1960s. "That particular group was anti-anything all the way through. With that particular grouping, it wasn't simply a matter of George, it was anything." Diamond was correct in his judgement that Pell's time as a prefect at Werribee coloured some slightly younger priests' views of him for the future.

Several priests who were seminary contemporaries of Pell never forgot their encounters with him on the football field. "There were better footballers, more talented players, but he was effective and would play in a certain way, the way the Brothers drilled fellows to play", the late Father Leo Saleeba said years ago. "He was very strong, and his arms tended to fly out; he was a bit awkward." Another priest found: "You tended to get a headache after playing against him."

Several priests, including Dixon, mentioned the antics of Pell and his friends on seminary outings, where they would roll up newspapers and whack others with them. "George was usually the initiator", Dixon insisted. He cited the incident as an example of the "bully" side of George Pell. Asked to provide more examples, Dixon mentioned his former boss' style of football and an incident decades later, when, as archbishop of Melbourne, Pell stopped a group of priests at an official archdiocesan priests' gathering from watching the film *Jesus of Montreal*. Pell's friends remember the newspaper "bashings" as "healthy high-spiritedness". "He enjoyed it and gave as good as he got; it was part of the fun", Diamond said.

Others took it all more seriously. Paul Connell, who began at Werribee in 1964, the year after Pell had left for Rome, said the Pell legend and folklore lived on at Werribee after him. "Dunking, bullying people, forceful, outgoing to the point of riding roughshod ... he was a legend in those days if one was talking about an overbearing bully." Thirty years later when Pell was appointed archbishop of Melbourne, Connell was seminary rector.

In his fourth year at Werribee, Pell was summoned by the seminary rector, who broke some news that was to shape his future. From September that year, 1963, he would be continuing his studies at the Pontifical Urban University in Rome. It would take some time to get used to the Latin of the lecturers, he was warned, but he would love the experience. At a time when the dynamism of the Second Vatican Council had gripped Rome, this opportunity for an outward-looking student in his early twenties from provincial Australia was more than a dream come true. Pell had good reason to be heartily grateful to his mentor, Bishop O'Collins. A late vocation to the priesthood after working as a plumber, O'Collins prided himself on his ability to spot up-and-coming talent and encouraged his priests to pursue university studies.

Before leaving Melbourne, Pell and two other seminarians, as was the custom for students going to Rome, put on their best black suits and ventured out to *Raheen*, a stately home on Studley Park Road, Kew, to pay their respects to Archbishop Mannix, then ninety-nine years old and a few months from death. In 2004, in a foreword to Australian author Michael Gilchrist's biography of Mannix, Pell recalled that the old archbishop "rather deflated our self-importance by asking if we had been working in the garden!" The seminarians each kissed the archbishop's ring—Pell little realizing that he would one day wear the same one. He would even sit in the same chair, which Mannix willed to his close confidant B. A. Santamaria, who in turn left it to Pell, who remembered: "Mannix had a rug over his knees and an Irish theological journal on a table next to him. He wondered who we were—we told him we were going to Rome to study—and he courteously wished us well. There was certainly no sign of any confusion."

George, then twenty-two, sailed from Melbourne on the final voyage of the *Stratheden*. By that time, Margaret was studying music at Melbourne University, and David, thirteen, was at Saint Patrick's College in Ballarat. Before air travel took over, ocean liner departures were quite an event. Hundreds of well-wishers gathered, holding streamers thrown from the ship by the European immigrants returning to their old countries for a visit and the young Australians embarking on the big trip to London and Europe. Clutching streamers thrown by Pell from the deck, all his family and some of his friends were there to see him off. David remembered the breaking streamers as the ship moved off.

His father fell silent, and Margaret's and his mother's tears flowed as the liner drew out from the dock to sail from mid-winter Melbourne, via Suez, to Naples in the European summer of 1963.

7

"Euntes Docete Omnes Gentes"

Few visitors to Rome see Saint Peter's Basilica and Square from a vantage point as panoramic as the grounds of the Pontificia Universitas Urbaniana, or, in English, the Pontifical Urban University. The university and its residential college stand on the Gianicolo (the Janiculum Hill) just behind the Vatican. In any light, the basilica's dome—Michelangelo's magnum opus—and the colonnade around Saint Peter's Square—designed by Bernini to suggest the welcoming arms of Mother Church—are strikingly beautiful. From the Gianicolo on misty mornings or at sunset, these architectural wonders take on an awe-inspiring, ethereal quality.

The Vatican's proximity, less than half a mile downhill, puts the university, known as Propaganda or "Prop" by its graduates (because it was under the direction of the Congregation of Propaganda, now the Dicastery for Evangelization) at the heart of the Church. Its main building is on Vatican, not Italian, territory, which partly explains why Jews were sheltered safely within its sturdy walls during the Nazi occupation of Rome. Entering the Propaganda grounds, it is impossible to miss the prominent lettering across the top of the building: "Euntes docete omnes gentes" (Go teach all nations), as Christ instructed His apostles. That, in a nutshell, is what the Pontifical Urban University is all about.

It began in 1627 as the Collegio Urbano de Propaganda Fide, named for its founder, Pope Urban VIII. The college coat of arms includes the papal crown and keys (to the kingdom of heaven) and the three bees that were part of the personal crest of Urban VIII. It was Urban's predecessor, Gregory XV, who established a new Vatican department, the Congregatio de Propaganda Fide, to spread the

Catholic faith to all corners of the world. Urban extended Gregory's vision by creating the school to train missionary priests.

Urban VIII also commissioned the papal summer residence outside Rome, at Castel Gandolfo—about a ninety minutes' drive from Rome—overlooking Lake Albano. In the 1960s, Propaganda had its own villa near the Castel, where Pell and his classmates spent most of their summers. Pope Paul VI would invite them into his villa once every summer for afternoon tea. Like all popes, Paul VI was presented with an extraordinary array of mementos and gifts, and these he would often give away to the students he met at the Castel. Pell received a statue of John the Baptist baptizing Christ, which had stood on Paul VI's desk for years. (The pope's baptismal name was John Baptist Montini.) Unlike his more austere predecessor, Pius XII, who rarely mixed, even in Rome, Paul VI also visited each ordination class at Propaganda Fide.

Senior students were allowed to venture farther afield during their holidays, and one year Pell won a scholarship from the French government and did a summer language course at the Sorbonne. He and another student spent an idyllic summer in Paris, living in a youth hostel.

Now as in the 1960s, Prop draws its students from all nations, especially the countries of Africa and Asia. They mix socially in small groups of about fifteen, known as *cameratas* (or fellows), drawn from different years and countries. The common language, Italian, is an effective leveler. In Pell's time, the English-speaking students got together once a week—on Sundays after lunch—and the Australians gathered for special events such as the annual Australia Day picnic and Anzac Day Mass and commemoration. That extraordinary spiritual melting pot/oasis was George Pell's home from 1963 to 1967, some of his most formative years and those of the modern Catholic Church.

When Pell arrived for the start of the academic year in September 1963, he was disappointed by his first sight of Saint Peter's. "In my Australian prudishness, I thought it looked very dirty from the outside." Most Australian students reacted the same way and felt rather shocked that the main church of Christendom was not better maintained. (Saint Peter's has since been cleaned extensively and is now flood-lit at night.) Pell had enjoyed his weeks of travel to Rome, stopping off at exciting ports and learning Italian. He would write home every week—the blue aerograms were eagerly awaited, and the family still has them all.

Pell's time in Rome coincided with the Second Vatican Council. Many of the two thousand bishops there for the council were Propaganda Fide alumni and would visit the students at the college and say Mass in the chapel. The lecturers would talk in detail about the council, enthusing about or occasionally berating its decisions. From the college gardens, the students could see long lines of bishops coming and going to and from the sessions, carrying briefcases. It was a time of ferment, expectation, excitement, and tension in the Church, and it set the stage for reforms, upheavals, uncertainties, and unforeseen conflicts for decades. The turmoil spilled over into the lives of Pell and his classmates. David Pell recalled that another seminarian in Rome wrote to his family just weeks before his ordination that he was not sure about his vocation. "I couldn't believe what I was hearing", said David. "He was ordained but resigned [left the priesthood] in later years." George, if anything, was even more committed.

Propaganda's English-speaking students had a Newman Society, which produced an annual journal, *Loquitur.* The title was taken from the motto of English Cardinal John Henry Newman: "Cor ad cor loquitur" (heart speaks to heart). The journal comprised articles and poems by the students on theological and contemporary questions or issues related to their own countries. The 1964/1965 volume, which saluted the memories of Pope John XXIII and President John F. Kennedy, pictured those men on the cover, with the domes of Saint Peter's Basilica and the U.S. Capitol. It was edited by two second-year students, George Pell and New Zealander Neil Darragh. After the straitjacket world of Pius XII and Dwight Eisenhower's 1950s, Kennedy's and John XXIII's brief, tumultuous times on the world stage caught the imaginations of young people. Most Catholics expected Pope John, elected in 1958 at the age of seventy-six, to be a short-term stopgap who would make little impression. These expectations could not have been more wrong. In calling the Second Vatican Council, John XXIII left an indelible impression that continues to unfold decades after his death.

The Pell/Darragh editorial, written, as they put it, to "catch the spirit of our times", paid tribute to the two Johns as "men of men, these men of God", who, they claimed with the naïve optimism of youth, "presaged the return of the Church to the centre of Western life". The edition included articles on black saints, African socialism, the Church in West Irian (now, Papua), Buddhist-Christian dialogue, an adaptation of Mark Antony's speech entitled "On Calvary's Top", and a prayer for the canonization of Cardinal Newman. George Pell contributed two pieces—a poem and a spirited attack on the Australian government's White Australia policy, which favoured and encouraged British migration (a stance that would have been controversial at home at the time). With shades of arguments to come thirty-five years later in the debate over Pauline Hanson's One Nation party, Pell branded the policy unjust and outdated: "Eleven million whites in an empty land surrounded by 1,500 million coloured Asians might have been a going concern when the Dutch, the French, and 'Mother England' held most of Asia under 'protective custody'. Today it looks suspiciously like an anachronism." Australia would pay a price for "preferring third-class Europeans to first-class Asians". As Australia was completely unprepared to replace the annual intake of 100,000 Europeans with 100,000 Asians, he argued,

> it would be best to start with a much smaller number, perhaps 10,000 a year, followed by consistent increases as the newcomers assimilated. The great unknown is the dark silent stream of prejudice, buried beneath the topsoil of Australian public life, born from cultural superiority and colonial achievement and strangely nourished by ignorance, fear, and a superiority complex; yet slowly and certainly losing itself in an ocean of changed conditions.

The following year, Pell wrote a critique of one of the most controversial plays in the world at the time—*The Deputy*, by German playwright Rolf Hochhuth, which condemns Pope Pius XII's response to the Holocaust. As Pell reported: "At the Basel première people rioted. In London, Evelyn Waugh sailed into the fray claiming bad theatre and worse history, while in America (where else, except perhaps Australia?) a prominent churchman condemned the drama and then admitted he hadn't read it." The critique concluded that while the play held together as drama, the character of the pope bore no resemblance to reality.

The play's thesis rests on the assumption that Pius XII could have stopped Hitler's persecution of the Jews. But Pope Paul VI, who at the time assisted Pius XII with diplomatic affairs, insisted, along with most others involved, that the situation could have been made worse by a papal protest against the Third Reich. An anti-Nazi statement by the Dutch bishops resulted in the deportation of Jewish converts to Catholicism living in the Netherlands, including Edith Stein (Saint Teresa Benedicta of the Cross), who was immediately killed at Auschwitz. No one could have predicted a successful intervention by the pope, and here lies the real issue. Was Pius XII, because of the enormity of the crimes, as the Vicar of Christ on earth, obliged to bear a public witness to the truth that was unlikely to improve the situation and that might have provoked further atrocities against the Jews and sent most of Catholic Europe back to the catacombs?

Propaganda has a rich history of colourful characters. Saint Oliver Plunkett, the primate of Ireland and archbishop of Armagh who was martyred at London's Tyburn tree in 1681, studied and was ordained at Propaganda and was its theology professor from 1657 to 1669. Cardinal John Henry Newman, the former Oxford don and convert from the Anglican clergy, also studied at Propaganda. In true Propaganda spirit, he went on to found the London and Birmingham Oratories, modelled on Saint Philip Neri's Roman Oratory, and to create the Catholic University of Ireland. In Newman's time, Propaganda was located near Rome's Spanish Steps (it was later moved to the Janiculum Hill), but the altar where Newman said his first Mass is still in use.

Vast numbers of Propaganda graduates have become cardinals, archbishops, seminary heads, pastors, and also martyrs. "Be faithful unto death, and I will give you the crown of life" (Rev 2:10), one of the inscriptions in the college chapel reminds students at daily Mass. Even in the early twenty-first century, Propaganda students from countries such as Angola knew they faced dangerous lives, possible imprisonment, or eventual death when they returned home, but most approached the future with a missionary zeal equal to that of any student from the college's 375-year history. Propaganda is highly influential in the rapidly growing Church in the developing world, from where most of its students are drawn. By the early 2000s, the university's library had 11,000 volumes in 530 non-European languages, including 270 African languages. Australia is no longer classed as a "missionary country" entitled to a free education at the college.

In George Pell's time, all university textbooks were in Latin, as were the lectures (officially), although the lecturers sometimes broke into Italian. Like most new students, Pell took several months to become used to the accents and idioms of the teachers. "Everyone had enormous trouble at first, but at least we had immediate access to the textbooks." (And sufficient grasp of Latin to read them.) Professors often taught from their own textbooks, which were widely used in seminaries throughout the world. Pell and his fellow Australian students did a little Italian study before they left for Rome and had a few lessons in the language at the college, but they mainly picked up the language themselves.

The university, just twenty yards from the college, across the driveway, was also attended by students who lived in other colleges throughout the city. Many of the Italian seminarians belonged to religious orders and were training to work in foreign missions abroad. They attended classes in their full religious habits. Lectures were held in large theatres, including the Great Hall (*Aula Magna*), a steep, five-hundred-seat, semicircular amphitheatre.

Many of the university professors were the international leaders in their fields. One of the unforgettable teachers of George Pell's time (and for decades of students before him) was Monsignor Antonio Piolanti, a lecturer at both the Pontifical Urban and Lateran Universities in Rome. Piolanti, "Pio" out of earshot, was a tall, solidly built man who taught Christology. He wore a long, black soutane and a Roman hat on his bald head. When he arrived for classes, he would toss the hat on the desk, say the customary opening prayer, and pick up where he had left off the last time with "Ut dicebamus" (as we were saying).

Blessed with phenomenal recall, Piolanti lived for his subjects and rarely, if ever, referred to a note or a textbook. In his lectures, he quoted the early Church Fathers and Church scholars through the ages, both those he admired and those he despised, with perfect accuracy and at length. His highest accolades were reserved for Saint Thomas Aquinas, whom he revered: "Saint Thomas Aquinas says and *we* say ..." It was clear what he expected in exams. Delving deeper into his subject, he would occasionally tell the students "Pro doctioribus inter vos ..." (for the more learned among you). Piolanti fascinated generations of students, including Pell.

A centralist at heart, Piolanti was aghast at moves by the council to give individual bishops more authority in their dioceses. On one memorable occasion, he made an impassioned speech about the "one, holy, catholic and Roman, apostolic Church". When a Spanish student dared to ask why he inserted "Roman" into this line from the Creed, he thundered, "Because to say Roman is to say apostolic."

In later years, Piolanti became something of a recluse. Before his death in 2002, he spent time studying the work of Pius IX, a fact that would surprise none of his former students. Pius IX, who died in 1878 after a reign of thirty-two years, was one of the Church's strongest, most traditional popes. Among other things, in 1854 he defined the dogma of the Immaculate Conception. He called the First Vatican Council in 1870, which defined the doctrine of papal infallibility. Upon his death, his Masonic enemies attempted to toss his body into the Tiber.

Delivering a paper at Boston University in 1991, Pell recalled how amazed he had been to learn that the reign of Pius IX "coincided with steady, and sometimes spectacular, spiritual regeneration in many places, and especially in the English-speaking world. This is a fact that I, as a young priest ordained immediately after the Second Vatican Council and deeply committed to its liberal reforms, found puzzling and indeed somewhat shocking. How could such intransigence have coincided with and helped to bring about such a genuine revival?"[1] Years later, with vast experience, Pell was not surprised by Pius IX's effectiveness. Over time, the liberal outlook of his student days gave way to a pragmatic conservatism.

Far more enthusiastic about Vatican II than Piolanti was a Slovenian lecturer Monsignor Janez Vodopivec, an accredited expert consultant to the council who played an important role in drafting one of its main documents, *Lumen Gentium*, a decree about the Church herself. George Pell recalled Vodopivec as "a very good lecturer on ecclesiology", with an enthusiasm for the council that was contagious among the students.

Another lecturer Pell respected for being "thorough and quite influential" was Father Roberto Masi, who taught sacramental

---

[1] George Pell, *Rerum Novarum: One Hundred Years Later* (Boston: Boston University, 1992).

theology. Amid the turmoil of the time, Masi brought out an important document defending the Real Presence against some of the Dutch theologians who were already, with the council barely closed, attempting to undermine that basic tenet of the faith. It was a foretaste of things to come. The Dutch Church, once one of the strongest in Europe, with more vocations per head of population than any other European country, including Ireland, was a wreck by the end of the twentieth century, with hardly any priests, religious, or parishes after destructive internal upheavals.

Redemptorist Father Jan Visser, however, who taught Pell moral theology in Rome, was a Dutch theologian who upheld traditional Catholic teaching. In the 1960s, Visser was a member of Pope Paul VI's commission of inquiry into the birth control pill—one of the minority on that commission who opposed the pill.

A young Italian, Father Carlo Molari, who taught dogmatic theology, was Monsignor Piolanti's assistant and a real Pell favourite: "He was a very exciting lecturer; I certainly liked his enthusiasm and ambition to speak to contemporary people." Dogma, canon law, Scripture, the Psalms, and patristics made up the remainder of the heavy academic program. An elderly, bearded Lebanese archbishop, Sfair, struggled to teach the students Hebrew.[2]

Propaganda's *Aula magna* was also the scene of some lively theatrical performances by the students, including a production of *The Mikado* in November 1965, when Pell, as he had at school, played Pooh-Bah. Students from Japan, India, and Senegal were the three little maids. Several performances were staged, with about five hundred people attending each one, including nuns and students from Propaganda and other English-speaking colleges (the English, Irish, Scots, and North American colleges). Many Australian bishops, in Rome for the Second Vatican Council, also came to watch.

A few days later, on December 8, 1965, the feast of the Immaculate Conception, Propaganda students crowded into Saint Peter's Square with tens of thousands of others for the historic closing ceremony of Vatican II. Such interludes were a welcome break from the rigorous timetable of the college. The students' days began at 5:30 A.M. (6:00 A.M.

---

[2] The descriptions of the Propaganda lecturers are drawn from conversations with Cardinal Pell, other Propaganda students of various generations, and Peter Brock's *Home Rome Home* (New York: Spectrum Publications, 2001).

Sundays), with prayer, meditation, and Mass before breakfast. Classes were held in the mornings, followed by lunch (the main meal of the day). After lunch there were times for a *siesta* (part of Roman life), recreation and sport, study, evening prayer, supper at 8:00 P.M., more study, and a Great Silence from 10:30 P.M.

George Pell was an enthusiastic player on the college basketball team. Much to his disgust, the old soccer field was later turned into a car park, but the basketball courts remained. His contemporaries say he played basketball with power and "sheer physicality" and had a "strong presence" both on and off the court.

In general, he was somebody whom the other students expected to make a significant mark, perhaps as a writer for academic and theological journals. Paul Bongiorno, whom George met at the boat at Naples when he arrived for the 1966–1967 academic year at Propaganda, remembered him as "an imposing figure with a real personality and an enormous intellectual capacity". Pell kept in close touch by letter with his friends at Corpus Christi Seminary in Werribee. "He wrote to me regularly, and I got the impression of broadening interests during the Second Vatican Council in Rome", Denis Hart said.

Margaret, having completed her bachelor of music degree, set sail for Europe in June 1966 to study the violin. Her playing secured her a place in the prestigious Santa Cecilia Academy Chamber Orchestra in Rome. She lived first with a Norwegian family as an *au pair* and later moved into an international student hostel. Margaret and George, always close, met up on Thursday and Sunday afternoons, when Propaganda students were allowed out to explore the city of Rome but were expected back at the college in time for the evening meal.

They travelled, in the summer of 1966, to East Germany and to Czechoslovakia, staying in youth hostels where even toilet paper was rationed, with four or five flimsy sheets doled out to each guest every day. They found life behind the Iron Curtain dull, grey, and heavily policed, with some trams dating back to the Austro-Hungarian Empire. They were fascinated by the experience, however, especially George. His secondary schooling coincided with a time when the Communist menace loomed large across the world. When he was a teenager, some of his heroes were the Catholic leaders of the Eastern bloc who kept their people's faith alive in the face of brutal repression. These included Cardinals Wyszyński of Poland, Beran in Czechoslovakia, Stepinac in Croatia, Slipyj in Ukraine, and Mindszenty in Hungary. Mindszenty was imprisoned for many years under Communism and later took refuge in the American embassy in Budapest. He was able to leave Hungary in 1971 and died in Vienna in 1975. Pell's first-hand experience of Communist countries brought home some of the political aspects of Catholicism that were not so evident in Australia.

8

You Are a Priest Forever

Friday morning, December 16, 1966, dawned a cold day in wintry Rome. Like most of his fifty classmates, who had spent three and a half years in Propaganda College, George Pell was surprised by how tense and churned-up he felt. Aged twenty-five, he was about to give his life to Christ as a priest: ordination day was the end point of many years of thought and study.

A few months earlier, on August 15, Pell and his classmates had become subdeacons. They had been given the breviary to read every day for the rest of their lives and the Roman collar to wear. They had also taken vows of lifelong celibacy. The sacrifice demanded by such a vow inevitably provokes soul-searching and even fear, and George Pell was no exception. His sister recalled her brother pouring out his anxieties about that vow one afternoon during a long walk over some of the bridges that cross the Tiber.

On their ordination morning, the class of 1966 walked together down the narrow footpaths and winding, cobbled laneways of the Janiculum Hill to Saint Peter's Basilica, watching for the odd speeding car or Vespa. They wore their spectacular Propaganda College uniforms, black soutanes with red buttons, red piping, and red waistbands, a style dating from the 1600s. A black Roman hat—a dome with a broad, flat brim—completed the uniform, much to the chagrin of some, who felt silly in it. They were very proud of the distinctive soutane, however, which according to student legend was designed by Michelangelo.

After a ten-minute walk, the group turned a corner, and in front of them was the largest church in Christendom. Inside, they headed for the Altar of the Chair, at the very top of the basilica, underneath the sole stained-glass window in Saint Peter's, which depicts the Holy

Spirit in the form of a white dove against a yellow and orange background. It was at the same altar, on January 14, 2023, that Cardinal Pell's Vatican funeral attracted one of the largest crowds of any cardinal's funeral in living memory.

Fifty-seven years earlier, one by one, dressed in white, the fifty young deacons from five continents were ordained priests by Cardinal Gregorio Pietro Agagianian, an Armenian who had come to Rome as a student at the age of thirteen and stayed for a lifetime. He was head of the Vatican Congregation for the Propagation of the Faith from 1960 to 1970, and his process for canonization opened in October 2022. The cardinal anointed each deacon's hands with oil and then wound fine white cloths around them.

Among the congregation were Pell's mother, his sister, Margaret, and their young brother, David, then aged sixteen, who was rapidly catching up to his brother in height, reunited with George after four years. His father, though fully reconciled to the idea of his son being a priest, had to remain in Ballarat to manage the hotel. For a mother with strong faith, the strength of feeling Mrs Pell would have experienced as she watched her beloved son being ordained a priest would be difficult to describe. Women in the same position have reported being overwhelmed with love, pride, gratitude to God, humility, faith, and wonder. The white cloths put around George Pell's hands that day would be wound around the hands of his mother after she died and be buried with her. The same has happened to the cloths of every other man ordained that day—a special honour the Church affords women who give birth to future priests. Margaret Pell remembered a lump in her throat during the ceremony and shedding some tears, knowing how hard George had worked and how well he was suited to the difficult vocation to which God had called him.

Sung in Latin, the verse "You are a priest for ever according to the order of Melchizedek" (Ps 110:4) swirled around the basilica, adding to the solemnity. Pell recalled Father Nicola Praglia's "Tu Es Sacerdos" being sung. But for him and many others, the music that evoked the strongest memories of Rome was Richard Wagner's "Pilgrim's Chorus" from *Tannhäuser*, sung by the Propaganda choir on special occasions. Its stirring words greeted the ordination class as they returned to the college for lunch.

The day after his ordination, Father Pell, surrounded by his family, friends, and passersby, chose the Roman Church of the Christian Brothers as the venue for his first Mass. The Mass was in the Tridentine Rite of the time, with the celebrant facing the altar.

Within the Propaganda family, the ordination class of 1966 stood out for an important reason—the vast majority of its members stayed the course as priests, unlike many in the years immediately before and after. Of those classes, only about 10 percent of the men from some countries, including Australia, stayed for the long haul. Either they were not ordained or they left a few years afterwards. Perhaps the class of 1966 had the best of both worlds—a solid grounding in the certainties and intensity of the preconciliar Church combined with what felt like a new springtime as the council unfolded.

A couple of days after his ordination, the annual Propaganda Fide versus American College basketball game was on. David Pell had never seen his brother play basketball, "let alone give the black American captain a mouthful at every opportunity. Aussie Cricketers could learn a thing that day! Talk about being competitive." In December, the Pells travelled to Paris, Lourdes, London, and Ireland, including Dublin, Cork, and County Clare, before returning to Rome. "We had an exciting trip. Mum twigged early on that when George suggested that we sit in front of a masterpiece in the Louvre 'to absorb the painting and to ponder on it' that he was actually having a rest!" David Pell recalled.

> George was in great form, and I think delighted that his brother had grown up—at least in size, anyway.
>
> George was never a great driver—so by 1966 December, I don't reckon he would have driven many miles since he left Australia—but that wasn't going to deter him! We hired a car in Dublin and went touring! What an event. He didn't believe in getting close to the centre white line; he straddled the left-hand side—so much so, that he clipped a protruding tyre of a parked car, in Cork's main street.
>
> Mum was on tenterhooks.... He drove up the side of Cashel Castle and realised that he could not get through and he couldn't turn around. Again, he was straddling the left-hand side up against the parapet walls. No idea and no hope. "Get out George and let David do it!" Mum ordered. Me, the sixteen-year-old, had to manoeuvre the car backwards down the side of the castle with the three occupants following on foot!

After a family Christmas in Rome in 1966, life at Prop for Father Pell went on its rigorous way. The ordination class still had its most important six months of study ahead, to complete the much sought-after licentiate in theology. Pell preached, heard confessions, and did some work at churches around Rome in his first six months after ordination, and he said daily Mass at one of the many altars in the college chapel. He spent his first Easter as a priest at Notaresco in the Abruzzi Mountains, helping out in the local parish. Study, however, was a priority. The licentiate was a stiff, searching exam, oral and written, covering 120 topics from four years of the course.

The previous year, as part of the course, each student had produced a written dissertation. Pell's dissertation delved into the controversial work of the French Jesuit Pierre Teilhard de Chardin. Hero or heretic, genius or muddled fraud, opinions among Catholics are sharply divided about this extraordinary priest, geologist, palaeontologist, and volunteer stretcher-bearer on the western front in World War I. Chardin attempted to reconcile theories, such as evolution, with Catholic theology. But his writing was fraught with obscure passages, some of which seemed to contradict the Church's unchanging teaching regarding the natures of both God and man. Thus, he met with constraints imposed by Church authorities, and the Holy Office issued a *monitum*, a warning, against his posthumously published works. Those works had serious flaws. In *The Future of Man*, Chardin claimed that modern totalitarian regimes, whatever their "initial defects", were in line with the "essential trend of the 'cosmic' movement". Some credit him with envisaging the creation of the internet, when he spoke about a "noosphere"—a kind of global network of minds facilitating trade, communication, and the exchange of knowledge.

In his dissertation, Pell lamented the Church's not allowing Chardin to publish freely during his lifetime and develop and refine his work under the stimulus of the criticism it would have attracted. "Those of us who know something of the priest-scientist's private life will not be surprised that he regarded much of his work as tentative ... yet another reason for sympathetic judgement."[1] While critical

[1] George Pell, *A Bird's-Eye View of Teilhard de Chardin in Christology*, third-year dissertation written under the direction of Rev. Father C. Molari, May 1966.

of aspects of his subject's writings, Pell concluded that Teilhard de Chardin's work was intended, not to compete with divine revelation, but rather to enrich its perspectives and to penetrate farther into its mysteries. "The frightening upsurge of secularism and the separation of the Church from so much of what is good in modern life show the need for something deeper than a scrupulous intellectual 'orthodoxy' and adherence to traditional formulas", Pell wrote. "We cannot expect that his answers be perfect. They are not. However, without slurring over his deficiencies, and without failing to warn if necessary, there is no doubt that the new Church coming to birth after Vatican II will regard him as one of our greatest prophets, accepting him as he is, with his prejudices and failings, and despite his slightly garbled message. A voice crying in the wilderness, condemned to wandering amidst a primitive people."

Three and a half decades on, a more experienced Pell regarded Teilhard de Chardin, no longer as "one of our greatest prophets", but as "an interesting writer who tried to reestablish the traditional alliance between science and Catholicism" and who made an important contribution to the Christian discussion on evolution. Pell read the works in their original French and could not have chosen a livelier topic to pursue en route to his licentiate.

Most priests who have studied in Rome regard the licentiate as their academic highpoint, harder to earn than a doctorate. Decades after leaving Rome, some priests still dreamed about facing up to Piolanti, Visser, and the other Propaganda examiners. Pell was deeply absorbed by the lectures and the subjects and worked very hard, but he was largely untroubled by the course once he adjusted to the language.

Of the fifty Propaganda College classmates who sat the licentiate, Pell came in fifth, his degree awarded *magna cum laude*, the second highest of the five grades. Among those ahead of him was Father Bartolomeo Adoukonou, who went on to be secretary of the West African Bishops' Conference and a member of the International Theological Commission. The Propaganda class of 1966 produced three cardinals (Pell, Felix Job of Ibadan, and Anthony Okogie of Lagos, Nigeria), as well as numerous bishops, seminary rectors, academics, and pastors. Because the future was unknown to graduates returning to Vietnam, Korea, and parts of Africa and the Middle East, and because many of the priests would probably not meet again after living so closely together for three years, their farewells after the licentiate in the summer of 1967 were very moving.

While many of his classmates prepared to face the difficulties of ministering amid Third World poverty, George Pell, temporarily, tasted life at the opposite end of the mission. That summer after ordination, Pell took the opportunity to spend three months working in Baltimore, Maryland, in the United States, where it was a tradition to bring young English-speaking priests to help out while the local priests took holidays.

At the wealthy cathedral parish of Mary Our Queen in the northern part of the city of Baltimore, the people were very friendly, and Pell found it a wonderful introduction to parish life. While there, he made lifelong friends with the Catholic Weigel family, who had two sons—John, who became a doctor, and George, still in high school at the time, who became an academic and writer, specializing in Catholic social teaching, religion and democracy, religious freedom, and the just-war tradition. George Weigel is best known today as the author of the definitive biography of Pope John Paul II, *Witness to Hope* and *The End and the Beginning*. Weigel recalled:

> We first met Father Pell in the summer of 1967. If memory serves, he was third in an apostolic succession of young Australian priests coming to the Cathedral of Mary Our Queen for the summer. I was about to enter my junior year of high school.
>
> My family was very involved in the cathedral parish; among many other things, my brother and I used to answer the phones in the evening, so we got to know the priests well. Father Pell became a friend of the family and even came to the Georgia shore with us for a few days that summer.
>
> We stayed in touch over the years, although my contact with him has been much more intense in the past ten years, as our work has intersected at many points. I think everyone who met Father Pell in 1967, shortly after his ordination, was impressed by his freshness, openness, and candor—qualities we often associate with Australia.

Years later, in an article marking fifty years of their friendship, Weigel observed that little did they know then that "the next half-century would lead us into the same foxholes in various ecclesiastical battles; or to a shared friendship with a Polish priest, pope, and saint;

or into synods, consistories, papal elections, and other adventures."[2] Pell's intellectual gifts, "might have marked him out for a scholarly career. But providence (and John Paul II) had other plans, and rather than teaching history full-time, George Pell made history, becoming the defining figure of twenty-first-century Catholicism in Australia."

Like many Propaganda students, Pell was keen to pursue a doctorate, but he was determined not to stay on in Rome for a doctorate in canon law. He had his sights set on Oxford and a doctorate in history. It was his good fortune that Bishop O'Collins supported the idea wholeheartedly. At that stage, Pell seemed destined for a life as a Church academic. Apart from all other considerations, Bishop O'Collins hoped Pell's years at Oxford would give the Australian Church someone who could beat the then-prominent liberal Catholic commentator Max Charlesworth at his own game. Some of Australia's bishops had long considered the articulate, controversial Charlesworth a thorn in their sides and were becoming increasingly aware that the Church needed to educate young priests to take the Church's message to the people through the mass media.

9

Campion Hall, Oxford

Pell arrived in Oxford in 1967 for the Michaelmas term, which runs from September to Christmas. For four years his home was Campion Hall, operated by the Jesuits. The Hall was originally opened in 1896 in the Saint Giles area of Oxford, and the present sandstone building, with quadrangle garden at its centre, was built in 1935. It has a dignified, scholarly atmosphere, and its walls are decorated with religious art. Most of its residents were Jesuit students from around the world, along with priests and seminarians from other religious congregations and some diocesan priests like Pell. The Hall is tucked away in Brewer Street, a quiet lane opposite Christ Church Cathedral. A blue plaque on the house next door commemorates writer Dorothy Sayers, who was born there in 1893, when her father was headmaster of the cathedral school.

Scholars were lecturing in Oxford on theology and canon law before 1150. By 1180, a large group of scholars were resident in the town, with the earliest schools growing up around the monastery of Saint Frideswide, where Christ Church now stands. From 1220, the new Catholic orders—the Dominicans and Franciscans—began teaching in Oxford. More established orders such as the Benedictines and Carmelites also moved in, setting up what were the forerunners of some of today's colleges.

In 1571, during the reign of Elizabeth I, the Thirty-Nine Articles of the Church of England were imposed on the university, excluding Catholics. Among those who conformed initially was Edmund Campion, then a much-fêted Oxford scholar, who deeply impressed the queen when she visited Oxford in 1566. Campion, however, began having second thoughts about the Reformation that soon turned into anguish. He fled to Ireland, Douai, and later Rome, where he joined the Jesuits. After his ordination in Prague, Campion risked his life returning to Britain in 1580. For thirteen months he travelled through England preaching, writing, and reconverting many to the Church before being captured in 1581. He was paraded through London with a label "seditious Jesuit" stuck to his hat en route to the Tower of London, where he was tortured on a rack. Brought before Elizabeth herself, Campion was given a final chance to renounce the papacy in exchange for his freedom, but his loyalty to the Holy See prevailed, and he was hanged, drawn, and quartered at Tyburn on December 1, 1581. He is known as "the Pope's champion", and his portrait adorns the foyer of Campion Hall.

While well-spoken Oxford tour guides often stand before the *Martyrs' Memorial* and lament the burning at the stake of the Church of England Bishops Ridley, Cranmer, and Latimer during Queen Mary's counterattacks on Protestantism, they rarely mention the fate that befell Campion and others who were executed for their fidelity to the Catholic Church.

Pell's time in Oxford coincided with the canonization of Campion by Pope Paul VI, on the initiative of Cardinal John Heenan of Westminster. At the time, Cardinal Heenan was worried that the Catholic Church was in danger of losing her identity in Britain in the rush towards ecumenism after Vatican II. To restore a sense of perspective, he decided to put forward forty English martyrs, including Blessed Edmund Campion, for canonization.[1]

Initially, in Oxford, Pell was interested in studying the life and times of Saint Augustine of Hippo. He was advised, however, that in order to study Augustine, it was essential to study the period before his life, when much of the Church's structure of authority was being formed. Pell was steered towards eminent Anglican academic Canon S.L. Greenslade, the Regius Professor of Ecclesiastical History, who was to supervise his thesis. The topic settled upon was "The Exercise of Authority in Early Christianity from about 170 to about 270". In hindsight, it was a useful choice for someone destined to wield authority as the archbishop of Australia's two largest cities, to serve on Vatican congregations, and to lead an important Vatican reform process.

[1] Cardinal John Heenan of Westminster told this personally to Father Tim Norris and his cousin, the late Bishop Patrick Casey of Brentwood.

The work involved years of poring over early Church documents in Latin and Greek and meticulous note-taking, as well as reading and analysing scholarly works already produced in the field, many of them in French and German. Oxford's Bodleian Library became Pell's second home (and his sister's, as well, when she visited and helped copy out copious pages of Latin and Greek). With some tuition in German, Pell delved into the world of the early Fathers of the Church's formative years—Cyprian, Irenaeus, Origen, Clement of Alexandria, and Tertullian.

His research brought him face-to-face with the influential Gnostic heresies of the early Church—theories, breakaway groups, and upheavals as ubiquitous and fundamentally anti-Christian in their time as the New Age movement (and just as hard to pin down and categorise). While the events he studied had happened more than seventeen hundred years before, it was a useful academic background for a modern Church leader. The early Fathers' handling of the Gnostics put many modern problems in context. Pell's intimate knowledge of such a sensitive period in Church history stood him in good stead in defending the Church and her structures against those desperate to see them changed radically.

The master of Campion Hall in Pell's time as a student was Father Edward Yarnold, S.J., whose academic specialty was classics and theology. Pell was deeply fond of him. Yarnold died in July 2002, six months after he was interviewed for the first edition of this biography, when he was staying in a nursing home on the outskirts of Cheltenham, an hour's drive through the Cotswolds from Oxford. He was recovering from a knee operation. His recollections of George Pell as a student were clear: "An imposing presence, he had leadership qualities, initiative, and a great sense of humor. He was a bit of a scholar, certainly a hard worker, and he had a strong ecumenical interest."

Yarnold said Pell stood out at Campion for the amount of priestly work he undertook in the Oxford district. Although Pell's parish experience at that point mainly extended to helping out occasionally in Rome and a summer in Baltimore, the instincts of a good pastor were already apparent. Apart from concelebrating Mass with his fellow students and the staff in the Campion Hall chapel every day, Pell also at different stages of his four-year stay served as a chaplain for the Catholic boys at Eton College, where he said the first Catholic Mass since the Reformation; said Masses and heard confessions for the Catholic boys at Summer Fields, a privileged, selective school north of Oxford, once attended by Ronald Knox and Harold Macmillan; taught catechism to Catholic primary school children at the request of the Notre Dame Sisters in Oxford; said Mass and coached soccer at Notre Dame Girls High School; said Mass for the students at the Oxford University chaplaincy; and regularly helped out his friend Father Cyril Murtagh in the nearby parish of Hinksey with Sunday Masses.

Yarnold remembered Pell daring to argue one evening with one of the most prominent and controversial theologians of the twentieth century, Father Edward Schillebeeckx, a Belgian Dominican and teacher of the history of theology at the University of the Netherlands. One of Oxford's strengths has long been the way its graduates and undergraduates are encouraged to speak up in lively, informed academic debate with regular and visiting professors. Yarnold recalled that Schillebeeckx, in his talk, touched on several points that Pell was examining as part of his thesis: "Everyone else just asked questions, but I remember George argued with him on one or two points."

Father Michael Tate, the former Australian federal attorney general, who left politics and became a priest, was an Oxford (Worcester College) contemporary of George Pell. Verbal dexterity, Tate explained, is part of the Oxford game. Tate, who also attended the Schillebeeckx lecture, recalled that Pell was "not belligerent, but not deferential either".

That was a telling episode for what it said about the assurance of a young priest with the confidence to argue with one of the world's most renowned theologians in front of his college master, senior fellows, and fellow students, at a time when Schillebeeckx was hailed as the voice of the future. Five decades on, Schillebeeckx is still revered by those who believe "relevance to the world" can improve on "divine revelation". Catholics well-grounded in tradition, however, recoil especially from Schillebeeckx' fiddling with terms such as "transignification" (Consecration achieves a change of meaning) and "transfinalization" (Consecration changes the purpose of the elements) to replace "transubstantiation" (Consecration turns the elements into the actual, physical Body and Blood of Christ). Aside from those serious issues and Schillebeeckx' influence on the fate of the Church in Holland, Pell in later years regarded Schillebeeckx as a "very substantial theologian" and admired his early work *Christ, the Sacrament of the Encounter with God*.

It was under the influence of modernist theologians such as Schillebeeckx that the Church in Holland (where he worked and taught) was to embrace radical theological change more ruthlessly than any other in the world in the 1970s. The roles of priests and laity were blurred to the point that they were often indistinguishable. Much of the Church's traditional sacramental theology and supernatural mystique was abandoned in the name of "relevance".

Pell, too, was touched by the tumultuous time the Church went through in the late 1960s and the 1970s, when many of his contemporaries were leaving. "As a young priest at Oxford once or twice I wondered whether I was in the right line of business", he admitted. But fleeting doubts about his vocation were never a significant crisis. He persisted with his study and priestly work and found things calmer going within a year or two.

Many others did not. Up to fifty thousand Catholic priests were laicized (released from their priestly vows) during the pontificate of Pope Paul VI as uncertainty took hold of both younger and older priests and the Vatican adopted a liberal approach to releasing them. Contrary to popular misconception, celibacy was not the central issue in many cases. As Pell observed among some of his contemporaries, it was more a question of a weakening of faith, a loss of the supernatural dimension of religion, and a loss of sight of the call to follow Christ. For many men, meeting a potential partner or wanting to carve out a different career might trigger the decision to leave the priesthood but was not the root cause.

Oxford, in Pell's day, retained a touch of the eccentric charm Evelyn Waugh captured decades earlier. One or two of the elderly Jesuits at Campion, for example, claimed to be "amazed" that some bishops would send their students to Rome before Oxford—and pointed out with some glee that baths and time out of the college were in short supply in Rome compared with Oxford. Father Vincent Bywater, S.J., in his eighties when interviewed in 2001, was a senior fellow of Campion Hall in Pell's day, teaching geography. He would not have been out of place around a luncheon table in the 1920s, sharing plovers' eggs with Charles Ryder and Sebastian Flyte of *Brideshead Revisited*. True Oxford students, Bywater contended, "live the life and pick up their degree on the way out". Chaps do not talk about what they are reading—"it just isn't done." Bywater advised new lay students to "hunt in packs" and not let their energies be drained by one-on-one relationships, especially with women.

His first impression of Pell was that he "looked like a Rugby player". Wrong code, correct sentiment. In fact, at Oxford, Pell did play rugby, for Corpus Christi College in the Cuppers, or all-college, competition. He also played tennis in a joint team for Campion Hall and Saint Benet's, the residential hall of the Benedictine Order. And he travelled regularly by train to London's Paddington Station to catch the tube on his way to an opera at Covent Garden. He occasionally drove to nearby Stratford-on-Avon to see the Royal Shakespeare Company perform. It was there, after a performance of *Othello* in 1968, that he met Father Eric D'Arcy, a philosophy lecturer from the Archdiocese of Melbourne, for the first time. They became lifelong friends, and D'Arcy was later named the archbishop of Hobart.

More important, in Bywater's scale of values, was the belief that Catholic bishops "should all have their blade". Pell passed muster on that score. For a sportsman, rowing on the beautiful Cherwell and Isis with their weeping-willow banks in summer twilight is an experience to treasure. Pell thought he was an awkward rower, not well taught, and that he lacked some of the balance needed to excel at the sport. He rated himself a "much better rowing coach", which he was several years after returning from Oxford, when he coached teams at his old school at Ballarat. In Oxford, he rowed for Corpus Christi College in what he called a "fat boys' team" (Campion Hall, with only about fifty students, did not have a team). The boat was apparently dubbed "Don't Feed the Vicar". Legend, and Bywater, suggested he was a little modest about his prowess on the water. The eight did so well in the university competition that they "won their blades" by achieving four "bumps"—overtaking four boats in front of them—over four days of racing. Along with his treasured doctorate, the Corpus Oar (dark blue with two red stripes) came home to Australia with Pell, checked onto the plane.

Bywater remembered little, if anything, about Pell's studies, but he did recall the effectiveness of his work with the Catholic boys at Eton and Summer Fields and how the boys responded well to the positive influence of the athletic young priest: "The boys looked up to him;

he was a kind of hero. The wrong priest in that role could have been a negative influence."

One night, in his first term in Oxford in 1967, Pell attended an Australian dinner at Rhodes House, centre of the Rhodes Scholarship scheme. There he met a theological student for the Anglican priest-hood from Melbourne, Peter Elliott, who already held two degrees in history from Melbourne University and was reading theology. He was part of Oxford's strong Anglo-Catholic subculture, which had flourished from the time of Newman 120 years earlier. Pell invited Elliott back to Campion Hall for dinner. Elliott recalled:

> What struck me, I remember, the first time I visited him was his devo-tion to the Holy Father, Pope Paul VI. He proudly showed me his beautiful bronze, the baptism of Christ by John the Baptist, that the pope had personally given to George in his last year at Propaganda.
>
> He was also very deeply immersed in the Second Vatican Council. I think some people today would be surprised, because he's been so bitterly criticized as a conservative. He was a great dining companion and told stories about Propaganda College and all the different ethnic groups and characters there and was very entertaining. What struck me also was his common sense and very broad intellect. He was not just focused on the early Christian centuries, which are his specialty, but his view of British history was intensely broad. Anyone who looks at his library can see this. He has got at his fingertips the basic sources of British constitutional, political, and social history.

Pell and Elliott became close friends, dining together regularly until Elliott did not call for a few weeks. One night, in October 1967, Elliott, who had been ill, sought out his friend: "I went to spill the beans to him. I said 'I've been through a crisis the last few weeks. I haven't been at all well, and what's come to a head is the fact that I've got to be honest with myself; I've got to seek instruc-tion in the Catholic religion.' "

Pell's first comment was: "I'm not surprised." His second com-ment was: "I'll stand by you." He also promised: "When the day comes, I will offer to be your sponsor." Those words, at one of the most important junctures of his life, had a moving effect on Elliott for decades afterwards. He became a Vatican official in the Pontifical Council for the Family, vicar for religious education for the Catholic

Archdiocese of Melbourne, head of Pell's religious-education-texts-for-schools project, auxiliary bishop of Melbourne, and one of Pell's closest friends.

Not surprisingly, as the son of an Anglican clergyman and as someone living in a high Anglican theological college, Peter Elliott's conversion was a lengthy process of seven or eight months.

> It had to be done at my own pace. George was there as the kind of person that I could go to when I was blue, and I often was. He could send you up, and be a bit silly if need be, but he was very gracious. He never pushed me; he never put pressure on me. George has a sense of freedom and great belief in the autonomy of persons to make their own decisions. His critics know nothing of that. George helped me have a sense of humour about it all. Through his father, he had a respect and a curiosity about Anglicanism, and that was a learning curve for him those years in Oxford.

Although they had never crossed paths in Australia, Elliott and Pell shared a strong abhorrence of Communism and considerable respect for B. A. Santamaria's "Movement". Both Elliott and his father supported Catholic social doctrine and the Democratic Labor Party (DLP), although many people did not realise that Anglicans were involved in the Movement. In the late 1960s, Marxist Catholics were active and vocal in Oxford, centred at Blackfriars, a residential hall operated by the Dominicans. This angered Pell and Elliott, who made a point of attending their public meetings and using their historical knowledge to ask pointed, awkward questions about the incompatibility of Marxism and Catholicism. Not surprisingly, being needled in public angered the hosts of the meetings, accustomed as they were to adulation from their followers. But there was little they could do about the pair they dubbed "the big Australian bastard" and "the little Australian bastard".

While still an outsider to Catholicism, Elliott, in late 1967, could sense the tensions building up within the Catholic Church. In his words, these "exploded" the following year, July 1968, when, against the expectations of the many liberals who regarded him as one of their own, Pope Paul VI issued *Humanae Vitae*. But that was after Elliott had become a Catholic.

On June 24, 1968, Pell stood behind his friend and put his hand on his shoulder as his sponsor as he was received into the Catholic Church. He teased Elliott about "going to Rome over Folly Bridge" after he had moved out of his Anglican College to live in a small, medieval flat over Folly Bridge. On December 8, 1968, the feast of the Immaculate Conception, Pell again stood behind Elliott as his Confirmation sponsor at Corpus Christi Church, Headington Quarry, outside Oxford. Elliott has vivid memories of the evening— for the wrong reasons. "I said to George, 'How are we getting up to Headington?' and he insisted 'We'll go up on my bike.'" The 50cc motorbike was no larger than a Roman motor scooter, a Vespa, and small for the six-foot-three Pell alone, let alone with a passenger. Following the ceremony, the Irish pastor put on a splendid dinner, after which the two Australians got back on the bike to return to Oxford.

> I was feeling elated, but as George hit the starter my foot slipped, and my heel went into the spokes of the wheel as it spun. It ripped the back off my shoe and the back of my heel, so I let out a loud expletive— very good after Confirmation—and was carried into the presbytery by George, with blood pouring out of me and my face pale. George was looking very embarrassed, and the pastor was reminding me I needed to have fortitude (one of the seven gifts of the Holy Spirit conferred at Confirmation). The scar's still there to remind me of my Confirmation and its indelible character, and George drove me back very gingerly, all bound up, to Saint Benet's Hall, where I was living by then.

His doctoral research going well, Pell took time out during the 1969 Christmas break to visit America. He went to Baltimore to see the Weigels, and then travelled to New York to see his old schoolmate Father Michael Mason, who was studying for a master's in theology at the Protestant Union Seminary. The year at Union was a preparation for his doctorate in sociology at Columbia University, which he began the following year. They were turbulent times, and not just for the Church. The United States was in the grip of the Vietnam War, the draft, student strikes, and turmoil generally. In contrast, Christmas had a touch of magic when the two old boys from Saint Pat's met up again. New York was especially cold, and with half a dozen Union students, male and female, Mason and Pell caught the subway and startled and entertained commuters by singing

Christmas carols. As Mason remembered: "It was to contribute a bit of Christmas spirit. We were always having to move on when we saw any subway cops, because busking wasn't allowed at that time, and they probably couldn't comprehend that we weren't collecting money. We took the subway all the way from Union to Battery Park and then went across to Staten Island. People were looking at us as though we were weird."

It was Christmas Eve, and after the concelebrated midnight Mass in the parish on Forty-Third Street, where Mason lived and worked, he and Pell went out for dinner. "To cap it off perfectly, we walked out onto Second Avenue, and it was snowing thickly. There wasn't anything moving on Second Avenue, and for both of us, it was the first time we'd seen snow at Christmas. It was really magic. So, we ran down Second Avenue like idiots, throwing snowballs at each other."

Pell's dissertation for his doctor of philosophy degree at Oxford University was due to be presented at Easter 1971. It sought to answer the question: In the centuries immediately after the death of Christ and His apostles, how did the Church as we know her continue to take shape? Pell described the theology of the succession of bishops following in the footsteps of the apostles in the early Church. His principal ancient sources were the writings of the early Church Fathers, including Clement of Alexandria's *Paedagogus*, *Opera Omnia* of Saint Cyprian, Hippolytus' *The Apostolic Tradition*, Saint Irenaeus' *Adversus Haereses*, Origen's homilies and commentaries, and Tertullian's *Opera*.

"There's no doubt that reading the basic sources so extensively at that period, they shape your way of thinking semi-consciously", Pell observed. The period he examined began as the Church was emerging from a crisis inflicted by the loose, heretical Gnostic movement. Much of the writing of the early Fathers was directed against Gnosticism, and the discovery of more than seven hundred pages of Gnostic writings in 1945 in Egypt vindicated the reliability of their descriptions of the movement.[2] Irenaeus, bishop of Lyons from about 178, was impatient with the Gnostics, declaring caustically: "Are not there as many heresies as philosophies?" While most heretics were

---

[2] George Pell, *The Exercise of Authority in Early Christianity from about 170 to about 270* (D.Phil. diss., Oxford University, 1971), p. 10.

condemned to a life of searching and never finding, others, he said, "claim to discover a new doctrine a day, while others went one better than even the Apostles and discovered another God!" For Irenaeus, teaching one and the same faith, drawn from Scripture and tradition, united the Church. At a richer and deeper level, the Church's unity is rooted in the Holy Spirit and so transcends history while participating in it: "Where the Church is, there also is the Spirit of God, and where there is the Spirit of God, there is the Church and every grace", Irenaeus wrote.[3]

Saint Cyprian, bishop of Carthage from 248 or 249 until his martyrdom in 258, was a pivotal figure in Pell's Oxford studies. He was a stable, self-assured character, capable of reducing complex arguments to a few basic points and then defending his position with force and clarity—a natural leader and a good writer. He articulated the loyalty Christians felt for the Church, which he repeatedly referred to as "Mother" or "Mother Church", a term still widely used. Mother Church, he taught, weeps over her lost children or rejoices "to welcome back the glorious confessors [people who had suffered for their faith by jail or other punishments but who were not martyred]".[4] Cyprian's preoccupations were promoting loyalty, a sense of duty, and unity within Mother Church—a mystical unity founded on the activity of the Holy Spirit, a unity of doctrine and in organisational cooperation. Pell noted: "On many of the intellectual problems then confronting interested Christians [like the literalist interpretation of Scripture], he [Cyprian] was deeply insensitive; a quality which he sometimes used to advantage in the struggles of his episcopate."[5] As Pell put it: "Cyprian's concern for unity is closely connected with his equally firm conviction about the unicity of the visible Church. God himself ordained that there be one Church, so that there is one God, one Christ, one Church and one (teaching) chair founded by Our Lord on St. Peter."[6] Cyprian was intransigent on matters of doctrine. At the same time, he was sensitive to the political subtleties of the many difficult situations that confronted him and pastorally had a great deal of common sense. In 250, he was the first bishop of his time

[3] Ibid., p. 37.
[4] Ibid, p. 305.
[5] Ibid., p. 290.
[6] Ibid., p. 309.

to permit the deathbed reconciliation of repentant *lapsi*, those who had left the Church. This magnanimous, compassionate gesture flew in the face of the traditions of the time and, as Pell explained, "is the first recorded and certain example of a Christian bishop acting alone in a monarchical fashion to resolve a new and significant problem".[7]

In October 1970, towards the end of Pell's research and writing, Father Gerry Diamond arrived in Oxford to pursue his master's studies. He found that he and "certain other characters had to put some pressure on to make sure deadlines [for the Pell dissertation] were met". It was due by Holy Thursday in April 1971, and if not submitted by then, Pell would have had to wait another two months. Diamond was in the thick of the last-minute flurry, helping with proofreading along with Pat Bearsley, a New Zealand Marist, and taking the dissertation back and forth to the typist at Wallingford (outside Oxford) for last-minute corrections. Pell then rushed it to the bookbinder and made the deadline.

The Melbourne Symphony Orchestra was in New York, so Margaret Pell flew to England to spend Easter with her brother. The Pells and Gerry Diamond visited Canterbury that weekend, and Pell defended his dissertation successfully on Easter Tuesday. (In 1975, when he had saved up the fare, Pell would return to Oxford for the presentation of his doctorate in the Sheldonian Theatre, wearing the blue and scarlet gown of an Oxford doctor of philosophy.) On the Wednesday after Easter, George Pell, S.T.L., D.Phil, left for Australia via a two-week holiday in the Holy Land and India, where he caught up with old friends from Propaganda Fide.

Only those who have been there and been awarded an Oxford degree fully understand the self-confidence the process and achievement bestow.

Back in Ballarat, Pell's mentor, Bishop O'Collins, had retired, and Bishop Ronald Mulkearns had succeeded him. At Oxford, Diamond and Pell had a standing joke that Pell could look forward to being appointed curate at Manangatang, one of the most remote outposts of the diocese. Since Manangatang had a curate, Pell was sent to the next parish, Swan Hill on the Murray River. After eight years in Europe, it was time for some pastoral experience in the bush.

[7] Ibid., p. 324.

10

Country Curate, Editor,
and the Battle for Aquinas

"This could only happen in Communist China", Paul Bongiorno, himself a Ballarat priest by 1971, remembered his old friend fuming about his appointment to Swan Hill. At the outset of their careers, young people with a lot to give are generally in a hurry to put their training and education to good use. George Pell was no exception, although, in hindsight, he conceded that his pastoral experience at Swan Hill was "one of the best things that ever happened to me".

He accepted that life would be very different after returning from Europe, and he was familiar with country Victoria. After getting out a map to pinpoint Swan Hill's exact location, Pell put his reservations to one side, packed up his books, and drove north, ready to dive into his first full-time job.

Ballarat is a large diocese, covering the western third of the state of Victoria. It stretches from the South Australian border in the west to the Murray River in the north and Bass Strait in the south. Swan Hill is about a five hours' drive from Melbourne and four hours from Ballarat through monotonous terrain that makes staying awake at the wheel a real effort. It is a service centre for the surrounding Mallee wheat-growing area, which also produces dried fruits, vegetables, some wine, and timber. While the town itself, on the Murray River, is well appointed and reasonably prosperous, most of Pell's work was to be in centres up to an hour's drive away.

Working in remote locations is the norm in country dioceses, but it can be a culture shock for newcomers. Country Australians are hospitable, and the people of the district gave their new curate a great welcome. He took to them immediately and quickly became absorbed in the pastoral work of the Church—saying Mass, preaching, hearing confessions, anointing and visiting the sick, conducting Baptisms, weddings, and funerals, and helping with religion in the schools. "You're confronted with all sorts of personal situations and personal sufferings", he recalled. "That was a very good time. I was very lucky. My parish priest [pastor], Father Bill Melican, was a good parish priest, very good company, a good talker and raconteur, and a good host. It was a very lively parish with a couple of out stations, and I looked after one end of the parish (Nyah West)." He also worked in Piangil (current population 190) nearby.

Father Pell was the best-educated priest in his diocese and one of the best educated in Australia. However, applying that knowledge to practical pastoral situations was something he learned on the job: "It wasn't just that you were confronted with the personal consequences of Church teaching, but in a certain sense I had to relearn all my theology, or reformulate it, so that I could make it accessible and understandable to people."

Like many before and after him, Pell found it surprisingly hard work. "I didn't write nearly as fast then as I do now under pressure, and a background difficulty was that I had done my theology in Rome, and the Roman world of theological formulation, at least as it was taught then, was very much a Continental world", he said in 2001. "It was quite different from the patterns of thought in the English-speaking world. To some extent, my four years in England had helped me to start that transition, but nonetheless it was solid work to get together a decent sermon."

He need not have worried. Numerous Swan Hill parishioners appreciated his early sermons and all aspects of his work. As his career unfolded over subsequent decades, they looked back on his time in the parish with affection, and were proud to have been his first parishioners, recognizing that grass roots experience is essential to any bishop. They also found him a lot of fun. "He loved swimming in the local pool with the youngsters; he loved kicking around a football with the boys. And he loved food—the cakes at parish socials always went down well—and he was sincere and very approachable", Claire Betts remembered. Margaret Jirik, a mother of five, including three sons who attended Saint Patrick's College, Ballarat, said Pell was "spot on". He had a few meals with the family, and Margaret remembered him urging her son, John, to aim high, even suggesting he try for a Rhodes Scholarship. Audrey Walsh, who served on the newly formed parish council with the young curate, found him "most unassuming; he threw himself into parish life—I felt the parish had a real buzz while he was with us."

At a time of upheaval following the Second Vatican Council, when parishioners were confused and a little apprehensive about the changes taking place, Pell organized a series of speakers to talk on the issues of the day. One of them was his old friend from Oxford, Peter Elliott, by that time a Catholic seminarian in Melbourne. Pell invited him up to give the people of Swan Hill and Nyah West a kind of teaching mission on successive nights. Elliott was not yet ordained a deacon, but he accepted the invitation and flew up on a "flibbity-jib plane from Essendon" and spoke. The people turned out in good numbers and rated the talks a success.

The people Pell served in the Murray region showed no signs of being impressed about his being an Oxford graduate; many people probably never even knew he was Doctor Pell. "He was never high and mighty; he was always very easy to communicate with", Jirik remembered. When he returned for a funeral years later, they found he was just the same. "If he had got too big for his boots, one of the women in the parish with twelve children would have had something to say. That lady treated him like one of her own children, anyway." Some people in the parish were more impressed when they learned that he had ventured behind the Iron Curtain.

It was in Swan Hill that Pell wrote his first published book, an account of the fifty years' work of the Sisters of Saint Joseph in the district from 1922 to 1972. The folksy, close-up portrait of the Church's fledgling days in the Mallee district captured the spirit of the pioneering Church and the tireless work of the Sisters. The order was founded by Saint Mary of the Cross MacKillop, who was "far ahead of her time in her conviction that the same educational opportunities should be available to all classes of people".[1] From the beginning, the Sisters opted out of educating the richer classes and concentrated their efforts on the poor, and especially the many thousands of Australian

[1] George Pell, *Success Story: Made in Australia: The Sisters of St Joseph in Swan Hill* (Maryborough, Australia: Hedges & Bell, 1972).

children living on farms and settlements throughout the bush, tens and sometimes hundreds of miles from a large town. "Not only were these children to be given an education at least equal to that of the State system, but they were to be prepared for the wider dimensions of life through instruction in their faith.... It was above all the Sisters who converted the largely ignorant and somewhat indifferent religious sentiment of last century into the robust and articulate commitment of so many of our 'over-thirties' today."[2] The Sisters, the book recalls, battled harsh conditions in their early years, including dust storms in the 1920s that were so fierce that visibility was limited to a few feet and flying sand cut the skin. On such occasions, they learned to keep the children overnight at school, and after one storm removed sixty pounds of sand from the convent when the storm settled.

As a tribute to the Sisters, Pell ended the book with an appropriate verse from priest/poet John O'Brien:

> Your name in dust is hid,
> No thought or word has earned you immortality;
> Immortal only are the kindly things you did—
> Amen I say, you did them unto me.[3]

In 1973, Pell's second appointment as a curate brought him home to Saint Alipius in Ballarat East. The church is an impressive bluestone Ballarat landmark, on the left-hand side of the wide, main street driving in from Melbourne. George and Margaret Pell senior, by then well into their sixties, were still working hard in the Royal Oak Hotel. Margaret junior was living in Melbourne, playing in the orchestra, and David was an accountant. Pell's mother, who had been unwell for some time, suffered a heart attack at her younger son's wedding in 1972. She recovered but had subsequent bouts of ill health.

Pell's pastoral work continued much as it had in Swan Hill. Ballarat East was a busy parish with four priests and five schools. In March, Bishop Mulkearns appointed Pell his episcopal vicar of education, a non-executive, part-time position representing the bishop

---

[2] Ibid.
[3] John O'Brien, "The Helping Hand" (1921).

on education matters. The main task was to chair the diocesan education board, an advisory group on policy.

Pell's time at Saint Alipius overlapped for twelve months with that of another curate, Gerald Ridsdale. Ridsdale's hidden, fiendish behaviour at that time, as well as before and after in a string of parishes—Apollo Bay, Ballarat, Edenhope, Inglewood, Mortlake, and Swan Hill—eventually led to his jailing as one of Australia's most notorious paedophile priests. In 1994, Ridsdale (Pope John Paul II had stripped him of his clerical faculties the year before) received an eighteen-year jail sentence in Warrnambool County Court. He pleaded guilty to forty-six charges, including thirty-six counts of indecent assault, five of committing unlawful sexual intercourse, four of gross indecency, and one of attempting unlawful sexual intercourse, against twenty-one children, aged nine to fifteen, between 1961 and 1982. In 1993, he had been jailed for three months on similar charges.

The court heard that Ridsdale had assaulted victims in toilet blocks, showers, beds, and in the confessional. He had allegedly carried a jar of Vaseline in his car and once rewarded an altar boy with sacramental bread after twice molesting him while driving home from Mass. Another victim underwent anal surgery after being sodomized by the priest. The court also heard that Ridsdale indecently assaulted a girl, aged ten, after officiating at her father's funeral. Ridsdale, the judge said, "heartlessly abused his power" by committing "wicked and appalling acts of debauchery". During his time at Saint Alipius, Ridsdale was the chaplain at the nearby Saint Alipius Christian Brothers primary school. The court heard that Ridsdale sodomized one boy in the school bike shed when he came to him for help after being molested by a Saint Alipius Christian Brother.

During the time he lived in the same presbytery as Ridsdale, George Pell had no inkling of his colleague's real nature. Other priests, and former priests, who had shared presbyteries with Ridsdale said the same thing. So did many parishioners from various parishes where he served. It was two decades later that the dark truth emerged. Such clerical abuse had been going on for decades in many countries, with few people—parents, teachers, or fellow priests—suspecting anything. Those who had tried to alert Church leaders to the problem were generally swept aside, probably due to a mixture of disbelief, indifference, and incompetence on the part of Church authorities.

Pell was not around the Saint Alipius parish for much of the time Ridsdale was in residence. He spent more and more of his time working for the Catholic Teachers College in Ballarat, initially known as Aquinas College, where he was appointed principal in November 1973, a job that also took him to Melbourne one or two days most weeks.

Also in 1973, with Pell looking on, Peter Elliott was ordained a Catholic priest during the Eucharistic Congress in Melbourne. The following year, Gerry Diamond returned from his studies abroad with a licentiate in Scripture from Rome as well as his Oxford M.A. He, George Pell, and Denis Hart, who had been working as a priest in Melbourne, had dinner together for the first time since George had left the seminary at Werribee in 1963. His friends were in the same financial straitjacket as Pell himself, so when they wanted to meet up, as they did several times a year, dining at a good Italian restaurant like Melbourne's Florentino, they saved up for weeks beforehand. They appreciated good food and wine, and it was worth the effort. Peter Elliott was also part of this close circle, referred to by some as "the gang of four". This camaraderie was important to them all at a time of upheaval and uncertainty in the Church. To their deep sadness, large numbers of priests were leaving the mission around that time, including Paul Bongiorno, who remembered Pell lending him a sympathetic ear and shedding a few tears when he went to tell him the news. The Church could ill afford such a loss of talent.

Despite years of service as archbishop of Australia's two largest cities, George Pell rated "saving Aquinas College, Ballarat, as one of the best things I have done"—an indication of the priority he afforded Catholic education. The college, now the Aquinas Campus of the Australian Catholic University (which also has campuses in Sydney, Melbourne, Brisbane, and Canberra), is located at 1200 Mair Street near the centre of Ballarat. It is a leafy campus with a striking focal point, a Guy Boyd sculpture of the Madonna and Child, commissioned by Pell. The campus' newer buildings are in sympathy with the stately Victorian home, Manifold House (circa 1881), with its wide, iron lace verandas, at the heart of the campus.

Catholic teacher training began in Ballarat around 1884, when the Loreto Sisters operated a training college until 1906. A few years later, the Sisters of Mercy stepped in, opening Aquin Training College in

1909, with some students sent as far afield as Melbourne University for academic studies and even overseas for expert music tuition. It soon became known as the Sacred Heart Training College because it operated in the same group of buildings as the secondary college of that name. Initially, the average number of graduates per year was around thirteen, rising by 1971 to thirty-seven. By that time, eighty-six students were enrolled in total, and numbers began to increase dramatically. This was due to several factors—the opening up of new Catholic parishes and schools, smaller class sizes that required more teachers, and the exodus of Sisters, Brothers, and priests from teaching, creating opportunities for lay teachers.

In 1972, Bishop Mulkearns and the Sisters of Mercy agreed that, to facilitate the necessary expansion, the Diocese of Ballarat would assume financial responsibility for the college, which the Sisters would continue to administer. By 1973, it could not accommodate the 180 students who wanted to enroll in 1974. An urgent meeting was called by Sister Clare Forbes, the acting principal of Sacred Heart, on July 5, 1973. Pell, as Ballarat's vicar for education, chaired the meeting, which was attended by other priests, lay officials of the diocese, and the Sisters of Mercy. It was agreed to rename the institution Aquinas College and to lease 1200 Mair Street. The property was once the stately home of businessman and mining engineer Cyrus Bath Retallack, who came to Ballarat from Cornwall in the middle of the nineteenth century and who had surrounded his mansion with a tennis court, a croquet lawn, an orchard, and stables. It later served as Queens Church of England Girls' Grammar School, but it had been bought earlier in 1973 by the Saint John of God Sisters, whose hospital was adjacent. Numerous meetings followed, and a deputation, including Pell, was sent to discuss the future of the college with the education minister in Victoria premier Rupert Hamer's Liberal Government, Lindsay Thompson. Later in the year, Pell was offered the position of director of the college and accepted it for three years beginning November 5, 1973. New lay staff were selected, and a crest for the new college was designed around the motto chosen by Pell—*Umbram Fugat Veritas* (Truth puts shadow to flight). Its crest included the many-pointed star symbolizing the patronage of Saint Thomas Aquinas.

Putting the interests of Aquinas ahead of her own, Sister Clare Forbes, who had been acting principal, was happy to stand aside to allow Pell to take the position, as she knew he had better academic qualifications. Pell appointed her as his deputy, and they forged a powerful partnership, earning the nicknames George and the Dragon. "Clare was one of my closest friends, and I think even our strongest enemies would concede we made a formidable pair", he said.

Forbes, from Bungaree just outside Ballarat, had entered the Sisters of Mercy in 1943, the year her only brother died at age ten. Two of her four sisters were also Mercy Sisters. In 1977–1978, when she finally had the chance to pursue postgraduate study, she completed a master of education degree at the Jesuit university Boston College, where she was inducted as a member of the Alpha Sigma Nu society, a Jesuit honour society reserved to those who made an outstanding contribution to the university. As Pell recalled at her funeral in Saint Alipius in 1992 (she died, aged sixty-seven, from a brain tumor), Clare was energetic, vigorous in argument, and passionate about her causes as only those with Celtic blood can be: "Speaking personally, words cannot express how much I owed her as friend and supporter, tactical adviser, and spiritual mentor. She reinforced, as no one else did except my mother, my own devotion to Our Lady. She was born on the feast of Our Lady of Perpetual Succor and believed it significant that she received the news the cancer had spread to her brain on the feast of Our Lady of Guadalupe, to whom she had a special devotion."

While it could have been coincidence that Forbes received the news on that day, many Catholics with devotion to a particular saint or to the Blessed Virgin Mary have noticed that major milestones in their lives, both positive and sad, occur on related days in the Church calendar. This is interpreted by the faithful as a sign that, as the poet Tennyson wrote, "More things are wrought by prayer / than this world dreams of."[4]

Regardless of the financial limits in which he operated, George Pell looked back on Aquinas in the 1970s and the early 1980s as a "most happy" tertiary institution, where the staff and students reveled in the casual, egalitarian atmosphere he encouraged. In later years, when he would sometimes encounter former students, they invariably remembered it that way too. As in some of the smaller liberal arts colleges in the United States, the thirty or forty staff and the students

<hr/>

[4] Alfred Lord Tennyson, *Idylls of the King* (1859).

mixed freely—not just the academic staff, but the administrative and support staff as well. Attendance at the fortnightly college Mass was voluntary, but around 70 percent of students were generally present. By 1975, the number of students had grown to four hundred.

As director, Pell, always more of a night owl than an early bird, started at the college about 9:00 A.M. and often continued until 9:00 or 10:00 P.M. At the height of battles for government funding, he was usually in Melbourne several days each week and often travelled to Canberra to put Aquinas' case to the federal government.

Michael Gilchrist, the former editor of *AD2000*, the Melbourne-based journal of religious opinion, taught at Aquinas while Pell was in charge. Gilchrist said his boss' style was "rugged Australian without excess authoritarianism. His staff meetings were a delight—he did not allow waffle; he kept things to the point and kept it moving. Once a month or so he would give the students a pep talk, commenting on any reports of serious misbehaviour, chiding them that excessive drinking or rowdy partying 'was not what we expect of future Catholic teachers'." Despite being only in his thirties, Pell was something of a father figure to the students and got on well with them, Gilchrist said, despite never being able to come to grips with what he termed their "barbarian music".

As well as running Aquinas, Pell taught moral education at the college. In 1979, to deepen his own understanding of the subject, Pell took four months' leave to begin researching the writings and influence of American psychologist Lawrence Kohlberg, whose theories dominated the discussion of moral education in the English-speaking world for many years up to the time of his suicide, at the age of sixty, in 1987. A former professor of education and psychology at Harvard University, Kohlberg was best known for his work in the development of moral reasoning in children and adolescents. Pell's research led to a 234-page scholarly evaluation of Kohlberg, with a ten-page bibliography of sources as diverse as Aristotle and Kant. While acknowledging that Kohlberg "was not entirely wrong" and praising him for resisting moral relativism, Pell concluded that he was

inconsistent and deficient in his treatment of morality and religion.... Despite his insistence on the separation of morality and religion, his highest form of moral reasoning requires and demands a post-conventional religious orientation, because the "why" of moral living is not resolvable on purely logical grounds. The fact that the religion he espouses involves a cosmic or pantheist type of divinity does not exonerate him from the flight from rationality into some religious orientation. The morally autonomous person cannot be religious, yet must be religious!

The thesis earned Pell a master of education from Monash University in 1982. He chose to focus on Kohlberg because he was well aware of the man's subtle but pervasive influence on teacher formation throughout the Western world, especially in relation to how people viewed issues of morality and religion in the broad curriculum. Taken too far, Kohlberg's approach was, in Pell's view, incompatible with some of the principles of Catholic education and therefore needed to be analysed and understood thoroughly.

Throughout 1975, 1976, and 1977, Aquinas staff and some Institute board members, including businessman Bernard Callinan, a close friend of Pell's, frequently lobbied parliamentarians and produced newspaper articles to argue for full recurrent funding for the college. The breakthrough came on July 6, 1977, when the education minister in the Fraser coalition government, Senator John Carrick, announced that Aquinas College would receive full federal recurrent funding from January 1, 1978. In making the announcement, he said, "The Government recognized that the distinctive character of non-government schools depends on the availability of teachers committed to the ethic on which the schools are founded."[5]

Pell also had to lobby for capital grants for buildings to accommodate the increasing numbers of students. This exhaustive effort met with only limited success, with Aquinas receiving minor works grants of AU$24,000 in 1978 (about US$18,500), AU$43,000 in 1979, and AU$30,000 in 1980. At the same time, he managed to have a new library built, raising funds from a variety of sources, mainly non-government, and being frugal with day-to-day spending. The substantial salary to which Pell had been entitled since the beginning of 1974, which he did not accept but plowed back into the

---

[5] Information on government funding for Aquinas and the formation of the Institute of Catholic Education and its entry into the State College of Victoria was drawn partly from J. N. Kellett, *Institute of Catholic Education—An Overview of Its Formative Years* (June 1987).

cash-strapped college, helped. The Callinan Library opened in 1980 and was expanded with an AU\$165,000 grant in 1982. A new administrative block, and the Forbes Student Centre, named after Sister Clare, soon followed, built in a style in keeping with the traditional beauty of the college's main buildings.

In naming the library after his great friend, Pell honoured an outstanding Australian. Knighted in 1977, Bernard Callinan, born in Moonee Ponds in 1913, qualified as an engineer in the 1930s and volunteered for duty at the start of World War II. As one of the commandos in the ill-fated Sparrow Force, which landed on Timor, Callinan and his three hundred comrades withdrew to the hills to fight on against odds that saw them outnumbered eventually by one hundred to one. The commandos, whom Callinan eventually commanded, did much to immobilize thirty thousand Japanese troops on Timor. As Nevil Shute wrote of them: "Few soldiers in history can claim to have done more than that."

As auxiliary bishop of Melbourne in 1995, Pell preached his friend's eulogy in Saint Patrick's Cathedral. He spoke of Callinan's Military Cross, which he won for leading "a small band of heroes, whose exploits will pass into Australian legend as the only Allied troops in 1942 between India and Eastern Papua who had not surrendered to the Japanese." He told how "Sir Bernard served Australia with distinction in six years of war; he served it with equal distinction in peace for almost sixty years ... [in] his leadership roles in the construction of the new Parliament House [Canberra] and La Trobe University." He said, "His Catholicism, among the best of its type and generation, was the informing principle of his life", that "he was devoted to the Mass, the sacraments, and the daily rosary", and that "he accepted the clear lines of religious authority" and "accepted, without hesitation, the proper religious authority of pope and archbishop."[6]

During his time at Aquinas, Pell produced two booklets on Catholic education. *Are Our Secondary Schools Catholic?* and *Bread, Stones or Fairy Floss* were published by the Australian Catholic Truth Society. These thirty-page booklets, which sold for twenty-five cents

---

[6] George Pell, "Sir Bernard Callinan", in *Be Not Afraid: Collected Writing* (Sydney: Duffy & Snellgrove, 2004), pp. 259, 261.

and were well received across the country, were significant in that they first drew the attention of Catholics outside Victoria to Pell. In a straightforward way, the booklets set out what Catholic education should be about—or rather, what Catholic parents of that time assumed it was about. Later generations of practicing Catholics became deeply concerned about the effectiveness of school catechesis. From today's perspective, those early books are middle of the road, but they helped establish Pell's reputation as an up-and-coming conservative in the Church. This was perhaps a reflection of the radical "new church" direction that was being taken in the late 1970s and 1980s.

As Peter Elliott pointed out, although *Bread, Stones or Fairy Floss* was very popular among conservatives, it put Pell in a middle position on catechetics. "He didn't fall for the old conservative line of 'just teach them the catechism and everything will be solved', which is impossible", Elliott explained. "That's what he meant by the stones. The fairy floss was the light situation ethics and sugar catechetics of the 1970s, and the bread was a good balance in doctrine and life and Scripture."

Under the heading "Fairy Floss", Pell argued: "Many of those graduating from our secondary schools are good people and good Catholics, but most of them are theologically illiterate.... Youngsters are encouraged to spend too much time talking about themselves and too little time talking about Christ and the gospel message." Catholic schools were not turning out enough people interested in God and religion, as distinct from those "with a vague interest in humanity and the fashionable concerns of the moment".[7]

He also called for greater professionalism and better education for teachers of religion: "There can be no viable answer in the simplicities in the past." However, while the Church had changed many things, such as the language of the Mass, "we should never imagine that she can abandon her claims to some absolute truths or turn away from her basic strengths." One religion was not as good as another, however soothing it might be to believe otherwise. "Ecumenism is not indifferentism."

[7] George Pell, *Bread, Stones or Fairy Floss* (Melbourne: Catholic Truth Society Publications, 1977).

In *Are Our Secondary Schools Catholic?* (1979), Pell wrote:

The ideal of a liberal education, formerly limited to the ruling elites, is now regarded as appropriate for the big numbers of pupils attending secondary schools in advanced Western society. Such an ideal requires not only a developed capacity for abstract thinking, and an acquaintance with and reverence for the achievements of the past, but a cultivated understanding of what is central and important. "A great intellect", says Cardinal Newman, "possesses the knowledge not only of things, but of their mutual and true relations; knowledge, not merely considered as acquirement, but as philosophy."

This probably seems a far cry from the concerns of those pimply creatures consigned to our care in lower secondary, obsessed with sport and barbarian music, but even then we can be developing an admiration for excellence and rationality (by demanding it), and helping to cultivate an absolute distaste for bigotry and ignorance.[8]

Each generation, he argued, gets the generation of young people it deserves.

Adolescence is our last best chance to influence people, to tap the idealism which is present in most cases, to provide models of leadership and service so that intellectually and politically, as well as religiously, we shall have people at a local and national level who will stand up and be counted. Many of our Catholic students can be interested in things higher than parties, money-making and being president of the local race club.[9]

These booklets attracted attention because they supported the notion that Catholic school students ought to be taught the fundamental theology of the Catholic religion and inculcated with an understanding of absolute truth. That was a far cry from the situation in most Catholic schools in the 1970s, where Catholic doctrine was barely taught at all. Students at that time might find themselves spending religion classes sitting in circles on the floor discussing the environment or the evils of capitalism, or lying on their backs with

[8] George Pell, *Are Our Secondary Schools Catholic?* (Melbourne: Catholic Truth Society Publications, 1977), p. 16.
[9] Ibid., p. 28.

their eyes closed listening to relaxing music as they "discovered their inner selves". In rare instances where issues such as the priesthood or *Humanae Vitae* were raised, students were generally treated to diatribes in favour of women's ordination and contraception. Pell might not have fully realised it at the time, but in penning those two booklets, he was taking the first steps in a much wider battle for the minds and hearts of Catholics and the future direction of religious education and much else in the Church.

In April 1980, Pell put on the vestments in the sacristy of Saint Alipius for one of the hardest tasks of his fourteen-year priesthood— saying the Requiem Mass for his mother, who had died after a long struggle with heart disease and breathing difficulties. He paid tribute to his mother as a woman of great strength and faith, a faith very typical of the west of Ireland in its certainties and its impatience with theological subtleties.

> She knew as well as Saint Paul and any of the Gospel writers that any human achievement meant hard work, struggle, and sometimes sorrow. She and Dad worked enormously hard that their children would have opportunities not open to themselves. Mum was very proud that her children, through the grace of God, and luck and strong management direction from her and Dad, to some extent availed themselves of their opportunities.

One consequence of a fairly long illness, Pell noted, is that it enables the family of the sick and dying to come to terms with what is happening.

> In fits and starts, slowly at first but inevitably, they come to realise that the time for birth, for planting and healing has passed, that now we are at the time for parting and for death.
>
> For Christians this cannot be just an occasion of sadness, or grief without hope. Just last night one of our parishioners from the East told me that it was hard to give condolences to a priest; with the clear implication that priests above all must take seriously the promise of eternal life. Wouldn't we all be delighted, he added, if our mother was to meet the Queen or the Pope—and of course the dead have gone to meet Someone much more important ... a God who loves us and is interested in us, and who has a task for each one of us.

This is true of course because we are sons and daughters of God, not slaves dominated by fear, but it is only one side of the coin. We are still waiting for the final revelation; we are still limited (probably a happier way of describing our lot than Saint Paul's references to our decadence!); groaning in one great act of giving birth as we wait for our bodies to be set free.

I ask you then to pray in the Mass a prayer of thanksgiving for the good she accomplished; to pray in the hope of the resurrection that she may be loosed from her sins.

By that time, the Catholic Church, with the charismatic Pope John Paul II at the helm, had become newsworthy in a way she had not been for decades. This period coincides with the beginning of Pell's journalistic career. In December 1979, Bishop Ronald Mulkearns appointed him editor of *Light*, the Ballarat Catholic news journal. During Pell's five-year editorship, it was published at first every two months and eventually ten times a year. In his first editorial, in March 1980, Pell summed up where the Catholic Church stood at the beginning of the new pontificate:

The Second Vatican Council was the most important event in the Catholic Church since the Reformation. It shook the Church out of her immobility, and headed her into the next millennium. There have been wonderful and new developments, but these have been purchased at a considerable price. In retrospect, some who appealed to the "spirit of the council" and justified their claims under this head are now seen to have been following aberrations. Just as surely some refused to accept any changes, or accepted them reluctantly or with bad grace.

To some extent the Church was polarized.... We must work and pray that the worst doubts and divisions are behind us.

Light under Pell was notable for its broad world view of the Church, the range of subjects it tackled in depth, and its book reviews (everything from detective thrillers and biographies to religious books). Such diverse characters as Malcolm Muggeridge, Caroline Chisholm, Mother Catherine McAuley, Mary MacKillop, Mary Ward, and Saint Thomas More were profiled.

The journal's regular contributors included Aquinas teacher Michael Gilchrist, who wrote a column on public life, and Babette Francis. Her organisation, Women Who Want to Be Women, was the *bête noire* of feminists at the time and something of a joke among female journalists. Decades later, however, it was interesting to note that her early health warnings in regard to the birth control pill, the IUD, and abortion became mainstream news.

Under Pell, many issues of the journal carried a special theme—teenagers, Australian Rules football, television, saints and heroes, life after death, abortion, prayer, the Eucharist, Christ, Lent, education, justice and peace, and Our Lady, with articles that stood the test of time. The journal's editorials also give a clear insight into Pell's view of the world and the Church in his late thirties and early forties. His editorial of August 1981 was about the spectacular wedding ceremony of the then Prince and Princess of Wales, with its "marvellous ritual and pageantry, organised to perfection with that mixture of dignity and showmanship that only the English can achieve". Pell went on, then, to predict that

an increasing percentage of Australians will see the British monarchy not simply as irrelevant, but also as not being in the best interests of Australia.

Australia will become a Republic, although whether it will be sooner or later cannot be predicted. The issue is not important enough to justify major bitterness in the Australian community. Much better will be a pattern of evolution.

An Australian Republic does not necessarily mean a change of flag, nor a withdrawal from the British Commonwealth; not even an increase of our fashionable anti-British sentiment. We owe most of our public institutions, and much of the basic stability of our Australian way of life, to the contribution that the British made to our country. We should be grateful for this.

However, our eyes should be towards the future. It would be ironic if the Catholics in a diocese which saw the Eureka Rebellion[10] and which was proud to be regarded as Mannix territory should now become, or at least be seen as, stalwart defenders of the British monarchy.

---

[10] On Sunday, December 3, 1854, Ballarat gold miners took up arms against the corruption and unfairness of goldfield authorities in a battle regarded as the birth of true democracy in Australia.

The following December, Pell set out the role he believed the pope, bishops, and priests should take in speaking out about moral and political issues, a foretaste of his approach as a bishop. Clerics, he said, have an obligation to speak out on moral issues in public life.

> The pulpit is never the place for partisan politics, although it can occasionally be used to discuss public moral issues.... In the long run, the separation of Church and State is good for both parties.... There is no single Catholic political ideal, no single model of Christian social life, any more than there is a single model for a Catholic school or parish. Some models of Government are, of course, clearly incompatible with basic Christianity; such regimes would be dictatorships of the left or right, who systematically violate human rights. Politics is for lay people. Clericalism in politics is wrong in principle and wrong in practice.

In a special supplement, *1984 in Australia*, published in June that year and built around the Orwell novel, Pell lamented that

> many Australians, and certainly many Australian Catholics, are proudly and persistently anti-intellectual, and this often takes the form of an hostility to education and schooling. In the world of tomorrow, the children of today could pay a bitter price for this stupidity.... No group of schools anywhere has a better record than our Catholic schools in educating children of parents who were not highly educated themselves and often not at all prosperous. We must do even better with this generation and the next, especially in country areas and for the children of our migrants.

As he observed, while larger numbers of students were staying in formal education for longer periods, "it is doubtful whether people are reading more, especially material of a more serious nature." In November 1983, to mark the centenary of Karl Marx' death, Pell had written, "We are all influenced, often unknowingly, by Marxist theory, and yet there would not be six Catholic secondary schools in Australia that teach about Marx!"

Pell's interest in history and literature was often to the fore in *Light*'s editorials. For Anzac Day 1984, he quoted English poet

Wilfred Owen, whose words capture eloquently the human cost of
World War I, a war in which sixty thousand young Australians died.

> Behold,
> A ram, caught in the thicket by its horns;
> Offer the Ram of Pride instead of him.
> But the old man would not so, but slew his son,
> And half the seed of Europe, one by one.[11]

The editorial observed that World War I produced the greatest war
poetry in the English language but little else that was good. Churchill, he noted, the main advocate of the Gallipoli landing, at least
learned from the defeat and made doubly sure of Allied superiority
before he allowed the Normandy landing in World War II. He also
noted that despite Archbishop Daniel Mannix' opposition to conscription during World War I, no less than fourteen Victoria Cross
winners, in uniform and riding grey chargers, and ten thousand soldiers in uniform marched with him in the 1920 Saint Patrick's Day
procession in Melbourne.

When Pell lived at Saint Alipius with several other priests, he was
often on hand when his niece, Sarah, then aged six or seven, would
knock on the presbytery door after school and ask whether "Georgie"
was at home. If he was, the curate and his little "Princess", as he called
her, would have afternoon tea together or go for a walk. A few years
later, Sarah's younger brother, Nicholas, would often visit his uncle
when he was administering the quiet Bungaree parish outside Ballarat.

Family holidays were spent in January at Torquay, a small town
with a superb surfing beach on the Victorian south coast, in a three-
bedroom house the Pell family had bought. Denis Hart spent the
summer holiday of 1975 there with Margaret and George and
returned every year for the next twenty-five years to "flop around"
in the surf they all enjoyed so much. The house was regularly full of
Pell family members—brother David, his son and daughters and their
friends, extended family, and parishioners. Hart remembered it as
a "constant flow of people—a complete kaleidoscope—what you'd
describe as the ordinary parish people, people with whom he had an
academic contact, many of the families of the young men and women

---

[11] Wilfred Owen (d. 1918), "The Parable of the Old Man and of the Young" (1920).

he lectured at Aquinas College. He seemed to strike a chord both at the highest intellectual level and at the most common human family friend level. He had to have a group of people around—he wasn't keen on it being quiet."

Hart remembered his friend encouraging the young students who came in their careers and their faith. He also encouraged a literary interest. Sometimes, the guests included one or two of the Saint Patrick's students Pell knew through coaching rowing at the school, including Peter Tellefson, principal of Saint Kevin's Junior School at Toorak; Tim O'Leary, a Melbourne businessman; and Michael Casey (who became his private secretary and is now director of the PM Glynn Institute at the Australian Catholic University and author of the philosophical work *Meaninglessness*). "I'm sure Casey's interest in philosophy and logic came from the way Pell nurtured him and gave him books to read", Hart said.

For years in summer, Torquay Catholics became accustomed to the two priests saying Mass together each weekday morning at 10:30 A.M. in the local church. On Sundays, they said a private Mass.

One of Pell's earliest and most important mentors in the Church was Sir James Patrick O'Collins, bishop of Ballarat from 1941 to his retirement in 1971, who lived on after his retirement in what was known in Ballarat as the Old Bishop's Palace, a large, grand old home with extensive grounds. Pell was happy to acknowledge that O'Collins was "a father and friend, source of strength and confidence and practical wisdom" to him. The bishop, who initially completed only primary school, worked at South Melbourne gasworks and as a plumber before completing his secondary education at night and studying for the priesthood. O'Collins was highly intelligent but dyslexic. Nevertheless, while he was in Rome, he managed to master Italian, and when Pell read O'Collins' diaries years later, he was struck by the excellent Italian as well as the man's deep spirituality.

In 1981, when O'Collins was nearing ninety, Pell left the presbytery at Ballarat East and moved into the Old Palace with him to give him company and to be on hand to look after the old man, along with his housekeeper, Nancy Nugent. It was a household with a bizarre mixture of formality (a gong was rung to announce that meals were served) and eccentricity, with the bishop, even in the freezing winter, insisting on sleeping on the outside veranda. This was probably partially penance and partially because he believed it was good for his health. After the limitations of preparing soft, chopped-up food for the elderly bishop, Nancy relished the chance to cook for the young priest and his friends. As a daily outing, Nancy and the bishop drove Pell's sandwiches for lunch over to him at Aquinas College, Mair Street, in the bishop's Mercedes-Benz.

Fathers Elliott, Diamond, and Hart made the trip up from Melbourne several times a year for a roast lunch at the Palace. Elliott recalled those times with affection, including the day the three Melbourne priests, all dressed in black for the benefit of the old bishop, were stranded on the highway with a flat tire. "The only practical one of the three of us was Denis Hart, who knew the basics of changing a tire. Gerry knew the theory, and I did the rhetorical encouragement, with people driving by laughing at the three hapless priests." These dinners in the Bishop's Palace were relaxing and, at times, sad. Occasionally, the bishop's mind wandered back through the years, deciding one day that the Melbourne visitors were all from Rome and it was about 1922. He began inquiring about Cardinal Fumasoni Biondi (the former head of the Propagation of the Faith in Rome) and other well-known characters from six decades earlier. Sad but also amused in an embarrassed kind of way, the four young priests did the only thing that seemed reasonable in the circumstances—they played along, reassuring him that those he asked after were exceedingly well.

After Bishop O'Collins died in November 1983, aged ninety-one, Pell moved again—this time to the small rural parish of Bungaree, just outside Ballarat, as administrator, a less permanent and less authoritative role than that of pastor. He took Nancy and her culinary skills with him as housekeeper. He ministered to the people of the parish and continued editing *Light* and running Aquinas College.

As director of Aquinas, Pell was responsible for the training of almost one thousand Catholic teachers. At graduation ceremonies, he stressed to the teachers the importance of their role, not just in education, but also within the Church. At one ceremony he said:

> The Australian temptation is to tame Christ, not to crucify him, to trivialise his life and mission, not to grant them significance by an act of repudiation.... The whole drift of our society is pressuring the Church to abandon her claims to any kind of exclusive connection with revealed truth.

> The religion we profess is not a general "do-goodism" or a gentle humanism, but one which makes difficult and particular moral demands and requires specific beliefs. [This was] as alien to the people of today as to the Jews and pagans of Christ's time.

He asked the female graduates (the large majority of students) to consider their role in terms of the "revolutionary change" that the role of women in Australia was undergoing. "The Church will be relying on you as teachers, and generally as wives and mothers, to accept the strengths of the women's movement, to resist its pagan excesses and occasional silliness, above all to adapt and retain the strength of Catholic family life."

Pell relished life as head of a tertiary institution and over the years became increasingly proud of Aquinas and its students, academic standards, spirituality, and environment. He said he had no further ambitions at the time, although his influence on Catholic teacher training in Victoria was further extended in 1980 when he began a three-year stint as principal of the Institute of Catholic Education. In that role he had overall responsibility for the Victorian Catholic teachers' colleges, which by that time were well established. As well as overseeing the Institute, Pell continued running Aquinas on a day-to-day basis. In later years, courses in nursing and business were introduced there and at other Catholic colleges, which became part of the multicampus Australian Catholic University.

In his decade at Aquinas, Pell took time out twice to recharge his own intellectual batteries—firstly as a visiting scholar at his former Oxford college, Campion Hall, in 1979, and again at Saint Edmund's College, Cambridge, in the Michaelmas term of 1983. In both places he caught up on reading, did a little writing, heard lectures, and participated in university and college life. At Cambridge, he attended a series of lectures on Aristotle by Catholic philosopher Elizabeth Anscombe, whose scholarship contributed to a revival of interest in Aristotle's definitions of virtue and of the good life. Anscombe, an eccentric genius and passionate Catholic, studied and taught at both Oxford and Cambridge and in 1970 was appointed to the Cambridge chair once held by her former teacher, analytic philosopher Ludwig Wittgenstein. When Anscombe died in January 2001 at age eighty-one, Pell, by that time in his fifth year as archbishop of Melbourne, paid tribute to her in *Kairos* as "a giant in the world of twentieth-century philosophy" and the mother of seven children.[12] "Anscombe became a convert to the Church in 1940, allegedly after reading G. K. Chesterton's Father Brown detective stories. I have nowhere encountered a more formidable exponent. This was seen dramatically in 1968 as she defended Pope Paul VI's teaching against artificial contraception. Always dressed in slacks, often with a Kimono-type top, she wore a monocle and often carried a small brown paper bag for her cigars."

In March 1984, preparing an editorial for *Light* on Pope John Paul II's apostolic letter *Salvifici Doloris* (On the Meaning of Human Suffering), a tragedy in one of the small country communities Pell was serving, near Bungaree, meant the pope's letter hit home extra hard. As he told *Light* readers: "A young mother and two of her three beautiful young children were killed in a car accident. A few weeks ago a schoolmate of the young mother had also died tragically on the road. These brute facts, which none of us can completely escape, added a new dimension to this small article. The families involved and all the local community were again confronted with one of life's great mysteries." The young woman also lost the unborn child she was carrying. Recalling the Requiem Mass he celebrated for her and for her children, Pell wrote later that the task was

> as difficult as burying my parents.... Like other helpers priests regularly have to confront suffering and evil, and try to help people to cope. This is not easy. Presence and support are important and few words are far better than too many words. Human suffering is a mystery, and the suffering of good people is a greater mystery still. For those without faith, suffering is a brute fact, without meaning, which many bear stoically and with dignity. For those people with faith in a personal God, who is good and has endowed life with pattern and purpose, suffering can seem to contradict the Good News.
>
> A sudden and unexpected death, or a massive injustice, can shake and test a faith lived out and supported by many years of prayer and good behaviour.... It is natural in the first shock to see little but our loss.... Christ's teaching repeatedly ruled out any necessary connection between suffering and personal or family guilt. The instinct of

---

[12] *Kairos Catholic Journal* was the official publication of the Melbourne Archdiocese from 1990 to 2015.

many people when stricken with misfortune to ask why God is punishing them is mistaken. The Old Testament book of Job wrestled with the fact that the innocent often suffer....

But it is no coincidence that the cross or a crucifix is the most powerful Christian symbol. It helps us when in trouble to know that the Son of God suffered too. Suffering can poison us, harden our hearts, confirm us in our obsession with self. But Christians believe that suffering can purify, spark unexpected growth humanly and spiritually.

We also believe that the scales of justice balance out in eternity, just as surely as this does not always happen in this life. Those who suffer more than their share will have redress. This is part of what Jesus meant when he said "Blessed are those who mourn, they shall be comforted."

In mid-1984, Peter Elliott came to stay with Pell while attending a conference in Ballarat. Elliott, who was secretary to Bishop John Kelly, Melbourne's auxiliary bishop, found his normally gregarious friend "a bit blue ... unusually quiet". Elliott suspected that his friend had the same thing on his mind that he did—that was, who would be appointed the new rector of Corpus Christ Seminary in Melbourne. Elliott, as a bishop's secretary, was privy to some of the intrigue surrounding the post. "But I kept my mouth shut, of course." As the seminary served the whole of Victoria, the rector did not have to be a Melbourne priest but could come from provincial or country Victoria. In fact, a large number of Ballarat students had recently dropped out of Corpus Christi, something that worried and annoyed Bishop Mulkearns of Ballarat and his priests, who were keen to have one of their own priests at the helm for a change. There was no doubt that Pell had the academic and administrative experience. While he would have been content to remain in academia for the rest of his working life, it was probably time to move on if he were ever to do so.

Bishop Kelly was deeply concerned about the liberal, free-and-easy direction the seminary was taking. With the post of rector falling vacant, the wily Kelly, who was known in Melbourne as John A., was determined to see Pell promoted to the position. Kelly also knew that his first choice would never be accepted by Archbishop Sir Frank Little and those around him, so he apparently drew up a short list of three names, with Pell as number three. Those in spots one and two were older, more conservative priests, whom Kelly supposed, correctly, that Archbishop Little and his colleagues would reject in favour of the "third way". "By the time they got down to number three they were ready to stop arguing and go home", was how one Melbourne priest, who was a seminarian at the time, related the story.

Elliott remembered that Kelly was working flat out to get Pell into the job: "The place was obviously falling apart; they needed a strong rector. Bishop Kelly knew George was a strong man who would inspire and discipline, but he also had the academic background. One night at Bungaree George said, 'Well, who is going to be the new rector, there are all these rumours?' and I just looked at him, and I don't think I said anything. I just pointed at him, and he said 'Oh'."

And sure enough, it happened. At age forty-three, with eleven years at Aquinas behind him, as well as almost five years as editor of *Light*, Pell prepared to leave Ballarat, to become rector of his Melbourne alma mater, Corpus Christi Seminary. Pell's father, for one, did not think the move was a promotion, with his son moving from running an institution with two thousand students to one with fifty students. On the other hand, seminary rectors, with the responsibility for training future priests, are entrusted in a very special way with shaping the future of the Church, and the job is considered a very important position. It was not a job Pell sought out. "I took the position because I was asked", he said.

At the seminary, on June 28, 1984, Archbishop Frank Little gathered the students together and announced that from the following year, Doctor George Pell, director of Aquinas College, Ballarat, would be their new rector. "That'll give you all something to talk about", the archbishop added.

It did. They were still talking about it decades later.

11

A Few Small Changes

The tall, dark-haired rector sat alone, facing his staff and students in a semicircle at Corpus Christi College in June 1985. The hostility in the room was palpable—almost all of those he was addressing opposed the changes he was announcing. The meeting was a follow-up to the memo he had posted on the notice board earlier, headed "A Few Small Changes". Despite the angst surrounding him, Pell looked utterly relaxed and in control, long legs stretched out comfortably in front of him. At this and other such meetings, one or two seminarians burst into tears.

A small minority of the students, who regarded the "few small changes" as long overdue to transform what had become a rather miserable student hostel into a house of prayer, were on the rector's side and aghast at some of their classmates' reactions. Fed up with the institution, one of those who supported the rector privately referred to the seminary as "the house of horrors". This small group knew it was high time someone tackled the malaise sapping life and strength from the Church in general and the seminary in particular. Now almost forty years into their priestly careers, the small group who favoured what the new rector was trying to do became some of the most successful priests of their generation. But as students they were in a tiny minority. While many students kept their views to themselves, a sizeable group was openly hostile. Monsignor Charles Portelli, pastor of Keilor Downs in outer suburban Melbourne, recalled: "George was really in the bear pit; none of his staff gave him any support in front of the students. He was sitting there out on his own, but he was not intimidated, not in the slightest."

Ordinary Catholics in the pews, the Mass-goers of Victoria and Tasmania whose generosity maintained the seminary, would have

147

been shocked to discover that the "few small changes" causing such a fuss included the introduction of a daily Rosary for the community, an extra community weekday Mass, and prayers before the Blessed Sacrament. Students were also to attend one of the daily Masses said at different times at the college. Most lay people would have assumed that daily Mass was a routine part of life in the seminary and been incredulous to learn that the new rector was facing such opposition as he tried to restore the practice. In the training of a priest, could anything else be more important than the Sacrifice of the Mass? What sort of priests would these students make? How would they cope in parishes with at least three weekend Masses as well as weddings and Baptisms, daily Masses on weekdays, devotions, visiting the sick, and working with different parish groups and parishioners? Another "small change" was that Sunday lunch was to be a more formal meal, preceded by drinks, with grace to be said.

Up to the mid-1980s, the ever-increasing chasm between the traditional and liberal factions in the Catholic Church had been peripheral to George Pell's work as a priest. If pressed, the people he had served as a curate in Swan Hill and Ballarat would have characterised him as a modern priest, in tune with the young in a changing world. The atmosphere at Aquinas had been egalitarian and liberal, and, since his student days in Rome and in Oxford, Pell had been an ardent advocate of the reforms of the Second Vatican Council.

By the 1980s, however, it was clear that in the name of the "spirit" rather than substance of the council, many in influential positions were determined to alter the essence of Catholicism by impugning its traditions and even important doctrines. At Corpus Christi, this split was evident long before Pell's arrival as rector. Several students, for instance, said they felt persecuted and "left out of the loop" because they preferred to receive Holy Communion on the tongue rather than in the hand. The Church afforded everyone that choice after the council, yet at Corpus Christi and elsewhere, those opting for the traditional method were ostracized and even abused verbally for their choice. Likewise, students who objected to theology lecturers criticizing the Church's opposition to artificial birth control felt powerless to deal with the derision this earned them from those in charge. As rector, Pell saw firsthand how and why the Church was heading for a serious crisis of faith.

Students who had felt persecuted up to that time welcomed his arrival. A few never accepted him, but most of those opted out of seminary training altogether. After a few months, most of the students got on well with him, and, in the words of one, they were "gobsmacked" (figuratively, not literally) when he took to the football field with them for a kick around. "He used to hit, push in the back with a real force, and was still incredibly fast even though he was twenty-five years older", one student remembered. "He never meant to hurt you playing football, but he played tough, and if he wanted the ball and you had it . . . well, that was how Brother O'Malley had taught him to play." In Pell's view, the seminary teams of the early 1960s, drawn from a much larger group of students, would have flattened those of the 1980s easily. "There were less of the muscular Christianity types coming through", Pell recalled. "When I was rector, one of the cultural shocks—it was a foolish, frivolous example, but nonetheless it did jolt me—was the low standard of the football. It was largely a function of numbers. In a large seminary of several hundred, it is not difficult to get thirty-six decent players." The encounters with his seminarians sometimes cost the rector two days of bandaged knees and painful genuflections, but to him it was worth it.

When the new students for 1985 entered Corpus Christi on March 1, the college in which their new rector found himself was vastly different from the one he had entered as a first-year student twenty-five years earlier. As he joked to a friend: "In my day we had night prayers and lights out. Now we have light prayers and nights out." Or rather, they did until Pell took the place in hand. The old seminary, at Werribee, had looked something like an English stately home. After refurbishment, it resembled a luxury hotel. The new seminary, near Monash University at Clayton, was modern in every way—from the grey concrete blocks of its buildings to the outlook of most of its staff and students. Peter Joseph, one of fifteen new students entering the college for the first time in 1985, thought it looked like an army barracks. Architecturally, and in more significant ways, the institution was not to the new rector's taste. Pell recalled an instructor from the Royal Melbourne Institute of Architects threatening to bring students to the college, because "he would tell his students you can see more building defects in a confined space here than in most other places."

Pell was responsible for the spiritual formation of the seminary students, who were training to be priests in Melbourne, Tasmania, and in Victoria's regional dioceses—Ballarat, Sale, and Sandhurst. He was not responsible for their academic program, which was undertaken by the Catholic Theological College. Pell regarded this program as "academically pretty solid, though it didn't have enough philosophy studies". Among other issues, he had to come to grips with the latest thinking in matters such as psychosexual development, which were relevant to the training of young men for lives of celibacy.

Charles Portelli was one of twelve men ordained from Corpus Christi College in Pell's first year as rector. Portelli remembered Pell's determined battle to have an appropriate image of Our Lady installed in the seminary chapel dissolving into high farce with the antics of one of the liturgists on the seminary staff. The rector, concerned by the absence of any image of Our Lady in the chapel, had decided to have an image of Mary at the foot of her Son's crucifix carved by the wife of the man who had carved the crucifix itself. The statue duly arrived, but some on the college staff wanted it mounted on the wall or in some other location well away from the crucifix. Portelli recalled standing at the chapel door, watching as one of the liturgists gestured and pointed at the unfortunate student holding the statue, ordering him to move it farther and farther back from the cross. Just as the hapless student would do so, Pell would order "No, no—closer, closer", and back it would come until the other staff member gestured for it to be moved in the opposite direction. Pell's wish prevailed—eventually—until he left as rector. The statue disappeared shortly afterwards.

Professionally and personally, 1985 was one of the hardest years of Pell's life. By the time he began work at the seminary, his father was dying, spending time in hospital and at Margaret's home in Melbourne, where she cared for him with love and devotion, despite his protests to his family to "Be on your way; don't be wasting too much of your time on me; I'm all right." He died on April 24, 1985, five years exactly after the funeral of his wife, Margaret. Like her, George senior was buried from Saint Alipius in Ballarat East, where his son preached the sermon, recalling his father's colourful career and personality. This time his sermon was more expansive than the very moving one he gave at his mother's funeral Mass. Family members say he was slightly closer to his mother and so cut up over her death that he felt unable to speak for very long. By 1985, he also had more experience of coping in the pulpit with sad occasions, and to some extent he was able to take his cue from his father, who "would not want us to be too troubled, too disturbed at this time. Recently he repeated many times that he had had a good innings [a cricket term meaning 'a long life'], had enjoyed a good life."

For twenty-five years in the Royal Oak Hotel, Pell said, his father

> dispensed hospitality, administered justice, kept the peace and incidentally built and maintained a sense of community which was as good as that in many of our parishes.... All who met him agreed that he was a great character, who regularly expressed himself colourfully and eloquently, sometimes with a pungent humour. I think he was a remarkable man. Dad was devoted to his family. Like most Australian men of his generation, he did not wear his heart on his sleeve (and was none the worse for this), but his devotion to his family was complete. I only realised fully how lucky I was in my parents as I grew older and saw a bit more of the world. Often in talks or sermons on the family I have told people that as a child and an adult it never once crossed my mind that my parents did not love me; I never doubted for a moment that they would do anything they could to help us. If every adult could say this honestly about his parents, our world would be a much better place. It is this quality of love which enables us to be sure that good people in their dying pass from death to life.

For the funeral, Pell chose scriptural readings that suited his father's life and outlook. "To the extent that he understood and accepted our teaching on life after death, he would have agreed that either there were many mansions in the Father's house or there were none at all." He recalled his father as a strong man, physically and personally, who told it as he saw it and who had high principles and kept to them.

> I know that he would have approved the second reading where Christ, in the Holy City, the new Jerusalem, is giving "water from the well of life free to anybody who is thirsty". He would have been pleased for another reason. Like most of us, he too affected to being anti-British, at least in unimportant matters like cricket matches; when it was a matter of importance, for example, war, things were different. In fact, he

was very proud of his origins, of the people and tradition to which he belonged. It is this scriptural passage, of course, which Blake used as one starting point for his marvellous poem on the New Jerusalem, which English people now sing just as we sing "Waltzing Matilda". Dad would have been pleased with this reading and thought it only right and proper.... It is a privilege as his son and as a priest, with faith and full confidence, to commend his soul to the care of our loving God.

A large group of senior students from Corpus Christi travelled to Ballarat for the funeral, en route to a "weekend of reflection" at the beach. Lunch was organized especially for them at a private home, but after the Mass only four of around thirty of them opted to stay behind—each one of them appalled and deeply embarrassed at their classmates' insensitivity.

Pell's family and close friends were also shocked by the attitudes of some of the seminary staff. At one seminary dinner, the priests organizing it seated the rector in a part of the room distant from the main action, with his back to those who had to speak. "It was unbelievably rude and hurtful", said someone who was there.

Why such open hostility? How much of it, if any, did Pell deserve, and if so, why? The basic problem was a deep clash of ideas. One of the priests on the seminary staff who predated Pell's arrival said that his "few small changes" amounted to "George's wish list" and that they had about as much intellectual sophistication as "the man of straw" from The Wizard of Oz. He and others resented the rector's determination to bring in the changes, believed his methods amounted to "bullying", and claimed he had a romantic notion of trying to recreate the Church of yesteryear.

The other side of the argument is that, for the sake of the students and their future parishioners, Pell was gently but firmly attempting to redress the slackness and lack of direction that had crept into the seminary. He believed that the first step in training priests is to focus them on their own personal relationship with God, ensuring it has the strength to endure whatever tests and tribulations lie ahead. Mass and devotion to the Real Presence of Christ in the Eucharist and to the Blessed Virgin Mary are central to the Catholic faith, and if young priests leave the seminary without a firm grasp of these building blocks, their faith and that of their people will suffer.

Weighty tomes have been produced on these questions, but the experience of the past fifty years suggests that the slackness of the 1970s and 1980s was a mistake. Those who disagree viewed Pell and his backers as conservatives "stuck in the 1950s". They would reject this and paste the "conservative" label on their critics for being "stuck in the 1970s".

The late Peter Cross was dean of studies at the seminary when Pell was rector. Like Pell, he had attended Campion Hall, Oxford, and had completed his Ph.D. in Rome. Father Cross said Pell's appointment as rector was "an initial shock for the seminary staff. I don't think anybody expected it." He was four years behind Pell in their student days and had been a member of the first-year rhetoric class that had sometimes clashed with Pell when he was their prefect. However, unlike some from that class, Cross did not nurse any grudges.

Cross said that as rector, Pell "could be fairly confronting" but that he had a "great way with the students", and he "impressed me greatly for talking so openly with them about issues concerning the college". He said staff and students "always knew where they stood with Pell" and also exactly what he wanted and expected. Accustomed to the Oxford culture of students speaking up and arguing with their lecturers, Pell never resented the Corpus Christi students for speaking their minds. Staff meetings, too, were sometimes fiery.

While Pell's "few small changes" were controversial, Cross agreed that they were basically that—small changes, even symbolic ones. "I was not opposed to them", he said. "As dean of studies, I was also concerned that the students should be doing a bit more work." Cross said that the few students not attending daily Mass had also been of concern to previous rectors. These, apparently, had not tackled the problem as directly as Pell, who stunned the students by scheduling Mass at 7:00 A.M. a couple of mornings a week (the students had been accustomed to getting up later and attending later Masses).

According to Cross, some of the students resented Pell because they believed he was accusing them of not praying. "I don't believe he was ever trying to say that, but he hurt a lot of them by insisting on prayer in the chapel", Cross said. As a spiritual director to some of the students, Cross said they were meditating regularly in their rooms, yet Pell wanted prayers in the chapel that could be "measured" by what could be seen publicly. He said some of the students also found some of the military imagery invoked by Pell in his talks too provocative. Such phrases as "soldiers for Christ" and "We're fighting a battle", used by Pell to provoke discussion, put the students off, Cross found.

Frank O'Loughlin served on the seminary staff from 1977 to 1990. He had graduated from Propaganda Fide three years after Pell and completed his doctorate at the Pontifical Urban University. Father O'Loughlin taught the seminarians sacramental theology and was a moderator for a group of eight or nine students. He and his colleagues found Pell "great fun socially", and he said there was an atmosphere of "good bonhomie among the staff having a drink at night". But when it got down to serious matters, he and Pell were usually diametrically opposed about what direction the seminary should be taking. Unlike Peter Cross, O'Loughlin did not view the "few small changes" as minor. "On the surface they looked minuscule, but in fact they meant a change of spirit that was quite significant", O'Loughlin said. "They took backwards a formation system that was trying to give a much more thorough formation."

O'Loughlin said with Masses at different times of the day, it was hard to know if and when students were attending. To the best of his recollection, most of the students were daily Mass-goers, but many of those who were not were probably in the process of making up their minds that the priesthood might not be for them. O'Loughlin said one of the difficulties he had with Pell was the rector's insistence on "what the eye sees and what the ear hears" in terms of community prayer for the students.

Sydney priest Peter Joseph was a first-year student at Corpus Christi when Pell was rector. Father Joseph became chancellor of the Maronite Diocese of Australia and wrote the updated version of the definitive Catholic reference book *Sheehan's Apologetics* during his time as vice-rector and theology teacher at Vianney College, the seminary for the Diocese of Wagga Wagga in New South Wales. Student meetings with Pell were open and frank, he recalled, with some students rude and presumptuous. Joseph looked back on his time under Pell with real affection, claiming in jest: "I was taught by George Pell, and I've got the scars to prove it." At the famous "few small changes" meeting, Joseph remembered one student complaining bitterly to Pell about the fact that one compulsory morning Mass would be held on a weekday, to be attended by the entire student body.

"I was hurt when I saw that notice", the student protested.

Pell replied, "You have got to ask yourself why you were hurt."

Even with eleven years' experience of running a tertiary institution behind him, Pell found the job as rector challenging. But the experience was to have a major impact on the future training of priests in Victoria and Tasmania when he became archbishop of Melbourne twelve years later, and in Sydney from 2001 onwards.

As rector, he was unsure of whether he would be able to secure the backing of the trustees of the seminary (the bishops of Victoria and Tasmania) for all the changes he wanted to make. His political skills, honed through eleven years of doing battle with politicians on behalf of Aquinas College, came to the fore. He was determined to "win" on major issues like daily Mass attendance by the students (only a few diehards held out, and they later left without being ordained). Joseph observed that Pell picked his battles carefully.

For example, Pell had also discovered almost no devotions in the college, although the students did meditate and read the morning and evening prayers of the Church individually. In Pell's own student days, Benediction had been held once a week and, at certain times of the liturgical year, once a day. At Clayton, despite trenchant opposition from some quarters, his efforts to encourage the students to pray the Rosary every day bore fruit, with half to two-thirds of the students joining in.

"And I did manage, eventually, to put on Benediction once", Pell recalled.

When asked, "Was that once a week or once a month?"

He replied, "Once in three years."

In time, Pell won over many students' trust and confidence. Most of them enjoyed the Church history that he taught them, and while many of them shied away from the "muscular Christianity" of the football field, they liked matching it with the rector on the tennis court, where sometimes they were able to beat him. Peter Elliott said that after a few rocky patches, the students accepted Pell

because they saw him as a man, and there was nothing devious about him. The packaging told you the product. You knew where you stood. He'd tell you off if you were wrong, and he was usually right, but he'd do it in a straight way without being too aggressive. He'd just let you know, and he'd also have options and advice for you. He'd never leave you up in the air. I don't believe the staff ever accepted him, they resented him.

The problem was, he couldn't change the staff, and there weren't enough bishops who could help him on that one. He had a couple of bishops supporting him, but not all. It slipped back after he left, of course, because the staff were still there.

It would be a mistake to assume that the problems of Corpus Christi were significantly different from those of any other Australian seminary at the time. In Sydney, for example, at Saint Patrick's Seminary, three senior seminarians were discovered to be active homosexuals and left shortly before they were due to be ordained. Church sources say their "secret" was discovered one day when they were having a bitter argument in the refectory.

In Melbourne, Pell said, the homosexual subculture at Corpus Christi "was not manifest" during his time as rector, although "a number of students who left quickly moved into gay life-styles. Two former students of the seminary died of AIDS."

The numerical decline in seminarians was also a major worry in Melbourne, as elsewhere. In 1973, the Clayton seminary opened with 144 students. Each subsequent year saw a steady decline of around 7 to 10 percent. By 1984, when Archbishop Little announced Pell's appointment as rector, student numbers had more than halved to sixty-three students. A larger than average intake of fifteen in 1985 saw an increase to sixty-eight. Pell's final year as rector, 1987, was another good year with sixteen students starting. Only eight newcomers, however, arrived in 1988. From that point, the downward trend accelerated, with just four students starting at the beginning of 1996, the year George Pell became archbishop of Melbourne, bringing the college total to twenty-one. Slow but steady increases in enrollments, and a much lower rate of attrition, later saw numbers almost double to forty-one.

"It was more than just ugly; it held no happy memories", one man said. "No wonder nobody complained when it was closed down and the seminary moved to Carlton [when George Pell became archbishop in 1996]." Another priest turned down the chance to undertake university studies while he was a seminarian at Clayton "because

it would have meant I had to spend an extra two or three years there."
This priest gave Pell full credit for his being ordained, "because if it
had not changed, I could not have stuck it out a moment longer."

Several former students claimed that before Pell, staff members
encouraged students to spy on each other, reporting their classmates
for anything negative they said about the administration. After Pell
arrived, staff members who disliked him accused students who did like
him of sneaking off "like Nicodemus by night" to tell tales of them.

Portelli remembered having a room on the "shady side" of one
block of the seminary. Of the seven students on the opposite "sunny"
side of the block, every single one left shortly before ordination.
Portelli said it is nonsense to blame the upheavals of the now long-
ago Second Vatican Council for the situation in the 1980s. Rather,
the policies and practices of the day in seminary training were simply
a failure, and students lost confidence in the place and also, sadly,
in many cases, in the ideal of the priesthood itself. "Seminary formation imploded. The transcendent, sacramental side of the priesthood was not emphasized at all." Nor were the students particularly
directed towards the social welfare aspects of the work of a priest.
Against such a backdrop, it took extraordinary faith and determination for students to persevere, and those who did generally emerged
as outstanding.

Melbourne priest Greg Pritchard recalled that "group night" in
the seminary was a "sacred cow". "You could be excused from
Mass, but not from group night." On one occasion he remembered,
group night consisted of ten students and a staff member whining
and complaining about how hurt and pained they felt by Pell. When
it came to his turn, Father Pritchard said that he did not feel he had
anything to complain about, and the staff member made it clear he
was out of line. One group even devoted an entire "recollection
weekend" at the beach to discussing, in largely negative terms, "the
effect of Father Pell in my life".

Other students, however, did not trust the teachers and formators
resisting Pell's changes. One man said that before Pell's time, he had
even stopped going to confession to any of them because "I felt I
couldn't trust them and didn't want to pour my heart out to them."
The most committed students helped each other, talking over problems and offering plenty of tea and sympathy when the need arose.

In one case, their support extended to a few friends encouraging a young man, who had given up seminary studies in disgust, to return.

Coming from Wagga Wagga in New South Wales, Father Peter Joseph would normally have studied in Sydney, but he had asked his bishop, William Brennan, to allow him to study in Melbourne under George Pell. Joseph said he had not been keen to study at the Sydney seminary because at that time Sydney students were subject to what was known as the Ira Progoff "intensive journal method" of Jungian psychology, which involved making copious daily notes about their personal feelings. Also, he had happened upon Pell's booklets *Bread, Stones or Fairy Floss* and *Are Our Secondary Schools Catholic?*. "I thought the booklets were intelligent and orthodox", Joseph recalled. "I hadn't heard of George Pell when I bought the booklets, but I read them and thought, 'He knows much more than he's saying.' " Peter Joseph spent eighteen months at Corpus Christi before Pell called him in one evening in mid-1986. "Have I done something wrong?" the younger man inquired. "Nothing you need confess", the rector reassured him. The news was, from September, he would be studying in Rome at Propaganda Fide. "You'll find it very difficult at first, but you'll love it", Pell said, just as he had been told by his rector two decades earlier.

Early the following year, 1987, Pell received some news of his own. After just two years and a few months at the helm of Corpus Christi, the apostolic nuncio (Vatican ambassador) in Canberra wrote him that the Holy Father wished to appoint him an auxiliary bishop of Melbourne and would like to know if he would accept the promotion. Pell replied that he would. He said he was "partly surprised" at the promotion, "because my views were certainly not the flavor of the month" in Australian episcopal and theological circles at the time. "It was a shock of course", he said. "It's one thing to have this sort of thing talked about; it's quite different to have it happen." He added that he had "mixed feelings" because he hadn't had long enough to do all that he wanted at the seminary. "But the other thing was that I was pleased to be out of the seminary because it was a difficult assignment. The majority of the staff and a goodly percentage of the students felt that I was heading in the wrong direction."

Several of his more cynical friends even suggested that he was "kicked upstairs" because he was having too much influence on the seminary. Others tell a different story, claiming that the archbishop of the day, Sir Frank Little, had asked Rome if he could appoint two auxiliary bishops, Hilton Deakin and Peter Connors, and that Rome had replied, through the nuncio, that yes, he could have two new auxiliaries, provided one of them was George Pell. Several priests mentioned that when he was in Melbourne in 1986, Pope John Paul II made a point of visiting the ailing Bishop Kelly at the hospice where he was living. It was not impossible that Kelly, an admirer of Pell, offered His Holiness a little advice. One of Pell's colleagues on the seminary staff long believed he was destined to be a bishop while running Aquinas and was sent to the seminary to broaden his experience. Asked in 2002 why he selected Pell as one of his auxiliary bishops, Archbishop Little made it clear: "Others do the choosing."

The announcement, made at noon Rome time, was broadcast on Melbourne radio at 9:00 P.M. Pell rang his friend Peter Elliott and asked him over to the seminary staff room for a drink. "I remember coming into the staff room and everyone sitting there and having a beer, but they all looked like stunned mullets," he said, "and you could read that they were trying to weigh up whether it was better to have him as their rector or auxiliary bishop." While Pell's "few small changes" at the seminary had been nowhere near as comprehensive as he believed necessary, he had learned invaluable lessons: "I learned how things should not be done in future." But most of all, he realised that a seminary could only be reformed with leadership from the very top of the Church—the archbishops or bishops at the head of the dioceses that owned it.

Pell was consecrated a bishop at forty-five years of age in Saint Patrick's Cathedral on May 21, 1987. It was reasonable to think, as many did, that his time in charge of a regional Victorian diocese—or perhaps the Archdiocese of Melbourne—would come. If and when it did, seminary reform would be one of his top priorities.

12

In Many Places No Birds Sing

"Evil is nearly as deep a mystery as saintliness, as heroic goodness, and much more of a problem. But in Cambodia nature did register a protest. Under Pol Pot, the misery and hunger were so great that the people, in their battle against famine, ate all the wild birds. More than ten years later there are very few birds in Cambodia; in many places no birds sing." So wrote Bishop George Pell in December 1989.[1] His visit to Cambodia, as chairman of Australian Catholic Relief (ACR)—the overseas aid agency of the Catholic Church in Australia, now known as Caritas—was one of his many working visits to lands torn apart by war, tyranny, natural disasters, or sheer poverty. He found war-torn Cambodia a world different from anything he had experienced before, where at that time trains on one of the few remaining railway lines travelled with two carriages ahead of the engine, in which passengers travelled free because of the ever-present risks of land mines.

Shortly after his consecration as a bishop in May 1987, Pell's fellow bishops elected him to the post of ACR chairman, a job that took at least a day a week. It was a major part of Pell's life for his nine years as an auxiliary bishop, although by no means the only part. His job was to ensure that the donations of Catholics to ACR were put to the wisest possible uses in countries where so many urgent demands were pressing—for food, water, shelter, infrastructure, medical supplies, education, and sustainable enterprises that, hopefully, could help people survive in the future.

ACR/Caritas, affiliated with its counterparts throughout the world, is funded from the donations of Mass-goers, who are encouraged by

---

[1] The sources for this chapter are George Pell's personal, handwritten, and never-published travel diaries, which he lent to the author during the writing of the first edition of this book.

their priests to give generously, especially during Lent, when even many children do their bit for the six-week Project Compassion appeal. The chairman's job was strenuous and demanding, with frequent visits to the world's trouble spots and poorest areas.

In 1987 ACR was a potential quagmire and a stern test for any new bishop. The Church's justice, peace, and humanitarian aid efforts were under a darkening cloud. For several years beforehand, sections of the secular media, and Bob Santamaria's National Civic Council, had been asking pertinent questions about monies donated in good faith being diverted to Communist organisations in the Philippines. The Australian Bishops' Catholic Committee for Justice and Peace had become extraordinarily anti-American, issuing a discussion paper for schools and parishes, *Work for a Just Peace: Reflections on Peacemaking in an Armed World*, calling for Australia to reappraise its military relationship with the United States. The publication drew a sharp written protest from the United States embassy in Canberra. As Santamaria observed: "The gulf between the Catholic bishops and the great majority of their people on this question is obvious."

Economic times were hard. On October 19, 1987, "Black Monday", the Dow Jones Industrial Average dropped 22.6 percent, and the Australian Stock Exchange followed suit. Despite such problems, in 1988, Pell's first full year as ACR chairman, Catholics donated just over AU$3 million to the Project Compassion appeal, allowing ACR to direct more than AU$4.7 million towards relief and development projects in Asia, Latin America, Africa, and the Pacific. In Pell's last full year as chairman, 1996, the appeal raised almost AU$4.5 million. Extra donations and government contributions allowed AU$6.8 million to be distributed to the world's greatest areas of need.

As chairman, Pell devoted the greater part of nine years to the poorest people on earth—some Christian, but the vast majority not—ravaged by starvation, natural disasters, and brutal regimes. Frequently, he flew to Sydney from Melbourne for a day or two a week to work at the organisation headquarters. Frequent travel to the places where ACR was working in partnership with local Catholic agencies was exhausting and emotionally draining. In his nine years at the helm, Pell visited India (three times—once immediately after a deadly cyclone), Cambodia (three times as it was rebuilt from the human rubble of Pol Pot's "Killing Fields"), Zambia, Thailand, Vietnam, Indonesia, and the Philippines. On such journeys, the bishop kept detailed diaries. He also attended meetings in Rome and Hong Kong of Caritas Internationalis, the worldwide federation of Catholic aid agencies.

Writing after his first visit to Cambodia in 1989, Pell recalled:

> American bomb craters are still visible on the approaches to the Phnom Penh airport, and the huge modern bridge over the Tuleg Sap river has three spans missing.... The American bombing of Cambodia produced a climate of hate, which helped the Pol Pot cancer to spread. Pol Pot himself was Western educated in France where he had been heavily influenced by French Stalinists. The Western tradition of revolutionary tyranny stemming from the Jacobins of the French Revolution of 1789, through Marx himself and then Lenin all contributed to making Pol Pot what he was, and is....
>
> Pol Pot drove most of the population of Phnom Penh into the countryside to be "re-educated". Today there are still a few rusting hulks of cars, abandoned by the side of the roads, without petrol, in this exodus. Evidence of higher education was often a death warrant. Some responsible estimates assert that one or two million Cambodians died or fled, out of a population of eight million....
>
> Six of the seven Catholic churches in the capital were destroyed, stone by stone, while the Khmers (Cambodians) who returned from France to join Pol Pot's revolution had to demonstrate their loyalty by working on the destruction of the Catholic cathedral. This site was later occupied by a telecommunications centre. The visit certainly affected me. I rarely dream, or, as the medical people tell us more accurately, I am one of those who do not remember dreaming. But I dreamt every night in Cambodia.

Pell penned his diary in haste during his visit to the country. On all of his ACR trips, he recorded his observations on planes and at the end of long days travelling by road and boat. He described the ACR-sponsored projects and pinpointed local needs for future ones. The Mass, prayers, and the Church feature prominently. Occasionally, his diaries mentioned the books Pell happened to be reading. At the end of a long day in Vietnam in 1993, staying in a Communist-run guesthouse, he took out Saint Gregory of Nyssa's *Life of Moses*, published in the fourth century, and Le Carre's *Night Manager*; during a long delay at the Bombay airport later the same year it was Owen Chadwick's *From Bossuet to Newman* on doctrinal development.

On December 12, 1989, Pell visited Site 2, a camp on the Thai/ Cambodian border that was home to 150,000 Cambodians, half of them under the age of fifteen and about one in five under the age of three. His guide was French-speaking Bishop Yves Ramousse, Cambodia's only surviving Catholic bishop still working in the region at that time, Pell recorded:

> Father Pierre, missionary in Asia for 50 years and history written on his brown, weather-beaten face, told me, as a child clutched his hands, that the children are God's blessing on the place!
>
> Camp divided into squares surrounded by ditches with bamboo shacks. Three rooms: kitchen with open fire, living space with table and benches and bedroom. Everything in bamboo, even sliding doors. Quite clean, and many attempts to plant flowers and trees. Visited 2 Catholic churches in north and south of camp. In northern church, Stations of the Cross on wall, picture of Holy Family. Building topped outside by white crucifix. Gaggle of small children ran to Bishop Ramousse and some of the women came forward too, straggling in for choir practice for Christmas. 100 Baptised Catholics in the group with 200 catechumens. The instruction is done by the people themselves, sometimes by the newly baptised. Preparation takes two years ... the rebirth of the Cambodian church!
>
> Two Khmer bishops and 14 priests martyred for the faith under Pol Pot. At his house R. [Ramousse] told me this and his usual jollity fell away to reveal immense sadness and someone near to tears. Other bishops including R. expelled. R. now responsible for Cambodian Church. Children friendly and many of the adults friendly, too. Every type represented in community of 150,000 including gangsters and war lords. Difficult to imagine such pleasant people being such murderers!

From Site 2, Bishop Pell travelled through Thailand and Vietnam to catch a plane for Cambodia.

> 14/12/89: By Russian plane from Ho Chi Minh City to Phnom Penh. 30+ passengers, tiny seats, front 5 or 6 rows full of luggage inc. cases of whiskey and beefeater gin. Noisy, no air vents, clouds of vapour from air-conditioner spewing up front. Jolted landing, drab, drab, drab.

16/12/89: Anniversary of my ordination. Spent morning visiting local fine arts institute (or school) and saw the youngsters practising Khmer dancing—older teachers, one with large stick which she beat upon the floor, were from former Royal Ballet.... Visited hospital, 50 km away. Many malaria patients and amputees, some of them 18 to 22, one or two looked about 15. One amputee friendly, others less so, not taking my hand when I offered it.

In afternoon visited former high school, which was jail and extermination camp for Pol Pot. Instruments of torture there. Enormity of crimes too much to take in. Barbed wire entanglements still on perimeter of school and some on verandas in one of buildings, where prisoners were confined in brick cells constructed in class rooms. Saw cell where Foreign Minister of Pol Pot executed, saw statues of Pol Pot. There has to be a heaven for those who died here, whatever their earlier faults, and the idea of hell for those who led and organized this barbarity has a certain logic. To what extent did the American bombing prompt this hate? 20,000 exterminated at camp.

In evening met with Maryknoll Fathers (USA) now working in Cambodia.... Earlier in evening, home Mass at Dario's house in suburbs. Only European there and protected by locals, Gregorian chant in background for Christmas.... Soldier on guard during night outside our hotel.

18–19/12/89: Choeung Ek is quiet and beautiful, near a lake, not too far from Phnom Penh, the capital of Cambodia. Nearby the peasants work the fields pretty much as they have always done since the jungle was cleared. The Cambodian countryside is still like the Garden of Eden, but the serpents of evil have swarmed there.

Choeung Ek is also the site of the killing fields, the mass graves where thousands of victims of the government of Pol Pot (1976–1979) were taken for extermination. 8985 corpses found, not all mass graves disinterred—perhaps 89 out of 139. Splendid Khmer monument to the dead, with layer upon layer of human skulls. Mythology tells us that Saint Patrick drove all the snakes from Ireland and Pol Pot drove the birds of the air from Cambodia. I remembered this as I marvelled about how so much evil and suffering could have occurred in such a setting of peace and beauty. Surely nature must have objected. Surely the wind or the trees must have murmured in protest at the outrages, at the barbarism.

Stayed overnight at two-storey Pol Pot residence at Takeo—in middle of lake, accessible only by narrow footbridge and now by a road for cars. Was home of Ta Mok, provincial Pol Pot governor, known as "the butcher". Slept like a log under mosquito net.... Visited Chief Buddhist Monk in Cambodia, Venerable Tep Vong in large hall with photo of Pope at one end. He did not support recognition of Catholics or freedom to worship, said time was not ripe. Ven prayed for us and we prayed the prayer of Saint Francis.

Some of the diary entries capture a sense of the Catholic Church's centuries-old missionary effort in southeast Asia and the high price it sometimes extracted:

Samray [one of the Catholic Relief workers] just out of hospital after a bad traffic accident. Scars on face and some brain damage affecting concentration. Quietly spoke in French, expressed his determination to request recognition of Catholics again and again from government until it is given! He used to travel to Vietnam to bring back the Blessed Sacrament. His wife and children fled (to camps?).... Has there ever been an age in which so many Catholics have suffered and died for their faith?

Visited Teachers' College at Takeo where ACR are building a dormitory which we saw incomplete.... In afternoon crossed Tuleg Sap by boat and visited former Carmelite nuns' monastery, now used as an orphanage with 100 orphans. Received by management at a long table in the derelict chapel—all religious symbolism removed but portraits of the President (20 years younger than he is actually!), Marx and Lenin. Statue of Sacred Heart, with no arms, had been replaced in room behind chapel within former cloister. Brought back after Pol Pot threw it out. Convent built in 1911 and bell of 1922 restored and used to summon children. Prayed at tombs of sisters at rear of convent. Immense niche in wall for crucifix had not been removed, so form still visible and derelict building still topped by cross visible from river.

Pell and ACR were satisfied that Cambodia's government in 1989, while Marxist and therefore far from perfect, was an improvement on the past, with sufficient basic food, limited small business, schools open, and infrastructure slowly being replaced. Pell wrote after the trip:

Cambodia is like a chessboard and the players are ruthless. But the signs of hope were strong. Children are everywhere and children are a sign of hope, a reaction to the slaughter. Some locals claim that Cambodia now has the highest birth rate in the world, except for the Cambodian refugee camps on the Thai border! Religious freedom has been restored to the Buddhists and the small Moslem minority, and the small Christian communities hope they too will receive similar recognition.

ACR, with the support of the Australian Government, has worked in Cambodia for nearly 10 years, not because we approved of the government, but because we wanted to answer human need, to lessen human suffering.

The Catholic Church's relief efforts in Cambodia reached out to the people in general, with no special concentration on the Catholic minority, in the provision of relief and development aid. Religious freedom for Christians was finally granted by the Cambodian government in May 1990—a step for which Australian Catholic Relief and George Pell deserved credit.

In 1992, Pell returned to Cambodia, accompanying Cardinal Edward Clancy, for the opening of a rural development centre in Takeo province, supported by ACR, to assist agricultural, health, water, and reforestation projects. ACR's efforts in working with and equipping local people to repair more than 260 feet of a vital retaining wall, which had been swept away by floods the previous year, had saved much of the area's water supply. By doing this, fifty to sixty thousand people were fed with rice for a year.

The three years since his last visit had made a real difference. Pell's diary entry dated February 29 recorded:

> Airport much changed with small terminal thronged with people ... big advertising billboards outside airport on road to Phnom Penh. Four or five times as much traffic as in December '89; cars, motorbikes and pushbikes. Many more houses, shops, etc., restored; great activity business-wise, around streets. Smell of hope in the air.... Mass with Maryknollers, quite public (unlike celebration for Christmas in Dario's room in '89).

On March 1, he was mobbed by an "immense throng of Vietnamese" Catholics in Cambodia, eager for blessings and to kiss his ring. He also met Sister Matilda, "who was the solitary religious working in the whole of Cambodia in the late 80s". On March 5,

Pell and Clancy were received by Prince Sihanouk in his beautifully restored palace.

> Sihanouk protected by 20 or 30 North Korean guards in grey tropical uniforms—about 30 years old, fit, strong, vigilant and like something from James Bond. Incidentally Onesta's number plate was 007 [Onesta Carpene was the woman in charge of ACR's operations in Cambodia]. Sihanouk beautifully dressed in Western suit, smooth and voluble. Allowed Cardinal to sit on couch with him as Cardinal ranks as a prince!
>
> Like many of the leaders we met, he spoke quietly, excellent English interspersed with a few French phrases.... Sihanouk spoke of the genius of the great and noble Catholic religion; of the pivotal role of Polish Catholics in overthrowing communism.... He spoke of Khmer Rouge deriving inspiration from the French Revolution and especially Robespierre and from the Chinese Cultural Revolution.... Stressed importance of justice and peace for long-term future. Acknowledged role of ACR and Christian work in helping the unfortunate.

The ACR-backed Agricultural Centre in Takeo had forged even farther ahead when Bishop Pell returned for a third visit on November 25, 1993. This time, the journey from Phnom Penh took ninety minutes on a good road, rather than three and a half hours on a goat track. After a 7:00 A.M. start from Phnom Penh, clogged with traffic, he arrived at Takeo to find:

> Enormous change in Agricultural Centre even from official opening 18 months ago. Gum trees much higher, banana trees now too, deep moat around field next to centre and variety of veggies, fruit growing. Locals now have three crops a year of rice and significant improvement in yields achieved. Attended meeting of team with 20 local leaders in afternoon ... very proud of work being done for health in the six local primary schools.

Most Australian Catholics in the pews, who faithfully contribute to Project Compassion year-in, year-out, have never heard of Takeo, but their contributions helped turn around the lives of a community that, a decade earlier, had been as desperate as any people have ever been in human history.

Pell's third visit coincided with Cambodia's colourful, joyous Water Festival and boat races. He found:

> Shops reopened, all sorts of food available including fresh fruit and vegetables. Two Western supermarkets open—including "Le Shop" managed by an Aussie! Children cheeky—many bright-coloured and western clothes about. The United Nations Transitional Authority in Cambodia forces—22,000 military and civilian personnel—had just left unlamented, with the tragic but accurate nickname of "United Nations Transmission of AIDS Commission".

Even nature, given time, had healed itself. Overhead, one day, Pell spotted something that brought the killing fields to mind—three or four V-shaped flights of birds. Even the beautiful ibises had returned. Slowly but surely, life and hope were triumphing over death.

On the other side of the world, new challenges for Caritas were opening up. Pell reported in 1996 that Caritas had committed itself to long-term housing reconstruction in Zaire, Rwanda, and Tanzania, after more than 1.5 million refugees began returning. The project provided homes and taught carpentry skills to local men and secondary school boys. Other projects undertaken were also lasting in their impact. In Peru in 1996, a small grant of US$6,000 helped the community of Tucucucho in Huancavelica build a sheep dip. "Sheep are the major source of income for these families, and the dip will increase their income by reducing animal loss from parasites and disease", Pell wrote in his annual report.

In 1994, Pell joined sixteen other Australian Catholic representatives as part of an ecumenical election-monitoring team during South Africa's first all-race elections, where he found the people's joy and spirit of optimism overwhelming. The following year Caritas drew together thirty-three Church agencies to promote awareness of the appalling death and injury toll and upheaval caused by the use of anti-personnel land mines. Pell was also one of a delegation of Australian bishops to Ukraine, led by Cardinal Clancy, to establish a practical partnership with Caritas Ukraine, as the Catholic Church in Eastern Europe reestablished her social mission after exclusion from all humanitarian work during the decades of Communist rule. It was during one such visit, to Eastern Europe in 1992, that Pell, at the age of fifty-one, who until that time had appeared to be in robust good health, suffered his first heart attack. He became unwell during the trip, and the problem was confirmed after he returned to Melbourne. He elected to keep the condition private and looked after his health carefully, while living life to the full, for the next thirty years. The seriousness of his condition, however, made his subsequent achievements, and tribulations, all the more remarkable.

As Caritas chairman, Pell sometimes worked at the "front line" in major emergencies, such as the Indian earthquake of 1993, one of the worst on the subcontinent. Before dawn on September 30, 1993, a series of earthquakes struck southwestern India, about 250 miles southeast of Bombay, razing towns and villages to rubble. The official death toll from the quakes and aftershocks was thirty thousand, but aid workers on the ground estimated the true figure at between fifty and sixty thousand. While most of the victims were at home in bed, many were in the streets before dawn celebrating the festival of Ganesh and immersing statues of the elephant-faced god in water.

The effects were most severe in two villages—Killari and Umarga Taluk. Homes with walls up to a foot and a half thick—large granite stones pasted with mud—tumbled down, killing those inside. Pell, along with representatives from Caritas France and Caritas Germany, was at the scene within two weeks, by which time not even half the dead bodies had been buried. Trauma and shock abounded. "We gave comfort 'being with', not with things", he wrote. "When people come out of shock then they can eat." He assisted, not only with Caritas relief efforts, but in long-term planning for rebuilding twelve hundred homes and infrastructure such as schools and health centres and water systems.

It was clear to Pell that the survivors would need food and medical supplies for the next six months and that local workers would be able to play a major role in rebuilding homes. At that point, daily rain, unusual for October, was hampering the burning of corpses and made life even harder for the survivors, some of whom insisted on sleeping out of doors in tents for fear of more aftershocks. Catholic relief workers had been among the first on the scene, with Mother Teresa's nuns allowed through the roadblocks before others. The Catholic teams concentrated on the isolated villages, as these were being largely ignored in the general relief effort that concentrated on villages easily accessible by road.

Pell's diary entry of October 15, 1993, began:

Mass for chapel full of nuns—Salesians, Fatima sisters and Missionaries of Charity. Preached briefly on *In your word is faith and life*, i.e., interdependence of faith and service. Travelled 90 km from Latur to Killari, richest village in the area, reduced to immense piles of rubble 15 feet high. Some of homes 200 or 300 years old—walls 18 inches or more thick with two feet of mud on roof to keep houses cool. Immense irregular granite stones held together simply by mud. Village reduced to a few doorways. In Killari, probably 12,000 died out of 22,000....

Met middle-aged man on top of his rubble, who had lost six or eight of his extended family in large house. Apparently a young girl found alive unconscious after being buried for five days—was under an iron cot....

Wondered how God allowed earthquakes (perhaps God not all powerful, even cosmologically—because of original sin and allowed scheme and potential of suffering). But God does leave room for us to act!!! May God help victims and my weak faith.

Destruction at Mangalore worse than Killari—not a stone upon a stone. In Mangalore 5,500 died out of 6,000. Especially at Killari, sight-seers and thieves ransacked village for gold buried in homes or on the victims. Soldiers now in charge in villages and on the approach roads.

At Nandunga met old grandma in green sari weeping because she had lost eight family members. Salesian sisters told how women flocked to talk with them because so few women among first visitors, e.g., soldiers, police relief workers. One brother told me he was battling for the untouchables. Spent 6:00 P.M. to 7:30 P.M. in rosary and then holy hour with nuns before Blessed Sacrament. Power off intermittently and news threatened another major quake between 7:00 P.M. and midnight. So far (9:50 P.M.) so good!

Bishop Pell travelled home via Bombay and Madras, with a detour to Wattala, outside Colombo in Sri Lanka, for Caritas meetings. In the 1980s and early 1990s, Caritas Australia contributed more than AU$1.5 million for relief and rehabilitation programs for victims of the civil war. In his Madras stopover, Pell hired a car and visited Saint Thomas Cathedral, where the tomb of "Doubting Thomas", the apostle, is believed to be located. "Of greater interest was an altar before which Saint Francis Xavier prayed. Prayed there that Jesuits be given another Ignatius and Xavier. They need them."

The ACR/Caritas annual reports from 1987 to 1996 show that administrative expenses were kept to a minimum—around 4 to 8 percent of expenditure a year. In such an organisation, allocating millions of dollars a year donated by practicing Catholics in good faith, a vital part of the chairman's job is to ensure the money is well spent. Even before he took over stewardship of ACR, Pell knew that a few administrative land mines needed defusing. Throughout the early 1980s, some ACR funding allocated for humanitarian work in the Philippines was finding its way to violent Communist-infiltrated organisations. At that point, Communism remained a force in Asia, including the Philippines. Such concerns were taken seriously both by the head of the Catholic Church in the Philippines, Cardinal Jaime Sin, and by Pell, who was determined to ensure that Australian Catholic aid money was not sidetracked. Following the money trail proved a complex, time-consuming, and expensive task, but it was essential to restore ACR's credibility, which was in dire danger of being compromised very seriously in the minds of donors.

In 1988, Cardinal Sin admitted that the Church's National Secretariat for Social Action in the Philippines had been "infiltrated, highly infiltrated", and that overseas funds had been diverted "to buy weapons and strengthen and develop" the Communist New People's Army (NPA). The NPA, founded in 1969, was the armed wing of the new Communist Party of the Philippines (CPP) established in 1968 under Jose Maria Sison in opposition to the corrupt United States–backed regime of Ferdinand Marcos. The CPP's aim was to rebuild the party securely on the revolutionary heritage of the teachings of Karl Marx, Vladimir Lenin, and Mao Tse Tung.

When Sison visited Australia in 1986, he was sponsored, incredibly, by the Catholic Commission for Justice and Peace, the Australian Council of Churches (a Protestant organisation in those days), and teachers' unions, among others. In the Philippines, the CPP's front organisation, the so-called National Democratic Front (NDF), was charged with the task of harnessing moral and financial support from the West, and, handily for the Communists, its international representative was a former Roman- and German-educated Catholic priest, Luis Jalandoni, who had left the priesthood to marry a former nun. Reports furnished to Pell in the second half of 1988 showed that Jalandoni, while still a priest, had channeled Church funds to the CPP/NPA when he was social action director in the Diocese of Bacolod, under Bishop Antonio Fortich.

In the 1970s, Jalandoni and his wife based themselves in Utrecht, Holland, to muster support from across Europe, boasting that by the end of that decade he had fifteen "solidarity" committees established in different countries from Ireland to Sweden, Greece to Austria. The CPP had numerous other off-shoot organisations, including the KMU, a far-left Filipino trade union, and these, too, set up support organisations in Europe. The NDF's European base remained in the Netherlands, with a range of non-government organisations and Catholic aid agencies from the Dutch Church providing generous assistance to a complex web of far-left Filipino organisations. That process, significantly, continued for years after the fall of the Marcos government and the accession of Cory Aquino as Filipino president in February 1986, threatening the emergence of the Philippines' then-fledgling democracy and free economy. In June 2022, in a controversial move, the Philippines Anti-Terrorism Council designated Jalandoni and five alleged members of radical Islamist groups as terrorists.

Australian aid agencies, including ACR, were enmeshed in the 1980s mess. As Pell wrote in Melbourne's *Advocate* Catholic newspaper: "Catholics are deeply resentful when priests and religious working for social reform are automatically dubbed as communists. They find it equally objectionable when those opposed to communism are presumed to be uninterested in social justice and fueling the violence of the civil war."

To see the situation firsthand, Pell, accompanied by Father Sam Dimattina, a Melbourne priest and a member of the ACR national committee, paid a nine-day visit to the Philippines in December 1988, travelling to Manila and north through the centre of the island of Luzon to Vigan, and south to Bacolod on the island of Negros. On his first night in Manila, the quiet was broken by occasional rifle and pistol shots. "Unemployment rate in Manila would be doubled if population law-abiding—reduction in no. of armed guards", he quipped in his diary. The following day, he found Cardinal Sin "expansive, humorous [as if he'd] kissed the Blarney Stone!" In Manila they visited Smoky Mountain, a vast rubbish dump, home for thousands of families in makeshift shacks, "where the rats and the stench would knock you over.... It gave me a jolt to visit some of the people who live on the suburban railway network in Manila and are helped by the St James Foundation, a joint venture of the Australian government and ACR. Tens of thousands of squatters live in shacks along the railway lines, with their main entrances often three or four meters from the passing trains."

On the island of Negros, Pell and Dimattina concelebrated Mass with Bishop Antonio Fortich, a "gnarled, fearless old lion" who spoke his mind as he smoked his pipe after Mass. His flock, the poorest of the poor—sugar workers earning US$1.50 a day—followed him with devotion and trust akin to that afforded Archbishop Daniel Mannix by Melbourne Catholics during World War I. "How much is he in control of underlings? How much is he used?" Bishop Pell wondered in his diary.

As Pell and Dimattina travelled around, every bishop they spoke with admitted that some aid money had gone to the Communists, though other projects financed were worthwhile. They found that the Filipino bishops were effectively remedying the situation. To ensure further that money donated by Australian Catholics was used for the purposes it was intended, Pell decided that, in future, ACR money given to the Asian Partnership for Human Development would be for non-Philippine projects only. Instead, ACR would make a grant of AU$400,000 a year for the next two years directly to revamped Filipino development work. That satisfied the Church's sternest critics on the matter in Australia, including Bob Santamaria.

Pell's visit to the Philippines convinced him more strongly than ever that Australian Catholics had an important role to play in assisting the country, 85 percent of which is Catholic. He told readers of Melbourne's Catholic *Advocate* after his visit: "Those of us who accept Christ's teaching about our obligations to the poor, who support the struggle for justice, who believe in democracy as the best form of government, who believe communism is an evil—we have a special regional and religious obligation to increase our help to this Christian nation."

Pell noted that the Catholic Church was the one institution in the Philippines that had grown in respect and standing during ten tumultuous years. "We have seen priests and religious in the Philippines, sometimes people we know, branded as communists when

this was clearly false, and we have been tempted to dismiss the communist menace entirely as a figment of right-wing imagination. This
is an elementary mistake.... In 1987, for instance, communist urban
guerrilla 'sparrow units' killed more than 100 people, soldiers, and
civilians in Manila alone."

In Vietnam, working with the Communist authorities was part
of a day's work for Pell and ACR. (Cardinal Edward Clancy and he
stayed in the guesthouse of the central committee of the Communist
Party in Hanoi in 1993.) It was a vast cultural leap for the Ballarat
boy from a Democratic Labor Party (DLP) background. But those
assisted by ACR/Caritas were grateful that the Catholic Church
cared enough about them to make such an effort with humanitarian
aid, irrespective of the religious beliefs or non-beliefs of the recip-
ients. In Hanoi in August 1993, Pell and Michael Whitley, ACR's
national director for eighteen years, visited the Blind Association.
"Somewhat unnerving at first because the president and vice pres-
idents are all blind! Both VPs in army-type uniforms with impene-
trable dark glasses. Impossible not to be impressed by the enormity
of their task. We help Blind Society with talking books program.
Were told story of blind woman whom the family had never heard
laugh until she heard a talking book! And when she laughed then
her family cried!"

Driving along Highway 1 outside Hanoi, Pell observed an exotic
landscape, with many fine Catholic churches left over from the French
colonial days. Some were being repaired. The surrounding countryside was "flat, fertile, irrigated land ablaze with recently planted green
rice". The flatness was interspersed with "sheer outcrops of layered
granite—a la Hanging Rock—but craggy, not smooth". In Ho Chi
Minh City (Saigon), Cardinal Clancy and Pell visited Archbishop
Paul Binh in Thong Nhat Hospital, which formerly belonged to
President Thieu and until a couple of years earlier had been reserved
for the Communist hierarchy. The old archbishop, a Propagandist
from 1933 to 1938, had suffered a stroke but was clear in his mind,
dignified, and shrewd. He assured the visitors that the Church was
intact, with three thousand converts a year.

The following day, Pell visited an orphanage for 250 street kids in
the Go Vap district of Saigon. "Boys and girls, lively, cheeky uninhibited, from 8 yrs. to 15 yrs. Short of affection, as they came around

us without hesitation. Clean but very poor, but seemed well run. 40,000 dong given for food monthly for child—120,000 needed."

Later in the day, the vicar-general of the Saigon Diocese arranged for Pell to say Mass at 5:00 P.M. in the Cathedral of Our Lady. "Striking and moving to see large statue of Our Lady still in place dominating large square in front of red brick cathedral. Sixty or more people present; a range of ages but many elderly. Applauded loudly at beginning and end, I preached in French...." Speaking French was invaluable for the ACR chairman both in Vietnam and Cambodia. Invaluable, too, was his background at Propaganda College in providing a network of contacts in the developing world.

From the killing fields in Cambodia to cities of Ukraine, where people were beginning to regroup after decades of oppression, from the orphanages of Vietnam to the rubble of southwest Indian villages after a severe earthquake, Pell's nine years of running Caritas were absorbing, at times exhausting, and rewarding. As he saw it: "I think things [like Caritas] are intrinsically worthwhile. It sounds a bit lofty, but my friend Michael Mason says that even when we make mistakes, what we are doing is of 'ultimate significance'."

By the time Pell relinquished the position of chairman of Caritas in April 1997, he had explored corners of the world, far from the beaten tourist tracks, that most people can only wonder about. Those visits strengthened his appreciation of Australia. "I never returned home from one of those visits without thanking God for the type of quality of life we have here in Australia, and I would often resolve to tell people of that and point out what an obligation we have to keep it good and to make it better."

13

Preparing for the Second Spring

George Pell's nine years as auxiliary bishop to Archbishop Sir Frank Little in Melbourne was a time of contradictions, for him personally and for the wider Church. He was often exceedingly busy, usually working seven days a week from early morning to late into the evening. In addition to his work at Caritas, he was also overseeing the creation of the Australian Catholic University (and spending five years as its foundation pro-chancellor), serving as a member of two important Vatican organisations, travelling, lecturing, attending meetings, visiting parishes, and conducting Confirmation ceremonies in the southern region of the Melbourne Archdiocese. His home was a house in the southern bayside parish of Mentone, where nominally he was the pastor, although the day-to-day work of running the parish was done by successive administrators, Fathers Ted Teal, John Murphy, and John Walshe.

Despite the sometimes frenetic schedule, the role of auxiliary bishop is strangely devoid of heavy responsibilities, prompting Pell to say to one of his friends: "The only decision I have to make every day is which side of bed to get out on." Tongue-in-cheek, but an accurate reflection of the power of any auxiliary bishop. In many ways, auxiliary bishops have less autonomy canonically and in practice than pastors, who are directly in charge of their parishes. Auxiliary bishops have no control over archdiocesan policy or finances and are subject to their archbishop, who may or may not delegate significant responsibilities to them. The archbishop, however, is the ultimate boss. Years later, when the Royal Commission into Institutional Responses to Child Sexual Abuse was inquiring into the Archdiocese of Melbourne during these years, the extent of Pell's influence as auxiliary at the time became an issue during his cross-examination.

PREPARING FOR THE SECOND SPRING

Archbishop Little, who retired to the leafy Melbourne suburb of Camberwell in a house Pell bought for him on behalf of the Church after succeeding him as archbishop in 1996, was uncomfortable with the description of himself as the "boss". "I liked to think of it as a team", he said. And did he and Bishop Pell make a good team? "Not as good as I had hoped", Archbishop Little admitted—and he did not just mean that they were at odds when Pell's beloved Tigers were up against Sir Frank's team, the Essendon Bombers. "Well, we never discussed theology—history was his area", Sir Frank said.

It was no secret that the two men, both graduates of Saint Patrick's Ballarat and Propaganda Fide, were often at odds over the Church's direction, especially in relation to issues such as seminary formation, school catechetics, and devolution of some of the traditional roles of pastors to lay administrators and nuns as paid pastoral associates. As Father Anthony Robbie, Pell's secretary from 2016 to 2020, noted in his obituary about Pell:

> It was well known that relations between the two men were somewhat strained, and Archbishop Little did not overburden his auxiliary with too many duties. These were the days when Pope John Paul II, still vigorous, and energetic, was calling for a sincere revival of traditional Catholic faith and practice. Bishop Pell threw himself wholeheartedly into the effort and became a focus of hope for many troubled Australian Catholics and something of a standard bearer for the movement. Unfortunately, in the process, he also became a target of those who were much more committed to the new winds of change, which had been blowing through the Church with mixed results for over two decades. Bishop Pell was blunt and direct and enjoyed the limelight, but he was also articulate and knew how to defend himself in a hostile situation. There were to be many of those as the years passed.[1]

Little knew that he and his auxiliary were not on the same page, theologically or pastorally. "I suppose that I found George ever ready to share his point of view quite strongly, and that is what I would want", Sir Frank reflected in 2001. Pell's forceful arguments, however,

---

[1] Anthony Robbie, "Obituary—His Eminence Cardinal George Pell", Order of Malta Australia, January 13, 2023, https://www.orderofmalta.org.au/obituary-his-eminence-george -cardinal-pell/.

were presented to his boss behind closed doors, and once specific decisions had been made, Sir Frank said, Pell supported them in public, regardless of how much he might have argued against them in private.

"One of the things for which I remain grateful was that he was ready to take on the tough assignments", Sir Frank said. He refused to elaborate on the nature of these "tough assignments", but one, undoubtedly, was Pell's walking notorious paedophile Father Gerald Ridsdale into court on Little's orders. That footage was to haunt Pell for years as the child abuse crisis intensified and the extent of Ridsdale's offending become known.

Interviewed in 2001, Pell described his relationship with Sir Frank from 1987 to 1996 as "cordial and correct", adding, "I was loyal to Frank." Their differences, he says, were never personal but related to their different views on the best way forward for the Church.

Denis Hart, at that point a priest in Melbourne, said that as Pell worked around the southern region of Melbourne, he became increasingly concerned about the serious laxity in religious education and at the inroads secularism and feminism were making into the life of the Church. "As auxiliary bishop he couldn't do a great deal about it, but he was a rock of strength to people who were troubled by what was happening."

Peter Elliott, who began work in the Vatican on May 1, 1987, a few weeks before Pell's consecration, said Pell "would not even confide in his friends about some of the anguish he went through when he had to at least tolerate things going on which he knew were wrong or that would not enhance the growth of the Church."

In the 1970s, 1980s, and 1990s, the majority of Australia's Catholic bishops, including the senior archbishops—Little in Melbourne, Leonard Faulkner in Adelaide, Francis Rush in Brisbane, and Edward Clancy in Sydney—while very different characters, were in broad agreement about the direction of the Church. They tended to give their Church bureaucrats, liturgical "experts", and Catholic education offices and seminary formation staff considerable rein in terms of experimentation and new ideas, and in turn, these people pushed the boundaries of liberalism well beyond what those archbishops would have approved of themselves.

For example, in many parts of Australia, the first rite of Penance, or individual confession, was replaced by the less demanding "general absolution", or third rite, where a large congregation

PREPARING FOR THE SECOND SPRING 179

of several hundred were absolved of their sins en masse without confessing individually. It was rarely, if ever, mentioned that the Church reserved general absolution for genuine emergency situations (such as an army going into battle) and that the penitents in such cases were obliged to confess serious sins individually as soon as possible afterwards. Priest meetings openly lauded some bishops for "turning a blind eye" in the face of opposition from Rome about the misapplication of general absolution.

In classrooms, Catholic teachers openly defied Catholic doctrine on matters such as purgatory and the virginity of Our Lady, some priests and nuns claimed it was not a grave matter to miss Mass on Sundays, traditional furnishings and statues disappeared as many churches came to resemble lifeless assembly halls. As regards the Mass, the emphasis in many places shifted from Christ's Sacrifice on Calvary to the mere commemoration of a special "meal". The ripping out of high altars reminded some of one of the edicts of the English Reformation under Edward VI: "All the altars in every church taken down, and in lieu of them a table set up." In some cases, people attending Masses were encouraged to stand around the altar holding hands—when some people objected, they were branded "snobs" and "conservatives". Many who wished to continue to receive Communion on the tongue rather than in the hand were shunned, as were those who wished to kneel. Some priests abandoned large chunks of the official Roman Missal and improvised parts of the Mass. Serious-minded Mass-goers cringed as the traditional, familiar introductory rite—"The grace of our Lord Jesus Christ, and the love of God and the fellowship of the Holy Spirit be with you all" gave way in many places to banal openings like "Hi everyone, nippy morning for getting up, wasn't it?" or "G'Day ... 'ow are y'all?" The mumbled responses of those gathered were usually followed by the priest urging them to turn around and have a chat with those nearby. Seminarians socialized more than ever before, and some took part-time jobs in hotels during the term. Vocations and Mass attendances plummeted.

Pell's ascendancy in Melbourne and later Sydney helped put the brakes on avant garde liturgical trends before they reached the levels of absurdity—admittedly unusual—that have been witnessed elsewhere in Australia, including children chomping into cream cakes near the altar after First Communion, priests "sitting out" most of the Mass and allowing laity to do everything until the Consecration, vast and important sections of the Mass left out, and poems and other works substituted for scriptural readings.

Against that background, there was no shortage of media interest and discussion in Catholic circles leading up to Whit Saturday, June 13, 1992, when Pell celebrated a Solemn Pontifical Mass (an Extraordinary Form High Mass said by a bishop) at Saint Patrick's Cathedral in Melbourne. It was the first Extraordinary Form Mass in a cathedral in Australia since the Novus Ordo Mass was promulgated by Pope Paul VI in 1969 to replace the Tridentine Mass of 1570, which had been last modified by Pope John XXIII in 1962. A surprisingly large crowd turned up that Saturday morning, encouraged, no doubt, by Pope John Paul II's wishes that the traditional Mass retain a place of honour and be available to those who wished.

It was the founding chairman of the Ecclesia Dei Society of Australia, Sydney lawyer Glen Tattersall (later Father Glen Tattersall), who had asked Bishop Pell to celebrate the Pontifical Mass, and he had readily agreed. Pell was a capable Latinist and set about learning the complex rubrics and movements of the old Rite in order to celebrate that High Mass. He was assisted, among others, by Father John Walshe, who ran the parish of Mentone, where Pell lived (and was nominally the parish priest) when he was an auxiliary bishop.

In his sermon in the cathedral, Pell explained the relationship between the *lex orandi* and the *lex credendi* (the law of praying and the law of believing) and their foundation in Christ as bequeathed to us in the Catholic, apostolic tradition. Thirty-one years later, as parish priest of Melbourne's Saint John Henry Newman, which attracts around seven hundred Catholics to its Sunday Masses in the Extraordinary Form, Father Tattersall, preaching at a Mass he offered for George Pell's soul, recalled the bishop's sermon on that historic morning in 1992.

"This is a precious inheritance; it is not ours to improve or to prune", Pell had said. "It is the source of faith and repentance, the source of everlasting renewal. To the extent that we depart from this central tradition of worship and conversion, that we damage or pollute this core, we are weakened and enfeebled. 'Without me,' says Christ, 'you can do nothing.' "[2] Father Tattersall reiterated the vision

---

[2] George Pell, *Test Everything: Hold Fast to What Is Good* (San Francisco: Ignatius Press, 2015), p. 143.

Pell had placed before the congregation at Saint Patrick's: "The Tridentine Mass has many virtues; it is part of a noble tradition of worship. Through prayers, ritual, and music it attempts very explicitly to convey the beauty of holiness, and especially through its decorum and dignity it helps to bring us to bow in worship before the invisible God, the All-Holy One."

There is an immense pluralism within the Church in many areas, Pell had said, "and it is not too strange to celebrate again, as is done regularly in Melbourne, that form of the Mass which predominated for nearly fifteen hundred years in the Western Church."[3] While the world that first produced Gregorian chant at the end of the sixth century and the world that witnessed the Tridentine reforms in the sixteenth century are gone, "the Christian mystery that inspired these great movements" is still with us, he said.

> I cannot promise you a second spring. I can only promise you a hard slog. The external pressures on us will remain formidable. The Counter-Reformation discipline that applied in the Church from Trent until the 1950s is gravely weakened. Our situation is closer to the theological variety and turmoil that existed in the Middle Ages, while the external threats are a bit like the Gnostic crisis in the second and third centuries that nearly destroyed the Church; when a bewildering variety of movements, both puritan and laxist, deriving from both philosophy and the Eastern mystery religions, struggled to make the Christian message contemporary, to improve it, to make it appropriate for the times. Even then in the second and third centuries, the chattering classes thought Christianity old fashioned and irrelevant![4]

When told after the Mass that he had been condemned for this retrograde step from a prominent and reliably liberal pulpit in the city, Bishop Pell smiled and replied, "Well, we must be doing something right then!"

Father Tattersall, in his sermon, said Cardinal Pell would agree with Saint Augustine that the truth is like a lion that, once it is released from its cage, can easily defend itself: "He was himself something of a lion. The fear of God delivered Cardinal Pell from the fear of men.

[3] Ibid.
[4] Ibid, p. 144.

But it was also the love of God that urged Cardinal Pell on—and it was the love of neighbour that embraces in and for Christ both friend and foe, and provided the best and most powerful of motives for George Pell to propose the Truth that can set us all free."

In a July 2022 interview with *Catholic World Report*, during the Sacra Liturgica conference at Saint Patrick's Seminary in Menlo Park, California, when the restrictions on the Extraordinary Form were causing controversy and heartache, Pell defended the value of the variety of rites in the Church as "part of the Catholic genius". "This has to be balanced around unity, of course, but unity does not have to mean uniformity or the suppression of traditional and established and indeed beautiful forms of worship", he said. "Many people like to pray according to the *vetus ordo* [old rite], and I think they're just too many and too numerous to be ignored. So I think the situation will slowly develop within the organic unity of the Church, and peace will return in some form or other."[5]

By the mid-1980s, when it was clear that Pope John Paul II intended to fight the encroaching malaise afflicting the Church head-on, many observers, including Pell, thought that the Church in Australia—under the leadership of a few archbishops--was digging herself deeper and deeper into a 1960s and 1970s rut. She was also being left behind the dynamic resurgence in spirituality emerging in some places overseas, he feared. In parts of the United States, including New York, where the seminary in Dunwoodie was filling up once again under Pell's friend Cardinal John O'Connor, the revival was known as "the second spring", an expectation that was to prove overly optimistic.

While heavily constrained by the limitations of his position as an auxiliary bishop in Melbourne, Pell led the way in putting important issues on the Catholic agenda in Australia. The forum he used effectively was *AD2000*, a glossy journal of religious opinion launched by B. A. Santamaria and the National Civic Council in 1988. Bob Santamaria was regarded as politically incorrect, but he was one of the few Catholics in Australia who had the capacity, intellectually and organisationally, to launch such a project. While Australian Labor

[5] "Cardinal George Pell Reflects on Celebrating (and Not Celebrating) the Mass" (interview with Paul Senz), *Catholic World Report*, July 20, 2022, https://www.catholicworldreport.com/2022/07/20/cardinal-george-pell-reflects-on-celebrating-and-not-celebrating-the-mass/.

Party (ALP) supporters and many members of the Liberal Party too—especially those who understood the benefits of economic rationalism—rubbished Santamaria's socioeconomic outpourings against free trade and globalization, many of those same people came to appreciate his magazine. In many parishes, however, the publication was outlawed as contraband, with a few priests even brandishing it in their pulpits as they condemned it as the "rag of the devil". Sir Frank Little hated it, as did almost all of Australia's bishops, with the exception of Pell and one or two others. In a letter to *The Age* in 1993, responding to a column by Michael Barnard, Little attacked what he called a small minority "who seek to set themselves up as the sole or the true and final arbiters of orthodoxy". He went on: "Theirs is the style of 'dissent' which has characterised the methodology of a minority group of 'traditionalists' who continue to alienate themselves from the Church. It is the style of innuendo, guilt by association, near slander and near character assassination which one finds paraded in fringe publications such as *AD2000* and *Fidelity* [another Catholic periodical]."

Santamaria, an old friend of Pell's earlier mentors, Bishop O'Collins in Ballarat and Bishop Kelly in Melbourne, had become close friends with Pell during his time as seminary rector, when Santamaria wholeheartedly approved of Pell's "few small changes". As rector and more often as auxiliary bishop, Pell often lunched at Santamaria's National Civic Council (NCC) headquarters in North Melbourne and regarded the older man as something of a father figure.

While Pell agreed with the broad thrust of many of Santamaria's economic and social views (such as bolstering the traditional family), he was far more of a political agnostic than Santamaria and did not share his entire critique of economic rationalism. The two men shared a love of history and a deep admiration for Archbishop Mannix (who had been Santamaria's mentor) and enjoyed lively intellectual exchanges. Pell also enjoyed mixing with Santamaria's large, bright family. The glue that bound their friendship, however, was a deep concern about the direction of the Catholic Church in Australia.

AD2000 readers noticed the contributions of George Pell, whom most Catholics outside Melbourne had not heard of before. His photograph suggested he was a generation removed from the older

Church hierarchy, and, while more conservative than that hierarchy on many issues, he appeared to be more in tune with the vision of Pope John Paul II, then at the height of his pontificate.

The magazine's readers also soon became familiar with the success of Bishop William Brennan in attracting students for the priesthood and launching Vianney College, a successful seminary in the small rural Diocese of Wagga. Pell and Brennan, though very different in style, were soon identified by Catholics across Australia—by supporters and opponents—as offering a vision different from that generally prevailing at the time. In January 1995, Pell wrote an article praising Wagga for taking the lead in Australia in producing a 530-page religious education syllabus, *We Belong to the Lord*, soon after the publication of the English-language edition of the new *Catechism of the Catholic Church*. The *Catechism* was one of the important initiatives of Pope John Paul II's papacy.

In *AD2000*'s first few years, Pell contributed more than half a dozen pieces. These struck a chord with those Catholics who were looking askance at the left-wing, anti-American stance of the Catholic Commission for Justice and Peace (the body set up by the Australian bishops to research and teach about such issues) and at emerging liturgical and theological trends and falling Mass attendances in most but not all parishes (mainly those that resisted modernism). In some parishes, liturgical dancing and even "clowning" had become part of Mass.

Overseas, especially in the United States, the battle lines were drawn sharply and the fight-back of the centre/right was well underway, especially through the books and magazines published by Ignatius Press in San Francisco, California, and through the cable TV programs of Mother Angelica's EWTN (Eternal Word Television Network). "Does Saint Bozo's Parish no longer amuse you?" asked one of the friskier advertisements, accompanied by a picture of a circus clown, for the publication *New Oxford Review*. Such a statement would have meant nothing in earlier decades, but it struck the right chord with those irritated by the outlandish liturgies pushed at them on Sundays, as most priests and bishops stood idly by.

Church teachings on marriage, contraception, and the all-male priesthood were increasingly ridiculed from within the Church's own ranks. More seriously, aspersions were cast in some clerical quarters about fundamental tenets of the Catholic faith such as the bodily Resurrection of Christ, His divinity, and the Virgin Birth. Many believed bishops needed to take a stronger line in upholding Catholic dogma. In Sydney, a young Rhodes scholar and seminarian by the name of Tony Abbott, who was later elected to Parliament and became prime minister in 2013, abandoned his studies and wrote about the Church's internal disarray in an article in *The Bulletin* news magazine.

Some in the Church wanted to differentiate the local community or church from the "official Church" and questioned the need for a ministerial priesthood as distinct from the priesthood of all the baptised. Others wanted to move towards a congregationalist-style or communitarian Church, led at local level by middle-level functionaries rather than parish priests. In Melbourne in 1996, Sir Frank Little hired a layman, Terry Curtin—a former public servant and the father of four children and the grandfather of three—on an AU$40,000 package to run the parish of Aspendale.[6] Such moves, ostensibly, were made to meet future shortages of clergy. But they also signaled a move towards a different kind of lay-led Church, one in which the vocations slide would only worsen. Similar issues flared again in Australia, Germany, Italy, and other nations in 2022 and 2023 as part of the Synod on Synodality process.

While far more restrained in his comments than most of those objecting to the move away from traditional Catholic teaching and practice, Pell in his articles in *AD2000* decades ago attracted attention and opened up important debates. As he said in 2001:

> I was certainly aware that I was offering something somewhat different. I don't think those articles were provocative—they didn't look for trouble—but yes, I had consciously decided that I should say something—in a prudent, unfolding sort of a way. I suppose my ideas developed as the years went along too. I think *AD2000* made an enormous contribution because it created a network of orthodox Catholics throughout the country. It gave them information, it gave them ideas and theology to support the Holy Father. I think it was one of Bob Santamaria's biggest achievements.

---

[6] Referred to in "Pell's Crusade" (a newspaper feature) in *The Age*, November 10, 1997.

As for his senior episcopal colleagues: "They weren't commendatory, as you can imagine. But nobody rebuked me." They were hardly going to, given the fact that the themes of the articles were, to use Pell's phrase, "four square" behind the pope.

Tensions boiled over in October 1993 when *Four Corners*, a television program of the government-funded Australian Broadcasting Corporation, hosted a debate, with audience participation, to discuss the then-recently released papal encyclical *Veritatis Splendor* (The Splendor of Truth) by Pope John Paul II. Pell was in the hot seat, defending the encyclical's reassertion that there exists a set of fundamental moral truths that are binding on the conscience of Catholics and that personal conscience may not override. The encyclical also called on bishops to defend those basic moral truths inherent in the Catholic faith and to ensure that those whom the bishops appoint to teaching positions will be men and women who can be trusted to proclaim and defend them. Bishops were being told by Pope John Paul II, Pell said, to "get out and correct rampant misapprehensions" about Catholic moral teaching.[7]

The studio audience was sharply divided, with the debate one of the most fiery on a religious theme seen on Australian television. In defending the encyclical, Pell not only clashed with Australian philosopher Peter Singer[8] but was opposed by prominent Catholic priests including Father Bill Uren, S.J., then the head of the Jesuits in Australia, Uren's colleague Father Michael Kelly, S.J., and Sister Veronica Brady, I.B.V.M. Uren admitted that a number of people "may be disappointed" with the encyclical if they had been hoping for an alteration of the Church's position on contraception, artificial reproduction, and women priests. While the language was diplomatic, commentator Andrew Olle was perceptive in his quip: "It sounds like theological civil war."

Compared with the sometimes rancorous arguments that erupted in the time of John Paul II, the process of establishing the Australian

---

[7] "Cardinal George Pell Debates Liberal Jesuit on Contraception and Women's Ordination", by Andrew Ollie, *Four Corners*, Australian Broadcasting Corporation, October 1993.

[8] In 1993, Peter Singer was the chair of philosophy at Monash University in Melbourne, where he became the director of its Centre for Human Bioethics and the codirector of its Institute for Ethics and Public Policy. In 1998, he was appointed the DeCamp Professor of Bioethics at the University Center for Human Values, Princeton University.

Catholic University was harmonious, if labourious. In 1988, education minister John Dawkins announced a new direction for tertiary education in Australia, promising extra funding to institutions that joined a unified national system and had at least two thousand equivalent full-time students—a process that resulted in amalgamations of colleges under the umbrella of existing universities and in the creation of new ones. The eight Catholic colleges in the eastern states—three in Victoria, three in New South Wales, one in Canberra, and one in Queensland—decided that in the interests of retaining their identities, they would merge with each other rather than with other colleges in their areas.

With eleven years' experience as a tertiary administrator at Aquinas, Pell was appointed by the Australian bishops to chair the Amalgamation Implementation Committee, which included his old friend and fellow warrior from Aquinas days Sir Bernard Callinan and representatives from each state/territory involved. Representatives of the colleges had first met with Dawkins in August 1988 to tell him of their plans to form a single institution, with one chief executive officer and a single governing body, a single academic board, and one set of academic awards. Such an undertaking was a vast challenge, with some 1,250 miles separating the several campuses of four Catholic schools: Catholic College of Education Sydney in New South Wales, Institute of Catholic Education in Victoria, McAuley College of Queensland, and Signadou College of Education in the Australian Capital Territory.

In October 1989, after winning federal government approval to create one new body with the status of a university, the Catholic archbishops of Sydney, Melbourne, Canberra, and Brisbane announced that the Australian Catholic University would begin operating in the 1991 academic year. The Implementation Committee oversaw asset and liability transfers, staffing structures and appointments, admissions procedures, communications infrastructure, libraries, administrative arrangements, and most importantly, academics. Six faculties were established: education, nursing and health sciences, arts and science, business and administration, social science, and theology, with both undergraduate and postgraduate degrees offered as well as diplomas.

The university opened on schedule at the beginning of 1991, with 5,668 students, including 2,303 first-year enrollments. Cardinal Clancy was the inaugural chancellor, while Bishop Pell was appointed pro-chancellor, retaining a close interest in the running of the university.

Pell was frequently invited to speak at university conferences in Australia and overseas. His paper to La Trobe University's Seminar on the Sociology of Culture in May 1988 was published as the book-let *Catholicism in Australia: Immortal Diamond on a Darkling Plain*. Not inappropriately, as he was speaking in Melbourne, Pell opened with a sporting analogy, comparing the Catholic Church with a game of Australian Rules football in which the Church was kicking against the wind:

> In this scenario we are only approaching quarter-time in the match. The wind is against us and conditions are muddy and difficult. We are a few goals behind, but there have been patches of good play, although some of the veteran players are rattled and another group inclined to play their own game.
>
> The captain-coach (Pope), a player of extraordinary strength and skill, is performing well but has not yet succeeded in imposing a coher-ent game plan on his team. Fewer supporters come to the home and away games, although there are big crowds for the finals at Christmas and Easter. As always, many of these supporters, some only interested spectators, give contradictory, often useless and occasionally damaging advice. But active support is vital even from those supporters. . . .
>
> Due to retirements and recruiting difficulties we are battling to field a good first 18, we do not have as many underage teams, although there are a number of youngsters coming through who are keen to have a go in the big time. Other teams from the same district are still in the competition, with many attractive, clever stylists, but they are not physically strong and the crowds at their games have fallen steadily.
>
> The Catholic team's opponents now play a different type of game, no longer applying heavy physical pressure, but moving the ball around freely and unexpectedly. Some Catholic key position players lack mobility, being better suited to the older, tougher, more direct type of encounter. However, the Catholic side has no alternative except to practise its strengths. The match is not lost, although the team has to regain confidence in its ability to play in its traditional style. Our opponents too are finding conditions harsher, their easy confidence shaken by developments elsewhere.
>
> In other words, the Catholic team has to slow the game down and close up play. We should start a few fights. This tight defensive play

will give us time to see which of our young forwards adapt best to the new conditions. As they grow in confidence, we will be better placed to take advantage of the wind change (which shall come certainly at some stage), to take more risks and regularly run the ball out of defence. The remainder of the first quarter should be quite exciting!

At a time when the pursuit of unity between Christian denominations seemed paramount to most Catholic bishops, Pell's talk threw a healthy dose of realism onto the subject, calling for "abandonment of the mirage of imminent church union". He made it clear that the ordination of women by other churches lessened the likelihood of Catholic participation in local church unions but advocated greater practical and sometimes political cooperation between the churches.

Nor did he mince words on the importance of the priesthood, insisting that a resurgence of vocations "is even more important than the continued expansion of lay activism for the future of the Church". The pope and bishops, he said, were the servants and defenders of a precious, two-thousand-year-old tradition, which they were not at liberty to dismantle.

> Certainly core doctrines, for example the divinity of Jesus, the central position of the Pope and important moral teaching on for example the indissolubility of the family, the defence of life and human dignity through social justice, cannot be jettisoned to gain adherents.
>
> In other words, Catholics need a style which is a mite more confrontational and certainly much less conciliatory towards secular values. The Cross is a sign of contradiction. The doctrine of the primacy of conscience should be quietly ditched, at least in our schools, or comprehensively restated, because too many Catholic youngsters have concluded that values are personal inventions, that we can paint our moral pictures any way we choose. This devastating illusion is one of the causes of the AIDS epidemic.

At the time the paper was given, Pell was one of Australia's most junior bishops, although he spoke as if he knew he would be guiding the Church in the future. While he could not guarantee that Catholicism would prove an effective long-term opponent to the "forces of disarray and darkness", he did promise that "the leadership of the Church will dedicate its best efforts to this end." There were, he acknowledged, "other approaches to Catholic life, with a different diagnosis and different prescriptions from mine", and he professed "no ambition to coerce independent parties to my point of view, only an ambition to do what I feel the Church needs". It will be Christ, he said, "who is the immortal and transforming diamond".

In terms of the battle inside the Church for the hearts and minds of Catholics, Pell's strongest comments came in an *AD2000* article in August 1994. No organisation, he insisted, could survive "Alice-in-Wonderland individualism" but would dissolve and disappear within a generation.[9] The Catholic Church was not a "group of free-thinking do-gooders" and should declare which beliefs and practices are Catholic. "Those who cannot maintain cabinet solidarity leave the cabinet", he said. "Bishops cannot remain silent when writers seek to build a consensus against official teachings, against the Pope, and teach regularly and publicly that Catholics can write their own tickets, can decide themselves the tenets of their Church."

The validity of Christ's teaching has never depended on popular approval—he was crucified for his opinions. The fundamental Catholic appeal is to the truth of Christ's teaching; this norm cannot be set aside by changing fashions. Dissent, he wrote, was being disguised or dressed up with the following ruses worthy of Orwell's "double-speak":

- Attack the Pope and then call yourself conservative and middle-of-the-road, redefining the "centre" in a heterodox fashion. The American priest Father Richard McBrien (author of *Catholicism*) is an old hand at this, but the line has been run in Australia.
- Claim that the Pope is divisive (or the *Catechism* is) when traditional truths are restated. . . .
- Claim that the Church is "authoritarian", as month in and month out you attack her while remaining safely in your position of leadership and responsibility.
- Claim that freedom of conscience enables you to choose your faith and morality, to contradict Christ and the Pope, yet claim to be as good a Catholic as the Pope. (The Church has never taught that conscience is supreme. Conscience is at the service of truth.)

[9] George Pell, "How Dissent Operates in the Church", *AD2000* 7, no. 7 (August 1994), https://www.ad2000.com.au/articles/1994/aug1994p9_833.html.

- Claim that the Church at the Second Vatican Council recovered a proper historical understanding of truth and escaped from the static, neo-Platonic world-view which dominated during the Counter-Reformation. Then go further and imply, rather than state, that fundamental dogmas and sacraments are liable to further change and development, and imply, rather than state, that fixed points of belief and practice are only for "fundamentalists".

However, he warned, the party is over. "The Pope has now delivered three massive blows against the forces of dissolution in the Church: *Veritatis Splendor*, *Ordinatio Sacerdotalis*, and the *Catechism of the Catholic Church*. As a result, it is no longer possible to claim that basic Catholic positions are unclear.... It is the opponents of Catholic teaching within the Church who now have the problems: do they accommodate themselves to these restated teachings inside the Church—or outside her?"

By November 1995, Pell had broadened his battlefront and taken his own advice about "starting a few fights" when he targeted controversial philosopher Peter Singer. Addressing a seminar at Sydney University on the recently released papal encyclical *Evangelium Vitae* (The Gospel of Life), he said that there was

only one serious candidate for the role of King Herod's propaganda chief in Australia, our most notorious messenger of death. This is Peter Singer, who for twenty years has never ceased to advocate abortion, euthanasia and infanticide.

Appointed Professor of Philosophy at Monash University, Melbourne, at the age of 31, he is a prolific writer and determined propagandist. His zeal for dispatching "sub-standard" humans is accompanied by great enthusiasm for animals, especially apes, while his 1975 book *Animal Liberation* is sometimes described as the bible of the animal liberation movement.[10]

Singer, Pell acknowledged, was "our best known philosopher overseas, author of the entry on ethics in *Encyclopaedia Britannica*, a

[10] George Pell, "Evangelium Vitae—Catholicism, the Media and the 'Culture of Death'", *AD2000* 8, no. 10 (November 1995), https://www.ad2000.com.au/articles/1995/nov1995p3_870.html.

regular contributor to quality journals such as the *New York Review of Books.*" On some issues, the bishop said, Singer was clear-headed; on others he was muddled.

> He admits that the foetus is a living human being and therefore claims that he and the Pope "at least share the virtue of seeing clearly what is at stake in the debate" on abortion.
>
> However, he puts the human foetus at a level much lower than a chimpanzee, even lower than a dog, with no right to life simply because it is human. It is self-awareness, in his view, which grounds a right to life. In 1988 his colleague at the Monash Centre for Human Bioethics, Helga Kuhse, compared the human embryo to a lettuce leaf.

Australia's moral decline, the bishop observed, "would need to slip a few more notches" for Singer's views on newborn children to be acceptable to public opinion. The Catholic Church, Pell argued, had to be at the forefront in the struggle for public opinion, "for there is no other non-government organisation with our Church's capacity for influence. We have many religious allies: a potentially huge number among nominal Christians and the recently unchurched, but unfortunately no Australian parallel to the strength of Protestantism in the USA, especially in the southern states. We bear a heavy responsibility for the defence and extension of Judeo-Christian influence in our public life."

For decades, the Church in Australia had drawn apathy rather than either passionate approval or disapproval. That was rapidly changing, as Pell took to the role of social commentator with a vengeance, telling the Sydney seminar:

> The "modern" spirit is deeply subjectivist and relativist, at least in the realm of general moral theory, although this is often married, in the same individuals, with fierce moral convictions on particular issues. It is not only traditionalist or orthodox moralists who are tempted to intolerance. *Webster's Dictionary* defines political correctness as "marked by or adhering to a typical progressive orthodoxy on issues involving especially race, gender, sexual affinity or ecology...."
>
> Earlier this year, a New York writer, George Sim Johnston, claimed that in our dreary decade of Clinton and Yeltsin the present Pope was

the only world leader with the stature of Churchill and De Gaulle. Certainly his role, with Ronald Reagan, in the collapse of communism dwarfs the efforts of Pope Leo the Great and then Pope Gregory the Great in the fifth and sixth centuries to defend Rome and the remnants of the Roman Empire in the West from the depredations of the barbarians. Most of Eastern Europe today is still far from the promised land, economically and politically, but they are free. It is not surprising that one magazine I saw spoke of the Pope as a second Moses!

But John Paul II, Pell argued, had set himself an even more difficult task: to help strengthen and revive the moral and religious sensibility of the Western world, setting in place much of the intellectual groundwork with the new Code of Canon Law, the *Catechism*, and his encyclicals. To date, the fruits in the West had been scarce. Pell told the seminar:

In *Gospel of Life*, the Pope has not just spelt out his intellectual arguments on the sanctity of life. I also believe that in his attack on the "culture of death", the soft nihilism which has settled over Western Europe and the English-speaking world, he has also struck a popular chord.... His is a message, not just for the Catholic community, but for all society. It is our task to exploit these opportunities and for this we shall need the media—print, radio and television....

It is one of the Holy Father's most important writings, an eloquent and passionate appeal to "respect, protect, love and serve life, every human life!"...

Why was the encyclical so well received? A couple of reasons come to mind.

In all societies influenced by the great religions there are huge reservoirs of respect for life, selective and imperfect as these enthusiasms always are. There are oceans of basic human decency, ripe for development and refinement, especially through the media, by Christians and all lovers of life.

The encyclical taps into a rich vein of human conviction and sentiment in favour of life, even among weak and sinful people who might no longer be regular church-goers, but whose moral imagination and even subconscious stirrings move to a rhythm established by generations of Christian liturgy and learning.

Those who have labored mightily to overturn community sensibilities on abortion and euthanasia, usually under the banner of personal autonomy and moral relativism, are well aware of this inconvenient moral bedrock....

The enemies of life do not like their deeds to be brought into the spotlight. Always the supporters of abortion will be among the most vocal opponents of any public showing of films which demonstrate what actually happens in the womb when life is extinguished.

Pell's arguments were noticed internationally. In 1990, Pope John Paul II appointed him to the Rome-based Pontifical Council for Justice and Peace, an international body of bishops and priests who advised him on matters related to social justice, international relations, and global conflict resolution. The pope also appointed Pell as a participant in the Synod of Bishops in Rome on the preparation of priests, where he was a synod spokesman and part of the committee that prepared the final synod message and set the course for priestly training for decades to come. His approach might not have been popular at Clayton, but the Vatican's Congregation for the Evangelization of Peoples appointed him to inspect the national seminaries of New Zealand (1994), Papua New Guinea and the Solomon Islands (1995), the Pacific (1996), and Irian Jaya and Sulawesi (1998).

In 1990, just two and a half years after his consecration as a bishop, the biggest surprise of his life arrived out of the blue from the secretary of state in Rome: a letter informing him that the Holy Father wished him to join the Congregation for the Doctrine of the Faith—the most influential body in the Church in terms of faith and morals. So certain was the Vatican of Pell's acceptance that his appointment was announced from Rome even before he had had time to reply to the letter. Bishop Pell, at forty-nine, was an up-and-coming figure in the universal Church.

Living in the Melbourne Parish of Mentone, Pell confided to his friend Father Walshe that he suspected his preferment in Rome might have been assisted by Belgian Jan Pieter Schotte. A former professor of canon law who had studied at the Catholic University of America, Schotte was ordained a bishop by John Paul II in 1984, had met Pell, and had served as secretary of the Synod of Bishops in the Vatican.

14

The Universal Church

The Palace of the Holy Inquisition (Palazzo della Sacra Inquisizione) was built by Saint Pius V when he was pope in 1571 to house the Sacred Congregation of the Universal Inquisition, which was founded in 1542 to defend the Church from heresy. This it did primarily through intellectual and legal endeavors. In its early days, the Sacred Congregation, in keeping with the times, imprisoned and tortured serious offenders and occasionally referred others to civil authorities for burning at the stake before the Church abandoned the execution of heretics in the 1640s. Such ruthlessness was part of the rule of law in European life. In England, for example, Catholics suffered from imprisonment, torture, and execution under both King Henry VIII and his daughter Elizabeth I, who was excommunicated by Saint Pius V. A strict and dedicated Dominican friar, Pius V was a key figure in the post-Reformation Church—implementing the decisions of the Council of Trent; forbidding the sale of indulgences; introducing a new catechism, breviary, and missal; reemphasizing the works of Saint Thomas Aquinas; and forming the Holy League with Spain and Venice, which defeated the Islamic Turks at the Battle of Lepanto.

In 1908, Pope Pius X discarded the term "inquisition" and renamed the body the Sacred Congregation of the Holy Office. It was renamed the Congregation for the Doctrine of the Faith (CDF) in 1965. Its duty, as defined by Pope John Paul II in 1988, was to "promote and safeguard the doctrine on faith and morals in the whole Catholic world; so it has competence in things that touch this matter in any way."[1] That understanding of the role of the congregation was

[1] John Paul II, Apostolic Constitution *Pastor Bonus* (June 28, 1988), no. 48.

195

changed somewhat by Pope Francis, who renamed the congregation the Dicastery for the Doctrine of the Faith in 2022. A year later he made Argentinian Archbishop Victor Manuel Fernandez, his some-time ghostwriter and the author of the provocative *Heal Me with Your Mouth: The Art of Kissing* and *The Mystical Passion: Spirituality and Sensuality*, the prefect. "Noting that the Dicastery in the past at times pursued possible doctrinal errors and questionable methods, [Pope Francis] underscored the fact that what he expects from the new leadership is something very different", *Vatican News* reported.

> He encouraged a renewed proclamation of the Gospel message, and called on the Dicastery to become an instrument of evangelisation, helping the Church to enter into conversation with the people of the world in a context that is unprecedented for the history of humanity.
>
> The Church, Pope Francis continued, needs to grow in her interpretation of the revealed Word and in her understanding of the truth, without imposing a single way of expressing it.
>
> A harmonious growth nurtured by respect and love, he said, will preserve Christian doctrine more effectively than any control mechanism.[2]

Some interpreted these statements as a thinly veiled criticism of Pope John Paul II and the man he chose as prefect in 1981, German Cardinal Joseph Ratzinger, who served in that capacity until 2005, when he was elected pope and became Benedict XVI.

Ratzinger was in charge of the congregation when George Pell, the first Australian appointed to the twenty-three-member body, attended his first meeting in 1990. Proceedings began with a con-celebrated Mass in Pius V's ornate chapel. The homily was given by another of the younger officials of the congregation—Dominican friar Christoph Schönborn from Austria, who was secretary of the committee that drafted the new *Catechism of the Catholic Church* and who later became the archbishop of Vienna and then a cardinal. The Congregation for the Doctrine of the Faith was regarded as the most influential of the Vatican's congregations, and membership was a rare honour. While the Vatican attempted to include bishops from

---

[2] "Pope Asks New Prefect of DDF to Guard the Faith in Unprecedented Context for Humanity", *Vatican News*, July 1, 2023, https://www.vaticannews.va/en/pope/news/2023 -07/pope-letter-new-prefect-dicastery-doctrine-faith-fernandez.html.

different parts of the world, members were selected primarily on the basis of their intellectual and theological stature.

The congregation was housed on the site of its original palace, which was vastly enlarged in 1930. The sturdy stone building with the smoky blue window shutters is almost beside Saint Peter's Basilica—a two-minute walk through the left-hand columns of the square. The top floor contains apartments of curial officials. A portion of the congregation's secret archives, a treasure trove of history dating back to the Middle Ages, was opened to scholars in 1998.

It was during one of his working visits to the CDF that Pell and a seminarian friend who was studying in Rome, Peter Joseph, visited the nearby tomb of one of congregation's most famous prefects, Cardinal Alfredo Ottaviani (1890–1979). Ottaviani, a baker's son from Trastevere in Rome, was a fierce opponent of most of the significant changes brought about by and after the Second Vatican Council, especially the introduction of the new Mass to replace the centuries-old Tridentine Rite. "Are we seeking to stir up wonder, or perhaps scandal, among the Christian people, by introducing changes in so venerable a rite, that has been approved for so many centuries and is now so familiar? The rite of Holy Mass should not be treated as if it were a piece of cloth to be refashioned according to the whim of each generation", he told the council in 1962, drawing the wrath of many bishops swept up in the mood for change.[3] He set out his objections in full in his Intervention (letter) to Pope Paul VI in 1969. "He probably needs our prayers", Bishop Pell quipped to Peter Joseph when they visited his grave. The inscription on Ottaviani's tomb, "Christum et ecclesiam vehementer dilexit" (He loved Christ and the Church intensely), now appears on Pell's own tomb in the Saint Mary's Cathedral crypt in Sydney. Pell regularly described himself as a "loyal son" of the Second Vatican Council, which he was. In his later years, impressed by the interest of some young Catholics and converts in the Tridentine Rite, he grew more interested in liturgical traditions that had been replaced or ignored after the council, not so much by the council fathers (the attendant bishops) but by those who attempted to interpret (and sometimes misinterpreted) their decisions "in the spirit of the council".

[3] Ralph M. Wiltgen, *The Rhine Flows into the Tiber: A History of Vatican II* (Devon, U.K.: Augustine Publishing, 1979), p. 28.

As a Congregation for the Doctrine of the Faith member for ten years, Bishop Pell was required to attend plenary sessions at least every eighteen months. Before such meetings, hundreds of pages of documents relating to different matters under investigation would be sent to each member to be studied in depth. Cardinal Ratzinger chaired the meetings so that every member had the floor in turn, to expound his views. Most, including Pell, spoke in Italian. Cardinal Ratzinger then summed up everyone's comments, demonstrating a rare breadth and depth of knowledge and an enormous capacity to synthesize and analyze various expert opinions.

Matters discussed by the congregation were strictly confidential, although some final judgements, outlining why a particular book or enterprise has been found not to have the Church's approval, are published. Pell regarded Ratzinger, a courteous, reserved man, as one of the most formidable intellectuals he had ever encountered. "His working relationship with the Holy Father has been one of the high points of papal history", Pell said when interviewed for the first edition of this biography in 2002. "The Church of John Paul II owes Ratzinger an enormous debt; his contribution has been invaluable, and the abuse heaped upon him is totally unjustified."

More of the hostility towards the soft-spoken, silver-haired German came from bishops inside the Church as much as from outsiders. In June 2002, for example, Canberra's auxiliary bishop Patrick Power branded the CDF's 2000 document *Dominus Jesus* (Lord Jesus) as "a deliberate regression from the teaching and spirit of Vatican II".[4]

From Galileo to Hans Küng, from Teilhard de Chardin to the seven women involved in the mock "ordination" on a moored boat on the Danube in July 2002, hundreds of scholars, clerics, religious, and lay people, including several Australian priests, faced the intellectual might of the congregation's examinations in different centuries. Diocesan bishops and archbishops visited it, often somewhat nervously, during their five-yearly *ad limina* visits to the Vatican. The congregation was the Church's final arbiter in matters of faith and morals, the body that drew the disciplinary line between what was

---

[4] Patrick Power, "Joy, Hope and Some Anxiety", *The Mix*, April 2002, quoted in "The Church Around the World", *AD2000* 15, no. 5 (June 2002), https://www.ad2000.com.au /articles/2002/jun2002p4_1024.html.

acceptable teaching/writing/behaviour within the universal Church and what was not. Some issues were clear-cut, others involved years of examination.

In Rome, congregation officials met regularly with their local consultors (priests with relevant expertise), and Ratzinger met John Paul II at least once a week. In the 1980s and 1990s the congregation issued many of the most important and controversial decisions of the time. In 1995, for example, after several years of argument in the United States, Australia, and other countries, the congregation issued a definitive ruling, approved by Pope John Paul II, that the Church's claim that she had no authority to ordain women to the priesthood was "to be held always, everywhere, and by all, as belonging to the deposit of faith".[5] In Australia, Pell had already set out that teaching in a pamphlet of which seventy thousand copies were distributed. The pamphlet was later incorporated into his 1996 book for upper secondary students, *Issues of Faith and Morals* (Oxford University Press and Ignatius Press).

As well as being appointed to the CDF in 1990, Pell was appointed for five years to the Vatican's Pontifical Council for Justice and Peace, a body comprising twenty-five men and women, lay and religious, that included bishops, social workers, a former South American president, academics, a priest who described himself as an old friend of the Communists, a specialist in the arms trade, and the vice president of a United States bank. The council's work, in which Pope John Paul II took a close, personal interest, was to promote and develop the Church's work for social justice. The campaign to relieve Third World countries of much of their crippling international debt was an example. Pell's time on the council coincided with the centenary of the Church's landmark encyclical on social teaching, *Rerum Novarum*, promulgated by Pope Leo XIII in 1891. The centenary occurred at a momentous time—shortly after disintegration of the Soviet Union, which had been committed to ridding the world of religion. To mark the centenary, Pope John Paul II issued a commemorative letter, *Centesimus Annus*, in which he wrote that the reasons for the collapse

---

[5] Congregation for the Doctrine of the Faith, *Responsum ad Propositum Dubium concerning the Teaching Contained in "Ordinatio Sacerdotalis"* (October 28, 1995).

of Communism were far deeper and more complex than economic inefficiency alone.

The centenary of *Rerum Novarum* was considered significant enough by three universities—Oxford, Boston, and Melbourne—to warrant an international conference called "The Worth of Nations" held at Boston University in February 1992. As a member of the Pontifical Council for Justice and Peace, Pell delivered one of the major papers, setting out the history of Catholic social teaching. He outlined how and why, at the age of eighty, Leo XIII, the author of eighty-six encyclicals—the most important contribution to papal teaching since the Middle Ages—gave qualified approval in *Rerum Novarum* to democracy and the modern age and urged Catholics to become involved in political life.

The encyclical, Pell said, had been written largely in response to the social situation of Catholics, many of whom belonged to the working classes. Leo set out to address the problem of the condition of workers, in order to find remedies quickly, such as a just wage and regulated working conditions, "for the misery and wretchedness pressing so heavily and unjustly" on most working people. These remedies would depend more on Church social teaching appealing to individual responsibility and conscience than on government intervention. While condemning greed and defending the rights of workers to form trade unions, the encyclical also defended the right of individuals to own private property and rejected socialism and government ownership of the means of production. "Leo XIII's sanctioning of trade unions was a decisive factor in their becoming an integral part of Western society", Pell told the conference. "The success of trade unions was, in turn, an important reason behind the failure of Marx's prediction about the increasing misery of the working class in capitalist society."

Pell reiterated John Paul II's resolute opposition, expressed in *Centesimus Annus*, to the Marxist version of Christianity, liberation theology. Looking at the then-recent revolutions in Eastern Europe and the burgeoning of freedom in the former Soviet republics, he, like the pope, found deeper reasons for the collapse of Communism than the rejection of Marxist philosophy and economics. Rather, the collapse of Soviet Communism was "the penultimate blow to the whole Enlightenment project" that had extolled the perfectibility of mankind and led to the "radical secularization of the European mind".

Pell argued:

The connection with the French Revolution is immediately apparent. More problematic is the connection of the Enlightenment with the darker side of that revolution and some of its terrible progeny in recent history—for instance the revolutionary violence of Lenin and Stalin, the Maoist crimes of the Great Leap Forward and the legacy of the Parisian Stalinists who trained Pol Pot for the Cambodian Genocide.

The communist collapse has been a massive blow to the Enlightenment myth that progress is inevitable ... that traditions can be ignored, or should be denied, and that human reason is all powerful. It is also another proof that without religious belief, it is difficult, perhaps impossible, for altruism to flourish and persist, and curb the selfishness and weakness of human beings. These would appear to be impossible attainments in the absence of belief in an intelligent and benign Supreme Being ready to reward and to punish and somehow to atone for and redress the worst human sufferings. If the collapse of communism is the denouement of the French Revolution, the beginning of that end may well have been marked by the issuance of *Rerum Novarum* in 1891.

Pell acknowledged that following Vatican II, the Church's efforts to cooperate with people of goodwill in different societies, including those behind the Iron Curtain, had brought mixed blessings for the Church. "Before his death in 1978, even Pope Paul VI spoke of 'the smoke of Satan in the Church'", he said. "There has been no resurgence of faith and practice throughout the West. Indeed, the Church has virtually collapsed in some countries such as Holland and has been severely damaged in parts of French-speaking Canada." This had been offset by rapid growth in central and Eastern Europe, in parts of Asia, like Korea, and in Africa (although the growth there was slower than the Muslim expansion).

While Australia's public debate on euthanasia was still some years away when Pell spoke at Boston University in 1992, his perceptions were prescient in view of the practice being legalized in every Australia state in subsequent decades, with the laws progressively becoming more and more liberal as the dominoes fell. By 2023, the

Labor-Greens government in Canberra, the national capital, was pushing to allow the practice for teenagers as young as fourteen, and in a move that many believed was connected, had taken over the Catholic Calvary Hospital. In his Boston speech, Pell cited the views of his friend Cardinal John O'Connor of New York as to what lay ahead: "I predict that the 'right to die' will dwarf the abortion phenomenon in magnitude, in numbers, in horror. As mothers have become legalized agents of the deaths of their children, so children will become legalized agents of the deaths of their mothers—and fathers. Fathers will have no more legal right to defend themselves than they currently have to defend their unborn babies."

Social justice programs in the English-speaking world, he argued, should involve constructive efforts to enhance and strengthen family life. "No civilized society can afford to be complacent about the evident growth of an underclass, riddled with gang warfare and broken families, single parents, uncontrollable children, alcoholism and drug abuse."

In a pluralist, secular, and liberal society, the Catholic Church was a continuing source of authority and tradition, able to provide hope, inspire service, and encourage self-restraint. On that point, Pell told the conference delegates, he was happy to leave the last word to a London journalist, not a Catholic, who had written about *Centesimus Annus* in the *Financial Times*: "The absence of all religion, as envisaged by the late Mr John Lennon, is a terrifying prospect. It would return humanity to the jungle, armed to the teeth. We all need the pope, and his encyclicals. If there were no such thing it would be necessary to invent him."[6]

The conference was one in an annual series of diverse gatherings from the worlds of science, philosophy, academia, business, and (occasionally) religion organized by Boston University professor Claudio Veliz, who was a good friend of Pell's. Veliz, a former economics history professor in Chile, came to Melbourne in 1972, when he was awarded the chair of sociology at La Trobe University. After La Trobe, Veliz taught at Boston University until mid-2002. Pell met Veliz early in his time as an auxiliary bishop, and he became

---

[6] George Pell, "Rerum Novarum 100 Years Later", Boston University, 1991, quoting Joe Rogaly, *Financial Times*, May 3, 1991.

close friends with him and his wife, Maria Isabelle, who had a vacation home at Lorne on the Victorian south coast, not far from Pell's. Veliz, who has a Calvinist background, said he was amazed to find himself "agreeing with nearly everything Pell says" despite their differences in beliefs and backgrounds.

Pell's work on the Congregation for the Doctrine of the Faith and the Pontifical Council for Justice and Peace put him at the very heart of John Paul II's pontificate, which he came to appreciate on a deeper level when he met people who understood all too well what Karol Wojtyła had suffered under the Nazis and Soviet Communists in his native Poland.

Pell made three visits to mainland China in the late 1980s and early 1990s. By far his most memorable encounter was in Shanghai, with Father Vincent Zhu Hongsheng, a gentle Jesuit then in his mid-seventies and part of China's persecuted underground Church. When Father Vincent wanted to kiss the bishop's ring as a sign of respect, Pell found it one of the most humbling moments of his life. It was 1989—just after the Tiananmen Square massacre—and Vincent had been released the previous year from seven years' imprisonment by the Communist authorities; still his every move was monitored. But after enduring pain and suffering as punishment for his faith for much of his life, Father Vincent had no fear left. "The Communists can't touch me—they know—because I'm not frightened of dying and I'm not frightened to go back to jail", he told Pell. Vincent had also been imprisoned and tortured from 1960 to 1978, surviving day and night for years in a tiny cell submerged in eighteen inches of filthy, freezing water—his "crime" was refusing to renounce the authority of the pope as the Vicar of Christ on earth.

Meeting Bishop Pell, the old priest was overwhelmed. He had given his all, including his freedom and comfort, for Christ, and this was the first time since his imprisonment that he had met one of the successors of the apostles from the West. It was one of the highlights of the old man's life—and one of the most unforgettable encounters of Pell's life as well. Father Vincent, who in his youth had studied in France, Ireland, and the United States, impressed Pell with his excellent English: "He was a marvellous man, full of life, quoting Thomas More and Cardinal Newman. He will be a saint—canonized—a man of outstanding piety, most impressive and absolutely fearless." Father

Vincent, who died 1993, was one of forty priests and bishops mentioned in a 1994 United Nations Commission on Human Rights report on religious freedom.

Pell's journeys to China were not connected to his ACR/Caritas work and were not funded by that organisation. But he gained the approval of the Australian Catholic Bishops' Conference to give all the money left over from the annual ACR Project Compassion collection, taken up every Lent in all Australian parishes, that had not been allocated to projects in other countries, to the Church in China, rather than investing it. Pell understood the struggles of Chinese Catholics who had remained loyal to the pope, and how important the Church in China would eventually become.

Before 1997, visits like his were often organized by missionary priests working out of Hong Kong. One of those who paved the way for Pell's first visit to China was Irish-born Columban priest Father Ned Kelly, who worked for years in Hong Kong and Taiwan. In later years, Hong Kong's reverting to China and the aggressive process of "sinicization" of religion under Xi Jinping have made missionary activity riskier, and arrests are not infrequent.

In his Requiem homily for Pell, Monsignor Charles Portelli recalled his old boss' visits to China, dressed "in a bad suit and collar and tie" to disguise the fact he was a bishop: "He was given powers by the Holy See so that he could reconcile to full communion with the Church those who had been separated from it. Only rarely would he speak of the living martyrs, especially those in the Chinese underground church. I think that there he learnt how to remain constant in his faith, regardless of the prevailing wind."

Pell kept his customary diaries on his China trips, with vast slabs written in Italian for a little extra protection in case he was detained. He brought moral and practical support to Chinese Catholics, including theology books on the post–Vatican II Church, which was yet to take shape in China. On one occasion, Pell entered China with US$20,000 strapped in his money belt, money provided by support organisations in the West to help the Church in China. On another occasion, when some of Pell's contacts in China were involved in setting up a factory in Wuhan (site of the COVID outbreak decades later), he sent in sewing machines to assist. Had the authorities examined the machines more closely to find out why they were so heavy, they would have found them packed tightly with Catholic theology books. While Pell and Father Sam Dimattina travelled to China "incognito" (their papers showed that they were teachers), the Chinese authorities knew they were Catholic priests. This was easily worked out from the people and places they visited in Beijing, Shanghai, Wuhan, and smaller centres in the far west of the country, close to the border with Tibet.

To understand the significance of these visits it is essential to understand that brutal persecutions have been suffered by Catholics in China, both before and after the Communists led by Mao Zedong took over the country in 1949. After years of sending Catholics, and other religious believers, to labour camps, the government established the Chinese Catholic Patriotic Association (CCPA) in 1957 (a development in which Xi Jinping's father, Xi Zhongxun reportedly played a role). This was designed to control Chinese Catholics and separate them from the Holy See. In 1980 the government set up a Catholic Bishops Council, also independent of Rome. Both organisations are under the control of the Chinese Communist Party (CCP), and the Vatican did not recognize either of them.

On October 1, 2000 (China's national day), Pope John Paul II canonized 120 Chinese martyrs—eighty-seven Chinese Catholics and thirty-three foreign missionaries—killed in China from 1648 to 1930. Even though these martyrdoms occurred before the revolution led by Mao, CCPA bishops protested that the canonizations were "an insult" and "a distortion of history".

At the time of Pell's visits to China, the lines between the underground Church (meaning those Catholics secretly loyal to the pope) and the CCPA were blurring, with considerable overlap, as Cardinal Joseph Zen, retired bishop of Hong Kong, described in the *New York Times* in 2018:

> From 1985 to 2002, Cardinal Jozef Tomko was the prefect of the Congregation for the Evangelization of Peoples, which oversees the Church's missionary work. He was a Slovak, who understood communism, and he was wise.
>
> Cardinal Tomko's position was that the underground Church was the only lawful Church in China, and that the official church was unlawful. But he also understood that there were many good people

in the official church. Like the bishop of Xian, who for a time was a vice chairman of the bishops' conference. Or the bishop of Shanghai, Jin Luxian, a Jesuit and a brilliant linguist, who had been interned in the 1950s.

Back then, the Holy See had a cautious policy that it implemented generously. It was amenable to reasonable compromise but had a bottom line.[7]

In 1615, Pope Paul V allowed missionaries in China to celebrate the Mass in Chinese, but later misunderstandings and conflicts led to the eventual removal of this permission. Because the Church in China had been isolated from the effects of the Second Vatican Council, in the late 1980s and early 1990s, the Tridentine Mass in Latin was commonly said, and priests and bishops loyal to the Holy Father prayed for him under their breath. Pell attended Mass at the old cathedral, run by the CCPA, in Shanghai, complete with tabernacle and altar, stations of the cross, and statues. He conducted many of his conversations with Chinese churchmen in Latin, as it was the only language he and they had in common.

At the time of his visits, Pell recognized that China would be the next great frontier for Catholics for evangelization. "In some parts of China there are double the number of Catholics now than when the communists took power", he said in 2002. "Red Guards destroyed a lot of the moral and intellectual framework so there is a great void amongst the middle classes and young people to be filled. Nobody believes in communist theory any more. In Shanghai a taxi driver refused to take me to [former Chinese Premier] Chou en Lai's house. He said there is no point in going there." Walking around the city, Pell found that Chinese authorities had hijacked a Christian image— the Madonna and Child—to promote the controversial one-child policy, since abandoned due to demographic decline, which in the early 1990s was enforced not only with compulsory contraception, abortion, and economic sanctions, but sometimes with infanticide. "Such a clever adaptation of a traditional motherly image for perverse purposes." Nevertheless, Christianity was spreading in China in

[7]Joseph Zen Ze-Kiun, "The Pope Doesn't Understand China", *New York Times*, October 24, 2018, https://www.nytimes.com/2018/10/24/opinion/pope-china-vatican-church-catholics-bishops.html.

much the same way as it had in the pagan Roman Empire, and "the whole Confucian ethos is not wildly incompatible with Christianity, despite a healthy agnostic tradition in Chinese upper-class life."

Pope John Paul II took a close interest in China, making Bishop Ignatius Kung, the underground bishop of Shanghai, a cardinal *in pectore* in 1979. In one swift raid on the Shanghai Diocese on September 8, 1955, Kung, along with several hundred priests and Church leaders, was arrested and imprisoned, as were hundreds of lay Catholics, including members of the Legion of Mary. They were sentenced to ten to twenty years' hard labour and "reeducation" at special camps as punishment for their evangelizing work. One woman, Margaret Chu, spent twenty-three years in various prisons, including one hundred hideous days in handcuffs, during which she was made to work in 95°F heat in the fields of a labour camp, not even allowed to wear a hat or change clothes or take off the handcuffs at night. Not surprisingly, she prayed for the gift of death.

While many priests and lay Catholics succumbed to the pressures and tortures inflicted upon them and agreed to renounce the pope of the time, Pius XII, many, like Bishop Kung and Father Vincent Zhu, did not and, despite imprisonment and "reeducation", managed to maintain contact and maintain the underground Church. Others, such as the then-teenage Joseph Zen and his family, anticipating the Communist revolution, had fled to Hong Kong years earlier.

Among those who did acquiesce to the authorities, two months after the mass arrests of September 1955, was Father Aloysius Jin Luxian, S.J., the rector of the Shanghai seminary, who made a tape recording, played in many prisons, urging Catholics to support the Communist government. For that effort, his sentence was lessened from life to eighteen years (including several in a forced labour camp). In 1985, he became the CCPA bishop of Shanghai. Four years later, Bishop Pell and Father Dimattina met him—a small, gentle man, an eighth-generation Chinese Catholic who was ordained a Jesuit priest in 1945 after studies in Europe. Bishop Jin insisted there was no division between the official and underground Churches. "There is only one Church in China—the Roman Catholic Church. Both are very loyal to the Pope. Every day, I pray for the Pope."[8]

---

[8] *Cardinal Kung Foundation Newsletter*, Easter 2002.

His predecessor in Shanghai, Bishop Kung, was finally released under house arrest in Shanghai in 1985 at the age of eighty-four. That year, watched closely by the Chinese government, he was allowed to meet Cardinal Jaime Sin of the Philippines, who had travelled to China to see him. While not allowed to converse in private, Kung got his message of loyalty to the pope out to the world by singing a song in Latin across the banquet table, "Tu es Petrus et super hanc petram aedificabo Ecclesiam meam" (You are Peter and upon this rock I will build my Church). In 1986, Kung travelled to the United States to settle in Stamford, Connecticut. Within a year he was well enough to travel to Rome to receive his cardinal's hat from Pope John Paul II, followed by an unprecedented seven-minute standing ovation from the crowd gathered in Saint Peter's as he returned to his wheelchair.

At the same time, the Vatican was showing a willingness to reconcile some of the CCPA bishops, especially those trained and ordained before the persecutions began. This, understandably, distressed some in the underground Church, who felt betrayed by those who joined the CCPA. The only eventual way forward, Pell believed, was for both groups to be allowed to practice their faith openly, as a united Church, in communion with Rome and free from domestic persecutions. That goal remains a distant one, with underground bishops arrested and spirited away and violent persecutions as recently as the 2020s. While Pope John Paul II was unable to succeed in his wish to visit China and celebrate Mass there, Pell was certain that the Middle Kingdom would be an even greater priority for later popes.

Twenty years later, despite his earlier high hopes for progress, Pell was deeply disappointed about the Vatican's 2018 deal with Beijing and the secrecy surrounding it. "I don't think we've gained anything", he told The Spectator in March 2022. "The persecutions seem to be continuing. In some places they've got worse." He said that nobody "outside a small circle" has any knowledge of the agreement's details, "which seems to me to be quite irregular."[9]

In October 2021, Pell took Secretary of State Pietro Parolin to task in The Australian newspaper and in the Italian press after Parolin

[9]Damian Thompson, "'I Don't Think We've Gained Anything'—Cardinal Pell on the Vatican and China", The Spectator, March 21, 2022, https://www.spectator.co.uk/podcast/i-don-t-think-we-ve-gained-anything-cardinal-pell-on-the-vatican-and-china/.

criticized Australia, the United States, and Britain over the AUKUS agreement, under which the United States and/or Britain would sell Australia nuclear-powered submarines to improve the security of the Pacific region in the face of an unprecedented arms build-up by China. "The Holy See is against rearmament", Cardinal Parolin said of the deal. "One cannot but be worried." Pell defended AUKUS, which was backed by both sides of the political divide in Australia. More collaboration was needed between democracies in Asia and the Pacific to balance the great power of China, which was not democratic, he said. That was "perhaps not well understood in Europe, but it is so".[10]

In contrast to the concealed piety he found in the Church in China, Catholics in Scala, the historic cathedral town behind Amalfi on one of the most beautiful strips of Italian coastline, gave George Pell a rapturous welcome when he accepted the mayor's invitation to visit in 1988. Because they do not have a diocese of their own, it is a tradition in the Catholic Church for auxiliary bishops and bishops working in the Roman bureaucracy to be given *titular* dioceses—old dioceses that have been suppressed or merged into larger dioceses. Under a quaint, antiquated rule in the old Code of Canon Law, bishops were never permitted to set foot in their titular dioceses, but this was relaxed in Pope John Paul II's new code, issued in 1983. Pell's titular diocese was home to various noble families of the Mediterranean coast and was the local bishop's seat from 987 to 1818. By 1988, Scala was a quiet village surrounded by chestnut and oak woods, with its 130 churches for thirty-five thousand inhabitants a reminder of more bustling, prosperous centuries.

Visiting Rome on Church business, Pell was staying with his old friend Peter Elliott, who was by then working in the Vatican curia. They borrowed a car and drove south through Naples and along to the glorious Amalfi coast. Elliott recalled that day:

> In the morning, it was all strictly arranged, and George had to wear his cassock and his cap, and as we drove into town there were signs up all over the place—"*Welcome Monsignor Pel*" (Italians tend to chop

---

[10] Paul Kelly, "AUKUS Alliance: Vatican Lacks Moral Authority on China", *The Australian*, October 6, 2021.

off double letters). He was ushered into the cathedral, then the mayor greeted him with a florid speech, and then they sat him on the throne and took photographs. It was the first time a bishop who was a real bishop of Scala had sat on the throne for almost two hundred years. The bishop of the area knew about it and let it all go ahead.

Then we went off to the sacristy and all dressed up for solemn Mass, and they gave George the most valuable mitre in Italy—parts of it dated back to the eleventh or twelfth century. It was remade about twenty times, and he came out wearing that and carrying a fifteenth-century crosier looking a million dollars, and the Mass proceeded (in Italian). At the exact moment of the elevation of the host, they exploded a bomb outside the cathedral to celebrate the sacred moment. It made a lot of noise—an unusual form of liturgy.

The celebrations after the Mass made for an extraordinary day. Pell and his party enjoyed a banquet inside the cloister of an enclosed order of nuns in the town, with the nuns performing eighteenth-century dances for the visitors—a tradition at recreation time in the convent for hundreds of years. "Then we were led out after going to visit the old sisters, I mean those who'd gone to God in the cemetery, to throw holy water over them, then we went out and the huge iron gates closed behind us." The visitors were then escorted from one place to another, plied with coffee and cakes, and, late in the day, left town loaded with gifts and feeling as though they had caffeine poisoning.

Eight years later, when George Pell was promoted to be archbishop of Melbourne, he had to relinquish his titular diocese. But when he moved into the large, comfortable archbishop's residence in a leafy street in Kew, one of Melbourne's eastern suburbs, he found that the house lacked a name, so he had a nameplate made. He called the house Scala.

15

Be Not Afraid

Important announcements from the Vatican generally come at noon sharp Rome time, 9:00 P.M. or 10:00 P.M. in eastern Australia. On the evening of Tuesday, July 16, 1996, morning newspapers scurried to get a major story into their first editions. "Archbishop in Shock Resignation" was the headline in *The Australian*, which reported:

> The Archbishop of Melbourne, the Most Reverend Frank Little, last night shocked the Catholic Church when he announced his resignation for health reasons. Archbishop Little, 70, who had served in the position since July 1974, is understood to have only informed colleagues of his decision early yesterday.
>
> The Catholic Church said last night that His Holiness Pope John Paul II had appointed the Most Rev George Pell, currently an Auxiliary Bishop in the Archdiocese of Melbourne, to replace Archbishop Little.[1]

Unavailable for comment when the story was written, Archbishop Little held a press conference the following day, where he said, "Will I start with the ingrown toenails? It's a little bit of everything." While expressing "a great sense of relief to be departing from the high-pressure job", Sir Frank admitted he also felt "a sense of sadness and no doubt will feel a sense of grieving. That will be something that I'll have to work through."

Was Sir Frank, who was five years younger than the retiring age for bishops, sending up the "health reasons" cited for his abrupt departure? The ingrown toenails line meant the explanation needed

[1] James Murray, "Archbishop in Shock Resignation", *The Australian*, July 17, 1996.

211

to be taken with a grain of salt. When bishops and archbishops retire, their dioceses are often left vacant for weeks, months, or more than a year in some cases, but the concurrent announcement of George Pell's appointment showed Pope John Paul II's determination to see him in a senior leadership position as soon as possible. Sir Frank Little said: "I don't know whether George was the logical choice, I knew he would be a very strong contender, he had shown qualities of leadership." Pell and Little kept up appearances during the changeover, being photographed together in a show of unity, with Sir Frank leaving gracefully, his dignity intact. Pell wished his predecessor "many years of peaceful retirement" and paid tribute to him as a man "admired and respected both within and outside the bounds of the Catholic Church". Sir Frank said Pell had been "very kind and thoughtful to me after I left, and I'll always be grateful."

From the outset, Pell had a clear set of priorities for his episcopate: priests, including the role of priests as leaders in parishes, seminary education, and encouraging vocations to the priesthood; proper formation in religious education, including better religious textbooks for schools; fostering the link between Melbourne and the Holy See; and an extensive building and restoration project for the areas surrounding Saint Patrick's Cathedral in East Melbourne. Writing in *Eureka Street*, the liberal magazine she edited for the Jesuits, Morag Fraser acknowledged that the morale of the clergy needed a boost but, in a shrewd prediction, said the job ahead for Archbishop Pell "makes heading Coles Myer [one of Australia's largest retail chains] look like a picnic at Albert Park".

Whatever the maneuvers behind closed doors in Rome that led to Pell's appointment, the problem of clerical paedophilia had, by that time, reared its evil head with a vengeance. Just seven weeks earlier, an Australian Broadcasting Corporation *Four Corners* program had focused on clerical sex abuse in the Catholic Church in Ballarat and Melbourne. The program left viewers shocked, particularly by the evasive and indifferent responses of Ballarat Bishop Ronald Mulkearns and Monsignor Gerald Cudmore, vicar-general of the Archdiocese of Melbourne, to serious allegations. Evidence was presented of rapes and indecent assaults against minors and adults, male and female, of offending priests being moved from parish to parish, of repeated cover-ups, and of a victim's suicide. One interviewee told the program, "This

really is Armageddon for the Church."[2] The matter featured prominently at George Pell's press conference the morning after his appointment had been announced. In what proved a major understatement,
he admitted that the Church's response to the problem had been "a bit
spotty". "There's no doubt it's been really damaging and perhaps the
worst blow to our prestige in the community that we've suffered for
quite a while." The media reported the press conference under such
headlines as "Clean-up Pledge", "Archbishop Vows Restoration of
Public Confidence", "Archbishop Vow on Paedophiles".

Pell officially took over as archbishop of Melbourne at Mass on
a chilly winter's night, August 16, 1996. Because Saint Patrick's
Cathedral was in the middle of a major restoration, the Royal Exhibition Building, where Australia's first federal parliament met, was
the venue, allowing a congregation of eight thousand people to join
Cardinal Edward Cassidy, the Rome-based head of the Council for
Promoting Christian Unity, fifty bishops, and four hundred priests
in welcoming Pell to his new role. Archbishop Little laid his own
crosier on the altar after he and the papal nuncio had led Pell to the
cathedra. Pell had come with his own crosier, which was a gift from
Saint Patrick's College, Ballarat, on his ordination as bishop in 1987.

Preaching in the sonorous voice that was about to become well
known across the nation, Pell set the tone for his episcopate, emphasizing the distinctive roles of the laity and ordained priests and stressing
the need for more priestly vocations. While Melbourne should be able
to provide its own priests, he made it clear he would also welcome
priests from abroad who wished to serve the city. He recalled his boyhood hero, Archbishop Daniel Mannix, consecrating the archdiocese
to the Immaculate Heart of Mary in May 1944 at the height of World
War II in the Pacific and once again placed the city of Melbourne
under Our Lady's protection.

It was a confident sermon, frequently interrupted by lengthy
applause. While his sentiments would have been standard fare for
a Catholic archbishop in other times and places, the sermon was
groundbreaking in the modern Church in Australia, where many
senior clerics were playing down the role of Mary, the Mother of

---

[2] "Twice Betrayed", by Sally Neighbour, *Four Corners*, Australian Broadcasting Corporation, aired May 27, 1996.

God, as they bent over backwards to pander to putative sensitivities of the Protestant churches. While reveling in their "liberal" labels, those same clerics were also proving to be anything but liberal on the question of welcoming priests from overseas who wanted to serve in Australia. Unlike Pell, who was well-disposed to newcomers from other races, many of the supposed liberals regarded the "cultural differences" of foreign priests as insurmountable.

Pell's determination to tackle the vocations crisis was not shared across the Church. Some senior clerics and Church bureaucrats (who perhaps had a vested career interest) viewed the looming shortage of clergy as an opportunity to develop a lay ministry or some form of congregationalism. But as Pope John Paul II told priests in Rome on Saint Valentine's Day 2002: "We must not be easily satisfied with the explanation that the scarcity of vocations is compensated for by *growth in the apostolic commitment of lay people*, nor even less that it is desired by providence to foster this growth. On the contrary, the more numerous are the lay people who intend to live their own baptismal vocation generously, the more necessary are the presence and pastoral work of the ordained ministers."[3]

Among those in the front row of the congregation at Pell's first Mass as archbishop was the dynamic Victorian premier Jeff Kennett, a non-Catholic who had become accustomed to receiving Communion from Archbishop Little, a practice not in keeping with the Church's teaching. While there was no incident at the Mass, Pell offered to go over to Kennett's office to explain the Church's position, but the premier declined the visit and requested that the explanation be sent to him in writing. Pell wrote and asked Kennett, as a non-Catholic, to refrain from receiving Communion in the Catholic Church. That stance annoyed Kennett, who branded it as "silly" and "petty". "If ever he [Pell] was hoping to get a convert, I would have thought that those who enjoyed participating in things Catholic were the first line of potential candidates", Kennett commented.

Pell concluded his first Mass as archbishop by inviting the congregation to "go forward together on the next stage of our journey towards God, who will become all in all, for all of us." His long walk down the aisle of the Exhibition was accompanied by the triumphant strains of Handel's "Hallelujah Chorus".

[3] John Paul II, Address to the Clergy of Rome (February 14, 2002).

For the motto on his archbishop's coat of arms, Pell chose, in English, "Be Not Afraid", echoing Christ's words to His followers and reiterating a constant refrain of Pope John Paul II. The coat of arms includes a *Pelican in Her Piety*, a traditional eucharistic emblem, based on the medieval legend that the pelican would feed its young with blood from its own breast, which it would lacerate with its beak—symbol of Christ feeding us with his own flesh and blood. The pelican is also a traditional emblem of the Pell family. *The Sun in His Splendour* is a traditional emblem of Saint Thomas Aquinas and served as a reference to Aquinas College Ballarat. It is also a eucharistic emblem. The monogram *MR*, with the coronet, is a traditional symbol of the Blessed Virgin Mary and was in the coat of arms of Pope John Paul II.

Pell took up the reins of the Melbourne Archdiocese the day after his liturgical reception, but the final, formal part of his accession was not completed until June 29 the following year—the feast day of Saints Peter and Paul—when he received the pallium from Pope John Paul II in Rome. A tradition dating back to the fourth century, the pallium is a circular cloth band, about two inches wide, worn by the pope and archbishops over their chasubles at Mass. It has two pendants, one hanging down in front and one behind, each about two inches wide and twelve inches long, weighted down with small pieces of lead covered with black silk. The pallium is made of white wool, part of which is supplied by two lambs presented annually to the pope. Decorated by six black crosses and a gold pin set with a precious gem, it symbolizes the archbishop's communion with and participation in the office of the pope.

Forty people journeyed with George Pell to see him receive the pallium—Margaret, his sister, David, his brother, David's daughter, Sarah, his cousin Mary, his friends Fathers Diamond and Hart and (then) Monsignor Elliott, some younger Melbourne priests, and several dozen friends. Twenty-nine archbishops received the pallium that day from the pope, from archdioceses as far afield as Kenya, Canada, Ireland, the United States, and Mexico.

Pell made good friends among the other prelates, especially Archbishops Francis George of Chicago and Charles Chaput of Denver, Colorado, who were in the vanguard of John Paul II's Catholic revival. Some Australian bishops, in contrast, for ideological reasons and because they recognized his potential for "stirring the pot", kept

Pell at arm's length, something that did not upset him in the slightest. As an archbishop, he stayed as close as ever to his old friends and
shared the occasional dig at the expense of his episcopal colleagues.
Bishops' conferences, he found, were "great for a snooze". One
bishop was so slow to pick up the tab for entertaining or shouting a
round of drinks that Pell reckoned he "still had his First Communion
money". Another colleague, he joked, had such an ego that Pell's
own robust ego "only came up to his ankles".

In Melbourne, long before he received the pallium, Pell was forced
to act on the issue of paedophilia. "It was mentioned in my first discussions with the premier, Jeffrey Kennett, and he made it very clear
to me that he wanted to get something in place to deal with it", Pell
recalled eight years later.

> And just before that at a fund-raising luncheon I was sitting next to the
> governor, Richard McGarvie, a former Supreme Court judge who
> had been a friend of mine for years, and I have always been very, very
> grateful to him for his advice. Now he said: "You are going to have
> to deal with this problem resolutely because if you don't it will bleed
> you dry for years—emotionally, and more importantly than that, it
> will bleed away the good standing of the Church. And of course,
> your first priority needs to be the victims of genuine attacks." So, he
> said, "Why don't you set up something akin to a royal commission,
> with a commissioner, and give him the power to deal with it?" I had
> an absolutely top flight body of senior lawyers and other professionals
> from around Melbourne, and we put a procedure into place.

Two months after his appointment, in October 1996, Archbishop
Pell announced the establishment of the Independent Commission
into Sexual Abuse, to be headed by Peter O'Callaghan, QC,[4] with
another independent legal panel assessing compensation payouts
for victims, up to a capped figure of AU$50,000. That figure, later
seen as mean, was arrived at because it matched the amount paid
by the state at the time for crime compensation. At the same time,
the Catholic Church was establishing a national program, Towards
Healing. While Melbourne was in touch with the Towards Healing

---

[4] QC is the abbreviation for Queen's Counsel, used when the sovereign is a queen (KC
stands for King's Counsel). It denotes a high-ranking lawyer in the British Commonwealth
who may represent a person in court.

program, Pell decided not to join it because he was satisfied that the urgency of the problem in Melbourne was being addressed by the comprehensive program of assessment, compensation, and counseling he had set up. "I was surprised later at the resentment that was generated amongst some of these other people [officials in other Catholic dioceses and religious orders], not because we didn't deal with the problem, but because we dealt with it another way", Pell said in 2001. "I've got no regrets about that at all because the proof of the pudding is in the eating. It has brought people to justice, provided counseling, and provided very substantial compensation to a whole lot of people."

Broken Rites, established in 1993 to assist clerical abuse victims and which has fielded thousands of complaints, branded the Melbourne scheme "the best of a bad lot". The backlog of cases facing O'Callaghan when his commission began was such that in its first six years, 126 victims received compensation from the Melbourne Archdiocese. In the vast majority of cases, the payouts were made after the victims' assailants had been arrested, charged, convicted, and jailed. Within five years, the process had cost the archdiocese more than AU$3 million in compensation and almost AU$2 million for counseling, with victims entitled to counseling for as long as needed. Among the many disgraceful and heartbreaking cases that came across Pell's desk in Melbourne as a result of the commission's work was one in which a woman had borne a Down syndrome child to a priest, who later deserted them. The woman finally accepted a payout of less than AU$25,000.[5]

Pell's predecessor, Daniel Mannix, and Mannix' Brisbane counterpart, Sir James Duhig, were nicknamed, in their heyday, "Daniel the politician" and "James the builder". A generation earlier Sydney's Irish-born Cardinal Patrick Moran, a keen writer of Church history, was known as "Moran the historian". George Pell's time as an archbishop probably entitled him to the three nicknames, and more besides. His enemies were delighted to suggest a few—"Pell Pot" (ironic in light of his Caritas work in Cambodia after the killing fields) and the "bully bishop from central casting" among them. Melburnians from August 16, 1996, to May 10, 2001, to make up their minds about George Pell. His contribution as archbishop included:

[5] *Inside the Vatican*, January 1999.

- boosting the number of seminarians studying for the priesthood for Melbourne from a paltry twelve to twenty-six (but still with a long way to go) and ordaining a dozen new priests during that time;
- reforming the seminary's spiritual life in accordance with Pope John Paul II's blueprint, *I Will Give You Shepherds*;
- overseeing the production of To Know, Worship and Love, a high-quality set of religious education school textbooks from kindergarten to senior secondary school, to redress the paucity of such materials not only in Australia but across the English-speaking world;
- establishing a new tertiary institution in the heart of Melbourne, the John Paul II Institute for Marriage and the Family, headed by internationally respected moral theologian and bioethicist Anthony Fisher, O.P., and allied to the Pontifical Lateran University in Rome, offering bachelor's and higher degrees to the doctoral level;
- creating a Catholic precinct in the heart of Melbourne, around Saint Patrick's Cathedral, by moving Corpus Christi Seminary and the Australian Catholic University into the area, opening Goold House as the administration centre for the archdiocese, with the John Paul II Institute and Mannix Library next door, and restoring and rebuilding the old parish buildings and church at nearby Carlton as a residence and chapel for the seminarians (Pell regarded that chapel, decorated and designed by Father Charles Portelli, his former student and master of ceremonies, as one of his finest achievements);
- appointing the distinguished philosopher Hayden Ramsay, a former lecturer in philosophy at the Universities of Edinburgh, Stirling, and Melbourne, as an adviser on his personal staff to produce scholarly articles, to teach in the seminary and the John Paul II Institute, and to "give the archdiocese some philosophical backbone";
- creating a sculpture garden and pilgrim path with cascading water around Saint Patrick's Cathedral and installing two tributes to indigenous people in and around the cathedral;
- being one of only three bishops in the world known to have issued a pastoral letter to mark the thirtieth anniversary of the most controversial papal encyclical of all time, *Humanae Vitae*;

- speaking out publicly on a wide range of issues, including Victoria's gambling culture, the One Nation political party, and rallying other churches behind his opposition to the exhibition of the controversial "art work" *Piss Christ* at the National Gallery of Victoria in 1997;
- buying and restoring the site of Mary MacKillop's birthplace in Brunswick Street, Fitzroy, for use as a support centre for the families of drug addicts; and
- leading four hundred young people to the Holy Land and Rome for a pilgrimage to mark the Jubilee Year 2000.

George Pell secured the appointment of Denis Hart, the man he regarded at the time as "probably my closest friend", as his auxiliary bishop and vicar-general in Melbourne. Pell's friendship with Father Gerry Diamond had also strengthened through the years. Diamond noticed a considerable improvement in morale among Catholics after Pell took over the archdiocese, believing they responded well to the archbishop taking his message to the wider community through the media and also to his preparedness to make hard decisions when required and stick to them. Remembering Pell's Oxford thesis, Diamond chuckled at the idea that Pell bears a passing resemblance to Cyprian, one of his heroes among the early Church Fathers: "The interesting thing is that where Cyprian can get what he perceives to be desirable through a conciliatory process, he goes through the process. When he considers that may not be possible, he goes for it directly."

Another friend Pell worked closely with in Melbourne was Steve Lawrence, a former Hawthorn Australian Football League (AFL) player, who was director of Melbourne's youth ministry in the early years of Pell's time in Melbourne. Lawrence and his wife, Annie, named their daughter Georgia after Pell. The Lawrences later lived and worked in Rome before returning to Sydney. At age four, Pell's namesake was giggling at the Australian accent she detected in his fluent Italian. Georgia Lawrence was the second girl named after Pell. The first was his niece Georgina Pell, who was a premature baby (only 5 lb., 2 oz. at birth) and looked even more fragile when her uncle held her for the first time. It was one of the rare occasions Margaret and David Pell saw tears in his eyes.

Once a week as archbishop, Pell heard confessions in Saint Patrick's Cathedral—not a routine practice for many modern bishops, some of whom have been known to forget the words for absolving penitents. True to his promise to support priests, Pell set aside Thursday afternoons to be spent alone in the cathedral presbytery, giving any priests who wanted to see him informally the chance to speak to him without an appointment. He also initiated a series of clergy dinners, working through Melbourne's long list of priests alphabetically. These were held at his home in Kew and brought together priests of a variety of ages, backgrounds, and viewpoints. At one such occasion, Father Martin Dixon livened up his outfit with a single, conspicuously large clip-on earring, worn to tease Monsignor Peter Elliott, sitting across the table, who had recently spoken out publicly against grunge fashion and body piercing among young people.

Dixon disagreed with many of Archbishop Pell's decisions in Melbourne and, to his credit, was prepared to put his name to his criticisms, which reflected the views of quite a few of his colleagues. Dixon said Pell was "dictatorial" and that under his regime, consultation days with priests became more a matter of "this is what we are going to do." He said authority was largely centralized in the archdiocese during that time, and some of the younger priests who strongly supported Pell "wanted to believe in a 'bells and smells' Church of the forties and fifties that had gone by that time". Dixon also disagreed with the archbishop's transferring the Australian Catholic University campus into the East Melbourne "Catholic precinct" near the cathedral because, he said, it disadvantaged students from the outer southeastern suburbs who had to spend twice as long each day travelling (although it was closer for those in the poorer western and northern suburbs).

Dixon did, however, have a few positive things to say about his old boss when interviewed in 2001. "I would love to say George was a bastard, but he wasn't. He is an enigma. He's very pastoral-hearted, very good with people; he's sociable and likes a drink, and he was generous with priests. He never wanted priests to have to worry about money, and we were most appreciative. He was also loyal to his priests in front of the laity. If one of them complained to him about you when he was visiting your parish, he backed you up."

After his own rough ride as rector of Corpus Christi seminary a decade earlier, Pell wasted little time in moving to alter that institution, agreeing, as he did, with Pope John Paul II's assessment that seminaries must be the *pupilla oculi* (apple of his eye) of every bishop. He was determined to press ahead with a new seminary regime from the beginning of 1997, rather than let everyone find his feet in the new episcopate and postpone any real action at the seminary until the beginning of 1998.

Pell had been at the helm exactly four months when Melbourne's Sunday *Herald Sun* broke this story on its front page: "The entire teaching staff of Australia's largest Catholic seminary has quit over suggested changes to the training of priests. The mass resignations at Corpus Christie [sic] were announced at a meeting of staff with Melbourne Archbishop George Pell, who is pushing reforms to make priests conform to stricter regimes." The brief page-one article pointed to a longer piece on page three, headed "Pell's Priests Quit— Staff Walk Out over Archbishop's Plans", which was very close to the mark:

> The head of Australia's biggest Catholic seminary and his entire teaching staff have resigned in protest at planned changes to the training of priests by Melbourne Archbishop George Pell. The five senior staff, including the rector, Father Paul Connell, announced their resignations at a meeting of staff and students attended by the archbishop on Thursday. It is believed to be the first mass resignation of staff at an Australian Catholic seminary. Corpus Christi, which takes in dioceses in Victoria and Tasmania, is Australia's biggest seminary.

According to the article, the resignations were sparked by reforms the archbishop wished to implement, including changes to daily devotions. "Also being planned is the relocation of the theology college from Clayton to Cathedral College in Victoria Parade, East Melbourne", the article revealed. One of the departing staff members told the *Herald Sun* that the reforms were a "subtle vote of no confidence" in the seminary and that the archbishop's stricter and more regulatory regime was not welcomed by the staff.

The paper quoted Pell as saying that the planned reforms were approved unanimously by the seminary's trustees, who included the Catholic bishops in Victoria and Tasmania, and that they were based on Pope John Paul II's pastoral letter dealing with the formation of seminarians. "I want them to be able to pray better, to celebrate the sacraments more devoutly and pray the word of God more devoutly, especially by example", the article quoted the archbishop as saying.

"They [the staff] are good people who have done a good job, but they have a different vision of seminary formation [the non-academic preparation of priests]. These changes are being made with the intention of strengthening the spiritual environment in the seminary."

Father Connell told the *Herald Sun* that the trustees of the seminary had invited the staff to continue running the seminary in the new style that the archbishop wanted. "We considered it and decided we weren't willing to do that, and we resigned", he told the paper. "The decision was taken very seriously and after considerable thought." The others who resigned were Dean of Studies Father Peter Howard, Spiritual Director Father Bill Attard, Director of Pastoral Formation Father Martin Ashe, and Sister Maria Bongiorno, I.B.V.M. Another staff member, Father Steve Bohan, the director of first-year formation, had recently come to the end of his term of appointment.

Opponents of the Pell style of seminary formation portrayed the former staff as intellectual martyrs sacrificed in a reactionary push to return to a 1950s style of priestly training. At the opposite end of the spectrum, others applauded the resignations, claiming the seminary had dropped its standards both intellectually and spiritually before the archbishop stepped in. On balance, it came down to a clash of priorities as to what mattered most in priestly formation—and the archbishop, who held ultimate responsibility for seminary formation, prevailed. Interestingly, some of those who resigned from the seminary stayed on at the Catholic Theological College (where both seminarians and lay theology students studied) in part-time teaching positions, including Paul Connell. The fact that he remained in a teaching position suggested the clash of visions between the seminary staff and Pell was more to do with the spiritual formation of the students than with their academic studies.

Pell insisted the staff were not sacked. It is plausible, however, that the archbishop saw from the outset that Connell and his staff had such a different view of seminary formation that, sooner or later, there would be a parting of the ways. Five years on, Connell defended the training system in place before Pell's reforms.

In many ways, the issue was a rerun of the issues raised in Pell's "Few Small Changes" memo from his own days as rector—compulsory, set prayer times versus voluntary participation at the student's discretion. His reforms, he later said, involved "the basic sorts of things that most

Catholics would already believe were happening in the seminary—
daily Mass, morning meditation, morning prayer of the Church,
night prayer of the Church, a holy hour once a week in front of the
Blessed Sacrament, private recitation of the rosary and devotions to
Our Lady in May."[6]

As Peter Elliott read the situation, the seminary staff were trying
to give Archbishop Pell an ultimatum: "Either you don't go ahead
with these proposals or we resign." "It was a threat", Elliott said. "He
will not take people doing that. You don't threaten George Pell and
get away with it and put ultimatums to him. They made a hideous
mistake. Another bishop would have buckled and said 'Please don't
go because I can't replace you.' Actually, that was the risk. They
were well-trained seminary staff; they'd been there for years, which
was part of the problem. It was an ingrained thing." Connell argued
that students can be made to attend Masses and services at particular
times, but that did not guarantee they were praying. His preferred
system, he said, while it appeared more "liberal" in that students
could choose their own times to pray, meant "a long-term interiori-
sation of the values that one wants inculcated in preparation for them
becoming priests".

Critics of the seminary pre-1996 point to its abysmally small student
numbers and the high rate of young priests leaving the priesthood in
Melbourne as signs that the system was failing. In both the United
States and Australia, seminaries that have restored some of the discipline and prayerfulness evident in seminaries decades ago have enjoyed
a stronger revival in vocations than other seminaries. Advocates of this
approach insist that young people called by God want the real thing
and that "relevance" to modern values will never match the power
of divine revelation. Opponents argue that while the more traditional
seminaries have seen an increase in student numbers, the type of students attracted tend to be rigid in outlook and unsuited to dealing with
people in the complex world of the new millennium.

Father Mark Withoos, ordained in 2000, saw both systems operate
at the seminary and preferred the system after the Pell reforms. Even
in the more liberal, pre-Pell days, Withoos said he found adjusting
to seminary life difficult at first, but he was surprised to find "very,

[6] Quoted in *The Age*, June 4, 2002.

very minimal prayer". "We didn't have adoration [of the Blessed Sacrament] or Benediction", he said. Some staff, Withoos explained, were "not necessarily loyal" to Church teachings like *Humanae Vitae*, and he heard "occasional snide remarks about the pope". Despite the presence of six staff for twenty-five students, he did not find the system of self-regulated prayer and accountability to a "mentor" satisfactory. "We were required to attend fifteen minutes of morning prayer every day, except Saturday, and I turned up regularly—so regularly that my mentor suggested that I take a second day off a week and sleep in." Mark Withoos felt he had to comply.

It was clear that Connell and his team were not the right men to implement Pell's vision of seminary education. Pell was scheduled to visit the seminary on Thursday, November 14, 1996 (the last week of the seminary year), to announce the new system of training for 1997. Connell and some of the other staff and their friends insist that as a group, the staff, after lengthy discussion, had decided not to resign just before Pell's November 14 visit but, rather, to "let Doctor Pell sack us and wear it". They say it was some of the other Victorian bishops, trustees of Corpus Christi along with Pell, who came up with the idea of the staff resigning to save face all around, both for themselves and for the archbishop. The staff, Connell said, were reluctant to accept the compromise at first and determined to tough it out, but when the crunch came, they buckled—or blinked—first and resigned. Pell probably was surprised and undoubtedly relieved.

The Age reported on November 30, 1996, that Pell was facing a backlash from his clergy over the changes, with "dozens of priests ... known to have contacted Corpus Christi seminary to express their dismay". The article quoted a nameless "liberal cleric" who said that conservative trainee priests were often misfits. "In four or five years Archbishop Pell might have forty or fifty people in the seminary, but if you gave them a Rorschach test you'd find most of them were at the neurotic end of the scale. You won't get the sort of people who are able to offer leadership in a complex society."

The other side of the argument is that a stronger emphasis on spirituality should help give the priests the strength of character to remain true to their calling when they begin working in the world outside the seminary. At that point and subsequently, the sheer numbers of seminarians in the more conservative United States dioceses show that at least in terms of numbers, the more traditional men are ahead, with some small conservative United States dioceses outnumbering much larger ones by fifty to one.

In the 1990s, the argument over seminary formation, while obscure to many, was (as it still is) at the heart of much conflict and division within the Catholic Church across the Western world. So deep were the divisions that in one Australian seminary in the 1980s (not Melbourne), students who wanted to say the Rosary told friends outside that they had to do so in private, for fear of being dismissed for not being "ecumenical" in outlook.

In subsequent years, Pell boosted the seminary's academic program, enhancing the philosophy component with the help of Hayden Ramsay. He also resumed the practice of sending occasional students to Propaganda Fide in Rome (which granted scholarships to the Melbourne students even though Australia was no longer a "missionary" country) as well as to other Roman universities.

By the start of the academic year in 2000, the old parish buildings in Drummond Street, Carlton, a short walk from Saint Patrick's Cathedral, had been restored and rebuilt as the new site for Corpus Christi. In March 2000, Pell opened the new Corpus Christi Chapel—a picturesque bluestone chapel that had started life as a church school in 1855 under Melbourne's first Catholic archbishop, Alipius Goold. Relics of prominent Catholic figures were installed in the chapel, including two saints—Saint Francis of Assisi and Saint Thomas Aquinas, whose "magnificent theology", Pell said, "is distilled in the hymns and prayers he wrote for the feast of Corpus Christi. He also wrote the hymn from which the college motto, *De Te Vivere* (To live by You), is taken." At the opening, Pell singled out Thomas Aquinas' faith, piety, intellectual genius, and application as an example to the young seminarians and the staff. The other relics imbedded in the chapel were of two prominent twentieth-century Catholics—Mother Teresa and Croatian Cardinal Alojzije (Aloysius) Stepinac, who spent fifteen of his twenty-two years of episcopacy in prison and under house arrest and who challenged the totalitarianism of both the Nazis and the Communists and refused to sever the Catholic Church in Croatia from the Holy See.

Archbishop Eric D'Arcy, the retired archbishop of Hobart, by then living in Melbourne, said at the opening that the seminary chapel was the most important space in any diocese. "Here the seminarian learns to pray regularly, or at least consolidates his patterns of prayer in good times and bad, in times of enthusiasm and times of dryness." Ramsay said the change of venue was a masterstroke by the archbishop. "The Clayton place had to be seen to be believed, the chapel was 1970s concrete—horrible." He said the beautifully restored chapel at the new seminary site in Carlton offered the students the richness of the Church's traditions.

Qualified seminary staff were difficult to find. In the wake of the events at the end of 1996, Monsignor Aldo Rebeschini, a Propaganda Fide graduate and the former secretary to Cardinal James Knox in Melbourne and Rome, took up the position of rector at the start of the 1997 academic year and with it the Herculean task of implementing the archbishop's desired changes in the face of fierce opposition from some of the older students. In his three years at the helm, Monsignor Rebeschini settled things down and saw a welcome increase in new students

The next rector, Father Michael McKenna, returned from a sabbatical at Harvard University and continued building up the seminary. In 2002, nine new students began their studies at Corpus Christi, compared with just one newcomer in 1996. By 2003, the seminary had forty-one students in total—thirty-one of them studying for the Archdiocese of Melbourne, and the others for Hobart, Ballarat, Sandhurst, and Sale.

The seminary crisis behind him, Pell's first Christmas celebrating midnight Mass in Saint Patrick's Cathedral was fast approaching, but festivities that year were tempered by an encounter he had the Thursday before Christmas when he blessed the body of a dead baby, Thomas Walter Joseph Ryan. Thomas had been born the day before in Melbourne's Mercy Hospital. His parents, Clare and Tom Ryan, knew their little boy's life would be brief—an ultrasound scan at eighteen weeks' gestation had detected a severe abnormality, anencephaly, and, as expected, the baby's head was incomplete, his fate sealed. The archbishop's vicar for health care, Anthony Fisher, a Dominican priest, was helping the couple through their ordeal. Thomas lived eighteen hours, and as Father Fisher said at his funeral Mass, "He packed so much into his seventeen or eighteen hours ... long enough to leave us many memories ... long enough to give

Clare and Tom some time with him, to celebrate little birthdays as he achieved each new hour and especially their private one with him at midnight when against all odds he saw a new day." At the saddest moment in Clare Ryan's life, a tall figure in black came quietly into her hospital room and blessed her dead baby as she cradled him in her arms. Pell said very little, but his closeness made a difference.

One of Pell's first initiatives as archbishop had been to establish an archdiocesan Respect Life Office. The office offers support, advice, and information to all those caught up in the tragedy of abortion—be it women who have had abortions or those considering one. It provides priests with material to handle the subject effectively and sensitively. For instance, one of its brochures addressed to women who have had an abortion says: "Allow me to speak for every minister of every denomination who has ever failed you: I'm sorry. Every minister of God tries to preach faithfully both God's law and his mercy. But so often we end up preaching more of one than the other, and the message becomes unbalanced. Please forgive our failings, just as God will surely forgive yours."

Thomas Ryan's story featured prominently in one of the office's newsletters. As Father Fisher noted, Thomas, in his short life,

> made opportunities for his health caregivers to show their respect and was photographed and delighted in by his parents. Again unconsciously he made a space for care at a time when their profession is under greater and greater pressures to show less and less care and respect.... Even while still in the womb Thomas was influencing others, creating opportunities for others, giving his parents a chance to give testimony to the preciousness of human life and to show courage and true love. That they did so with such natural, unaffected heroism is surely the action of grace.

Thomas' story had an interesting postscript. His parents, Tom and Clare, went on to have four other healthy children. They wrote Pell a letter of support when he was in Barwon Prison in February 2020, in which Tom wrote that the family "are all praying for you, and I'm tipping my deceased son, Thomas Walter Ryan, whom you visited, will be praying for you also."

16

"Si Monumentum Requiris, Circumspice"

After exploring the Pilgrim Path and sculpture garden Archbishop Pell created beside the bluestone cathedral, Melbourne education consultant Christopher Bantick, a member of the Church of England, wrote in an email to the author:

> Many thanks for the suggestion that I take a walk around the water gardens of St Patrick's. In early evening Autumn light, they were stunning. I must say that I was deeply moved by the statue of St Catherine of Siena carrying the crown of thorns. She was dutiful and dignified. Then there was the pensive and gentle St Francis of Assisi calmly acknowledging my presence.
>
> Besides the golden lamb in a pool of water with a verse from the Apocalypse, what struck me—apart from the design—was the vision that Archbishop Pell had for Melbourne in this. I mused long on McAuley's words:
>
> > Incarnate Word, in whom all nature lives,
> > Cast flame upon the earth: raise up contemplatives
> > Among us, men who walk within the fire
> > Of ceaseless prayer, impetuous desire.
> > Set pools of silence in this thirsty land.[1]
>
> This is a special place. I will bring my family here. It made me think of the need for children to understand the context of public monuments, religious statues and iconography. Otherwise, they are being denied a rich and extensive cultural heritage.

"Si monumentum requiris, circumspice" (If you seek his monument, look around) is the inscription on the tomb of Sir Christopher Wren in Saint Paul's Cathedral, London. He was the architect of the building.
[1] James McAuley, "A Letter to John Dryden" (1936–1938).

On a sunny day or even in the gentle drizzle of a dark afternoon, the Pilgrim Path is an inspiring place to be, with often only the distinctively Melbourne sound of the Collins Street trams rattling past to break the silence. The Pilgrim Path, opened in the Jubilee Year 2000, has a trail of cascading water, pouring over a selection of quotations cut with gold inlays into bluestone structures. Some are biblical quotations; another is the poem by James McAuley, quoted above.

After the Pilgrim Path was opened, Pell explained the selection of quotations:

> I've long had a great admiration for McAuley. I think that's a particularly beautiful Australian piece of poetry. Even the Scripture quotes, I ran them past a whole range of people, learned people, but I also very explicitly ran them past devout Catholics who weren't at all learned, just to see—we had a few others that were possibilities—which ones they preferred. I was always particularly pleased to see so many of the tourists standing looking at McAuley's poetry or looking puzzlingly at the texts.

At the top of the Pilgrim Path are a number of sculptures of saints drawn from some of the ethnic communities that comprise the Catholic Church in Melbourne. Pell himself commissioned the first two statues—fresh, interesting sculptures of the patron saints of Italy, Saint Francis of Assisi (1181–1226) and Saint Catherine of Siena (1347–1380). Sculptor Louis Laumen, who years later sculpted the crucifix in the chapel of Domus Australia in Rome, depicts them identifying with the sufferings of Jesus—Francis with the stigmata of Jesus' wounds, Catherine holding up the crown of thorns.

The statue of Croatian Cardinal Stepinac was commissioned and paid for by Melbourne's Croatian community as a reminder, not just of his heroism and faithfulness, but also of the contribution of the Croatian community to the life and culture of Melbourne. Born in 1898, Aloysius Stepinac was a World War I conscript in the Austro-Hungarian Army. He was ordained in Rome in 1930 and became archbishop of Zagreb in 1937. During the Second World War, Stepinac helped Croatian, Jewish, Serbian, and Slovenian refugees and openly criticized the Nazi regime. From July 1943, the British Broadcasting Corporation (BBC) and the Voice of America broadcast his sermons to occupied Europe. At the end of the war,

however, Stepinac was found guilty of Nazi collaboration at a mock
trial staged by Communist Yugoslavia and was sentenced to sixteen
years' hard labour in 1946. After five years' jail, Tito released him
and confined him to the village of Krasic. Although forbidden to
resume his duties, Stepinac was named a cardinal by Pope Pius XII
in 1953, and he died in 1960. In 1985, his trial prosecutor, Jakov
Blazevic, admitted that Cardinal Stepinac had been framed and that
he was tried only because he refused to sever the thousand-year-old
ties between Croatians and the Catholic Church. Pope John Paul II
beatified the cardinal in 1998.

The Irish were already well represented around the cathedral, not
just by its name, but with the statue of the "liberator" Daniel O'Connell, the lay parliamentarian responsible for Catholic emancipation in
Ireland (and England) in 1829, whose view it was that Irish liberty,
while a vitally important cause, was not worth "the shedding of a
single drop of blood". In the latter part of Little's time as archbishop,
some in Melbourne's Irish community feared that the statue would
be moved out of the cathedral grounds. Pell had O'Connell's statue
restored and moved to a new spot facing out onto Albert Street,
where Irish president Mary McAleese rededicated it. The archbishop
also commissioned another statue—of his Irish-born predecessor,
Daniel Mannix, who once wrote of his homeland: "A hundred bonds
stronger than steel bound me to the dear old land, from which so
many of you, like myself, have come."[2]

The ten-foot bronze statue of Mannix, on a bluestone plinth by
English sculptor Nigel Boonham, was commissioned for the cathedral
forecourt, and those who remembered Mannix attested that it was an
excellent likeness. The statue exudes a monumental presence over
Eastern Hill, much as its subject did for half a century. It was unveiled
in March 1999 by the then-governor of Victoria, Sir James Gobbo,
who praised Mannix as an intellectual, scholar, man of prayer, international figure, educationist, orator, and wit who dominated the life
of Melbourne through his long tenure as archbishop. The Italian-
born Gobbo, a scholarship winner educated in the Catholic schools

---

[2] Danniel Mannix, *Advocate*, March 29, 1913, quoted in Race Matthews, *Of Labour and
Liberty: Distributism in Victoria, 1891–1966* (Notre Dame, Ind.: University of Notre Dame
Press, 2018), https://www.google.com/books/edition/Of_Labour_and_Liberty/EoFSDwAA
QBAJ?hl=en&gbpv=1.

of Mannix' time, is a prime example of the success Mannix wished for the Catholic children of his archdiocese.

Also part of the Pell legacy is the Aboriginal message stick installed in the cathedral on Aboriginal Sunday in July 1998 and an Aboriginal stone inlay in the cathedral forecourt. The stone inlay depicts the Creator Spirit, a continuing source of life in both Aboriginal and Christian spiritual traditions. Encircled by a border of greenstone and a larger surround of basalt, the design of the stone inlay is based on the conceptual understanding that meaning is multilayered. Each symbol in the design—the dove, the eagle, the snake, and the water—has dual meaning, and the interpretation of the work depends on the perspective of the viewer.

In Aboriginal culture, the message stick was a means of communicating with other groups. The message stick installed in Saint Patrick's by Pell and various Aboriginal elders and people on Aboriginal Sunday, July 1998, depicts symbols representing Australia's Aboriginal Catholic communities. "For too long the indigenous people of this country have been left on the margins of our society, and sadly this has often been true of the Church as well", Pell said at the time. "My intention in encouraging the installation of the message stick and the stone inlay was to acknowledge the wrongs of the past and to highlight the special place that Aboriginal people occupy in the Church."

In her message published to mark the occasion, Wurundjeri Elder Joy Murphy said her people's story was similar to that of Catholics.

> Your story is by your chosen faith, our story is by the Dreaming. We both have creators and we believe in our creators. Ours is Bunjil the Eagle. In the creation story we say we belong to the land, that we are part of the land and the land part of us. Wurundjeri also say that there is a place for everyone and everyone has a place on this land.
>
> Saint Patrick's Cathedral provides a beautiful place and a comfortable environment. We feel happy here too. Today and always we will share this space as the symbol of creation in the lives of all people. We are honoured to form this partnership in respect of your reconciliation of the Aboriginal people and their lives.[3]

---

[3] Joy Murphy, "Aboriginal Culture: Message from a Wurundjeri Elder", Catholic Archdiocese of Melbourne: Saint Patrick's Cathedral, accessed April 29, 2024, https://www.cam1.org.au/cathedral/Aboriginal-Culture/Article/13413/message-from-a-wurundjeri-elder.

Beyond Saint Patrick's Cathedral, the Catholic precinct extends along Victoria Parade, where Pell had the Australian Catholic University's Melbourne campus relocated on the corner of Young Street. On the opposite side of Victoria Parade is Goold House, bought by Archbishop Little and converted by Pell into the archdiocesan and Catholic education offices. The archbishop's office was on the top floor, with sweeping views across central Melbourne. Near Goold House was the John Paul II Institute building, housing, not only the institute and its chapel, but also the Mannix Library, the Catholic Theological College, where both seminarians and lay people studied philosophy and theology at undergraduate level, and the Catholic Pastoral Formation Centre, where non-degree courses were offered in adult education and pastoral care.

Just around the corner at 7 Brunswick Street, Fitzroy, was the Mary of the Cross Centre. It was opened in 1999, on the site where Alexander and Flora MacKillop lived in the nineteenth century. Their first child, Mary Helen, was born there on January 15, 1842. That girl would become the first canonised saint of Australia. The property was put up for sale in 1997, and the archbishop was determined that a site of such significance in the Catholic story should be preserved and, more importantly, that it should become a place where Saint Mary of the Cross' pioneering work for the poor and marginalised would continue in a new context, in a new millennium. The centre was established to provide support for families who struggle with the sad and often tragic consequences of substance abuse.

Although a staunch opponent of Church involvement in so-called "safe" injecting rooms, where addicts could take drugs under supervision and with legal immunity, Pell was keen for the Church to become more active in responding to Melbourne's drug problem. To explore the different possibilities, he set up an archdiocesan drugs task force in June 1999, which identified the need for such a centre. The Mary of the Cross Centre worked with all comers, regardless of religion, race, background, sex, or age. Many of those it helped came from non-English-speaking backgrounds. Pell considered it one of his best contributions to developing the Church's mission to be an instrument of healing and reconciliation.

Addressing a joint sitting of the Victorian Parliament about the drug problem in 2001, Pell said heroin deaths were only the tip of an iceberg of misery and depression, some of which was also caused by other drugs, such as alcohol and marijuana. He said:

> The Australian youth suicide rate, one of the highest in the world, is a related, overlapping problem. This is not just a problem for the government and the police. Community money as well as government money will be needed. Nor can it be dealt with effectively by handing over the whole load to the schools and churches. The problem is too big. All community organisations, and especially the media and leaders among young people themselves, at school, work and university, will need to combine effectively if we are to change youth attitudes to drug usage, as we have made drinking and driving generally unacceptable.
>
> Knowledge by itself rarely changes behaviour. A spiritual framework (in the broadest terms), a vision, or a system of meaning, perhaps around the Golden Rule (treating others as we wish to be treated ourselves) is needed as the context for information and argumentation, appropriate to the youngster's level of development. This is easily fitted, at a variety of levels, into the ongoing health education units, and units of moral education and religious education when they exist.

Or in other words, education about the devastating health effects of drugs will often be insufficient to steer young people away from them. A solid foundation in religious and moral belief can play a major part in helping prevent young people from becoming drug users or help those who have become involved to break the habit.

Early in his pontificate, John Paul II created the Pontifical Council for the Family in Rome, to promote the traditional family—father, mother, and children. George Pell was one of a number of international archbishops, bishops, clergy, and lay people who were consulters to the Pontifical Council, and Peter Elliott worked there until he returned to Australia in 1997. As part of the Pontifical Council's efforts, the pope established a new Pontifical Institute for Studies on Marriage and the Family. This was to be announced during his Wednesday audience in Saint Peter's Square on May 13, 1981 (the anniversary of Our Lady's first appearance at Fatima, in Portugal, in 1917), but before he could do so that day, the Holy Father was shot by Mehmet Ali Agca. The institute was finally established the following year, entrusted by the pope to the care of Our Lady of Fatima, to whose intercession he attributed his miraculous survival on the day the institute was to have been born. The institute was a postgraduate academic institute, linked to Rome's Pontifical Lateran University, offering diplomas, master's degrees, licentiates, and doctorates in bioethics and marriage and family studies. Full branches of the institute were established in Rome, Washington, D.C., Valencia (Spain), Mexico City and Guadalajara (Mexico), Cotonou (Benin), and Salvador da Bahia (Brazil). Campuses later formed in India, Austria, and Ireland. In response to the pope's express wish that the institute be present on all continents, the Archdiocese of Melbourne took up the challenge, and the John Paul II Institute for Marriage and Family opened in July 2001 in Melbourne, in a collaborative arrangement with the University of Notre Dame in Perth.

The Washington John Paul II Institute had begun with nine students. Melbourne's opened with twenty-seven students, and in less than two years the numbers rose to forty. All candidates already held undergraduate degrees and, after graduation, could expect to be employed as teachers in seminaries and theological colleges, as leaders in community and Church organisations, or as ethicists in the healthcare industry. It was a rigorous institution academically. To enroll in the Licentiate in Sacred Theology (Marriage and Family) course, for example, applicants needed at least a credit in previous theology degree courses, a strong background in philosophy, and an adequate knowledge of scholastic Latin and/or biblical Greek and at least one modern European language.

Pell named his vicar for health care, Father Anthony Fisher, O.P., then forty-one, as director of Melbourne's John Paul II Institute. Fisher was one of the Catholic Church's bright young talents whom Pell later appointed as his auxiliary bishop in Sydney and who eventually succeeded Pell as archbishop of Sydney in 2014. After arts (honours) and law degrees from Sydney University and a first-class honours degree in theology from the Melbourne College of Divinity, Fisher completed a doctorate in bioethics at Oxford in 1995. While studying in England, he worked as adviser to the British bishops on bioethics.

At first glance, Fisher (who wore a full, floor-length religious habit for work in his quaint attic office in Melbourne and still wears it as archbishop of Sydney) could have been a medieval Dominican scholar in a monastery. He specialized, however, in the moral theology of the future, in the cutting-edge medical-science issues where ordinary Australians were increasingly looking for answers—stem cell research, reproductive technologies, genetic engineering, and cloning. Along with contraception, abortion, and euthanasia, those were the pressing moral issues of the time, before widespread controversies flared on transgender issues.

Two years into his time as archbishop, Pell took on the issue of contraception by marking the thirtieth anniversary of Pope Paul VI's *Humanae Vitae*. He, Archbishop Barry Hickey of Perth, Australia, and Archbishop Charles Chaput of Denver, Colorado, were among the few bishops in the world who issued pastoral letters to mark the anniversary of a document that has been accused of being anti-woman and a contributor to overpopulation and abortion.

Pell argued that the Church's stand against artificial birth control was respectful of women. In a contraceptive culture, women mostly carry the burden of limiting births, often with negative consequences to their health and happiness, he wrote. The years since 1968 had revealed that both oral contraceptives and the intrauterine device (IUD) pose serious risks to women's health. Long-term use of the Pill has been linked to cardiovascular disease as well as breast and cervical cancer. And despite the widespread use of these and other contraceptives, abortion and teenage pregnancy rates had escalated around the world, including in Australia, which in 1998 had an abortion rate in excess of Great Britain and Holland. At the same time, more and more professional women were speaking openly about their grief at being unable to conceive after putting off motherhood for too long.

Pell argued the case for *Humanae Vitae* along prudential lines, in tune with medical and social concerns. First, he urged Catholics to read the encyclical in a spirit of openness. To that end, he made copies freely available at all Catholic churches, pointing out that the document was about far more than contraception and was "probably the most famous and least understood encyclical in history".[4]

The archbishop admitted that many Catholics honestly believe

> that Pope Paul VI was wrong to reaffirm the traditional Christian teaching against artificial contraception, common to all Christian churches until early this century. However this may be argued, the Holy Father was right on two scores; on the dignity and beauty of

[4] George Pell, *On Life and Love*, July 25, 1998, https://www.catholicculture.org/culture/library/view.cfm?recnum=463.

married love and on the dire practical consequences of the contraceptive mentality, of selfishness at work.

The widespread use of the Pill unlocked the sexual revolution
in Australia and the Western World, which brought an increase in
abortions, marriage breakdowns, the number of single mothers and
homeless children. These dark consequences of casual sex are hidden
from view, while sexuality itself is debased in films, magazines, and
advertising, and young men and women, their relations often troubled
by a lurking mistrust, are more reluctant than ever to commit themselves to each other unconditionally for life. Individuals are asking the
Church to legitimize homosexual activity, to bless single-sex unions.
We have now the tragic AIDS epidemic ... the signs of the times
have validated Paul [VI's] pessimism about the future, and like the
true prophets of the Old Testament he was derided and denounced
for his predictions.

It was important, Pell argued, to examine the benefits of faithful
married love and natural methods of family planning.

Since 1968 ... medical scientists have developed the knowledge for
couples to manage their fertility without the use of harmful drugs, surgery or artificial devices. In the past thirty years, great advances have
been made in the area of natural family planning. Sadly, many of our
people are unaware of them and still talk dismissively of what are in
fact very effective techniques...

Advances in natural methods of family planning have ... empowered women to take a greater role in decisions about their reproductive health, enhancing self-confidence and self-esteem.

His initiative sparked an enormous debate on family issues in Melbourne's two major newspapers, *The Herald Sun* and *The Age*, with
front-page news stories, features, and letters to the editor for and
against the statement. In an editorial *The Herald Sun* praised Pell for
suggesting that the trappings of the 1990s might have made Australian
society materially better off, but in a spiritual and psychological sense
life had become much harder for many people.

Dr Pell's comments will prick many a conscience. Perhaps it is time to
pause and try to balance our obsession for material wealth against the
need for spiritual contentment. In a perfect society people would think
less of themselves and more about family, friends and those needing

help. Dr Pell was right to express concerns about the direction society was heading, that "... the general direction in marriage breakdowns, extra-nuptial births, divorces is quite clear and irrefutable."[5]

Pell was also put to the test that year on the issue of homosexuality. In many people's minds, his refusing Communion to homosexual activists who protested the Church's teaching by wearing rainbow sashes to his Masses had defined him as a hardline conservative. Those who better understood Catholic teaching, including clerics and Church bureaucrats who disagreed with Pell on other issues, say he had no alternative but to refuse Communion to sash-wearers.

Rainbow Sash protests began in London at Westminster Cathedral in 1997, when a young man in a sash was refused Communion by Cardinal Basil Hume, a gentle, scholarly, Benedictine monk widely regarded as a liberal on social and moral questions. An Australian homosexual activist and former Franciscan seminarian, Michael Kelly, then helped organize a similar protest at Saint Patrick's in Melbourne, when New York's Cardinal John O'Connor presided as the papal delegate at the reopening of the cathedral that October. Kelly said he and his friends regarded O'Connor as "a notorious homophobe". Until his death, O'Connor was one of the most widely respected prelates in the world, well known for his tough anti-abortion stance and a good friend of Pell, who kept O'Connor's picture in his Sydney office.

The next protest in Melbourne happened on Pentecost Sunday 1998, when seventy people attended Mass wearing brightly coloured rainbow sashes over their clothes. Pell was the principal celebrant of the Mass, and the group notified him of their plans in advance. They also notified the local and national media, who turned up in droves, and the story drew international attention. When the time for Holy Communion came, the sash-wearers approached the archbishop, who refused them the Sacrament unless they took off their sashes. Instead, he proffered a blessing. Michael Kelly told *The Age* that Pentecost Sunday had been chosen because "that was when the Holy Spirit touched every tribe, nationality and tongue, 'but apparently not gay and lesbian people'."[6]

[5] "Life in the fast lane", editorial, *Herald Sun*, August 3, 1998.
[6] Margaret Easterbrook, "Archbishop Denies Communion to Gays", *The Age*, June 1, 1998.

That Sunday, one of those wearing the sash was Nan McGregor, who, the newspapers reported, was the mother of a gay son. After the Mass, McGregor told the press that being denied Communion was "an extremely emotional" experience. "Archbishop Pell said he couldn't give me Holy Communion until I took the sash off. I said I was a heterosexual mother, but he said he couldn't until I took the sash off because the sash indicated I rejected the teachings of the Catholic Church", she said. "I feel sorry for him. I think he is lost in his own bigotry and small-mindedness."[7]

In the next few years, Michael Kelly and others repeated the exercise several times in Melbourne and once in Sydney, with Pell's reactions varying from telling him "repent and believe" to standing silently and not offering a blessing. Had Kelly approached Pell for Communion without the sash, Pell would have given him the Sacrament "because I don't know, he might have been to confession. I've never asked anybody when they come up to Communion what they do. If I'm asked what are the Church teachings, I will tell them. Receiving the Sacrament is the ultimate expression of our Catholic faith. It's not a question of refusing homosexuals or someone who is homosexually oriented. The rule is basically the same for everyone."

The people in the pews in Saint Patrick's seemed firmly on Pell's side on Pentecost Sunday 1998, and they broke into loud applause when the archbishop took the sash-wearers to task at the end of Mass. In contrast, the crowd at Saint Mary's in Sydney remained silent after a similar speech the first time the protest was staged there. Despite these varied reactions, among the Australian hierarchy the issue was clear-cut. In Canberra, the liberal auxiliary bishop Patrick Power, while making the protesters welcome for discussions, also refused them Communion. At the time of the Melbourne protests, the then-archbishop of Sydney, Cardinal Edward Clancy, said he also would have had no choice but to refuse Communion as the protesters were openly defying long-established teachings. "All Catholics are assumed to know what the necessary dispositions are if they are to receive Holy Communion", Cardinal Clancy said. Archbishop of Brisbane John Bathersby and Archbishop of Perth Barry Hickey both said they would have refused Communion to those wearing the

[7] Ibid.

sashes. Bathersby said he was sad that an act of worship was being used to make a political statement. As he pointed out, the Catholic *Catechism* says homosexual acts can be approved "under no circumstances", but "every sign of unjust discrimination" against homosexual people should be avoided and homosexual people must be received "with respect, compassion and sensitivity".[8] Hickey said, "If a bishop comes out frequently about Church teaching, that does not make [the Church] more conservative. When an issue of public morality comes up, one must speak publicly about it.... If we have made ourselves unpopular, it does not mean we are wrong."

Pell said neither he nor other bishops had the authority to alter Church teaching on the matter. "In wearing the sash, they're trying to get the Church to change the teaching on that subject, which we can't and won't do", he said after yet another demonstration on Pentecost Sunday 2000, when three security guards attended the Mass in case of disruption. "The Church's view on sexuality ... is clear and unequivocal and derives from natural moral law, which we believe is unchanging."[9]

After the Rainbow Sash protests, Pell noted that homosexual activity posed a much greater health risk than smoking because one sexual encounter with an infected person could cause AIDS. The epidemic of AIDS around the globe—by late 2000 health authorities estimated that HIV was infecting new victims at the rate of more than one every eight seconds—prompted the National Academies Forum to hold a major symposium on the problem. Archbishop Pell was one of the main speakers, along with medical specialists, scientists, and leaders of gay organizations and AIDS support teams. He shared the platform with Ian Rankin, former president of the National Association of People Living with HIV/AIDS, who also made a speech. Afterwards, both men fielded questions from the audience.

Given the confusion prompted by the Rainbow Sash controversy, Pell's speech spelled out the Church's position on homosexuality. "I am grateful for the opportunity to discuss the scourge of AIDS; to set out Christian moral teachings, hard as they can appear, as they

[8] *Catechism of the Catholic Church*, 2nd ed. (Washington, D.C.: United States Catholic Conference, 2000), no. 2358.
[9] George Pell, Statement on Homosexuals Receiving the Eucharist, June 2, 1998, https://www.catholicculture.org/culture/library/view.cfm?recnum=373.

surround and defend our central claim to the importance of love and
compassion; to deny the charge that Christian teaching is homopho-
bic; and to deny any suggestion that AIDS is divine retribution", the
archbishop said. "God always forgives, humans sometimes forgive.
It is nature which is ruthless and never forgives. Against that Christ
asked all those who are burdened to come to him and find rest; the
yoke is easy and the burden light."[10]

The Church, he said, had a clear right and a duty to comment on
public policy. "So often decisions that affect our lives are seen to be
merely 'social' and 'economic'; there is clear advantage for everyone in
the contributions towards public policy of a group such as the Church
whose concern is with moral truth. The Catholic Church proposes; she
can no longer impose or prescribe. People accept or reject our truth
claims." In a climate of easy agnosticism among Australian opinion
makers, he added, it was necessary to explain Christian perspectives.

> Catholics believe that Christ is Son of God as well as son of Mary.
> Because of this divine origin, we think our moral and faith teaching
> has a unique authority, founded as it is on access to truth. We believe
> these truths are reported to us reliably in the New Testament, writ-
> ten within early Christian communities and authorized by the early
> Church as an accurate witness to the lives and preaching of Christ and
> the apostles.
>
> Christian teaching on the moral legitimacy of sexual behaviour
> has always been clear, founded on our Judeo-Christian moral frame-
> work and proclaimed out of concern for the ultimate happiness and
> well-being of the individual and society. Simply put, sexual activity
> belongs within the framework of heterosexual marriage and exists for
> the procreation of children and the mutual love of the couple. There-
> fore, certain sexual behaviour is considered by Christians to be clearly
> inappropriate (and if committed with knowledge of the evil involved,
> sinful). Such behaviour includes adultery, pre-marital sex, masturba-
> tion, and homosexual activity.

No moral blame, he said, attaches to a person simply because he
is inclined towards disordered sexual behaviour. Personal culpability

---

[10] George Pell, "Discussion on AIDS: Private Morals and Public Policy" (speech, National
Academies Forum, Australian National Library, Canberra, Australia, November 29–30, 2000).

requires understanding of and consent to the prohibited activity, not just inclination. For Christians, just because a course of activity is regarded as difficult—even almost impossibly difficult—is no reason to reject or abandon the ideal. "We all know some will not—and some cannot—live up to good moral standards, but this is not a sufficient reason to abandon the standards. Christians believe in forgiveness and acknowledge human weakness, but Christianity requires the Cross."

The Church's first response to the sick was to love them and care for them, he said.

Everywhere followers of Christ are doing this for AIDS victims. However, we need also to invoke Christ the Teacher for there are difficult lessons to be learned from HIV/AIDS.

Christian teaching on sexual activity is much more difficult for some to live up to than others, but that does not make it false, irrelevant, or wildly unrealistic. The social and personal effects of promiscuity, contraception, abortion, and marriage breakdown show its relevance and support its truth. Moral standards have an important function even when they are beyond the reach of some, because they point out what should be the direction of our striving.

Catholic teaching, especially sexual teaching, is not arbitrary. It is based on long and careful reflection on what really contributes to human happiness and what really makes a society flourish. Compassion does not proclaim what it knows to be false: that would violate human dignity and add to the tragedy of HIV/AIDS. Instead, it reaffirms the truth and looks for new ways to formulate and communicate it, since we have certainly not done all we could have here.

This did not mean the Church wishes to see homosexual activity made a criminal offense again as it was in the past, he said.

Government has limits to its authority, and there are good common sense reasons too for thinking that legislation and public intervention do not always help (whereas good moral education always will). The Church, too, in every society, but especially in a religiously pluralist society, has limits to its authority, e.g., the Church traditionally has not insisted that brothels be closed and does not ask today that homosexual activity be criminalized. Where human motivation is complex, the proper public response is a complex issue too, and different cases will be best handled in different ways, respecting the separation of Church and state.

Young adults and teenagers deserve to be told the truth about AIDS, he said.

Many youngsters have only the fragments of a framework left over from the "me generation" of their parents; many do not even have that. Most appreciate at least hearing about a strong, sound, ethical position that claims to be based on ultimate human happiness, presented clearly and charitably....

Secondly, they should be told the truth, the advantages of waiting, the advantages of monogamy. The truth, however, is not a "safe sex" advertisement. The only safe sex is no casual sex. The truth about condoms should be told: they are unreliable, they encourage sterile sex for gratification among the young, and they are a public health hazard because of the practice they encourage and promote. Sexual addiction is possible and damaging. Twenty-five percent of sexually transmitted diseases in the USA occur among adolescents.

While resolute in his views that rainbow sash wearers should not be offered Communion, Pell rejected any suggestion that he was a "homophobe", pointing out that he had often spoken with people who were openly homosexual and had visited his share of AIDS patients.

17

Salt of the Earth, Not Sugar
or Artificial Sweetening

In December 1998, George Pell told Fides, the Vatican news agency, that Catholic bishops, as Cardinal Joseph Ratzinger had recently reminded the Australian prelates visiting Rome, were called to be the salt of the earth—not the sugar. Or, Pell added, "the artificial sweetening".[1] For the benefit of his episcopal colleagues, he did not need to repeat the rest of Christ's comment in the Bible—that when salt loses its flavour it should be thrown out and trampled underfoot. After a stressful month in Rome, they were well aware of the warning in Cardinal Ratzinger's words.

From mid-November to mid-December, the entire Australian episcopate, along with other bishops from around the South Pacific, had been in Rome for the Synod of Oceania and to pay their regular five-yearly *ad limina* visits to the pope and the Vatican congregations. *Ad limina* means "to the threshold", and that is exactly where the bishops felt they were.

The Australian bishops, some more than others, were admonished for what was viewed in Rome as encroaching liberalism and modernism in the Church in Australia. In his *ad limina* address handed to the Australian bishops in the form of a letter, Pope John Paul II suggested that the Australian sense of equality, when taken too far, could be problematic. "While it has many positive elements, tolerance of and openness to all opinions and perspectives on the truth can lead to indifference, to the acceptance of any opinion or activity as long as it does not impact adversely on other people." The worldwide

[1] Quoted in *The Courier-Mail*, December 19, 1998, p. 27.

crisis of faith was "manifested in Australia by the rise in the number of people with no religion and the decline in church practice". At stake were many of the issues George Pell had been addressing for years—and more besides: orthodox seminary training; religious education, particularly in relation to the sacraments, in Catholic schools; the importance of maintaining clear distinctions between the roles of priests and laity; nuns returning to their convents and traditional habits and work; and liturgical abuses. These could include priests leaving out important parts of the Mass or using their own words or, in extreme cases, encouraging lay people to stand around the altar and say the words of Consecration with them, adding in their own bits and pieces. At the conclusion of the month-long visit, a twenty-page Statement of Conclusions was signed. It was co-authored by the Australian bishops and curial officials, including Cardinal Ratzinger and the prefects of five other Vatican congregations: Divine Worship and Discipline of the Sacraments; Bishops; Clergy; Institutes of Consecrated Life; and Education.[2]

This stormy, controversial visit was reported widely in the Australian media. Newspapers in Europe and North America also covered it. Some of the headlines of the time told the story: "Why Vatican Cuffed Bishops", "Reformists See Papal Rebuke as Setback", "Back to the Old Faith", "How the Papal Hit Squad Brought Priests to Heel", and "Bishops Told to Get Tough".

When they returned to Australia, some bishops vented their spleen in public, admitting they were "hurt, angry, and depressed" about the reception they had received at the Vatican and about the letter written to them by the pope. A few, including Pell, were more accepting, saying that if the Statement of Conclusions and *ad limina* address contained stern words, it was to remind Catholics that the Church was not open to change on central issues. "What [the statement] is saying is these aren't going to change and ... in a polite sort of way people can't have their cake and eat it", said Pell. "I am not suggesting that anybody who might disagree with the Church on any one or two particular issues, that their membership ... is called into question. But if you disagree with the Church on a

<hr />

[2] Joseph Ratzinger et al., *Dichiarazione finale dell'incontro interdicasteriale della curia romana con una rappresentanza dei vescovi della conferenza episcopale dell'Australia* (December 14, 1998).

whole raft of things, a legitimate question is to what extent do you remain a Catholic?"[3]

In a written statement, widely distributed in Melbourne along with the lengthy Statement of Conclusions document, Pell spoke of a widespread crisis of faith in society as a whole and a related crisis of Christology among believers. God, he said, was much more than the mighty forces of nature, and only man is made in God's image. "The Second Person of the Trinity became a man; not an angel or a cabbage." Problem areas had to be confronted and errors corrected by persuasion and dialogue, not blunt use of authority. The Church in Australia, Pell warned, "must not be like a husband and wife who deny the early signs that their marriage is in trouble; not like a bank manager who will not admit that his Branch is losing money and customers." The decline in worship by Catholics, he said, was significant. He branded the trend the "rise of the R.C.'s—resting, relaxed or reluctant Catholics." The truths of Catholicism, he said, were spelled out in the Creeds, "and the possibilities of innocent misunderstandings are legion when we speak of God. This is why home-written creeds are forbidden at Mass, even for home or school Masses."[4]

The Statement of Conclusions covered sixty-three issues. Much of the battle, however, centred on one issue in particular—the Sacrament of Penance. In almost every diocese of Australia in the previous decade, including Melbourne, the traditional practice of Catholics confessing their sins individually to priests had been largely overtaken by highly popular "general absolution" ceremonies, generally held during Advent and Lent. At these liturgies, several hundred people were absolved of their sins at once, after prayers, hymns, a communal examination of conscience, and a communal act of contrition. A communal penance, such as everybody reciting a Hail Mary or two, was usually given. The Church's canon law, however, reserved general absolution (or the third rite) for genuine emergency situations, such as soldiers going into battle or an airplane being hijacked, with the onus on penitents to confess their serious sins individually at the earliest opportunity if possible. Its routine use in parishes, while

---

[3] "Why Vatican Cuffed Bishops", *The Australian*, December 26, 1998, p. 3.
[4] George Pell, "Introduction to the Australian Bishops' Statement of Conclusions", March 19, 1999, https://www.catholicculture.org/culture/library/view.cfm?recnum=1044.

popular, is illicit under Church law, although the vast majority of those in the pews were unaware that this was the case.[5]

Pope John Paul II had reiterated the Church's teaching to the bishops on their 1998 visit: "The personal nature of sin, conversion, forgiveness, and reconciliation ... demands personal confession of sins", he told them.[6] Pell had always been a strong advocate of the traditional, or first rite, practice of individual confession. Earlier in his episcopacy, however, he displayed an ambivalence about whether he should ban general absolution in the parishes, although he was leaning towards that course. When asked by a journalist if he would abolish the third rite, he replied:

> It is undoubtedly popular.... It was introduced as a way of encouraging people back to individual reconciliation and penance. That, I think, has been a spectacular failure. The question is, whether by having the Third Rite we are reinforcing the disappearance of individual confession. That's the crucial issue, and I'm not sure which way we should go on that....
>
> The opinion of church-going Catholics is a very important consideration, but not necessarily the primary consideration. The teaching role ... is given first of all to the pope and the bishops, and we are very, very much the spokesmen for tradition.[7]

In Sydney, Cardinal Edward Clancy banned general absolution in his parishes before Easter in 1998, and in late October that year Pell took the same action, announcing the decision at a gathering of Melbourne priests. Catholics in other cities, however, were assured in the secular media that it would be business as usual with general absolution before Christmas and that nothing would change despite the moves in Sydney and Melbourne. But in Rome a few weeks later, Pope John Paul II ordered all Australian diocesan bishops to stop abusing the third rite, declaring that individual confession remained "the only ordinary way for the faithful to reconcile themselves with God and the Church".[8] Most of the bishops complied, albeit some with bad grace, and one or two ignored the edict—at least initially.

[5] *Code of Canon Law*, cann. 961–63.

[6] John Paul II, Address of the Holy Father Pope John Paul II to the Bishops of Australia on Their "Ad Limina Visit" (December 14, 1998).

[7] Geoffrey Barker, "Defender of the Faith", *Australian Financial Review*, May 29, 1998.

[8] John Paul II, "Ad Limina Visit".

Pell continued to follow up the Statement of Conclusions and urged a return to individual confession by Catholics long after the fuss had died down. Preaching to his priests before Easter 2001, he mentioned the pope's concern about "a certain dwindling of our enthusiasm and availability" for the demanding work of hearing confessions. "We must always, each week, be regularly available, and we must teach and explain, especially if customers seem to be scarce and every sinner in the parish seems to be over the age of fifty!" he said. "Basic human needs are never cancelled out by crises of culture, much less by passing fashions. The Sacrament of Penance meets the deep human need for forgiveness, and the need for this to be both ritualised and deeply personal."[9]

The emergence of these conflicts into the public arena in 1998 stunned many Catholics and non-Catholics, most of whom had no idea that theological divisions were running so deep, although the issues at stake had worried Pell and others for years. Preaching at the state funeral for his old friend B. A. Santamaria, in March 1998, Pell elaborated on some of those concerns:

> The Catholic community in Australia owes B. A. Santamaria a great debt for his leadership in the fight against communism in the unions; for his indispensable contribution in obtaining financial justice for all Christian schools from state and federal governments; for his authorship of fifteen of the Bishops' statements on social justice; for his brilliant alliance with Archbishop Mannix....
>
> However, some would believe that his greatest religious contribution has been during the last ten or fifteen years as different forces contended for the soul of Catholicism. Here B. A. stood squarely with the Holy Father.[10]

Informing Australian Catholics of the nature of the challenge they faced, he said, was Santamaria's last great struggle, and the conflict was far from over. "There are minority forces in Australian Catholicism who want to subordinate gospel morality to individual conscience.... Others see the ministerial priesthood as one relic of a vanished clerical

---

[9] George Pell, "The Priest: Mediator between God and Man", *AD2000* 14, no. 5 (June 2001), p. 20, https://ad2000.com.au/articles/2001/jun2001p20_482.html.

[10] George Pell, "Archbishop Pell's Tribute to B. A. Santamaria" (March 3, 1998), *AD2000* 11, no. 3 (April 1998), p. 10, https://ad2000.com.au/articles/1998/apr1998p10_560.html.

age. Even more seriously some do not see Christianity as a revealed religion. So the divinity of Christ is impugned, the Trinity redefined, and the worship of the one true God relativised and minimised. It is increasingly hard work to convince our youngsters of the evils of abortion and euthanasia, let alone contraception."

For those in authority, the divisions posed the challenge of trying to keep a divided family together, balancing both the need for charity and the demand for truth. As Pell said in a 1998 radio interview, "Human beings have rights, these have to be respected. So, as the pope said in one of those great moral encyclicals, the individual conscience is a proximate norm, it's indispensable, there's no substitute for sincerity. But it is not the last word, we stand under the truth, and for Christians we stand under the Gospel and the solemn teachings of the Church."[11]

Though he met with resistance from some within his own flock, some of Pell's strongest stances captured widespread popular support. In October 1997, the National Gallery of Victoria staged an exhibition of works by the American artist Andres Serrano, including a photograph named *Piss Christ*, depicting a crucifix immersed in a jar of urine. Pell was outraged: "The National Gallery should be a temple of beauty; not a home for sleaze." Determined to fight back, he organized a coalition of Christian church leaders to object to the blasphemous work. Jewish and Moslem leaders joined the effort. A phone-in poll in the *Herald Sun* newspaper showed that 93 percent of respondents agreed with the archbishop's stance. The incident drew international attention, and in a speech afterwards to the Oxford University Chaplaincy in England, Pell recounted:

> I contacted the gallery and asked them to remove the blasphemous photo to a private gallery. I explained that a publicly funded institution had no right to insult Christians in this way.
>
> The judge ruled against us, but Catholics and other Christians gathered each day outside the gallery, some praying the Rosary; some were secondary Catholic students. On the second or third day a man from Sydney pulled the photo from the wall; on the next day a

[11] "Archbishop George Pell", interview by Stephen Crittenden, *Encounter*, Australian Broadcasting Corporation, May 17, 1998, https://www.abc.net.au/listen/programs/encounter /archbishop-george-pell/3480104.

couple of youths attacked the Perspex covering of the photo with a hammer.

There was big press coverage; then unexpectedly the gallery cancelled the entire Serrano exhibition. I am not entirely sure why! I never began the operation thinking we would achieve this result. It was not earth shattering; undoubtedly the result was helped by the mild violence, which did not come from rank-and-file Catholics. But it was a victory for decency. The moral of the story is that we struggle because it is right and proper. Whether we win or lose is secondary; but we can and sometimes will win against the odds.

Just as newsworthy was his outspoken opposition to Pauline Hanson's One Nation Party, which, before it disintegrated for the first time, captured 23 percent of the vote in the 1998 Queensland state election. In May that year, the archbishop condemned One Nation for policies that "set groups of Australians against one another". "Racist policies are a recipe for strife and for misery", he told a Melbourne gathering.[12] "We commend those political leaders, especially the leaders of the three main political parties in Victoria, who have spoken out clearly against the policies of the 'One Nation' party, who are political opportunists and adventurers."

Many people, he acknowledged, had voted for One Nation, not because they were racist, but because they believed the simple solutions proposed would help them. Governments and others needed to protect Australians from the most drastic consequences of globalization. Hard-line economic policies were chipping away at the social cement built up over generations in Australia and tempting people struggling in life to embrace simple, mistaken solutions and to scapegoat minorities, such as the Aborigines and Australian Asians. All Christian churches, he said, had an obligation to oppose this "demonization of small groups" and encourage policies that embraced the poorest 20 percent of the nation in both the countryside and the cities. Pell said:

All Australians have a right to a "fair go", just as all of us have an obligation to work and contribute. We must resist effectively any set

[12] Quoted in "Triumph, Disaster, and the Fearless Disciple", obituary, *The Australian*, January 11, 2023.

of policies which would take us even some small distance towards the tensions, hate, and violence between races that have poisoned Southern Africa and even the southern states of the USA. We should beware. Long journeys often start with small steps. Racism, whether it be anti-Aboriginal or anti-Asian, must never be given a respectable face. We have left that behind us in earlier stages of Australian history.

Pell used to describe himself as "a political agnostic", though he was intensely interested in politics. He voted Labor, Liberal, and National Party in his time and years earlier for the Democratic Labor Party (DLP), and he had friends in all the main parties, but not the Greens. "It depends on the issues, but often I am more interested in what I think are the core beliefs and personal attributes of the individuals." As archbishop, he was forceful in his criticisms of policies he disagreed with, not with particular parties as such. He was against the Liberal government's encouragement of gambling in Victoria. He was just as outspoken when the Labor government pursued the idea of "safe" heroin injecting rooms, commenting that Jesus Christ had not gone around "handing out condoms and syringes, literally or metaphorically". Harm minimization, the archbishop argued, was never right, because a good result could not be achieved by performing an evil action. When the Labor government moved to ban twenty-four-hour poker machine clubs in country towns and tighten up advertising rules for gambling, Pell wanted it to go much farther and restrict gambling times to twelve to fifteen hours a day and move ATMs well away from pokies, or slot machines. "The more we can get people into the fresh air the better. The more time they have to think about what they are doing the better." The archbishop himself played the pokies "once or twice", but found them boring: "I put these 20 and 50 cent pieces in the machines, but I'd have just as much fun putting them down the toilet", he said. "Many people get themselves into diabolical trouble. I've seen the results as I travel around parishes. I've spoken to families who have lost houses, and it's not just confined to poorer suburbs. The Catholic Church does not believe that having a bit of a gamble is in itself morally wrong. What is wrong is when it damages you and your family life."[13]

[13] Interview for first edition of this biography.

On federal politics, while many Catholic agencies attacked the Howard government's proposals for a goods and services tax that was a major plank in the Liberal Party's 1998 election platform, Pell made the point that the complex issue was not one on which the Catholic Church could or should present a single viewpoint. In terms of the Church's concern for social justice, strong arguments could be made for and against the tax.

In 1998, Prime Minister John Howard, an avowed constitutional monarchist, appointed Pell as a delegate to the Constitutional Convention to be held at old Parliament House in February the following year. At the convention, he served on the resolutions committee responsible for drafting motions put to the convention and moved the motion in support of the republican model that was finally adopted by the convention. On the eve of the republican referendum in November 1999, Pell issued a statement appealing to "all Australians whatever their religious or politician convictions to vote Yes to a republic to complete our long and peaceful evolution to independence and maturity." Acknowledging that there was no one Catholic view on the issue, he argued: "The proposed change will preserve all the strengths of the present system, all the present guarantees for our freedom. It continues the Westminster system of government, with our prime minister accountable to parliament. Those who believe in this system will never have a better chance to preserve it."

For all that, Pell retained an affection for the monarchy, especially Queen Elizabeth II. When she died on September 8, 2022 (a date traditionally celebrated as the birthday of Mary, the Mother of God), Pell expressed an interest in attending the coronation of King Charles III in Westminster Abbey the following year.

By August 1999, Pell had a stronger national profile than any other Church leader in a generation, which prompted a Sydney think tank, the Centre for Independent Studies, to invite him to deliver its inaugural Acton Lecture, named after Lord Acton, an intellectual barred from entering Cambridge in 1850 because of his Catholicism but who was eventually appointed Regius Professor of Modern History at that university in 1894. Acton was a man of immense erudition, best remembered for his aphorism that "power tends to corrupt, and absolute power corrupts absolutely."

The lecture took place on August 4 at the Customs House, and several hundreds of Sydney's most influential business leaders, judges, lawyers, academics, and journalists turned up. For George Pell, it was new ground. Many of those there were not Catholic and had previously shown little interest in religious leaders, but they all wanted to hear the archbishop of Melbourne who had helped them realise that the Catholic Church had something of value to contribute to contemporary debate.

As a historian, George Pell quickly put Acton in context for the audience: "In September 1964, as a student in Rome during the Third Session of the Second Vatican Council, I remember Cardinal Cushing of Boston reminding the Council Fathers of Acton's claim that 'freedom is the highest political end', a sentiment which the Council partly endorsed in its Declaration on Religious Freedom."[14] However, unlike most late twentieth-century Western thinkers, Acton's liberalism was rooted in Christianity.

Turning his attention to the twentieth century, the archbishop said that by most conservative estimates, at least one hundred million people were killed by Communist governments in the twentieth century. While it was appropriate to regard the Holocaust as the crime of the century, he regretted the silence surrounding the mass murder and torture of various Communist regimes. "Nearly all the twelve-year-olds I speak to know of Hitler; very few have heard of Stalin. I could not even obtain a tax deduction for donations to the descendants of the prisoners of the Gulag, who survive today—millions of them—in Siberia, originally from many different nations."

Catholic intellectual tradition, he said, had an important contribution to make to the debates on freedom and human rights in the contemporary world. "Most Australians would interpret liberty in the classical English sense, following John Stuart Mill (unknowingly), as doing our own good in our own way, without hurting others, and without too much government interference, much less imprisonment or other forms of violence", he said. Such notions, he argued, posed interesting dilemmas: "Should a person be free not to wear a

<hr>

[14] George Pell, "Catholicism and the Architecture of Freedom" (lecture, Customs House, Sydney, Australia, August 9, 1999), https://www.cis.org.au/wp-content/uploads/2015/07/op70.pdf.

seat belt in a car? Should a woman be free to have an abortion? Does the father of the child have any rights here? Does the embryo, foetus, human being, or unborn child (however defined) have any rights?... To what extent should governments be morally neutral or indifferent, leaving the strong to triumph and the poor to go to the wall?... Is business constrained by virtue as well as by economic necessity?"

From his earliest days as a young philosophy teacher, Pope John Paul II was preoccupied with freedom, Pell said, and its connection with truth, particularly the truths expressed in the natural moral law: "The Pope's own view is that there is no true conflict between freedom of choice and moral law. All Christians believe, despite Freud, that each human person has a rational intellect and a free will, rather than being 'a jungle chaos of hidden emotions and inner conflicts with an irrational character'." Human beings are free, Pell said, "to build slowly an integrated personality, without gross contradictions. But this is a lifelong spiritual quest." God-given law consists of truths meant to free people from subservience to their feelings and to help them make good moral choices.

Among the notions that had to be rejected firmly, he said, was the "Donald Duck heresy", which "rests squarely on the fallacy of overwhelming natural virtue. All you have to do to fulfil yourself is follow your natural impulses. Donald Duck always does this and always gets into trouble. It is a heresy which sanctifies mistakes, provided one is genuine, being oneself." The fact that he is a cartoon character should not blind Australians to the dangers around them, including from trends in North America that are often imported later.

Shortly before Pell's lecture, the thirtieth anniversary celebration of Woodstock in America had seen rioting, arson, looting of US$170,000 from a mobile bank, drug-taking, and gang rapes. This, Pell said, was an inevitable progression from the first Woodstock concert and love fest and as clear an indication of social disintegration as the Columbine High School massacre. Those who attended both Woodstocks had rejected their parents' values, he said. "This time it was the pacifism of the sixties which was spurned.... Either the restraints of thirty years ago were no longer effective; or the self-hatred, anger, and alienation of the destructive minority were stronger and were incited, rather than restrained, by the music. The last song of the gathering, as the ambulance sirens wailed through the smoke and the mayhem, boomed out from a group called 'Cracker'. Its chorus summed up the scene, 'Don't f— me up with peace and love.'"

The most controversial and widely reported aspect of the Acton lecture was Pell's contention that Catholics, in the face of subjectivism and relativism sweeping society, should abandon the notion of the primacy of conscience. "This has never been a Catholic doctrine (although this point generally cuts little ice)", he told the audience. Pell was sailing against the prevailing wind, but the pursuit of popularity was never his objective. If he polarized people, so be it: "Christ was crucified for his opinions," he later said. "It's not as though he was a disciple of Dale Carnegie and set out to massage the population into coming along with him."

Among Mass-goers, however, the archbishop found support. In a radio interview he said, "My job is to do my duty, is to serve the people, to preach the good news, and I'm quite confident (I'm out into two or three parishes a week) that amongst the Mass-goers there's very, very considerable support; no doubt about it in my mind, the majority support me."[15]

For all that, a few ultratraditionalists were dissatisfied with Pell, branded him a "liberal", and complained that he was too gentle in his shake-up of the Melbourne Archdiocese. Hard-liners who had looked forward to a clean-out of Church bureaucrats were disappointed. Father Anthony Fisher said there was an expectation early on that heads would roll. "Not a lot of that happened", he said.

> George had this view that people should not be made unemployed by the Church, so he never pushed anyone out, even the ones who were really shocking, and some of them were pretty rotten eggs. He wanted to keep the Church intact. There's a very generous, compassionate side of him, which I think people should know about. It's softly, softly catchy monkey rather than sack all the people at the top of the bureaucracies and make radical changes immediately. This is a very pastoral father figure, a man of very great charity.

At the other extreme, Pell's "new Church" critics, including some priests and nuns, labeled him "a man of the eighteenth century" or

[15] "Archbishop George Pell", *Encounter*.

"a reactionary trying to recreate the Church of the 1940s or 50s". Pell responded to such charges:

> I fully accept all the major teachings of the Second Vatican Council—collegiality, the great liturgical changes into the vernacular.... The doctrine that the State does not have the right to coerce an individual conscience. The other great advance of the Second Vatican Council in which I have been an active participant is ecumenism.... It's quite impossible to take the Church back anywhere, and it's never entered my head to take it back into the 1950s, although I think it's a convenient term of abuse for those who disagree with me.[16]

Philosopher Hayden Ramsay, who worked for Pell in Melbourne and later in Sydney, said that, compared with the diffident, media-shy Church leaders of the past, it was impossible to call Pell traditional in terms of his pastoral style. Just as priests and bishops traditionally learned the techniques of good preaching in the pulpit, Pell has been "media trained within an inch of his life", according to experienced public relations insiders. Ramsay said: "He has a genuine belief in the media; he's a very modern man. George's picture, I think, for the survival and thriving of the Church in the new century is that it has to be engaged in all the major social issues. It can't afford to go quiet and disappear into the rubble to become a remnant of the past, just running parishes and schools. So he's out there fighting about how we're going to deal with drugs, he's making statements on divorce which are absolutely provocative."

Ramsay sensed, when Pell employed him, that the archbishop would have enjoyed undertaking scholarly work such as writing for academic journals himself; he had the requisite academic training, but not the time. As a substitute, he was keen to have someone on his staff contributing to the cutting edge of philosophical analysis and writing.

More than a dozen Melbourne priests interviewed during the writing of this book, from the strongest Pell supporters to some of his most vehement critics, agreed that he was always well received by the vast majority of people as he visited two or three different parishes

---

[16] Barker, "Defender of the Faith".

a week in his time as archbishop. The late Father James Staunton, the Irish-born former pastor of Blackburn South, said Pell was "a towering figure intellectually who lifted the morale of Catholics". Staunton said people in the pews appreciated the archbishop's writings and television appearances in which he presented the Catholic point of view well and succinctly. Staunton said Pell went out of his way at clergy dinners and gatherings to show the archdiocese's Irish priests and those from other overseas countries that he valued their presence and work. "He was a great priests' man. The worst thing about his period as archbishop was when he left", Staunton said. "He was always in charge of the situation, but he had the brain and brawn to do it well."

Pell forged close links with all of Melbourne's main Catholic communities from overseas—the Italians, the Serbs and Croatians, the Coptics (from Egypt), the Maltese, and the Vietnamese. He predicted that "the grandchildren of today could see the first Vietnamese-Australian archbishop of Melbourne, and there will be many such ethnic bishops before then." In 1999, Pope John Paul II appointed Maltese-born Father Joseph Grech as Pell's auxiliary bishop.

In 2001, Frank O'Loughlin, the former pastor of Sandringham, while widely regarded as belonging to the Church's liberal wing and most definitely not in the Pell camp, cited positives and negatives from the Pell legacy in Melbourne. "I think the worst effect was a sense of disenfranchisement among people who didn't share his views, lack of consultation", O'Loughlin said. However, he praised Pell for acting "firmly and well" early in his term to deal with the scourge of paedophilia. And O'Loughlin believed Pell had no option but to turn the sash-wearers away from the altar. "It's extremely difficult and conflict is inevitable, but what else can an archbishop do?" O'Loughlin's view on that matter was largely echoed by priests across the spectrum, from the most conservative to the most liberal.

18

A Whirling Adventure

Across Australia, Mass-attendance surveys conducted for the Australian Catholic bishops showed a downward trend from 1994 to 2001 to an average attendance rate of 15.9 percent of nominal Catholics, with both Melbourne (17 percent) and Sydney (17.8 percent) doing slightly better than average, and three centres—Hobart, Darwin, and Geraldton—falling below 10 percent. By 2024, especially in the wake of the COVID pandemic, attendance figures were far worse.

In Pell's time as archbishop of Melbourne, it was already evident across the city's parishes that a sizeable proportion of those attending regularly are older people, well into their sixties and beyond. This trend has worsened. Blaming rampant materialism, encroaching secularism, or Sunday shopping for the atrocious trend is wrong. Those factors were probably even more strongly at play in the United States, where Pell knew that attendance rates were often 50 to 100 percent higher than in Australia.

On one side of the debate in Australia, some argue that turning around the poor attendance rates must involve building better, more welcoming Church communities and offering ever-more modern "relevant" liturgies and upbeat music that "speaks to young people". On the other hand, it is argued, no church will ever attract and maintain adherents by trying to outdo popular entertainment—substance, rather than style, must be the key. George Pell and others of his ilk see the problem primarily as a deep crisis of faith, one that cannot and will not be solved by gimmickry, peddling counterfeit compassion, or caving in to the prevailing mores of society in a quest for relevance. "Catholic lite has been advertised and sold in some places for years now", Pell said twenty years ago, "It has been a failure. Young Catholics won't buy it. The taste is off."

So off, in fact, that the Church has melted away as a force in the lives of the vast majority of Catholics in their twenties, thirties, and forties, who are disinclined to return to regular practice. Given the religious education offered in most Catholic schools from the 1970s onwards, many nominal Catholics know very little about the Church, her history, her doctrines and teachings, and have little foundation on which to build any kind of prayer or faith life. While some make a conscious, studied decision to embrace atheism or agnosticism, many more dabble in the various manifestations of New Age spiritualism and/or indifferentism, which expanded exponentially in the 1990s and the early years of the new millennium, suggesting a religious vacuum and a dormant but unsatisfied yearning for deeper meaning in many people.

That many nominal Catholics have opted for this path is hardly surprising. For much of the 1970s and 1980s, Catholic students spent many a religious education class sprawled around classroom floors listening to music such as John Denver's "Sunshine", Neil Diamond's "Be", or Simon and Garfunkel's "I Am a Rock". Relaxation tapes lulled us to sleep as we "discovered our inner selves" (or snatched a quick catnap to be ready to get on with subjects that mattered). Annual "retreats" were the ultimate joke in some schools—the chance for an illicit nip of Bacardi and Coke or a cigarette while wandering along the beach "contemplating" at retreat centres run by religious orders. Despite religious faith being heavily reliant upon intellect and will, students were rarely challenged but were subjected to group sessions of psychobabble and touchy-feely waffle. Paraliturgies (prayer sessions) were usually made up on the spot, usually focused on God made visible in the sun, the stars, and the ocean. The Mass, the Trinity, Our Lady, Church tradition and doctrine barely rated a mention. When many students gave up Mass as a form of teenage rebellion, they had little foundation to which to return.

Evangelizing young Catholics and drawing them directly into the life of the Church was one of Pope John Paul II's strongest endeavors. As an archbishop, George Pell adopted the same priority, extending his efforts well beyond the normal parish visitations and meetings with Confirmation classes. From the start of his episcopacy in Melbourne, Pell tackled the problem from the angle of religious education from kindergarten to year twelve by initiating the writing and production of a comprehensive set of religious education textbooks for schoolchildren, one for every year level. Within a few months of his appointment in 1996, he arranged for his old friend Peter Elliott to be released from his duties as an official in the Pontifical Council for the Family in Rome to head the project.

Religious education textbooks—especially well-written and well-presented ones—were almost nonexistent, not just in Australia, but also in many places overseas. Most of the available primary school booklets were flimsy in content, dull in appearance, and incomplete in many aspects of the faith. Teachers had to supplement them from whatever sources they could. In secondary schools, the situation was even worse, with religious education in many schools devoted to "comparative religion" courses (examining Christianity alongside Islam, Judaism, or Buddhism, for example) to the exclusion of Catholic doctrine.

"When people heard the word *textbooks*, they went ballistic, they were horrified", Elliott recalled. "It's not something that many people would have thought of immediately, but George used his pragmatic mind and went straight to a practical solution to a long-term problem." Elliott was determined to produce lively, colourful texts that were "not some boring old things from the dark ages". The archbishop was clear about what he wanted—a mixture of life, doctrine, and Scripture—with good artwork and pictures. After five years' work, half of the series To Know, Worship and Love was published in 2001, and the remainder in 2002. The books for each year level came with a detailed instruction guide for teachers. In-service training in using the materials was provided. The debate also presaged years of argument and problems among secular educational authorities over curriculum in such basic subjects as mathematics, English, science, and history, which, a quarter of a century later, remains largely unresolved.

Pell was satisfied that the completed text project met his main specifications. Generally, the works were well received. However, after years of freedom in selecting their own materials almost at will, some teachers, themselves graduates of a much flimsier system of religious instruction, bitterly resented being "dictated to" in terms of what to teach. The more militant Melbourne teachers threatened to (and for a time actually did) lock the books up in school cupboards and refused to use them.

Once they were in use, however, many teachers and parents found the books helpful and appealing to children. The early childhood books, subtitled "The Good Shepherd Experience", set the foundations for the child to start building a lifelong intimate relationship with God. Content for the older students is rigorous, detailed, and interesting, exploring, not only religion, but the place of the Church in the world historically and at the present time. The series makes good use of classic art reproductions, photographs, timelines, Scripture passages, and prayers. As its three-pronged name suggests, To Know, Worship and Love combines doctrinal learning with Scripture and prayer and an understanding of the place of religion in the everyday world as an influence for good.

Many priests in favour of the books argued then and still do now that they would be far more effective if the training of religious education teachers was similarly overhauled within the Australian Catholic University. Pell admitted that the university, which he did so much to create, did not live up to his hopes in terms of training teachers to impart solid Catholic teaching. The institution's independence, however, left bishops with little option to apply direct pressure. They could only hope to extract effective changes through encouragement and persuasion.

Pell also took his message directly to the schoolchildren in their tens of thousands. On September 5, 2000, he filled the Rod Laver Arena at the National Tennis Centre in Melbourne Park with high school students for a special Jubilee Mass. Archbishops rarely have the chance to speak directly and at length to a captive audience of twenty thousand sixteen- and seventeen-year-olds. Pell was determined to single out this group for special attention at a highly impressionable point in their lives. "As young Catholics today about to leave school and enter the wider world, the torch is being passed to you", he challenged them in his homily. His sermon that day was crafted around some of the themes and ideas of popular teenage culture:

> Many of you will have seen the film *Gladiator* set in the second century under Marcus Aurelius, one of the most enlightened of the pagan Roman emperors. The brutality of the amphitheatre was mirrored by the brutality of Roman daily life.
>
> My thesis is simple. Christ's teachings were like a river of life-giving water, nourishing and strengthening those who believed in

him in this hostile and savage environment. Christian faith, lived out
in daily life, produced a movement of cure and renewal responding
to the misery, chaos, fear, and oppression of daily life in Rome. They
came much closer to a civilization of life and love through Christian
living. The improvement was a result of Christian faith.

Sexual experimentation, he assured the students with candor, was
nothing new. Sexual life in ancient Rome, he said, "was a jungle
where the strong oppressed the weak. We know from the mosaics
of Pompeii that nothing was off limits; women, men, boys, girls, and
animals, and all this was portrayed on the walls of the bathhouses
before the eyes of even the youngest." So, did the early Christians go
with the flow, conform to the fashions of the time because everyone
was doing it? "Enough of them, the best of them, refused to do any
such thing. With invincible obstinacy, they stuck to Christ's teachings; they sometimes fell, as we do, but they persevered", Pell said.
Appealing to the students' strong belief in equality of the sexes, he
pointed out:

> The Christians taught a new concept of sexuality, not as an escape,
> not as a recreational right, not as another opportunity for the strong
> to oppress the weak; but sexuality linked to love; the love between
> a husband and wife, open to fertility, life, and children. Therefore, in a
> society where the male head of the household had a literal power of
> life and death over its members, where women were oppressed, almost
> legally powerless, Christianity required men to love and respect their
> wives as they respect their own bodies. This was a revolution.
>
> This was a society where men regularly fought each other, or ani-
> mals, to the death—and hundreds of thousands of spectators delighted
> in this spectacle. Rome was a city which rarely produced sufficient
> babies to keep the population stable and relied on regular migrations.
> These congregated in mutually antagonistic ghettos, and race riots
> were not uncommon. This was a society where abortion was com-
> monplace, as was infanticide, the killing of the newborn, especially if
> they were girls. There was a significant imbalance of the sexes. Pagan
> society did not want baby girls.

The Church offered kindness, charity, and a sense of community
to even the poorest, loneliest, and most marginalized people:

To cities filled with the poor and homeless, Christianity offered charity as well as hope. To cities filled with immigrants and strangers, the Christians offered community, friendship. To cities filled with orphans and widows, Christianity offered help and a wider sense of family. To cities torn with ethnic strife and riots, Christianity offered social solidarity. To cities faced with epidemics, fires, and earthquakes, Christianity offered effective nursing services. Even Galen, the most famous ancient physician, fled to his country house away from the plague. The Christians stayed and nursed their sick.

The long struggle of the Cross, with its hundredfold reward even in this life, "is passing into your hands", Pell told the students.

Continue to ponder and pray on the strange life of Jesus Christ, whose jubilee we celebrate.... Think on the achievements of the early Christians; of all the good Christians over 2,000 years. Remember always that they, like us, got their strength from this same Christ, the living water, which can bring life and health to any spiritual desert. Continue to drink from this stream, work and pray that it continues to bubble up in your heart too, taking you into eternal life. May you say "Yes" with courage and without hesitation when Christ calls you.

A few weeks later, a Jubilee Mass for younger children at Melbourne's Colonial Stadium broke the previous attendance record of 46,000 for an Australian Football League match. Television commentator and Collingwood team president Eddie McGuire welcomed the crowd of 70,000 year four to year ten students on November 15, a warm, sunny day, saying: "It wasn't the Bombers and it wasn't the Magpies that broke the attendance record. It was the Catholics!"

Four choirs and a 150-piece orchestra sounded as though they could raise the stadium's closed roof. Archbishop Pell, wearing gold vestments and magnified on large-screen televisions, concelebrated the Mass with his three auxiliary bishops. Governor General Sir William Deane, Deputy Prime Minister John Anderson, and Victorian Premier Steve Bracks were among the few adults invited. The theme of the Mass was "Who Is My Neighbour?" The archbishop, in his homily, challenged the children to seek to serve rather than to be served and spoke to them about the different "good Samaritans" who had befriended other Australians in the past. Younger children watched the Mass on television back at their schools.

Pell also staged large get-togethers with children every Saint Patrick's Day. The cathedral would be packed for Mass, followed by a picnic lunch in Fitzroy Gardens. On March 17, 2001, he told the children gathered in Saint Patrick's Cathedral:

> Our country of Australia has been compared to a beautiful patterned carpet of different colours, like a wonderful tapestry. Another comparison is to say Australia is like a happy neighbourhood, many different groups of people, minding their own business, but getting on well together. But one of the most beautiful and colourful pieces of the carpet is our Catholic community, to which we all belong. I hope each and every one of you is proud to be a Catholic; proud to say, "Yes, I believe in the one true God. Yes, I believe in Jesus, who died for us. Yes, I am proud to belong to the Catholic Church, which is led by the pope and bishops." So today on this Saint Patrick's Day we want you youngsters to join us older people in thanking God for all the good things we have in Australia. I want each one of you to realise, to feel that you belong to a Church which has contributed a lot to Australian history and Australian society, and I want you this morning to decide that you too will do your bit, when you grow up, to keep Australia good and make it a better place.

First-hand encounters with young Catholics were one of the hallmarks of the long pontificate of John Paul II. World Youth Days were his idea, drawn partly from his own excursions with young people in Poland when he was a young priest and partly from the enthusiastic reception he received from young people in a Paris park during his visit to the city in 1980. The first World Youth Day in Rome in 1985 attracted 250,000 visitors, and the events—which extend over a week—grew from there, being held in a different venue every two years in cities in Europe, South America, North America, and Asia.

From the vigor and strength of his early pontificate to the infirmities of old age and ill health, John Paul II was the star attraction of each gathering, arriving by popemobile or helicopter to chanting and singing. These unique events, usually held in the Northern Hemisphere summer, are more pilgrimage than holiday and generally involve extreme discomfort—crowds of several hundred thousand, sometimes several million people, blazing heat, long walks to vast outdoor arenas, pelting rain, mud, sleeping outdoors or in church halls, and a mixture of chaos and precise organisation. Participants pray together, participate in vast outdoor Masses, sing and dance together, enjoy each other's company across language and cultural barriers, receive catechetical instruction from various bishops from around the world, and explore different parts of the Catholic world. The pope's closing Mass of the 1995 gathering in Manila attracted what was estimated as the largest crowd in history—between five and seven million people. As well as being an international celebration of youth and Catholicism, World Youth Day, and the efforts the young people make to raise money to pay their way there, is designed to strengthen and deepen their long-term bonds with the Church. As Pope John Paul explained in his apostolic letter preparing for the upcoming Jubilee in 2000:

> The future of the world and the Church belongs to the *younger generation*, to those who, born in this century, will reach maturity in the next, the first century of the new millennium. *Christ expects great things from young people*, as he did from the young man who asked him: "What good deed must I do, to have eternal life?" (*Mt* 19:16).... If they succeed in following the road which he points out to them, they will have the joy of making their own contribution to his presence in the next century and in the centuries to come, until the end of time: "Jesus is the same yesterday, today and for ever".[1]

More than one thousand young Australians were among the two million young people from 120 nations who attended the Jubilee 2000 World Youth Day in Rome. For that event, George Pell, his three auxiliary bishops, and nine young priests led the Melbourne contingent of four hundred, the largest from any Australian diocese. Around 250 members of the group left Australia early for a twelve-day pilgrimage in the footsteps of Christ, from Bethlehem to Golgotha, en route to Rome. Some, including Pell, found it a more powerful and moving experience than the time in Rome afterwards.

In the Holy Land, the group stayed in two places—in Bethlehem, birthplace of Jesus, and at Daganya Kibbutz in the north of Israel near the Sea of Galilee. Each day began with prayer and Scripture

---

[1] John Paul II, Apostolic Letter *Tertio Millennio Adveniente* (November 10, 1994), no. 58.

readings about the places being visited, and daily Mass was celebrated at one of the many sacred sites that figured in the life of Jesus. The group travelled around on four buses, with priests and bishops assisting the tour guides. They visited the Incarnation Grotto inside the Nazareth Basilica, the place where Mary learned she was to bear a son she would name Jesus; Christ's birthplace—the Church of the Nativity in Bethlehem; Mount Tabor, site of Christ's Transfiguration before three of his apostles; Cana—site of Christ's miracle with the wine at a wedding feast and where the married pilgrims renewed their wedding vows; Qumran, where the Dead Sea scrolls were discovered; Caesarea—where Christ founded His Church "upon this rock"; the mount of the Beatitudes; the Dead Sea, where they had a swim; the old city of Jerusalem; and the Jordan River, where Christ was baptised and where members of the group renewed their own baptismal promises.

Pell remembered praying quietly in the darkened Gethsemane church, with the young people spread around him, in the place where tradition has Jesus suffering the agony in the garden. His favourite memory was of the choir lads informally leading the group in singing "Were You There When They Crucified My Lord?" around the cross in the basilica at Golgotha, site of the crucifixion.

> For 20 or 30 minutes the group sang as we passed the Cross and waited to enter the Tomb. It was a golden moment. The group sang again at the Cenacle, the traditional venue for the Last Supper, while we had a beautiful solo, deep down in the jail room under Caiaphas' house, where Jesus might have spent time before his crucifixion....
>
> It is interesting to ponder why the good God chose such a hot, difficult spot as the homeland for his Chosen People. And a small nation surrounded by larger, more advanced and powerful neighbours, who were often at war. Perhaps to try to teach us the lesson that growth and survival come from God, not from our efforts.[2]

Many of the Melbourne pilgrims who travelled overseas with Pell were tertiary students. Others took leave from their jobs; a few were married couples (one woman was six months pregnant with her

---

[2] Reminiscences drawn from *Testimonies to the Glory of God: World Youth Day Pilgrimage AD2000*, ed. Helen Hedigan (Melbourne: Buxton Printers, 2000).

GEORGE CARDINAL PELL

second child); and quite a few were still at school. At age fourteen, twins Brendan and Brad Rowswell (Brad, a Liberal Party member of Parliament is now the shadow treasurer for the State of Victoria), both altar servers from Beaumaris in Melbourne, were the youngest in the group: "Highlights of the Holy Land for both of us, we agreed, were the Wailing Wall of the Temple, the Church of the Nativity, and finally both the spiritual experience and watching the archbishop come down a waterslide."

The waterslide was in a park beside the Sea of Galilee, where Jesus often walked with his disciples. In searing hot weather, it was a welcome sight for everyone, including the archbishop, who did not hesitate to follow his disciples in tumbling down. Father Mark Withoos, ordained a priest by Pell in July 1999 after studies at Corpus Christi College, Melbourne, and Propaganda Fide, was one of the priests on the trip. He remembered Pell being very open to the young people and them warming to him: "He's very fatherly."

In Italy, the Melbourne pilgrims stayed in parishes about twenty-five miles outside Rome at Ostia and Vitinia. Pell, an old hand in Rome, said the city had never seen anything like the two million young people who crammed in for World Youth Day with Pope John Paul II.

The police chief put it nicely on TV—"From what magic box did these happy young people come?" Droves of them swarmed all over Rome, usually walking in groups, chatting, laughing and singing; greeting one another across ancient enmities and language barriers. There were no arrests; remarkable patience and good humour in the heat; no drugs.

On the Circus Maximus, where Christians were martyred, hundreds of priests heard confessions every day, and platoons of young helpers prepared their peers to confess properly. Hundreds of thousands went to confession, the Sacrament of Reconciliation, including most of the Melbourne pilgrims. Four hundred thousand attended the Stations of the Cross at the Colosseum. Nearly every registered pilgrim queued up patiently in Saint Peter's Square to go through the Holy Door, past Peter enthroned (on a statue near the main altar) and around his tomb. Some waited for over an hour in the heat and were doused with freezing water when the authorities put the fire hoses on them. Many groups put on street concerts, watched by hundreds at a time.

It could probably only have happened in Rome, but August 15, the feast of Our Lady's Assumption into heaven, was traditionally a public holiday, and in spite of two million visitors in town, the authorities stuck to the usual public holiday timetable—which meant almost no transport. Marc Florio, the director of Catholic youth ministry in Melbourne, and about forty other young people found themselves stranded at night in the centre of Rome, unable to return to their billet in a church hall in a parish twenty-five miles outside the city. They did the only thing they could and phoned the archbishop where he was staying at a clergy house near the Piazza Navona. "The archbishop opened the doors, and thirty or forty of us slept around the apartment on the floor, under the tables, on the couches." Marc said the young people on the trip found the archbishop "blokey, warm, down to earth, and not up there in an ivory tower".

Archbishop Pell, Archbishop Desmond Connell of Dublin, and Cardinal Edward Cassidy of the Pontifical Council for Promoting Christian Unity provided three sessions of religious instruction for the Australian pilgrims. Father Paul Stuart, who was then the director of vocations, took many of the Melbourne group on a guided tour of Rome, with Father Stuart celebrating Mass in the crypt of Saint Peter's Basilica, followed by breakfast in a café along the Via della Conciliazione, where just a few hours later more than one million people would crowd in to see the pope officially open World Youth Day in Saint Peter's Square.

Seeing the pope, even amidst a crowd of a million in Saint Peter's or two million at Tor Vegata University on the outskirts of the city, was the highlight of the week in Rome for most of the pilgrims. That was in spite of the twelve-mile walk to Tor Vergata in 104°F heat to see Pope John Paul II arrive in a white helicopter for a vigil of prayer and rejoicing, followed by fireworks and a giant outdoor "sleepover". The pope returned the following morning for Mass to complete the World Youth Day.

Towards the end of Pell's time as archbishop of Melbourne, one of his more controversial moves was his inviting Opus Dei (Work of God) to work in the archdiocese. Opus Dei, founded in 1928 by Spanish priest Monsignor Josemaría Escrivá, is a predominantly lay Catholic organisation that had grown phenomenally both in membership and in property. Pope John Paul II strengthened its hand by making it a personal prelature—meaning that, administratively,

it answers, not to local bishops, but to its own bishop and head. It
began working in Sydney in 1963.

The first that many Melbourne Catholics, including many priests,
knew of Opus Dei's entry into the archdiocese was an article in the
Sunday *Age* on April 1, 2001, which said Pell had invited Opus Dei
to supply a priest to run Saint Mary's Star of the Sea parish in West
Melbourne. The parish church, one of the largest in Australia that is
not a cathedral, was in dire need of restoration but had great potential to be restored, which was accomplished with expertise and style.
Many were far from happy with Pell's invitation to Opus Dei. Even
parish priests regarded as "conservative"—men who agreed with Pell
on 99 percent of other matters—expressed reservations.

Pell acknowledged that Opus Dei was "not everyone's cup of tea"
but made no apologies for its entry into Melbourne during his time as
archbishop. "I invited them, I thought they were a good thing, they're
heading in the right direction", he said. Pell was well aware of the criticisms of Opus Dei, including those of former members, and strongly
rejected any suggestion that members had joined Opus Dei with anything less than full, informed consent. He did not share the Opus Dei
asceticism, but neither did he hold it against them; he believed that their
Spanish flavour should be welcomed and tolerated within the broad
Church in Australia. He found Opus Dei members "very strict, very
disciplined but friendly and certainly not aggressive". He praised their
loyalty to the Church's teachings and their deep, sincere spirituality. Pell
agreed with those who saw Opus Dei as taking up, in modern times
and in a different way, the role that Ignatius Loyola formed the Jesuits
to fulfill in the sixteenth century—that of an elite, self-disciplined, and
self-sacrificing "spiritual army", fiercely loyal to the papacy. Later, as
archbishop of Sydney, Pell said he agreed with the stand taken by the
late Cardinal Basil Hume of Westminster, who banned Opus Dei from
recruiting members under the age of eighteen. "If I thought they were
bullying young people, I would stop it, yes", he said.

The article about Opus Dei's move into Melbourne appeared at a
time of heightened media interest in the Catholic Church. Just a few
days earlier, on Monday, March 26, 2001, the apostolic nuncio in
Canberra, Archbishop Francesco Canalini, had made an announcement unprecedented in the history of the Church in Australia: "His
Holiness Pope John Paul II has accepted the Resignation of His Eminence Edward Bede Clancy for reasons of age and has appointed as

Archbishop of Sydney His Grace Most Reverend George Pell, until now Archbishop of Melbourne. The news will be made public in Rome on Monday, 26 March, 2001 at 12 noon, Rome time."

The promotion of the seventh archbishop of Melbourne to be the eighth archbishop of Sydney surprised many of Pell's supporters and opponents. On ABC radio, former Human Rights Commissioner Chris Sidoti told *AM*: "The church in Sydney is headed back to the Middle Ages." The normally talkative ABC religious affairs commentator and former priest Paul Collins said: "I'm speechless."

Letters and faxes of support arrived at Pell's office and home by the hundred, and talk-back radio lines in both Sydney and Melbourne ran hot. The retired archbishop of Hobart, Eric D'Arcy, admitted he was stunned because he regarded Melbourne, a larger archdiocese than Sydney, as a more important job. Numerically, it is. The Archdiocese of Melbourne, with one million Catholics, had 232 parishes compared with Sydney's 137 parishes. Sydney, however, is the oldest and most senior archdiocese in Australia, with its archbishops traditionally elevated, within a few years of their appointment, to the College of Cardinals. Because George Pell was only fifty-five when he was appointed archbishop of Melbourne, Catholics reasonably expected that he would lead their archdiocese for two decades— unless he was promoted to Rome as head of a Vatican congregation such as Education or Evangelization of Peoples. Rumours of an imminent appointment to both positions circulated in Melbourne before he was announced as the new archbishop of Sydney.

Long-time Vatican watcher Desmond O'Grady shrewdly observed in *The Age* that

> George Pell was almost certainly hand-picked by Pope John Paul II for the job of Catholic Archbishop of Sydney. The reasons the controversial cleric was chosen, however, may be more complex than has so far been acknowledged.
>
> Pell fits the model for new church leaders that the Pope has been applying to key appointments. And conservatism is not the prerequisite for promotion. The most important quality he seems to seek is strength of personality....
>
> The Vatican wants leaders who will make their presence felt in and beyond their sees. Many of the appointees are conservative— but not all of them. But the point about all of them is that, while you may disagree with what they say, you know they are there. The

Vatican believes Catholics generally are far less alienated from the church's thinking than its middle management and the media convey. This assumption seems to derive partly from the reception John Paul receives on his overseas trips, particularly to the United States.

Those assumptions suggested the Vatican was seeking bishops who were vigorous and forceful, traditional but slightly populist, conservative as regards doctrine and discipline, but well abreast of current social issues.

Pell's appointment also needed to be seen against the background of Vatican concern about the Church in Australia, such as the low rate of Mass attendance and vocations and the survival and Catholic character of institutions such as schools and hospitals. It believed, correctly, that Pell was the best hope for tackling those problems.

On the day after the announcement, Pell spent a full day in Sydney with Cardinal Clancy, holding a media conference and giving interviews. Marc Florio, director of the Catholic youth ministry in Melbourne, recalled that Pell had a prearranged meeting with young people in North Melbourne for that night: "He was the number one news item for that day, and everyone wanted time with him. Yet despite all this, the archbishop rushed back to Melbourne for his 7:00 P.M. meeting with young people. He looked exhausted, yet he enthusiastically and energetically participated in the meeting. The fact that he did not cancel the meeting (which he could easily have done and all those present would have totally understood) certainly demonstrated his commitment to young people."

Tributes—and more than a few tears—flowed around the Melbourne Archdiocese as the archbishop was bid farewell by his friends and flock at a special Mass in Saint Patrick's Cathedral and a variety of social gatherings. Youth worker Ana Snjaric spoke for the young people of the archdiocese at their farewell party for Pell:

> No matter how busy he was he always seemed to make time for us; whether it was for youth leader dinners, joining us quietly in prayer at the Holy Hour on Thursdays or playing pool with the cathedral choirboys. None of it went unnoticed.
>
> Many people talk about the youth of today but few actually do something to help young people and encourage them to love and actively participate in the Church. He helped us to be the best we can be. Archbishop Pell is an exception.

Pell thanked his priests for their faith, leadership, and service at the annual Mass of the Oils (where the oils to be used during the coming year for Baptism, Confirmation, Ordination, and Anointing of the Sick are blessed in the cathedral), with a large number of priests in attendance. "God has chosen us, gratuitously (I am sometimes tempted to think, personally, perhaps a little bit capriciously), to be his ambassadors, to act as his representatives especially through the sacraments. We must never forget the mystical, supernatural dimension of our priestly identity and work, which is nourished by our lives of action, liturgically and in service, but especially by our regular personal prayer." He also urged the priests to maintain unity. "The maintenance of the public unity and mutual respect of the clergy is the first external defence of this spiritual treasure and that public unity should never be breached in any circumstances."

That comment was especially pointed. Just eleven days earlier, in the media frenzy generated by Pell's promotion to Sydney, a column in *The Age* claimed that the Vatican II generation of priests (men then in their fifties) were speaking derisively

of a group of conservative younger priests they call the "Spice Girls", who, they say, have been loyal Pell supporters and have acquired considerable influence in the archdiocese. Asked what the term means, most will reply with an embarrassed "no comment". Others are coyly suggestive: "The 'Spice Girls'? They're the group who prance around George when he's at the altar in Saint Patrick's." But some say it bluntly: "They're a bevy of younger clergy who are strongly supportive of George Pell." They're gay—I'm speaking about orientation, not practice—and they are very focused on elaborate ritual and dressing up in clerical garb, in a way that has not hitherto been typical among Australian Catholic priests. The priests who complain about the "Spice Girls" insist that they are not motivated by homophobia. They say their objection is to what they see as the group's undue influence in the Melbourne archdiocese, and they claim that the number of gays in the clergy is now disproportionately high.[3]

It is not unusual for strong public figures to be the subject of snide innuendos, and Pell was no exception. The troublemakers behind

[3] Ray Cassin and Ian Munro, *The Age*, March 31, 2001.

such rumours often hide from scrutiny behind a cloak of anonymity, and so it was with the priest or priests who gave the "Spice Girls" story to *The Age*.

In another era, that catty wisecrack, with no substantiating evidence, might have produced an uncomfortable laugh or two and been quickly forgotten by everyone but the person who thought it up. Priests' nicknames for each other are nothing new—in preparing this book I heard about or encountered "Weed", "Monsignor Grunge", "Precious", and "Smoky Pete" to name just a few. While the "Spice Girls" wisecrack might have started out as an in-club joke, the public leaking of the moniker, in a tense climate, after years of devastating revelations about clerical paedophilia, millions of dollars in payouts, and the priesthood's reputation in tatters, was going to cause havoc. It is hard to conclude anything other than that it was spiteful, orchestrated to wreak maximum damage to the reputations of Pell and the priests cooperating with his program to restore dignity to the celebration of the sacraments, which is probably why the perpetrator of the insult has never put his hand up.

In the following months, the matter was picked up by various pro-gay websites with claims that "progressive" gay priests "worked very hard in their parishes", suggesting, perhaps, that the leak stemmed from that direction. But in the poisonous atmosphere that the "Spice Girls" article engendered, it was impossible to know.

Apart from a lot of angst, the "Spice Girls" crack produced some banter among some of Pell's priest friends who teased each other about who was Posh, Baby, Scary, and so on—and who qualified as "Old Spice". Most priests, including those not involved, were incensed at the cowardly attack from a fellow priest. At a priests' meeting shortly afterwards, Pell was "as passionate as I've ever heard him", according to Anthony Fisher.

Father Fisher, who doubted very much that he was one of those being targeted (but as the "Spice Girls" were not named, he could not be certain), was impressed by one of the younger priests who spoke at the meeting. "He wouldn't have been regarded as one of the 'Spice Girls', but he felt his whole generation had been attacked by fellow priests." The solemn Mass in Melbourne, said every Sunday by the archbishop, was an important weekly occasion, Fisher explained, and if younger priests concelebrated with the archbishop, it was a positive sign that they wanted to be there. In fact, very few priests concelebrated on most Sundays at the cathedral because they were busy in their parishes. The "Spice Girl" slur, Fisher argued at the time, was akin to an "abortion" mentality among some middle-aged priests in regard to younger priests. Despite years of a "contraceptive" mentality in regard to vocations, where little was done to encourage new recruits, young men had begun coming forward again, only to be tarred with the "Spice Girls" brush. "Some of the priests want no children, no new generation. We've actually got the vocations; we've got the young priests. Now we want to run them out, to get rid of them."

The matter flared again on the *Sunday* television program in a profile of Pell just before he took office in Sydney, about a month after the initial article. He made his anger clear: "I thought it was most insulting and most misleading and a gratuitous slur. I totally reject those anonymous sorts of comments."[4]

The irony of pointing the finger at Pell and his friends in regards to "bells and smells" is that many of his friends, including Fisher and Peter Elliott, an internationally respected author on liturgy, had often quipped that "George doesn't have a liturgical bone in his body" and sometimes has trouble remembering where to stand, where to put his hands, and many of the other complex rubrics of Catholic liturgy. "Just like Pope John Paul II, it doesn't interest him", Fisher said in 2002.

By comparison with some of the elaborate, solemn High Masses in overseas churches, the 11:00 A.M. High Mass at Saint Patrick's could seem a little simple and flat, which suggests that the perpetrator of the "Spice Girls" label has seen little of the universal Church and is hampered by a limited, parochial vision. While an effort was made with the singing and other aspects of the liturgy at Saint Patrick's, the participants during Pell's time as archbishop were dignified and prayerful, certainly not "prancing". They wore the standard garb of any priest saying Mass—white alb over black trousers and shirt, with a standard chasuble in the liturgical colour of the day over the alb.

Sensitive to the comments sometimes made about elaborate "bells and smells" liturgies, Pell said that early in his episcopacy, he instructed

[4] *Sunday* was broadcast nationally by Channel Nine on Sunday mornings from 1981 to 2008.

the cathedral liturgists to simplify the trimmings at the High Mass. It seemed extraordinary that an archbishop needed to have such concerns, but the damage done anonymously by an ordained priest, apparently with decades of experience, in giving the "Spice Girls" story to the newspaper was a telling insight into the tensions gripping the Church.

At the archbishop's Easter Sunday High Mass at Saint Patrick's Cathedral, his last Sunday Mass presiding at Saint Patrick's, protesters from the Queer group staged a farewell of their own outside the cathedral grounds, hanging nooses on the fence palings and chanting for Pell to "go to hell" as he greeted Easter Sunday churchgoers leaving the church. Pell, as always after Mass, stood on the cathedral steps. His back was to the rally as he exchanged Easter greetings with members of the congregation, who at one point competed with the demonstrators with three cheers for the archbishop.

George Pell bade farewell to Melbourne's one million Catholics in a "thank you" letter in *Kairos*, the archdiocesan newspaper, in which he identified the faith practice of the young and middle-aged as the Church's greatest pastoral challenges. "I am more convinced than ever of the beauty and usefulness of the first rite of penance, perhaps because of my weekly stint in the box at the cathedral", he wrote. "The pilgrimage to the Holy Land and Rome for the World Youth Day last year brought me encouragement and inspiration, as did the number and quality of the Melbourne seminarians and young priests. There are many good memories."

For his Mass of thanksgiving at Saint Patrick's Cathedral on the evening of April 24, Pell chose the same scriptural passages that had been read at his Mass of reception at the Exhibition Building five years earlier. "God writes straight in crooked lines", he told the congregation. "There is a lesson here for all of us; to use whatever time we have, because we can never be sure how much time remains to us. *Carpe diem*—seize the day. We must seize our opportunities for prayer and for action, rather than relying on good intentions to be implemented tomorrow!"

Whatever other mistakes he might have made as archbishop, Pell said, he had not erred in placing Christ at the centre of his efforts and preaching; Christ, not as another good man, a prophet, a martyr, although He is all these things, but Christ the God-man, our

Redeemer and Savior. "There have even been one or two voices in the Catholic community who would reduce Christ to the most perfect human. These have to be resisted, and I am sure they will continue to be resisted, because they destroy the special claims of Christianity. Our Lord would not be our Redeemer, but another brave hero, like many thousands of other men and women. If Christ is not risen, Paul wrote, then our religion is in vain; we are dupes, unfortunate, mistaken do-gooders."

Referring to a passage he admired by G. K. Chesterton in his 1908 book *Orthodoxy*, Pell concurred with the English convert that orthodoxy never takes the tame course or accepts the conventions. It is always easy, Chesterton said, "to let the age have its head; the difficult thing is to keep one's own.... To have fallen into any of those open traps of error and exaggeration would indeed have been simple." Avoiding such traps as archbishop of Melbourne, Pell said, had been, to quote Chesterton's eloquence, "one whirling adventure; and in my vision the heavenly chariot flies thundering through the ages, the dull heresies sprawling and prostrate, the wild truth reeling but erect."

19

Archbishop of Sydney

Pell was liturgically installed as archbishop of Sydney in Saint Mary's Cathedral, in the heart of the city, on the evening of May 10, 2001. His reputation had preceded him, and that night, the cathedral, like the city itself, was abuzz with expectation, some excitement, and some derision. Saint Mary's, not surprisingly, was packed with three thousand people, including Australia's head of state and Queen Elizabeth II's representative, Governor-General Sir William Deane; Prime Minister John Howard, who was to become a good friend of Pell's; Opposition Leader Kim Beazley; and leaders and members of other denominations and non-Christian religions.

Outside, a children's choir sang with joy, just yards from a vocal group of homosexual-rights and pro-abortion protestors howling, hissing, and waving placards: "George Pell, go to hell." As the mob lurched forward, three were arrested. This was a big story, and the media were out in force. Sydney is one of the world's most racy, secular cities, home of the annual gay Mardi Gras, a reputation Pell would address in his homily.

At his first press conference in Sydney after the announcement of his appointment, expectations had been running high about what Pell might say about the city's famous annual gay Mardi Gras parade. Eager for a quotable response, and expecting the archbishop would admonish the event, members of the Sydney media were bowled over with laughter by Pell's deadpan, witty response when quizzed about the event: "I don't think we'll be entering a float."

Most of the laity in the pews were delighted. So were many of the three hundred priests, although a few agreed with the disgruntled Church bureaucrat who had grumbled to the press: "Melbourne's gain is Sydney's loss." Most of the Sisters, hard to pick out in ordinary clothes with no religious insignia, were wary, although the few Sisters dressed in any semblance of habits were happy. Seated around the altar, the faces of most of the fifty Australian bishops present were inscrutable, although a couple could not hide their hostility. More than half, certainly, would have preferred to see somebody else taking on the role, either a liberal or an innocuous functionary who would not rock any boats. Pell was neither.

At almost six feet three inches tall, with an athletic strength that matched his height, and a formidable intellect and personality, Pell was respected throughout the universal Church. Pope John Paul II regarded him as one of the leading English-speaking bishops of the world. He was also a highly controversial figure, recognized by many Australians, few of whom lacked an opinion about him. Pell's ideological enemies, those determined that secular humanism would have the last word in Australian public life, recognized in him a formidable, credible opponent—a caliber of Church leader not seen in Australia for half a century.

As well as five years behind him as an archbishop in Melbourne, Pell, then fifty-nine, had nine years' experience as an auxiliary bishop, three years as a seminary rector, eleven years at the helm of Aquinas College in Ballarat, and plenty of pastoral experience. He had just completed ten years as a member of the Vatican's Congregation for the Doctrine of the Faith in Rome.

He had come through some enormous battles—and, although nobody realised it that evening, a few more horrendous ones lay over the horizon, the kinds of battles that remind Catholics very sharply that Christ reserves some of His heaviest crosses for His closest friends.

For a few minutes before his installation Mass, George Pell summoned his reserves of interior silence, shut out the atmosphere around him, and faced his Lord in the Blessed Sacrament, asking for the grace he needed to undertake the job. Only a handful of priests, seated in the front pews beside the back of the main altar, saw the tall, impressive figure at close quarters as he knelt in his soutane and faced the tabernacle. One priest recalled: "For those few minutes it was just George and God, alone. The cathedral might as well have been empty; he was oblivious to it all. He was so intent on praying to our Lord, so still."

The Gospel reading at George Pell's installation Mass was not a scriptural passage generally chosen for such occasions. It was Saint John's story of the woman taken in adultery, whose accusers were told by Christ that he who was without sin should cast the first stone. One by one the accusers slunk away, until only the woman and Christ were left, and He did not condemn her, but told her to go and sin no more. In the days leading up to the Mass, much of the media coverage of the archbishop's promotion had centred on how Sydney, with its exaggerated reputation for brashness, hedonism, and a strong gay culture, would respond to the new archbishop. "In contrast with these scriptural perspectives, one or two local writers seem to suggest that sin is a recent Sydney invention", Pell remarked in his inaugural sermon. " 'Sin City' or 'Tinsel Town' has a contemporary local resonance! However, human weakness also flourishes in other parts of Australia, and the beautiful passage from Saint John's Gospel reminds us that human perfidy is as old as the Garden of Eden." The Gospel story, he said, represented a "supreme teaching moment highlighting the delicate balance between Our Lord's justice in not condoning the sin and his mercy in forgiving the sinner." God would always wipe the slate clean for genuine sorrow and amendment.

As in Melbourne, Pell made the recruitment and nurturing of vocations to the priesthood a key priority. "Without priests our parishes will wither and die", he said. "These stark realities should not be hidden from young Catholics, from young parents. A priest-less parish is a contradiction in terms, because there is no parish without the sacraments, without Baptism, Eucharist, Reconciliation. We should pray tonight that in the years ahead a sufficient number of young men will be on a wavelength that enables them to hear Christ's call to the priesthood, to join those gallant priests expending themselves in faithful service and prayer in the archdiocese and elsewhere."

Only a few of those in Saint Mary's that night, and even fewer watching the Consistory in Saint Peter's Square two years later, in October 2003—George Pell's family and close friends—knew what a reluctant starter he had been for a life in the Church. Despite a professional football contract at age 18 and the prospect of a lucrative career in law or medicine, he had taken a leap of faith, sensing that God wanted him to dedicate his life to doing His work.

Many Sydney Catholics had had their first close look at their new archbishop the Sunday after his liturgical reception, when reporter John Lyons presented a detailed profile on Channel Nine's *Sunday* program. Lyons put a number of descriptions to the archbishop for his reactions:

LYONS: A bully Bishop.

PELL: I think that's misleading and insulting, and there's no evidence to justify it whatsoever.

LYONS: A right-wing fundamentalist.

PELL: I describe myself as radical centre. I'm very committed to the use of reason. I believe in some fundamentals, but that's quite different from being a fundamentalist.

LYONS: A homophobe.

PELL: No, I reject that completely. In the Archdiocese of Melbourne, I've regularly spoken with many homosexuals. We have two hospices for HIV victims. I've visited both of those regularly. I'm certainly no homophobe.

LYONS: A careerist.

PELL: No, not in the slightest.

LYONS: The pope's man in Australia.

PELL: I hope so.

LYONS: A misogynist.

PELL: No, that's insulting. As a matter of fact, the person who most recently made that claim had to withdraw the claim that she'd alleged ... I'd made about women's ordination. No, I'm certainly not a misogynist.

LYONS: She withdrew under threat of legal action, did she?

PELL: She did, yes. Because I think a fair comment is fair comment, but if people are purveying lies, I think they should be challenged.

How could the only man ever to hold the reins of both the Melbourne and Sydney Archdioceses, who many predicted, correctly, would go on to head a Roman congregation as a cardinal prefect, be anything other than an ambitious careerist? In the secular world, ambition is a virtue rather than a vice, but Pell was adamant that he never had any ambitions to rise through the clerical ranks and said he was "extremely surprised" to be asked to become archbishop of Sydney. Years earlier, however, one of Pell's closest priest friends recalled him pointing out that "ambition is not a bad thing."

Interviewed in 2001, Pell acknowledged that people sometimes
speculated that he took the public positions he did during the late
1980s and early 1990s in an effort to distinguish himself from the
other bishops in a carefully orchestrated plan to secure promotion.
"The overwhelming probability would be exactly the opposite", he
said. "Moreover, my basic perspectives are in fundamental continuity
with my teaching and writings at Aquinas and as seminary rector."

But did not those points of difference set him apart just at a time
when the Church was changing under the influence of Pope John
Paul II?

"It wasn't changing here in Australia at the time", Pell said.

Surely it was clear that it would, given the trend in the United
States at the time and the appointment of strong pro-Roman prelates
like Cardinal John O'Connor in New York?

"I didn't think in those terms", Pell said. "I worried that the
Church in Australia was slipping from bad to worse, and that was
the basis of my decisions to point out a few things."

Pell was fully cognizant of the daily struggle of priests in dioceses
who continued to defend the fullness of Church teaching and refused
to sell out in the face of pressures to trivialise it or reduce the Christian message to a bland, lowest-common-denominator level in pursuit of peace at any price. He had been prepared, he said, to spend his
entire working life as a parish priest in rural Victoria or as a Church
academic and enjoy it.

In Sydney, Pell generally visited two or more parishes a week,
sometimes for Confirmations and sometimes for two-day midweek
visitations, where he spoke to different parish groups and schoolchildren, followed by a return visit for the Saturday evening vigil Mass.
In recent years, some Australian Catholic dioceses had moved to confirm children before their First Communion at age eight, restoring
the original sequence of the sacraments of initiation: Baptism, Confirmation, Eucharist. Pell understood the theory behind it, but in
practice he regarded it as a pastoral disaster. He strongly preferred
delaying Confirmation until the final year of primary school, or even
into secondary school, when candidates were better able to grasp the
significance of the sacrament. The detailed instruction given at that
time is designed to boost the candidates' faith for the years ahead. As
an auxiliary bishop in Melbourne, Pell always made time to meet and

instruct Confirmation classes before conferring the sacrament. As an archbishop, this was much more difficult.

As he did in Melbourne, Pell celebrated High Mass most Sunday mornings in his cathedral, except for when he was visiting a parish. He also said the evening youth Mass at the cathedral once a month. On weekdays, if not visiting a parish or school for Mass, he offered the Holy Sacrifice in his private chapel, on the first floor of the cathedral presbytery. That building, erected during Cardinal Edward Clancy's reign, looks like a neo-gothic showpiece: its highly polished downstairs reception rooms more stylish than homey. Some people would feel they were in a goldfish bowl, with large mirrored windows looking to the cathedral surrounds.

Pell's rooms upstairs were less lavish but more comfortable. They were dominated by the bookshelves holding his vast, well-thumbed library (around three thousand volumes by 2001 and growing), which covered theology, philosophy, literature, history, and much else. Other shelves housed the escapist, detective stories Pell enjoyed. He had read most of Agatha Christie and P.D. James and all of Frederick Forsyth and John le Carré. His other favourites included Brian Moore, an Irishman who emigrated to Canada, the English Catholic novelist Piers Paul Read, Alan Furst's books set around the start of World War II, Australia's Christopher Koch, and poet Les Murray. His perennial favourite poets were Wilfred Owen, killed in action at age twenty-five shortly before the 1918 Armistice, and Australia's James McAuley. Piled up around the rooms were the theological, philosophical, and social commentary journals he read avidly, including the *Spectator*, the *New York Review of Books*, the *Times Literary Supplement*, the *Tablet*, *First Things*, *Origins*, *Homiletic and Pastoral Review*, *Quadrant*, *Annals*, and *Australasian Catholic Record*.

The archbishop's eclectic art collection ranged from Rembrandt prints and an ink drawing of Our Lady penned by a German soldier during the siege of Stalingrad to modern Australian paintings and prints. He had the print from Sidney Nolan's Ned Kelly series he bought after returning to Australia in the early 1970s, watercolours by Milada Kessling, a Polish-Australian artist, landscapes by Max Wilks and Patrick Carroll, and a magnificent replica of the Vladimir *Madonna* by the Polish-Australian artist, Andrew Molczyk. One wall of Pell's private chapel was dominated by a striking print of John

Coburn's *Fifth Day of Creation* (one of a tapestry series that is Australia's gift to the Kennedy Center in Washington).

George Weigel, senior fellow at Washington's Ethics and Public Policy Center and Pope John Paul II's biographer, was impressed over the years by the breadth of Pell's reading and study. "Go into his sitting room, and you'll find files of every important opinion journal in the English-speaking world", Weigel said. "He's far more attuned to what's really going on in the world of ideas than many of his critics, who tend only to read each other's articles and books. George Pell is in close touch with everybody's thought."

The one trapping missing from Pell's desk in Melbourne, Sydney, and later Rome was a computer. "I'm still at the stage of the quill", he said in 2001. Years later he applied to do a course in jail, but was released before he got the chance. Margaret, his sister, related how he took a brand new laptop to the beach one year, before any software had been installed, turned it on and was disappointed when the internet was not there. And Peter Elliott, who shared Pell's Melbourne house for a time, claimed he never did master the remote controls for the television and video.

Though lacking in computer skills, Pell wielded his pen with dexterity, turning out complex sermons, speeches, and newspaper columns at a rapid pace, often after settling down to read and write for a few hours late into the night after an evening out. Despite years of early rising in the seminary and for early Masses, Pell by nature was a night-owl rather than an early-bird. "If he was ever grumpy, it was in the morning", one of his former staff in Melbourne remembered. "If he had an early appointment and came out to the car with his hair still wet, you shut up and didn't turn the music up too loudly on the way."

Pell was the first to admit he didn't "suffer fools easily" and could be impatient under pressure, but those who dealt with him frequently and those meeting him for the first time invariably found him warm, courteous, and good company. In private, he was as articulate and opinionated as he was in public, in saltier language, though he rarely resorted to swearing. He once described an Italian curial cardinal as "a greasy wog" and another as "Hopalong" because of his fondness for guns. "George loved that nickname", Terry Tobin recalled. "He told us that Hopalong collected firearms, guns of all kinds. He kept a revolver in his desk. It was never used in anger. Didn't have to be. He just waved it around at recalcitrant underlings." Pell called another colleague, with whom he was good friends, "a big baby". Another reminded him of a "kangaroo hopping about the place".

Pell's childhood friend Father Michael Mason observed he was "very stable and secure" and "very loyal at keeping up with his friends and keeping in touch". Years after leaving Swan Hill, his former parishioners were amazed and touched when he made the long trek back for the funeral of someone he had known well. He also turned up to support old friends on important occasions in Ballarat. Those who knew him well say he was extraordinarily generous both to charities like Caritas and to others in need and remarkably unattached to money, although he liked to be surrounded by good furniture, art, and books. Pell's cousin, Chris Meaney, remembered that when they visited Valencia in Spain for a conference on families, Pell was confronted by an angry, homeless man in a street, who was railing against the Church, provoked by the sight of Pell in his roman collar. Most people, in that situation, would move on as quickly as possible. Pell stopped, opened his wallet, and handed the man €150. "That might change his view of the Church", he told Meany. Judging by the man's reaction, it did. When Pell's family sold their Torquay beach house in Victoria, he gave most of his share of the proceeds away. His family said he put a lot of thought and imagination into choosing Christmas presents for them.

In Sydney, as in Melbourne, Pell made friends and took the time for a social life (unlike some bishops who seldom mix socially with members of the laity) and received plenty of invitations. He especially enjoyed the barbecues and Sunday night "sgetties" (as the grandchildren of his old friend Bob Santamaria called pasta evenings) at the home of his close friends Bernadette (Santamaria's daughter) and Terry Tobin.

While Pell was the leader of the conservative wing of the Church, he was friendlier with many priests and lay people on the Church's liberal wing and in the centre than many of his more conservative friends, who took Church politics far more seriously than he did. After his installation in Melbourne, Pell had a group of his most loyal priest friends to dinner at his house in Gellibrand Street, Kew, to celebrate. One of the younger priests was struck by the archbishop's lack of rancor towards those who had given him and his friends a hard time previously: "Those of us who were there were looking forward to important changes in the diocese, but George also said we could afford to be magnanimous to other priests, and he was." Several priests and family members said he could not bear the rather Celtic tendency of keeping up long-running grudges and resentments. "If he's got something to say, he'll say it, probably in the forceful, colourful language of the pub he grew up in, and then forget it", one old friend said. "In other ways he could be very Irish, a bundle of contradictions. You sometimes got the feeling that the left hand didn't know what the right hand was doing."

Pell could cook and preferred trying his hand at dishes that were "quick and simple", especially steak. But he rarely did so after becoming a bishop, preferring to return friends' hospitality by taking them out for dinner, where he enjoyed a glass of wine and the odd after-dinner cigar—the only times he ever smoked. While generally gregarious, according to Pell's family and friends who holidayed with him, it was hard to get a word out of him at breakfast, when he disappeared behind the daily newspapers, which he read cover to cover. He was fascinated with politics, international news, sport, and the arts, but looked through the lifestyle and popular culture sections to be aware of what his flock, including teenagers, were interested in. As an archbishop, he was probably better informed about pop music, most of which he disliked, than most parents whose children were fans of singers such as Eminem, whom Pell took to task for singing of "killing women, nuns and gays, carving them up like cantaloupes". Eminem's "turgid incoherence", Pell argued, was "a return to barbarism, grossly offensive and pornographic, with not a flicker of intelligent vulgarity or salacious charm", causing a coarsening of sensibilities among young fans. He went so far as to suggest governments had scope for tight, clear legislation to curb the worst expressions of hate, including that found in the entertainment industry.

In his first few months in Sydney, one of Pell's most important addresses was his speech to the Quadrant Dinner in August. To the surprise of the audience, who were mostly devoted economic rationalists, he began with a look backward to a time when, he said, the family in Australia enjoyed a privileged place in law and in social and economic policy: "Nothing epitomized this more than the 1907 landmark judgement of Henry Bourne Higgins, president of the newly established Commonwealth Court of Conciliation and Arbitration, in the case that established the basic wage, to support a working man, his dependent wife and three children 'in frugal comfort'", Pell said. As it became more difficult for families to maintain their standard of living on one income, feminism and new opportunities in the workforce came to the rescue, he noted, enabling families to maintain and often improve their standard of living, at least initially, although many poorer families found that even two incomes were not enough, and parents had to seek a "third income"—part-time work at nights or at the weekend to make ends meet. "This sort of thing is not always good for workers—at whatever level of responsibility, although some love it—and it is certainly not good for families or for children waiting for their parents to come home."

While many in the room took this opening, and his subsequent answers to questions, as an attack on free-market economics, Pell insisted he was not being nostalgic for the basic wage and centralized systems of the past but was focusing on the problems of the present and future: "I am not saying that the collapse of the family was the consequence of some sort of unholy alliance between feminists and radical free-marketeers. It is only when we become a little bit like Marxists and insist that if only we can get the economics right everything else will look after itself that the blindness of the market becomes a problem."

Despite the number of divorcees in the room, and in the general community, Pell briefly floated the notion of a tax on parents who divorced as a means of helping to defray the costs to the general community. Politicians, lawyers, and commentators roundly condemned the notion as impractical and unfair. Even Pell himself admitted a few months later, in an address to the Pontifical Council for the Family in Rome, that it would probably be impossible to implement given the difficulties in establishing who was the guilty party in each marriage breakdown. The media fracas overshadowed all of Pell's other points in his Quadrant speech, which drew on research on family issues— most of which supported the Church's position that to preserve social stability it makes good sense to buttress the stability of the family.

He said:

In Australia, 46 percent of marriages end in divorce. The impact on
both parents and children is significant, with rates of mortality and illness much higher than in families which stick together. Children of
divorced families are more prone to poor results at school and to depression and low self-esteem. One of the most important recent studies of
the effects of divorce on children reported that 90 percent of children
react to divorce with strong feelings of fear, anxiety, and abandonment.
The old slogan that divorce is better for both parents and children than
staying in an unhappy marriage no longer has credibility.

He also used independent research to debunk the notion of "trial
marriages" as a means of preventing separation and divorce, pointing out Australian Bureau of Statistics figures showing that divorce
is actually twice as likely for people who cohabited before marriage
compared with those who did not. "Cohabitation before marriage
has increased from 23 percent of couples in 1979 to 69 percent in
1999", he said. "My fear is that we are setting ourselves up for a
vicious circle where family breakdown is perpetuated by behaviours
which make it all the more likely."

Pell said that "without crticising any individual or making judgements about people's situations or experiences", it was time to accept
that divorce and births out of wedlock come with high social costs.
Social policy should address the underlying causes and, if possible,
reverse the trends with what he called "a preferential option" for the
family in law and in social and economic policy. He agreed with the
suggestion by Barry Maley at the Centre for Independent Studies
for reintroducing fault as an element in determining the custody of
children and property settlements. "I do not see why marriage should
be the only contract people can walk away from without penalty",
Pell said. "The weakness of the family is now at the point where it
is beginning to undermine the strength of the state. The state needs
children just as much as any couple living in a village in India. As
falling fertility rates in the West make very clear, we need to start
re-thinking this attitude if we want enough people around when we
are old to care for us, pay taxes to support us, and if necessary, go to
war to defend us." Pell supported the right of all women, including
mothers, to undertake paid work outside the home and to receive

equal remuneration for that work, along with subsidized child care. However, he noted that surveys repeatedly showed that many mothers of young children worked, not for fulfillment, but out of economic necessity and would prefer to spend more of their children's early years with them at home.

He pushed the envelope even farther, arguing that government policies were not enough to reverse the decline of the family and that religion has a role to play: "True and effective love of one's children requires sacrifice, making a gift of oneself to others, and it is this sacrificial love that maximizes the chance of an encounter with the transcendent. We may not realise it yet, but the great and now rather dated experiment in radical secularism has failed, and the failure of the family is one of the most important manifestations. It is time for a radical change of outlook, and we need it to come soon for our own good." In other words, individuals and families ignore the spiritual or religious side of life at their peril.

With a daily schedule akin to that of a cabinet minister or private sector CEO and a position and outspokenness that saw him enmeshed frequently in controversies, Pell admitted that he could sometimes find it difficult to step back and switch his concentration to his own prayer life. That was something he made time to do every day, regardless of the demands of the schedule. Prayer, he admitted, could be "a very considerable relief" from the pressures of work and controversies. In addition to Mass, the archbishop's daily prayer included the breviary and meditation. While many Catholics have their favourite saints to whom they pray regularly, Pell prayed "almost exclusively to Christ". "That's just the way it's evolved with me", he said. He also had a strong devotion to Our Lady and said the Rosary several times a week—often during one of his frequent walks through the Botanic Gardens to Mrs Macquarie's Chair (a stone bench with a view of Sydney Harbor, named in honour of Elizabeth Macquarie, the wife of the Lachlan Macquarie, an early governor of the colony from 1810 to 1821) or along the surrounding streets. On other days, he swam at an indoor pool or, on days off in summer, surfed at a beach to the north of Sydney where he had a condo. Golf was a favourite pastime of many priests, but not Pell. He said it would take up too much time, and after playing a variety of sports well, he was not keen on the idea of dabbling at the edges and playing the game badly. He would have loved to be able to ski but was never free to accept the invitations of families who asked him to go with them.

Shortly after Pell arrived in Sydney, Jeni Cooper, editor of Australia's biggest-selling newspaper, the *Sunday Telegraph* (circulation of seven hundred thousand plus, readership of two million plus), offered him a weekly column. He delivered it on time and by fax, covering religious and general topics, ranging from stem cells, euthanasia, saints, and the pope to movies, Harry Potter, and sport. His first column was about Sydney:

> When I was leaving Melbourne for Sydney, people warned me I was coming to a very different place. I always asked what these differences were and murmured that I was not going to Afghanistan. Central Sydney reminds me of New York; the crowds, the bustle, the tall buildings, and the conviction of Sydneysiders that theirs is the premier city. And so it is.... Most people in Sydney are not shy. Students will often say hello to me; even three skateboarders from the square came up to shake my hand....
>
> "Sin City" is secularist spin. There are fewer unbelievers in Sydney and more Christians. Melbourne is a place where Catholics and unbelievers flourish.
>
> The Sydney-Melbourne rivalry is long-standing. To the dismay of their respective champions, the cities have much in common. Sydney and Melbourne Catholic parishes are indistinguishable, and even the clerical stories overlap, with only the names of bishops changed. I love both cities, but I now call Sydney home.[1]

Somewhat to the archbishop's amusement, the column that drew the greatest response in the early years was a pre-Christmas column in 2001 about Harry Potter, the world's best-selling children's character ever. While some Protestants and Catholics objected to the book's positive portrayal of witchcraft, the archbishop enjoyed it and said so, putting many parents' minds at rest and infuriating a few others. "To my mind there is not much danger of this (glamourizing witchcraft) because the world of fantasy is so extreme, such a clever and unusual

[1] George Pell, "A Great Religion Offers Meaning to Multitudes", *Sunday Telegraph*, October 16, 2001.

stimulation of the imagination. It is clearly unreal; interesting and totally peculiar."[2]

He read the first book, bought a sequel for his nieces, and saw some of the films. "I like a good different escapist read, which has to be well written, to take me into other worlds", he wrote.

> Would Harry's magic work with me too? I still read a lot; all sorts of things. I probably owe this gift to a young Christian Brother, my teacher in grade five, who launched us into the many kingdoms of fiction. Being able to read easily is the key to all knowledge, and we have to be grateful to any new author who can entice millions of young readers into this adventure and expand their imaginations. . . .
>
> Harry Potter is an eleven-year-old wizard, whose parents were killed in the struggle against evil. When he goes to Hogwarts, the boarding school for witchcraft, this struggle is resumed. . . .
>
> Often when we read a book beforehand, we don't like the characters in the film version, but most viewers seem to have liked the way Harry and his friends Ron and Hermione (the film taught me how this name was pronounced) were cast. So too with the adults.
>
> The headmaster Dumbledore, a venerable patriarch, the deputy Minerva McGonagall (what a great name), the giant Hagrid, the nasty teacher Snape are all well-known English character types, populating an unusual Gothic school building set in an exotic countryside.
>
> More importantly the book (and the film, which differs slightly) are full of good moral teaching just like traditional fairy stories. Harry learns that his parents were killed by the evil Lord Voldemort, and the story tells how he and his two friends continue this fight, conquer their fears, and put themselves at risk for one another as loyal friends.
>
> I happen to believe that it is important for all us, and children, to learn that good and evil are real spiritual forces, that each of us has to commit himself against evil. Voldemort lied to Harry that there is no good or evil, only power, that his parents were cowards; and in a final violent physical struggle Harry triumphed and good prevailed. All of us, and especially the young, need to be reminded good is more powerful and will have the last word.
>
> When Harry was obsessed by the image of his dead parents, his headmaster explained there was neither knowledge nor truth in that apparition. But there is a good dose of moral truth in Harry Potter, book and film. And it is a great yarn.

[2] George Pell, "Harry Potter and the Christians", *Sunday Telegraph*, September 23, 2007.

In his first Christmas column, Pell did not miss the chance to hammer home a few truths:

> Ours is not a safe secular Christmas, a kindly festival of gifts and goodwill for the children, which temporarily creates a dream world, where problems and sickness and strife are put to one side. We believe that the Christ Child grew up to be a great man, teacher and healer, who redeemed us; set us on the path which brings human fulfilment.
>
> Seventy percent of Australians are Christians, and there is very little anti-Christian sentiment. All groups are accorded religious freedom. It is therefore a great pity that so few Christians choose to use Christian symbols for their Christmas decorations. I am not against giving, much less receiving gifts. Indeed to give is deeply Christian. I am not even opposed to Father Christmas, although I think he only became popular about the 1920s, after a Coca-Cola advertising campaign. I can understand non-Christians using only holly and reindeers. But why do Christians avoid the crib with Mary and the Christ Child in their business advertising? In the Philippines you would never think Santa was the main person at Christmas; Mary and Jesus have central billing there.[3]

For the first time in a quarter of a century, Pell holidayed at a different place in January 2002, leaving behind Torquay west of Melbourne for the New South Wales central coast. During the break, Pell also kept an eye on one of his priorities for the Archdiocese of Sydney—the renovation of the Good Shepherd Seminary chapel at Homebush. Unlike the tension and acrimony surrounding his changes to the Melbourne seminary a few years earlier, similar reforms in Sydney went smoothly. Before Pell's appointment to Sydney, the seminary rector, Father Michael Foster, had indicated that after six years he was ready to move on at the end of 2001. Foster left the seminary with nine first-year students—considered a healthy intake. Pell appointed Sydney-born and educated Father Julian Porteous, formerly pastor of Dulwich Hill, to the position of rector, effective in January 2002. Before his official starting date, Porteous, at Pell's initiative, oversaw an extensive renovation of the seminary chapel.

---

[3] George Pell, "Season of More than Reindeer", *Sunday Telegraph*, December, 12, 2001.

Nothing illustrates the competing and contradictory visions in today's Catholic Church better than its "before" and "after" images. Before the renovation, the chapel was bare in the extreme—no sanctuary, no fixed altar, no fixed crucifix, no stations of the cross, no statues, and the tabernacle unadorned and tucked away in an alcove to the side. Decoration was minimal—a painted icon of the Blessed Virgin Mary and two coloured windows with swirling, abstract patterns, one blue, one red. Porteous said the red one was possibly for Christ, the blue one possibly for his Mother, but it was impossible to be certain. The old chapel had a wooden tablelike altar in the centre, a movable lectern, and seats for the students placed around the "table" in a horseshoe arrangement, with no fixed kneelers but mats to be put down as needed.

Under Porteous' supervision, the chapel was transformed by Sydney architect John O'Brien and Opus Dei priest Father Victor Martinez, a trained architect with a doctorate in theology and experience at designing chapels. The basic vision for the renovations, however, was that of Pell, who insisted on a traditional sanctuary, a fixed, solid altar (made from Sydney sandstone and granite), a life-size crucifix, a fixed lectern, a tabernacle given pride of place in the centre of the sanctuary, a statue of Our Lady, and four stained-glass windows depicting Saints Peter and John, Mother Mary MacKillop, and Mother Teresa.

At the end of 2002, the Good Shepherd Seminary had thirty-four students, and twenty-five of those were in first and second years. Half the students were training for the Archdiocese of Sydney, and the remainder for other New South Wales dioceses and for Adelaide, which had closed its seminary due to lack of numbers in the latter years of Archbishop Leonard Faulkner's reign as one of Australia's most liberal archbishops.

The younger students who entered in 2001 and 2002 and those who followed in 2003 and 2004 belonged to a "post-postmodern" generation of devout young Catholics who were largely untouched by the post-Vatican II struggles in the Church. At the time, Pope John Paul II was the only pope many of them had known. His vitality and initiatives like World Youth Day had given them a Catholic vision of life and a sense of the significance of the Catholic Church in the world. Most were in their early twenties when they entered and had worked in a variety of previous occupations—builder, gem merchant, engineer, and teacher, among others. The devotional piety and orthodoxy of some of the younger students impressed and surprised some older Sydney priests more accustomed to the liberal approach of the 1960s.

Like Pell at Corpus Christi in 1985, Porteous introduced "a few small changes" to the Good Shepherd Seminary from the start of 2002. While he did so on the specific instructions of Pell, he fully agreed with the program the archbishop set out. They were of one mind on key issues of seminary training. On weekdays, Sydney seminarians got up at 6:00 A.M. and said the morning prayers of the Divine Office, followed by half an hour's meditation before a communal Mass at 7:30 A.M. After breakfast, they began classes and came together again at 5:00 P.M. for evening prayer and again at 9:15 P.M. for night prayer. The evening Rosary was optional but well attended. Saturday was the day off, with morning Mass optional, but the students were expected to return to the seminary in the evening (under previous regimes they were allowed to spend Saturday nights away). The Sunday Mass was at 9:30 A.M., and on Sunday evening the Blessed Sacrament was exposed for an hour for adoration, followed by Benediction and the Divine Office. Students traditionally cooked Sunday lunch themselves, experimenting with different ethnic cuisines or the dishes of their cultural traditions. First-year formation involved a solid spiritual grounding, a study of the Scriptures and their place within the tradition of the Church, and a detailed study of the *Catechism of the Catholic Church*. While some of the older students found the regime restrictive, the rector and the archbishop were convinced it provided the most solid foundation for future priests.

At the beginning of the 2002 school year, a small number of Catholic primary schools in Sydney began using the Melbourne religious education textbooks on a trial basis. The trials proved successful, and the series was reprinted and adapted for use across Sydney, with local photographs replacing some of those of Melbourne churches.

In April 2002, Australia's Catholic bishops as a group were in the glare of the national spotlight when the High Court ruled on their application, backed by the federal government, to prevent single women, including lesbians, from accessing *in vitro* fertilization technology. Opposing the application, which dated back to October

2000, were the Human Rights and Equal Opportunities Commission and the Women's Electoral Lobby.

The test case centred on the long-standing efforts of a Catholic Melbourne woman, Leesa Meldrum, to conceive a child by way of the technology. Meldrum, who had failed to conceive in an earlier heterosexual relationship and was diagnosed infertile, had devoted ten years and AU$40,000 in medical expenses to her quest to have a baby. "I want a baby more than life itself", Meldrum told the news media at one point. "I would go to any length to have a baby. I guess I have gone to every length."[4]

In July 2000, the Federal Court had upheld as a right Meldrum's access to the public in-vitro fertilization (IVF) program, thereby forcing a change in state law in Victoria, which had previously restricted single women from using the technology, prompting the more determined women to travel across the border to Albury in New South Wales for treatment. It was then that the bishops appealed to the High Court, which ruled seven to zero to reject their bid and awarded costs against the Church.

Legal commentators gave the bishops' case little, if any, chance of success, although their advice from a variety of senior legal practitioners was that it was worth pursuing. Pell supported the Church's application and had made his views clear earlier in the debate: "We are on the verge of creating a whole new generation of stolen children." Prime Minister John Howard echoed his concern, insisting on "the fundamental right of a child within our society to have the reasonable expectation, other things being equal, of the care and affection of both a mother and a father".

To some it seemed the Catholic bishops were singling out a *small proportion* of IVF applications for opposition when the Church's moral teaching that all human lives be equally respected suggested that a far graver issue—the manufacture of human embryos, many of which are frozen for years, then destroyed—was at stake with IVF technology in general. Life begins at the moment of conception, and this fact is central to the Church's opposition to all violations of the dignity of human embryos, including abortion, experimentation, and the harvesting of cells or organs.

---

[4] David Marr, "Babytalk", *Sydney Morning Herald*, September 1, 2001.

Yet in the High Court battle, the Church appeared to be directing her resources and wrath at a very small number of women wishing to access the technology, while leaving the bigger picture alone. Pell did not see the issue that way. The bishops' prime concern, he said, was defending the traditional family and the ideal of heterosexual marriage from another form of undermining. "A child has the right to a normal sort of family life." Pell denied that he, as an unmarried male, was romanticizing the benefits of traditional heterosexual marriage. He said his pastoral experience with ordinary families had shown him time and again the unhappiness and consequences, especially for children, that often stemmed from the breakdown of the traditional family.

In an interview with the U.S. think tank the Acton Institute, around the time of the High Court ruling, Pell elaborated on the difficulties Church leaders face when they address important public policy issues:

> The Catholic bishops—and many other Christian leaders—have recently spoken out on the question of refugees attempting to enter Australia. The political and cultural Left has universally welcomed this intervention, whereas some of those on the Right have told us that the church should stay out of politics. On the other hand, we are currently awaiting a decision from our High Court [the equivalent of the United States Supreme Court] on an appeal lodged by the Catholic bishops. This appeal challenges a court decision striking down a state law restricting access to assisted reproductive technology to married and de facto couples and giving access to single women and lesbians. Broadly speaking, the bishops' intervention in this matter has been supported by the political and cultural Right, while those on the Left have told us to stay out of politics.
>
> My view is that very few people are consistent in saying that the church should stay out of politics, because there will always be an occasion where they will welcome the clergy's support on one issue or another. If, as church leaders, we believe that there are occasions where our contributions to the moral debate are necessary, we have to accept that almost every time we speak—on whatever issue it may be—someone, somewhere, will tell us to stay out of politics.[5]

[5] George Pell, "Christianity's Indispensable Social Teaching", *Religion & Liberty* 12, no. 2 (July 20, 2010), https://www.acton.org/pub/religion-liberty/volume-12-number-2/christianitys-indispensable-social-teaching.

At the same time, Church leaders should assess carefully whether an intervention is necessary and appropriate, and they should frame their comments in terms of principle rather than politics. "It is sometimes difficult to know when to speak and when to keep silent", Pell admitted. In the Catholic tradition, he said, priests and bishops were not permitted to hold public office, and, as a matter of practical prudence and professional integrity, they should refrain from using their positions to advance the political interests of any party, except in extreme situations. "We encourage lay people to be actively involved in their communities, and practical party politics is their business, not the business of the clergy", Pell said. "We live in democratic societies, and Christians and Christian churches have the right to be heard, like everyone else."

Contrary to some people's expectations, the Catholic Church is not an enemy of the market, he said. A great deal depends on what is meant by a free-market economy. "If we mean 'an economic system which recognizes the fundamental and positive role of businesses, the market, private property, and the resulting responsibility for the means of production, as well as human creativity in the economic sector', then the church supports the free market", he said. "But if we mean 'a system in which freedom in the economic sector is not circumscribed within a strong juridical framework which places it at the service of human freedom in its totality, and which sees it as a particular aspect of that freedom, the core of which is religious and ethical', then the church opposes it." The Church could do better, he added, in encouraging business people to consider their role in the wider society. "There are many fine Christians who are senior and successful business leaders, and their witness and example to their colleagues are invaluable. But I think we could do more to develop the idea of business as a vocation and to deepen business people's understanding of the importance of their work—not just for themselves and their families but for society as a whole. Business people could be more aware of the moral imperatives that drive and restrict their activities."

In Pell's first fifteen months in Sydney, his progress getting around to all of Sydney's 137 parishes and the city's Catholic schools was hampered by his spending significant periods working overseas, mainly in Rome. His first trip to Rome as archbishop of Sydney was in 2001, to receive a new pallium from Pope John Paul II, on June 29, the feast day of Saints Peter and Paul. Popes have been conferring the pallium on bishops since the fourth century at least, and it is given to archbishops of major cities to symbolize Catholic unity around the pope. The white wool used in the pallia comes from lambs blessed in Rome on the feast of Saint Agnes (January 21), who are cared for by Benedictine nuns in Trastevere (a Roman suburb little changed in centuries in the ancient Jewish quarter). The pallia are blessed by the pope and placed overnight on the eve of the feast on the tomb of Saint Peter in Saint Peter's Basilica.

During the ceremony, the archbishops, from thirty-six cities as far afield as Washington, Delhi, and Acapulco, promised allegiance to the pope. Their promises were read by Denis Hart, the new archbishop of Melbourne, because he was the last archbishop appointed before the ceremony. Having two archbishops receiving the pallium on the same day was an Australian first. Rome was fine, clear, and hot for the entire week—except for the half hour during the open-air Mass in Saint Peter's Square, when fierce thunder rolled across the sky and rain bucketed down. "A squeal ran through the crowd", Pell recalled in his *Sunday Telegraph* column.

We were drenched. Umbrellas arrived late, and as the Mass continued I spent fifteen minutes huddled under one in the papal colours with the archbishop of Florence.

By coincidence June 29 was also the day when Doctor Peter Jensen, the new Anglican Archbishop of Sydney, was consecrated. I prayed during our ceremony and beforehand when I visited Peter's tomb, under Bernini's spectacular 'Baldacchino' that God might bless him and his Archdiocese. The original Saint Peter's was built by Constantine, the first Christian emperor in the fourth century, over Peter's traditional burial place. Today you can walk through this ancient Roman cemetery, first excavated during the Second World War.

It is always a moving experience to concelebrate and pray with the Pope, bishops, priests and people from many different cultures, often leading lives more difficult than ours. It reminds us that we have only a small, brief part in an immense and age-old tradition of worship and service centred on Jesus Christ.

This was true on this occasion too, but it is harder to pray when you are sopping wet. With the red dye from our outer vestments

staining the white albs, one had to work harder for reverence and recollection. But life is like this. Christ was born in a stable and crucified
on a rubbish tip. I am sure he would have needed a sense of humour.[6]

From Rome, Pell paid a brief visit to the Polish city of Kraków,
where Pope John Paul II was once priest and bishop, to look in on a
three-week seminar on Christians in a free society, organized each year
for ten years by a Polish Dominican priest, Father Maciej Zieba, formerly a lay leader of Solidarity. Two of Pell's American friends, George
Weigel and former Lutheran-turned Catholic priest Father Richard
Neuhaus, a prolific author and editor of the New York–based monthly
journal of religion and social commentary First Things, also attended,
and they went out to dinner in a city they found much changed—for
the better. "I first visited in 1990 soon after the fall of communism
and the city was drab and polluted", Pell told Sunday Telegraph readers.

> Poland has done better than any other ex-communist State, and it
> is wonderful to see brightly dressed children, restored buildings, and
> the debates, bustle and colour of a free society. However, unemploy-
> ment remains at fifteen percent and the challenge of agrarian reform
> still lies ahead....
>
> Poland, like Ireland, has the strongest Catholic life in the Western
> world. Contrary to some fears, in the twelve years since liberation
> there has been no pattern of radical secularization. I stayed in the
> monastery of the Dominican priests, founded about 1224, which is
> now a vibrant centre for students from the Jagiellonian University.
> The Sunday evening Mass I attended was packed with youngsters.
> It was not always like this; in the 1970s only five percent of students
> from some faculties worshipped regularly.

Pell was back in Rome in October 2001 as one of 250 bishops
attending a synod on the role of bishops with Pope John Paul II. Pell
spoke about the duty of bishops to teach about good and evil, heaven
and hell, the afterlife, and genuine Christian hope:

> One could say that there is considerable silence and some confusion
> on such Christian hope especially as it touches the last things, death

[6] George Pell, "When in Rome Do as Sydneysiders Do", Sunday Telegraph, July 8, 2001.

and judgement, heaven and hell. Limbo seems to have disappeared, purgatory has slipped into limbo, hell is left unmentioned, except perhaps for terrorists and infamous criminals, while heaven is the final and universal human right: or perhaps just a consoling myth.... Christian teaching on the resurrection of the body and the establishment of a new heaven and earth, the heavenly Jerusalem, are a vindication of the values of ordinary decent living, while the final judgement, the separation of the good from evil, marks the establishment of universal justice not found in this life.

The synod's theme was "The Bishop: Servant of the Gospel of Jesus Christ for the Hope of the World". Among other issues, the synod addressed the following questions: Were bishops presenting the fullness of Catholic teaching in language people could understand? Were they practicing what they preached? Was their service real and consistent? Was there a need for formal training for bishops? Pope John Paul II, while physically ailing, told the bishops, "I'm OK above the shoulders."

In his *Sunday Telegraph* column, Pell described how John Paul II's synod

> met in the shadow of the September 11 attacks, and while the war commenced in Afghanistan on October 11 our usual morning prayer, mostly Old Testament psalms sung to the ancient Gregorian chant, was dedicated to the theme of peace and justice, and we prayed the rosary together in the afternoon for the same purpose. I was also taken by the terribly difficult situation of some bishops. Three million Sudanese have died in the last 20 years in the continuing war there. In some African countries 30–40 percent of people are infected with HIV.[7]

Like many Australians, Pell had learned of the September 11 attacks on the United States the following morning, from the newspapers. Stumbling down to breakfast after saying some morning prayers, he noticed the headlines, and his first thought was that it was a spoof or an advertisement. That afternoon, he led a Mass in Saint Mary's

---

[7] George Pell, "Peace and Justice Dominate Bishops' Prayers", *Sunday Telegraph*, October, 28, 2001.

Cathedral to pray for those killed and injured and their families, and the following day he led a packed service for schoolchildren in the cathedral. "Religious people pray when there is trouble, even when the trouble is not, strictly speaking, their own", he told the children.

> Prayer gives us strength and patience in tribulations. We ask God to convert the spiritual energy generated by our prayers to give strength and consolation to the family and friends of the victims. And we pray that those who died will be purged, cleansed of the effects of their sins, even the misguided zealots who caused these catastrophes.
>
> We have all suffered a brutal shock, but the shock probably has been greatest for you, our young people, too young to remember even Vietnam, let alone World War Two. This should be a terrible lesson for you that evil and violence don't belong only in nasty, escapist adventure films, but sometimes erupt in spectacular and destructive real life situations. We pray not to be put to the test in extreme situations. We practice in small ways to do good so we can answer the big challenges.

He warned the children against singling out the local Islamic community for blame.

> All of us will have to take more care that this catastrophe overseas does not worsen our pressure points here in Australia. We do have some racial and religious tensions; not bitter and deep by world standards, but trends to be reversed. Hostility towards aborigines; violence and threats of violence against Jewish synagogues; Moslems, even their children, insulted and threatened; violence from race-based gangs, and propaganda hostile to our traditions of public tolerance and diversity. We need to pull together; without exception. It is unjust to scapegoat the local Islamic community: they too reject these murders.

The October synod of bishops in Rome elected Pell to its follow-up working party preparing the final report, a task that took him back to Rome several times in 2002. He also made a week-long visit in January to speak at the Opus Dei conference in honour of the centenary of the birth of Josemaría Escrivá. Pope John Paul II also attended, addressing participants at the end of the event.

20

Vox Clara

In March 2002, following publication of the third Latin edition of the Roman Missal, the next step was to make vernacular language editions available, including in English. To this end, on April 20, Pope John Paul II established a new body, known as the Vox Clara (clear voice) Committee "to assist and advise the Congregation for Divine Worship and the Discipline of the Sacraments in fulfilling its responsibilities with regard to the English translations of liturgical texts".[1] The twelve members of Vox Clara include bishops and cardinals from the United States, Canada, England, Ireland, Ghana, India, and the Philippines. The Congregation for Divine Worship and Discipline of the Sacraments appointed Pell as chairman. It was a sign of confidence in his leadership in a delicate and vital challenge.

The committee was established because the pope and Cardinal Jorge Medina Estevez, the former prefect of the Congregation for Divine Worship and Discipline of the Sacraments, were dissatisfied with some of the previous work undertaken by the official body charged with producing uniform translations of liturgical texts— the International Commission on English in the Liturgy (ICEL). The use of politically correct, "inclusive" language and poor translations, which altered the meanings of liturgical ceremonies subtly but in important ways, were among the problems identified. The Vox Clara Committee's brief was to help ensure that the Latin was translated as accurately and as authentically as possible, according to the principles set out in the Vatican document *Liturgiam Authenticam*, issued a few days later with the endorsement of John Paul II. It specified: "The

[1] John Paul II, Message to the Prefect of the Congregation for Divine Worship and the Discipline of the Sacraments (April 20, 2002).

greatest prudence and attention [are] required in the preparation of
liturgical books marked by sound doctrine, which are exact in wording [and] free from all ideological influence."[2]

While it hardly seemed unreasonable for the pope and his curial
cardinals to ensure that the English translation of the Mass be as au-
thentic and accurate as possible, *Liturgiam Authenticam* drew squeals
of protest from influential liturgists. In the Brisbane Archdiocese's
liturgical magazine, which was widely read across Australia, Father
Thomas Elich, the head of liturgy for the archdiocese, was critical of
the *Liturgiam Authenticam*'s emphasis on words and expressions that
"differ from usual and everyday speech" in order better to convey
"heavenly realities".[3] He was concerned that "inclusive language is
dismissed as an inauthentic development", adding: "If we use in liturgy language which reflects an unjust world view or the sinful structures of a culture, then the liturgy will be compromised." *Liturgiam
Authenticam*, he said, "betrays the hard-won devolvement of responsibility for liturgical translation to bishops' conferences" with the
Holy See reserving "to itself the right to prepare translations into
any language and to approve them for liturgical use". He concluded:
"Taking these various elements as a whole, one cannot escape the
conclusion that the collegiality and local responsibility for liturgical
translation have been seriously compromised by this document."

The Vox Clara Committee defined its role as serving "as an instrument of consultation to assist the Congregation for Divine Worship
and the Discipline of the Sacraments in its work for English-language
translations of liturgical texts and to enhance and strengthen effective cooperation with the Conferences of Bishops". Pell, as chairman, wholeheartedly backed the pope's insistence that the vernacular
translations of the official Latin texts be precise and theologically
faithful, as well as beautiful.

What intrigued some Mass-goers about this row is whether Pell
and his episcopal colleagues would take the next logical step and
assert their authority to ensure that priests stick to the official text
of the Mass and other liturgical celebrations. Catholics in some parts

---

[2] Congregation for Divine Worship and the Discipline of the Sacraments, Instruction on
the Use of Vernacular Languages in the Publication of the Books of Roman Liturgy *Liturgicam
Authenticam* (March 28, 2001).

[3] Thomas Elich, *Liturgy News*, June 2001.

of Australia are accustomed to priests using their own words even for
the most solemn parts of the Mass, including the Eucharistic Prayer;
leaving out the Creed or substituting a different one that talks about
the environment and the Church's weaknesses instead of "the one
holy catholic and apostolic Church"; substituting different biblical
passages or non-scriptural readings for the scriptural readings of the
day; and the regular omission of significant sections of the Mass, such
as the preparation of the gifts for the Consecration.

Like the then-Cardinal Ratzinger, Pell saw merit in the tradition of
the priest facing east or its spiritual equivalent, the tabernacle, during
certain parts of the Mass. Facing the people throughout the Mass, he
said, could put too much emphasis on the priest at the expense of
concentrating on God. Facing "east" and facing the people are both
licit options. It was important, he said, that bishops set an example to
priests by following the rubrics when saying Mass and celebrating all
the sacraments.

Pell took on the presidency of Vox Clara for the long haul, and it
was not until 2010 that the committee brought the revised English
edition of the Roman Missal to fruition. Barbecue lingo it was not, as
Pell said in an interview at the time. It was one of his major achievements, through which he and his fellow English-speaking cardinals
struck a powerful blow in the culture wars against postmodernism and
meaninglessness in favour of scholarship and precision of language.

Benedict XVI approved the translations from the official Latin
Roman Missal and associated prayers on March 25, 2010, the feast
of the Annunciation. A month later, the committee joined the pope
for a celebratory lunch at Casina Pio IV, a small sixteenth-century
palace in the Vatican gardens. It was the culmination of nine years of
work by Vox Clara. In order to strengthen the quality and rigour of
the new translation, Vox Clara and the new ICEL, headed by Arthur
Roche, the then-bishop of Leeds, worked in accordance with the
2001 Vatican instruction *Liturgiam Authenticam*, setting out what was
required. ICEL, in turn, was guided by broad sets of guidelines prepared by Vox Clara.

The full project was scrutinized and approved twice, by bishops'
conferences from the United States, Canada, Australia, Britain, Ireland, India, Africa, and the Caribbean. It reflected the determination
of John Paul II and Benedict XVI to reassert doctrines and beliefs
after forty years of upheavals. Too often, in practice, the changes to

the Mass after the Second Vatican Council were turned into something never intended: outlandish, avant-garde liturgies and an erosion of doctrine, ostensibly "in the spirit of the council".

As mainstream Protestant churches lurched leftward, ordaining women and actively homosexual men as priests and questioning long-held doctrines about the Resurrection, the Virgin Birth, and the need for salvation, Pope Benedict held steady in his conviction that richer, more reverent liturgies are essential to strengthening religious belief and practice.

In Australia, the new Mass text was introduced on Pentecost Sunday 2011. It replaced the one with which congregations had become familiar during the last forty years, but which Pell said was too colloquial and "a bit dumbed down".[4] The new document was not a literal translation but a more accurate one, employing powerful words such as *venerable, compassion, sacrifice, victim, consubstantial,* and *everlasting salvation.* "The previous translators seemed a bit embarrassed to refer to angels, sacrifice, and perpetual virginity", Pell said. "They went a bit softly on sin and redemption." The version he oversaw did not. Instead of confessing they have sinned "through my fault", priests and people had to admit they had sinned "through my fault, through my fault, through my most grievous fault".

For people in the pews, one of the most noticeable differences was their response, several times during Mass, to when the priest says, "The Lord be with you." Instead of "And also with you", they now answered, "And with your spirit"—a direct translation of the Latin "Et cum spiritu tuo". The latter form acknowledged that priestly ordination affects the spirit of a man, affording him the power to consecrate bread and wine into the Body and Blood of Christ. "It is not a question of moral virtue but of ontological difference." A subtler yet important change is when the priest says, "Pray brethren, that my sacrifice and yours may be acceptable to God, the almighty Father." The previous translation was "that our sacrifice may...." As well as adhering to the Latin "meum ac vestrum sacrificium", the change avoids blurring the roles of priests and laity.

As a whole, the new translation had "a different cadence", Pell said. "It is powerful, dignified, and beautiful, and people will grow to love it." He was right. In Australia, the people in the pews accepted

---

[4] Tess Livingstone, "Fresh Embrace of Everlasting Salvation", *The Australian,* May 22, 2010.

it well, and most embraced its dignity and reverence. At the time it was finalised, Pell was unconcerned if people initially found the wording, with its emphasis on the sacred and the transcendent, a bit daunting. He compared the Mass text to a good children's book in the sense that it would stimulate thought and broaden Mass-goers' knowledge. That, he said, would lead to a deeper understanding of theology as people encountered the occasional unfamiliar word such as "oblation", a theological term for offering or gift.

"If someone writes a scholarly article, a few hundred people will read it", he said. "A few thousand people read a theological book, but the Mass, a celebration in which tens of millions will participate repeatedly across the decades, is a highly effective form of catechesis. Before receiving Communion, for example, one of the congregation's responses is "Lord, I am not worthy that you should enter under my roof, but only say the word, and my soul shall be healed." Pell said the earlier version, "Lord, I am not worthy to receive you, but only say the word and I shall be healed" lost the richness of the scriptural reference, which is drawn from the response of the centurion in Luke's Gospel, as Christ approached his house to heal his dying servant.

One of the most controversial changes came at the heart of the Mass, with the revised translation saying that Christ's Blood would be "poured out for you and for many" instead of "all", as in the previous version. Pell said that while Christ died for everyone, the new translation, which adhered to the official Latin wording *pro multis* (for many), reinforced the point that individuals were free to choose or to refuse God's mercy and eternal salvation.

For the cardinal, the printing of the missal was the end of a challenging but immensely rewarding chapter of his life, even if it cost him the need for a pacemaker in 2010 after collapsing in Rome after one of his long-haul flights. As Vox Clara president, he chaired all twenty meetings in Rome, studying thousands of pages, and in an exercise unlikely to be repeated for generations, he clocked up more than 650,000 kilometres (more than 400,000 miles) in flights to and from the Eternal City.

21

Darkening Days

In May 2002, a year after his appointment, Pell was at home in his new city and turning his attention to the appointment of a third auxiliary bishop for Sydney. His predecessor, Cardinal Edward Clancy, had had three auxiliaries, but one of them, Bishop Peter Ingham, had been promoted to his own diocese, Wollongong, in July 2001 shortly after Pell arrived in the city. A year after his own appointment, Pell was beginning to know Sydney and its parishes, and his reputation internationally was growing through his work for the synod of bishops and Vox Clara. He was also in demand as a speaker at international conferences and had engagements booked for later in 2002 in Rome, New Zealand, and Washington, D.C. Close friends had never seen him as relaxed and healthy, compared with his time in Melbourne, when he had often looked tired and strained. In Sydney, he exuded the self-assurance of someone enjoying a very fulfilling job. Some people even thought he had toned down his more controversial statements a little. "It might just be that I'm behaving", he quipped. His appointment of an Opus Dei priest and experienced university chaplain, Father John Flader, to head Catholic adult education in Sydney drew a generally positive reaction, with many seeing merit in his bringing Opus Dei more into the mainstream life of the archdiocese. Asked if he would object to Flader or others encouraging vocations to Opus Dei, Pell said he would not, provided those involved were over the age of eighteen. "But I'd far rather they went to the seminary to become [diocesan] priests", he said.

Although Saint Mary's Cathedral and Pell himself had been caricatured on a float or two in the Sydney Gay Mardi Gras in February, Pell's expected clash with the city's powerful gay lobby did not eventuate in his first year. The first Rainbow Sash demonstration in

Sydney took place in Saint Mary's Cathedral on Pentecost Sunday, May 19, 2002, with Pell refusing Communion to a small group of sash-wearers, including Michael Kelly, who had travelled up from Melbourne. After the Mass, Pell addressed the congregation, reiterating his earlier statements that the Catholic Church had no authority to give those staging such a protest Communion.

American members of the Rainbow Sash movement, who were reportedly given Communion while wearing the sash in churches in New York, Rochester, Chicago, and Minneapolis on the same day, branded Pell's stance "antagonistic" and "ridiculous". "The impression [in America] is that Pell is 25 to 30 years behind the rest of the world", Brian McNeill, a member of the Minneapolis Rainbow Sash, told Sydney's gay newspaper.[1] "McNeill said that American Catholics had not heard such language from Church leaders in decades. 'The bishops here are too smart to say that kind of thing because they know just how antagonistic and insulting that is to a lot of people—not just to gay people, to society.'" Rainbow Sash spokesman Michael Kelly complained that Pell's response to the protesters, "I can't help you", was made in "a tone of rebuke. There was no sense of warmth, understanding, or compassion in the way he handled the issue."

Despite extensive media coverage, the protesters were not the centre of attention at the cathedral that Sunday. Pell confirmed several dozen adults who had recently entered the Church and released a major statement on Christian hope, written after lengthy consultations with 250 high school seniors and graduates from Sydney. "Nearly everyone, even the irreligious, at different times is aware of the power of the Spiritual, of the Mystery behind everyday existence, of the power and majesty of the invisible God", he wrote. Some of the young people, Pell reported, felt that human beings were most open to God "when we are at our lowest ebb", while others said that "we can hope to encounter God, too, in the emptiness of success. Something is missing, because, to quote Saint Augustine, 'Our hearts are never at rest until they rest in God.'" It was Christian hope,

---

[1] Staff Writers, "U.S. Catholics Blast Pell", *Sydney Star Observer*, April 20, 2008, https://www.starobserver.com.au/news/national-news/new-south-wales-news/us-catholics-blast-pell/6224.

he said, that gives us courage to participate in the eternal struggle between good and evil, confident of final victory.[2]

Preaching on Christian hope on that sunny late autumn Sunday, Pell had no idea that a few days later he himself would face the beginnings of an ordeal that would test his own inner strength and hope like never before. He could not have imagined that by the time spring came to Sydney just a few months later, his name would be spread across the world, from Iceland to South America, from the BBC in London to national newspapers in Japan, as the archbishop who had stood aside awaiting the results of an inquiry into allegations that he had sexually abused a twelve-year-old boy forty-one years before. It was also the beginning of protracted controversy that was to dog Pell for more than twenty years, culminating in his wrongful imprisonment in 2019.

In 1996 in Melbourne, Pell established a process to handle sex abuse complaints against clergy, and the national process, Towards Healing, was adopted by the rest of the Church in Australia a few months later. Scores of tragic cases of abuse and heartless, irresponsible cover-ups by Church authorities came to light. The processes, flawed as many victims, victims' families, and support groups found them, were at least there and provided help for victims. They also prevented the wholesale meltdown of Church credibility seen elsewhere, especially in the United States, where bishops buried their heads in the sand for years longer than their Australian counterparts.

The year 2002 was a crisis year for the Church in the United States, with stiffer jail terms for offenders and higher court-awarded compensation payouts for victims than anywhere else. In Boston alone, the Church set aside US$18 million for victims of just one priest, John Geoghan, accused of molesting 130 children over thirty years. This case sparked a crisis that saw another three hundred civil lawsuits filed in sixteen states, and 250 Catholic priests out of 46,000 removed from public ministry from January to October. In 2002, when the most senior United States bishops were summoned to the Vatican and ordered to devise a system to handle the problem, some estimated the Church would pay out well over US$1 billion before the crisis was resolved. (By the end of 2015, it had paid out almost US$4 billion.)

[2] George Pell, pastoral letter *Hope* (May 19, 2002).

From Poland to Hong Kong, Ireland to South Africa, it would be hard to find a diocese untouched by this issue. Nor is the problem confined to the Catholic Church. In early 2001, in the lead-up to the queen's Golden Jubilee Australian tour, Governor-General Peter Hollingworth was under intense pressure to resign over his handling of such matters during his time as Anglican archbishop of Brisbane. In mid-2003, Hollingworth resigned. He was finally stripped of his right to practice ministry in 2023. Smaller churches, too, have occasionally come under the spotlight for a problem that also afflicts schools, sport organizations, and institutions that care for children, the sick, and the elderly.

Figures collected by the Australian Institute of Health and Welfare present a shameful picture of the problem across society at the time.[3] In 2000/2001, the number of child-abuse cases investigated and substantiated across all states and territories in Australia was 27,367. That figure covered sexual, physical, and emotional abuse and neglect, with sexual abuse comprising 13.8 percent of the total. The true figure was far higher, as many such crimes go unreported for years and are often never reported. While biological parents, as well as step-parents, de facto step-parents, siblings, and other relatives are overwhelmingly the main perpetrators, the revelation that some priests, Brothers, and Sisters, who had supposedly dedicated their lives to God, were and are guilty of this terrible crime deservedly drew headline treatment.

While girls are more vulnerable to abuse than boys, it is boys who are more likely to fall victim to paedophile Catholic priests, a fact that prompted suggestions that homosexuals should be kept out of seminaries. While homosexual priests are a minority (it is assumed), they have been convicted of far more paedophilia offenses than heterosexual priests. In March 2002, Pope John Paul II's spokesman, Joaquin Navarro-Valls, told the New York Times, "People with these inclinations [homosexuality] just cannot be ordained ... you cannot be in this field."[4] Pell "broadly agreed" with Navarro-Valls, although he qualified that by saying one or two exceptions could make very worthwhile priests. In response to the crisis, seminaries around the world stepped up the psycho-sexual screening of potential candidates.

[3] Australian Institute of Health and Welfare.
[4] Melinda Henneberger, "Vatican Weighs Reaction to Accusations of Molesting by Clergy", New York Times, March 3, 2022.

As long ago as 2000, critics were demanding a Royal Commission, the highest form of public inquiry in Australia, into the issue. It was finally called by Labor Prime Minister Julia Gillard in 2012. The cases detailed in the lead-up to that Royal Commission made gruesome reading, with most clerical perpetrators setting a pattern of sinister, calculated behaviour, preying upon and seducing child after child, mainly boys but sometimes girls, in dozens of parishes, moved on frequently by Church authorities after complaints and rumours about their behaviour.

The crisis gave enemies of the Church powerful ammunition, and some seized the opportunity to try to bring down an organisation they wanted to see destroyed. Twenty years ago, for example, a lengthy internet list of clerical sex abuse offenders and their crimes appeared under the name of *Antichrist*. It prominently displayed a quote attributed to Émile Zola: "Civilization will not attain to its perfection until the last stone from the last church falls on the last priest." Although the overwhelming majority of sex abuse happens within families, the site argued: "Forget Osama bin Laden, Saddam Hussein and the renegade Muslims. Our real terrorists live much closer to home. They're in our churches, in our schools, in our community centres—and up our kids' backsides! They're called Christians. For humanity's sake, pray that they are stopped!"

The backlog of unresolved abuse allegations, many of them involving numerous complainants, was so chronic and so enormous when Pell took over Melbourne that he pressed ahead with the Independent Commission run by Peter O'Callaghan, QC, rather than waiting to join the national Towards Healing process established later. Under the scheme, twenty-two priests were barred from ministry in six years and more than 120 people compensated.

On Thursday, May 30, 2002, George Pell called an extraordinary press conference as a preemptive strike against allegations set to be aired three days later on Channel Nine's *60 Minutes* program. He issued a statutory declaration and a statement denying that in 1993, while auxiliary bishop of Melbourne under Sir Frank Little, he had attempted to conceal the sexual abuse of a young man by the name of David Ridsdale by his uncle, Father Gerald Ridsdale, by offering the victim financial assistance in return for his silence. "The allegation

I attempted to silence a victim or cover up allegations is unfounded and untrue and is anathema to me", Pell told the assembled, startled journalists at Saint Mary's Cathedral. "I emphatically and totally deny the allegation that I made any attempt to buy David's silence. It was also alleged that I offered to buy David a house or a car.... The allegations that I made any such attempts or offers are not only unfounded, but also implausible."[5] The banner headline the day after his press conference in Sydney's high-circulation *Daily Telegraph*, "Sex Scandal Engulfs Pell", was a taste of what was to come for the following fortnight.

On Sunday evening, the heavily promoted story went to air, with *60 Minutes* reporter Richard Carleton's opening: "It's hard to imagine a graver charge. It's against one of the most powerful men in Australia, the man who is now the Catholic Archbishop of Sydney. Now, the accusation is simply this—that ten years ago, Doctor George Pell attempted to bribe a distressed young man who had been sexually assaulted by a priest, and that Doctor Pell did this to cover up a potential scandal to protect his church."[6]

The young man making the allegation had grown up in Pell's hometown, Ballarat, and was the nephew of Father Gerald Ridsdale, a defrocked, disgraced Catholic priest serving a lengthy jail term for a string of paedophile crimes (see pages 126–27). According to the program, Ridsdale began assaulting David when the boy was eleven, and the abuse lasted until he was fifteen. "Sick as it may sound, the abuse would sometimes occur when the priest was driving the altar boy to the next town to say Mass", Carleton reported.

David Ridsdale claimed that George Pell was one of the few individuals he had trusted as a young man, and he phoned him in early 1993 to tell him of his ordeal and to ask for help: "I was getting so confused and so psychologically agitated and depressed and angry I had to deal with this issue. And I believed at the time that he was the best way for me to go." Ridsdale claimed that Pell took control of the conversation and said, "I want to know what it will take to keep you quiet."

---

[5] "Archbishop George Pell's Statutory Declaration", June 3, 2002, https://australianpolitics.com/2002/06/03/archbishop-pell-statutory-declaration.html.

[6] "Richard Carleton Exposes Cover Up of Paedophile Priests", *60 Minutes Australia*, 2002 (date unknown), https://www.youtube.com/watch?v=V4_hoy_fJWc&t=2718s.

Ridsdale's sister Bernie backed up her brother, insisting that David had rung her later that day and related how he had made a phone call to Pell and how "George had asked him what it would take for it to go away, to make it go away." Another of David's sisters, Trish, concurred: "David told me that after he had told George about the abuse, George asked him what it would take to keep him silent. In fact, David's words to me were, 'The bastard tried to offer me a bribe.'" That same day, the program reported, David Ridsdale phoned the police to report his uncle, who, unbeknownst to David, was already being investigated. A day later, the priest was charged over the sexual assault of David and a number of others. In 1997, Bishop of Ballarat Ronald Mulkearns had resigned amid accusations that, as head of Ballarat Diocese, he had covered up Ridsdale's offenses.

When Father Ridsdale walked into court in May 1993, George Pell walked beside him—an image played repeatedly on television for decades. Was this a piece of foolish, misplaced loyalty to a former colleague that sent the wrong message to victims of men like Ridsdale and to the shocked public in general? Or was it a magnanimous gesture by a man big enough to be there with "one of the least of my brothers" at his lowest point, when the Church and the public shunned him? Should the bishop have entered the court with the victims rather than the accused? In June 2002, in the media storm that ensued after David Ridsdale's claims, Pell conceded that walking the priest to court, something he did with "considerable reluctance" at the request of Ridsdale's lawyers, was a mistake. "I did so in priestly solidarity. This was a mistake as it misled people about my basic sympathies for the victims, borne out by all my subsequent work to root out this evil."

What he did not say publicly, but revealed off-the-record in our first interview for this biography in 2001, was that he walked Ridsdale to court because his then-boss, Archbishop Little (a close friend of Bishop Ronald Mulkearns in Ballarat), had ordered him to do so. The cardinal's brother, David Pell, confirmed the point in his eulogy at Pell's funeral. "I need to remind you that all ordained priests take a vow of obedience to their bishop", he told the congregation. "That is what George was doing when he accompanied that perpetrator to court. He [Ridsdale] was not his friend. [George] was appalled at what he heard in court and did not go back the

next day."[7] Several others, including two of his former private
secretaries, Michael Casey and Father Anthony Robbie, also knew
about Little's order, which a cynic might believe had been given
to undermine Pell's reputation. Little, when interviewed for this
book in 2001, did not hide his dislike of Pell, though he conceded
that George had done some "tough jobs" (which Little refused
to elaborate on). Over the years, when that footage with Ridsdale was replayed time and again, I asked Pell whether he should
set the record straight. He said the "honourable thing to do was
to keep quiet", although he admitted that walking Ridsdale into
court had been a mistake. It coloured many Australians' view of
him, unfairly.

In an early interview for this book, months before the *60 Minutes*
program, Pell also said that at Ridsdale's first trial, the priest's defence
lawyer had asked him to give evidence in court for his client. "He
urged me, explaining it could help Ridsdale avoid being sent to jail",
Pell said. However, the lawyer later withdrew the request.

> This was because I said: "If I appear in court I would say, 'I'm not
> commenting in any shape or form on the truth or otherwise of the
> accusations against Ridsdale.' And secondly, 'Ridsdale has done
> immense damage to the victims, to himself, and to the Church.' All
> I would say is that 'there was another side to Ridsdale too; he did
> good things.'"
>
> I said if I appeared in court, I would insist on saying those three
> things, and they didn't ask me to appear. Also, at that stage, I had no
> idea of the extent or the gravity of the offences; I knew they were bad
> enough, but I knew none of the details of the cases. I never knew then
> just what an enormous range of offences was involved.

An unredacted 2017 report of the Royal Commission into Institutional Responses to Child Sexual Abuse said of David Ridsdale:

> We consider Mr Ridsdale to be an honest witness. We accept that he
> genuinely believes that Bishop Pell said, "I want to know what it will
> take to keep you quiet", in an effort to keep Mr Ridsdale's allegation
> from becoming public.

[7] Staff writers, "David Pell's Eulogy for Cardinal Pell: A Good and Holy Man, and a
Proud Australian", *Catholic Weekly*, February 2, 2023, https://www.catholicweekly.com.au
/david-pells-eulogy-for-cardinal-pell-a-good-and-holy-man-and-a-proud-australian/.

However, we are not satisfied that Bishop Pell said the words attributed to him or otherwise sought to obtain Mr Ridsdale's silence. It is more likely that Mr Ridsdale misinterpreted an offer by Bishop Pell to assist as something more sinister. There is no compelling reason for the then bishop to make such a statement.[8]

In claiming that Pell and Father Gerald Ridsdale had known each other as seminarians and even shared a house, the *60 Minutes* report gave the impression of some closeness between the two. Gerald Ridsdale, born in 1934, was seven years older than Pell. They seldom encountered each other at Saint Patrick's College, Ballarat, and they were not in the seminary at the same time. They overlapped in the Ballarat East presbytery for twelve months in the early 1970s, not out of choice, but because they were assigned to it, along with at least two other priests. Ridsdale was forty at the time, and Pell thirty-three.

Pell never attempted to conceal this. In the interview for this book months before the *60 Minutes* controversy broke, he said: "I didn't dislike him. In retrospect, you'd say he was tense and he had a somewhat unusual personality, as events more than amply demonstrated, but it never for one moment entered my head that he had problems of this order." That was hardly surprising, given the secretive nature of Ridsdale's predilections. A former priest of the Ballarat Diocese, who also spent a year under the same roof as Ridsdale—in Warrnambool—said that he, too, had no idea of his colleague's behaviour.

At the height of the crisis, Pell met with his priests at Saint Mary's presbytery. "He spoke well, but he's bleeding inside", one priest who admired him said. "If nothing else, this has underlined for him the power of the false accusation." In the climate then, as now, a false accusation is something many priests fear, as do male teachers.

The archbishop's fellow *Sunday Telegraph* columnist, Leo Schofield, could not resist a sharp dig at Pell, whom he branded "Melbourne's gift to Sydney". Schofield wrote what a lot of Pell critics said privately: "Consider two media images of His Grace. In one he is telling a group of Catholic gays, the rainbow-sash people, 'I

[8] Catholic Church Authorities in Ballarat, *Report of Case Study no. 28: Catholic Church Authorities in Ballarat* (unredacted) (Australia: Royal Commission into Institutional Responses to Child Sexual Abuse, November 2017), p. 350, https://www.childabuseroyalcommission .gov.au/sites/default/files/file-list/un-redacted_report_of_case_study_28_-_catholic_church _authorities_in_ballarat.pdf.

can't help you.' In the second, the good prelate is seen accompanying Father Gerald Ridsdale, a self-confessed paedophile, to court 'in priestly solidarity'. Ridsdale is a criminal. The only crime of the group of gay Catholic men and women was to peaceably approach the altar for communion."[9]

Pell cancelled a working visit to Papua New Guinea to deal with the matter, and the *Sunday Telegraph* gave him extra space to tell his side of the story. He began by recounting a recent question he had been asked: What would Jesus say to those who put the image of the Church before the welfare of abuse victims? The Church response to sexual abuse must always have justice and compassion for the victim as first priority, he replied, and the image of the Church must always rank much lower than the needs of the people—especially the victims and their families. Loyal Catholics, he acknowledged, grieve for the victims and the crimes committed and the "disastrous mistakes by Church leaders in dealing with them". Outsiders who do not know the Church have their darkest fears strengthened by the scandals, he said. As for David Ridsdale, the archbishop reiterated his sympathy for the abuse he had suffered but denied his central allegation.[10]

Much of the controversy after the *60 Minutes* program centred on whether the compensation payments made through the Melbourne scheme, and also some made through Towards Healing, were "hush money". Pell stumbled over the issue on *60 Minutes*. Later, after media revelations about confidentiality clauses imposed on some victims who went through the Towards Healing process in New South Wales, he reviewed the processes with the help of his friend John McCarthy, QC, a prominent Sydney barrister.

On June 9, McCarthy, president of the Saint Thomas More Society, a guild of Catholic lawyers, told the press that he had "received many messages of concern relating to clauses in deeds of release for victims of clerical sex abuse" that "seem to be the standard nondisclosure clauses in damage settlements".[11] These clauses, McCarthy said, seemed to be "completely at variance with what Church leaders, including Archbishop Pell, believed was happening under

[9] Leo Schofield, "Double Vision", *Sunday Telegraph*, June 9, 2002.

[10] George Pell, "My Accuser's Memory Has Played Him False", *Sunday Telegraph*, June 16, 2002.

[11] Kelly Burke, "Church Fails Its Own Sex Abuse Rules", *Sydney Morning Herald*, June 11, 2002.

the Church's current process, Towards Healing, for those who had been victims". Towards Healing, he said, had been in operation in all the dioceses of New South Wales for some years, and "since 2000 the program's charter in Clause 41.4 states: 'No complainant shall be required to give an undertaking which imposes upon them an obligation of silence concerning the circumstances which led them to make a complaint, as a condition of an agreement with the Church authority.'" McCarthy said that, after making inquiries, he had found that Clause 41.4 had not been appropriately implemented in deeds of release for settlements with victims. "Customary confidentiality clauses have been maintained", he said, adding Pell had authorized him to state that, in regards to the Archdiocese of Sydney (for he could not speak for other dioceses or religious orders), in all cases where Clause 41.4 had been breached, such cases would be reviewed and victims would be relieved of any obligation of silence that might have been mistakenly imposed.

A week later, Pell asserted in the *Sunday Telegraph*: "There has never been a confidentiality clause in the Melbourne 'release' document for victims. The compensation procedures are designed to allow victims to avoid legal confrontation and legal costs."[12] However, he agreed with McCarthy that "elsewhere in Australia the picture is more confusing as the confidentiality clauses used everywhere in out-of-court settlements have often been applied." In December 2000, he said, the Australian Catholic bishops following the Towards Healing protocols had agreed that there should not be an obligation of silence, imposed by the Church, on the circumstances around the complaint. But he acknowledged that there had been "uncertainty and inconsistency in implementing this policy".

In the article, Pell rejected allegations that a compensation offer to a young woman (featured on *60 Minutes* with her parents) from the Melbourne Archdiocese solicitors was "hush money" to keep the incident quiet. "At that stage, the priest perpetrator had been tried, convicted, and was in prison", he said. "There was huge publicity." There was, because John Kevin O'Donnell, at seventy-eight, was the oldest Victorian to be sent to jail. O'Donnell, a Jekyll-and-Hyde character who made friends with children and bought them milkshakes and hamburgers, had pleaded guilty to abusing two girls and

[12] George Pell, "My Accuser's Memory".

ten boys from 1946 to 1977 in several parishes including Chelsea, Seymour, Dandenong, Hastings, and Oakleigh.

The mother of the girl featured on *60 Minutes* was understandably angry. Two of her daughters had been abused by O'Donnell, and much of her anger, and that of other victims' families, was directed at Pell, despite the fact that Archbishop Little was still in charge when O'Donnell went to jail. Interviewed for this book in 2001, the woman said she and her family had been regular Mass-goers until they found out about the abuse. She said she and her husband had expected more understanding and warmth from Pell when they met him privately at the presbytery at Oakleigh after he became archbishop. "He was arrogant and a bully", she said. When asked what she meant by that, exactly, she answered: "He wasn't on our side; we'd say something, and he'd say 'That happened before my time.'" The woman said the three met in a cramped room. Space was so tight that she and her husband had had to sit up straight, while Pell, who is six feet three inches, had crossed his long legs and one of his feet was near her knee, the woman said, although not touching it. "I looked at him and said, 'Will you move your foot', and he had to uncross his legs and sit up straight like we were. He looked really cut, genuinely upset." Pell remembered the encounter well. "This was a really difficult interview", he said. "Nothing I said helped the situation."

The controversy had died down by the time Pell left for Mexico with one hundred young people from Sydney. They were the advance party en route to World Youth Day in Toronto, Canada, where another two hundred young people from Sydney joined them. Pell and the young people were impressed by the crowds visiting the shrine of Our Lady of Guadalupe, which dates from 1531, ten years after the Spanish conquest. At that time, as Pell explained,

> Mary appeared to a young Indian convert, Juan Diego, and left a miraculous image of herself as a young Indian woman on his cloak to convince a properly sceptical bishop.
>
> More than fifteen million pilgrims now visit this shrine every year, so that it ranks second only to the Vatican as a Christian pilgrimage centre. The local rulers, the Aztecs, were a highly developed civilization in many aspects; trade, mathematics, astronomy. But it was an incredibly cruel society, regularly practicing human sacrifice, including

child sacrifice, sometimes with thousands of victims.... Mary told Juan Diego that she loved his people and would protect them. They converted in millions to follow her God and her only Son Jesus.

In Toronto, the people from Sydney, from sixteen to thirty-five years old, joined up with another one thousand from around Australia, 250,000 from around the world, and 550,000 North Americans for Mass with Pope John Paul II, then eighty-two. The pope looked frail and ill compared with the dynamic energy he had projected years earlier. If anything, Pell found that the pope, persevering in his teaching and travelling in spite of his infirmities, had an even more powerful effect on the young people than before. "A new generation of young people probably loves him more than their elder brothers and sisters did in his heyday", he said. "Suffering and perseverance also give powerful witness, especially to those who believe in redemption through the Cross."

Pell himself made world headlines when Canadian journalist Michael Valpy picked up on one of the catechesis sessions he gave to five hundred young people in a suburban Canadian parish as part of World Youth Day.

Archbishop Pell taught his listeners about a Jesus who promises punishment for those who stray from the church's teachings on premarital sex, abortion and euthanasia—as well as on social justice and looking after the poor.

He taught them: "It's important for you to defend Catholic tradition as coming to us from Christ and the apostles." He taught them: "The function of the Pope is to protect that tradition, to say, 'This belongs to Catholic tradition and this doesn't.'" He taught them: "We are not free to decide for ourselves what is right and wrong. Our conscience can be wrong."[13]

What he taught them, Valpy wrote, was "everything that growing numbers of liberal progressive Catholics, mainly in the West, are rebelling against—from papal authoritarianism to the church's rejection of [artificial] birth control and the ordination of women.

[13] Michael Valpy, "Schisms of Theology Run Silent, Run Deep", *Globe and Mail*, July 25, 2003.

Several theologians have called the increasingly fractious dissent a silent schism, a reference to the millions who have left the church because they can't accept its teachings."

Yet the archbishop received a standing ovation from his young audience. World Youth Day is not just a sunny gathering for a couple of hundred thousand kids to sing and join hands and let their spirits soar. It was designed as a time for promulgating the official teachings of the Church. As Pell had previously told the international Catholic newspaper *Tablet*: "Liberalism has run its course and has nothing to offer the Church."

Valpy commented: "As Archbishop George Pell of Sydney told 500 young Roman Catholics yesterday that abortion is a worse moral scandal than priests sexually abusing young people, it became clear why the church is heading in two different directions." He explained that Pell made the comparison between abortion and priestly sex abuse in response to a question from a Kentucky man, Greg Rickert, who wanted to know what Catholics should say when someone asks them about the sex scandal currently afflicting the Church in the United States. Pell replied that the truth of the scandal had to be faced. There were two levels, he said, the abuse itself and the sometimes inadequate way the Church authorities dealt with it. But there were other scandals that received little coverage. Valpy wrote, "I asked the archbishop afterwards what he meant by saying abortion is a worse moral scandal. 'Because it's always a destruction of human life', he said. Then he said: 'I'm not in any way attempting to downplay abuse. I'm saying there's been a lot of attention on sexual abuse, but not on other things. That's all I'm trying to say.'"

Valpy concluded his article by quoting Australian author Thomas Keneally, who had recently written a *New Yorker* article saying he had left the Church because of priests such as Archbishop Pell. "I have long since abandoned any expectation that the institutional church will begin to listen to its people", Keneally wrote. "With such men in charge [as Archbishop Pell], men who wield their authority as an instrument of exclusion, I cannot return to the generous mystery of my boyhood faith."

Valpy's story was given widespread airtime and newspaper coverage in Australia, to the extent that one media crew staked out the

Sydney airport to speak to Pell as he arrived at the crack of dawn after an all-night flight across the Pacific. Later that day, he issued a statement insisting that he was not in any way downplaying the seriousness of sexual abuse.

> There are many terrible wrongs that people can suffer, often with lifelong consequences. But Christian teaching is at one with the law and secular ethics in holding that the supreme wrong that can be done to a person is the taking of his life. This claim does not make any other evils less evil.
> This was the context in which my remarks were made and in which they should be understood.... Sexual abuse is evil, but there are other serious evils in society as well.
> Where innocent or vulnerable people are hurt, honesty and compassion are essential. The Church has accepted the challenge to respond in this way to sexual abuse. It is important that our community should do the same on the issue of abortion.[14]

Pell acknowledged that many in society do not share the Catholic Church's view of abortion, "but for Christians, abortion represents the destruction of innocent human life."

The sharp division between the view of the majority of Catholics and many others was underlined in September 2002, when Pell was voted the "worst of the worst" at the annual Ernie Awards for sexist remarks in Sydney. Around four hundred women joined the New South Wales upper house president Meredith Burgmann at the tenth awards ceremony, where the audience votes for the winners on the loudness of their "boos". According to the Australian Associated Press news wire, Pell earned the Gold Ernie from a field of seven category winners. He also took the clerical category award, the Fred, "from a distinguished line-up that included Governor-General Peter Hollingworth" and was singled out for his comments on abortion in Canada.

To commentators like Pope John Paul II's biographer George Weigel, the fact that Pell attracted such criticisms simply meant that he was doing his job in a way that "confounds the hoary media script,

---

[14] Peter Westmore, "Power without Responsibility: The Vendetta against Dr Pell", *AD2000* 15, no. 9 (October 2002), https://ad2000.com.au/articles/2002/oct2002p3_1142.html.

which is that orthodoxy is dour, uncompassionate, uninteresting, etc. Cardinal Pell proves by his preaching and his life that orthodoxy is far more interesting than the alternatives—and a lot less stifling than secularism, which builds a world without windows or doors." Weigel said that Pell was "one of the great signs of hope for the Church in the twenty-first century" with the capacity to "invite others to join in that great adventure of orthodoxy".

A few hours after flying in from Canada, Pell was working at his desk in Polding House, Pitt Street. He resumed his program of parish visitations, Confirmation ceremonies, meetings, and speeches, including one at the unveiling of a painting of one of his favourite saints, Edith Stein (a Jewish scholar who became a Catholic and a Carmelite nun and was put to death by the Nazis at Auschwitz), Masses in other parishes, and a lunchtime visit to Saint Ignatius College, Riverview, to mix with the students. On Sunday afternoon, August 11, with the House of Representatives due to debate the federal government's embryonic stem cell legislation, Pell addressed a crowd of 1,300 people in Sydney at a rally against the use of human embryos for such a purpose. He and other speakers, including William Hurlbut, a medical doctor from Stanford University and a member of the United States President's Bioethics Council, spoke in favour of the use of adult stem cells, which, they argued, were showing more promise.

In mid-August, Pell spoke in favour of paid maternity leave at a conference on "Working Time, Families, Communities" for the Australian Centre for Industrial Relations Research and Training at the University of Sydney. (His comments at that gathering in favour of maternity leave drew national media coverage.) He was scheduled to preside over Adoration of the Blessed Sacrament at 9:00 P.M. on Friday, August 23, followed by Benediction at 11:30 P.M. at the Chapel of the Resurrection, City Road, Chippendale, an occasion that would underline the importance Pell attached to that form of devotion.

But it was Pell's auxiliary bishop, Irish-born David Cremin, then seventy-two, who led the devotions at Chippendale, because on Tuesday afternoon, August 20, Pell stood aside from his duties as archbishop of Sydney in a fight to prove his innocence of an allegation that he had sexually molested a boy forty-one years before.

22

The Age of the Martyrs Is Not Yet Dead

At 5:30 P.M. on Tuesday, August 20, 2002, George Pell stood outside Saint Mary's Cathedral Presbytery and in fading light read out a statement.

Certain allegations have been made about my conduct when I was a seminarian over 40 years ago.

The allegations against me are lies, and I deny them totally and utterly.

The alleged events never happened. I repeat, emphatically, that the allegations are false.

An independent inquiry to investigate these allegations has been set up by Archbishop Philip Wilson, Acting Co-Chairman of the National Committee for Professional Standards, which supervises the Church's "Towards Healing" protocols. The inquiry will be conducted, I understand, by a retired Victorian Supreme Court judge.

I will, of course, co-operate with this independent inquiry in every way possible—frankly, openly, and unreservedly.

For the good of the Church and to preserve the dignity of the office of Archbishop, I will take leave from today as Archbishop of Sydney until the inquiry is completed.

I repeat that the allegations are lies and that I am determined to refute them.

I welcome the inquiry and a chance to clear my name, recognizing that I am not above civil and Church law.

I have taken a leading role in condemning and exposing sexual abuse within the Catholic Church in Australia. Six years ago, in Melbourne, I set up Australia's first Independent Commission to inquire into sexual abuse by members of the Catholic clergy.

To allege that I am now personally implicated in this evil is a smear of the most vindictive kind. I truly wish I could say more right now. However, it is important that I do not say anything that could be seen to prejudice the inquiry. Therefore, I am unable to make further comment.[1]

He then headed upstairs to his private chapel.

Every major morning newspaper in Australia led with the story the next morning, filling in details missing from Pell's statement. The complainant alleged, it was reported, that at a holiday camp for under-privileged children on Phillip Island in 1961, he was molested at age twelve by a seminarian known as "Big George". The story dominated television and radio news all over the country and received promi-nent coverage internationally. Retired Victorian Supreme Court Judge Alec Southwell, QC, who was not a Catholic, was appointed to conduct the inquiry, which occurred in early October.

The complainant could not be named for legal reasons. What lit-tle was known of him was that he was about eight years younger than Pell—fifty-three at the time the story broke—and that he had children and grandchildren. In the 1980s he featured in the report of Royal Commissioner Francis Xavier Costigan, QC, who was inquir-ing into the activities of the Federated Ship Painters and Dockers Union. Among other matters, the report mentions a Supreme Court writ issued against the complainant for unpaid taxes, interest, and costs of more than AU$110,000. The report also details involvement in SP (starting price) bookmaking, a system of illegal gambling on horse races, which he used to augment his wages while employed at a Melbourne dockyard. He gave his occupation as "bookmaker" when applying for a credit card.

The transcript of the commission shows the complainant repeat-edly refusing to answer questions, branding the Royal Commission "a farce", talking back to the commissioner, and accusing him of "squandering taxpayers' money" when he, the complainant, claimed to be "virtually paying your wages". As Andrew Bolt wrote in the *Herald Sun*, "The royal commission also grilled Mr X about a surprise visit he paid to a nervous witness who was in the middle of giving

[1] "Dr George Pell's Statement on Sex Allegations", *The Age*, August 21, 2002, https://www.theage.com.au/national/dr-george-pells-statement-on-sex-allegations-20020821-gduih4.html.

evidence in which it was hoped he would name names. Mr X refused to explain why he dropped in on the witness—a man he'd never met before—at his Sydney hotel after flying up from Melbourne."[2]

Co-chairman of the Church's National Committee for Professional Standards (NCPS) Brother Michael Hill and members of Broken Rites condemned the leaking of the complainant's criminal history to the media.

It was clear that a number of Catholic figures in Sydney and Melbourne knew about the complaint for weeks before Pell was told. The complainant first approached the Church's sex-abuse complaints authority, the National Committee on Professional Standards (NCPS), in June—just over a week after David Ridsdale's appearance on 60 *Minutes*, alleging that Pell had tried to bribe him to keep quiet. The complainant was interviewed in Melbourne by Sister Angela Ryan, NCPS executive director, who forwarded the details to NCPS co-chairman Bishop Geoffrey Robinson—one of Pell's two auxiliary bishops in Sydney. Both urged the complainant, repeatedly, to go to the police, but he refused to do so.

The NCPS other co-chairman, Brother Michael Hill, was overseas in July and first became aware of the complaint in mid-August. Hill said it had been "awful, really awful" for senior members of NCPS to know about the complaint and have to withhold the information from Archbishop Pell. The fact that Robinson was Pell's auxiliary bishop had been "another horrific complication", Hill said, explaining that the NCPS heads were unable to inform Pell "because until you are sure the complainant is not going to the police and you get a definite complaint your hands are tied". He said that maintaining confidentiality, even from the person accused, was standard practice while those taking details of the complaint were urging the complainant to go to the police. This was because in some cases, telling the alleged perpetrator about the matter could mean repercussions that "bounce back on whoever was making the complaint".

One of the mysteries about the complaint is who posted details of it on the Sydney Independent Media Centre website August 7, a fortnight before Pell stood aside. Publication on the web was followed swiftly by the posting and faxing of copies to selected journalists,

---

[2] Andrew Bolt, "Why Pell Can't Win", *Herald Sun*, August, 22, 2002.

lobby groups, and victim support groups around Australia. The detailed account of the allegation was published under the by-line "Xavier O'Byrne, Parramatta". The material suggests that the author either had detailed contact with the complainant or someone he had confided in or someone with access to the NCPS process.

According to "Xavier O'Byrne", Bishop Robinson decided that the Church could not investigate this complaint under its sex-abuse protocol, the 1996 document Towards Healing, because Pell was an archbishop under the authority of the pope.[3] The website article continued:

> The complainant was left with the impression that the church was not eager to act on this complaint. The complainant still believed that his complaint needed to be investigated by someone. But, if not by the church, who then? The complainant was considering taking his complaint to an investigative journalist of a leading newspaper, so that the journalist could make the necessary inquiries that the church had failed to do. As soon as the National Committee for Professional Standards heard about this intention, they decided—urgently—to initiate a church investigation after all, although (said Robinson) a church investigation would not have any teeth because Pell is too big.

The alleged instances of indecent touching by the man the complainant referred to as "Big George" made appalling reading. Since the material was posted before any inquiry was launched, let alone anyone prosecuted or found guilty, the article was intended to do serious damage to Pell. Such an attack on the reputation of any citizen would be a grave matter. Against an archbishop whose preaching on issues of faith and morals had made him a well-known public figure, the potential damage to his reputation and good name, should any of the mud stick, could be catastrophic.

Pell's solicitor Richard Leder of Corrs Chambers Westgarth in Melbourne, wrote two letters to the Adelaide-based operators of the internet site, which were also posted. "The assertions in the article are scurrilous and without foundation", the first letter said. "Archbishop Pell rejects the allegations entirely. The article is highly defamatory

---

[3] "Big George Would Grab Me from Behind and Molest Me", Sydney Morning Herald, August 21, 2002, https://www.smh.com.au/national/big-george-would-grab-me-from-behind-and-molest-me-20020821-gdfk6q.html.

of the Archbishop. You would, no doubt, be well aware of our client's standing in the community and the strong stand that he has taken against sexual abuse within the Catholic Church. The damage that our client will suffer as a result of the publication of the article is incalculable. We are instructed to demand that the article be removed from your website immediately." The second letter said that Pell had "received further advice that as well as giving rise to a civil defamation action, the article also constitutes a criminal libel".

It was impossible to determine what links, if any, existed between the anonymous complainant and "Xavier O'Byrne's" internet article. The complainant's solicitor, Peter Ward of Galbally and O'Bryan in Melbourne, said he was "quite confident" his client had nothing to do with the internet item. Ward said he had a professional, rather than personal, relationship with the man and did not know whether he owned or could operate a computer, but doubted very much if he would seek to draw attention to the case, even with his name protected.

Galbally and O'Bryan agreed to represent the complainant for nothing after they found out that Towards Healing would not pick up the legal costs. Nor did the Church pay Pell's legal costs. Ward, a practicing Catholic, said he was astonished by that but decided to continue to work for the complainant to ensure he got a fair hearing. "Pell probably wouldn't agree but I think we did him the greatest favour [in representing the client for nothing] by giving him the chance to clear his name", Ward said. The ethics of his profession, he explained, meant he would prepare the strongest and most thorough case possible for his client to ensure he received a fair hearing. Ward has also represented the complainant in other matters. As a Catholic, Ward had no qualms about lining up against an archbishop, although he said he admired Pell for speaking out the way he did when he was archbishop of Melbourne. "He was conservative and that upset a number of people, but you knew where you stood with him", Ward said. "He was an excellent spokesman for the Church."

Ward said it was "no secret" that South Melbourne parish pastor Father Bob Maguire knew the complainant. "By that I mean he assisted him, told him where to go." Father Maguire, who died three months after Pell, in April 2023, was well known in Melbourne's inner suburbs for his hands-on help to drug addicts, street children, and gamblers. He was, initially, in no mood to talk to me when I called him in late 2002, venting his spleen over the telephone about Archbishop Denis Hart and his administration of the archdiocese. "And now you're torturing me with questions", Maguire said, before I had asked any. He referred to an ongoing row with Hart over funding for the range of welfare projects run from South Melbourne, for which, he pointed out, he had been awarded the Order of Australia. Maguire described himself as both orthodox and orthopractic (practicing the faith at street level). Was Maguire close friends with the complainant? He refused to speak publicly about the matter until the man was named. "We don't know who he is, officially."

So he liked Pell, then?

"Some people are running off at the mouth talking about a saint and an icon. George is all right as a human being. He gave us dough. He also said he'd back anyone who was doing things."

Did he respect Pell's background running Caritas, the Church's aid agency?

"Any fool can run things. It's about being hands on and getting your feet wet."

The late Father Gerry Diamond, then pastor of Glenhuntly in Melbourne, was one of the first priests to speak up publicly for Pell in print, branding the allegation against him as "preposterous", given the kind of seminarian Pell was in 1961. "The routine of the seminary was designed to foster growth in faith and in moral virtue", Diamond wrote. "This was facilitated by daily Mass, meditation, spiritual reading, and daily examination of conscience as well as by weekly confession and spiritual conferences."[4] As a seminarian, Pell was serious and self-disciplined and, in 1962, was chosen by the Jesuit rector of the college as rhetoricians' prefect to guide the first-year students in their growth in self-discipline. He also was noted for his prowess on the sporting field and in debating. At the end of each academic year, seminarians were reminded of their responsibilities during the holidays and of the need to continue their daily spiritual life. They also were specifically called upon to watch for and not place themselves in imprudent situations that could serve as "occasions of sin". At times, during the summer holidays, students assisted with camps run at Phillip Island, camps that were intended to enable boys, especially from deprived

[4] Gerry Diamond, "Heavy Cross to Bear", *The Courier-Mail*, August 22, 2002.

areas of Melbourne, to spend a week at the beach, which otherwise would not have been possible. These camps were supervised strictly and consisted mostly of team games. The accusation appeared to be groundless and reflected behaviour totally out of character with the one anonymously accused.

Diamond's description of the strictness and discipline of seminary life in the 1960s was echoed in some pulpits around Australia by other priests from the same era, who said students as serious and dedicated as Pell did not commit the kind of offenses alleged. Another Melbourne priest disagreed with Diamond's analysis of the times: "There was so much testosterone around that it's a wonder they weren't all at it."

The night of the announcement, Prime Minister John Howard defended Pell strongly as a person of honour: "I believe completely George Pell's denial", he said. "I rang him this evening and spoke to him. They are, of course, very serious allegations, and he's done the right thing in standing aside, and the church has done the right thing to have the allegations fully investigated." Howard said someone in his position had to make personal judgements from time to time about people. "You either believe somebody or you don't."[5]

A few hours later on the Australian Broadcasting Corporation's *Lateline* program, Patrick Power, the auxiliary bishop of Canberra, one of Pell's staunchest ideological opponents within the bishops' conference, was more circumspect. Asked by Tony Jones if he would be prepared to say the same thing as the prime minister, Power replied, "I think I would say that given that there is going to be an inquiry, I think it is best to leave it to the inquiry to make those judgements, rather than to try and pre-judge or pre-empt what Judge Southwell will come up with." John Howard, Power said, was "in the situation that any friend of Archbishop Pell would be in. Namely, that they would see him as a person of great integrity and in that sense express their support for him in this difficult situation. I think, as I say, he's come to the defence of a good friend of his, and I think many of Archbishop Pell's other friends would take a similar stance." Asked whether the accusation would damage Pell's chances of being promoted to the rank of cardinal in future, Power surprised many

[5]John Howard, Doorstop Interview, Parliament House Canberra, August 20, 2002, https://pmtranscripts.pmc.gov.au/release/transcript-12579.

Catholics, accustomed to previous archbishops of Sydney being promoted to the ranks of cardinal, when he said: "Could I say that all the presumption that he was ever going to be a cardinal, I think, is simply presumption. I don't think that that ever necessarily followed in any case."[6]

In Brisbane, Labor Premier Peter Beattie, an experienced lawyer, praised Pell for stepping down with dignity and told the Queensland Parliament that people who made false claims should feel the full force of the law and that his government was considering upgrading criminal defamation to an indictable offense. In a plea for a level of censorship that newspapers and the electronic media would regard as dangerous, civil libertarian and prominent Brisbane lawyer Terry O'Gorman went farther, arguing that people accused of sexual abuse should not be identified unless they have been found guilty, to avoid reputations being irretrievably damaged. Sexual abuse allegations, he said, were "very easy to make and very hard to defend".

Speaking from London, David Ridsdale, who had accused Pell of trying to buy his silence about the abuse he suffered at the hands of his uncle, urged the complainant to go to the police to have the matter dealt with properly. Ridsdale also said that, while "there are plenty of reasons why I do not believe that George Pell should be a spiritual leader", he also held a deep respect for the right of people to the presumption of innocence until they were proven guilty.

A Melbourne priest who was supporting the man who claimed he was abused by Pell portrayed the complainant as a "deeply sensitive, wounded man, who was never looking for money or publicity or to embarrass Pell publicly, but rather was a reformed character who has left behind his life of crime and wanted a quiet, private meeting with Archbishop Pell and a 'rapprochement', after which they'd each go their separate ways." The man likened the complainant to a hypersensitive little boy, outwardly tough, who was frightened by a "large spider" when young and has carried irrational fears and aversions ever since.

According to that priest, the late Father Bob Maguire, the complainant never wanted to damage Pell's career, but, rather, he was

---

[6] *Lateline* was a television news program aired by the Australian Broadcasting Corporation from 1990 to 2017.

acting out of a sense of personal injustice and out of a sense that Pell was too hard on people over issues like premarital sex, abortion, and homosexuality: "He simply wanted to make the point that Pell isn't above everybody else—remember George that thou art but a man, a human being flawed like other men." Maguire said the complainant said he first noticed George Pell on television in the late 1990s and recognized him from the long-ago camp.

In *The Age*, Martin Daly also reported that the complainant had not been after publicity, quoting him as saying: "I did not think it would even make the Melbourne papers. That [publicity] was not what I wanted. George Pell made it public, not me."[7] But Pell had little option after the internet posting; he believed that going public was the only thing to do.

Daly reported that the man "feels vilified by the Catholic Church and its sources who allegedly revealed to the media his criminal history". He also quoted a friend of the alleged victim, who asked not to be named. "He [the alleged victim] is very angry. Our intention was for reconciliation and healing for both parties", he said. "But what has happened is as far away from that as you could possibly imagine. We are in shock. He does not deserve to feel this bad a second time around. It is not what we expected. This all flies in the face of the spirit of Towards Healing. This is Goliath talking down to David." Daly reported, however, that "the alleged victim took the first step on May 2, 2000, in the process that this week forced George Pell to stand aside."

According to Daly, Broken Rites, the Melbourne-based advocacy and support group for victims of Church abuse, said the complainant had telephoned them. He alleged he had been abused at a Phillip Island camp for altar boys by George Pell, who was a seminarian at the time. Bernard Barrett, of Broken Rites, said: "He gave his first name. But we did not press him. We told him to call us back when he wanted." The alleged victim called again on June 8 and repeated his claims. He rang back a few days later, saying that, on the advice of his parish priest, he had contacted Sister Angela Ryan, the Melbourne-based executive director of NCPS, which supervises the Church's Towards Healing

---

[7] Martin Daly, "Pell Accuser: I Won't Back Down to Bullying or Smears", *The Age*, August 24, 2002.

process. Sister Ryan interviewed the man in June and sent him a copy of his statement, which he returned with corrections to parts that were not in sequence. Sister Ryan, Bishop Geoffrey Robinson, and Broken Rites all advised the man to contact police. "But I estimate 90 percent of them [complainants] still go through the Church process, rather than the police", Barrett said.

Daly said that the complainant wrote to Bishop Robinson on July 17, expressing concern about the lack of progress in his case and threatening to take his case to the media unless something was done. On July 20, Daly said, Bishop Robinson wrote to the man offering a process of inquiry. "He also promised that if the complaint was proven, the accused person would be confronted with the findings, 'and the difficulties of his situation would be pointed out to him as forcefully as possible' ", Daly wrote. "The man agreed to the inquiry offered by the bishop."

The Age report claimed that the complainant did not want publicity but wanted the matter dealt with by the Church. As Daly reported, the allegations were leaked to an Adelaide website. *The Age* submitted a series of questions to Pell on the night of Monday, August 20, and on Tuesday Pell stood down. Pell's announcement came shortly after Archbishop Philip Wilson of Adelaide, the acting co-chair of NCPS, announced publicly that there would be an inquiry.

The breaking of the story triggered an avalanche of well over a thousand letters, cards, emails, and telephone good wishes for Pell, which poured in for weeks from around the world, including a personal message of support from Pope John Paul II sent via a senior Vatican cardinal. Sydney's senior auxiliary bishop, David Cremin, was appointed to oversee the archdiocese during Pell's leave. For several weeks, Cremin was the only bishop functioning in an archdiocese that has long had an archbishop and three auxiliaries. Apart from Pell's leave, Bishop Robinson was ill and took holidays, and the third vacancy had not been filled.

Not surprisingly, those who suffered the most anger and grief about the allegations were Pell's family. At the height of despair one day, one close relative admitted: "Coping with a death would be easier." The weekend after his announcement, Pell headed off to his beachside unit with his sister, Margaret, and their cousin from Melbourne, for four days. He walked on the beach but rarely went out otherwise, and he said Mass every day. Back in Sydney, one of his close friends spotted him walking around the cathedral presbytery grounds early one morning praying the Rosary with an intensity not seen before. When Pell ventured outside the grounds for walks, people in the street were invariably friendly and wished him well.

Among dozens of letters to the editor published at the time was one in *The Australian* by Brian Haill, president of the Australian AIDS Fund, Inc., who told of Pell's kindness to AIDS patients. The archbishop had quietly visited many of the people with HIV/AIDS whom Haill's organization cared for. "He brought gifts and laughter and offered himself openly to intense questioning at each of these meetings", Haill wrote. "The metropolitan media never knew of this side of him, but these meetings revealed a deeply compassionate side to a really caring pastor. For those reaching to throw stones, take care—this is a good man. Justice too must be served. But let there not be a rush to judgement beforehand."

From the time of his announcement, George Pell made himself incommunicado to journalists. Pell's anonymous accuser also kept his head down. His Melbourne solicitor, Peter Ward, said the man was very distrustful of strangers and would not be interviewed by someone he did not know. Nor would he answer questions put to him in writing, Ward said.

In Australia, Pell's leadership was sorely missed by Catholics. The week he stood aside, debate in the House of Representatives indicated that the government's legislation permitting embryonic stem cell research on unwanted, frozen embryos was likely to pass easily on a conscience vote. That same week, also in Canberra, the Australian Capital Territory Legislative Assembly voted by a majority of one to become the first Australian state or territory to remove abortion from the criminal code.

While Pell stayed out of sight, many of his friends and foes were only too willing to be interviewed, although only a few would speak on the record. One or two of the complainant's friends and associates were also cooperative. Some of the claims made by people on both sides were impossible to check, although they were indicative of the passionate feelings the issue provoked. One usually reliable source even claimed that embittered families of victims of a convicted Melbourne paedophile priest had put a private investigator on Pell's tail for a time hoping to discover something that could be used against him. Little of interest was uncovered, the source said, and the information, such as it was, was passed to an organisation opposed to the Church.

Several people sympathetic to the complainant and who also appeared to be fully informed about details of the case made it clear that they disliked Pell and traditional Catholic teachings on sexuality. They said that had Pell been a Uniting Church minister, a Jewish rabbi, or anybody else but an outspoken Catholic archbishop, the matter would never have arisen. Why not? Was some kind of New-Age sectarianism taking hold? Did this mean that the complaint was partially motivated by some kind of ideological conflict with Pell? No, but exposing what the complainant and his supporters regarded as "hypocrisy" was a factor, one of the complainant's priest friends claimed. The priest, who said he believed the complainant "97 percent", also said he believed the incident had been a one-off "flash in the pan" and that Pell did not deserve to lose his career but should "tone down the holier-than-thou rhetoric". The priest was being either naïve or disingenuous in the extreme. In the prevailing climate of concern around the world over clerical sex abuse, it was utterly fanciful to suggest that any bishop convicted of such an offense could hold his position. Another man closely associated with a sex-abuse victims' support group said Pell had set himself up "to be taken down a peg" by speaking loud and long about "no sex before marriage" and making "other statements that don't gel or that are out of kilter with people".

All the members of victim-support groups interviewed stressed that the complainant deserved to have his story heard. So why did he not come forward earlier? Why did he not pursue his right to have his day in court, report the matter to police, and work through the legal system? It was impossible to ask him, but one woman with years of experience assisting sex-abuse victims said she believed he was "hedging his bets" by pursuing several avenues—he was in contact with Broken Rites and his parish priest and had kept *The Age* in the background as well.

Not surprisingly, several of Pell's friends, including people with children, leapt to his defence, insisting "he just wouldn't have it in him" to abuse—or hurt—a child. Parents who know him well say he has encouraged their children to excel and to practice the faith and that he has played sport with children, listened to them, read to them, taught them, recommended books for them, and helped them all of his adult life without even a suggestion of scandal. "I've watched him with my child; he's open, warm, and really loves children, and they love him, they respond to his goodness", one mother said. Another friend thought it ridiculous even to suggest that Pell was gay. It was well known among his circle that had he not been a priest he would have liked to have married and to have had children. In one of the first interviews for this biography, late in 2001, Pell said that he favoured the retention of mandatory celibacy for clergy. He also said that he had found the hardest part of keeping that vow had not been living without sex but "living without the love and close companionship of a wife and children".

Two decades ago, hard-headed supporters of Pell, in Australia and overseas, especially in the United States, did not underestimate the hatred some of his opponents held for him and for bishops like him. Such people feared that after the allegations were settled, others would materialize as part of a calculated process to render his position untenable and intimidate less brave Church leaders into compromising, or remaining silent, on the harder aspects of Church teaching. As events twenty years later proved, it was a prescient apprehension.

Had Australia really become so secular and so insular by 2002 that Church leaders whose views contradicted the prevailing social mores could not go about their work without derision, harassment, or worse? The loud "boos" at the Ernie awards in 2002 for Pell's anti-abortion statements gave those who care deeply about such matters pause for thought about what has, by degrees of encroaching secular humanism, become socially acceptable and what has not. It was clear that the Church faced a long, uphill battle for her teachings on marriage, family, and society to gain widespread credence, especially while the Church struggled to put her own badly shaken house in order. In September 2002, Archbishop Jozef Zycinski, fifty-four, of Lublin, Poland, an archdiocese with 190 seminarians, visited Australia. Zycinski praised Prime Minister Howard for supporting Pell, but he rather startlingly compared modern-day Australia's attitude towards the Church to that of the Communists who formerly ran Poland. "Under the Communist system we used to repeat the joke that to become innocent, one has to prove that one is innocent. Because the basic principle was that everyone is guilty", he said. "But I am afraid that in a free, civil Australian society, what was a joke in Poland is a reality here."[8]

In a November 2001 interview, Pell explained why some people saw him as such a divisive figure. "I think one of the functions of a bishop is to try and ensure that the fullness of the Catholic faith is taught", he said. "It has been a temptation for twenty or more years to try to improve the situation of the Church by going silent on some aspects or underplaying other challenges." The Church, he said, was not a sociological institution "or a shop selling a variety of merchandise, and if some brands aren't selling we just cancel that brand. I believe that we're basically about something that is supernatural, revelations from the Son of God. Some of his teachings were hard and provocative, but they have been proved to bring life in the long run even in human terms, and we don't have any warrant or authority to change them." One of the prices to be paid for leadership, he recognized in a later interview, on the eve of his thirty-fifth anniversary of ordination in December that year, was "opposition from people who conscientiously feared that you were mistaken in what you stand for".

> It can become a bit more irritating if in fact they fear that you're making progress than if they think you're a complete dope. Now the other thing is, and I will be careful how I say this because not everybody who opposes me by any means falls into this category, but I do feel that if you're going to bat for what is good and for the faith, you might be opposed by what euphemistically might be described as evil. I think that once in a while there has been a dimension of that in the opposition team.

In the lead-up to the inquiry into the allegations by the anonymous former painter and docker, the dean of Saint Patrick's Cathedral, Melbourne, Father Gerard Dowling, reminded radio listeners on September 8, 2002, and *Kairos* readers in print that one of the

---

[8] James Murray, "Faith in Physics: Zycinski Says the Narrowness of Some People's Vision of God Is Expanded by Science", *The Australian*, September 24, 2002.

hardest aspects of Jesus' final hours was the false accusations directed at him. He was sentenced to death on trumped-up charges, with false statements sworn against him. Those who heard or read the rector's words drew comfort from them as they prayed and waited in the expectation that Pell would be cleared. Father Dowling said:

> As a priest in today's society, I am only too well aware that I could be falsely accused. The same can be said of my brother priests and quite obviously of one of those who bears the added responsibility of being a bishop in this critical climate. To make this claim is not to put any of us above reproach, nor beyond the requirements of justice, if we have failed. Nevertheless, it does put the spotlight on the inherent vulnerability of anyone who is game enough to take up Jesus' cross and follow him, be that as a lay person, a religious, deacon, priest or bishop.... The age of the martyrs is not dead.

At the time, the Sydney archdiocesan website invited all people "to pray for the Archbishop and his accuser, that the truth will prevail and that justice be done". At sixty-one, Pell was just beginning what was to be his most productive decade in the Church. Like anyone on the wrong side of middle age, Pell said at the time that he occasionally thought of death and dying, but it did not bother him. When it happened, he said, he would want his friends and flock to thank God for his life as well as pray for his soul, that he be loosed from his sins in purgatory and enter heaven.

23

Cleared

George Pell and the former painter and docker who accused him of sexual abuse that had allegedly taken place more than forty years before had one direct exchange during the inquiry into the allegation. The two came face-to-face outside the first-floor boardroom of the Rydges Hotel in Exhibition Street, Melbourne. "Day of reckoning, George", those nearby heard the complainant say. Pell looked his accuser directly in the eye. "Yes, it is", he replied. The real day of reckoning came later, on Monday, October 14, 2002, when former Victorian Supreme Court Judge Alec Southwell, QC, released his report. "Bearing in mind the forensic difficulties of the defence occasioned by the very long delay, some valid criticism of the complainant's credibility, the lack of corroborative evidence and the sworn denial of the respondent, I find I am not 'satisfied that the complaint has been established', to quote the words of the principal term of reference", Southwell wrote. He described the investigation, which heard evidence for five days, from September 30 to October 4, as similar to a royal commission or a statutory board of inquiry. Southwell said: "The complainant, when giving evidence of molesting, gave the impression that he was speaking honestly from an actual recollection. However, the respondent [Pell] also gave me the impression that he was speaking the truth."[1]

The report was released two days after the bombings of two Bali nightclubs, which killed almost two hundred people and maimed many others—including eighty-eight Australians. Pell said the lunchtime Mass that Monday in Saint Mary's Cathedral for victims of the attack.

[1] A. J. Southwell, "Report of an Inquiry into an Allegation of Sexual Abuse against Archbishop George Pell", p. 15, http://www.bishopaccountability.org/news555/2002_10_14_NCPS_Report_of.pdf.

336

His appearance at the altar, in green vestments, was the first many of the congregation knew of his exoneration.

Soon afterwards, he held a press conference and released the following statement:

> I am grateful to God that this ordeal is over and that the enquiry has exonerated me of all allegations. The Honourable A.J. Southwell, QC, was appointed to determine, under specific Terms of Reference, whether or not the complaint was established. In his findings released today the Commissioner has gone as far as the Terms of Reference allowed him to go in exonerating me.
>
> When a person is under extreme pressure, personal values may crumble. However my Catholic convictions sustained me during those dark weeks. I found a great strength in regular prayer and in reflecting on the great Christian teachings about suffering, death and resurrection. My confidence that God loves us all without exception, and that He asks of us justice, truth and a compassion which bears no one ill will, was never shaken. In addition, I was immensely consoled by the love, support and loyalty of family and friends.
>
> As you are well aware I submitted myself to the rigorous scrutiny of this five-day enquiry, which produced 561 pages of transcript. It heard from fifteen witnesses and considered statements from another seventeen witnesses. I have faxed to Archbishop Philip Wilson, co-chair with Brother Michael Hill of the Towards Healing process and co-appointer of the enquiry, my consent to the public release of the full transcript of the enquiry and all the exhibits.
>
> I am deeply grateful to all those who supported me in many different ways: my family and friends, my defence team, the Catholic community, lay people, bishops, priests and religious, and Christians of all other denominations, people of other religions, people of no religion and, in a particular way, people who explained to me that, although they differed from me in matters of religion, morality or social life, they wished to offer me their support.
>
> I have just celebrated Mass for all those caught up in the tragedy of Bali, and look forward to being in the office tomorrow, resuming my work of spreading the Catholic faith and celebrating Mass on Sundays, as usual, at Saint Mary's Cathedral.

Would any of the mud stick, one of the journalists asked at his press conference. "There's no mud to stick", Pell said, "I've been exonerated." He had no criticism of the inquiry but was disappointed there were "a lot of leaks". "I had nothing to do with them", he said. "I don't know who did." The complainant's solicitor, Peter Ward of Galbally and O'Bryan in Melbourne, said his client also had no complaints. "He reckons he got a fair hearing", Ward said. "We are delighted with the hearing. We have been vindicated." Ward accepted that Southwell had found in the archbishop's favour but pointed to the paragraph where the judge said the complainant gave the impression that he was speaking honestly.

Pell said that he bore his accuser no ill will and that "after a little interval of time" he had been able to pray for him and continued to do so. He said he would be happy to meet the complainant if the man so wished. "I think I'd say, well, this is a great mystery to me. These things didn't happen. How it's developed like this, I just don't know." Pell said it was "a bit of a mystery" whether the complainant's accusations were "the product of a delusion or a violation by somebody else or lies or a combination of all three". Asked if he was considering legal action for defamation, Pell said: "Well, I've never sued anybody. Bishops don't normally sue. I'm aware in the United States that, as people falsely accused, some of their ministers of religion have sued for defamation. I wouldn't rule it out forever and a day as a general principle, but it's not part of my thinking at the moment." Asked should there be changes to a situation where people could make anonymous allegations against public figures and remain anonymous when the charges were not substantiated, Pell said, "I think that's one of the factors we should be looking at." Rejecting suggestions that the inquiry was not transparent, Pell pointed out that he did not set it up and that it was closed in order to protect the complainant's anonymity. Had the complainant gone to the police, he said, and "in the unlikely event that it had got to court", proceedings would have been open. So intent was the complainant on preserving that anonymity that he swung a punch at a Melbourne *Herald Sun* photographer who tried to photograph him.

Pell criticized the conveners of the Church's Towards Healing process, noting it was "remarkable" that it took two months from the time the complaint was lodged with them until he was informed of it. "I think I would've anticipated that I would've been informed earlier than that." Asked if the delay had harmed his case, he replied, "It certainly didn't help it." In an extraordinary twist, one of the main targets of that criticism is a man who should have been one of the archbishop's closest associates, Bishop Robinson, the then Sydney-based chairman of the Church's National Committee for Professional Standards (NCPS). The archbishop knew nothing of the matter until August 8, when he was told by his lawyer, Richard Leder, that defamatory claims had been posted anonymously on a website.

Sydney traditionally has three auxiliary bishops. For more than a year, the archdiocese had had only two—Robinson and David Cremin, then seventy-two, who ran the archdiocese in Pell's absence. Appointing a third auxiliary was undoubtedly high on Pell's "to do" list.

As for the complainant, what he stood to lose after the verdict was ... nothing. His good name was unaffected, and his legal team, unlike the archbishop's, acted for nothing after the Church made it clear she was not paying the legal fees for either party. In contrast, Pell had everything to lose—his reputation, his position as head of Australia's most senior Catholic archdiocese, and a probable cardinal's hat in the future. Australia's Catholics stood to lose their strongest leader in fifty years. As Southwell noted: "Although this is not a criminal proceeding requiring proof beyond reasonable doubt, I must bear in mind that serious allegations are involved and that an adverse finding would in all probability have grave, indeed devastating, consequences for the respondent."[2]

Southwell said that early in the hearing it became apparent there was considerable doubt whether the alleged molestation took place at a camp in 1961 or 1962. While the complainant's recollection was that he attended only one camp, "between schools" in 1961, Church records show he definitely attended the 1962 camp. To ensure that the merits of the complaint could be properly investigated, Southwell had the terms of reference amended so the matter related to "1961 or 1962". As to motive, Southwell said extensive inquiries made on behalf of Pell had unearthed "no evidence of any other matter or incident which might have aroused spite or malice on the part of the complainant towards either the respondent or the church".[3]

Ward said it was clear that the complainant had been vindicated against suggestions he was acting out of some vindictive motive. "The fifteen-page report is a well-compiled, well-weighted document",

[2] Ibid, p. 6.
[3] Ibid., p. 11.

Ward said. Southwell said that the complainant's credibility was subjected to a forceful attack during the hearings but that his record was
"notable more for alcohol and violence than dishonesty". However,
Southwell continued,

> there is sufficient evidence of dishonesty to demonstrate that the com-
> plainant's evidence must be scrutinized with special care. It would be
> difficult to be satisfied about his version against that of the respon-
> dent unless some support were to be found in the evidence of other
> witnesses, or in circumstantial evidence. The complainant had been
> before the court on many occasions, resulting in thirty-nine convic-
> tions. Most of these were for drunk-driving and assault, between 1969
> and 1975, but there were also three convictions for illegal betting, two
> fines for contempt, and a three-year jail sentence in 1995 for traffick-
> ing amphetamines. The complainant had also evaded taxation.

Ward admitted that the complainant was responsible for one
of the leaks from the inquiry—that of Pell's opening statement,
reported in *The Age* in Melbourne by Martin Daly. Ward agreed
that he had spoken to Daly in the foyer of the hotel during the
inquiry, "but that doesn't mean I was leaking to him; I wasn't."
Ward also complained about the leaking of part of a transcript of the
inquiry to Andrew Bolt, leading columnist with another Melbourne
newspaper, the *Herald Sun*. That section of the transcript detailed
evidence given to the inquiry by the complainant about his relationship with the former state historian of Victoria, Bernard Barrett,
who worked with Broken Rites, an advocacy group for victims of
clerical sex abuse. According to the published transcript, the complainant told the inquiry that he and Barrett met to discuss "victim
impact statements and how much money I was going to get". But
the complainant made it clear he was not after money. In response
to this, Barrett told the inquiry he had only explained the maximum
amount the Church might pay. The complainant said he thought
Barrett leaked this part of the transcript, but Barrett denied doing so.
It seems that whoever posted the information on the internet and
circulated it to various journalists and organisations was intent on
inflicting maximum harm on Pell.

At his press conference, Pell said he was looking forward to resum-
ing work and regaining his equilibrium. During his month in exile,

Pell said Mass and read the breviary every day as usual and took comfort from doing so, but, not surprisingly, he found meditation difficult. Instead, he worked his way slowly through the Gospel of Saint Matthew. He returned to full duties on Tuesday, October 15, the feast of Saint Teresa of Ávila, whose famous quotations include: "We always find that those who walked closest to Christ were those who had to bear the greatest trials."

In February 2003, Archbishop Pell led a concelebrated Mass in the chapel of the Good Shepherd Seminary for the opening of the seminary year. The Sydney seminary had twenty-one new students—seven studying for the Sydney Archdiocese, seven for the regional and country dioceses of New South Wales, and another seven belonging to the recently opened Neocatechumenal Way seminary in Sydney, who study alongside the Good Shepherd students and who are destined to work as priests throughout Australia and Oceania. Also present were nine second-year students, plus a smaller number in the senior years. The size of the first-year class had not been seen anywhere else in Australia for at least twenty years. To Pell, the promising turnaround in vocations in Sydney was evidence that "God writes straight in crooked lines." After all, it came about immediately after the worst year for publicity the Church had ever seen.

Unlike a few of his colleagues in the Australian episcopal conference, who appeared comfortable with the idea of a lay-led Church, Pell acknowledged that the need for more priests is "probably the single greatest need of the Church in the next twenty-five years." He was optimistic:

> Vocations have always been somewhat scarce. The priesthood is a great life and not a refuge for those who cannot make it in the wider world. It holds many consolations, attracts great support from many people, and provides many opportunities for service and leadership in faith.
>
> We know the Holy Spirit will continue to flow where He wills, but one constant in all Catholic history is the need for priests, for vocations to the ministerial priesthood. Our Lord himself appointed the Twelve, called forth the shepherds, the fishers of men. Saint Paul underlined the importance of ambassadors for Christ. Without priests, our parishes will wither and die. The call of Christ to young men to be priests is a call to a great adventure.

Later in 2003, Pell received two new auxiliary bishops who shared his understanding of the importance of nurturing vocations to the priesthood. One was Bishop Julian Porteous, rector of the Good Shepherd Seminary—one of the more successful men in such a position in Australia for decades. The other new bishop was Anthony Fisher, O.P., the director and a former professor of bioethics and moral theology at the John Paul II Institute for Marriage and Family in Melbourne, which under his leadership was flourishing with 150 students.

After a rough 2002, the archdiocese was looking strong.

24

Raising God's Profile

News of George Pell's promotion to the College of Cardinals broke in Australia on Sunday evening, September 28, 2003, moments after Pope John Paul II read his name and those of twenty-nine others from his balcony to the crowd gathered in Saint Peter's Square for the Angelus. A thirty-first cardinal, whose name was never revealed, was created *in pectore* (Latin for "in the breast", meaning, "in secret"). He was presumably from a country hostile to the faith, where revelation of his name might have endangered him or others.

The consistory was set for October 21, which caught many by surprise. With only three months to go in the year and a heavy schedule ahead of the Holy Father, with the beatification of Mother Teresa and his own Silver Jubilee celebrations for his remarkable term as pontiff, many were expecting a February consistory.

The announcement threw Rome's ecclesiastical tailors into a frenzy as orders poured in by telephone and fax from the thirty cardinals from twenty-two countries for the distinctive crimson red robes they would need in time for the big day. "Usually we have at least two months' notice, but this time the pope caught cardinals and tailors off-guard", said Gabriele Masserotti Benvenuti, one of the partners at Barbiconi, a tailor shop that has served the Vatican for more than two hundred years.

George Pell's statement was short and to the point:

It is a signal honour to be appointed a Cardinal of the Catholic Church. The ancient College of Cardinals reflects the unity and universality of the Catholic Church, both wonderful blessings.

As Archbishop of Sydney, my appointment also recognizes the contribution of the Catholic community to Australian life. I will continue working to maintain and deepen this tradition of service.

Like Pell, most of the new cardinals were serving as archbishops of major episcopal sees; they came from all corners of the Church: the United States (Justin Rigali of Philadelphia), Canada (Marc Ouellet, P.S.S., of Quebec), and Hungary (Peter Erdo of Budapest), as well as Italy, Scotland, Mexico, India, Brazil, Guatemala, Spain, Nigeria, France, Sudan, Ghana, Croatia, and Vietnam. Four of the new cardinals were priests rather than bishops—from Switzerland, Belgium, Poland, and the Czech Republic—whom the pope honoured for outstanding service. As Pell said: "I'm sure that my story today is repeated amongst the overwhelming majority of the thirty-one new cardinals. That is, local boys, people who worked as priests and bishops from right around the world and who are now called to this office."

Some of the group were colourful characters. Cardinal Tomas Spidlik, S.J. was born in the Czech Republic in 1919, a year before Pope John Paul II, and like the then-Holy Father endured forced labour under the Nazis. He was ordained in 1949 and later taught Czech and Russian at a secondary school and lectured in Rome. For more than half a century from 1951, he worked with Vatican Radio, preparing homilies in Czech—an invaluable service for Czech Catholics who suffered for decades under Communism. He also led retreats for the Holy Father and the Curia.

On the weekend his appointment as a cardinal was announced, George Pell's office desk in the cathedral presbytery was weighed down with even more books and scholarly journals than usual as he wrote out by hand a major paper he would give the following Saturday to the symposium on "Catholic Moral Teaching in the Pontificate of John Paul II" at Philadelphia's Saint Charles Borromeo Seminary. Like most skilled writers, Pell focused best with a looming deadline. Largely overlooked in the excitement of his promotion to cardinal, the Philadelphia paper is one of his best pieces of writing, drawing upon the wisdom he gained in his many battles for the Church.

Pell began the speech with Pope John Paul II's observation in his 1993 encyclical *Veritatis Splendor* (The Splendor of Truth) that the Church was facing a crisis touching the very foundations of moral theology. "This crisis was no longer a matter of limited and occasional dissent but of an overall and systematic calling into question of traditional moral doctrine", Pell told the symposium. Traditional moral doctrine was under widespread attack in ways that were unimaginable to most people when Pope John Paul II was elected as the Vicar of Christ a quarter of a century earlier, Pell said. He cited the rush towards legally binding "gay marriages", partial-birth abortion, human cloning, and genetic engineering as examples.

Much of the speech centred on the role of conscience and the Christian understanding of human rights. "I believe in both conscience and human rights," Pell said, "but I believe the doctrine of the primacy of conscience is incompatible not only with the Christian concept of human rights, but with any concept of human rights."

Pell laid bare the erroneous notion that primacy of conscience advocates have Cardinal John Henry Newman on their side. The passage often cited to support that claim is Newman's declaration at the end of his *Letter to the Duke of Norfolk*: "Certainly, if I am obliged to bring religion into after-dinner toasts (which indeed does not seem quite the thing) I shall drink—to the Pope, if you please—still, to Conscience first, and to the Pope afterwards." In that letter, Pell explained, Newman was concerned about Ultramontane claims of extreme infallibilists and was facetiously explaining that if the pope told the English bishops to order their priests to work for teetotalism or to hold a lottery in each mission, they would not be obliged to do so. There was no doubt, Pell said, that Newman's understanding of conscience was specifically Christocentric, within the Catholic tradition.

The denial of God's truth, Pell argued, makes an enduring concept of justice that genuinely serves human life and love impossible:

> The practical meaning of this can be seen in the contradiction [John Paul II] identifies between a growing awareness of human rights and a repudiation of the fundamental rights of some of the most vulnerable members of the human family. We are so familiar with talk of the "right" to an abortion that it can be difficult for us to recall what a shocking and absurd debasement of the language of rights this is. And now, as medical science continually pushes back the age at which premature babies can be saved, including babies who have survived abortion, abortion activists are beginning to insist that abortion is not just the "right" to terminate a pregnancy, but the "right" to "the extinction of the foetus".

Pell's insights in Philadelphia were a shock to many Australian Catholics, educated in the 1970s and later, who grew up in a Church that emphasized ecumenism and particular areas of social justice to the virtual exclusion of all else. For about fifty years, few Catholic

secondary school students in Australia had heard anything about the
binding truths of Catholic moral teaching. At times, the twists on
ecumenism and social justice even undermined those truths. For
example, social justice classes on anti-discrimination and the need
for fair legislation often left the impression that one type of lifestyle or relationship was as good as another, or that Catholics could
argue the case for "reproductive rights". At worst, abortion was
seen as "sad" rather than "wrong". Strong words like "wrong" were
reserved for "social sins" such as intolerance. The rare student who
did try to argue for a more traditional Catholic understanding was
patronized as "narrow-minded" or "fundamentalist". In the same
way, the intrinsically good practice of ecumenism became confused
in many young people's minds with the idea that all the churches
were equally good. This was regardless of their stance on moral
issues or more important questions like the divinity of Christ or
transubstantiation, which were rarely mentioned.

For decades, the tendency in Australia had been for bishops and
priests to make the public argument for Catholic moral claims and
social teaching on the basis of reason, with little reference to God.
Over the years, Pell had largely relied on that approach himself. In
the secular media, where he fought many of his battles, it was easier
to gain traction against heroin injection rooms, the use of condoms,
and the unfettered access to reproductive technology by using prudential arguments rather than by citing the will of God. In a nation
of twenty million people in 2002, with an abortion rate of more than
eighty thousand a year, the bishops tried to use arguments that would
gain airtime and be listened to by the young women tempted to
undergo such a procedure.

The prudential arguments against many of the practices opposed
by the Church—such as the threat to the elderly of the encroaching
acceptance of euthanasia—are sound. That is no surprise. There can
never be a contradiction between truth and reason. But by October 2003, Pell had decided that such an approach had its limitations.
"Relying on this approach too much can be a mistake", he said in
Philadelphia. "I think we should follow the example of Saint Thomas
More and Saint Catherine of Siena and others—including the pope—
and make God a central part of the case we make to the world."

That refreshing admission from an officer on Christ's front lines
gave many of Pell's episcopal colleagues around the world food

for thought. It was sound advice, going straight to the heart of the Church—Christ himself. It also demonstrated the need for the Church's senior bishops to have the intellect and skill to make a convincing case in media that lacked understanding of Catholic teaching and were often hostile to the Church. For thirteen years, Pell himself wrote about God and current issues in Australia's biggest-selling tabloid newspaper, the *Sunday Telegraph*, read by around two million people every week—a tenth of Australia's entire population. The column was effective in a cutthroat media world, where column inches were at a premium, attracting plenty of feedback, positive and negative.

In a 2003 column, he had posed the question:

> Is it important to know the difference between right and wrong? Nearly every Australian would say yes. To know that God exists? Probably most Australians would agree. To know that God loves us? The number would be smaller, but still substantial.
>
> Is it important to know that Jesus Christ is divine and the only Son of God? I don't know how many Australians would answer yes, and some who believe it wouldn't be sure what difference it made. Some claim that there is no point in giving answers to questions nobody is asking. This seems reasonable, but there can be situations where questions should be asked, even when there is silence.[1]

The following week he went on to discuss Australia's uneasy silence about abortion, equating it with the many years few people questioned slavery or the ill treatment of Australia's Aborigines. In a later column, he warned that the ubiquitous New Age movement had "no God capable of hearing our prayers, much less capable of answering them". The warmth of Mother Earth, so prominent in the New Age, removed the threat of judgement by the Father-God of Judaism and Christianity, he said. "But it also removes all possibility of justice and redress in the next life for those who have suffered."[2]

In his 2003 Philadelphia speech, Pell acknowledged the enormous pressure on the Church to mind her own spiritual and religious business and to leave the question of which values the community should

---

[1] George Pell, "Ask the Big Questions to Find Big Answers", *Sunday Telegraph*, December 14, 2003.

[2] George Pell, "The New Age", *Sunday Telegraph*, December 21, 2003.

adopt to those who could consider it in a secular way. "This is not a position that the Church can ever accept", he said. The Church should never concede that secularism was the only basis for public discourse. Pope John Paul II was right, he added, to claim that "the Christian faith gave form [to Europe], and some of its fundamental values in turn inspired the democratic ideal and the human rights of European modernity."

In Australia, Pell's promotion to cardinal drew warm congratulations from many people in public life. Prime Minister John Howard, a Protestant, praised him as "a great intellectual, a person of great determination and strength".[3] New South Wales Premier Bob Carr put on a civic reception for the cardinal, and thousands of letters, faxes, and emails streamed in from around the world.

Despite the many well-wishers, Auxiliary Bishop of Canberra Patrick Power said publicly that the appointment "further shows the Church to be representing many elements that I think are not doing the Church very much good at the moment".[4] He went on: "Many of the values that I think are dear to Australian Catholics, such as the dignity of the human person, the primacy of conscience, the theology of communion, the need for dialogue in our Church, reading the signs of our times—I don't think that they're values that are particularly clearly enunciated by Archbishop Pell."

Perhaps Bishop Power forgot that loyalty is another value Australians hold dear. In Rome, a cardinal in charge of a major congregation said he had never heard of such a public reaction by one bishop to another's promotion anywhere in the world. Pressed by journalists to respond, Pell, ever the team player and reluctant to sink the boot into a brother bishop, opted for diplomacy:

> The Catholic Church is not a small sect. There are a billion Catholics throughout the world and obviously there are different schools of theology. I hope I preach Christ. I certainly try to explain that the Christian teachings are true and beautiful and useful for people in this

---

[3] "Pope Makes Pell a Cardinal", *The Age*, September 29, 2003, https://www.theage.com.au/world/pope-makes-pell-a-cardinal-20030929-gdwfl5.html.

[4] "Bishop 'Disappointed' over Pell's Promotion", *Sydney Morning Herald*, September 29, 2003, https://www.smh.com.au/national/bishop-disappointed-over-pells-promotion-20030929-gdhhex.html.

life and the next. I'm a loyal son of the Second Vatican Council. I don't run around making up teachings. I've got no mandate from the Church to correct or improve Christ's teachings, but I've got to try to understand them more deeply and explain them.[5]

Pell also promised to continue to speak out on issues such as the Australian government's hardline but very popular stance in detaining asylum-seekers from abroad in detention centres. "I've said many times I think the policy of the government is too hard and too tough", he said. "But I also recognize the reality of Australian public opinion, the constraints on the government, but it's certainly not our finest hour." Many of Pell's supporters thought that argument was not his finest hour either. Apart from the Green-Left political fringe, most Australians expect their national leaders to keep control of the nation's borders and are prepared to vote them out if they fail. Since then, the debate over migration has intensified worldwide as millions of people have crossed the Mediterranean into Europe, the English Channel into Britain, and the deserts of Mexico into the United States. Most Australian Church leaders agreed with Pell's view. But when questioned on the matter, they were not prepared to specify how many unauthorized arrivals were too many.

Writing of Pell's promotion to cardinal in 2003, Bishop Anthony Fisher, O.P., said: "The word *cardinal* comes from the Latin *cardo*, meaning 'hinge'. It means someone in a pivotal position; a leader 'outstanding in doctrine, morals, piety and prudence in action' according to the canonical job description. When the Pope appoints a Cardinal, he sets the bar high on the kind of leader God requires and we deserve."[6] Fisher's wry humour put Pell's critics into perspective: "The usual suspects were rounded up to make the usual tut-tut noises. Some pretended surprise. Others thought it typical of a church going the wrong way. But they agreed on this: church or state, our leaders should agree with us. They should follow the polls and lead from behind. Otherwise they are out of step with the community."

[5] "Pell Dismisses Criticism of Appointment", *The Age*, September 29, 2003, https://www.theage.com.au/national/pell-dismisses-criticism-of-appointment-20030929-gdwfpr.html.
[6] Anthony Fisher, "The Human Wish for Leadership", *Sunday Herald*, October 12, 2003.

Asked about his chances of being elected pope, Pell, who enjoyed the flutter on the horses, answered as only an Australian could: "We've got the Melbourne Cup in a month or so ... and a little bit of form on the country course doesn't signify you should be a major challenger for the Melbourne Cup."[7]

[7] "Pope Makes Pell a Cardinal".

25

Witnessing Christ in Crimson

The bells of Saint Peter's Basilica rang out across the Eternal City at 10:10 A.M. on Tuesday, October 21, 2003, and shortly afterwards, thirty new cardinals walked into the square for the ninth consistory of the extraordinary pontificate of John Paul II. Each cardinal was accompanied by a priest, and walking beside George Pell that morning was his cousin Monsignor Henry Nolan from Ballarat, who had also accompanied him when he entered the seminary forty-three years earlier. Monsignor Nolan was the eldest of the twenty-seven cousins on Pell's mother's side of the family. Pell's sister, Margaret, was there. His brother, David, attended with his wife, Judy, and their four children: Sarah, Rebecca, Georgina, and Nicholas. They were happy that the pectoral cross Pell was wearing was the one they had made for him when he became a bishop in 1987. The ruby at the centre of the cross and the diamonds at the four points were from his mother's engagement and eternity rings. The day before, Margaret had bought her brother a set of cuff links when they found that the white shirt made to go under the red soutane needed them.

As Pell told *Sunday Telegraph* readers:

> The Pope created thirty new cardinals, twenty-six of us bishops along with four priests from twenty-two nations. The ceremony was celebrated outside in Saint Peter's Square in beautiful sunny weather, cooled by a slight breeze. This was welcome, as five layers of clothes and vestments make it easy to build up a head of steam. On Tuesday there was no Eucharist as the Pope conferred the red hat on each cardinal in a ceremony of music, Scripture readings and prayer. The office of cardinal does not derive from the Scriptures, so there is no ordination ceremony. When the list of names is announced by the

Pope, and the red hat is conferred, the Pope's decision becomes effective. The spectacular crimson red vestments are to remind us that the cardinals should be prepared to die in witnessing to Christ's person and teaching, as the early martyrs did in the pagan Roman Empire. Actually the century just concluded produced more Catholic martyrs than any other. Faith and heroism are still flourishing, usually in situations of great adversity.[1]

It was a sunny, unusually hot autumn morning, and the square looked its best, brightened by the red and gold tulips, the red of cardinals, the purple of bishops, and a crowd of faithful people from many races and cultures, who filled the square close to its two hundred thousand capacity. At the centre of it all sat a frail old man in gold vestments and gold miter with the pallium, symbol of his authority, around his neck. Unable to stand, walk, or sit straight and struggling to speak and just to breathe, the Holy Father, two days earlier, had beatified Mother Teresa of Calcutta and, a few days before that, had celebrated his silver jubilee as Vicar of Christ. At that point, he was the fourth-longest-serving pope in history behind Saint Peter, Pius IX, and Leo XIII.

The thirty new cardinals from twenty-two nations and their tens of thousands of supporters speaking different languages were the perfect illustration of what Bernini's colonnade expresses so beautifully. The basilica, as the Holy Father would remind the crowd at the next day's Mass, "opens its arms wide to all humanity, as if to show that the Church is sent to proclaim the Good News to all men and women without exception".[2] The old and the new Church of Christ, he said at the consistory, "shines out today, assembled round the successor of Peter".[3] Many of the faithful would not have understood the Italian language in which the pope's address was read out, but even the children present were moved by the old man's courage and mere presence and sensed they were witnessing history.

[1] George Pell, "Receiving the Crimson as the Holy City Plays Host to Saintly Ceremonies", *Sunday Telegraph*, October 26, 2003.

[2] John Paul II, Homily at Eucharistic Celebration with the New Cardinals (October 22, 2003).

[3] John Paul II, Homily at Ordinary Public Consistory for the Creation of New Cardinals (October 21, 2003).

In the distance, to the left of the square when facing the basilica, stood the proud vista of the Pontifical Urban University atop the nearby Janiculum Hill. Four of the thirty being elevated to the office of cardinal that day were graduates of that one institution. The twenty-first-century cardinals following in the footsteps of Saints Oliver Plunkett and John Henry Newman were Stephen Fumio Hamao of Japan from the ordination class of 1957, George Pell and Nigeria's Anthony Okogie from the class of 1966, and India's Telesphore Toppo from the class of 1969.

The vast congregation had a sense of involvement with the ceremony, cheering loudly as the name of each cardinal was read out. Pell's name drew loud cheers, and a startling "Aussie Aussie Aussie, Oi Oi Oi" (a popular sporting cheer) from a special scallywag from Down Under—his brother, David. About one hundred of Pell's friends from Australia were there, as well as friends he had made over the years from Canada, England, Ireland, and the United States. His party included his auxiliary bishop from Sydney, Anthony Fisher, O.P., Archbishop Philip Wilson from Adelaide, South Australia, and priests from Sydney, Melbourne, Ballarat, Brisbane, London, Dublin, and Rome. An additional ninety Australians who attended were in Rome on a pilgrimage for Mother Teresa's beatification, led by Archbishop Barry Hickey of Perth, Western Australia.

In the Gospel reading, James and John were wanting to be the first in the Kingdom, and Jesus told his disciples: "Whoever would be first among you must be slave of all. For the Son of man also came not to be served but to serve, and to give his life as a ransom for many" (Mk 10:44–45). As the pope reminded the cardinals in his homily, read out for him by Archbishop Leonardo Sandri of the Vatican Secretariat of State:

> Only after his death, however, would the Apostles understand the full meaning of these words and, with the help of the Spirit, fully accept their demanding "logic".
>
> The Redeemer continues to propose this same programme to those who, through the sacrament of Orders, are most closely associated with his mission. He asks them to convert to his "logic" that contrasts starkly with that of the world: to die to oneself, to become humble, disinterested servants of one's brethren, shunning every temptation to make a career and to seek personal advancement....

This is undoubtedly a difficult ideal to achieve, but the Good Shepherd assures us of his support. We can also rely on the protection of Mary, Mother of the Church, and the Holy Apostles Peter and Paul, the pillars and foundations of the Christian people.

As for me, I once again express my esteem to you and accompany you with constant remembrance in prayer. May God grant, in the various offices he entrusts to you, that you spend your whole life for souls.[4]

Before approaching the pope one by one to receive their official appointments and red birettas, the new cardinals took the oath of fidelity in Latin:

I, N., Cardinal of Holy Roman Church, promise and swear, from this day forth and as long as I live, to remain faithful to Christ and his Gospel, constantly obedient to the Holy Apostolic Roman Church, to Blessed Peter in the person of the Supreme Pontiff, become members of the Roman clergy and cooperate more directly in N. and his canonically elected successors, always to remain in communion with the Catholic Church in my words and actions, not to make known to anyone matters entrusted to me in confidence, the disclosure of which could bring damage or dishonour to Holy Church, to carry out diligently and faithfully the duties to which I am called in my service to the Church, according to the norms laid down by law. So help me Almighty God.[5]

The crimson of a cardinal's attire, Pope John Paul II reminded the thirty new cardinals receiving their birettas from him in Saint Peter's Square, "symbolizes the colour of blood and recalls the heroism of the martyrs. It is a symbol of a love for Jesus and for his Church that knows no bounds".[6] Vast screens in the square provided close-up footage of each cardinal kneeling before the Pope and receiving the biretta and the Holy Father's blessing. Later, as the cardinals were embraced by more than one hundred of their fellow cardinals, the pope appeared to wipe a few tears from his eyes before the crowd bade him farewell

[4] Ibid.

[5] Holy See Press Office, Ordinary Public Consistory for the Creation of New Cardinals, The College of Cardinals General Documentation.

[6] John Paul II, Consistory.

with enthusiastic applause, waving and cheering as he was wheeled in his chair from the square.

"I'd like to say how honoured and delighted I am to have been made a cardinal during the pontificate of our present Holy Father", Cardinal Pell told a crowded press conference at the Vatican radio centre after the ceremony.

I'm a great admirer of Pope John Paul II, and, talking about Australia as part of the Western world, I think that his diagnosis is basically correct. And I worked for years to support and implement that.

Certainly in Australia and in most parts of the Western world, those religious communities who preach the message of Christ more faithfully and strongly and have real service and create genuine community, they're going better than those communities who have a much more liberal sort of approach, or radical approach. Many of those are just slipping away and dissolving. Now even if we were preaching Christ and following Christ and we weren't getting the results that we have now, we'd still be obliged to do so. But we believe that Christ is the Son of God. We believe that His teaching is not just cumulative human wisdom, but a divine revelation, and I don't find it surprising therefore that when we preach it truly, when we live it, people are attracted by it today as they have been for two thousand years.

But how would he reconcile such conservatism with the need to attract younger people to the Church, he was asked.

I think it's very difficult for a Catholic or a vital Christian not to be conservative, because our basic teachings come from the great teacher who we believe was the Son of God two thousand years ago, and one of the great tasks of every bishop, and certainly a cardinal, is to preserve the apostolic tradition and to present it in a way that people can understand it. It comes at a cost; we have to take up our cross; but it works, and I think it works much, much better than the neo-pagan mix that is often presented, which is superficially attractive but, over a longer term, has brought considerable suffering to our society.

In Australia, some of the press comment about the new cardinal's promotion remarked on the distance George Pell had travelled in his sixty-two years from his parents' hotel in the Victorian country town of Ballarat to Saint Peter's Square. His story, he said—sports-loving country boy from an ordinary family who grew up to be a priest and then a bishop—"would not be untypical of the variety of backgrounds of the different new 'princes' of the Church".

Cardinal Pell's press conference was packed with journalists from religious and secular publications from Australia, the United States, and Britain, and from Australian television networks. He admitted that it had been hard to take in all the details of the ceremony in the square. "I listened attentively, but I was slightly distracted." It had all been touched by a "hint of sadness" with the obvious decline in the Holy Father's health. It would be wonderful, he said, if the next pope was "like the present Holy Father". And did he take any personal pride in all of this, he was asked. "I hope I don't allow myself too much pride, but I'm certainly very pleased and grateful to be a cardinal of the Holy Roman Church."

One great Protestant theologian, he recounted, said that "when preaching you should have the Gospel in one hand and a newspaper in the other", he said. "We've got to talk to the needs of people today. We've got to support the communities and form communities, especially with young people, we've got to get young people to bear witness to other young people. That's one of the most potent of all sorts of witnesses for youth."

He identified the erosion of faith, especially among the young, as one of the Church's major challenges:

> We have a slow erosion of church practice. In Australia the Catholics are not dissociating from the Church, but there are about 18 percent who worship weekly; we'd like that to be more than that, and as always of course we've got to practice what we preach, and we have to work as well as we can so that the flame of faith will catch, especially in the hearts of young people and younger middle-aged people.
>
> Sometimes young people drift away, at least temporarily. With those drifting away after being Catholic-educated, I want them to know what our basic claims are, and I want them to know the basic rationale we give for those claims. I think if we can get that across, it's a better basis for the flame of faith to catch, but it's also a better basis from which people might return after they drift away.

The neo-pagan mix, afflicting every Western society, had to be resisted, Pell said: "Very easy, slack rules on sexuality, suggestion that the question of God is irrelevant, very little regard for marriage and the family, very little regard for clear moral teachings, the suggestion we can all paint the moral picture any way we like. This is the sort of mix that is breeding a lot of unhappiness in the Western world, and in other places."

In relation to his role as chairman of the Vox Clara Committee advising the Congregation for Divine Worship and Discipline of the Sacraments on the English translations of the liturgy, Pell said it was important for the translations to be faithful to the original Latin. "The language will be, you might say, slightly more sacral, not everyday language, but given the significance of what we're enacting, especially in the Mass, in the Eucharist, it's my ambition to see beautiful and faithful translations of the Roman Missal, and I hope we'll have a translation of the Roman Missal closer to two years rather than three or four or five."

That afternoon, as gentle rain began to fall, each of the new "princes" spent two hours greeting visitors and imparting blessings to them. Pell was one of those positioned in the Paul VI Audience Hall. Others were seated in even greater splendor in the Vatican palace. Pell later joined about 150 friends for a reception in his honour hosted jointly by his friend John McCarthy, QC, a Sydney barrister, and the Knights of the Holy Sepulcher, a Catholic chivalric order dating back to the first Crusades.

Rome's severe summer drought broke with a vengeance the following morning, Wednesday, October 22, and the concelebrated Mass scheduled for Saint Peter's Square was shifted to the papal altar inside the basilica, beneath Michelangelo's dome and the bronze canopy of Bernini's baldacchino. Cardinal Joseph Ratzinger, prefect for the Congregation for the Doctrine of the Faith and dean of the College of Cardinals, was the principal celebrant, with Pope John Paul II, resplendent in gold vestments reading some of the prayers and presenting each cardinal with a gold ring bearing an image of the crucifixion. The pope's sermon, read out for him, encouraged the new cardinals: "If at times fear or discouragement surface, may the comforting promise of the divine Teacher console us: '*In the world you have tribulation; but be of good cheer, I have overcome the world*'! (Jn 16: 33)."[7]

[7] John Paul II, Eucharistic Celebration, italics in the original.

Despite his struggles to breathe and speak, the pope read the Latin formula before presenting the rings. "Receive the ring, sign of dignity, of pastoral zeal, and of a firmer communion with the See of Peter. Receive the ring from the hand of Peter and be conscious that in loving the Prince of the Apostles your love for the Church is reinforced." The Holy Father amazed those with a view of the altar by kneeling during the Eucharistic Prayer and other parts of the Mass. The thirty cardinals, in cream vestments with gold trim, concelebrated the Mass.

That evening, Pell hosted a dinner for his family and friends at Rome's Orazio restaurant, with the cardinal taking delight in organizing the seating plan himself, mixing up his extraordinary range of friends from around the world. "Having the family and a lot of my friends and priests there made it a really lovely week", he said later. "It was a wonderful time. One friend says a little bit like heaven. We were praying and feasting and seeing new things and enjoying one another's company, it was great."

On Thursday morning, the cardinal was able to present his three nieces and nephew to Pope John Paul II. Like all who met the Holy Father, the youngsters were impressed by his warmth and gentleness. "I just felt like hugging him", one of Pell's nieces told her aunt, Margaret Pell. "May your time in the City of the Apostles confirm you in faith, hope and love", the pope said at the audience.

Pell himself was lucky to make it to that papal audience. Early that morning, he and around a dozen priests in his party had concelebrated an early Mass at one of his favourite places in Rome, the fourth-century Basilica of Saint Clement, built on top of two buildings dating back to the Roman Republic before the time of Christ, one of them a temple to the pagan goddess Mithra. "There is a tremendous feeling of history in Rome", Pell said at the Mass. "The history of Europeans in Australia is so brief, we very much appreciate being in such a holy place, a sacred site where people have prayed for more than 1500 years."

The church has been cared for by Irish Dominicans since 1667 and comprises three Catholic churches built on top of one another dating from different eras; it was first mentioned by Saint Jerome in his writings in 392. It is named after Saint Clement, Christianity's fourth pope (88 to 97), who, according to legend, was banished from

Rome to the Crimean mines, where he converted so many soldiers and fellow prisoners that the exasperated Roman authorities tied an anchor to his neck and threw him into the Black Sea.

After Mass, Pell and his party explored the church until it was time for him to return to Cardinal J. Francis Stafford's residence in Trastevere to dress for the audience. A torrential rainstorm, however, meant finding a taxi was harder than walking on water, so the Dominicans' gardener set off with the cardinal in his car, only to be delayed with a flat tire. Pell was drenched and arrived at Cardinal Stafford's only just in time to change and make it to the audience.

After six exhausting, exhilarating days in Rome, Pell flew to Lebanon en route home. "This land has been a centre of civilization from well before the time of Christ", he told readers of his *Sunday Telegraph* column.

> Here the alphabet was invented, a simple development with immense consequences linking symbols to sounds, which made literature accessible to people generally....
>
> Many Lebanese of different religious traditions have migrated to Australia since the 19th century, making a wonderful contribution. More recently they have come here to bring up their children in peace, especially after the Lebanese civil war, where local factions and eventually foreign armies fought one another, killing about 150,000 people between 1975–1990. More than one million Lebanese left the country during this time.

He was welcomed to Lebanon by President Emile Lahood, the Maronite Catholic bishops, the leader of the Shiite Muslims, Sheik Kabalaan, and the leader of the Sunni Muslims, Mufti Rasheed Kabbani. Pell wanted to see the small chapel and residence where the Maronite patriarchs lived in the Valley of Saints for 450 years until about 1850. With no road leading to the historic centre, he joined other pilgrims in walking the last half mile. He found the simple, poor buildings an "eloquent testimony to an unconquerable faith". Pell had a natural authority, but despite his recent elevation as a prince of the church, his Lebanese hosts found he did not stand on ceremony. At one function, he impressed them by serving himself from the buffet, something most Lebanese bishops would not do, considering it *infra dignitatem* (beneath their dignity), one of Pell's friends from the Maronite community said. Pell considered it more about hunger than humility. In Sydney, Pell was close to the Maronites, whose young men served as bouncers at his first public function in the city, in case troublemakers turned up. Years later, a group from the community threw black paint over an offensive mural depicting him, within hours of its appearing.

Back home in Australia, Pell spent a busy fortnight in his archdiocese before heading back to Rome (a twenty-hour plus plane journey from Sydney) for meetings. This was his third long-haul flight since the beginning of October, and Pell's friends could only admire his stamina. "It seems as though Pell is doing two jobs, his work in Sydney and fulfilling his obligations in Rome to the various bodies and committees on which he serves", one man observed late in 2003. That is not unusual for a cardinal, but what makes it so demanding for an Australian cardinal is the distance from Australia to Europe. After the consistory, Pell was appointed to two more Vatican bodies—the Pontifical Council for Justice and Peace and the Pontifical Council for the Family. It was not a life for the faint-hearted.

On his last Roman trip for 2003, Pell visited, for the first time, his titular church in the Diocese of Rome—Santa Maria Domenica Mazzarello, a modern church built in 1997 in an outlying Roman parish created in 1982. The church is dedicated to the Salesian saint Maria Domenica Mazzarello, canonized by Pope Pius XII in 1951 for her work, along with that of Saint John Bosco, of founding the Salesian nuns, the Daughters of Mary Help of Christians. The order was one of the largest of women religious in the world, with fifteen thousand members in eighty-seven countries—including more than five thousand in North and South America. Our Lady Help of Christians, by coincidence, is patroness of Australia.

After a frenetic year, Pell returned to Australia in time for the Australian Bishops' Conference bi-annual meeting, which gave approval for Sydney to bid for the 2008 World Youth Day, an event with the potential to eclipse the 2000 Olympics in visitor numbers. Sydney's natural beauty and mild winter climate, Pell envisaged, would lend itself to the event.

At home, he was celebrating at least four Masses a week, often more, in different Sydney parishes, visiting several schools, and celebrating Mass for many different groups from the Chinese community to the

Italian community (marking fifty years of service by the Scalabrinian Order in Australia). In early December he conferred the Sacrament of Confirmation according to the Tridentine Rite at the Maternal Heart Chaplaincy at Lewisham, conducted by the Fraternity of Saint Peter, and joined Catholics at Saint Ambrose Church, Concord West, for First Saturday devotions. Getting out and about in his archdiocese was his way of practicing what he said at his Roman press conference after becoming a cardinal: "I think as a bishop, it's my task to encourage those movements or parishes or people where there is life and vitality."

It was also his task, he said that day, to be "vigilant to see that the teachings of Christ are presented accurately and comprehensively, especially to our young people". In many parts of Australia, like the rest of the world, it is harder to think of an issue that causes practicing Catholic parents as much angst as the weak catechetics in Catholic schools.

For all the glory of the October 2003 consistory in Rome, it was a smaller, quieter event late in the year that could ultimately touch many more lives and, possibly, save many more souls. On December 4, Pell's old friend Peter Elliott travelled north to Sydney from Melbourne for the launch of the To Know, Worship and Love series in Sydney. The series had grown to eleven books ranging from early childhood to tenth grade, with more added later. By 2004, Catholic schoolchildren, not only in Sydney and Melbourne, but also in regional New South Wales were learning from the colourful, well-produced textbooks. And in parts of Australia less fortunate, some families ordered sets to help their children at home. The children are encouraged to learn and understand four points Pell himself insisted be printed on the back of each book:

> We believe in one God, Father, Son and Holy Spirit who loves us.
> We believe in one Redeemer, Jesus Christ, only Son of God, born of the Virgin Mary, who died and rose from the dead to save us.
> We believe in the Catholic Church, the Body of Christ, where we are led in service and worship by the Pope and Bishops.
> We believe that Jesus, Our Lord, calls us to repent and believe; that is, to choose faith not doubt, love not hate, good not evil, and eternal life in heaven not hell.

Through those books, in leading tens of thousands of Catholic children every year to grasp these important tenets of the faith, Pell, in life and now in death, will continue fulfilling the vision of his hero Saint John Paul II, who urged Church leaders to "live as witnesses to a hope that never disappoints and as missionaries of a life that conquers death".[8]

---

[8] John Paul II, Address to the Pilgrims Devoted to Saint Rita of Cascia on the Centenary of Her Canonization (May 20, 2000), no. 4.

26

Death of Pope John Paul II

Eighteen months later, Pell was with a group of Neocatechumenal leaders and seminary rectors at Domus Galilee on the Mountain of the Beatitudes overlooking the Sea of Galilee when he heard the news of Pope John Paul II's death. "My reactions were mixed", he said in Rome on the eve of the late pope's funeral. "We were saddened by the loss of this extraordinary leader, [yet] we were relieved that his suffering was over and aware that we were Christian people who believed in life after death. But there was certainly sadness and an awareness of a great loss."[1]

The overwhelming majority of Australians, Pell said, aware of John Paul II's pivotal role in the overthrow of Soviet Communism, would have agreed with the posters put up around Trastevere in advance of his funeral: they featured a large photo of John Paul II with the simple message "Un Bravo Uomo" (a great man). "I think for the overwhelming majority of Australians, they would have said that—a good man and a great Catholic."

Pell mentioned a *Wall Street Journal* column by Peggy Noonan, a former speechwriter for President Ronald Reagan, which summed up well how mainstream practicing Catholics felt about Pope John Paul II. She had written a few years earlier that he "made her and many, many Catholics feel secure that the Church was in good hands—that they were safe." They did not feel safe from "external threat or misadventure or scandals or crises", Pell explained. Rather, they had confidence that the pope could deal with these things. "This is exactly the way I felt", he said, "from the first time I heard him in

---

[1] "Cardinal Pell on John Paul II" (interview with Zenit), Catholic Online, April 8, 2005, https://www.catholic.org/featured/headline.php?ID=2014.

his inaugural sermon." That was in October 1978, when Pell was at home in a presbytery in Ballarat and listened on the radio to the new pope, speaking in Italian.

The Holy Father's last years, Pell said, had been filled with suffering, and were "probably his best sermon". One of the differences between the Christian and the secular attitudes towards suffering, he said, "is that those without a belief in God tend to flee from suffering and pretend it doesn't exist. We as Catholics confront suffering and try to help those suffering, but we also believe that through suffering and death, primarily of Christ, we were redeemed and saved. In other words, good can come out of suffering.... And that beautiful teaching of Jesus'—that whatever we do for the least of our brothers and sisters to help them in their suffering, we do to Christ himself—is spectacular."

The late pope's great moral encyclicals *The Gospel of Life* and *The Splendor of Truth* had marked him as "an extraordinary teacher because he pointed out that not just particular doctrines but the very basis of morality are being challenged in our society. In a postmodern world the basic claim is that there are no moral bases and the most we might be able to achieve would be a temporary consensus."

John Paul II was also "the first Pope to deal adequately with the advantages that capitalism had brought us ... a spread of prosperity and not just in the West but also to many parts of China, for example, which is absolutely unprecedented", Pell said. He had also "endorsed democracy as a highly desirable form of government more explicitly than any other Pope in the past. I think he did well to do that."

Pell, a man not prone to hyperbole, said that John Paul II was

probably the most extraordinary Pope in Christian history in 2,000 years. Now that's a large claim and it's something that I don't make lightly. Because of the modern means of communication and travel, he's moved on a stage that's absolutely gigantic.

We speak of Leo the Great in the middle of the fifth century and Gregory the Great at the end of the sixth, but the canvas within which they moved—the Italian peninsula; across the Alps; across to North Africa and Greece to some extent—was a world that was much more confined in comparison to today.

And of course, political leaders ... realize that his role in the over-throw of communism, bringing freedom to the peoples of Eastern

Europe and Russia, was absolutely pivotal. It was his visit to Poland in 1979 that really awoke the Polish people and when Poland started to move, the whole pack of cards came down.

Recognising this, some of the Communist leaders tried to stop people from attending the pope's Masses. But as a visiting English bishop observed, even when the buses were stopped, Poles walked for miles, sometimes through the night, to worship with the pope. "He [the pope] told them that they were living a lie", Pell said. "And through a most unusual conjunction of forces"—Ronald Reagan running the States and Margaret Thatcher leading the United Kingdom and John Paul II spiritually guiding the Church, the lie was overcome by the truth. "The [dissolution] of the Soviet empire without violence was a miracle," Pell said, "and I think it was the president of Poland who said just recently, 'We wouldn't be free today without this Pope.' So, basically, I don't think it's surprising that they're talking about a million and a half Poles coming for the funeral. It's for all these sorts of reasons that so many heads of state are coming. It will be one of the most extraordinary funerals in history."

It was. It drew about four million mourners including U.S. President George W. Bush and Prince Charles, who delayed his wedding to Camilla Parker-Bowles for twenty-four hours in order to attend.

The subsequent conclave, which elected Joseph Ratzinger as John Paul's successor, was short; the white smoke appeared on the afternoon of the second day. The bells of Saint Peter's pealed at 4:10 P.M., and half an hour later, when Cardinal Ratzinger appeared as Benedict XVI, George Pell was on a nearby balcony, standing beside Cardinal Francis George of Chicago. Pell and George, who never confirmed it, were widely credited as being among Benedict's leading supporters at the conclave. The runner-up, reportedly, was the Jesuit Cardinal Archbishop of Buenos Aires, Jorge Bergoglio.

27

Evangelization at Barangaroo

In August 2005, Pell and his fellow Australian bishops led 2,500 young Australian pilgrims to World Youth Day in Cologne, Germany, where they joined about a million other young people from around the world. The event was significant for Germany, where pressures against religion were strong, Pell wrote in the *Sunday Telegraph*:

> In ex-communist East Germany, 70 per cent or even 90 per cent are not baptised, and the culture of death flourishes there.
>
> Because of abortion and unemployment in the East, houses are unoccupied and suburbs are being turned into parkland.
>
> As always, the pilgrims were well behaved, patient and friendly, marching across the cities, singing hymns, smiling.
>
> They were clear evidence faith makes a difference, that goodness is life-giving, that clear consciences and community bring joyfulness. It is encouraging to see young people full of hope. Christianity at its best.
>
> The pilgrims always camp out on the Saturday night after the Vigil. Rain meant that Marienfeld was muddy and brought out the small mice, while the Vigil service was subdued, with traditional music (Ave Maria) and concluded with adoration of the Blessed Sacrament. Thousands of candles, lifted high, twinkled in the darkness as we sang "Alleluia".
>
> The final Mass was also beautiful and a small miracle. There were plenty of small difficulties: some couldn't see much, some were distracted. But it was awe-inspiring looking down on this immense gathering, like an army prepared for battle—not for destruction, but for the future, for faith and for goodness. Above all, it was the silence

that provoked the awe. Reverence and prayer during the whole Mass and especially after Communion. I would not have believed a million young people could be so still, and I thanked God for it.

Just before the Angelus at noon on Sunday, Pope Benedict made the announcement the Australians had been anticipating: "And now, as the living presence of the Risen Christ in our midst nourishes our faith and hope, I am pleased to announce that the next World Youth Day will take place in Sydney, Australia, in 2008. We entrust to the maternal guidance of Mary Most Holy, the future course of the young people of the whole world."[1]

So began three years of planning and organisation. Pell and his auxiliary bishop Anthony Fisher, whom Pell appointed coordinator of the event, hoped that large numbers of young Catholics from Europe and North America, as well as those who lived closer in Asia and Oceania, would brave the tyranny of distance and make the journey Down Under. They need not have worried. World Youth Day 2008, the first held in the Southern Pacific, where Sydney's mild, sunny winter lent itself perfectly, was like no other.

Pell, then sixty-seven, was in the prime of his life and career, and he set the tone for the week at the opening Mass on the shores of Sydney Harbour at a site called Barangaroo (named after an indigenous woman who lived in the area at the time of British colonization in 1788). Bennelong Point, the headland where the Sydney Opera House stands, is named after her husband.

The setting for the opening Mass, on Tuesday, July 15, 2008, in what felt like an outdoor cathedral, was extraordinary—ferries, hovercraft, and water taxis skimmed by as winter sunshine gave way to sunset, then city twilight, reflected on the gleaming water. In a crowd of several hundred thousand, the spirituality was palpable. It is one lost sheep, however, that attendees remember years later. In his then forty-one years of priesthood to that point, Pell had preached at least 2,000 sermons—but rarely one that punched home a message as powerfully. Those who had heard him preach many times thought it was his best, and in private, he agreed.

---

[1] Benedict XVI, Apostolic Journey to Cologne on the Occasion of the XX World Youth Day, Angelus (Cologne—Marienfeld, August 21, 2005).

Welcoming the flock to the precinct in Italian, French, German, and Spanish, as well as English, Pell singled out anyone, anywhere "who regards himself or herself as lost, in deep distress, with hope diminished or even exhausted".[2] Although the lost sheep was usually left behind, Jesus told his followers the parable of the Good Shepherd to show that God knows each one of His sheep and goes searching for the lost one, especially if he is sick, in trouble, or unable to help himself. Touching hearts and bringing more than a few tears to young and not-so-young eyes, Cardinal Pell showed why Christianity remained such a force millennia after the death of its founder. "Young or old, woman or man, Christ is still calling those who are suffering to come to him for healing, as he has done for two thousand years", the cardinal said. "The causes of the wounds are secondary, whether they be drugs or alcohol, family breakups, the lusts of the flesh, loneliness, or a death. Perhaps even the emptiness of success."

On top of his vestments, Pell wore his pallium, the woollen stole that symbolises his authority as the metropolitan archbishop. Three years earlier, in April 2005, Pope Benedict, when receiving his pallium as pastor of the Universal Church, had explained: "The lamb's wool is meant to represent the lost, sick or weak sheep which the shepherd places on his shoulders and carries to the waters of life.... The human race—every one of us—is the sheep lost in the desert which no longer knows the way. The Son of God will not let this happen; he cannot abandon humanity in so wretched a condition. He leaps to his feet and abandons the glory of heaven, in order to go in search of the sheep and pursue it, all the way to the Cross. He takes it upon his shoulders and carries our humanity; he carries us all."[3]

At the opening Mass, Pell also wore the pectoral cross and ring of the first archbishop of Sydney, English-born Bede Polding, and carried the crozier of Cardinal Francis Moran, the first Irish-born archbishop of Sydney. He urged those present not to spend their lives "sitting on the fence, keeping your options open, because only

---

[2] "Cardinal Pell Tells Young Pilgrims to 'Be Open to the Power of the Holy Spirit'", *Catholic News Agency*, July 15, 2008, https://www.catholicnewsagency.com/news/13244/cardinal-pell-tells-young-pilgrims-to-be-open-to-the-power-of-the-holy-spirit.

[3] Benedict XVI, Mass, Imposition of the Pallium and Conferral of the Fisherman's Ring for the Beginning of the Petrine Ministry of the Bishop of Rome, Homily (April 24, 2005).

commitments bring fulfilment".[4] Happiness, he said, comes from "meeting our obligations, doing our duty, especially in small matters and regularly, so we can rise to meet the harder challenges.... Self-control is necessary to develop and protect the love in our hearts and prevent others, especially our family and friends, from being hurt by our lapses into nastiness or laziness", he said. "We will bring forth good fruit by learning the language of the cross and inscribing it on our hearts.... Following Christ is not cost-free ... because it requires struggling against what Saint Paul called 'the flesh', our fat relentless egos, old-fashioned selfishness. It is always a battle, even for old people like me!"

In a Mass concelebrated by eighty cardinals, four hundred bishops, and thousands of priests, the sermon drew powerful applause, especially from the young pilgrims who came from 170 countries. Regardless of whether they were from France or Latin America, Poland or South Africa, the United States or Asia, many identified with Pell's comment that they had travelled so far that they had arrived at the ends of the earth. "If so, that's good, for our Lord told His first apostles that they would be his witnesses in Jerusalem and to the ends of the earth."

In Sydney in 2008, Pope Benedict XVI, eighty-one, who had arrived two days earlier, was far from the crowd at the opening Mass. He was in seclusion at a retreat centre, surrounded by bushland, on the fringe of the city, where he took time to recuperate from the long flight, rest and pray, in preparation for what proved to be an extraordinary week. Two days later, on Thursday, the pope arrived at Barangaroo by boat, welcomed by a flotilla of ships. On Friday, he blessed the hundred actors who staged the Stations of the Cross around the inner city, starting with the "Last Supper" on the steps of Saint Mary's Cathedral. On Saturday, in perfect sunny winter weather, the pilgrims walked the ten kilometres (about six miles) from the chapel of Saint Mary of the Cross MacKillop across the Sydney Harbour Bridge to camp at Randwick Racecourse. There, despite the vast crowd gathered for Benediction by candlelight, it was possible to hear the proverbial pin drop during the adoration of the Blessed Sacrament. Earlier in the day, during Mass at Saint Mary's

[4] George Pell, "Homily for World Youth Day 2008 Opening Mass", EWTN, July 15, 2008, https://www.ewtn.com/catholicism/library/homily-for-world-youth-day-2008-opening -mass-3817.

Cathedral, where the pope blessed a new white marble altar sculpted by Nigel Boonham, he apologized publicly to victims of sexual abuse at the hands of rogue clergy. He also called on the Church hierarchy to provide a safer environment for the young. "I would like to pause to acknowledge the shame which we have all felt as a result of sexual abuse of minors by some clergy ... in this country", he said. Then, in words that were not included in advance copies of the speech, the pope added: "Indeed, I am deeply sorry for the pain and suffering the victims have endured, and I assure them that as their Pastor, I, too, share in their suffering. These misdeeds, which constitute so grave a betrayal of trust, deserve unequivocal condemnation. They have caused great pain, they have damaged the Church's witness. Victims should receive compassion and care, and those responsible for these evils must be brought to justice."[5]

On the Friday, Cardinal Pell took Benedict XVI to Australia's first Catholic medical school at the University of Notre Dame, at Darlinghurst, a near-city suburb. The pope visited the school's medical library (named in his honour) and joined Pell for a prayer ceremony in the restored Sacred Heart Church, which was an integral part of the medical campus. The Sydney campus of the University of Notre Dame Australia (UNDA) is one of Pell's significant legacies, exemplifying his talent for reviving and overseeing the transformation of old churches and church buildings for new uses. The university was first established in Western Australia in the second half of the 1980s, and in 2003, two years after his appointment to Sydney, Pell implemented a suggestion from the university's vice-chancellor, Peter Tannock, to invite UNDA to establish a campus in Sydney, close to the city centre and easily accessible by students in the area.

Pell was keen to invite Notre Dame to Sydney because he wished to diversify and expand Catholic higher education in his archdiocese and to foster healthy competition with the Australian Catholic University. He wanted to see a Catholic medical school and a Catholic law school established. He was equally enthusiastic about Australia's first liberal arts college, Campion College, that had been established two years earlier at Old Toongabbie, west of Sydney,

[5] Benedict XVI, Apostolic Journey to Sydney (Australia) on the Occasion of the 23rd World Youth Day (July 12–21, 2008), Eucharistic Celebration with Bishops, Seminarians and Novices, Homily (Saint Mary's Cathedral, Sydney, July 19, 2008).

in the Diocese of Parramatta. Campion, which Pell described as a "pearl in the desert', was partly modelled on U.S. Catholic liberal arts schools, such as Christendom College, in Virginia, which had a core humanities curriculum.

With Notre Dame, Tannock recalled, Pell

> also wanted to see the revival and maximum effective use of the very important but badly degraded parish facilities at Broadway and Darlinghurst. The cardinal was deeply committed to the idea of a substantial Catholic university education sector and saw it as crucial to the future of the Church in Australia. He was a visionary leader of the Church in this area. UNDA accepted the invitation because it perceived it as a "call to mission" and because it believed that a Sydney Campus would take it to a new level of national significance.

In an intensely secular country, initiatives such as Campion and Notre Dame, championed by Pell, have offered Australians a coherent intellectual framework, which is able to contend with the modern ideologies that have captured the nation's universities and other institutions.

From an initial enrolment of 450 students in 2006, when it was blessed by Cardinal Pell and opened by Prime Minister John Howard, Notre Dame Sydney had grown to 1,700 students in 2008, mainly school-leaver undergraduates. Foundation Schools of Arts and Sciences, Business, Education, Law, Medicine, Nursing, and Philosophy and Theology were established. The Howard government supported the new Sydney Medical School for Notre Dame and provided capital funding for new facilities at Broadway and Darlinghurst and Commonwealth-funded places in teaching, nursing, and medicine. Beautiful facilities were built around the old parish churches at the university's heart.

Benedict's visit was especially memorable because it included his talk to a special group of invitees, participants in the Sydney Archdiocese's program for disadvantaged young people, Alive+, some of whom were homeless. Citing the Gospel parable of the Prodigal Son, the pope told them:

> Many of you must have had personal experience of what that young man went through. Perhaps you have made choices that you now regret, choices that led you down a path which, however attractive it

appeared at the time, only led you deeper into misery and abandonment. The choice to abuse drugs or alcohol, to engage in criminal
activity or self-harm, may have seemed at the time to offer a way out
of a difficult or confusing situation. You now know that, instead of
bringing life, it brings death. I wish to acknowledge your courage in
choosing to turn back onto the path of life, just like the young man
in the parable. You have accepted help—from friends or family, from
the staff who run the "Alive" programme: from people who care
deeply for your well-being and happiness.[6]

On the final Sunday of the week of World Youth Day, Pope
Benedict's Mass drew a crowd of at least four hundred thousand to
Randwick Racecourse, the largest gathering in Australian history.
"This is a good time to be Catholic", the cardinal wrote a week later.
"They are days to remember. Tens of thousands of happy young
people make the rest of the population happy too. All Sydney, and
not just Catholic Sydney, has taken the pilgrims to their hearts. I see
a city that has re-flourished."

Young Australians gathered in Rome with Pell on Palm Sunday
2009 to hand over the World Youth Day cross and icon of Mary,
the Mother of God, to the young people of Spain, where World
Youth Day was to be celebrated in 2011. Like other Australians in
Rome, Pell was "moved by the tributes foreign delegates paid to the
joyfulness, faith, and efficient organisation of the Sydney gathering",
he told them.

While looking back at a happy time, when Sydney was at the centre of the Catholic world, Pell and his flock were also looking ahead.
They gathered for the first Australia-sponsored Eucharist in the shell
of what was to become Domus Australia—Australia House—in
Rome. It would be built from refurbishing a nineteenth-century
Marist student house, study centre, and chapel in one of the oldest
districts of Rome. Ancient ruins had been discovered at the site in
2008, early in the construction process.

Pell, a historian by training, liked innovations and ideas placed in
their historical context. He read the young people a quotation, whose

[6]Benedict, XVI, Apostolic Journey to Sydney (Australia) on the Occasion of the 23rd
World Youth Day (July 12–21, 2008), Meeting with a Group of Disadvantaged Young Peo-
ple of the Rehabilitation Community of the University of Notre Dame (Church of the Sacred
Heart, Sydney, July 18, 2008).

author only one staff member at ten seminaries he had inspected outside Australia a decade earlier had been able to identify:

> Although the Church is spread throughout the world to the ends of the earth, it received from the apostles and their disciples the faith which it professes.... The Church believes these truths as though it had but one soul and one heart, it preaches them and hands them on as though it had but one mouth....
>
> The Church founded in Germany believes exactly the same and hands on exactly the same as do the Spanish and Celtic Churches, and the ones in the East, those in Egypt, and Libya and Jerusalem, the centre of the world.... Since faith is one and the same, the man who has much to say about it does not add to it and the man who has less does not subtract from it.[7]

The author, Pell revealed, was Saint Irenaeus, bishop of Lyons, writing in about A.D. 180. "Even then, Christians were conscious that they had inherited in a different and special way the promises the good God made to his people Israel in the prophecies of Ezekiel", he preached. "So too, gathered tonight from Australia here in Rome, eighteen hundred years after Irenaeus and more than twenty-five hundred years after Ezekiel, we see ourselves as the spiritual inheritors of the promises made to Ezekiel. Different from one another, but united in faith."

The principal reason for building Domus Australia, Pell told the young people, was "to strengthen the bonds of unity between the Church of Rome, the Church of Peter's successor, and the Catholic Church in Australia, which was almost as far away geographically from Rome as it is possible to be. "Only New Zealand is a bit farther, but when we move past New Zealand. We begin to approach Rome from the West!" Domus Australia, he said, would follow in a long tradition of national communities building pilgrim centres in Rome:

"In A.D. 726, Ine, the king of Wessex in England, founded a church in Rome for Saxon pilgrims, which still exists but was rebuilt in 1540. English Catholics founded a pilgrim house in 1362, the Scots College began in 1600, and the Irish College in 1628." He asked the young pilgrims to pray it would be blessed in the years ahead "so that the house becomes a home away from home for visiting Australians, a cultural and national as well as religious centre, a place with daily

---

[7] Irenaeus of Lyon, *Adversus Haereses*, bk. 1, chap. 10, nos. 1–3.

Mass, which will encourage tourists to become pilgrims and will offer a variety of help to both those who stay and those who visit. May God bless our work."

Just over two years later, Pell was one of more than twenty Australian bishops who led four thousand young Australians to World Youth Day in Madrid in August 2011. En route, one of several contingents of young Sydneysiders, led by Pell, travelled through the Holy Land in the footsteps of Christ, the prophets, and his apostles. They visited Coptic Cairo, where Mary and Joseph are believed to have taken refuge when they fled the murderous King Herod; the Dead Sea; and the Basilica of the Transfiguration atop Mount Tabor. In Jerusalem, the group prayed and meditated in the Church of the Holy Sepulchre, the Cenacle, and the Garden of Gethsemane. At the Sea of Galilee, Pell and his auxiliary bishop Julian Porteous offered Mass on a boat for the young pilgrims.

Pell's group occupied seven buses, and he sat at the back of a different bus each day, mixing and chatting with the young people. They found him easy to talk to, fatherly, and fun. "No photograph ever captured the warmth in person", one young woman, who was twenty when she was on the pilgrimage, remembered. Travelling up the steep, rugged terrain of Mount Sinai, in the south of the Sinai Peninsula in eastern Egypt, where Moses received the Ten Commandments, was one of the most unforgettable experiences for all, including the cardinal. They travelled in the dead of night, to be in time for the sunrise. "We left our hotel at 12:30 A.M., travelling by bus to the foot of the mountain before mounting camels for the one-and-a-half-hour trip in the darkness up the rough, steep, zigzagging nineteenth-century route, which the camels negotiated faultlessly", he wrote in his *Sunday Telegraph* column the next week.

> Far away from any city lights, the thousands and thousands of stars in the northern sky were revealed. It was like a cosmic cathedral, with the added bonus of shooting stars. This was the sky Abraham, Moses, and Elijah saw and the stars indicating Abraham's followers over the millennia, now looked down on a few more Southern pilgrims. Why did the one true God choose to reveal himself to Moses through the burning bush on this ugly and remote mountain? While Elijah also found God in the gentle breeze, not the earthquake or tumult, on this mountain, God's choice of locale is still a mystery.

28

A Corner of a Roman Street
That Is Forever Australia

Later that year, 2011, Pope Benedict XVI was at Pell's side for the opening of Domus Australia, the thirty-two-room hotel-guesthouse and chapel on the Via Cernaia near Termini in Rome. The property had been bought at a rock-bottom price in the wake of the Global Financial Crisis. Refurbished and decorated as Pell envisaged, it was a testament to his determination and drive, and one of his proudest achievements. While inspired by traditional pilgrim centres in Rome, it was built for lay visitors as well as clergy and religious, and those of all faiths or none. "The ambition is to encourage tourists to become pilgrims and to deepen their faith, to deepen their goodness", Pell said at the October 19 opening. "There will be Mass every day, regular opportunities for confession."

When Benedict blessed and opened the complex, on the first anniversary of the canonization of the Australian saint Mary of the Cross MacKillop, he said it had brought "a little corner of Australia to Rome". The Church, like good parents, the pope said, should provide her children with "roots and wings". For Australians unfamiliar with Rome, Domus Australia provided both, as well as four-to-five-star comfort at two-star prices.

The project, for about AU$30 million, was funded by Australian Catholics, primarily those of the Archdioceses of Sydney, Melbourne, and Perth and the Diocese of Lismore in northern New South Wales. It quickly made its mark as a going concern and was often booked out due to its popularity among Europeans as well as Australians.

During the excavation process, a treasure trove of Roman flooring and pipes from a large first-century building that originally stood on the site were uncovered. The chapel, restored and decorated by Pell's friend, Melbourne priest Charles Portelli, features bronze kangaroos around the foot of the ambo. The tabernacle is covered in green Russian malachite that caught Monsignor Portelli's eye. Australian gemstones—turquoise from Queensland, jasper from Western Australia, and crystalite from Victoria—adorning the gold cross on its door were donated by Portelli as his contribution to the project.

As Archbishop Fisher said in his homily at Pell's Requiem Mass:

> It took more than a bit of Christian shamelessness for the son of a Ballarat publican to take a Roman monastery with church, renovate it to Australian comfort standards, radically redecorate it, and so establish an Aussie watering hole—er, pilgrim house—in the heart of the Eternal City. It took boldness to get the Bishops of Australia and St Mary's Cathedral Choir there for the opening. And it took sheer importunity to bang on the door of the Pope, asking him to bless and open the place—perhaps the only hotel ever opened by a pope![1]

Domus Australia, the archbishop said, is a high-standard hospitality centre and it means a great deal to the Australian Catholics who have discovered it, especially on occasions such as Anzac Day when Australians and New Zealanders in Rome come together to pray for their war dead.

To tour its chapel and public spaces is also to revisit the history and faith of the Church in Australia and to peer into the soul of George Pell, Fisher said. The piety of earlier generations is seen in the architecture and the rather sentimental paintings inherited from the Marists, such as *The Holy Family, Our Lady of the Rosary,* and *The Souls in Purgatory.* The altarpieces by Paul Newton (one of Australia's leading portrait artists) are *Our Lady of the Southern Cross* and *The First Catholics Praying before the Blessed Sacrament in 1818.* The sanctuary is decorated with Aussie emblems, flora, and fauna. Around the house are images of the two Aboriginal novice monks who joined Saint Paul's in Rome and many pieces of indigenous Australian sacred art.

---

[1] Anthony Fisher, "Homily for the Solemn Pontifical Funeral Mass of George Cardinal Pell AC" (Saint Mary's Basilica, Sydney, February 2, 2023), https://www.sydneycatholic.org /homilies/2023/homily-for-the-solemn-pontifical-funeral-mass-of-george-cardinal-pell-ac/.

"So, while he rose to international prominence and roles, the Cardinal remained very much an Australian to the end", Fisher said. "As the Church had made enormous contributions to this great nation, he was convinced it has many strengths and will yet do much more good if it remains faithful to the apostolic tradition. So, all around Domus we see representations of St Mary MacKillop and Australia's first bishops, priests, nuns, and laity, of First Australians, convicts, and migrants, and what they built."

The chapel features portraits of contemplatives such as Saint Brigid (whose face is that of Pell's old friend from Aquinas College, Ballarat, Sister Clare Forbes), Thérèse of Lisieux, and Bishop-Abbot Salvado (a Spanish Benedictine monk who served as a missionary for Indigenous Australians in the nineteenth century). Irish-born Father John Joseph Therry (one of the penal colony's earliest priests) is there, as are legendary Archbishops Daniel Mannix (archbishop of Melbourne from 1917 to 1963) and James Duhig (archbishop of Brisbane from 1917 to 1965), whose portraits are popular with visitors from those cities and from Ireland, where they were born within a few years and a few miles of each other (in Charleville, County Cork, and Broadford, County Limerick, respectively). The English strand in Australian Catholicism is represented by nineteenth-century humanitarian Caroline Chisholm, who worked with immigrant women and families in the early days of the colony, and English Benedictine John Bede Polding, the founding archbishop of Sydney.

Cardinal Pell's coat of arms, featuring its distinctive pelican and reassuring motto "Be Not Afraid" is displayed on the wall of the sanctuary. As Fisher said in his funeral homily, the pilgrim house "gives us a peek into what drove George Pell the man and priest: his passions for evangelisation, education, welfare, worship, and witness". It is their company that the cardinal hoped to join in heaven and their communion in which he strived to live on earth.

Numerous martyrs are depicted around the walls of Domus, including Saints John Fisher, Thomas More, Edmund Campion, Paul Miki, Andrew Kim, and Peter Chanel. But the most powerful portrait, Fisher said, is that of the white martyr Cardinal Francis-Xavier Nguyễn Văn Thuận with his arms outstretched, kneeling in prayer in his prison cell where he spent thirteen years. "Little did Cardinal Pell know, when he commissioned the work, that his turn would come to spend 404 days in solitary confinement on what he would wryly joke was his 'extended spiritual retreat'." When that terrible time came, Nguyễn Văn Thuận was one of his inspirations; his faith, example, and writings helped Pell survive his own ordeal. "What all these saints and heroes had in common, of course, is faith in Jesus Christ", Fisher said. "They spent their lives conforming themselves to His teachings and graces, above all to His life, death, and resurrection. And so, in the courtyard at the heart of the Domus Australia complex stands a life-sized bronze of The Risen Christ."

29

Controversies and Insights in the Public Square

A week after Benedict blessed Domus, Pell flew to London to deliver one of the most contentious speeches of his career, the annual lecture of the Global Warming Policy Foundation, chaired by former British chancellor in the Thatcher government, Nigel Lawson, who died in April 2023 at the age of ninety-one, three months after Pell. In Westminster Cathedral Hall, the cardinal argued his case on rational rather than religious grounds. "Mine is not an appeal to the authority of any religious truth in the face of contrary scientific evidence", he said.

> Neither is it even remotely tinged by a post-modernist hostility to rationality. I reject emphatically the claim that most science can be dismissed or at least downgraded as socially constructed by the great and the powerful, although the enduring power of a paradigm, of established patterns of reasoning can help the self-interested to distort science for a time. My appeal is to reason and evidence and in my view the evidence is insufficient to achieve practical certainty on many of these scientific issues. Much less is there validation to justify huge public expenditure on these phantoms.... [1]

Pell questioned the assumption that global warming is happening in an unprecedented way and that it is primarily caused by human activity putting increasing amounts of carbon dioxide into the atmosphere. He looked at climate conditions in the past. In many places, he said, most of the 11,700 years since the end of the last ice age were warmer than the present by up to 2°C (35.6°F).

[1] George Pell, "One Christian Perspective on Climate Change" (lecture, Westminster Cathedral Hall, London, October 26, 2011), p. 11, https://www.thegwpf.org/images/stories /gwpf-reports/pell-2011_annual_gwpf_lecture_new.pdf.

Between 1695 and 1730, the temperature in England rose by 2.2°C, a period of rapid warming, unparalleled since, that occurred long before the Industrial Revolution.

Pell's scepticism about current claims about the climate was based not only on the facts. "My suspicions have been deepened over the years by the climate movement's totalitarian approach to opposing views, their demonising of successful opponents and their opposition to the publication of opposing views even in scientific journals. As a general rule I have found that those secure in their explanations do not need to be abusive."[2] He compared climate alarmism to religious fanaticism.

> The immense financial costs true-believers would impose on economies can be compared with the sacrifices offered traditionally in religion, and the sale of carbon credits with the pre-Reformation practice of selling indulgences. Some of those campaigning to save the planet are not merely zealous but zealots. To the religionless and spiritually rootless, mythology—whether comforting or discomforting—can be magnetically, even pathologically, attractive.[3]

Instead of favouring costly measures aimed at trying to control the climate, Pell said, he supported the view of Danish environmental writer Bjorn Lomborg that money should be used to raise living standards and reduce vulnerability to catastrophes and climate change, in whatever form. "We need to be able to afford to provide the Noahs of the future with the best arks science and technology can provide", Pell said. "In essence, this is the moral dimension to this issue. The cost of attempts to make global warming go away will be very heavy. Efforts to offset the effects on the vulnerable are well intentioned, but history tells us they can only ever be partially successful."[4]

> My request is for common sense and more, not less; what the medievals, following Aristotle, called prudence, one of the four cardinal virtues: the "recta ratio agibilium" or right reason in doing things. We might call this a cost-benefit analysis, where costs and benefits are defined financially and morally or humanly and their level of

[2] Ibid., p. 19.
[3] Ibid., p. 21.
[4] Ibid., p. 32.

probability is carefully estimated. Are there any long term benefits from the schemes to combat global warming, apart from extra tax revenues for governments and income for those devising and implementing the schemes? Will the burdens be shared generally, or fall mainly on the shoulders of the battlers, the poor? Another useful Latin maxim is "in dubio non agitur": don't act when in doubt...

First of all we need adequate scientific explanations as a basis for our economic estimates. We also need history, philosophy, even theology and many will use, perhaps create, mythologies. But most importantly we need to distinguish which is which.[5]

Depending on what day he was asked, Pell's views on man-made climate change ranged from agnostic to sceptic. He was especially keen that measures imposed to counter it would not devastate economies and societies. Unlike Pope Francis and many others, he did not regard the cutting of greenhouse emissions as an article of faith or a moral obligation, a position that drew the wrath of some in the Church, though many Catholics in the pews agreed with him.

While Pell had made it clear he was speaking as an individual and not presenting an official Church stance, prominent clergy were quick to attack. Members of the Columban Missionary Society and Father Joe Ryan of Westminster Justice and Peace pointed out that just five months earlier, the May 2011 report of the Pontifical Academy of Sciences, "Fate of Mountain Glaciers in the Anthropocene", had listed "numerous examples of glacial decline around the world, and the evidence linking that decline to human-caused changes in climate and air pollution".[6] The report showed that the way of life of many people in the regions dependent upon glaciers and snow packs for water was under grave threat and called for immediate action to mitigate the effects of climate change, Father Ryan said. True to form, Pell was ready and able to defend his position.

When Pope Francis released his 2015 environmental encyclical, *Laudato Si'* (*Praise Be to You*), Pell told the *Financial Times* the following July that it had "many, many interesting elements" and that "parts

[5] Ibid., p. 33.

[6] Ajai et al., "Fate of Mountain Glaciers in the Anthropocene", in S. Benner, G. Lax, P.J. Crutzen, U. Pöschl, J. Lelieveld, and H. G. Brauch, eds., *Paul J. Crutzen and the Anthropocene: A New Epoch in Earth's History*, vol. 1, *The Anthropocene: Politik—Economics—Society—Science* (New York: Springer, 2011).

of it" were beautiful. But, he said, "the Church has no particular expertise in science.... The Church has got no mandate from the Lord to pronounce on scientific matters. We believe in the autonomy of science."[7]

Laudato Si' also worried Pell on economic and national sovereignty grounds, especially its call for "enforceable international agreements", which are "urgently needed", Francis said, because "local authorities are not always capable of effective intervention."[8] Pell disagreed with the pope over the need to create "stronger and more efficiently organized international institutions, with functionaries who are appointed fairly by agreement among national governments and empowered to impose sanctions". Francis quoted Benedict XVI in support of this position: "To manage the global economy; to revive economies hit by the crisis; to avoid any deterioration of the present crisis and the greater imbalances that would result; to bring about integral and timely disarmament, food security and peace; to guarantee the protection of the environment and to regulate migration: for all this, there is urgent need of a true world political authority, as my predecessor Blessed John XXIII indicated some years ago." It was wrong when John XXIII and Benedict XVI wrote it, Pell said, and it was wrong when Francis repeated it, because it would compromise national sovereignty at the hands of world government.

In his last major speech in Australia (appendix 1), at the August 2022 Campion College fundraiser dinner in Sydney, Pell emphasised that there could not be a single obligatory Catholic position on climate change, although he introduced a few facts to challenge climate-change activism. There could not be one Church position on secular political issues, he added. As the archbishop of Melbourne and Sydney, Pell had never used the pulpit to tell Catholics how to vote unless matters of faith and morals or religious freedom were on the line. In Melbourne, that principle was clear in the lead-up to the 1998 federal election, when he refused to join many clerics and social justice advocates in condemning John Howard's proposed tax

---

[7] Rachel Sanderson and James Politi, "Reformer Tries to Bring Light to Closed World of Vatican Finance", *Financial Times*, July 16, 2015, https://www.ft.com/content /7f429c28-2bc6-11e5-acfb-cbd2e1c81cca.

[8] Francis, encyclical letter *Laudato Si'* (May 24, 2015), nos. 173, 175, quoting Benedict XVI, encyclical letter *Caritas in Veritate* (June 29, 2009), no. 67.

reform, which introduced the goods and services tax (GST), similar to sales tax in the United States, in return for reducing personal income tax rates.

Politics and culture, along with the importance of Catholic moral reasoning to Western society, was one of Pell's abiding interests. That interest led him to follow most of the significant international journals from the right, the left and the centre of the Anglosphere. At most times he had three books on the go—a theological tome, the latest significant secular biography or social-political tome, and a spy thriller. For more than thirty years, from his time as an auxiliary bishop in Melbourne onwards, Pell was much sought after as a speaker and as an author on cultural as well as religious issues, in Australia and around the globe. The breadth and depth of his reflections are evident in several of his books and anthologies including *Issues of Faith and Morals* (1997); *Be Not Afraid* (2004); *Test Everything. Hold Fast to What Is Good* (2010); *Contemplating Christ with Luke* (2012); and his three-volume *Prison Journal*, which many regard as his best spiritual writings. Pell was no shrinking violet in speaking and writing on issues he thought important, but he picked his topics carefully.

In the wake of 9/11 and two deadly terrorist attacks that killed dozens of Australians and others on the Indonesian island of Bali, a tourist hotspot, Pell became interested in the issue of Islamic jihad. Writing in *First Things*, Pell explored the question: "Can Islam and the Western democracies live together peacefully?" The essay was rich in historical context and theological contrasts between Christianity and Islam. Pell, who as archbishop of Sydney had good relationships with the city's imams, praised Indonesia as a successful democracy, but he said he was wary of unfettered Islamic immigration to the West. "I suspect one example of the secular incomprehension of religion is the blithe encouragement of large-scale Islamic migration into Western nations, particularly in Europe", he wrote. The history of Muslim relations with Christians and Jews did not offer reasons for optimism in the way that some people easily assumed.

> The claims of Muslim tolerance of Christian and Jewish minorities are largely mythical, as the history of Islamic conquest and domination in the Middle East, the Iberian Peninsula, and the Balkans makes abundantly clear. In the territory of modern-day Spain and Portugal, which

was ruled by Muslims from 716 and not finally cleared of Muslim rule until the surrender of Granada in 1491, Christians and Jews were tolerated only as dhimmis, subject to punitive taxation, legal discrimination, and a range of minor and major humiliations.[9]

The West's highly secular elites were "handicapped in comprehending the challenge that Islam poses", Pell wrote. "Western secularists regularly have trouble understanding religious faith in their own societies, and are often at sea when it comes to addressing the meaninglessness that secularism spawns. An anorexic vision of democracy and the human person is no match for Islam." Fighting against terrorist organisations was only one aspect of the challenge posed by modern Islamic jihadists, Pell continued. "Perhaps more important is the struggle in the Islamic world between moderate forces and extremists, especially when we set this against the enormous demographic shifts likely to occur across the world, the relative changes in population-size of the West, the Islamic and Asian worlds and the growth of Islam in a childless Europe."

Every great nation and religion has shadows and indeed crimes in their histories, he said. This was certainly true of the Catholic Church and of all Christian denominations. So, is it "legitimate to ask our Islamic partners in dialogue whether they believe that the peaceful suras of the Koran are abrogated by the verses of the sword. Is the program of military expansion to be resumed when possible? Do they believe that democratic majorities of Muslims in Europe would impose shari'a law? Can we discuss Islamic history and even the hermeneutical problems around the origins of the Koran without threats of violence?" Those issues needed to be discussed, Pell said. "Useful dialogue means that participants grapple with the truth and in this issue of Islam and the West the stakes are too high for fundamental misunderstandings."

The place of Catholic culture in the world was a theme close to his heart, as he told members of the Pontifical Council for the Family in a memorable sermon during a 2008 Mass at the Altar of the Chair in Saint Peter's Basilica (where he had been ordained forty-two years earlier and where his Requiem would be celebrated fifteen years later).

---

[9] George Pell, "Islam and Us", *First Things*, June 2006, https://www.firstthings.com/article/2006/06/islam-and-us.

Saint Patrick's College, Ballarat. Brother William O'Malley (old Bill) and George Pell (third player from the right) and other members of his championship Australian Rules football team of 1959.

Family portrait of 1963 before George sailed for Rome. David, George, and Margaret (top) with their parents, Margaret and George Pell senior, and Aunt Molly Burke.

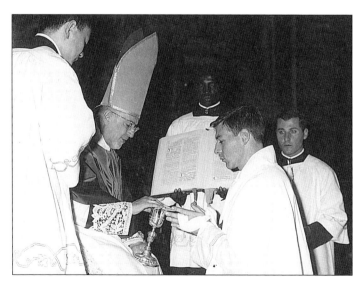

Ordination Day, Saint Peter's Basilica, December 16, 1966. Cardinal Gregory Peter XV Agagianian anoints George Pell's hands.

George Pell and his sister, Margaret, at his graduation from Oxford in 1975. He had received his D.Phil. in 1971 but had needed to save up for four years to return for the ceremony.

June 29, 1997. The archbishop of Melbourne receives the pallium from Pope John Paul II in Saint Peter's Basilica, Rome, on the feast day of Saints Peter and Paul.

Archbishop Pell (left), with Cardinal Joseph Ratzinger, prefect of the Congregation for the Doctrine of the Faith (center), and Pope John Paul II in the late 1990s.

Archbishop Pell addressing the Parliament
of New South Wales.

October 21, 2003, David and Margaret Pell with their
brother on the day he became a cardinal.

World Youth Day 2008 in Sydney with Pope Benedict XVI.

Holy Land pilgrimage en route to World Youth Day 2011 in Madrid.

Cardinal Pell on the World Youth Day mission trip
to Lima, Peru, 2013.

Cardinal Pell with his successor in Sydney,
Archbishop Anthony Fisher, (left), and
Melbourne Archbishop Peter Comensoli.

Cardinal Pell in handcuffs
during his trials in 2019.

Offering the Holy Sacrifice
of the Mass at Saint Mary's
Cathedral, Sydney.

In the Roman Empire, he said, Christianity was an underground Church, with sacraments celebrated in private houses. Christians took over pagan symbols such as the good shepherd, the fish and the dove, an anchor or a ship, and gave them Christian meanings. Only later, especially with religious freedom under Emperor Constantine, did specifically Christian symbols develop, such as the cross. "Now we have magnificent cathedrals, beautiful churches, a splendid patrimony of Church music, art, and literature, which help sustain our faith."[10] From the earliest times, Christians celebrated Easter once a year and a special Eucharist every Sunday rather than the Jewish Sabbath. In 321, Emperor Constantine declared Sunday a public holiday, with immense long-term consequences. "We should not be aiding and abetting those who want to make Sunday just another day" he said.

As an archbishop, Pell harnessed the faith and the energy of various ethnic groups in Melbourne and Sydney to enrich the wider Catholic community, and he would often join those communities in worship. In his book *Be Not Afraid* (2004), he wrote of celebrating Mass for Melbourne's Vietnamese Catholics at the Shrine of Our Lady of Lavang and the Vietnamese Martyrs. At the end of the Mass, on a clear, still night in 1999, he was deeply moved when the people turned to face north, toward Vietnam, to pray in silence. "It was a very beautiful moment", he wrote, "to see so many people in a country so far removed from their home, remembering things that most Australians cannot imagine." Many of the people, he recalled, had sheltered under a nearby gum tree—"a symbol of how the Vietnamese community has found shelter in a freer country".

Pell also travelled far and wide, visiting Japan in 1997 to commemorate the four hundredth anniversary of the martyrdom of twenty-six Catholics in Nagasaki. "Their sad, moving story is lent special poignancy by the countryside in which it took place, where the gardens and architecture and even the landscape speak at once of mystery and emptiness, of transcendence and human insignificance", he wrote. "It is interesting to recall the point when these martyrdoms occurred. A little over one hundred years earlier, Columbus had discovered America, and forty years before that Constantinople had fallen to the

Turks. The rise of British power was over two centuries away. In 1610, the Church founded the first university in Asia, the University of Saint Thomas in the Philippines."[11]

> The cathedral in Nagasaki is large, with the front adorned by burned statues salvaged from the wreckage of the old cathedral after the atomic blast. There is a simple, eloquent monument in the Catholic kindergarten attached to the Catholic Centre in the city commemorating two hundred students and twelve teachers conscripted to work producing armaments in a nearby school building, who died a fiery death when the bomb was detonated. It is a monument raised in the hope and with the prayer that such an event will never happen again.

Pell was also well respected in South Korea, where he was awarded the inaugural Mysterium Vitae (Mystery of Life) award in January 2008 by Cardinal Nicholas Cheong, the archbishop of Seoul. A like-minded Church leader, Cardinal Cheong had invested US$10 million to set up a Catholic Institute of Cell Therapy in Seoul to further adult stem cell research. While there, Pell and Chris Meaney visited the demilitarised zone, and at lunch afterwards, Meaney affectionately remembered, Pell struggled to get his long legs under the low table and chased beans around his plate with chopsticks. Pell received the AU$120,000 award for his strong stand against abortion in public debates and for initiatives such as founding the Australian campus of the John Paul II Institute for Marriage and the Family, the establishment of "life offices" in Melbourne and Sydney, which provide support services for pregnant women, and the Archdiocese of Sydney's annual AU$100,000 grant to support adult stem cell research in Australia. Pell used the prize money to fund pro-life initiatives. "Discriminating against individuals or destroying human life on the grounds of race, sex, religion, disability, illness, or stage of development is not only a grave injustice—it also undermines human rights and social justice, and makes the task of building good societies harder", he said, receiving the award.[12]

[11] George Pell, *Test Everything: Hold Fast to What Is Good* (San Francisco: Ignatius Press, 2015), p. 249.
[12] "Pell Honoured for Anti-Abortion Stand", *Sydney Morning Herald*, January 18, 2008, https://www.smh.com.au/national/pell-honoured-for-antiabortion-stand-20080118-1mra.html.

In Australia, Pell honoured the contributions his country had made to defend freedom-loving peoples throughout the world. He viewed its most important national observance, Anzac Day, through the prism of faith. Commemorated every year on April 25, the anniversary of the Australian Army's landing at Gallipoli, Turkey, in 1915, the day honours not only those who died in the First World War (sixty thousand from a population of about four million), but also the hundred thousand Australians in total who have sacrificed their lives defending the nation and its allies in World War II, the Korean and Vietnam Wars, and other conflicts against totalitarian regimes.

In Pell's own words, Anzac Day is

> the only national day to rank anywhere near Christmas and Easter. Hearing the Last Post never leaves me unmoved. As a Catholic priest, I think of this day of remembrance differently from when I was young. The battles of World War II, as well as the prisoner-of-war camps, were much closer then. But I never thought Anzac Day glorified war. It has always reminded us how terrible war is, but it also tells our national story of courage, idealism, self-sacrifice and spirit. It would be a betrayal of the dead if the Anzac spirit was smothered or forgotten.[13]

The Commonwealth of Australia was only a teenager, naive and innocent, when the Allied troops landed at Gallipoli. But the romance of war and the grandeur of empire were changed irrevocably when the scale of Australian losses, dead and wounded, hit home. The World War I death toll, proportionately, he wrote, "would be about a quarter of a million dead today—something beyond our imagining. It is no wonder that almost every small Australian town has its war memorial."

In 2012, Pell achieved his lifelong ambition of attending the annual Dawn Service at Anzac Cove, Gallipoli, when he joined a group of forty Sydney teachers, as chaplain, on a pilgrimage in the footsteps of Saint Paul. Dan White, the executive director of Sydney Catholic Schools, and some of the teachers were dismayed, initially, when they found out Pell would be on the trip. Having been influenced by his stern media persona, they did not have a favourable view of him at the outset of the trip. But they warmed up to him as they travelled

[13] George Pell, *Sunday Telegraph*, April 29, 2007.

together through Greece and Turkey, with him sitting in the centre seat at the back of the bus so that he could stretch his long legs. After a few hours of his repartee and insights, his fellow passengers were keen to crowd around him for the rest of the journey.

At the Shrine of Our Lady in Ephesus, believed to be the house where Mary, the Mother of God, spent her final years, Pell preached on entering heaven. If someone were met by Saint Peter at the gate and asked why he should be let in, the best answer, he told the teachers with characteristic, laconic Australian humour, might be "I was a mate of the boss's son." Mateship (close friendship with intense loyalty), traditionally, is a virtue Australians prize above most others. It was writ large at Gallipoli, where Pell and his fellow pilgrims gathered in the dark. At "the first blink of sunrise"—the time of the original landing—White remembered, "all were overcome with a spirit of prayer and awe."

From attending school ceremonies as a boy to offering Mass at the Allied war cemetery near Rome to visiting the Australian war memorial at Hyde Park in London, Pell had witnessed many Anzac Day celebrations, but the one at Gallipoli in 2012 moved him the most. On that occasion, Prime Minister Julia Gillard reminded the crowd of "the boys of Federation [achieved in 1901] who became the men of Gallipoli"[14] and started a new story for a new nation. Despite their defeat after eight months of stalemate and massive loss of life, Pell wrote, "we still take pride in their bravery (seven Victoria Crosses were won at Lone Pine) as we struggle to come to grips with the misery and slaughter." In an age of sectarianism, he noted, common suffering drew the Protestant and Catholic communities of Australia closer. "Ancient wrongs and mutual antagonisms were seen in a new light and Christian forgiveness encouraged greater tolerance. Only a nation with deep Christian roots and belief in redemptive sacrifice could set this Anzac failure at the heart of its legends."[15]

---

[14]Julia Gillard, "Lone Pine Ceremony, Gallipoli" (April 25, 2012), Australian Government, Department of the Prime Minister and Cabinet, PM Transcripts, https://pmtranscripts.pmc.gov.au/release/transcript-18533.

[15]George Pell, Sunday Telegraph, April 29, 2012.

30

Pious Fools Need Not Apply

George Pell was indignant, and he did not hide it. "We elected him for life", he said in astonishment and annoyance to two priest friends he was with in Sydney when one of them received a text message on February 28, 2013. Pope Benedict had resigned, the first pope to do so since Gregory XII in 1415. Benedict, eighty-six, had told cardinals in Rome, in Latin, that he was too old and too frail to lead a church with 1.3 billion members. Despite the stability of the John Paul II/ Joseph Ratzinger years, the Church was divided over her worship, teaching, and disciplines. The gravity of the Vatican's financial corruption and the clerical sex abuse scandals around the world were becoming ever more apparent. Pell realised at once that Benedict's departure would disturb the balance.

In his obituary for Benedict, initially written in 2018 and published across two broadsheet pages of *The Australian* just ten days before his own death, Pell noted:

> Benedict did commission a secret report on corruption in the Vatican, which has never been published, was not made available to the Conclave which elected his successor, but was consigned to Pope Francis. My personal conjecture, which is not supported by evidence, is that when Benedict saw the report, he concluded that he did not have the organisational capacity, nor the energy at eighty-five to cleanse the Vatican stables.
>
> Whatever his reasons,... it was an extraordinary decision for a prelate and scholar deeply versed in Church history, aware of the challenges in maintaining unity in a worldwide Church; for a pope who in every other way was the champion and exponent of Catholic tradition.

It is unlikely that Benedict anticipated that Pope Francis would be his successor, or that he would live more years in retirement than as pope to see some of the consequences of his decision.[1]

In private, Pell later told friends that he believed Benedict may have been misled by some senior people in the Vatican he had trusted but, in hindsight, had been unwise to do so. As Pell prepared to fly out for another conclave, where he was to be Australia's sole representative among 117 voting cardinals, he was reminded of what sixteenth-century Spanish Carmelite nun Teresa of Ávila said about confessors. She favoured "a competent theologian" over "a pious fool", he said. When he cast his ballot in the Sistine Chapel, he said, he would be supporting "not necessarily the most holy person, but the person best equipped for the job", regardless of nationality or colour. If that person happened to be from the United States, however, Pell believed it unlikely he would be elected. The reluctance to appoint a pope from the prevailing superpower, he said, dated to the fourteenth century, when a series of seven popes resided at Avignon in southeastern France, which was then a superpower.

In matters of Church governance, cardinals sometimes think in centuries. A keen Church historian with a doctorate in the subject from Oxford and years of teaching experience behind him, Pell named his three papal heroes: John Paul II, for whom he had "enormous admiration", Pius V, who led the Counter-Reformation and excommunicated Elizabeth I of England—a decision Pell regarded as a mistake—and Pius XII, who "was dealt an appalling set of cards" and contrary to widespread criticism "battled hard to help the Jews directly and indirectly so that a higher percentage survived in Italy than in any other place". He also admired fifth-century pope Leo the Great as well as Gregory the Great, who served from 590 to 604.

The man to be elected the 266th pope, the direct successor to Saint Peter, would face myriad challenges in the wider world and within the Church. In Pell's words, he would need to be "more of a prime minister than a governor-general". Pell named the need to counter the secularism of Europe and the West as a priority. Other challenges,

---

[1] George Pell, "Pope Benedict Was a Good Pope but Not a Great One", *The Australian*, December 31, 2022.

he said, included defending Christianity in parts of the world where religious adherents are under direct attack, such as Syria, Egypt, Pakistan, and parts of India; helping the Church to develop in China; and building cooperation with the Orthodox churches.

Continuing the clean-up after child sexual abuse scandals that did much to destroy the Church's credibility, especially in matters of personal morality, would remain ongoing. And after years of service on the quaintly but aptly named Council of Cardinals for the Study of the Organisational and Economic Problems of the Holy See, Pell also cited "the importance of continuing the reform of the Vatican finances".

In one of his final decisions as pope before his ring was smashed on February 28, 2013, to mark the end of his pontificate, Benedict appointed German lawyer and businessman Ernst von Freyberg president of the Vatican Bank, officially known by the title of the Institute of Religious Works. Partly because of fallout from the global financial crisis on its investments, the Vatican had ended 2011 with a deficit of almost €15 million, with the biggest spending on its 2,832 staff members and communications. Just as the twenty-four-hour news cycle shapes modern politics and international relations, it also has been a game-changer for an institution as ancient as the papacy. "Being subject to twenty-four-hour scrutiny and visibility is now a significant factor for the pope and for the Church", Pell said.

In Rome, as well as farewelling Benedict XVI, Pell attended a series of preliminary, pre-conclave meetings, known as general congregations, with his brother cardinals. There, mainly speaking Italian, they got to know each other better and outlined their views on the direction the Church should be taking. Cardinals regarded as theologically conservative, including Pell, reportedly favoured Cardinal Angelo Scola, a philosopher and a theologian who was the archbishop of Milan and the former patriarch of Venice (who had been elevated to the College of Cardinals on the same day as Pell in 2003). The Italians within the conclave were split, however, and many from outside Italy did not want an Italian. On the first ballot, on March 12, the Jesuit-run *America* magazine reported, twenty-three prelates received at least one vote, with the top place-getters Scola (30), Bergoglio (26), Canadian Marc Ouellet (22), and American Sean O'Malley (10). Pell reportedly scored two votes, as did New York's Timothy Dolan and Vienna's Christoph Schönborn.

On the evening of the second day of voting, March 13, with the Italians still split, Cardinal Bergoglio was elected with eighty-five votes to Scola's 20, from a group who had been appointed predominantly by John Paul II and Benedict. Taking the name of Francis, the cardinal-archbishop of Buenos Aires set the tone for his pontificate by declining to put on the *mozzetta*, the shoulder-length cape of red velvet trimmed with white fur traditionally worn by popes when they first appear on the balcony. He greeted the crowd with a simple *Buona sera*.

During the general congregations, Francis had won support among his brother cardinals when he emphasized the importance of being a Christo-centric Church, rather than an inward-looking Church. He also struck a chord with some when he endorsed the need to clean up the Vatican's finances. Within a month of Francis's election, in mid-April 2013, he appointed Pell to his new "kitchen cabinet", or Council of Cardinals, to be coordinated by a close friend of the pope, Honduran cardinal Oscar Andrés Rodríguez Maradiaga. It included German cardinal Reinhard Marx and U.S. cardinal Sean Patrick O'Malley of Boston. Pell was to remain in Sydney, but would commute to Rome as needed, as he had done for years, with increasing frequency serving on a variety of Vatican bodies. The council's focus was to be reform of the Curia. "I think different perspectives will be useful, and a few English-speaking perspectives won't hurt," Pell told Australian media when the appointment was announced. "I am very sure the Holy Father will be working for a better discipline. There has been a spot of bother, as we know, in the Vatican, with the butler leaking the papers and other allegations. Most of the people working in the Curia are very, very fine people, but there were one or two mishaps." Masterful understatement.[2]

Benedict had wanted to appoint Pell to lead a major Vatican department, the Congregation for Bishops, in the first half of 2010. Pell had travelled to Rome for the announcement, which had been set in type at the Tipografia Vaticana, ready to be made public at noon. That morning, Pell paid a brief visit to Benedict to let him know that the controversy over the mishandling of clerical sex abuse

[2] "Pell Jets to Rome after Appointment", *News.com.au*, April 14, 2013, https://www.bishop-accountability.org/news2013/03_04/2013_04_14_Newscomau_PellJets.htm.

was becoming more prominent in Australia and that he and the heads
of other archdioceses would be in the firing line in coming weeks.
It was not an insurmountable problem, he believed, but he wanted
to let the pope know out of courtesy. Benedict, who hated controversy, changed his mind about the appointment there and then. Staff
in the Tipografia, who later spoke to an Australian priest friend who
was working in Rome, were surprised when the announcement was
scrapped shortly before it was due to be released. Journalists covering
the Curia who were expecting an announcement were told that Pell
was not proceeding due to health concerns and that Canadian Cardinal Marc Ouellet, the archbishop of Quebec, was appointed prefect.

Four years later, Francis had no doubts he wanted Pell in a powerful
Vatican role. On February 24, 2014, the pope announced the estab-
lishment of the Secretariat for the Economy, to be headed by Cardinal
George Pell. Underlining the urgency and importance of the task, the
Vatican announcement said, "The prefect of the new Secretariat for
the Economy has been asked to start work as soon as possible."[3]

Pell welcomed the establishment of the new secretariat as an
"important and very significant [move] in the right direction". Showing he shared Francis' concern for the poor and his determination to
weed out financial corruption, he said, "If we make better use of the
resources entrusted to us we can improve our capacity to support
the good works of the Church, particularly our works for the poor
and disadvantaged.... I am looking forward to implementing these
recommendations as requested by the Holy Father."[4] The announcement was well received in many corners of the world. Rupert Murdoch, the executive chairman of News Corp, tweeted: "Pope Francis
appoints brilliant Cardinal Pell from Sydney to be no. 3 in Vatican.
Australia will miss him but world will benefit."[5]

True to the pope's request, Pell's start date was set for Monday,
March 31, with Pell booked to fly on Saturday, March 29. At least

---

[3] Sala Stampa della Santa Sede, "New Coordination Structure for Economic and Administrative Affairs of the Holy See and the Vatican State", press release, February 24, 2014.

[4] Australian Associated Press, "George Pell Called to Vatican to Oversee Budget as Pope
Looks to Cut Waste", *The Guardian*, February 24, 2014, https://www.theguardian.com
/world/2014/feb/25/george-pell-called-to-vatican-to-oversee-budget-as-pope-looks-to-cut
-waste.

[5] Rupert Murdoch (@rupertmurdoch), X (formerly Twitter), February 4, 2014, 8:50 P.M.,
https://twitter.com/rupertmurdoch/status/438128746034241536.

initially, he intended to live at Domus Australia. Leaving Sydney, which had become the longest appointment of his career and where he had made many good friends, was a wrench. In an interview after his appointment was announced, Pell did not hesitate when asked what he regarded as his most important achievements within the Catholic Church in Australia: "The young priests and the new RE [religious education] program", he said. The "young priests" were the generation of thirty- to fifty-something priests throughout New South Wales and Victoria who emerged from the seminaries he reformed and rebuilt after the upheavals and the slump in vocations of the 1970s and early 1980s. With a few exceptions who proved singularly unsuited to priestly life, their contributions, in the main, proved that restoring prayer, doctrinal orthodoxy, and academic rigour to seminary life paid off.

While many Sydneysiders wanted to say farewell and thanks to Pell, his final weeks in the city as archbishop were tough, due to his appearances before the Royal Commission into Institutional Responses to Child Sexual Abuse. In November 2012, former prime minister Julia Gillard had announced a royal commission (Australia's highest form of public inquiry, with power to summon witnesses) to investigate the sexual abuse of children in both secular and religious institutions. Tensions had been running high as more and more examples of abuse, within Catholic, other religious, and secular institutions including sporting organisations, surfaced. Pell's friend Tony Abbott, the Opposition leader and aspiring prime minister, promised Gillard bipartisan support for such an inquiry.

Two years earlier, Pope Benedict had apologized for years of physical and sexual abuse suffered by Irish children at the hands of priests, after a government inquiry there had exposed horrendous wrongdoing and cover-ups by bishops. "I openly express the shame and remorse that we all feel," he said.[6] He also rebuked Irish bishops for their failing "at times grievously, to apply the long-established norms of canon law to the crime of child abuse".[7]

Pell had no illusions, either, about the Church's woeful record, overall, in handling such a grave problem, which he once referred to as a "cancer" in the Church. People who claimed to be victims of

[6] Benedict XVI, Pastoral Letter to the Catholics of Ireland (March 19, 2010), no. 6.
[7] Ibid., no. 11.

child sex abuse were once viewed dubiously by Church authorities, he said during testimony before the royal commission, because in the past, enemies of the Church would accuse priests of crimes they had not committed. As recently as the mid-1990s the Vatican's attitude towards the sex-abuse claims was inadequate; but that view changed, he said, when a deputation of U.S. bishops visited the Vatican in the 1990s. "They explained vigorously to the Vatican that it wasn't just the enemies of the church who were doing this [accusing clergy of sexual abuse] for some political purpose, as the Nazis had done and possibly the communists, but that in fact there were genuine complaints, and good people, people who loved the church were saying that it's not being dealt with well enough."[8] He admitted that he was "uneasy" about the way child sex abuse claims were investigated, and that was why he pushed for improvements after he was appointed as archbishop of Sydney in 2001. "I think everybody was uneasy about the situation, and they were increasingly clear about inadequacies before 1996."[9]

Royal commissions do much of their work through public hearings, and in March 2014, shortly before his departure for Rome, Pell, along with several priests and officials of the Archdiocese of Sydney, appeared before the commissioners regarding Case Study 8. By then, the commission had completed other case studies concerning different arms of the YMCA, a Catholic special school in Adelaide, the Boy Scouts, the Salvation Army, the Catholic Church's Towards Healing Protocol to assist victims of child sexual abuse, and a Catholic school in Toowoomba, Queensland. While the commission looked at a variety of institutions, it focused heavily on Catholic and Anglican organisations, including the non-government school sector. (It paid too little attention, critics have argued, to state schools, where problems have also been uncovered.) The commission revealed an ugly underbelly of society that many Australians had not realised existed. No doubt the people of Ireland, France, the United States, and other

---

[8] *Case Study No. 8: Mr John Ellis's Experience of the Towards Healing Process and Civil Litigation*, transcript (Day 60), March 24, 2014, Royal Commission into Institutional Responses to Child Sexual Abuse, p. 12, https://www.childabuseroyalcommission.gov.au/sites/default/files/file-list/Case%20Study%208%20-%20Transcript%20-%20Mr%20John%20Ellis%20Towards%20Healing%20and%20ocivil%20olitigation%20-%20Day%20060%20-%2024032014.pdf.

[9] Ibid., p. 25.

countries, especially Catholics who, in the main, had looked up to their priests, Brothers, and Sisters, felt the same way as similar, shocking revelations unfolded around the world. Clergy, too, including Pell, were aghast to be confronted by details of behaviour they would have previously believed was too dreadful to contemplate.

Case Study 8 of the royal commission concerned the abuse of a Sydney man and former altar boy John Ellis and the Church's mishandling of the matter. From about 1974 to 1979, Ellis had been sexually assaulted by Father Aidan Duggan, an assistant priest at the Christ the King Catholic Church at Bass Hill in Sydney. Ellis had been between thirteen and seventeen years old and Father Duggan fifty-four to fifty-nine. He continued to abuse Ellis in his early adult years. The royal commission recorded: "In 2001, Mr Ellis disclosed to his counsellors for the first time that he had suffered abuse as a teenager at the hands of Father Duggan. Mr Ellis found it very difficult to talk about the abuse. The memories were painful and frightening and they came with strong physical memories of the abuse. The memories made him feel ashamed and sick."[10]

The case was a train wreck. It had dragged on for years and was acutely painful and unfair for Ellis, as well as severely damaging for the Church and, in some quarters, for Pell's standing, despite the fact the abuse took place decades before he was appointed archbishop of Sydney. Like many bishops of his generation around the world, he was left to pick up the pieces from evil that was almost incomprehensible. Being a high-profile, strong figurehead, he was expected to exercise leadership. As Gerard Henderson, executive director of the Sydney Institute, wrote in his book *Cardinal Pell, the Media Pile-On, and Collective Guilt*, most of the offences examined at the royal commission had occurred forty years earlier.

> Yet much of the media coverage implied that what was being examined were contemporary crimes.... In his final address to the Royal Commission, Justice McClellan did mention that he and his fellow commissioners had spent five years investigating what were primarily crimes of an historical nature, but this was not obvious to those who

---

[10] *Report of Case Study No. 8: Mr John Ellis's Experience of the Towards Healing Process and Civil Litigation* (Australia: Royal Commission into Institutional Responses to Child Sexual Abuse, 2015), p. 4, https://www.votf.org/wp-content/uploads/Report-of-Case-Study-8.pdf.

followed much of the media's coverage of the Royal Commission—
with its emphasis on Cardinal Pell.[11]

In relation to the Ellis case, the commission papers recount that
during the years the abuse took place, Father Duggan was a Benedictine monk on leave of absence from the Abbey of Saint Benedict of
Fort Augustus in Scotland. He had moved from Australia to Scotland
in 1942 and was ordained as a priest in 1950. During his leave of
absence from his abbey, he was incardinated in Sydney in 1990.

The sexual abuse began, the royal commission recorded, with
Father Duggan touching, hugging, and fondling Ellis. That contact
graduated to kissing, masturbation, and sodomy. It occurred regularly and frequently in Father Duggan's bedroom and sitting room
at the presbytery of Christ the King Catholic Church. On at least
two occasions, it occurred away from the presbytery when Father
Duggan was on vacation. In later years, a central issue was whether
Father Duggan (who had developed dementia) was able to respond to
Ellis' complaint. Ellis was told that "Father Duggan ... has no capacity to understand the full implications of a decision." The Towards
Healing protocol, followed by the Archdiocese of Sydney, gave clear
guidance: where the accused was unavailable to give a response, the
director of professional standards should appoint one or two assessors.
But an assessor was not appointed.

On the advice of his officials, Archbishop Pell wrote to Mr Ellis
on December 23, 2002, advising him that, as Father Duggan could
not respond to the "charges against him" and there were no other
complaints against him, under the "circumstances I do not see that
there is anything the Archdiocese can do." Ellis received this letter on
Christmas Eve. Cardinal Pell told the royal commission it was not his
intention to "convey to Mr Ellis that there was nothing the Archdiocese could do about resolving his complaint overall". Ellis construed
the letter to be a "clear statement that the archbishop considered the
matter to be at an end" despite the fact there had been no formal
assessment of his complaint.[12]

---

[11] Gerard Henderson, *Cardinal Pell, the Media Pile-On and Collective Guilt* (Redland Bay,
Australia: Connor Court Publishing, 2023), p. 304.

[12] *Case Study No. 8*, p. 5.

As reported by the Australian Broadcasting Corporation, during the royal commission's hearing, Cardinal Pell said he regretted the approach that had been taken by the archdiocesan lawyers. "Any reservations I might have about particular stands of our lawyers, I would not want to suggest that they did anything improper", he told the commissioners. "But from my point of view, from a Christian point of view, leaving aside the legal dimension, I don't think we did deal fairly." Pell explained that at first he doubted that Ellis had been abused by Father Duggan. "He presented so well. He's such a senior lawyer; he was represented by two very high-profile lawyers", he said. "I understood insufficiently just how wounded he was. We would never have run this case against many of the victims who came forward because they're manifestly so wounded. That was not apparent to me at this stage." Pell said he regretted not entering into mediation with Ellis. In addition to the harm that was done to Ellis, by the time the case was over, the court costs far exceeded his original request for compensation.[13]

Pell spent all of Monday (after being ambushed by protesters on the way in to the hearing), all of Wednesday, and Thursday afternoon of his last week as the archbishop of Sydney in the royal commission witness box. His ordeal ended in an apology to Ellis:

> As former archbishop and speaking personally, I would want to say to Mr Ellis that we failed in many ways, some ways inadvertently, in our moral and pastoral responsibilities to him. I want to acknowledge his suffering and the impact of this terrible affair on his life. As the then Archbishop, I have to take ultimate responsibility, and this I do. At the end of this gruelling appearance for both of us at this royal commission, I want publicly to say sorry to him for the hurt caused him by the mistakes made and admitted by me and some of my arch-diocesan personnel during the course of the Towards Healing process and litigation.[14]

[13] Thomas Oriti, "George Pell Tells Sex Abuse Royal Commission Case against John Ellis Was Unfair 'from a Christian Point of View' ", *ABC News*, March 26, 2014, https://www.abc .net.au/news/2014-03-26/lawyers-instructed-to-defend-church-to-send-a-message/5346110.

[14] Thomas Oriti, "Child Sex Abuse Royal Commission: George Pell Publicly Apologises to Victim John Ellis", *ABC News*, March 27, 2014, https://www.abc.net.au/news/2014-03 -28/george-pell-public-apology-to-sex-abuse-victim-john-ellis/5349910.

NTNews reported that Pell's apology was "a dramatic and public end to his 13 years as Sydney's archbishop as he conceded that Mr Ellis, who was repeatedly abused by a priest as a teenager, had not been 'unreasonable or lacked judgement' in taking on the trustees". The cardinal did not look at Ellis while reading the statement, the news website said. "He walked from the hearing room, passing Mr Ellis without a glance. Observers became agitated during the statement, with some people calling out 'look at him'."[15] It was to be the first of Pell's three appearances before the royal commission. He knew he would be called again to testify about the Melbourne archdiocesan response to clerical sex abuse and his time in Ballarat, thirty years earlier.

That evening, Pell's farewell Mass in Saint Mary's Cathedral had a subdued undertone, although the reception afterwards was warm and supportive, with Pell's flock from across the city sad he was departing. The royal commission hearing had received saturation media coverage, and many attendees had been watching proceedings intently. Most understood it was Pell's misfortune to be forced to pick up the pieces after years of inaction. Pell returned to the issue in his sermon, apologizing yet again to victims: "I apologise once again to the victims and their families for the terrible suffering that has been brought to bear by these crimes." [16]

From sporting organisations to Boy Scouts, the findings of the royal commission were devastating for most institutions examined. After surveying data from Church authorities, and based on its own firsthand research, it concluded that between January 1, 1980, and December 31, 2015, 4,444 claimants alleged incidents of child sexual abuse in 4,756 reported claims, with most allegedly occurring in the 1970s. While 90 percent of alleged perpetrators (1,880 known and 530 unknown) were male, so were 78 percent of claimants. The average age of the claimants at the time of the first alleged incident of child sexual abuse was approximately 11.4 years. Of all known

[15] Janet Fife-Yeomans, "Contrite Cardinal George Pell Ends His Reign with an Apology to Abused Former Altar Boy John Ellis", *NTNews*, March 28, 2014, https://www.ntnews.com.au/news/national/contrite-cardinal-george-pell-ends-his-reign-with-an-apology-to-abused-former-altar-boy-john-ellis/news-story/2466c5193c736033ddaoe3c9acc06da9.
[16] Ibid.

400 GEORGE CARDINAL PELL

alleged perpetrators, 37 percent were nonordained religious (32 percent were religious Brothers; 5 percent were religious Sisters); 30 percent were priests, and 29 percent were lay people. A total of 3,057 claims of child sexual abuse resulted in payments totaling AU$268 million, an average of about AU$88,000 per claim.[17]

The commission found that of all the Catholic priests included in the survey, who ministered between 1950 and 2010, taking into account the duration of ministry, 7 percent were alleged perpetrators, and most of them were in religious orders. The weighted proportion of alleged perpetrators in specific Catholic organisations was the Saint John of God Brothers (40.4 percent); the Christian Brothers (22.0 percent); the Benedictine Community of New Norcia (21.5 percent); the Salesians of Don Bosco (20.9 percent); the Marist Brothers (20.4 percent); the Diocese of Sale in Victoria (15.1 percent); the De La Salle Brothers (13.8 percent); and the Archdiocese of Adelaide in South Australia (2.4 percent).[18]

Pell's next appearance before the royal commission would be in early March 2016 via video link from Rome. It was to be no easier than the Sydney hearing.

[17]Royal Commission into Institutional Responses to Child Sexual Abuse, *Final Report: Religious Institutions*, vol. 16, bk. 1, pp. 19, 35, 113, 333, https://www.childabuseroyalcommission.gov.au/religious-institutions.
[18]Ibid., p. 35.

31

The Ordeal Begins

Australians were anticipating Christmas when a startling item appeared on newspaper websites and radio and television programs on Wednesday, December 23, 2015. Melbourne's best-selling *Herald Sun* reported:

> Boys as young as 14 were allegedly sexually abused at St Patrick's Cathedral in East Melbourne while Cardinal George Pell was in charge.
>
> Sano Taskforce detectives are investigating claims of assault at the Catholic church between 1996 and 2001—the same period when Cardinal Pell was archbishop of Melbourne.
>
> Investigators are appealing to anyone who was a victim or with any information relating to any alleged sexual assaults committed at the church during this period to contact them.
>
> The Sano Taskforce detectives specialise in investigating historical sexual assault and child abuse matters.[1]

The Sano Taskforce, which had been set up to probe child abuse cases surfacing from the work of the royal commission, provided no further details about the allegations and did not suggest that Cardinal Pell was directly involved in them. The communications director for the Archdiocese of Melbourne, Shane Healy, offered no comment on the claims and urged people to contact the taskforce if they had information related to the investigation.

The reports mystified cathedral and other archdiocesan staff, past and present, as well as Pell himself, who was preparing to celebrate

---

[1] Rebekah Cavanagh, "Sex Abuse Claims at St Patrick's Cathedral in East Melbourne under Police Investigation", *Herald Sun*, December 23, 2015, https://www .heraldsun.com.au/news/law-order/sex-abuse-claims-at-st-patricks-cathedral-in-east -melbourne-under-police-investigation/news-story/6633cab3e77f51ab891f45ac08955c31.

Christmas in Rome. He had been due to return to Australia in December 2015 to give more evidence to the Royal Commission into Institutional Responses to Child Sexual Abuse, but he had delayed the trip on the advice of his cardiologist and with the approval of the commissioners. Medical evidence in support of the delay had been tendered as a confidential exhibit, and it showed that Cardinal Pell suffered from high blood pressure and heart disease and that in his condition at the time, travel to Australia could induce a heart attack, which would be difficult to treat on board a plane. After having reviewed and accepted the evidence, the commission had postponed Pell's testimony until February.

Media reports referring to an "alleged" illness were therefore "misleading and mischievous", Pell said in a statement released to the media. "Claims that Cardinal Pell is refusing to attend the royal commission or to face victims of sexual abuse are false and ridiculous", the statement said. "Cardinal Pell's whole career is a story of stepping up to meet challenges, not avoiding them."[2]

Before Pell could appear again before the royal commission, the *Herald Sun* reported:

> A Victoria Police taskforce has been investigating allegations that Cardinal George Pell sexually abused between five and ten boys.
>
> Detectives from Sano Taskforce have compiled a dossier containing allegations that Cardinal Pell committed "multiple offences" when a priest in Ballarat and when archbishop of Melbourne. It has been alleged the 74-year-old, now in charge of finances at the Vatican in Rome, sexually abused minors by "both grooming and opportunity".[3]

The allegations spanned four decades, between 1978 and 2001. Legal sources had told the newspaper that more than a dozen detectives from Sano Taskforce had worked on the investigation for the past year, interviewing "numerous" alleged victims. Sano detectives, reportedly, also revisited the 1961 summer camp case, which had

---

[2] "Cardinal George Pell Labels Reports Casting Doubt on Legitimacy of His Illness 'Misleading and Mischievous'", *ABC News*, December 13, 2015, https://www.abc.net.au/news/2015-12-14/pell-attacks-reports-casting-doubt-on-legitimacy-of-his-illness/7024616.
[3] Lucie Morris-Marr, "Victoria Police Investigating Cardinal Pell", *Herald Sun*, February 10, 2016.

been investigated in 2002 and found lacking in evidence. The complainant in that case, however, declined to become involved in any new investigation of Pell.

Cardinal Pell released a statement saying that the allegations were "without foundation and utterly false" and calling for an inquiry into how the *Herald Sun* got the story, given that the article was how Pell, in Rome, first learned of the new allegations. His statement continued: "Cardinal Pell is due to give evidence to the Royal Commission in just over one week. The timing of these leaks is clearly designed to do maximum damage to the Cardinal and the Catholic Church and undermines the work of the royal commission."[4]

Since his health was still considered too precarious for international travel, Pell testified before the royal commission via video link from the Hotel Quirinale in central Rome, from February 29, 2016, to March 3, 2016. Afterwards he told reporters, "It's been a hard slog, at least for me, I'm a bit tired." The hardest part of the process, he said, was "reading the transcripts of the way the victims suffered, in preparation for this.... I hope my appearance here has contributed a bit to healing, to improving the situation."[5] For some it did, but not for all.

The commission asked Pell about Gerald Ridsdale's involvement with children while serving as a priest in the Diocese of Ballarat between 1961 and 1988. At the time, Ridsdale had been in prison since 1994, serving a maximum thirty-nine-year sentence for abusing dozens of child victims at multiple schools and churches across Victoria. While police had suspicions as early as 1975 that Ridsdale was abusing children, he was not charged until almost two decades later, and in the meantime he had been moved from one assignment to another.

In an emotional postscript to the hearings, Pell met with a group of abuse survivors who had travelled to Rome from Ballarat to watch him giving evidence. They agreed to explore the possibility of establishing a research centre in Ballarat to "enhance healing and improve

[4] "Statement from the Office of Cardinal George Pell", in "Cardinal Pell Hits Back at Claims He Is 'Under Investigation' over Child Abuse Allegations", *The Guardian*, February 19, 2016, https://www.theguardian.com/australia-news/2016/feb/19/cardinal-george-pell -hits-back-at-claims-he-is-under-investigation-over-child-abuse-allegations.

[5] "Sex Abuse Commission: Pell Promises Counselling for Victims", *The Australian*, March 4, 2016.

protection".[6] Pell said, "I am committed to working with these people from Ballarat and surrounding areas. I know many of their families and I know the goodness of so many people of Catholic Ballarat; a goodness that is not extinguished by the evil that was done."[7] Not all survivors who travelled to Rome wanted to meet Pell. In a short statement, published by *The Guardian*, those who did said: "We've had an extremely emotional meeting with Cardinal Pell. We met on a level playing field."[8]

During twenty hours of evidence over the course of four days, Pell stumbled verbally once or twice, especially in relation to Ridsdale's abuse of children in the small township of Inglewood, 115 miles northwest of Melbourne. His comment that it was "a sad story and of not much interest to me" drew gasps in Rome and from some watching proceedings in Sydney.[9] The following day, Pell made it clear to the commission that he regretted his choice of words and "messing up this sequence completely.... I was very confused, I responded poorly."[10] In general, however, during the gruelling process he was measured and thoughtful, displaying excellent recall, as the public, especially practicing Catholics, listened and watched in horror at the revelations that emerged.

These included the disturbing fact that Vatican officials had tried to stop bishops from removing paedophile priests such as the cruel and grotesque Father Peter Searson. His case is relevant to Pell's story for several reasons. First, it demonstrates how, as an auxiliary bishop, Pell was able to do next to nothing about it. Second, it shows that after he

[6] "Pell Says Meeting with Australia Abuse Survivors Was 'Hard and Honest'", *The Guardian*, March 3, 2016, https://www.theguardian.com/australia-news/2016/mar/03/cardinal-pell-meeting-australia-abuse-survivors.

[7] Rosie Scammell, "Cardinal George Pell, Top Vatican Official, Meets Abuse Victims after Testimony", *Washington Post*, March 3, 2016, https://www.washingtonpost.com/national/religion/cardinal-george-pell-top-vatican-official-meets-abuse-victims-after-testimony/2016/03/03/d6c2f332-e16d-11e5-8c00-8aa03741dced_story.html.

[8] "Pell Says Meeting".

[9] David Marr, "George Pell Wasn't Much Interested in Stories of Abuse by Priests. Which Was Lucky for His Career", *The Guardian*, March 1, 2016, https://www.theguardian.com/australia-news/2016/mar/01/george-pell-wasnt-much-interested-in-stories-of-abuse-by-priests-which-was-lucky-for-his-career.

[10] "George Pell Tells Royal Commission Walking Gerald Ridsdale to Court Was 'a Mistake'", *Sydney Morning Herald*, March 3, 2016, https://www.smh.com.au/national/george-pell-tells-royal-commission-walking-gerald-ridsdale-to-court-was-a-mistake-20160303-gn902u.html.

became archbishop, Pell acted swiftly and decisively in dismissing the priest, incurring the wrath of Roman authorities for doing so. And third, the case revealed what faithful Catholics and their children had been forced to endure for years.

Searson, reportedly, was the fifth abusive priest during a period of about thirty-five years in the small parish of Doveton, which years ago was one of Melbourne's poorer suburbs. Its people deserved far better. The fiendish record of one of Searson's predecessors in the parish, Father Wilfred Baker, was also covered by the commission. Baker held a number of appointments throughout the archdiocese between 1961 and 1997. In 1999 he was sentenced to four years' imprisonment for child sex offences. He was laicised in 2012 and died in 2014, when other criminal charges against him were pending. Baker's case, Archbishop Denis Hart told the commission, was one of the "Archdiocese failing to act on credible information about criminal abuse by a priest, which failure resulted in more children being abused, and resulted in a long delay in developing widespread awareness of the incidence and the risk of sexual abuse by some members of the clergy, and in preventing its occurrence."[11] But it was Searson who broke the hearts of the people of Doveton, as reported by one of Australia's major news websites on November 2, 2016:

> He was a paedophile, a psychopath and a thief who despised women, had a fetish for children and a sneering hatred for the locals of the tiny community.
>
> The creepy Father Peter Searson, who wore his yellow fingernails long and manicured, liked dressing up in an army uniform and carried a pistol he sometimes pointed at parishioners.
>
> He stole $40,000 from the parish finances, killed or tortured animals in front of children and showed them a dead body in a coffin.
>
> He got children to touch his penis, made them kneel between his legs, loitered around the children's toilets and audio-taped primary schoolers in the confessional box.[12]

[11] Report of Case Study No. 35: Catholic Archdiocese of Melbourne (Australia, Royal Commission into Institutional Reponses to Child Sexual Abuse, 2017), p. 30, https://apo.org.au/sites/default/files/resource-files/2020-05/apo-nid303709.pdf.

[12] Candace Sutton, "Unholy Family: The Psychopath Who Was the Fifth Paedophile Priest Sent to Town", News.com.au, November 2, 2016, https://www.news.com.au/lifestyle/real-life/news-life/unholy-family-the-psychopath-who-was-the-fifth-paedophile-priest-sent-to-town/news-story/e23032a3a1e03721086bee8750a653a0.

A former Marist Brother, Searson wreaked havoc and devastated young lives in two parishes, Sunbury and Doveton, for decades. Before the royal commission, Pell accepted partial blame for the failure of his predecessor, Sir Frank Little, to remove Searson, regretting he had not been pushier. But Little, who knew about Searson's abusive behaviour, was intractable, and his inaction on such grave matters was a contributing factor to his early retirement. It was Pell, in his first twelve months as archbishop of Melbourne, in May 1997, who finally stripped Searson of his priestly faculties. Searson beat Pell on a point of canon law in Rome, but the archbishop, rightly, defied the Vatican and refused to let Searson work again.

In one memorable exchange during the hearings with commission counsel Gail Furness, SC, Pell said that when he was an auxiliary bishop, Catholic Education Office officials in Melbourne withheld vital information from him about child sex abuse in the archdiocese. They did so, he said, because they knew he could be outspoken and they "wanted to keep a lid" on the situation. Furness said she found that explanation "completely implausible". In reply, Pell said, "I can only tell the truth." It was, he said, "an extraordinary world, a world of crimes and cover-ups, and people did not want the status quo to be disturbed."[13]

Nevertheless, the commission concluded:

> Cardinal Pell's evidence was that he could not recall recommending a particular course of action to the Archbishop. He conceded that, in retrospect, he might have been "a bit more pushy" with all of the parties involved.... On the basis of what was known to Bishop Pell in 1989, it ought to have been obvious to him at the time. He should have advised the Archbishop to remove Father Searson and he did not do so.[14]

In interviews after the hearings, Pell defended himself. A myth had been perpetrated, he said, that he had turned a blind eye to

---

[13] Tess Livingstone, "Cardinal Pell Should Be Praised for Daring to Rock the Boat", *The Australian*, March 3, 2016.

[14] "'He Should Have Done More': Key Findings from the Newly Released George Pell Reports", *The Guardian*, May 7, 2020, https://www.theguardian.com/australia-news/2020/may/07/he-should-have-done-more-key-findings-from-the-newly-released-george-pell-reports?CMP=gu_com.

claims of child abuse while working as a priest in Ballarat in the 1970s and early 80s and as Auxiliary to Archbishop Frank Little in Melbourne from 1987 to 1996. In Melbourne, he said, he did meet a delegation from Doveton Parish in 1989, who were rightly unhappy with the kooky and frightening Father Peter Searson. However, sexual assaults were not mentioned. And despite a litany of complaints about Searson, Little was resolute.[15]

After being appointed archbishop in 1996, Pell did what Little should have done years earlier: "The buck stopped with me," he said, "and I removed Searson within months of taking office."

The archbishop's willingness to act, where others had dithered and ducked, was also evident in his efforts in 1999 to persuade Pope John Paul II to strip another clerical paedophile, Michael Glennon, of his status as a priest. That was recounted in *The Age* when Chip Le Grand reported that "a lawsuit involving Aboriginal victims of a jailed priest could have international implications for the Vatican as they seek to protect the pontiff [Francis] from being drawn into a civil damages claim."[16] Despite being sentenced in 1978, Glennon remained an ordained priest until Pell moved to have him defrocked.

Unfair as it was, the accusation that Pell had not done enough to tackle abuse when he was Little's auxiliary paled alongside the accusation, preposterous as it was, that he abused children himself. Just how preposterous became clearer in an extraordinary, later revelation, when it emerged that Victoria Police launched Operation Tethering against the cardinal in March 2013, without any crimes or allegations of wrongdoing on his part being reported to them. In March 2018, during a Magistrates Court hearing into whether Pell should be sent for trial on historic sex abuse charges, his barrister Robert Richter, QC, questioned Detective Superintendent Paul Sheridan about Operation Tethering. Sheridan said it was an "intel probe" to see whether there were unreported serious crimes, *The Australian* reported. Richter asked him, "Operation Tethering, that wasn't a 'get Pell' operation was it?" Sheridan responded, "I guess you could term it the way you did, but I wouldn't term it that way."[17]

[15] George Pell, Rome interview by Andrew Bolt, *Sky News*, March 4, 2016, and Tess Livingstone, "Cardinal George Pell Should be Praised".

[16] Chip Le Grand, "Pope Seeks Immunity in Australian Court over Notorious Paedophile Priest", *The Age*, April 6, 2024.

[17] "George Pell: The Trial of the Century", *The Australian*, May 2, 2018.

Operation Tethering unfolded at a delicate time in the history of police work in Victoria. In March 2014, Melbourne's *Herald Sun* broke the story that Nicola Gobbo, a barrister known as Lawyer X, and the police force had agreed to a deal in which Gobbo, who represented many gangland figures in Melbourne at the time, would inform on clients including drug lords and gang bosses. It did not occur to senior police, evidently, that a barrister informing on client criminals could imperil convictions against them.

Pell only learned the details of the allegations against him when he was interviewed by Victoria Police in Rome in October 2016. At that stage, he had a sense of incredulity, as well as bemusement and anger, about the matter. That was clear to those who knew him and his mannerisms, especially when he was upset or angry, when his recorded interview was released after it was played as evidence at both his trials. Questioned by the police about allegations that he had abused two choirboys in the sacristy after Sunday Mass at Saint Patrick's Cathedral, Pell, arms folded, showed his annoyance but was confident and collected in his responses. "Are we in the archbishop's sacristy or the priest's sacristy?" he asked the police. Told that the boys found some wine in a cupboard in the room and took a swig or two, Pell said, "Well, that's not in the archbishop's sacristy. There is a formidable safe which is in the priest's sacristy, where the wine was locked."[18]

Most things in the story, Pell said, were "counter factual and with a bit of luck I will be able to demonstrate it". The first point was that "after every Mass I would stay out at the front of the cathedral and talk to people." When he was told it was alleged that he planted himself between the boys and the door and prevented them from leaving the room, moved his "robes" to one side and exposed his penis (an impossibility for any priest wearing a floor-length alb with no splits) while standing with his back to the door, Pell answered, "Stop it. What a lot of absolute and disgraceful rubbish. Completely false. Madness. All sorts of people used to come to the sacristy to speak to the priest. The sacristans were around. The altar servers were around."

After the police detailed the allegations of sexual assault on both boys, Pell replied: "Completely false. This is in the sacristy at the

---

[18] Carl Hamill, "George Pells Police Interview Video Full", March 3, 2019, https://www .youtube.com/watch?v=N5PdLiOO_dA&t=1984s.

cathedral after Sunday Mass. Need I say any more? What a load of garbage and falsehood and deranged falsehood. My master of ceremonies will be able to say he was always with me after the ceremonies until we went back to the car or to the presbytery. The sacristan was around. The altar servers were around. People were coming and going." Pell said the fact the allegations concerned the period immediately after Mass was good for his defence because it made them "all the more fantastic and impossible".

A further instance of alleged abuse was said to have occurred at least a month later. It purportedly involved the complainant walking along the corridor, still in robes after Mass, on his way back to the choir room, when Pell allegedly pushed the boy against the wall and grabbed his genitals in an attack lasting only a couple of seconds. Pell was flabbergasted by the story. "I was always out the front of the cathedral; I never came back with the kids", he said. Such behaviour by the archbishop of Melbourne, or any priest, in a corridor of the cathedral after Mass, with dozens of people milling about, would have prompted uproar among eyewitnesses and caused enormous fallout.

After months of speculation about whether the police would press charges, Victoria Police Deputy Commissioner Shane Patton called a press conference on Thursday, June 29, 2017, and read the following statement:

Today Victoria Police have charged Cardinal George Pell with historical sexual assault offences.

Cardinal Pell has been charged on summons and he is required to appear at the Melbourne Magistrates Court on July 18 this year for a filing hearing.

The charges were today served on Cardinal Pell's legal representatives in Melbourne and they have been lodged also at the Melbourne Magistrates Court. Cardinal Pell is facing multiple charges in respect of historic sexual offences. There are multiple complainants relating to those charges.

During the course of the investigation in relation to Cardinal Pell, there has been a lot of reporting in the media and a lot of speculation about the process that has been involved in the investigation and also the charging.

So for clarity, I want to be perfectly clear, the process and procedures that are being followed in the charging of Cardinal Pell have been the same that have been applied in a whole range of historical sex offences whenever we investigate them.

The fact that he has been charged on summons, we have used advice from the Office of Public Prosecutions and also we have engaged with his legal representatives is common and standard practice.

So there has been no change in any procedures whatsoever. Cardinal Pell has been treated the same as anyone else in this investigation.

Advice was received and sought from the Office of Public Prosecutions, however ultimately the choice to charge Cardinal Pell was one that was made by Victoria Police.

It is important to note that none of the allegations that have been made against Cardinal Pell have obviously been tested in any court yet.

Cardinal Pell, like any other defendant, has a right to due process and so therefore it is important that the process is allowed to run its natural course.

Preserving the integrity of that process is essential to all of us and so for Victoria Police it is important that it is allowed to go through unhindered and allowed to see natural justice is afforded to all the parties involved, including Cardinal Pell and the complainants in this matter.

Because of that, I am not in a position to take any questions here this morning and in moving forward, Victoria Police won't be making any further comments in respect of this matter.[19]

In Rome, June 29, the feast day of the Eternal City's patron saints Peter and Paul, is a public holiday. But Pell held a press conference in response to the news, hours after Patton's announcement of the charges. Sounding calm and collected, Pell, who could have claimed diplomatic immunity and remained in Rome, explained that he would return to Australia to defend himself. "I want to say one or two brief words about my situation", he said.

These matters have been under investigation now for nearly two years. There have been leaks to the media, relentless character assassination and, for more than a month, claims that a decision on whether to lay charges was "imminent."

[19] "Victoria Police's Full Statement Concerning Charges against Cardinal George Pell", *Sydney Morning Herald*, updated June 29, 2017, https://www.smh.com.au/national/victoria-polices-full-statement-concerning-charges-against-cardinal-george-pell-20170629-gx0xh5.html.

I'm looking forward, finally, to having my day in court.

I'm innocent of these charges. They are false. The whole idea of sexual abuse is abhorrent to me.

I have kept Pope Francis regularly informed throughout this lengthy process, and have spoken to him in recent days about the need to take leave to clear my name. I am grateful for his support in granting me this leave to return to Australia. I have spoken to my lawyers about when I need to return home, and to my doctors about how best to do this.

I have been consistent and clear in my total rejection of these allegations. News of these charges strengthens my resolve, and court proceedings now offer me an opportunity to clear my name and then return to my work in Rome.[20]

News of what had befallen the third-highest-ranking Vatican official spread like wildfire around the world. And it was clear, from the outset, that the Australia legal system (or specifically the legal system of the State of Victoria) would be on trial as well as Pell. It failed, abysmally.

What was not clear was whether there was any link between the charges against Pell and the forced resignation of Vatican Auditor General Libero Milone less than a fortnight earlier, when Vatican police launched a sudden raid on his office. They shouted at Milone, seized several computers, and threatened him with arrest if he did not sign a resignation letter. Many in Rome believed there was a link between the predicaments of Milone and Pell. Pell suspected it but had no proof.

Milone, a former chairman and chief executive of Deloitte in Italy, was and is held in high regard in financial circles. Pell (together with Cardinal Reinhard Marx, coordinator of the Council of the Economy, and Cardinal Pietro Parolin, secretary of state) had engaged Milone in June 2015 as the Vatican's first auditor general. His work became more important the following year when efforts to have the Vatican's books audited externally by PricewaterhouseCoopers were stopped, reportedly, by the Secretariat of State. Pope Francis had said financial reform was one of his priorities, but he did not interfere

[20] "Statement from the Cardinal George Pell Following Announcement of Charges by Victorian Police", in "Updated: Cardinal Pell Facing Historic Abuse Charges", *Catholic Weekly*, June 29, 2017, https://www.catholicweekly.com.au/updated-cardinal-pell-facing-historic-abuse-charges/.

when the audit was stopped. He later promoted the deputy secretary of state Archbishop Giovanni Angelo Becciu to cardinal but moved him sideways, to run the Congregation for the Causes of Saints. "That's good, Saints has no clout", Pell quipped at the time.

After news of the charges against him broke, Pell, travelling with his friend Chris Meaney, took the journey home in stages, on the advice of his doctors. They stopped in Tokyo and Singapore, where they sat down for an ice cream (one of Pell's favourite treats) at an outside table of a café; Pell, looking relaxed in a blue shirt and cream slacks, refused to huddle inside. They were snapped by a photographer, and an Australian passerby told them he had just called his mother, who "wants to know whether you are innocent". "Tell her that I am", Pell responded.

One of the first international Church leaders to speak up for Pell was his longtime friend Cardinal Timothy Dolan, the archbishop of New York. Pell's response to the charges, and his acknowledgment that he is not above the law, "shows the mettle of a great man", Cardinal Dolan told *Crux*. "He's the kind of man about whom I would find such reports to be completely contrary to everything he stands for", he said. "I feel terribly sad for my good friend Cardinal George Pell, sad for him and sad with him. I want to be very supportive, because I have immense admiration for him ... and I want to stick with him."[21] He did, most generously, in various ways, for which Pell was profoundly grateful.

Canadian priest and commentator Father Raymond de Souza, writing in London's *Catholic Herald* a week after Pell was charged, recognised the case would test the Australian criminal justice system and the Church in Australia. Because Pell refused to cooperate in the Church's marginalization, de Souza wrote, he was the target of a nefarious campaign that brought shame upon Australians, "who otherwise are quick to tell you of their sense of fairness, that everyone is entitled to a 'fair go'".[22] More than Pell's official assignments,

[21] "Dolan: Pell's Response to Abuse Charges Shows 'Mettle of a Great Man'", interview by John Allen, *Crux*, July 4, 2017, https://cruxnow.com/interviews/2017/07/dolan-pells-response-abuse-charges-shows-mettle-great-man.

[22] Raymond de Souza, "The Australian Church Must Hold Its Nerve", *Catholic Herald*, July 6, 2017, https://catholicherald.co.uk/as-cardinal-pell-goes-on-trial-the-australian-church-must-hold-its-nerve/.

de Souza added, his "clarity and courage have been an indispensable inspiration to tens of thousands of priests and lay leaders. In a certain sense, he assumed the mantle of Cardinal John O'Connor of New York as the most prominent voice in the English-speaking Catholic world. Cardinal O'Connor had, in fact, been an inspiration for Pell himself, a model of the bishop in a hostile culture."

The Vatican press statement on Pell's charges expressed "esteem" for the Australian criminal justice system responsible for finding out the truth, de Souza wrote. But, presciently, he did not share this confidence. The anti-Catholic climate in Australia is hard to appreciate without visiting the country or being in regular contact with locals, he argued. "The Victoria police insisted that Cardinal Pell has been treated 'no differently' from anyone else. That is only the most recent of their lies. The police have spent two years searching for characters who are willing to 'remember' assaults from 40 years ago. There will be more lies to come, and a wrongful conviction cannot be excluded." At that stage, Pell did not share this concern.

Pell and Meaney arrived back in Australia on July 10, 2017. His successor as archbishop of Sydney, Anthony Fisher, said the archdiocese would help with Pell's accommodation while he was in Australia, but it was not responsible for his legal bills. Supporters quickly organised appeals to fund his legal fees, and donors and supporters large and small, in Australia and overseas, made contributions. Pell also had to dig deep into his own pockets, which "just about wiped me out", he said.

Pell turned his attention to the charges he was facing. There was one complainant involved in the cathedral case. The second boy Pell was alleged to have attacked and abused had reportedly died of a heroin overdose a few years earlier, at the age of thirty-one. Six days after Pell was sent to jail on February 27, 2019, the family of the complainant said that it wasn't until after he attended the funeral of the other alleged victim that he told his mother what had happened.[23] She called Bernard Barrett, of the victims' group Broken Rites, who

[23] "Family of George Pell's Victim Describes How Their Son Changed after Abuse", *News.com.au*, March 5, 2019, https://www.news.com.au/national/victoria/courts-law /family-of-george-pells-victim-describes-how-their-son-changed-after-abuse/news-story /f037edd36ccaa45858674ee1e17293e5.

said, "I answered the phone and she explained that her son, who was a former choirboy, he was very upset because he'd had a troubled life since his teens, and he was telling her for the first time, at the age of 30, about having been abused by a priest."

Both boys had choral scholarships to attend Saint Kevin's College. The family of the one who later died said that he had been happy at school before the alleged abuse, but that afterwards his life changed for the worse. "He went from being this lovely boy who used to come to the football with me, who used to go and help his grandparents and helped around the house, to this boy wanting to go out all the time", his father said. "His whole attitude changed. His whole being just, he was a different boy." The boy started using heroin about a year after the alleged abuse, family members said. "At 14, he would spend nights where we wouldn't see him," his father said. "He would disappear for a day or two, and then turn up as though nothing had happened. His schooling, of course, became erratic." The school was threatening to expel the boy because of his behaviour.

His mother also told about how the boy's life took a sudden turn. "Looking back, as a person, he changed. He did. He wasn't the same person as what he was beforehand", his mother said. "I once asked him if he was ... I can't exactly remember the words I used, whether he was touched up or played with. And he told me no. . . . And I was just so angry with him for not telling me. So angry. Sometimes I'm still very angry. It's hard when you think a child can't come out and say, 'This has happened,' because most times they're not believed. I would like to think I would have believed my son."

The man's sister described her brother's life spiralling out of control. "It's very hard to explain to people that my brother struggled for half his life with a drug abuse problem. It's devastating because it helps to explain a lot of incidents in his life."

In total, Victoria Police charged Pell with twenty-six offences involving nine persons. Pell was particularly disturbed by the claims of one complainant, which drew heavy media coverage. That complainant alleged that Pell had raped him in the Ballarat movie theatre while they were watching the Steven Spielberg film *Close Encounters of the Third Kind*. Pell said that he had never seen the movie at all. The man also claimed Pell had raped him at night on the altar in the chapel of the orphanage where the boy had lived, a place Pell never worked. Pell staunchly denied the accusation and in private said such an action would have been "demonic". Pell had no fears that the matters would go to trial, but he was deeply disturbed about the well-being of the complainant involved.

Pell entered the Magistrates Court of Victoria facing twenty-six charges; he left facing ten. Charges 20 to 26, concerning the alleged abuse at the cathedral, went to trial and led to his conviction in December 2018. The other remaining charges, regarding alleged abuse in Ballarat swimming pools, were dropped by prosecutors in February 2019.

Charges 20 to 26 involved a single prosecution witness, J.J. Delivering her findings, on May 1, 2018, Magistrate Belinda Wallington said: "The prosecution rely on the evidence of J.J. whose statements were tendered as his evidence-in-chief of sexual offences alleged to have been committed against himself and M.R. There is no statement from M.R., who died of a drug overdose in 2014, having never spoken to anyone of having been sexually assaulted and having specifically denied it when questioned by his mother. J.J. alleged a second incident where he was alone."[24]

Magistrate Wallington, who committed Pell for trial on charges 20 to 26, also discussed the evidence given by former choir master John Mallinson, Pell's master of ceremonies Monsignor Charles Portelli, sacristan Max Potter, and others, including eleven choristers:

> Here was a preponderance of evidence that the archbishop spent time speaking with the congregants on the steps prior to returning to the sacristy. If a jury accepted the evidence of Monsignor Portelli and Mr Potter that the archbishop was never in the sacristy robed and alone, and that choirboys could never access the sacristy keys because they were always locked when unused, a jury could not convict.
>
> Their evidence may not be as high as that, however even if it is that high, the submission that a properly instructed jury could have no ability to put their evidence or part thereof, to one side, cannot be accepted. The jury has the fundamental function of weighing the evidence and the unfettered ability to accept or reject it. A committing magistrate may not usurp that fundamental role.

[24] Gerard Henderson, *Cardinal Pell, the Media Pile-On and Collective Guilt* (Redland Bay, Australia: Connor Court Publishing, 2023), p. 57.

The evidence of J.J. is evidence capable, as a matter of law, of supporting a finding of guilt and it is not for this court to impose its own view, if held, that a jury would be unlikely to convict. Having found there is evidence of sufficient weight that a properly instructed jury could convict, the accused is committed for trial on Charges 20 to 26.

Magistrate Wallington also committed Pell to trial on three charges involving alleged abuse of two boys at a swimming pool in Ballarat in the 1970s. Those allegations had been the first to be raised publicly and had attracted a lot of attention and were, as mentioned earlier, later dropped.

32

Time of Trial

Pell's incredulity towards the charges and his confidence about being able to clear his name were obvious to most people who knew him in the video recording of his Victoria Police interview in Rome on October 19, 2016. Robert Richter, QC, an experienced barrister in criminal law, whom Pell had selected to represent him because of Richter's powerful advocacy skills, had been with Pell in Rome for the lead-up to the police interview. In an interview for this book, Richter said he felt "terribly relieved" after the interview. Pell's answers were clear and "absolutely right", the barrister said, and it would "give him a better defence" if the matters ever made it to court. Richter knew that in the event of a trial the interview would be played to a jury, and the quality of Pell's responses were a significant factor in Richter's advising Pell not to take the stand. Pell was free to reject that advice. But Richter believed that if Pell allowed himself to be cross-examined in front of a jury, he would run the risk of "things going downhill from there". Pell's strong intellect and faith would not necessarily appeal to jurors, Richter said, "and the police interview, which was played in court, said it all."

Richter is well aware that many of Pell's friends and supporters believed he should have taken the stand. But, he said, the whole legal team

believed we had it won by the time the prosecution case closed. As the High Court ruled 7:0, we were clearly right, and calling Pell to the witness box would not have made a difference unless the jury was not, in any event, already disposed to convict because of years of media influence. It must follow that had we called him to the stand, it might have detracted from what we clearly achieved at the trial. Hindsight is not, in these circumstances, a guide into what the advice should have been.

Pell's confidence was also evident during the first proceedings against him, in the Magistrates' Court, and at the outset of his first trial. That trial was subject to a suppression order, put in place by the court, on the basis that media coverage of the "cathedral trial" could prejudice a second trial on the "swimming pool" charges. Pell was comfortable with the suppression order. In some ways, he told friends, it lessened the "circus maximus" atmosphere surrounding the first trial. Others were deeply uneasy, however, believing transparency would serve him better in the long run. It was the law and made sense insofar as he had been committed for trial on two distinct sets of charges, which allegedly occurred decades apart. But the misgivings of those who would have preferred transparency were legitimate. Day-to-day, transparent coverage of the trial would surely have highlighted the weakness of the case against Pell. Father Frank Brennan, S.J., a qualified lawyer who had clashed with Pell over theological issues, followed the trial closely and summed up the effects of the suppression order:

> Pell faced criminal trials which were conducted under suppression orders. This meant the public was not able to follow the evidence in the trials day by day. The public was simply presented with a final verdict followed by an internationally live televised public sentencing at which the trial judge had to operate on the basis that the jury had made the right decision. Once the suppression orders were lifted, three books with popular appeal were published, all critical of Pell and the Church. Only now are books more attentive to the evidence and therefore supportive of Pell starting to appear.[1]

While journalists had no alternative but to honour the suppression order, the County Court was not closed. The same had applied in the Magistrate Court, apart from specific instances when alleged victims were called to give evidence. Members of the public, including journalists, were free to attend proceedings and did so, though few media organisations could afford to keep reporters tied up for weeks on end without daily copy to publish or broadcast.

[1] Frank Brennan, "Where Has Cardinal Pell's Case Brought Us in the Australian Church?", *Studies: An Irish Quarterly Review*, spring 2021.

The cathedral trial began on August 15, 2018—the feast of the Assumption of Mary, an auspicious day in the Church calendar—and Pell arrived at court after celebrating Mass (as he did every morning). Most nights he was sanguine after proceedings, but a few who gave evidence, or who went along to watch, were less so. Monsignor Charles Portelli, for example, who had brought the cathedral vestments to court, was uneasy that the jury missed the full effect of seeing the archbishop being fully robed in the straight, seamless alb, held tightly in place by a cincture (long rope belt), and overlaid by a heavy chasuble as well as a microphone. Others were concerned that the jury were taken around the cathedral to see the sacristies on a quiet afternoon (when the corridors resembled Hogwarts during a school holiday) rather than on a Sunday morning amid the hurly burly surrounding the Solemn Mass. "That would have been so inconvenient for everyone", Pell told one of his friends who raised the matter. As usual he was thinking of the Church's best interests, and it was also a sign of how relaxed he remained, probably too much so.

A sore point with some was the fact that two former teachers, who were metres from where Pell was accused of sexually assaulting the choirboys, J and R, were not called to give evidence. Jean Cornish, a former principal of Good Shepherd Catholic School, at Gladstone Park in Melbourne's northwest which had about a thousand students, and teacher Lil Sinozic both worked in the cathedral in late 1996. Cornish was seconded to run the cathedral in early 1996 in preparation for its centenary celebrations, which began in late 1996 and stretched across 1997. Sinozic, who had taught in the school run by Cornish, joined her as assistant in 1996 and was also executive assistant to Portelli, Pell's master of ceremonies. Both women were on duty every Sunday morning in late 1996, after the cathedral had reopened after renovations in November that year.

Cornish's desk at the back of the cathedral was metres from the priests' sacristy. "Those hallowed halls were as busy as Bourke Street on a Sunday morning after Mass", she said. As a teacher, she was deeply aware of the importance of safety "from the child's perspective" and would not have hesitated to blow the whistle had she noticed anything amiss. "But this has been a travesty of justice, it could not have occurred", she said. While her desk looked directly out to the corridor beside the priests' sacristy, she was always "up and about" and "on the alert" around the sacristy area, where busloads of tourists who visited the cathedral on Sundays were not allowed but sometimes tried to enter. She said two choirboys swigging wine, as the complainant in the case claimed, would have been noticed by herself, the sacristan, Max Potter, his deputy, Michael Mahony, and altar servers returning chalices, candles, and crosses to the sacristy. At that time, she said, Pell was always outside on the main steps to the cathedral, greeting worshippers for up to thirty minutes. "Father Portelli was always with him, he never left his side, and they always returned to the sacristy together", she said.

Interviewed by *The Australian* at the time the cardinal's High Court appeal was being prepared (he referred to the story in his prison diaries after his friend Father Paul Stenhouse, M.S.C., reproduced the article in his final edition of *Annals* magazine), Sinozic said that she was livid that she and Cornish, who had been in the best position of all to see what was going on, were never called as witnesses. "Charles (Portelli) never let him (Pell) alone for a second," she said. "There were about twenty people around after Mass, including florists who were attending to flowers for the next show (the next Mass)."[2]

Victoria Police knew about Cornish's role. Under cross-examination from Richter, during the cardinal's committal trial in March 2018, Monsignor Portelli gave evidence that the door of Cornish's office, which looked out onto the corridor of the sacristies, was "always open" on Sunday mornings. He said Cornish would be "patrolling the corridor" for tourists and others who were not allowed in that part of the cathedral.

Among Pell's friends, opinions were divided as to whether he should have taken the stand. The court was closed during the complainant's evidence.

Sydney Institute executive director Gerard Henderson recounted in his book on the trials of Pell that the presiding judge, Chief Judge Peter Kidd, who had led the Country Court of Victoria since September 2015, stressed the important principle that a verdict of guilty had to be beyond reasonable doubt. "He summarised the prosecution's case—namely that A's account [Pell's accuser] should be

---

[2] Tess Livingstone, "Cathedral Workers Back George Pell's Appeal Application", *The Australian*, September 30, 2019.

accepted because he was a 'powerful and persuasive witness'."[3] Chief Judge Kidd also summarised the defence's case—that there was no evidence that could lead to a jury being convinced of the defendant's guilt beyond reasonable doubt, Henderson wrote.

Many of Pell's supporters, certain this was the case, were convinced it would all be over by the weekend, as was Pell himself, who saw the matter as "so clear cut". In essence it was, but it did not always come across that way in the courtroom. Staying with his friends Tim and Anne McFarlane, who drove him to and from the court each day, he enjoyed the company of their family, including their new granddaughter, Matilda. On the mornings Tim and the cardinal arrived at the court early, they would pull over in the city and say the Rosary. In the evenings, after dinner, Pell would chat to friends on the phone. He was relaxed and confident. Several friends who had attended the trial intermittently were nervous, however. The scenarios discussed seemed hard to follow at times, even for Catholics familiar with cathedrals. They wondered what the jurors would make of it all.

The jury retired to consider its verdict on Thursday, September 13, 2018. After deliberating for only ninety minutes, it requested the video recording of the claimant's evidence. On the Friday afternoon, the trial was adjourned for the weekend. On Wednesday, September 19, the foreman indicated that the jury had reached an impasse, and the judge instructed the jurors to continue their deliberations. The following morning, the foreman indicted that the impasse had not been resolved.

Chief Judge Peter Kidd advised jurors that they could reach a majority decision—in Victorian law this is eleven out of twelve for conviction or acquittal. At 4 P.M. on Thursday, September 20, 2018, they again returned, some looking devastated. Would one more night help? the judge reportedly asked. Observers remember the forewoman shaking her head. "No", she said and burst into tears. Stalemate. Three other female jurors also cried, and a male juror wiped away tears. Chief Judge Kidd had no alternative but to dismiss the jury. He thanked the jury warmly for its efforts, excused them from further jury duty for ten years, and strongly urged that whatever took place in the jury room "must stay there".

[3] Gerard Henderson, *Cardinal Pell, the Media Pile-On and Collective Guilt* (Redland Bay, Australia: Connor Court Publishing, 2023), p. 67.

By that point, Pell had "fully expected to be cleared", his close friends knew. He made the same point to Gerard Henderson, on the record, on July 25, 2020, after emerging from 407 days in jail. Recalling the hung jury, Pell told Henderson: "I was a little naïve . . . and so it wasn't the worst, but it wasn't good. The staff was handing out tissues because there were four or five of the jurors crying. And I thought they were crying because they believed deeply that I was innocent. And I was. I think it's highly unlikely they would have been crying because I hadn't been convicted."[4]

Following the first trial, Richter applied on Pell's behalf for a discontinuance of the cathedral trial. The application was succinct and pertinent. Quoted by Henderson, it said, in part:

Evidence led from 22 prosecution witnesses other than Mr J [i.e. A] demonstrated that if the normal practice of Cardinal Pell, his Master of Ceremonies, the altar servers, the sacristan, and the choir were followed, the assaults could not have occurred for a series of reasons. Even on those rare occasions when Pell may have deviated from his practice to stay on the front steps to greet parishioners after Sunday Solemn Mass, the evidence demonstrated that he would not have been in the sacristy alone while robed at all let alone for the time required to have committed these offences undetected. The prosecution did not challenge this evidence. It came from numerous honest witnesses.

The prosecution evidence also included a compelling record of an interview of Cardinal Pell [in Rome]. He learns for the first time during the interview that the allegation is that he sexually assaulted choirboys immediately after Mass in the sacristies and expresses relief that the allegations, once investigated, will be so easily shown to be completely fanciful. Each exonerating point made by Cardinal Pell in that interview has been corroborated by unchallenged evidence. If she has not done so already, the Director [of Public Prosecutions Kerri Judd QC] should watch the record of interview in order to do justice to this application.[5]

The application was rejected, and Pell's retrial began on November 7, 2018. As a result, the swimming pool trial, also scheduled for

---

[4] Ibid., p. 69.
[5] Ibid., p. 71.

that month, was postponed to March the following year. The swimming pool charges, however, were dropped by prosecutors in February 2019.

Richter recalled a surprising fact about the new jury. Every one of them, he said, chose to swear on the Bible that they would fulfill their duties. Over five decades of practice, Richter said, it was usual that some jurors would swear on a different religious book or simply make an affirmation if they were not religious.

Pell thought long and hard about taking the stand personally at his second trial, but in the end, he again followed the advice of his legal team. Brennan, for one, was surprised, and Pell, while he was languishing in jail, believed he had made the wrong call. He wrote in his *Prison Journal*:

> Frank Brennan was always keen for me to be in the box, especially after the hung jury decision. Eventually I decided I should give evidence, despite the entire legal team and my own advisers being opposed. Terry Tobin came around to my point of view. I only decided not to take the stand after the prosecutor had dealt with Charlie Portelli and especially Max Potter. I was so cross with the treatment they both received, I was frightened that my hostility might turn a majority for acquittal into a split decision. The basis of my reasoning was quite wrong.[6]

Pell's interview with Victoria Police, recorded in Rome, was played to the new jury. The complainant was not required to reappear or resubmit to cross-examination. His evidence and cross-examination from the first trial were also replayed. "Would the verdict have been different if Pell had given evidence?" was a question Brennan posed in *The Australian* later. "Who can tell? All that one can say is that, although the defence seemed to be on strong ground, in submitting that the circumstances made the narrative advanced by the prosecution manifestly improbable, that failed to secure the acquittal."[7]

[6] George Pell, *Prison Journal*, vol. 1, *The Cardinal Makes His Appeal* (San Francisco: Ignatius Press, 2021), p. 64.

[7] "Father Frank Brennan on Cardinal George Pell Guilty Verdict: 'I Still Hope for Truth, Justice'", *The Australian*, February 28, 2019, quoted in Frank Brennan, *Observations on the Pell Proceedings* (Brisbane: Connor Court Publishing, 2021), p. 21.

Friends of Pell's who sat through parts of the two trials agreed with
Brennan when he said in an interview with Sky News in April 2020:

> My own hunch has always been that a big factor was that Pell himself
> did not give evidence. And I suspect that a lot of the jurors sat there
> looking at a defence barrister like Richter who had a fearsome repu-
> tation, cross examining the complainant, I think for over a day. But
> then Pell just sitting there silent. And I suspect that some of the jurors
> thought: we're sick of the Catholic Church having money available
> to employ flash lawyers and they then just sit there silent. Now, that's
> only speculation on my part, but that was the hunch that I had as I sat
> through some of the proceedings.

The trial proceeded, again unreported, for three weeks, with prosecutor Mark Gibson, QC, beginning his final address to the jury on
Friday, November 30. He wrapped up the prosecution case on Monday, December 3, *News.com.au* later reported, telling jurors opportunities did exist for the offending to have occurred as the jury had
heard directly from the surviving victim, by then in his thirties.[8]

In his summing up, Robert Richter said on Tuesday, December 4:
"There is no support by a single witness for (the complainant's) version
of events.... Only a madman would attempt to rape boys in the priest's
sacristy immediately after Sunday solemn Mass." Pell had volunteered
to be questioned by police in Rome after he was confronted with the
allegations, Mr Richter told the jury, and they could see from video
footage of that interview that he experienced "genuine shock" and a
sense of "I can demonstrate that's impossible."

The jury retired and after almost four days, on December 11,
2018, returned a verdict of guilty, beyond reasonable doubt, on all
charges—on one count of sexual penetration of a child and four charges
of committing indecent acts with or in the presence of a child. As the
jury foreman read out the verdicts, Pell frowned and hung his head
low. There were gasps around the room. Richter felt "shattered".

As Henderson recounted, after he had thanked the jury, Chief Judge
Kidd made it clear it would be inappropriate for him to comment

---

[8] "The Timeline of Cardinal Pell's Trial", *News.com.au*, March 3, 2019, https://www
.news.com.au/national/courts-law/the-timeline-of-cardinal-george-pells-trial/news-story
/4016aac84126940efbbcb84798e6f3ec.

on their verdict: "That's your decision and yours alone." The judge then "took the unusual action of stepping down from the bench and headed to his chambers for what turned out to be a break of ten minutes. When he returned to court, the Chief Judge granted Pell bail for medical reasons and advised the convicted man that when he returned to court, he should be prepared to face a term of imprisonment."[9]

While out on bail until the following February, Pell had both knees replaced. He also used that precious time to be with family and friends, including over Christmas, tend the garden of the house near the Sydney seminary where he hoped to retire one day, and catch up with friends including from interstate, whom he enjoyed taking to the Australia Club. From coffee shops to news agents, he generally received a warm reception in and around the city. He said little to his friends about the ordeal ahead, but he did tell one of his closest priest friends: "Someone has to pay [for widespread paedophilia and cover-ups], and it looks as though it's going to be me." He was deeply concerned about the effect of his upcoming imprisonment on those close to him, especially his family, saying "I wish they didn't have to go through it." Apart from the blatant hatred of anti-Catholic protesters who had demonstrated each morning outside the court, the trial also stirred up painful memories for survivors of child sexual abuse, including by priests. Some victims looked on quietly and shed tears. Many of them, however, were able to separate their own past ordeals from the accusations against Pell and wanted to see him afforded a fair trial and the presumption of innocence.

The suppression order remained in place, which meant his conviction was not reported by mainstream media in Australia. It was widely reported outside Australia, however, and relayed on social media, so it was widely known, which underlines the folly of such suppression orders in high profile cases in the cyber age. In February 2019, in a widely reported final address to a four-day Vatican summit on child protection, where he brought together bishops from every continent, Pope Francis called for the "abominable crimes" of child abuse to be "erased from the face of the earth".[10]

---

[9] Henderson, *Cardinal Pell*, p. 84.

[10] Francis, Eucharistic Concelebration, Meeting "The Protection of Minors in the Church" (February 24, 3019), no. 8.

On February 27, 2019, Pell was back in court, for his sentence plea hearing, his bag packed for jail. Nobody was prepared to admit it, but his friends knew, as did he, that he might never leave prison in his lifetime. "Isn't this surreal?" was as emotional as he got at lunchtime that day, in the small room his team used during breaks.

It was surreal. To anyone who understood priestly vestments and the realities of busy Cathedrals after Solemn Masses it was obvious that he could not have done what he was accused of doing. How could it have come to this? He was going to jail, after a gross miscarriage of justice. Australia no longer felt as safe as it used to be. How could the rule of law have gone so wrong in modern Australia?

A gentleman as always, he wanted to struggle to his feet when one of his friends came in, but it was just as easy to give him a hug when he was sitting down. He quickly turned his attention to the new Winston Churchill biography, *Walking with Destiny* by Andrew Roberts, which he had mentioned when the friend had asked if there were a book he would like. By the time his bail was revoked an hour or two later, and he was taken into custody, ahead of his sentencing on March 13, the dam wall had broken, the phony war was over.

That night, alone in his cell, he began what has already become a modern classic, his three-volume *Prison Journal*. To read those three volumes is to know the man Pell was—his faith, beliefs, ideas, interests, quirks, likes and dislikes, and sense of humor—as well as to understand how he coped with the gross injustices heaped upon him. The journals also reveal the layers of his intellect and his phenomenal memory for religious and philosophical passages of consequence. Working in his cell with few books at hand, he was able to recall various writings, read over may years, that had mattered to him. One of his early entries expressed his feelings after his sentencing:

> A good deal of the sentence discussion was surreal and Kafkaesque, as the judge listed the many reasons why the attack was implausible and then tried to conjecture my motivation! According to Ruth [defence barrister Ruth Shann], even the prosecutor—and we know of the judge's views, too—believed me innocent.
>
> Remanded into custody, I was strip-searched [the first of many strip searches, which Pell understandably found disconcerting and distressing] by two Filipino guards, both respectful. One told me he had sat in court for the case and knew I was innocent, while three

members of the protection service who had looked after us during the trials wished me well and said they were pleased to know me.... I almost forgot to bow to the judge on leaving the court.

Handcuffed for the drive to the assessment centre. On arrival, I went through a series of registrations and a thorough medical quizzing. All courteous, but a series of delays behind locked doors.

As I was judged to be at some risk of self-harm, I was under regular observation during the night. Among the other prisoners, whom I will not see, all in their own cells, a woman wept occasionally (or so it seemed), while one or two others cried out with anguish and repetitive profanity. I only scored a couple of honourable mentions.

I was a bit exhausted and slept deeply until woken by the observer. I tried my usual rosary to get back to sleep, but only dozed.

In every way, it is a relief the day is over. I am now at the quiet heart of the storm, while family, friends, and wider Church have to cope with the tornado.

God our Father, give me strength to come through this, and may my suffering be united with your Son Jesus' redemption for the spread of the Kingdom, the healing of all the victims of this scourge of paedophilia, the faith and well-being of our Church, and especially for the wisdom and courage of the bishops, who have to lead us out of the dark shadows into the light of Christ.[11]

On the outside, reaction to the verdict and the cardinal's jailing was intense. Banner headlines proclaimed: "Cardinal to Convict", "George Pell Guilty: Catholic Church in Crisis", "Convicted Cardinal", "Pell's Name Scraped from his Australian Hometown", "Cardinal Sin", "Guilty as Sin", "Prey to God". Journalists speculated about whether Pell's Companion of the Order Australia (the nation's highest secular honour) would be stripped from him.

The Vatican reportedly said Pell had been forbidden from having contact with minors or serving as a minister until his appeal had been heard (which was impossible anyway as he was in jail). And in a stinging blow that registered with Pell, even amid the drama, his old school, which he adored and where he was a legend, Saint Patrick's College Ballarat, did not wait for the appeal process but struck Pell's name from a building that had been named in his honour. Along with several other Saint Patrick's old boys, including Archbishop

---

[11] Pell, *Prison Journal*, vol. 1, pp. 16–17.

Little and the former auxiliary bishop of Brisbane, Brian Finnigan (against whom there had never been accusations of abuse, but they were blamed for their handling of the issue), a black line was drawn through Pell's name on the special honours board that listed the 350 priests who had been educated at the college. A notice near the board said the line was "a symbol of respect for the bravery of victims of sexual abuse and their families, and for the College's deep remorse for the pain and suffering caused by the actions of this individual". The school renamed the building, formerly known as the Pell Wing, the Waterford Wing, after the Irish home county of Christian Brothers founder Edmund Rice. More unfairly and controversially, the school did not restore Pell's name to the wing or remove the black line through his name on the priests' honours board after Pell was cleared by the High Court in April 2020.

Shortly after Pell's death, Saint Patrick's principal Steven O'Connor told *The Australian*:

> I understand there are different opinions across our school community about Cardinal George Pell and his legacy. While I respect the diversity of these opinions and recognise there might never be a time when we are all in agreement, St Patrick's College has no plans to reinstate the Pell Wing.
>
> This has been renamed the Waterford Wing, which ties the school closely to its history and traditions by recognising the home of Blessed Edmund Rice. Additionally, we have no plans to reinstate Cardinal Pell's name on the honour roll, and we are not exploring any additional opportunities to integrate Cardinal Pell's name to our school property or processes.[12]

Other organizations also censured Cardinal Pell. After news of his conviction first broke, the Richmond Football Club in Melbourne removed Pell as a club vice-patron. The club told the media it had "formed a view that his association is neither tenable or appropriate".[13]

[12] John Ferguson, "School Stares Down Bid to Restore Pell's Name", *The Australian*, February 21, 2023.
[13] Tom Morris, "Richmond Removes Cardinal George Pell as Club Vice Patron Following Child Sex Crime Conviction", *Fox Sports*, February 26, 2019, https://www.foxsports.com.au /afl/richmond-removes-cardinal-george-pell-as-club-vice-patron-following-child-sex-crime -conviction/news-story/b7fa3681fb5d80c11d44a3346a78a2a7.

Another immediate response was the threat of a lawsuit. Pell was convicted on the word of one witness; the other young man in the case, who had died four years earlier of a drug overdose, never made allegations against the cardinal. But at the time of Pell's conviction, the dead man's father said he would sue the cardinal or the Church, and four years later, the day after Pell's death in Rome, he reiterated his intention to pursue the case. In July 2022, he filed a civil case against the Catholic Archdiocese of Melbourne and the cardinal, *The Guardian* reported, "suing for damages for psychological injury he claimed to have suffered after learning of the allegations his son had been sexually abused".[14]

The day after Pell was jailed, pending his sentencing on March 13, Robert Richter apologised wholeheartedly for describing the crimes of which the cardinal had been convicted as "plain vanilla" sex acts. Mr Richter said he had spent "a sleepless night reflecting upon the terrible choice of phrase" he had used in court during the course of a "long and stressful process". He offered his "sincerest apologies to all who were hurt or offended by it" and said the description was "not intended to evade the seriousness of what had been done". The seriousness of the crime was acknowledged, he said, "at the outset by the concession that it merited imprisonment".[15]

From the *Washington Post* to the *Times of Israel* and every publication large and small in-between, Pell's sentencing fourteen days after he went to jail drew saturation coverage. Rarely do liberal-left commentators have so much to write about as the painful hour (for Pell and countless supporters) in which Chief Judge Peter Kidd sentenced the cardinal to six years in jail on the five counts of child sex abuse for which he was found guilty. His non-parole period was set at three years and eight months. In his black shirt without his clerical collar, Pell looked older and frailer than he had just a fortnight earlier as the offending of which he had been found guilty was broadcast in

---

[14]Benita Kolovos, "Father of Ex-Choirboy Who George Pell Was Accused of Abusing Will Proceed with Victorian Lawsuit", *The Guardian*, January 10, 2023, https://www.theguardian.com/australia-news/2023/jan/11/father-of-ex-choirboy-who-george-pell-was-accused-of-abusing-will-proceed-with-victorian-lawsuit.

[15]Simone Fox Koob, "'Terrible Choice of Phrase': Robert Richter Apologises for 'Plain Vanilla' Comment", *Sydney Morning Herald*, February 28, 2019, https://www.smh.com.au/national/terrible-choice-of-phrase-robert-richter-apologises-for-plain-vanilla-comment-20190228-p510zy.html.

detail to the nation and the world. He was also required to sign the sex offenders' register, an indelible fall from grace.

"I must at law give full effect to the jury's verdict," Chief Judge Kidd told Cardinal Pell at his sentencing. "It is not for me to second guess the verdict. What this means is that I am required to accept, and act upon, J's account. That is what the law requires of me and that is what I will do." Pell, the judge said, had acted with "venom", had been "brazen" and "nasty", and had shown "staggering arrogance".[16]

Given the cardinal's age and state of health, the judge said that he was "conscious that the term of imprisonment, which I am about to impose upon you, carries with it a real, as distinct from theoretical, possibility that you may not live to be released from prison. Facing jail at your age in these circumstances must be an awful state of affairs for you."

Before delivering the sentence, he concluded: "On the one hand I must punish and denounce you for this appalling offending; yet, on the other hand, I am conscious of the heavy reality that I am about to sentence you, a man of advanced years, who has led an otherwise blameless life, to a significant period of imprisonment, which will account for a good portion of the balance of your life."

As was his wont, Pell kept his cool under pressure, not looking around the room, into which about two hundred people had packed. Surrounded by five prison officers, three security guards, and two police, he looked straight at the judge, his mouth set in a straight line.[17]

[16] "George Pell's Full Sentencing, as Issued by Chief Judge Peter Kidd", *ABC News*, March 13, 2019, https://www.abc.net.au/news/2019-03-13/george-pells-full-sentencing,-as -issued-by-peter-kidd/10897650.

[17] The full sentencing is available on YouTube: ABC News (Australia), "Cardinal Pell's Sentencing in Full", March 13, 2019, https://www.youtube.com/watch?v=7BBppZNrjeY.

33

Prisoner 218978

While not allowed to offer Mass, Cardinal Pell, like all prisoners, was entitled to see a chaplain, and he enjoyed welcoming Good Samaritan Sister Mary O'Shannassy once a week, on a Tuesday, at the Melbourne Assessment Prison. A former primary school teacher who was working as a parish pastoral associate when Pell was archbishop of Melbourne, Sister Mary regarded prison ministry, which she had provided for twenty-nine years, as a "privilege". As director of prison ministry for CatholicCare Melbourne, she led a team of chaplains and volunteers across Victoria's sixteen jails. "We are not entitled to see the prisoners, but they are entitled to see us", she said.

Pell greeted Sister Mary each week looking "spick-and-span", she remembered, always with a smile and a handshake. She would bring him Holy Communion, and together they would read the Sunday Mass Scripture readings for the week followed by some theological commentary on the readings by American theologian Mary McGlone, whose insights Pell appreciated. "His faith sustained him", Sister Mary observed.

So did the letters he received, many of which contained prayers he had not seen before. Sister Mary and Pell would talk about the letters and the books he was reading, including *War and Peace*, which he had wanted to tackle for decades but had not had the time. After arriving in jail in late February 2019, he finished it by July.

In Rome, about a year before Pell died, he met Texas sociology professor Mark Regnerus, who asked him if there was anything he missed about jail. "Ever the data collector, I bluntly asked him if he missed anything about prison", Regnerus said. "He responded that he did, in fact. He had appreciated the unscheduled time (a rarity in his life up to that point, no doubt), the freedom, you could almost say, of being incarcerated." On another occasion, Pell described the experience overall as "thoroughly unpleasant".

Literature had always meant a great deal to Pell, which stood him in good stead. Growing up, his favourite novel was *Wuthering Heights*. After preferring Graham Greene's novels as a young man to those of Evelyn Waugh, he favoured Waugh in later years, rereading *The Ordeal of Gilbert Pinfold* in jail. As he grew older, the poem that most touched his heart was English Cardinal John Henry Newman's "Lead, Kindly Light", a prayer to the Holy Spirit asking for guidance "o'er moor and fen, o'er crag and torrent, till / the night is gone; / and with the morn those angel faces smile, / which I have loved long since, and lost awhile." Pell frequently included poems in his sermons and speeches. He began his address to the Oxford University Newman Society in late 2002, "The Suffering Church in a Suffering World", quoting Matthew Arnold's poem "Dover Beach" (see appendix 2).

Pell's hardest time, spiritually, Sister Mary said, was Easter 2019, when he sorely missed the Masses and Holy Week ceremonies he had attended for at least seventy years and had led for more than fifty years—the Evening Mass of the Lord's Supper on Holy Thursday; the Reading of the Passion, the Veneration of the Cross, and the Stations of the Cross on Good Friday; the Easter Vigil Mass, with its Baptisms and Confirmations; and Easter Sunday Mass. Pell and Sister Mary became friends, and he kept in touch with her after his release, in time for Easter 2020.

Three weeks after being jailed, Pell received a handwritten letter from Benedict XVI. "Your Eminence. In this difficult hour in your life I wish to let you know that you are not alone", the pope emeritus wrote.

> Through all the weeks, with my prayer and my sympathy, I remained with you on this difficult way, always hoping that you would be free at last.
>
> Now a sentence has been made that can only fill us with great sadness. You have helped the Catholic Church in Australia, with great success, to come out of a destructive liberalism, guiding her again to the wideness and beauty of the Catholic faith. The World Youth Day in Sydney continues to shine as a token of faith for the whole of Christianity.
>
> I am afraid that now you have to pay also for your unshaken Catholicity, but thus you are very close to the Lord. I pray with all my

heart that the Lord may let you sense His closeness. Sending you my heartfelt best wishes, I assure you of my constant closeness to you in prayer. Sincerely yours in Christ.

Pope Francis also sent a personal, supportive letter, which Pell greatly appreciated.

Another memorable letter he received was written under the pseudonym of "Eugenio Pacelli", the name of Pope Pius XII, who governed the Church from March 1939 until his death at Castel Gandolfo, outside Rome, in October 1958. There the pope, who had served as the Vatican ambassador to Germany from 1920 to 1929, sheltered thousands of Jews from the Nazis during World War II. I walked through those bunkers with Pell one memorable winter afternoon in 2009. The letter from "Eugenio Pacelli" to prisoner 218978 in the forbidding-looking Melbourne Assessment Prison in Spencer Street, West Melbourne, contained a small booklet, *Five Loaves and Two Fish* by the late Vietnamese Cardinal Francis-Xavier Nguyễn Văn Thuận, who spent thirteen years in Communist prisons in his homeland. Pell, missing the spiritual succour of offering daily Mass, found the book a powerful testimony of faith. He worked out that the sender was his friend, former student, and former master of ceremonies, Monsignor Charles Portelli. Pell was deeply touched by the book's cover. It was the portrait of Nguyễn Văn Thuận, painted by Australia's Paul Newton, which graces Domus Australia, where Monsignor Portelli decorated the chapel in his inimitable style.

Cardinal Nguyễn Văn Thuận was promoted to cardinal in 2001 by John Paul II, two years before Pell. The book was drawn from the Vietnamese cardinal's remarks to young people at the 1997 World Youth Day in Paris, where Nguyễn Văn Thuận reflected on his life and his relationship with God and his Church. "Like the boy in the Gospel passage, I will recall my experience in seven points: my five loaves and two fish", he wrote. "These are nothing, but it is all I have. Jesus will do the rest." Like Saint Paul, who was also imprisoned for his faith, Cardinal Nguyễn Văn Thuận argued that a life devoted to God is the only one worth living, regardless of the circumstances.

The booklet was one of more than four thousand letters, books, and cards prisoner 218978 received during his 407 days in mostly solitary confinement. These came from every continent, and from places Pell had to research, such as the Faroe Islands, an archipelago of eighteen rocky islands between Iceland and Norway in the North Atlantic Ocean. Fishing and tourism are two of the main sources of income for the islands' fifty thousand residents. The well-wisher was a carpenter, historian, and president of the local Catholic association who invited Pell to visit "after you have been liberated" to offer Mass and see the islands' historic sites. The correspondence helped offset Pell's sense of isolation, sadness, loss of freedom, the indignity of strip searches before his family and friends were allowed in, and a life where two squares of Cadbury fruit and nut chocolate, bought out of a meagre allowance that had to cover (monitored) phone calls and newspapers, were a luxury.

Partially because he could not afford many stamps, and letters to other inmates were free, and partially because he sensed a deep pastoral need, Pell mainly replied to the hundreds of letters he received from other "guests of Her Majesty", offering them the encouragement they sought. As he wrote to one friend: "Many prisoners like to write and I now understand why Solzhenitsyn's books are so long!" Independent of the cost of stamps, he wrote "I had decided to reply to all of them—and have done so with one or two exceptions. I have some interesting correspondents."

Pell also described himself as "surprisingly well, on a pretty even keel spiritually and psychologically, thanks be to God". He developed a new self-reliance and appreciation for some of the simpler things in life—washing his socks in the shower, heating a meat pie for Saturday lunch in a microwave, and sweeping out his small exercise area because he enjoyed being outside "just to hear the birds". He had a daily routine of shower, prayer, meals, exercise, coping with the mail (which increased to about fifty cards and letters a day at Christmas), reading, and writing seven hundred to nine hundred words a day. He continued to follow developments in the Vatican. "Fascinating Roman news on the financial scandals, with a lot in the Italian papers also.... If our advice had been followed, it would have saved at least euros100 million", he wrote to a friend who was barred by authorities from visiting him because she was a journalist. "God bless and God speed to you and yours. Thanks for all the friendship and support. In the Lord, George (prisoner 218978)." This author will keep that precious letter forever.

34

Appealing for Justice

Much of Pell's time during his first few months in the Melbourne Assessment Prison, on the edge of the downtown area, known as West Melbourne, was taken up making notes and working with his legal team towards appeal, which was heard by three judges on June 6 and 7, 2019. The judges were Court of Appeal president Chris Maxwell, Chief Justice of Victoria Anne Ferguson, and Mark Weinberg, a former Commonwealth Director of Public Prosecutions and Federal Court judge, with a strong background in criminal matters. A key point of interest was whether the court would overrule a jury verdict. "I have said in previous judgements that juries almost always get it right," Justice Weinberg reportedly said, "but the word is almost."

By that time, Pell and Richter had become firm friends, enjoying many a theological discussion. Richter, a Jewish atheist, sparked Pell's interest in the Bible's Book of Job, which Pell wrote about extensively in the first volume of his *Prison Journal*. In looking ahead to the appeal, Pell and Richter jointly agreed that Richter should step back. Richter said he was "too close to the case to conduct the appeal" and feared he would become too passionate and unreserved if he did so. Thus, Pell was represented by Sydney barrister Bret Walker, SC, one of Australia's leading advocates, whose client was well satisfied with the case made on his behalf. Christopher Boyce, QC, led the prosecution.[1] Footage and photos of a handcuffed, unusually dishevelled Pell being led to and from a prison van to court symbolised his predicament. He was not allowed to mix with any friends and family members who attended in support. He kept his focus on the proceedings.

[1] SC is the abbreviation for Senior Counsel, and QC stands for Queen's Counsel. Both designations indicate top barristers in Australia.

Walker set out the gross improbability of the case against Pell. According to the complainant, the archbishop of Melbourne had been in full ceremonial robes at the time of the alleged crime. But these vestments, Walker pointed out, consisted of an alb, an ankle-length tunic with no opening down the front that was tied in place with a cincture (a rope or belt worn around the waist). On top of this was a chasuble, a knee-length over-robe, like a poncho. "Incidental to that proposition [of what the archbishop had been wearing] are matters of physical improbability to the point of impossibility of the simple pulling aside of those robes in order to commit the alleged atrocious acts."[2]

Walker also told the judges that witnesses gave alibi evidence for the cardinal. After Mass, at the time of the alleged crime, Pell "was greeting the congregation at the cathedral's front door, distant from the sacristy."

Feeling confident that such arguments proved the impossibility of the crimes he had been was accused of, Pell did some packing back in his cell on Tuesday, August 20, the day before the Court of Appeal verdict was due. He figured he could always unpack later if his appeal was unsuccessful. In his heart he expected to succeed. He had ordered a newspaper for Wednesday, "but, please God, I won't be reading it here", he wrote in his journal.[3] He did, unfortunately, because the Court of Appeal verdict, delivered early in the morning of Wednesday, August 21, and live-streamed, went against him in a split decision, 2–1. The reactions it provoked—protesters baying, "Hallelujah. Proof there is a God", outside the building—were cruel. Media speculation was rife: Would Governor General David Hurley, a former Army general and chief of the Defence Force, strip Pell of his award as a Companion of the Order of Australia? Would the Vatican allow Pell to remain a member of the College of Cardinals? Decisions would be made when the appeal process was exhausted, the Church made clear.

As the court's decision was read out by Chief Justice Anne Ferguson, Pell sat as if turned to stone. He was astonished and badly upset,

[2] Mark Bowling, "Judges Retire to Consider Pell Appeal", *The Tablet*, June 6, 2019, https://www.thetablet.co.uk/news/11762/judges-retire-to-consider-pell-appeal.

[3] George Pell, *Prison Journal*, vol. 2, *The State Court Rejects the Appeal* (San Francisco: Ignatius Press, 2021), p. 103.

he said later, though his legal team and close supporters, especially the lawyers among them, saw good reasons for an appeal to the High Court, the highest court in the land, especially with the points raised by the dissenting judge, Mark Weinberg. The summary of the split judgement released by the Court of Appeal highlights the contrasting views between Justices Ferguson and Maxwell, on one hand, and Justice Weinberg, on the other:

Each of the three judges sitting on the appeal has watched record-ings of the evidence given by 12 of the 24 witnesses at the trial. They have also watched recordings of the view the jury were taken on, the walk through of the Cathedral by the complainant and the recorded interview of Cardinal Pell before he was charged. Those re-cordings went for more than 30 hours. The judges have watched some of those recordings more than once. The written transcript from the trial is approximately 2000 pages in length. Each of the judges has read that transcript, some parts of it multiple times. Like the jury, the judges were taken to St Patrick's Cathedral to be shown what the jury had seen ...

Having reviewed the whole of the evidence, two of the judges of the Court of Appeal (Chief Justice Ferguson and Justice Maxwell, President of the Court of Appeal) decided that it was open to the jury to be satisfied beyond reasonable doubt that Cardinal Pell was guilty of the offences charged. In other words, those judges decided that there was nothing about the complainant's evidence, or about the oppor-tunity evidence, which meant that the jury 'must have had a doubt' about the truth of the complainant's account....

The Chief Justice and Justice Maxwell accepted the prosecution's submission that the complainant was a very compelling witness, was clearly not a liar, was not a fantasist and was a witness of truth....

Part of Cardinal Pell's case on the appeal was that there were 13 solid obstacles in the path of a conviction. The Chief Justice and Justice Maxwell rejected all 13. By way of example, one of the 13 'obstacles' was said to be that the acts alleged to have been committed by Cardinal Pell in the first incident were 'physically impossible'....

It was a matter for the prosecution to prove beyond reasonable doubt that there was a realistic opportunity for the offending to take place. That involved showing that the offending was not impossible. The prosecution also bore the burden of proving beyond reasonable doubt that the particular sexual acts took place. The Chief Justice and Justice

Maxwell stated that while the defence for Cardinal Pell maintained
submissions based on 'impossibility' in the appeal, they bore steadily
in mind that there was and is no onus whatsoever upon Cardinal Pell to
prove impossibility, that is, that it was impossible for the offending
to have occurred.[4]

The summary then covered Justice Weinberg's dissenting judgement. He found that, at times,

> the complainant was inclined to embellish aspects of his account. He
> concluded that his evidence contained discrepancies, displayed inade-
> quacies, and otherwise lacked probative value so as to cause him to have
> a doubt as to the applicant's guilt. He could not exclude as a reasonable
> possibility that some of what the complainant said was concocted, par-
> ticularly in relation to the second incident. Justice Weinberg found that
> the complainant's account of the second incident was entirely implau-
> sible and quite unconvincing. Nevertheless, Justice Weinberg stated
> that in relation to the first incident, if the complainant's evidence was
> the only evidence, he might well have found it difficult to say that the
> jury, acting reasonably, were 'bound' to have a reasonable doubt about
> the Cardinal's guilt. He went on to note, however, that there was
> more than just the complainant's evidence. In Justice Weinberg's view
> there was a significant body of cogent and, in some cases, impressive
> evidence suggesting that the complainant's account was, in a realistic
> sense, 'impossible' to accept. To his mind, there is a significant possi-
> bility that the Cardinal may not have committed the offences. In those
> circumstances, Justice Weinberg stated that in his view the convictions
> could not stand.

Nevertheless, the appeal on the unreasonableness ground was dismissed because the other two judges took a different view of the facts.[5]

Writing in *The Australian* on the day after the judgement was delivered, lawyer and legal affairs journalist Chris Merritt, in what proved
to be a prescient comment, said: "Weinberg's detailed and compelling dissent almost guarantees that the High Court will be asked to

---

[4] Victoria Supreme Court, *Summary of Judgment* Pell v The Queen *[2019] VSCA 186*,
August 21, 2019, pp. 2–4, https://www.supremecourt.vic.gov.au/sites/default/files/2019-08
/pell_v_the_queen_judgment_summary_-_web_0.pdf.
[5] Ibid, pp. 4–5.

re-examine this case."⁶ Despite writing in dissent, Judge Weinberg "dominated yesterday's decision in George Pell's appeal with a 204-page argument that can be summed up in one line: the cardinal's conviction is unsafe", Merritt wrote. It "cannot be permitted to stand" because there was a significant possibility that the cardinal was innocent. "The majority disagreed but ... this massive dissent is expected to become a guide for any special leave application", Merritt added. "Even if special leave is refused by the High Court, Weinberg's rejection of much of the prosecution's case is set to ensure the community's deep divisions over this cleric are unlikely to be healed."

Legal academic Mirko Bagaric said he had been surprised that the two judges who formed the majority had not followed Weinberg, because the dissenting judge was "clearly the brightest bloke on the Victorian Court of Appeal". Bagaric, a professor at Swinburne University, said that Weinberg was a "powerhouse" on criminal matters and more experienced in this area than the two judges who formed the majority. Weinberg would have acquitted Pell because he believed the jury verdict convicting him of historical child sex abuse was unreasonable and could not be supported having regard to the evidence. "On occasion [the claimant] seemed almost to 'clutch at straws' in an attempt to minimise, or overcome, the obvious inconsistencies between what he had said on earlier occasions and what the objective evidence clearly showed", Weinberg wrote.

The ruling came at a time "when a growing number of decisions by the Victorian Court of Appeal have been overturned by the High Court", Merritt noted. Were it not for Weinberg's dissenting judgement and the High Court, Pell's last remaining years would have been very different, despite the fact he would still have been every bit as innocent. Almost certainly His Eminence would not be buried in Saint Mary's Cathedral.

Pell, conscious of legal fees piling up and still smarting from the disappointment of the decision, thought long and hard about appealing to the High Court. After his eventual release, in an article for *First Things*, he said: "After I lost my appeal to the Victorian Supreme Court, I considered not appealing to the Australian High Court,

⁶ Chris Merritt, "Legal Experts Add Weight to Opinion of Dissenting Judge", *The Australian*, August 22, 2019.

reasoning that if the judges were simply going to close ranks, I need not cooperate in an expensive charade. The boss of the prison in Melbourne, a bigger man than I and a straight shooter, urged me to persevere. I was encouraged and remain grateful to him."[7] The strength of Justice Weinberg's dissenting opinion, which Pell studied closely, was also a factor.

The day after the Victorian Court of Appeal decision, Pell noted in his *Prison Journal* that he had been known to say that if there was one Church history book he would like to have written it was Peter Brown's *Augustine*. "To that list of material I would like to have written, I would now like to add Weinberg's judgement."

> It is explicit, clear, methodical, and wise. Some details in particular I loved. He wrote that "the complainant's account of the second incident seems to me to take brazenness to new heights, the like of which I have not seen. The use of the term 'madness' may have been a rhetorical flourish".....
>
> He acknowledged that the charges against me were implausible: an archbishop, still in his vestments, in a sacristy after Mass in his cathedral, grossly violating two young servers whom he did not know, at a time when the sacristy was full of other servers (adults) and he was with his master of ceremonies on the front steps of the cathedral. Justice Weinberg was particularly struck by the bizarre nature of the second incident, but it would also be an interesting exercise to find other cases as bizarre as the first set of accusations. Even the Billy Doe charges are not quite as spectacular.[8]

In April 2019, *Quadrant* magazine editor-in-chief Keith Windschuttle, author of the book *The Persecution of George Pell*, recounted a 2011 story in *Rolling Stone* magazine about "Billy", a ten-year-old student and altar boy who was caught in the sacristy in 1998 sipping leftover wine after a morning Mass. Rather than get angry, however, the priest poured Billy more wine, showed him some pornographic magazines, told him it was time he became a "man" and that they would soon begin their "sessions". A week later, Billy found out

---

[7] George Pell, "My Time in Prison", *First Things*, August 2020, https://www.firstthings.com/article/2020/08/my-time-in-prison.

[8] Pell, *Prison Journal*, vol. 2, pp. 106–7.

APPEALING FOR JUSTICE 441

what the priest meant. After Mass, the priest allegedly abused the boy. The priest was prosecuted, convicted, and died in jail. "What is the difference between this account of child sex abuse in a Catholic church in Philadelphia and the evidence given by the sole accuser in the Victorian court case that convicted Cardinal George Pell of sexually abusing a thirteen-year-old choirboy at St Patrick's Cathedral, Melbourne, in 1996?" Windschuttle asked. "Not much."[9]

Even with knowing that he had the truth, an increasing number of commentators, and Justice Weinberg in his corner, Pell was still daunted by the costs of his ongoing defence. In July 2021, a year after his exoneration, he revealed that he had incurred AU$3 million in legal fees and that a "significant" amount of the huge bill was yet to be fully paid off even after supporters, both rich and poor, had pitched in to fund the expert legal team that helped end his 407-day incarceration. A spokesman for the Archdiocese of Sydney said that the cardinal had received AU$390,000 from the State of Victoria to offset legal fees after the hung jury of the first County Court trial and that his legal defence had not been covered by the Church.[10]

While the costs were mounting, so was the support for Pell's side of the story. A month after the cardinal failed to clear himself before the Victorian Court of Appeal, *Herald Sun* columnist and Sky News television host Andrew Bolt, one of Australia's most independent-minded and incisive journalists, produced a telling commentary that put the matter in clear perspective for all confused by the legal details of the matter. Bolt wrote: "Last Sunday, I walked the route a man says he took as a 13-year-old choirboy before he was raped by Cardinal George Pell. I timed it. And I am stunned. Did Victoria's most senior judges make a terrible mistake in their maths when they ruled against Pell last month?"[11] Bolt asked the same question before his television audience, and his investigative work convinced many

[9]Keith Windschuttle, "Borrowed Testimony", *Quadrant Online*, April 29, 2019, https://quadrant.org.au/magazine/2019/05/borrowed-testimony/.
[10]John Ferguson, "George Pell's $3m Legal Bill to Clear His Name", *The Australian*, July 3, 2021.
[11]Andrew Bolt, "Pell Case: I Walked the Route of the 'Victim': It Couldn't Have Happened", *Herald Sun*, September 26, 2019, https://www.heraldsun.com.au/blogs/andrew-bolt/pell-case-i-walked-the-route-of-the-victim-it-couldnt-have-happened/news-story/0a58247f5af24c0a3a7d3cfa90a191ec.

Australians, of all faiths and none, that Pell's convictions should not stand. As Bolt noted:

> Pell's 12-page application makes a powerful case that Chief Justice Anne Ferguson and Court of Appeal president Chris Maxwell set an impossibly high hurdle—and a legally mistaken one—by effectively making Pell prove his innocence.
>
> The two judges in effect ruled that as long as it was possible Pell did one highly unlikely thing after another, it was open to a jury to declare him guilty beyond reasonable doubt—even though taken together the unlikely may seem impossible.
>
> So the jury could reasonably believe Pell slipped away from his procession after Mass, didn't stay to talk to parishioners as usual, escaped the MC who always accompanied him, found and raped two boys he didn't know and raped them in the normally busy sacristy with the door open.

Bolt concentrated on what the two judges in the majority argued— that the only time Pell could have assaulted the two boys in the sacristy was in the five or six minutes of "private prayer time" immediately after Mass finished. After that, the servers would be going in and out, bringing back vessels used in the Mass and stored in the sacristy. This private prayer time started when the choir (including Pell's accuser) formed a line, led by five servers, and processed to the cathedral's front door.

Bolt walked the route and timed it. Up the centre aisle with the procession: one minute. Around the cathedral with the procession to the gate at the back of the cathedral: two and a half minutes. Back to the cathedral's side door, running much of the way: forty seconds. Walking to the sacristy: twenty seconds. "Poking" around, opening a cupboard, finding altar wine and taking a "few swigs": one minute. All of which added up to five minutes and thirty seconds. "That leaves just 30 secs at most for Pell to allegedly find the boys, rape one, abuse the other, fondle himself, dress and leave—an assault the prosecution agreed must have taken about five minutes", Bolt wrote. "That's the maths. And it adds up to this: this rape could not possibly have happened." Father Frank Brennan, S.J., among others, had come to the same conclusion.

In terms of Pell regaining his freedom and justice being done and seen to be done, the biggest test was coming.

35

Last Chance at Vindication

There was never any guarantee the High Court, based on the shores of Lake Burley Griffin in Canberra, the national capital, would hear Pell's case. Nevertheless, on September 17, 2019, Bret Walker, SC, and Ruth Shann filed an Application for Special Leave to Appeal against the decision of the Victorian Court of Appeal. The proposed grounds of appeal were the following:

- The majority erred by finding that their belief in the complainant required the applicant to establish that the offending was impossible in order to raise and leave a doubt.
- The majority erred in their conclusion that the verdicts were not unreasonable as, in light of findings made by them, there did remain a reasonable doubt as to the existence of any opportunity for the offending to have occurred.

The application said:

Weinberg JA (dissenting) had a genuine doubt as to the applicant's guilt. He found there was a significant body of cogent evidence casting serious doubt upon A's account, both as to credibility and reliability. In order for A's account to be capable of being accepted, a number of the "things" had to have taken place within the space of just a few minutes. In that event, the odds against A's account of how the abuse had occurred would have to be substantial. The chances of "all the planets aligning", in that way, would, at the very least, be doubtful. This suggested strongly that the jury, acting reasonably, on the whole of the evidence, ought to have had a reasonable doubt as to the applicant's guilt.[1]

---

[1] Pell v. the Queen, M112/2019 (Court of Appeal, Supreme Court Victoria [2019] VSCA 186, March 11–12, 2020), https://www.hcourt.gov.au/assets/registry/case-summaries/2020/SPAppealsMar20.rtf.

The application was successful: of the twenty-two charges listed for determination that day, November 13, 2019, twenty-one were reportedly "dismissed". But Justices Michelle Gordon and James Edelman referred *George Pell v The Queen* "to a Full Court for argument as on an appeal". It was to be heard in the early months of 2020.

Still in jail, Pell did not comment, nor did any of his team. The Australian Catholic Bishops' Conference president Mark Coleridge said he hoped the High Court could bring clarity to the subject. "All Australians have the right to appeal a conviction to the High Court. Cardinal George Pell has exercised that right, and the High Court has determined that his conviction warrants its consideration", he said. "This will prolong what has been a lengthy and difficult process, but we can only hope that the appeal will be heard as soon as reasonably possible and that the High Court's judgement will bring clarity and a resolution for all."[2]

The former choirboy who made the allegations against Pell and whose evidence was key to the conviction understood that the appeal was part of the legal process, his lawyer Vivian Waller told *The Australian*. "He understands it has to happen, but his preference would be that it's over", she said.[3]

In January 2020, news media reported that Pell had been moved from the Melbourne Assessment Prison to Barwon Prison, a high-security jail housing some of Victoria's most dangerous criminals. It was about sixty kilometres (about thirty-seven miles) southwest of Melbourne, near the regional city of Geelong. The move, during which Pell's wrists and ankles were shackled, was made after a drone was spotted hovering over a visitors' garden where Pell had sometimes sat and worked at the first prison. But the drone was on a commercial operation, not connected with him.

In Barwon, Pell had a larger room, clear windows through which he could see the outside (unlike in the Melbourne Assessment Prison, where the windows were opaque), and sometimes the company of

[2] Gerard O'Connell, "Vatican Restates Trust in Australia's Judiciary as Cardinal Pell Set to Appeal Abuse Conviction", *America*, November 13, 2019, https://www.americamagazine.org/politics-society/2019/11/13/vatican-restates-trust-australias-judiciary-cardinal-pell-set-appeal.

[3] Tessa Akerman, "High Court Throws George Pell Sex Abuse Appeal Lifeline", *The Australian*, November 13, 2019.

several other inmates, including two Muslims who liked to discuss religion with him.

Close to the start of the COVID pandemic, Pell's hearings in the High Court in Canberra were held on Wednesday and Thursday, March 11 and 12, before a full bench of seven judges. The court's task, wrote John Ferguson at *The Australian*, was to determine "whether the Victorian Court of Appeal erred when it decided, 2:1 last year, that the County Court jury was within its rights to convict Pell of five sexual assault charges that occurred in the priests' sacristy at Melbourne's St Patrick's Cathedral in 1996 and in a corridor in 1997. Or whether there should have been a reasonable doubt."[4]

Of the multiple charges filed against Pell at the outset, the cathedral claims were among the most unlikely to have progressed. As Ferguson wrote: "Those with deep understanding of the cathedral, Catholic rituals and Pell's practices are incredulous that the archbishop could ever have been left alone for the five or six minutes upon which he was convicted of forced oral sex and other abuses." But the prosecution's submissions were firm in their view that the jury decision should not be overturned.

Justice Weinberg had effectively raised the spectre in his dissenting judgement of an innocent man having been wrongly convicted, observing: "These convictions were based upon the jury's assessment of the complainant as a witness and nothing more." He was especially damning of the conviction of Pell on the fifth and final charge, which was that in 1997 the then archbishop assaulted A in front of others, grabbing him on the testicles in front of dozens of people. "I would have thought any prosecutor would be wary of bringing a charge of this gravity against anyone based upon the implausible notion that a sexual assault of this kind would take place in public and in the presence of numerous potential witnesses", Weinberg ruled.[5]

[4]John Ferguson, "High Drama and Even Higher Stakes: It's the Moment of Truth for George Pell", *The Australian*, March 7, 2020, https://www.theaustralian.com.au/inquirer /high-drama-and-even-higher-stakes-its-the-moment-of-truth-for-george-pell/news-story /7db1f00d1f29d8f75d8f253a715709ae.

[5]Gerard V. Bradley, "Cardinal Pell's Unsuccessful Appeal—and Reason for Hope", *National Catholic Register*, August 12, 2019, https://www.ncregister.com/commentaries /cardinal-pell-s-unsuccessful-appeal-and-reason-for-hope.

During the High Court appeal, Pell's habit of talking to parishioners on the front steps of Saint Patrick's Cathedral emerged as a defining factor—just as Pell had described in his interview with Victoria Police in Rome in 2016. As Bret Walker, SC, agued, Pell spent ten to twenty minutes on the steps, engaged in conversation, leaving insufficient time for the alleged offences to be committed. No one, he said, had pointed to evidence that Pell spent just a few minutes on the steps. Nor was it possible for him to offend, as he was never left alone. "If the full bench of the High Court accepts that Pell did spend this much time on the steps, then it would have been impossible for him to have abused the boys in the priests' sacristy as he wouldn't have had the five or six minutes needed to commit the offences", *The Australian* reported.

> Mr Walker cited evidence from Pell's former right-hand man, Monsignor Charles Portelli, and the church's former sacristan, Max Potter, as examples of people who had testified in a way that supported Pell's innocence.
> He said it was not possible for the crimes to have occurred in the five to six minutes the court found that Pell had abused the children.
> "There is simply not the available time for it to occur. We cannot eliminate the possibility the archbishop was on the steps for too long not to have offended", he added, therefore excluding "beyond reasonable doubt".
> As Justice Bell said, if Pell was standing on the steps of the Cathedral for 20 minutes after Mass, "if that were the evidence, it would provide an alibi."[6]

At the end of the appeal arguments, the court reserved giving its decision to a later date.

While careful not to get his hopes up after the bitter disappointment of the Victorian Court of Appeal outcome, Pell was encouraged and quietly hopeful after the accounts of the High Court appeal given by his legal team and friends who had attended. After a few days, he also had the chance to watch it on an iPad in the jail, which added to his confidence as "Bret systematically demolished the

[6] Olivia Caisley and John Ferguson, "George Pell 'Didn't Have Time to Abuse Boys', High Court Hears News Story", *The Australian*, March 11, 2020.

arguments of the Victorian majority ... and demonstrating against them that showing X is possible is not the same as proving X is true beyond reasonable doubt."[7] In the last hour of Walker's summing up, Pell noted, he lived up to his promise to be in "hunt and kill" mode, something he accomplished with logic and precision, denouncing the "improvised and rickety construction of a Crown case to make something fit that will not fit".[8]

It was the beginning of April, 2020, the weather was turning cold, wet, and windy, and visitors were barred from the jail due to the rapid spread of COVID, of which a million cases had been recorded around the world. Holy Week and Easter were approaching, and Pell's thoughts and prayers were turning to the Passion, death, and Resurrection of Christ; the light and darkness of the season; and the struggle between good and evil. It was a time of year when he especially missed saying Mass.

That longing to offer the Holy Sacrifice was one of the most painful aspects of his incarceration, a theme he pursued at the Sacra Liturgia Conference in San Francisco from June 28 to July 1, 2022, in a talk entitled "The Daily Mass in the Life of a Priest: Reflections after 406 Days without It". "It was a radical change of program for myself. It was very different," he told the *Catholic World Report* in an interview during the conference. "But I didn't feel abandoned by God. I kept up a daily routine of prayers. I realized that I just couldn't say Mass. And so that was the way it was. And so I just got on with where I was and made the most of it."[9]

He was able to attend just five Masses in more than four hundred days in jail, he revealed. "A young priest came in twice when I was in Melbourne. And then an older priest, a friend of mine, came three times when I was down in Barwon." Pell said he was "one of that school that thinks that daily Mass is one of the hallmarks of a priestly

[7] George Pell, *Prison Journal*, vol. 3, *The High Court Frees an Innocent Man* (San Francisco: Ignatius Press, 2021), pp. 314–15.

[8] Ibid., p. 319.

[9] "Cardinal George Pell Reflects on Celebrating (and Not Celebrating) the Mass", interview by Paul Senz, *Catholic World Report*, July 10, 2022, https://www.catholicworldreport .com/2022/07/20/cardinal-george-pell-reflects-on-celebrating-and-not-celebrating-the -mass/.

life. It's an explicit act of worship, and thanksgiving, and adoration. It's the best prayer we have available. And it's a very ancient custom, daily Mass, going back to the first centuries. And I think it should be one of the hallmarks of priestly devotion." Even on days off, offering Mass remained his practice. He also saw the importance of prayer outside of Mass.

> I think also to help focus on the sacraments, or to properly order the priorities in a priestly life, you've got to pray outside Mass: pray the breviary and perhaps devotions; certainly, try to meditate regularly. Without prayers outside Mass, it is difficult to focus on the central things, and it's not too difficult to become distracted. I think Eugene de Mazenod, who founded the Oblates of Mary Immaculate, said it's not impossible for a priest to live day to day life like that of an agnostic. And the remedy for that, certainly, a daily prayerful celebration of Mass helps. But on top of that, the breviary and meditation and regular devotions are a great amount of help.

Over almost fifty-six years as a priest, thirty-five as a bishop and eighteen as a cardinal, Pell said, he had always appreciated the importance of daily Mass. "But after a period of priestly life that became even clearer to me, and as a bishop and as I moved around and as I looked at a little bit of work in liturgical circles, and as I started to read the writings, perhaps particularly of Cardinal Ratzinger on the liturgy, I realised just how closely related good, prayerful liturgy is to vitality in parish life", he said. "There is certainly a correlation, probably a causality, when the liturgy is poor in the true spiritual sense, then almost certainly the Christian life of the parish is poor."

At busy times in his working life, he admitted, it was challenging to maintain this rhythm of prayer of daily Mass and the Divine Office. "And when I was busy, as I was certainly as an archbishop and later, in a way that I'm not busy now, I found it was important to get to do your praying early in the morning, because often, as the day went along, you had many good reasons not to pray," he said. "So it meant that your life had to be organized and with a pattern of life and with prayer in the morning, particularly."

While the celebration of daily Mass was not "absolutely commanded by canon law", Pell urged any priest not celebrating daily to do so, as a good anchor for daily priestly life and the source and summit of the Christian life. As Anthony Fisher quoted at the ordination of Cardinal Pell's former assistant Father Joseph Hamilton in 2016, French soldier and priest Charles de Foucauld (1858–1916) wrote: "One Mass gives more glory to God than do the deaths of all the martyrs and the collective praise of the angels; for, whereas the martyrdom of men and the homage of angels have no more than a finite value, the Mass possesses an infinite value."

In the event of Pell's appeal being successful, it was decided he would stay, for a night at least, at the Carmelite monastery in Kew, an inner, eastern Melbourne suburb, close to where he had lived when he was archbishop of the city. He did not have much longer to wait. On April 2, a prison official told him his lawyers had phoned to say the High Court decision would be handed down the following Tuesday, April 7, at 9:30 A.M., in Holy Week.

It was—and he was cleared by a seven-to-zero judgement.

Perhaps he had an inner confidence that this time, all would be well, for Pell was awake until midnight the night before, tidying and packing documents. The court was sitting in Brisbane, and Pell learned the result from the television, when the unanimous decision in his favour was reported. From somewhere outside his cell a loud cheer went up, and two guards congratulated him through the window on his cell door. Like many who have come through a long war, Pell felt "no surge of elation", but he punched the air a couple of times and prayed the Te Deum, the traditional prayer of thanks. "Then a rosary in gratitude," he wrote in his *Prison Journal*, "as once again I did not want to be like the nine lepers."[10]

His ordeal had been a long haul. It was more than 1,500 days since he had found out in 2016 that Victoria Police were investigating him. He had penned about three hundred thousand words in thirteen months, much of it about the case, some of it about life inside prison, and some of it about other topics. His *Prison Journal* will stand the test of months, years, and decades, perhaps far longer, as his spiritual magnum opus. Writing it was a catharsis and a comfort, he found, and he hoped it would be a comfort to others.

On the morning he was to be freed, as three officers walked him to the central office of Barwon jail, one of them remarked, "Miracles

---

[10] Pell, *Prison Journal*, vol. 3, p. 329.

will never cease!" Pell replied, "This was no miracle. It was justice." His convictions, his jailing, and his losing his first appeal, in contrast, were gross miscarriages of justice.

"State power has been recruited in an effort to destroy Pell", Paul Kelly wrote in the *Weekend Australian* the following Saturday, "This situation cannot be swept under the carpet." Pell had not been given fair treatment in his trial and his first appeal, Kelly wrote. But the Victoria criminal justice system did not merely fail Pell, it also failed his complainant, who was put through a personal trauma for years only to see the case against Pell collapse in the final court that matters. The High Court has verified what many people believed the more they studied the case against Pell—that it was inherently unconvincing. Most people who read the minority Court of Appeal judgement by Justice Mark Weinberg would have grasped this. "Only the High Court, in its wisdom, halted the abuse of the justice system. The force of its judgment raises the inevitable question: if this case had been treated on merit Pell would not have been charged. The evidence was inherently implausible."[11]

This case was not a referendum on the Catholic Church or the failure of the Church over sexual abuse. But its sustained depiction on this basis has been, ultimately, a grave disservice to victims everywhere, Kelly wrote.

> The problem is that Pell's guilt or innocence became hopelessly entangled with the crimes and sins of the Catholic Church that he led and symbolised. Pell became a hate figure in a culture justifiably angry at the church's systemic child abuse but this situation was compounded when other institutions succumbed under pressure.
>
> Victoria Police adopted a 'Get Pell' mentality and failed to conduct a proper investigation of evidence. This was followed by a critical blunder—the highly dubious decision by the Victorian Director of Public Prosecutions, to charge Pell.
>
> The Court of Appeal subsequently failed in its 2-1 rejection of Pell's appeal as documented in the High Court judgement. Beyond these institutions, many opinion-makers made grievous mistakes. But none remotely has the culpability of the ABC in its relentless, biased and prejudiced campaign against Pell lasting for many years.

[11] Paul Kelly, "Travesty of Justice: 'Trusted' Institutions Fail Pell, Public", *Weekend Australian*, April 11 2020.

These institutions served neither justice nor the interests of victims of child sexual abuse. Putting up and campaigning for such a flawed case carried the high risk of this outcome—years of trials, appeals, personal aggravation and disputes that diminished everyone.

The High Court judgement highlighted the absurdity of the entire case against Pell, especially the fifth charge, that he allegedly attacked J. for a second time, weeks after the alleged first incident. As Frank Brennan, S.J., later wrote: "This second incident should have sounded to the police like the 13th strike of a clock, alerting them that the complainant's recollection of the event was fundamentally wrong, regardless of his apparent honesty and credibility."[12] This absurd, fifth charge, Brennan argued in a *Quadrant* article in June of 2023, was also a key to the "shoddiness of the police investigation, the dogged persistence of the Director of Public Prosecutions to prosecute any charge, no matter how weak and uninvestigated, and the bewildering thinking of the two most senior Victorian judges".[13]

On the day in question, Pell had presided at the Solemn Mass said by Father Brendan Egan, who would have been standing immediately in front of the archbishop in the corridor

> before Pell [allegedly] broke from the procession making his way through the throng of servers and choristers to assault the complainant. Chief Justice Ferguson and President Maxwell accepted that the assault was proved beyond reasonable doubt with this observation: "[A] fleeting physical encounter of the kind described by [J] can be readily imagined. Jurors would know from common experience that confined spaces facilitate furtive sexual touching, even when others are in the same space. And the act of squeezing the genitals is, itself, unremarkable as a form of sexual assault." They said: "We would accept, of course, that the sight of Cardinal Pell at close quarters with a choirboy might well have attracted attention but we would assume—as did cross-examining counsel—that all of the others in the corridor were intent on completing the procession, and removing their ceremonial robes, as soon as possible. In that state of affairs, it seems to us to be

---

[12] Frank Brennan, *Observations on the Pell Proceedings* (Brisbane: Connor Court, 2021), p. 148.
[13] Frank Brennan, "Cardinal Pell at the Hands of the Victorian Justice System", *Quadrant Online*, June 30, 2023, https://quadrant.org.au/magazine/2023/07/cardinal-pell-at-the-hands-of-the-victorian-justice-system/.

quite possible that this brief encounter was not noticed. At all events, the evidence once again falls well short of establishing impossibility." So much for the prosecution having to prove the case beyond reasonable doubt. Now it was a matter of an accused person having to establish impossibility.[14]

While Victoria police knew the identity of Egan, who had left the priesthood but was living and working in Melbourne, they reportedly did not interview him or any other person other than the complainant about the alleged second incident. That included Monsignor Portelli, who was also beside Pell. Portelli remembered the morning well. Pell was due home from Rome, but then-Father Egan was listed to say the Mass because the cathedral staff were unsure what time Pell would arrive. As it happened, he was in time for the Solemn Mass. But with a second Mass scheduled for that afternoon, Pell was happy to be present while Egan offered it. However absurd the charge, Pell was convicted and sentenced to eighteen months in jail as part of his overall sentence.

Quashing that conviction, the seven High Court judges observed: "The assumption that a group of choristers, including adults, might have been so preoccupied with making their way to the robing room as to fail to notice the extraordinary sight of the Archbishop of Melbourne dressed 'in his full regalia' advancing through the procession and pinning a 13 year old boy to the wall, is a large one.... The capacity of the evidence to support the verdict on this charge suffers from the same deficiency as the evidence of the assaults involved in the first incident."[15]

Pell was driven out of Barwon prison by Kartya Gracer, his lawyer, flanked by two helicopters, the media, and police cars. After settling into the chaplain's apartment at the Carmel in Kew, Pell celebrated Mass in the convent chapel—for him the most important aspect of his first day of freedom. It was a fortunate coincidence that in the chapel were the relics of one of his favourite saints, Thérèse of Lisieux, the Little Flower, and of her parents, Saints Zélie and Louis Martin. That evening, the Sisters served steak and three vegetables, and Chris

[14] Ibid.
[15] High Court of Australia, Pell v The Queen [2020] HCA 12, April 7, 2020, nos. 124–125, Jade, https://jade.io/article/724774.

Meaney brought a bottle of good red wine. Pell was disappointed to find he did not enjoy it. "Please God this distaste is not permanent", he wrote in one of his final diary entries. "That would be a blow!"[16]

The next morning, after Mass, he and Meaney left for Sydney, and they were followed by the media all the way, about 860 kilometres (more than 500 miles), to Good Shepherd Seminary in Homebush. Having anticipated that they would be followed and conscious of COVID restrictions, Pell decided not to detour and stop off in Bendigo, where his brother and sister lived. He had phoned them both the previous day, after his release; he would wait for a better time to visit them in person. Never inclined to speculate about private revelations, Pell later revealed that Margaret, living in a retirement home, believed (mistakenly) that he had visited her briefly the previous day, given her a kiss, and apologised for not being able to stay long. "Whether it was a dream or imagination or a small gift from God," he said, "it is a lovely story and a small recompense for her suffering and prayers."[17]

In unanimously allowing Pell's appeal to the High Court, Chief Justice Susan Kiefel and Justices Virginia Bell, Stephen Gageler, Patrick Keane, Geoffrey Nettle, Michelle Gordon, and James Edelman found that the jury in the lower court, acting rationally on the whole of the evidence, "ought to have entertained a doubt as to the applicant's guilt with respect to each of the offences for which [Pell] was convicted". The jury having failed to do this, there was "a significant possibility that an innocent person has been convicted because the evidence did not establish guilt to the requisite standard of proof". Thus, the High Court "ordered that the convictions be quashed and that verdicts of acquittal be entered in their place".[18] As John Ferguson wrote in *The Australian*: "It doesn't matter what you think of the man. But it matters if an innocent man has been jailed."[19]

A lot remained to be reckoned with in the aftermath of this case, which bore all the tawdry hallmarks of a witch-hunt, as George

[16] Pell, *Prison Journal*, vol. 3, p. 330.

[17] Ibid., p. 333.

[18] High Court of Australia, *Pell v The Queen [2020] HCA 12* (summary), April 7, 2020, https://www.hcourt.gov.au/assets/publications/judgment-summaries/2020/hca-12-2020-04-07.pdf.

[19] Ferguson, "High Drama".

Weigel argued in the *Catholic World Report* shortly after Pell's release. The vicious public atmosphere surrounding the cardinal, especially in Victoria, the state where he was born and grew up, was "analogous to the poisonous atmosphere that surrounded the Dreyfus Affair in late-nineteenth-century France. In 1894, raw politics and ancient score-settling, corrupt officials, a rabid media, and gross religious prejudice combined to cashier an innocent French army officer of Jewish heritage, Captain Alfred Dreyfus, for treason, after which he was condemned to the hell of Devil's Island." The Melbourne Assessment Prison and Her Majesty's Prison Barwon, Weigel wrote, are not Devil's Island.

> But many of the same factors that led to the false conviction of Alfred Dreyfus were at play in the putrid public atmosphere of the State of Victoria during the past four years of the Pell witch-hunt. The Victoria police, already under scrutiny for incompetence and corruption, conducted a fishing expedition that sought "evidence" for crimes that no one had previously alleged to have been committed; and by some accounts, the police saw the persecution of George Pell as a useful way to deflect attention from their own (to put it gently) problems. With a few honorable exceptions, the local and national press bayed for Cardinal Pell's blood.
>
> Someone paid for the professionally printed anti-Pell placards carried by the mob that surrounded the courthouse where the trials were conducted. And the Australian Broadcasting Corporation—a taxpayer-funded public institution—engaged in the crudest anti-Catholic propaganda and broadcast a stream of defamations of Cardinal Pell's character (most recently in a series coinciding with the deliberations of the High Court).[20]

The question of how any of this could have happened in the first place remained to be adjudicated, Weigel noted. "And it is imperative for the future of the Australian criminal justice system, and indeed for the future of Australian democracy, that a serious examination of conscience followed by a serious public reckoning take place." Four years later, there is no sign of that reckoning, on the horizon.

---

[20] George Weigel, "Justice, Finally", *Catholic World Report*, April 6, 2020, https://www.catholicworldreport.com/2020/04/06/justice-finally/.

Writing in *The Australian*, Greg Craven, a constitutional lawyer, a retired vice-chancellor of the Australian Catholic University, and a friend of Pell's, noted that the spectacular seven-to-zero decision of the High Court in favour of the cardinal was impossible to describe in conventional terms of winning or losing:

> It can be understood only in terms of impact. The impact of wrongful imprisonment and vile insult in the case of Pell. The impact of years of legal anxiety, and the final crushing collapse for the complainant.
>
> But the greatest impact will be on the Victorian criminal justice system. How could that proud system get something as important as this so legally wrong so consistently through so many steps over a process that lasted years?
>
> In the final analysis, the decision of the High Court came down to the most basic proposition of the Australian criminal law. Nobody can be convicted of a criminal offence unless that offence is proved beyond reasonable doubt—no matter how much they, or the organisation they represent, may be loathed.
>
> Facts pointing to a reasonable doubt cannot be overcome by anything, even the perception that the person making the allegations presents as highly believable.
>
> And appeal courts are not entitled to ignore factual doubts through deference to the view of a jury that a complainant was deeply convincing.
>
> Because facts, in criminal law, beat impressions. To justify the decision of the High Court, no one has to believe that the complainant was lying. It simply was the case that his evidence could not legally meet the facts.
>
> This is a major part of the tragedy of this case. No one is going to emerge unscathed.
>
> On the one hand, we have a man who has been unjustly imprisoned and reviled. True, his enemies will never again be able to call him a "convicted paedophile"—the High Court has substituted a verdict of acquittal—but his life and reputation have been trashed.
>
> Then we have another man, his accuser, who has been dragged through the thorns of the same justice system over a period of years to what looked like triumph but now is a bitter end.
>
> How could all this have happened?
>
> The grim answer is that the beginning of this disaster was the same as its end: the concept of a reasonable doubt. This never was a case where charges could be proved beyond reasonable doubt.

There always were too many witnesses who were in the right place but saw nothing. Too many mathematical failures of timing. Too many improbabilities of opportunity and action.

Yet it has taken the highest and final court in the land to state the flatly obvious.

While the High Court salvaged the last vestiges of credibility of the Australian legal system, reminding the nation and the world that the rule of law is not yet dead, some in responsible positions refused to acknowledge the problems. While the conduct of the case violated principles recognised as sacrosanct in every civilised society, Premier Daniel Andrews, the state's political leader, released a brief statement after the High Court decision: "I have a message for every single victim and survivor of child sex abuse: I see you. I hear you. I believe you."[21]

The people who mean the most, Andrews said, were "the victims". The only victim in this gross miscarriage of justice was Pell, who was wrongly convicted and jailed. Even after his release from an unjust imprisonment, some prominent figures in the Church sat on the fence. Francis Sullivan, the former chief executive of the Church's Truth, Justice, and Healing Council, said the High Court decision would leave some people relieved, some confused, and some angry. Cardinal Pell, Sullivan said, was "a divisive personality, not particularly popular, a bit of an ideological warrior and a lightning rod for discontent for a long time". Pell would not have shied away from Sullivan's description.

In legal circles, as Craven wrote, there was virtually no dispassionate observer who thought the charges against Pell could stick: not in terms of being prosecuted, let alone to the point of conviction. "Lonely dissenters hated Pell so much they did not care, said he certainly was guilty of other crimes anyway or that he was the right person to be punished for the general crimes of Catholic clergy. In other words, they had abandoned their legal ethics."

The inescapable conclusion, Craven argued, was that Pell was prosecuted on an unwinnable charge for two reasons: first, that there were those within the justice system, particularly the police, who were

---

[21] Greg Craven, "The Case against George Pell Was Misguided, Unreasonable and Vile", *The Australian*, April 8, 2020.

determined to destroy him; and second, that there was a large seg-
ment of the media, fuelled by the police and "victims' lawyers", that so
clamoured for Pell's conviction that the weaknesses of the case against
him were drowned out by howls of accusation. At the same time, a
self-congratulatory media had acted as a mob rather than journalists,
doing their best to create an atmosphere conducive to a conviction.
The Australian Broadcasting Corporation, funded by taxpayers to the
tune of more than AU$ billion a year, was particularly virulent.

Craven also reminded readers of a peculiar twist in the tale. The
same police force that stalked Pell from 2013 onwards was, at the
time Pell was cleared, the subject of a royal commission investigation
into their use of a defence barrister, Lawyer X (Nicola Gobbo), as
an informant. In June 2023, *The Australian* reported that senior Victorian police officers involved in the Lawyer X matter, and Gobbo,
were likely to escape criminal charges over their roles in the scandal,
despite five years of legal investigations costing taxpayers an estimated
AU$125 million. In a report to parliament, special investigator Geof-
frey Nettle, KC, (a former High Court Judge who had been one of
the seven judges who overturned Pell's conviction) threatened to
resign and said the state's chief prosecutor had refused to lay criminal charges, despite his office recommending key players, including
senior police, be prosecuted for offences including misconduct in
public office.[22] While in prison, Pell had wondered to what extent, if
any, his case had been a useful distraction for police from the Lawyer
X scandal.

Emerging from jail, Pell was deeply conscious that it was Holy
Week, and he valued the chance to commemorate it. In his last entry
in his prison diary, he wrote: "In a few days on Holy Saturday night
during the Easter Vigil, the Paschal Candle will again be blessed and
dedicated to the man-God, whom I love and serve, whom I have
followed for all my life, just as saints and sinners, firebrands and the
lukewarm have done for nearly two thousand years."[23]

Two days after his release, Pell accepted an invitation to write
an article on Easter for the *Weekend Australian*, which he did at an

---

[22] Damon Johnston and Rachel Baxendale, "Lawyer X Investigator Comes Out Firing,"
The Australian, June 22, 2023.
[23] Pell, *Prison Journal*, vol. 3, p. 333.

outdoor table in the peace of his garden at home in Sydney, safe from COVID and the prison routine. The piece was classic Pell, resonating with his spirit, his faith in the messages and mysteries of Easter, history, philosophy, insights into modern life, and wisdom:

> Every person suffers. None escapes all the time. Everyone is confronted with a couple of questions. What should I do in this situation? Why is there so much evil and suffering? And why did this happen to me? Why the coronavirus pandemic?
>
> The ancient Greeks and Romans thought the gods were capricious, liable to punish without reason. It is claimed that when we wrap up our Christmas presents we are following the ancient practice of those offering a sacrifice to a particular god who would cover it so the other gods would not be jealous.
>
> The atheists today believe that the universe, including us, is the product of blind chance, that no transcendent Intelligence exists to help explain our DNA sequence, the 10,000 nerves connected to an eye, the genius of Shakespeare, Michelangelo, Beethoven and Albert Einstein.
>
> Another option is a radical agnosticism. We don't know and perhaps we don't want to know. Here the agnostics can battle against fate with a Stoic dignity or turn furious, journey into the night 'raging against the light'.
>
> Easter provides the Christian answer to suffering and living. Christians are monotheists who developed from within the Jewish revelation; they too follow the God of Abraham, Isaac and Jacob. They believe that nearly 2000 years ago a young Jew was crucified on a hilltop in Jerusalem, one Friday afternoon, despised and rejected. Everyone saw him die, while a limited number, those with faith, saw him after a miraculous bodily resurrection on the next Sunday. The claim is not that Jesus' soul goes marching on. It was a return of his entire person from death, breaking the rules of health and physics, as Christians believe this young man was the only Son of God, divine, the Messiah. Jesus' bones will never be found. To the dismay of many this was a Messiah who was not a great monarch like David or Solomon, but Isaiah's suffering servant, who redeems us, enables us to receive forgiveness and enter into a happy eternity.
>
> "Behold the wood of the cross on which hangs the Saviour of the World."[24]

---

[24] George Pell, "In the Suffering, We Find Redemption", *Weekend Australian*, April 11, 2020.

Pell wrote that his generation and those younger were passing through a unique moment, with the pandemic. It was not, however, unprecedented.

> We were not alive for the Spanish flu pandemic after World War I, somewhat comparable so far, and we have heard of the terrible Black Death in the 14th century, where one-third of the population died in some places. What is new is our capacity to fight the disease intelligently, mitigate the spread.
>
> The sexual abuse crisis damaged thousands of victims. From many points of view the crisis is also bad for the Catholic Church, but we have painfully cut out a moral cancer and this is good. So too some would see COVID-19 as a bad time for those who claim to believe in a good and rational God, the Supreme Love and Intelligence, the Creator of the universe. And it is a mystery; all suffering, but especially the massive number of deaths through plagues and wars. But Christians can cope with suffering better than the atheists can explain the beauty and happiness of life.
>
> And many, most understand the direction we are heading when it is pointed out that the only Son of God did not have an easy run and suffered more than his share. Jesus redeemed us and we can redeem our suffering by joining it to His and offering it to God.
>
> I have just spent 13 months in jail for a crime I didn't commit, one disappointment after another. I knew God was with me, but I didn't know what He was up to, although I realised He has left all of us free. But with every blow it was a consolation to know I could offer it to God for some good purpose like turning the mass of suffering into spiritual energy.

The health services, Pell wrote, are deeply rooted in the Christian tradition of service, of charitable healers working long hours amid a lively danger of infection.

> It wasn't like this in pagan Rome where Christians were unique because they stayed with their sick and nursed them in times of plague. Even Galen, the best-known ancient physician, fled to his country estate during the plague.
>
> Kiko Arguello, co-founder of the Neocatechumenal Way, claims that a fundamental difference between God-fearers and secularists today is found in the approach to suffering. Too often the irreligious want to eliminate the cause of the suffering, through abortion,

euthanasia, or exclude it from sight, leaving our loved ones unvisited in nursing homes. Christians see Christ in everyone who suffers—victims, the sick, the elderly—and are obliged to help.

That is part of the Easter message of the Risen Christ.

In the same paper, writing from London, commentator Brendan O'Neill argued that what was done to Pell was "monstrous" and that it wasn't only him on trial—it was Catholicism more broadly. O'Neill contrasted this with the kid gloves treatment of accused offenders of other faiths. "Would someone take it upon themselves to daub a mosque with anti-Islamic slogans along the lines of the anti-Catholic bigotry that was spray-painted on to the door of St Patrick's Cathedral in Melbourne following the quashing of Pell's conviction?" O'Neill wrote. "Would the supposedly progressive sections of society turn a blind eye to such foul mosque desecration, as they largely did in relation to the hateful anti-Catholicism painted on to St Patrick's? 'Rot in Hell, Pell', the graffiti said—a disgusting anti-Catholic hate crime."[25]

Those who knew George Pell well, such as Sydney parish priest Father Anthony Robbie, who served as his secretary in Rome from 2016 to 2020, found him, in some ways, a changed man after his experience in jail. "The old character was still there; warm, gregarious and social, but softened and spiritualised", Robbie wrote in his obituary of Pell for the Order of Malta, in which he was an honorary chaplain and Pell a long-standing member. "He was devoid of any degree of self-pity or of hostility towards his accusers, He claimed that the experience had drawn him closer to God and it seemed the heavy humiliation had allowed qualities of tenderness and gentleness to come much more to the fore than had been apparent earlier."[26]

Pell's old friend Bishop Peter Elliott also said he found Pell more serene, with a stronger spirituality, after his ordeal. "He fell back on the spiritual riches he had received as a seminarian, especially from the Jesuits at Werribee, where his deep intellect had absorbed so much",

---

[25] Brendan O'Neill, "The Twisted Passions of the Anti-Catholics", *Weekend Australian*, April 11, 2020.

[26] Anthony Robbie, "His Eminence George Cardinal Pell", *2022 Australian Hospitaller: The Annual Review of the Australian Association of the Order of Malta*, 2022, p. 75.

Elliott noticed. Apart from his Bible and breviary, Pell had no access to other spiritual resources, but he remembered much of what various saints and Church scholars had written over the centuries, and many prayers, which he included in his *Prison Journal*. As he told William Cash in *The Catholic Herald*, "I've said to a number of friends, with my tongue in cheek, I don't see any improvement as a result of my time served, but I think it's reasonable to say my faith was strengthened."[27]

In Rome, Pell sustained his richer spiritual life after leaving jail. In Rome, as well as attending early evening Vespers at the Institute of Christ the King chapel within walking distance of his apartment in Rome, he was a regular at the Adoration of the Blessed Sacrament at Santo Spirito in Sassia (the Saxon district, as it was known when it was founded in the twelfth century). "We used to call the Church Santo Spirito in Pissidia", one of his priest friends remembered. "While we were there for a Holy Hour one night in winter (I used to sit behind the cardinal) I felt something warm against my leg. A homeless guy that was drunk lost control and peed in the bench. The cardinal thought it was hilarious."

During Pell's time in jail, the possibility that he could die there, without the chance to clear his name in this life, crossed his mind. He found comfort in beliefs he had held for more than sixty years. "In my youth, we were encouraged to pray for a happy death, to ask Jesus, Mary, and Joseph to assist us in our last agony", he wrote in the first volume of his *Prison Journal*.

> I remember sixty years ago visiting my uncle Tom dying in hospital with cancer and loudly repeating the prayer aspirations he learnt as a child.
>
> All of us, no matter the age, should "ponder our last end", try to be glad that we will be with Christ in glory, try to remove any large obstacle blocking God's love, and evaluate again, in our heart of hearts, whether our goals and activities are worth all our striving, directed in faith and hope to love.
>
> To conclude, from a prayer of St Francis de Sales (1567–1622).

---

[27] William Cash, "The Ordeal of Cardinal Pell: An Interview", *Catholic Herald*, January 11, 2023, https://catholicherald.co.uk/the-ordeal-of-cardinal-pell-an-interview/. This article originally appeared in the December 2021 issue of the *Catholic Herald*.

My God, I thank you now for the moment and circumstances of my death. I want to offer this moment to you with the hope that I will be departing this world in your peace. At death may I have no grudges or resentments. May I have forgiven all my enemies and have sought and received your forgiveness.

I want to affirm now the gift of faith, hope, and love you have given me through the Holy Spirit, to renew my baptismal promises, and to thank you for the eternal life promised by Jesus for those who eat his Body and drink his Blood.

P.S. pie for lunch—almost hot. Bravo.[28]

[28] George Pell, *Prison Journal*, vol. 1, *The Cardinal Makes His Appeal* (San Francisco: Ignatius Press, 2021), p. 231.

36

Kangaroo Courts? Failure of a System on Trial

Australia's reputation as the nation of the "fair go", in which the rule of law was a bedrock value, took a beating before, during, and after Cardinal Pell's legal saga. Writing fifteen months after Pell's death, Gavin Silbert, KC, a barrister with forty years of experience, who was chief crown prosecutor for Victoria between 2008 and 2018, said that Victoria's legal system was in a parlous state. "It is difficult to imagine a more devastating criticism of the majority of the Victorian Court of Appeal than that delivered by a unanimous bench of the High Court when it granted special leave to appeal, set aside the appellant's convictions and entered verdicts of acquittal stating there was a significant possibility that an innocent person had been convicted because the evidence did not establish guilt to the requisite standard of proof. In doing so, the court criticised the submissions of the Victorian Director of Public Prosecutions as specious."[1]

Pell's acquittal, *The Spectator*'s associate editor Damian Thompson wrote in London soon after his release, ended "one of the most despicable miscarriages of justice in the history of Australia". For five years, Thompson wrote, "Catholics and countless impartial observers all over the world have watched in horror as Pell was accused by the State of Victoria and then convicted on the basis of evidence riddled with implausibilities and impossibilities".[2]

From "Operation Tethering" onwards, until Pell was cleared by the High Court, the conduct of the case, by Victoria Police and the

---

[1] Gavin Silbert, "Victoria's Justice System Has Been Compromised by Its Police", *Weekend Australian*, April 5, 2024.

[2] Damian Thompson, "Cardinal George Pell Is the Victim of a Shameful Miscarriage of Justice", *The Spectator*, April 7, 2020, https://www.spectator.co.uk/article/cardinal-george-pell-is-the-victim-of-a-shameful-miscarriage-of-justice/.

state's justice system, shocked many around the world who followed it. One of the most articulate and incisive observers was George Weigel in the United States, who on June 29, 2017, the day the charges were laid against Pell, wrote that many Australians, including some in influential positions, including in the media, were "caught up in an atmosphere of hysteria and persecution that inevitably invites comparison to Salem, Mass., in the 17th century".[3] Anyone witnessing the snarling, yowling, and visceral hatred of some protestors on the streets outside the courts in Melbourne throughout the saga could see that was no exaggeration. The professionally painted placards that protestors were waving raised the question: Who was paying for them?

Waiting for the first trial to resume after lunch one afternoon at the County Court in William Street, Melbourne, I saw the face of a grandmotherly woman, who could have appeared on knitting patterns, transform into flint as Pell, stretching his legs in the corridor, walked by. "You don't like him?" I asked the woman. Her reply captured a common vengeful attitude toward the Catholic hierarchy: "I don't care whether he did it; I want him locked up." The Church's abysmal handling of the evil of child sexual abuse (though Pell was one of the first and few among Australian bishops to tackle the problem head on) combined with media coverage (much of it deserved, some of it hysterical and deeply unfair to Pell) had undoubtedly fuelled such opinions, a point Pell recognized. Someone from the Church was going to have pay the price for decades of abuse and cover-ups, Pell told a friend after his release from jail.

Responding to the verdict in the second trial, which resulted in Pell's jailing on February 27, 2019, Weigel noted:

> Has it occurred to anyone else debating the perverse verdict rendered against Cardinal George Pell, which convicted him of "historic sexual abuse," that the cardinal did not have to return to his native Australia to face trial? As a member of the College of Cardinals of the Holy Roman Church and a Vatican official, Pell holds a Vatican diplomatic passport and citizenship of Vatican City State. Were he guilty, he could have stayed put in the extraterritorial safety of the Vatican enclave, untouchable by the Australian authorities. But because

---

[3] George Weigel, "The Persecution of Cardinal George Pell", *National Review Online*, June 29, 2017, https://eppc.org/publication/the-persecution-of-cardinal-george-pell.

Cardinal Pell knows he is innocent, he was determined to go home to defend his honor—and, in a broader sense, to defend his decades of work rebuilding the Catholic Church in Australia, the living parts of which owe a great deal to his leadership and courage.[4]

As Pell prepared to appeal the conviction, he accepted the assault on his character with serenity and equanimity while spending time in a Melbourne jail "on retreat", as he put it to friends. He was not the only one being put to the test; the Australian justice system was being sorely tried, a process summed up by Weigel:

The case against Pell has been fraught with implausibility and worse from the outset. The Victoria police went on a fishing expedition against Pell, a year before any complaint had been received from an alleged victim. The committal hearing, which dismissed many of the charges the police brought, ought to have dismissed all of them; but amidst a public atmosphere that bears comparison to Salem, Massachusetts, during the witchcraft hysteria of the seventeenth century, a criminal trial was decreed. At that trial, and after Pell's defense demonstrated that it was physically impossible for the crimes with which he was charged to have occurred, a jury voted 10-2 to acquit him; but that meant a hung jury (several of whose members wept as their verdict was read), and the Crown decided to proceed with a re-trial. At the re-trial, Pell's defense team demonstrated that ten implausible and improbable things would have had to have happened simultaneously for him to be guilty of the charges; there was no corroboration of the complainant's charges; there was ample refutation of the very possibility of the vile acts with which Pell was charged having occurred by others present that day; the police were shown to have been grossly negligent in investigating the alleged crime scene—and yet the second jury voted 12-0 for conviction, after what can reasonably be supposed to have been their refusal to take seriously the trial judge's instructions on how evidence was to be construed.

And when the media-suppression order that had banned Australian press coverage of these trials was lifted and the second verdict was revealed earlier this week, a Niagara of calumnies was poured

---

[4] George Weigel, "The Pell Affair: Australia Is Now on Trial", *First Things*, February 27, 2019, https://www.firstthings.com/web-exclusives/2019/02/the-pell-affair-australia-is-now-on-trial.

over Cardinal Pell from both political and media circles, despite the fact that a few brave Australian journalists and Father Frank Brennan (a prominent Australian Jesuit on the other end of the ecclesiastical spectrum from Pell) pointed out the gross injustice of his conviction.

Something is very, very wrong here.

The term "kangaroo court' was raised by Father George Rutler, while he was the pastor of Saint Michael's Church in New York City. He noted:

Etymologists have traced the term "kangaroo court" to the make-shift jurisprudence of an Australian immigrant in the United States at the time of the 1849 gold rush—but Australia is the homeland of the marsupial. Cardinal Pell stood against politically correct policies such as contraception, abortion, the Gnostic revision of sexuality, and attempts to teach anthropogenic climate change theories as dogma. These are not welcome opinions in the courts of secular correctness. He also began with unprecedented vigor, not typical in Rome, the task of cleaning the Augean stable of Vatican finances.[5]

It was these unwelcome opinions, along with the clerical sex-abuse problems, that put a target on Pell's back.

During the years Pell was pursued, tried and jailed, Victoria led the nation in encouraging so-called "gender fluidity" among children and teenagers. It boasted Australia's most liberal abortion laws—which other states copied—and put permissive euthanasia laws into effect. Like other Australian states, it imposed mandatory reporting legislation requiring priests to violate the seal of confession in regard to matters of child sexual abuse. Premier Daniel Andrews signed up the state with the Chinese Communist Party's Belt and Road initiative, a move that was overturned federally. Pell's opinions on all of these matters were well-known.

So, the cardinal already had enemies before his trials began, but the way some media covered them increased hostility toward him. His

---

[5] George Rutler, "What Newman Can Tell Us about the Cardinal Pell Verdict", *Crisis*, March 14, 2019, https://crisismagazine.com/opinion/what-newman-can-tell-us-about-the-cardinal-pell-verdict. Cleaning the stables of King Augeas was one of the twelve Labours of Hercules.

sentencing was broadcast live, for example, which is not normally done. Given the public mood at the time of Pell's trials, Irish journalist Melanie McDonagh noted another aspect of Victoria that was to the cardinal's disadvantage. It was one of the few Australian states not to have the option of judge-only trials. "That, at least, should change", she argued. "I am usually a fervent admirer of the jury system, but this wretched case shows its limits, where the public atmosphere is febrile to the point of hysteria and the allegations involve a celebrated public figure."[6]

[6] Melanie McDonagh, "Why I Find the George Pell Verdict Hard to Believe", *The Spectator*, February 26, 2019, https://www.spectator.co.uk/article/why-i-find-the-george-pell-verdict-hard-to-believe/.

37

The Corruption Fight Continues in Rome

George Pell's arrest in 2017 interrupted his pursuit of hundreds of millions of euros in alleged financial corruption that had hollowed out the finances of the Vatican. Even during his imprisonment in Australia and after his release, Pell's work in Rome was slowly bearing fruit. Three years after Pell left Rome to stand trial in Australia, Pope Francis stepped up to implement significant reforms the cardinal and his team had recommended to improve the Vatican's finances, and this resulted in, among other actions, the sacking of Cardinal Giovanni Angelo Becciu.

In September 2020, five months after Pell was cleared by the High Court, Cardinal Becciu, then seventy-two, who was serving as the prefect of the Congregation for the Causes of Saints, was accused of fraud, embezzlement, and other forms of financial misconduct. Pope Francis then removed Becciu from his position at Saints and took away his privileges of being a cardinal. It was a major fall from grace. He had been the second-highest official in charge of the Secretariat of State, where, according to Pell and many other observers, he had been an opponent of financial reform efforts requested by Pope Francis, an assertion Becciu has strongly denied. At a press conference in Rome, Becciu said that Pope Francis "told me that he no longer has trust in me because a report came from the magistrates that I allegedly committed acts of embezzlement. In our meeting, the Holy Father told me that I favoured my brothers and their companies with money from the Secretariat of State."[1]

[1] Tess Livingstone and Tessa Akerman, "Nemesis Gone, George Pell Flies Back to Vatican", *The Australian*, September 29, 2020.

On hearing of Becciu's resignation, Pell, still in Australia, said: "The Holy Father was elected to clean up Vatican finances. He plays a long game and is to be congratulated on recent developments. I hope the clean-ups of the Augean stables continue, both in the Vatican and in Victoria."

Francis appeared to retain some affection, or was it concern, for Becciu. On Holy Thursday 2021, Francis celebrated the evening Mass privately with Cardinal Becciu in the chapel of the cardinal's apartment. "A fatherly gesture like this, on a day like Holy Thursday, does not seem strange", a Vatican spokesman said.[2] Francis delegated the task of offering the main public Mass of the day to the dean of the College of Cardinals, Giovanni Battista Re, who did so in Saint Peter's Basilica with restricted attendance due to COVID-19.

In July 2024, Cardinal Becciu emphatically denied that he had been an opponent of Pell's financial reforms. He acknowledged that he had some "differences" with Pell but said they had nothing to do with financial reforms. He said his "so-called opposition to the changes were 'invented' by those who had an interest in portraying him as 'his enemy' ".

"I had no title and no power in this", he said in a statement reported by the Italian newspaper *Il Giornale* and by Paola Totaro in *The Australian*. "I received instructions solely from the Secretariat of State and the Pope. However I did make clear that despite their reforms, spending and outgoings of the Holy See showed no signs of decreasing ... but if someone was opposing the changes, it was certainly not me," Becciu also said it was false to claim that he was behind the decision to abandon a PricewaterhouseCoopers audit. If Libero Milone believes this to be true, he said, "he should show me the letter on which my signature appears to do this."[3]

Pell did not live to see one of the most significant results of his work. On December 16, 2023, the fifty-seventh anniversary of his ordination to the priesthood, a Vatican court sentenced Cardinal

[2] Tess Livingstone, "Pope Holds Mass with Cast-Out Cardinal", *The Australian*, April 2, 2021, https://www.theaustralian.com.au/world/pope-francis-holds-mass-with-cardinal-he-cast-out-of-the-vatican/news-story/d83of2b685981c1fo728e51dbo23doe4.

[3] Paola Totaro, "Convicted Cardinal Angelo Becciu Lashes Out at 'Demonisers'", *The Australian*, July 8, 2024, https://www.theaustralian.com.au/world/convicted-cardinal-angelo-becciu-lashes-out-at-demonisers/news-story/16d326e17baff4ab48b5636790513e24.

Becciu, who by then was seventy-five, to five years and six months in jail on three counts of embezzlement. The sentencing concluded a historic trial that ran for two-and-a-half years. Becciu, who once described himself as a papal contender, insisted he was innocent and appealed the verdict.

Becciu was one of ten defendants in a trial focused on the Vatican's disastrous investment in a London building at 60 Sloane Avenue, Chelsea. The purchase of the building, according to Agence France-Presse (AFP), resulted in losses of between €140 and €190 million, which the Vatican claimed dipped into resources intended for charity. "Becciu was found guilty of embezzlement over the decision to invest $200 million in 2013–2014 in a fund run by financier Raffaele Mincione, which the judges said was hugely risky", the wire service said. "Some of this money went to buying part of the Sloane Avenue property." Becciu was also found guilty over a €570,000 payment to Cecilia Marogna, which he claimed was to help negotiate the release of a Colombian nun kidnapped in Mali. Marogna was sentenced to three years and nine months in jail. Becciu is appealing all convictions. In the Italian legal system, defendants are not jailed until appeals have been heard.

The others accused of financial crimes were also found guilty, with the court president Giuseppe Pignatone reading out sentences ranging from a fine to more than seven years in jail. The court ordered the confiscation from those convicted of €166 million and required that they compensate civil parties—including four Vatican entities—more than €200 million, including for moral and reputational damage.

The Vatican News Service reported that, in addition to jail time, Becciu was sentenced to perpetual disqualification from public office and an €8,000 fine. Enrico Crasso, a former financial adviser to the Secretariat of State, received a sentence of seven years' imprisonment and a €10,000 fine. The court sentenced financier Raffaele Mincione to five years and six months' jail, an €8,000 fine, and disqualification from public office. Fabrizio Tirabassi, a former employee of the administrative office of the Secretariat of State, was sentenced to seven years' imprisonment, a €10,000 fine, and disqualification from public office.

AFP reported that the trial "involved more than 80 hearings in the dedicated room within the Vatican Museums, where a portrait of a smiling Pope Francis hangs on the wall."[4] The week before the sentence was handed down, the pope had referred to Pell's episcopal motto, "Be not afraid", as a motto for the Vatican officials carrying on his work of finance reform.

After his return to Rome, following his release from jail, Pell, focused on a particular transaction he suspected could have been used to further the case against him, although he had an open mind on that matter. In May 2022, Dennis Shanahan, one of Australia's most experienced political reporters, the national editor of *The Australian*, and a frequent visitor to Italy with his wife, Angela, reported that Pell had raised concerns about more than AU$2 million sent to Australia from the Vatican during the period of the police investigation against Pell and his trial on historical sexual abuse. He publicly challenged Becciu to explain the "mystery of the funds".[5]

Pell told Shanahan: "My interest is focused on four payments with a value of $2.3 million made by the Secretariat of State in 2017 and 2018 to Neustar Australia (a tech security firm in Melbourne), two of which with a value of $1.236 million were authorised by Monsignor Becciu on 17/5/2017 and 6/6/2018. Obviously, these are different payments from those of 11/9/2015 which I allegedly authorised. What was the purpose? Where did the money go after Neustar?"

In Rome, Becciu confirmed previous reports that the $2 million he authorised to the office of Neustar were for the registration of an internet domain name. Pell responded:

> No one disputes that the Pontifical Council for Social Communications paid amounts to Neustar Australia for their expensive services and to ICANN, the registry, for the reservation of the title "Catholic" in 2012, 2015, 2016, 2017 and 2018.
>
> Doubts, of course, are removed by facts, by evidence, not by assertions. Unfortunately, I do not have information on payments to

[4] Agence France-Presse (AFP), "Cardinal Sentenced to 5.5 Years in Vatican Fraud Trial", *France24*, December 16, 2023, https://www.france24.com/en/live-news/20231216-historic-vatican-fraud-trial-to-deliver-its-verdict.

[5] Dennis Shanahan, "George Pell Challenges Cardinal Angelo Becciu to Explain 'Mystery' of More Than $2m Sent from Rome to Allegedly Adversely Affect His Trial", *The Australian*, May 8, 2022.

Neustar Australia in 2015 beyond US$150,000 the Council for Social Communications paid as a deposit. It was not my usual practice to sign off on payments from the Secretariat of State.[6]

Pell was open to be convinced either way as to whether funds from Italy played any part in encouraging the cases against him in Australia as a means of getting him out of Rome for as long as possible. The motivation for any such skullduggery, he believed, was fear of what he and his team might uncover about Vatican corruption totaling hundreds of millions of euros.

Whatever role, if any, dark forces associated with Vatican financial scandals played in worsening Pell's legal predicament is yet to be uncovered definitively. It is unlikely, however, that the trouble originated from that source. Operation Tethering, after all, the "get Pell" operation, was launched by Victoria Police in 2013, a year before Pell left Sydney to take up his role as prefect of the Secretariat for the Economy.

Interest in the mystery flared in December 2021, after Monsignor Alberto Perlasca, a senior official at the Vatican Secretariat of State, claimed funds were sent to the Australian Conference of Catholic Bishops for Pell's expenses during his trial and imprisonment. That was plain wrong. The Church in Australia did not financially support any priest accused of child sexual abuse, including Pell. And the Conference of Bishops confirmed it received no such payment. "The conference of bishops has said 'no such money ever arrived, certainly, we didn't receive it'", Pell told the Catholic News Agency. "So the unanswered question is: If the money wasn't sent for something to do with my case, why was it sent?" If "a good reason can be given" for why the funds were sent to Australia, he said, "then we can get on with our lives and investigate other directions." But it remained a major unanswered question. "And as I said," Pell added, "Cardinal Becciu confirms that the money was sent, and he believes it's none of my business as to why it was sent."[7]

---

[6] Dennis Shanahan, "One Question Left for Jailed Cardinal Angelo Becciu: Did He Adversely Influence the Trial of the Late George Pell?", *The Australian*, Dec. 17, 2023.

[7] Christine Rousselle, "Cardinal Pell to Becciu: What Was That $2M Payment Actually For?", *Catholic News Agency*, December 17, 2021, https://www.catholicnewsagency.com/news/249924/cardinal-pell-becciu-payment-australia.

Unusual money transfers to Australia were not the only reason Pell wondered if his Australian judicial problems had been exacerbated by parties within the Vatican. Pell was told, by a reliable source, that on the day of the Vatican Police raid on Auditor General Libero Milone's office, Monday, June 19, 2017, a high-ranking layman, who was later a defendant in the financial scandal trials, was heard boasting that the raid and the resignation was "bomb number 1, soon to be followed by bomb number 2, after which it will be clear to everyone where the power lies in the Vatican".

The formal charges against Pell in Australia were made on Thursday, June 29, 2017, ten days after the raid on Milone's office. Just weeks before these events, the auditor general had announced to the president of the Administration of the Patrimony of the Holy See (APSA), Cardinal Domenico Calcagno, his intentions of auditing APSA's foreign real estate holding companies in France, Switzerland, and the United Kingdom, whose boards of directors included APSA employees and consultants. Meanwhile, Pell would begin a Pope Francis–approved investigation into APSA's relationship with a Lugano-based Swiss bank, which had come under scrutiny for alleged illicit activities. Discussing his work, in a limited way, with friends during his years as prefect for the economy, Pell had sometimes said he was "looking to the north", recognising Swiss bank accounts as part of the problem.

Pell thought that certain transfers of Vatican funds might have been directed to his detriment through a web of offshore companies, anonymous trusts, and banks controlled by potential beneficiaries of his demise. He hoped that Vatican investigators would take advantage of their access to these bank statements to determine if any such malicious transfers were made. But this has not happened.

At the time of his arrest by Victoria Police, on June 29, 2017, Cardinal Pell had been on the trail of "something enormous" pertaining to Vatican corruption, said one of his closest priest friends in Rome. "About three months earlier, when I was called into his office in March 2017, he took me outside and we walked along the corridor", said the friend, who remains well placed in the Vatican. (Vatican staff had learned to discuss sensitive matters in corridors to avoid listening devices. Some curial cardinals, entitled to chauffeurs and drivers, preferred paying for their own transport or driving themselves to avoid being tracked.) "George was very pumped up", the priest recalled. "He had a report in his hand, and he was taking it somewhere, perhaps to the pope. He believed he had cracked 'one of the big tentacles' of corruption. He didn't tell me what it was."

By April 2017, suspecting that his time at the financial helm in Rome was almost up, Pell was alarmed by the state of play in the Vatican. In an internal memo to trusted colleagues, dated April 3, 2017, and headed "The Suffocation of Pope Francis' Reforms and the Bertonian Reconquest of the Vatican" (a reference to Cardinal Tarcisio Bertone, former Vatican secretary of state, who was linked to various financial scandals), he set out his fears that the hardwon financial gains of the previous three years were being reversed. "Since 2014 the scope of work of the Secretariat for the Economy, its authority, and the number of its staff, have been steadily reduced. It is without economic resources, it has limited authority and the fine work accomplished by its Administrative Section, parts of which now transferred back to APSA, is dissolving into chaos and running weeks, perhaps months, behind schedule", he wrote.

APSA, its powers strengthened by a series of papal motu proprio documents, remained untouched, unrepentant, and often inefficient, Pell believed. This was contributing to chronic delays in reviewing and improving the Vatican's financial situation at the behest of Pope Francis. APSA, Pell wrote, stonewalled the newly established controlling bodies, such as the Secretariat for the Economy and the Office of the Auditor General, and refused to adopt their new procedures. Figures from the past were still in place, controlling the finances, including Cardinals Domenico Calcagno and Attilio Nicora, both senior figures in APSA. (Nicora died a fortnight after Pell wrote his memo.)

The memo also suggested that the heads of the Vatican Bank, known officially as the Institute for the Works of Religion (IOR), had halted investigation of alleged past abuses and had effectively stopped efforts to redirect €30–40 million of alms given to Peter's Pence away from covering Vatican expenses and towards supporting its philanthropic and charitable works.

One of the major, original tenets of the reform process had been that the Secretariat for the Economy was to answer to the pope and was not to be subject to the Secretariat of State. The autonomy of the Secretariat for the Economy, which was to report to the Holy Father directly and whose cardinal prefect (Pell) was to act "in collaboration with the Secretary of State", was set out by Francis in his Apostolic Letter of February 24, 2014. The letter established the Secretariat for the Economy, the Office of the Auditor General, and the Council for the Economy, a fifteen-member body, comprising eight cardinals and bishops and seven finance professionals, lay men and women. Its role was to be oversight "for the administrative and financial structures and activities of the dicasteries of the Roman Curia, the institutions linked to the Holy See, and the Vatican City State".[8] The council was chaired by German cardinal Reinhard Marx, the archbishop of Munich and Freising, and included cardinals and bishops from Budapest, São Paulo, Quebec, Newark, Stockholm, and L'Aquila.

In his memo, Pell mentioned that the office of the Promoter of Justice and the Tribunal (Vatican judicial bodies with the power to hold wrongdoers to account) were giving little or no sign of processing the more than forty cases delivered to them by Vatican agencies. "The international agency Moneyval will be returning soon to examine progress in this area", he said.

Moneyval, established in 1997, is the Council of Europe's body for monitoring member states' compliance with international accounting standards to counter money laundering and the financing of terrorism. It makes recommendations to national authorities about ways to improve the accountability and security of their financial systems. By 2017, as Pell and his staff in the Secretariat for the Economy knew well, it had been watching the Vatican closely for years.

Pell also wrote that hostility towards Libero Milone and his staff had been devised by those opposed to reform, with the hope and expectation that they would resign. "No respectable professional would be willing to succeed Libero Milone as Auditor General without changes to the system," he added, "and without changes, no cardinal, competent and committed to the reforms, would be willing to succeed me as Prefect of the Secretariat for the Economy."

The Vatican had been running an annual deficit, Pell warned.

---

[8] Francis, Apostolic Letter Issued Motu Proprio Fidelis *Dispensator et Prudens* (February 24, 2014), no. 6.

This deficit should not be met by taking money from the poor, from Peter's Pence. This situation needs to be addressed seriously. It is necessary to choose between the worsening situation of today, and the Reforms.

The present situation is dysfunctional and dangerous for the reputation of the Church. As it stands today, opponents to the reforms surrender only after repeated pressure is put upon them. Furthermore, it results in a significant waste of energy and patience, this in order to achieve minimal results. This chronic reluctance to cooperate with the implementation of the reforms must be actively rejected, so that work can be normalized and conflicts reduced down to healthy debate.

One of the long-time Vatican staffers who consistently supported Pell said that while he and many of those dedicated to the reform efforts, past and present, would deny it for fear of repercussions, the blame for many of the problems rested with the way Pope Francis handled the cardinals resisting the use of international best accounting practices. "Great hopes were placed on his 2013 arrival and leadership in the Reforms project. Instead, he soon became, and remained all the way through, the worst enemy of his own reforms, through a series of unexplainable blunders."

The Cardinal Becciu case was not the only problem Francis tried to address in 2020. Spurred on by the loss of revenue from the Vatican Museums, which had been closed during the COVID-19 pandemic, the pope introduced new rules for procurements in order to cut costs and opportunities for corruption. The Vatican Museums are the Vatican's biggest revenue source, providing about €40 million in a normal year, from more than six million visitors. The pope did well in prohibiting age-old practices, such as favouring suppliers with family and other ties to particular sections of the Vatican, to prevent inflated pricing that was gouging into the bottom line. Francis also barred companies with convictions for fraud, tax evasion, and money laundering and those with links to organised crime or who were being investigated on suspicion of illegal activities from bidding for Vatican contracts. "That'll be a lot of them", one insider quipped. Companies based in internationally recognised tax havens or involved with child labour exploitation were also banned.

Vatican sources said the new rules were recognised in Rome as a "massive vindication" of the efforts of Pell and his staff to bring modern financial standards, transparency, and accountability to the Vatican. Three years earlier, one of Pell's last acts as prefect of the Secretariat for the Economy had been to propose such measures to avoid corruption. But as the Vatican press corps wrote three years later, the cardinal and his staff were often blocked by the Vatican "old guard", who were deeply enmeshed in the practices of the past, including nepotism. When the changes were announced, Pell said the pope's measures "represent a wonderful advance". On their own, they would not "solve the grave financial problems facing the Vatican", he said, "but they spell out the methodology which must be followed: transparency, proper control, and competition amongst suppliers with competitive costing and pricing to the benefit of the Holy See. Regular independent auditing will be needed to ensure that these norms are being followed."

Under Pell, the Secretariat for the Economy had also sought to have independent auditing for all Vatican offices and a single fund, tightly monitored, to handle all Vatican investments. The auditing system has not been adopted, as has been illustrated elsewhere in this book, but Francis established a single investment fund.

"For much of his pontificate, Pope Francis unfortunately appeared to have listened less to reformers like Pell and more to what have been called the 'old guard' resistant to financial reform, as well as allowed officials incompetent in financial affairs to inflict massive losses on Vatican finances." That is what Vatican commentator Edward Pentin of the *National Catholic Register* told Father Mark Withoos, Pell's former Roman secretary. "Now [the pope] seems to have recognised these errors," Pentin added, "and that Cardinal Pell, whom he has admired for his honesty, was right all along."[9] Pell and the pope had their differences, but when Pell returned to Rome for the first time after his acquittal by the High Court, Francis welcomed him to the Apostolic Palace with a cohort of Swiss Guards. Pell was stunned, for this privilege is normally reserved for visiting heads of state. There were no further one-on-one meetings, however, despite the fact Pell would have had much to contribute to the ongoing reform.

[9] Mark Withoos, "Cardinal Pell, the Living Martyr", *Crisis*, October 16, 2020, https://crisismagazine.com/opinion/cardinal-pell-the-living-martyr-2.

38

Remembering

The guilty verdicts against Cardinal Giovanni Angelo Becciu, nine other individuals, and four companies in the Vatican City courtroom came on an auspicious day. Saturday, December 16, 2023, was the fifty-seventh anniversary of the ordination of George Pell to the priesthood and the second anniversary of the death of his sister, Margaret.

That afternoon Saint Mary's Cathedral looked beautiful, peaceful, and welcoming as visitors waited for confession and looked around, enjoying the twinkling Christmas tree lights and the choir practising carols. A few paid their respects at the memorial to the fallen: *Pax Invictis*. Downstairs, about a hundred friends from near and far gathered at Pell's grave, where Archbishop Anthony Fisher offered Mass for the cardinal and Margaret and blessed his grave. Its headstone reflects his life—prayerful, colourful, and packed with achievements. "Prefect of the Secretariat for the Economy 2014–2019", the second to last line reads.

From Pell's perspective, his battles with Vatican officials were never personal. As always, he played the ball, not the man. A year earlier, he was arguing that Cardinal Becciu and the others accused of financial crimes deserved due process and a fair trial.

Accountant Danny Casey, who worked beside Pell for years in Sydney and Rome, attended the Mass. What drove Pell's work in Rome, he said, was his desire to see Vatican funds managed properly to help the Church's mission to the poor and vulnerable. That demanded modern, transparent accounting practices. The verdicts, Casey said, will be a powerful warning to others inclined to work against the reform process. December 16, 2023, will be recognised as a turning point.

What is indisputable, as Archbishop Fisher said that afternoon, is that "no Australian has done more for the Church internationally" than Pell. The Church in Australia will not see his like again, for a long time, if ever. Pell deserved far better, especially from his home state of Victoria and also his adopted state of NSW, where his working with children check was never approved after his release from jail. It hurt him and it severely limited what pastoral work he could carry out in Australia.

Within a year of Pell's death, his grave had become a popular place of pilgrimage and prayer. That probably would have amazed him in his lifetime. His burial spot, which he selected when he was archbishop, is beside a set of stained-glass windows depicting the image of Mary, Mater Admirabilis (Mother Most Admirable). Her father, Saint Joachim, is on her left, and her mother, Saint Anne, on her right. The windows are based on a fresco on the walls of the Convent of Santa Trinità dei Monti, at the top of the Spanish Steps in Rome. It was painted in 1844 by a French novice in that convent. God the Father is shown wearing a coronet and holding an orb; God the Son with coronet and sceptre, and the Holy Spirit, in the form of a dove, is emanating rays of grace towards Mary. It is an appropriate image and theme beside the grave of a man born on Trinity Sunday.

The windows were commissioned by Jack F. Hennessy, who was the architect responsible for Saint Mary's Cathedral after the death of William Wardell in 1899. Beside Pell's grave is a small altar for Masses. His tombstone features his coat of arms and episcopal motto, "Be Not Afraid", an image of roses, which he loved nurturing. Some of his roses were still flourishing on the balcony of the cathedral presbytery. The gravestone, at Pell's request (said cathedral dean Father Don Richardson), asks visitors "please pray for me." And its main message is "Christum et Ecclesiam vehementer dilexit" (He loved Christ and the Church passionately).

A few weeks later, on January 10, 2024, the first anniversary of Pell's death, the minor basilica of Santi Celso was packed by everyday Roman Catholics for a memorial Mass for Pell in the Extraordinary Form offered by Father Hamilton. In his short, off-the-cuff homily, Father Hamilton said Santi Celso e Giuliano was where Pell the Confessor had his daily Holy Hours when he returned to Rome after his release from prison. The evening before, Father Hamilton told the congregation, a Mass for Pell, "the great global prelate", had been concelebrated at Domus Australia. The principal celebrant was

Cardinal Gerhard Müller, and it was attended by Pell's friends among the College of Cardinals, including Americans Raymond Burke, James Harvey, and Edwin O'Brien, and Italians Angelo Bagnasco and Camillo Ruini.

Preaching in English, Cardinal Müller said in his homily that "the enemy does not sleep." In the case of faithful servant George Pell, he said, Jesus' words were proved shockingly true: "If they persecuted me, they will persecute you.... But all this they will do to you on my account, because they do not know him who sent me" (Jn 15:20–21). According to patristic standards, Müller said, Pell's trials would have placed him, even during his lifetime, among the ranks of the confessors who immediately follow the martyrs in the communion of saints. "*Prison Journal* is, to my mind," he said "of comparable literary value to Boethius' *On the Consolation of Philosophy*, written in the dungeon of the Gothic king Theodoric in Pavia, Italy, in 523. It was translated into English by Elizabeth I and Geoffrey Chaucer. I also think of the Protestant pastor Dietrich Bonhoeffer, writing letters from his jail cell, where he was imprisoned by the atheist German Nazi government." The persecution of George Pell, Müller said, was "the same persecution of Christians that recurs throughout history in different guises".

In the case of Pell, it was inflicted on a brave, honorable man, who had decided, at eighteen years of age, to devote his life to Christ rather than to law, medicine, or sport, which, he suspected when young, he might have enjoyed more. Over time, his trials will be recognised for what they revealed about the weaknesses of the justice system in the Australian state of Victoria in the second and third decades of the twenty-first century. The significance of his contributions, both inside and outside the Church, will also be increasingly acknowledged. His reputation will endure.

ACKNOWLEDGMENTS

Thank you to Ignatius Press and its founder Father Joseph Fessio, S.J., for the opportunity to refresh and complete the life story of George Pell, whose kindness, wisdom, and faith I will never forget and never stop missing. After a twenty-year gap, it has been great to work with editor Vivian Dudro again. The writings of George Weigel, Distinguished Senior Fellow of the Ethics and Public Policy Center and a close friend of George Pell's, are always compelling, and I thank him most sincerely for his brilliant foreword. He knew the cardinal well, for many years, and brought an important global perspective to the book. Thank you, too, Teresa DeMaria, for your generous support of the project.

Dozens of men and women in Australia, England, and Rome shared their insights for the original version of this biography in 2001 and 2002. Some of them, including Margaret Pell, Monsignor Gerry Diamond, and Oxford priest Edward Yarnold, S.J., have since gone to God, but the information and memories they provided were invaluable. Likewise, this time, was the help of Cardinal Raymond Burke, Archbishop Anthony Fisher, and Bishop Peter Elliott. Also very helpful were Fathers Frank Brennan, S.J.; Joseph Hamilton, who is now the rector of Domus Australia; Robert McCulloch, S.S.C.; Shawn Murphy, I.B.P.; Terence Naughton, Don Richardson, Anthony Robbie, Alexander Sherbrooke, Glen Tattersall, John Walshe, and Mark Withoos. I am especially grateful to Monsignor Charles Portelli, one of George Pell's closest confidants, for suggesting that the title be based on the war memorial with the inscription *Pax Invictis*, which Pell used to admire outside Saint Peter's Anglican Church, Eastern Hill, when they would walk near Saint Patrick's Cathedral in Melbourne. He also told me about George Pell's unforgettable visit to Cardinal Aloysius Stepinac's home in Croatia, his fondness for Magnum ice creams and much else. The Cardinal could have had no better friend, and he realised it. Thank you also to Victoria's Catholic prison chaplain Sister Mary O'Shannassy, S.G.S., photographers Bob and Peter Armstrong, Danny Casey, Michael Casey, Anthony Cleary, Mathew De Sousa, Katrina Lee, John McCarthy, KC, Tim and Anne McFarlane, Marcus Middleton, Libero Milone, David Pell and his family, Robert Richter, KC, Professor Tracey Rowland, Bernadette and Terry Tobin, KC, Kieran Walton, Dan White, and especially, a certain deep throat in Rome who prefers anonymity but whose abacus was highly useful to Cardinal Pell in detecting all manner of financial chicanery. If this deep throat ever pens a memoir, it will top the *New York Times* bestseller list.

I also thank Fathers Peter Joseph in Sydney and John Gillen, S.M., in Brisbane for their meticulous proofreading and excellent suggestions.

Sky News host Andrew Bolt's programs and Herald Sun articles were definitive in establishing George Pell's innocence while he was alive and stand as a testament to intelligent, independent-minded journalism. Father Frank Brennan's analyses of the cardinal's trials and tribulations and the Royal Commission into Institutional Responses to Child Sexual Abuse, gathered in his book *Observations on the Pell Proceedings* (Connor Court), are a must-read for anyone interested in the details of that shocking saga and who values the rule of law, the presumption of innocence, and a fair trial. The is true, also, of Gerard Henderson's meticulous, informative *Cardinal Pell, The Media Pile-on & Collective Guilt* and Keith Windschuttle's *The Persecution of George Pell.*

Personal bias aside (I work for *The Australian* and love it), the newspaper's coverage of George Pell's controversies, trials, appeals, exoneration by the High Court, and finally his death led the rest of the Australian media by light years. It was interesting, while researching, to discover how much the paper is followed online in Rome and around the world. Articles by Paul Kelly, Professor Greg Craven, Father Brennan, John Ferguson, Chris Merritt, Angela Shanahan, Dennis Shanahan, Paola Totaro, Henry Ergas, and others informed readers in a fair and balanced way about the complexities of the cardinal's legal case and his battles against financial corruption in the Vatican. The consistent quality of that coverage owes much to the professional leadership and bravery of editor-in-chief Michelle Gunn, editor Kelvin Healey, and deputy editors Petra Rees and Georgina Windsor. I thank them and the colleagues I work with every day in producing the paper's editorials for their support and for doing so much to make the newspaper a compelling read. After only being able to afford it a couple of days a week in jail, reading "the Aus" cover-to-cover, every day, was one of George Pell's enjoyments after his release. Had he not been a priest, he once told me, he would have enjoyed writing for a living in "a corner of the Aus", something he occasionally did as an archbishop and cardinal, and always enjoyed it.

Tess Livingstone
Assumption of Our Lady
August 15, 2024

APPENDIX 1

Campion College in Australia—
Pearl in an Eroding Landscape

Cardinal Pell's last major speech in Australia was for the Campion College Fundraising Dinner at the New South Wales Parliament in Sydney, August 17, 2022. Since Pell was a strong supporter of Campion from its inception, it is likely that a fair share of his vast library of theology, philosophy, history, and literature will be placed in the Gina Rinehart Library at Campion, where the books that had belonged to his good friend Father Paul Stenhouse, M.S.C., were installed in August 2023. Since Pell's death, the generosity of an anonymous benefactor has already seen a scholarship established in his name at Campion.

> The time is out of joint; O cursed spite
> That ever I was born to set it right.
> (*Hamlet*, Act 1, Scene 5)

I was born and then educated in the olden days of the nineteen forties–fifties, when La Niña was also operating, and the Ballarat of my youth was regularly wet and cold. We had no central heating.

It was a primitive time with Bob Menzies as prime minister sustained by Democratic Labor Party second preferences. A government was in peril if unemployment rose beyond 3 percent. Some of the cognoscenti, like Patrick White and Sidney Nolan, fled to London, then Dame Edna escaped from Moonee Ponds, but most Aussies enjoyed their good fortune and refused to acknowledge their lack of sophistication or feel inferior, to the dismay of their betters. I suspect this was one cause of D. H. Lawrence's earlier exasperation with Australia. I was educated at Saint Pat's in Ballarat, run by the Christian Brothers, to whom my generation and earlier generations are eternally grateful; or should be! The Brothers and the nuns worked for pocket money as no government funding was available for nongovernment schools. Without their sacrifices, many young Catholics between 1870 and 1970 would not have received a Catholic education.

It was a primitive time. Men only married women. Husband and wife usually stayed together and during those times when marital bliss evaporated. Most did not live together before marriage and many went regularly to Church. Probably more than half of the Catholics were at Sunday Mass. During the Second World War, a group called the Communists dominated many Australian unions, damaging the war effort considerably until Hitler invaded his Communist ally Russia. A group of Australian patriots, including many Catholics, threw the Communist union leaders out. This was a good thing.

It was a primitive age as multiculturalism had not been invented and the Greek and Italian migrants had to assimilate. The "wogs" and "wops" were expected to know their place, but even in primitive times there were turn-ups, the unexpected. The most powerful group of Catholic activists was led by a Melbourne man, an Italian-Australian, and almost all his foot soldiers were Irish-Australians. It worked well, although one or two conceded in a whisper that a name like "Santamaria" was not ideal in every circumstance.

Saint Pat's was not an academic school as few of the Brothers, our only teachers, had university degrees. Our school was renowned for producing Aussie Rules footballers and priests, over three hundred in fact since 1893, more than any other Australian school. When I was welcomed back as a new bishop in 1987, the headmaster explained to the boys in the cathedral that the college was renowned for producing two Brownlow Medal winners (the best and fairest player in the Victoria Football League) and two bishops. The achievements were mentioned in that order.

It was a primitive age. I, and a large cohort of my class (we had ninety boys under one teacher in year seven), studied Latin and French each year from year seven, and we had external written government exams for years ten to twelve. The results of such examinations were, of course, irrefutable evidence of achievement for those in less reputable high schools and Catholic schools.

We also studied a play of Shakespeare each year from year nine, starting with *Julius Caesar*, wrestling with the antique language, probably not understanding too much of the drama and variety of human experience presented to us, but being regularly exposed to the greatest writing in our language. My cohort also studied Chaucer and Milton, Browning and the Romantic poets, Emily Bronte, Hemingway, etc.

It was a primitive age. We had no television until 1956, the year of the Melbourne Olympics; there were no drugs available to students in Ballarat, but plenty of alcohol; no internet pornography, although *Man* magazine could be purchased from below the counter; no mobile phones, no computers, no internet.

The Second Vatican Council had not taken place. The Irish-born Dr. Daniel Mannix, a great tribal leader, was still archbishop of Melbourne, before dying at the age of ninety-nine in 1963. He provided reassurance to his followers, whom he encouraged into the middle class, a probably unmatched example of social mobility, and he did not disturb the Protestant majority as much in his later years as he did, e.g., in the great First World War debates on conscription. Vocations to the priesthood and religious life were plentiful (there were approximately two hundred seminarians for the diocesan priesthood of Victoria and Tasmania when I entered Corpus Christi seminary in 1960), while the Catholic community was clear-headed, confident, and narrow-minded.

Protestant churchgoing rates were not as high as ours (we took consolation in this), but the Protestant schools (known as Public Schools) were still imparting a Christian moral framework to their students for public life and indeed family life. It was the invention of the contraceptive pill and the consequent sexual revolution of the 1960s spread by, e.g., the music of the Beatles and the Rolling Stones, which upended this.

As a grumpy old male, entering into his ninth decade of life, and emerging from the ancient provincial setting I have described, some would claim that it is not surprising that I would echo the words of Hamlet, the prince of Denmark, that "the time is out of joint."

At this stage, to bolster my disreputable credentials and explain the disadvantages of my early environment, I cannot refrain from pointing out that Kentucky Fried Chicken opened their first Australian outlet in Ballarat in the 1970s, I think, working from the premise that if they could be successful in Ballarat, the most conservative city in

Australia in their estimate, they could sell their chicken anywhere in the nation. Are my origins, in the ancient provincial mists, sufficient to explain away my suspicion, with Hamlet, that "something is rotten in the state"? Am I blinded by sentimental nostalgia for a simpler, vanished past? After all, I was born during the Second World War, and now we have no World War, only the naked Russian aggression in distant Ukraine and clumsy, but disturbing Chinese belligerence as it attempts to reestablish the Middle Kingdom as the world's number one power. A possible Chinese naval base in the Solomon Islands is still some distance away.

I don't think Australian life is rotten at the core, but times are changing, and not always for the better. The inevitable royal commission of the future into Victoria could find a situation parallel to that of Joh Bjelke-Petersen's Queensland in the 1970s and 80s,[1] and too many Australians were content with the overreaction of bossy nanny states during the COVID crisis, when the churches were closed before the casino (at least in Victoria). Many in the Catholic leadership were too docile.

But hundreds of thousands of immigrants want to come to Australia each year (there are not too many clamouring to migrate into China). Before COVID Australia had four of the world's top ten liveable cities, and returning from Rome and travelling around Sydney's suburbs I marvel at the prosperity, the fine homes, continuing mile after mile.

Campion has been born, and the two Catholic universities provide something of a bulwark against the worst. But the times are changing, and many are uneasy, especially the social conservatives, regularly assailed by the woke activists even in sport (as we saw in the controversy over Folau and in the bravery of the Manly Seven).[2] Some leaders in big business have buckled or enthusiastically embraced

[1] Joh Bjelke-Petersen became the National Party premier of Queensland in 1968. Under his leadership, his party won enough votes in the 1983 election that he was able to form a one-party state government. But conflicts within his party led to his resignation in 1988. On September 23, 1991, he stood trial for corruption and perjury. The case ended in a hung jury.

[2] Israel Folau is a professional rugby player whose contract with Rugby Australia was terminated in 2019 after he tweeted statements against homosexuality with quotes from the Bible. The Manly Seven refers to seven members of the Australian Manly Warringah Sea Eagles rugby team who boycotted a 2022 game that required players to wear "pride" jerseys with a rainbow design.

anti-Christian measures. Corrs, the lawyers,[3] recently dumped the Melbourne Archdiocese as a client, without consultation and after being retained for more than sixty years.

It was under a Federal Liberal government that official forms replaced the term "mother" and "father" with "birth persons". I had spoken with a succession of the Labor leaders about the importance of maintaining a situation where pro-life and pro-family candidates could still be endorsed (unlike the Democrats in the USA), but I have been surprised by the exuberance of so many woke activists in the coalition parties. I did not anticipate such a rapid collapse. The presence of Dutton and Taylor[4] offers hope, unless they are heavily outnumbered, but I am tempted to claim that the only conservative blow struck by the last federal government was to reduce substantially the numbers of students doing poisonous arts courses, although they did protect the maths curriculum against the woke nonsense.

The Catholic vote is fractured, but a good number could be mustered to defend Catholic schools. However, the significant grouping for the future is the gospel Christians in all the Christian churches, especially the Catholics. Many, but not all of these, are migrants, and there are significant groupings in some places, e.g., Western Sydney.

In my youth I remember Archbishop Mannix explaining that in democracies, unlike the autocracies of the past, Christians can defend themselves through their votes. Our opponents are hoping that Catholics will keep silent in the public square after the shame of paedophilia. Such a Christian silence on the moral issues of the day would be a serious dereliction of duty, following one massive failure with another, an abuse of the abuse. However, it is not sufficient to speak, as people need to listen, and I suppose the anti-Christian forces on both sides of politics will only be tamed when they are shown Christians have votes, which they will sometimes use.

Population has drained from the countryside, union membership has fallen, and parliaments are dominated by a tertiary-educated meritocracy, increasingly secular, where the two major parties do not differ too much, at least on noneconomic measures. This is the context for the taming of the social conservatives, exemplified in the

[3] Corrs Chambers Westgarth is a leading law firm in Australia.
[4] Peter Dutton and Angus Taylor are Australian politicians who belong to the Liberal Party.

New South Wales Parliament, where the main parties are led by two good men—believing, practising Catholics—and produced the most draconian euthanasia legislation in Australia.

Despite all this, I am not an ecclesiastical Tim Flannery predicting religious collapse, complete disaster in the next decade or so. Nor do I think much of Flannery's insights into climate.[5] This bizarre conviction that we can change the earth's climate patterns is one piece of evidence that the times are out of joint. It is a billion-dollar, perhaps a one-trillion-dollar juggernaut, probably heading in the wrong direction.

Tim seems to have been a bit down in 2004. Australia was for him particularly vulnerable: "We are going to experience conditions not seen for 40 million years."[6] And he also thought, "There is a fair chance Perth will be the 21st century's first ghost metropolis."[7] In 2006, the threat of rising sea levels joined the dangers of drought. In an article entitled "Climate's Last Chance", he exhorted us to "picture an eight-storey building by the beach, then imagine waves lapping its roof".[8] Two thousand and seven was a mixed year, because while he felt Australia was in a "one-in-1,000-year drought" and that Brisbane and Adelaide could run out of water by year's end,[9] he was optimistic about the embedded energy in South Australia's hot rocks. The Rudd Labor government invested AU$90 million of taxpayers' money in this Cooper Basin geothermal project. Surprise, surprise, the project failed, was abandoned; and money was lost; a smaller sum, however, than the Vatican lost on the Sloane Avenue, London, purchase (that was €150 million). Something is not right, is off-key, when a man with Flannery's views can be published and published regularly in reputable journals. We joined Alice in Wonderland when Tim was declared Australian of the Year.

In the post-Christian vacuum which is developing, the esteem for freedom, the linchpin of the Liberalism project, from which society and the Church have received substantial benefits, is also under sustained assault. The renamed climate change movement against carbon

---

[5] Tim Flannery is an Australian scientist, activist, and writer, whose work on environmental issues earned him the 2007 Australian of the Year award.

[6] Ian Plimer, *Green Murder* (Brisbane: Connor Court Publishing, 2021) p. 190.

[7] Ibid., p, 189.

[8] Ibid., p. 191.

[9] Ibid., p. 192.

dioxide (which not only enhances the growth of vegetation, but is essential for it) has many of the characteristics of a low-level, not too demanding, pseudo-religion. When religious belief is lost or deconstructed, the survivors like to embrace some grand narrative and seem to need something to fear. Almost unconsciously they seek to appease the higher powers (of nature, in this case) with the sacrificial offering of fossil fuels, of coal and oil. Unfortunately for them, most modern economics will continue to need coal and oil. Democratic majorities in Australia and throughout the First World will not consent to regular electrical blackouts, power failures at the height of summer or winter. And of course our foes and allies in the Third World need coal and oil for their industrial and modernising programmes, just as we did in the past and continue to do so.

They are sensible and clearheaded on this point and would be bemused by Western virtue signalling. In 2021, 1,893 new coal-fired power stations were being constructed around the world: 446 in India, 1,171 in China, and none in virtuous Australia, which also abstains from developing nuclear power stations.[10] Australia has resources of coal and uranium, apparently sufficient for thousands of years, and I am sure these will be developed and exploited to the benefit of our descendants for many generations when our aberrant enthusiasms have lapsed.

There is no one obligatory Catholic position on climate change, because we are a religion, teaching faith and morals, and do not impose any scientific straitjacket. Every person has a right to be foolish, if he thinks it wise (this is also true of myself). The climate challenge is not one of my major concerns, although I enjoy introducing a few facts into the hysteria, e.g., no computer programme has accurately predicted future weather patterns and some historical facts about the warming periods around the time of Christ's birth and the Medieval warming from 900 to 1300, when Australia suffered from some terrible droughts. The worst lasted for thirty-nine years between A.D. 1174 and 1212, and a later mega drought lasted for twenty-three years between 1500 and 1522.[11] My major concerns are elsewhere: with the Catholic Church and the rise of a belligerent China.

[10] Ibid., p. 46.
[11] Ibid., pp. 286–88.

The 2021 census in Australia showed a spectacular rise in the number of those who declared that they subscribe to no religion, now numbering 38.9 percent; an equally spectacular drop in the numbers of the Uniting and Anglican churches, with losses of 22 percent and 20 percent respectively and the substantial, unprecedented decline by 4 percent of Catholic Church membership in five years. All this slippage followed significant Christian losses in the previous five years.

A point to be pondered is that the Catholic decline was so much lower than the Protestant percentages, although Catholics bore the brunt of the hostility from the media and the activities of the royal commission on institutional paedophilia.

All of those who love Christ and the Church are dismayed by these losses, but differ, sometimes acrimoniously, on how they should be addressed. We have a clear division between those who believe that we are the servants and defenders of the apostolic tradition, with no power to change substantially the doctrines that come to us from Christ and the apostles through Scripture and the Catholic magisterium. Opposed to them is an older cohort, generally a little bit younger than myself, who give the last word to modernity, who believe we are masters of the apostolic tradition and can amend it, e.g., to bless homosexual unions and to create women priests. Some also reject the basic Christian teachings on sexuality.

The recent plenary council has come and gone and was largely irrelevant to the preaching of the gospel and the threat of decline, being more concerned with the redistribution of power.[12] Australia's finest theologian [Tracey Rowland], a woman who happens to be orthodox (a position now regarded as conservative), was not invited to be a delegate. The nation's leading Catholic academic and an outstanding public intellectual [Greg Craven] (he was vice-chancellor at ACU [Australian Catholic University]), was barred from writing any council documents. There were no young priests, who are in fact one of the hopes for the future with their zeal, their theological discrimination, and intellectual firepower, and of course few [Roman Catholic] ethnic parishioners.

Council members requested that the priesthood, family, and education be discussed; to no avail, and naturally there wasn't a squeak

---

[12] The Fifth Plenary Council of the Catholic Church in Australia, which ended in July 2022.

on the approaching threats to religious freedoms in our schools, hospitals, and retirement homes. A goodly percentage of the council's pacemakers (fixers?) were self-absorbed, not interested in missionary expansion, isolated from the real world, from the clash between good and evil, faith and darkness. One can see how the Church disintegrated in Belgium, Holland, and Quebec. Jesus got a few mentions, more than Jesus Christ, and faith was hardly mentioned at all, much less evangelisation or the unborn.

The council seemed unaware of the causes for the revolution in manners and morals, which has also built up in Australia, exemplified in the brutal incivility and power plays of the social media, and the spread of pornography into every section of society, male and female. The tribal power politics of the advancing "cancel culture" is threatening to overthrow the foundations of liberalism, which has allowed the churches to survive in Australia even as the Judaeo-Christian legal foundations on life, marriage, family, and sexuality were undermined.

In the new politics of gender and race, white males, and especially old white males, represent the worst of the past, of the detested racism, colonialism, sexism and patriarchy, etc. To quote Paul Kelly (whom I have found regularly helpful in trying to understand what is happening in our wider society because of the decline in Christianity), these forces are bitterly opposed, not just to Christian civilization, but to the foundations of our traditional Western consensus "that all people, regardless of race, religion, sex, or gender, are equal before the law and share a common dignity".[13] The issues in dispute could scarcely be more basic. Reason, freedom, truth, risk banishment, while notions of Divine Law, immutable natural law have a quaint antiquated ring about them and are seen as expressions of a failed mythology.

Some writers, e.g., Larry Siedentop in *Inventing the Individual: The Origins of Western Liberalism* recognise liberalism's debts to Christianity (Harvard University Press, 2014). Most do not. My suspicion is that the links are even more profound, and any Western society which is based on the premise of equality before the law for all people and ascribes a common dignity to each and every person, citizen

---

[13] Paul Kelly, "Contemporary Liberalism: The Source of the Crisis", *Conversazione*, March 3, 2022.

or foreigner, productive or dependent, young and healthy or old and dependent—such a society can only continue when sustained by Christian ideals of universal love, often expressed as human rights, derived from a Creator God. One does not need to be a Christian for this, as a post-Christian instinct or sympathy can suffice, but this too is declining, savagely dismissed in our universities.

The brutal forces driving evolution, the law of the jungle, the economic and intellectual inequalities among humans, the differences between the strong and the weak, the sick and the healthy, all fly in the face of any claims of universal human dignity. Already a significant section explicitly endorses tribalism, revenge, raw power, and domination rather than any movement to consensus. In a hostile post-Christian Australia, sustaining the liberalism ideal might be as difficult as planting democracy in Iraq or Afghanistan. I do not believe that the battle is over, that the field has been lost. Recently a senior public figure told me that the only option now for Christians in Australia is to head for the catacombs and that the rot could only be stopped by a few martyrdoms. I hope and believe that this is a misreading of the situation, excessively pessimistic. But the situation is on the turn, and mighty tides are running against many, but not all, Christian teachings. Most Australians still believe "everyone has a right to a fair go." Just as certainly if the situation is not to worsen, not only Christians but all those who value our Western way of life need to "have a go", which is the second bedrock of the Australian consensus, the common sense of our ancestors which gave us our decency and prosperity.

Before I begin to commend what Campion is doing and try to relate it to the societal changes I am describing, we must turn our attention briefly to a recently perceived danger, a game changer in every respect: the belligerence and hostility towards Australia of China on the rise, rich and powerful.

War is a real possibility in the next decade, more probably over Taiwan, but not necessarily. Jim Molan's recent book *Danger on Our Doorstep* (Harper Collins, 2022), even when taken with a stiff pinch of salt, warns against a second Pearl Harbour and provides little comfort. I strongly recommend you read it.

One of the few vitally important tasks of the Albanese government is to increase our capacity to defend ourselves, inflict damage on any aggressor in the short term, and for the next twenty or forty years. We hope and work for peace, but if the worst was to happen, or even big trouble occurred, largely fought out to the north, present high levels of rhetoric would then be of absolutely no use. Deeds are needed, not words. China regards us as a weak link in the American alliance, because of our trade dependency with them and because of our military weakness. A power vacuum and an unprotected and frivolous society are temptations for dictators especially if they are wanting to distract their citizens from local problems such as poverty and inequality, oppression and discontent, 35 or 40 million surplus males and the prospect of over 200 million fewer people in the workforce in 2050.

China will refocus the Australian national conversation, however the situation develops, and I am not just talking about increased taxes for defence spending or the introduction of national service. Australia might be forced to decide whether we love our nation sufficiently to be prepared to defend it; whether we believe in freedom and democracy enough to resist a powerful dictator. Almost inevitably Australia will be forced to draw on the strengths of her Western civilisation in the centuries of dialogue or struggle, which will accompany the rebirth of the Middle Kingdom, a once mighty civilization, as old as Greece and older than the Roman Empire; but very different from our way of life, and presently very oppressive towards her citizens.

Another significant factor is that Christianity, mainly Protestantism, is spreading in China as it spread in the hostile pagan Roman Empire. Already China probably has 60 to 90 million Christians and is one of the largest Christian countries in the world. It is a reasonable proposition that the Australians of the future, on at least some occasions, will have more to interest them than the "State of Origin" matches and the Melbourne Cup. But in any event, Australia will need clearheaded, capable patriots. Where and how does Campion fit?

Campion College is a very small community of students and teachers and, in some senses, needs to be small to enhance the question and answer, objection and response, the dialogue, which is at the heart of all genuine tertiary education, especially in the humanities.

Campion is not practical, as its main B.A. course does not provide any specific professional preparation or qualification.

Campion College is not contemporary, as it is ahead of its time, although it is a bright example of political incorrectness. It is dedicated to the study of Western civilization, that magnificent flowering from the fusion of the ancient traditions of Jerusalem, Athens, and Rome that produced Constantinian Christendom, which lasted until the Reformation, the Reformation itself, the Renaissance, the Enlightenment, and the Scientific Revolution. New nations were set up by the Europeans: the Spaniards and Portuguese and then the French and English in America, Australia, and New Zealand, and colonial rule was established in Africa and parts of Asia. This came at a price, sometimes at huge moral cost. But there were also gains in education, health, law, transport, the spread of democracy to balance out the dark side of the French Revolution, Nazism and Communism, and Colonialism. The century of humiliation suffered by the Chinese is deeply felt there and fuels their assertiveness, but Hong Kong, until its recent takeover, with Singapore are remarkable human achievements.

Campion studies history through Christian spectacles—evaluating the right and wrong, the good and evil—rejects any notion of a whitewash, and works to diminish prejudice. But it inculcates a love for and pride in our tradition, just as we love our families while recognising their failures.

Their liberal arts programme aims to impart to the students "an integrated understanding of the events, ideas, movements, personalities and works which have shaped the development of Western Culture, in the four key disciplines of history, literature, philosophy and theology. Optional units are also offered in science, mathematics, Latin and Ancient Greek."

In other words, students are introduced to the wisdom of the ages through our tradition, the Western tradition. They learn of the central virtues, about faith and reason, about the search for meaning. They learn to analyse and synthesize, to say what they mean and mean what they say, to write and think logically and clearly, and to have practical wisdom, something worthwhile to say on the basic human issues beyond whatever profession they might choose to follow.

This is an ideal personal base for any professional career and for that unmentionable role, which is vital to society, of wife and mother, the nurturing of children. It can even help the despised males of our species to be good fathers—and husbands.

Because this education is good for individuals, it follows that it is good for society. Much of what Campion College now strives to do was done 100 or even 50 years ago for the elite and the battlers by family, school, church, university, and even much of the media. No longer.

One can describe what society needs in a variety of ways, e.g., tradition, ritual, and cult; confident, modest people not fearful and therefore not tempted to authoritarianism. One could say that society needs religious faith, a respect for order and hierarchy, patriotism, an awareness of original sin—the flaw that runs through every human heart and community—and an equal awareness that the human capacity for improvement is limited; progress is difficult, because success is not guaranteed by good intentions. Every society to avoid going backwards needs social conservatives from across the spectrum to transmit to the young what is worthwhile from the past. Our society is already suffering from a slowly spreading domestic chaos, damaged families, fragile children, alcohol, drugs, porn. Children need adults who will bring stability, set down boundaries so that love and respect can flourish and where the concepts of duty, honour, and compassion are exemplified.

Youngsters need to be shown that there are moral truths, of right and wrong, which we do not invent, just as there are truths of maths, physics, ecology, and public health. Society needs to understand that behind evolution is the Creator God, who is not only rational, stupendously intelligent, but good, kind, and interested in us. Our society needs to remember that we believe in free speech because we believe in truth; that things can be known as they are, however imperfectly. If there is no truth, there is no endpoint in debate or discussion. The more powerful tribe simply decides and imposes its solution by force. The knowledge of God's final judgement, that each person will be obliged to answer for his life's work, that there is a heaven and hell—all this knowledge is stabilizing for society, and it is a consolation to the victims of history to know that the scales of justice will balance out in eternity.

Campion College is not alone in this struggle, which is carried forward by many agents, millions even in Australia; most of them working quietly, unseen. The Ramsay Centre's contribution is especially valuable, and all the forces of righteousness should strive to co-operate, whatever the problems in the past.

The culture wars continue, and while our losses are considerable, the field has not been lost. The many victims of the chaos will be increasingly open to our message and appreciative of your help. Campion has joined the fray and is contributing steadily. It is a pearl in the desert. I congratulate the college's founders for their vision and perseverance as I commend the work of Dr Paul Morrissey and his staff and students. They all deserve our support, and I am sure that you, the Campion family, will continue to provide it.

APPENDIX 2

The Suffering Church in a Suffering World

This address to the Newman Society at the Oxford University Chaplaincy on October 29, 2021, was originally entitled "The Suffering Church in a Post-Christian World". Reluctant to endorse the notion of a post-Christian world, Cardinal Pell changed the title after he arrived in Britain.

In 1868, Matthew Arnold wrote the beautiful poem "Dover Beach" dedicated to two themes, the first of which is the decline of faith.

> The Sea of Faith
> Was once, too, at the full, and round earth's shore
> Lay like the folds of a bright girdle furled.
> But now I only hear
> Its melancholy, long, withdrawing roar,
> Retreating, to the breath
> Of the night-wind, down the vast edges drear
> And naked shingles of the world.

And then he turns, with prophetic insight, to the consequences of this departure:

> For the world, which seems
> To lie before us like a land of dreams,
> So various, so beautiful, so new,
> Hath really neither joy, nor love, nor light,
> Nor certitude, nor peace, nor help for pain;
> And we are here as on a darkling plain
> Swept with confused alarms of struggle and flight,
> Where ignorant armies clash by night.

What might a Catholic say about each of these themes? The world has changed mightily since 1868. The British and French Empires

499

are gone, the United States is the only superpower, to be joined by a resurgent and aggressive Middle Kingdom, the Republic of China. The two major forces hostile to Christianity, and faith of any sort, Communism and Nazism, have both been defeated in Europe and the former Soviet world.

Living standards, health and education, travel, longevity, and literacy have improved dramatically. We have nuclear bombs and nuclear power. The centre of the world is now found in the Pacific Ocean, not the Atlantic. How has faith coped?

Before describing and analyzing some aspects of faith, speaking as a Catholic leader, I would like to stake my claim, set out our basic position in this ancient, now secular, university, founded from even older monasteries, often by bishops and Catholic princes. We Catholics are here to stay; in England, in my country of Australia, and on every continent.

Popes come and go, with different gifts and strengths, but the papacy is still in Rome, the ancient capital of the empire, home of the successor of Peter and bishop of that eternal city. The roar that you hear is not the melancholy sound of a once mighty kingdom departing into oblivion. It is the roar of the Lion of Judah, embattled in many parts, humiliated and often reduced in the Western world, but absolutely devoted to its precious tradition, received from Christ and the apostles and deeply convinced of the life-giving power of this inheritance in even the most poisonous environments. The gospel Protestants, the Evangelicals will be with us in these mighty battles. We are here to stay and to struggle. We are not going away.

I was born during the Second World War on the other side of the world and grew up with those stories of heroism and suffering. As a churchman, I have sometimes wondered how appropriate it is to use war stories for gospel purposes because Jesus, unlike Mahomet, was not a warrior and soldier. But I have continued to do so; once in a while.

A favourite story I have used a few times with university students is an incident from the military career of Field Marshal Bernard Montgomery, the United Kingdom's finest soldier from the Second World War, a great man but an unusual personality by any standards.

In 1942, the Allies, including some Australian troops, had been pushed eastward across the top of North Africa by Rommel in a succession of defeats. When Montgomery was appointed, he discovered that plans had been drawn up to retreat further south towards the source of the Nile. After a short interval, he called together his headquarters staff, burnt publicly all the plans for withdrawal, and announced that they would take their stand where they were and fight there, when they were prepared and ready.

I think my listeners understood the general point I was making, but just to avoid misunderstanding, I want to make clear that our situation will be worsened, numerically as well as religiously, if we abandon our unseemly Christian claims to the importance of worship, prayer, and forgiveness; to the healing power of redemptive suffering; to the stark life-giving truths of Christian teaching on abortion and euthanasia; on sexuality, on monogamous, heterosexual marriage, on heteronormativity, on the importance of children.

On many occasions, I have urged believers to reject all claims to the primacy of conscience (only truth has primacy because while the right of each individual's conscience is important, even sacred, they are often in conflict) and to avoid the excess of inculturation, where, as in some parts of Japan, this doctrine has been used to prohibit the preaching of the gospel as something foreign and to be avoided. We stand and struggle under the rule of faith. I will return to this theme, to the elements of godliness today, later in this paper.

My second initial point is to spell out some basic perspectives on modernity, and I believe those of us in the Anglosphere must acknowledge a new development in Catholic history because most of the best commentators on faith and modern life are now writing in English. One might rightly claim that this simply continues the tradition established by our own Saint John Henry Newman, continued by Chesterton and Belloc, C. S. Lewis, and the Oxford chaplain Monsignor Ronald Knox. Tolkien's marvellous contribution stands in parallel to this, but today we are blessed with writers whose contributions are essential to identifying where the Catholic community is in the marshes and whirlpools of our often frantic prosperity. The Anglophone ascendency is also explained by the fact that the theological giants from continental Europe at the time of the Council, e.g., Congar, Rahner, von Balthasar, de Lubac, Danielou, Schillebeeckx are no longer with us and have not been replaced. We have George Weigel from the United States, Father Raymond de Souza from Canada, Ross Douthat at the *New York Times*, Rod Dreher with his Benedict option, Damian Thompson here in the U.K., Greg Sheridan from Australia, who is writing well on religion today, and perhaps most perceptively of them all, Mary Eberstadt, also from the United States.

This short paper is indebted to her teaching. I recommend particularly her marvellously titled book *Adam and Eve after the Pill*, which sets out to explain how the invention of the contraceptive pill has produced a revolution in daily life with consequences as important as those which followed the Marxist-Leninist triumph in the Russian Revolution in 1917. This is a large and controversial claim which outlines the challenges we confront.

I wish to recommend an address Eberstadt gave to the Catholic Social Scientists on September 18 of this year, entitled "The Cross amid the Crisis", and I would like to begin by highlighting an insight she used from an interview Evelyn Waugh gave to a newspaper in 1930, giving reasons for his conversion to Catholicism. He said, "In the present phase of European history, the essential issue is no longer between Catholicism, on one side, and Protestantism, on the other, but between Christianity and chaos."

I had long realised, as do nearly all the Protestants, that the issue is no longer between the English and the Irish in the Anglosphere, between the Proddies and the Micks. Indeed, the gospel Protestants will be indispensable allies in the Christian survival and revival when it comes, as is the case in the pro-life battles in the U.S.A. Neither do I anticipate that the millions of Muslims in Western Europe will be a major factor in the immediate future of our religious struggles, although Michel Houellebecq's novel *Submission* on the first Islamic president of France might be more prescient than myself. I guess that the secular capitalists who needed a labour force had presumed that they could paganize these Muslim immigrants in a generation or so and benefit from their anti-Christianity on the way. Indeed, the movement in the successive generations has been in the opposite direction with the development of a widespread radicalism and of a small core of violent terrorists who also work to intimidate majority Muslim opinion, which is for moderation. I have long described the confrontation as being between the Judeo-Christians and the secularists. I was well aware of organized and financed secular campaigns, generally using the media in a sophisticated fashion, often highlighting the particular sufferings attendant on the hard cases that make bad laws as they systematically demolished the Christian legal foundations on issues such as divorce, abortion, heterosexual marriage, and now euthanasia and gender. Only in the United States has there been significant progress with public opinion on the pro-life cause, by highlighting the realities of eliminating the unborn human babies.

We should not underestimate the long-term significance of the present U.S. Supreme Court, which has already begun returning abortion decisions to the individual states, where they will legislate as their citizens vote.

What struck me was Waugh seeing chaos as the alternative in 1930 and Eberstadt adopting this term to describe our situations today.

I have come to admire more and more Evelyn Waugh's insight into the hearts of so many different persons. Perhaps ten years ago, I was asked by the library at Sydney University to give a paper on Constantine, the first Christian emperor in the Roman Empire. He is one of my heroes because I believe we should continue to work and to harness whatever sociological forces we can to help carry the semi-religious, like myself, in the right direction. At this stage, I am not a supporter of the Benedict option for the wider Catholic community, of a flight to small isolated monastic-type communities of families, much less of a pre-monastic web of tiny family cells as the predominant Christian presence. Here or there, in different countries, the Catholic community might be so reduced eventually, but here and now, we should continue to support political and legal initiatives to maintain our religious freedoms, widely understood. In my view, Constantine did a lot of good work for the Kingdom of God through granting religious toleration, favouring Christianity through some tax reforms and the building of churches such as Saints John Lateran and Peter in Rome, through the public recognition of priests and especially bishops, and cautious legal enactments such as prohibiting fights to the death in the games and the branding of slaves on the face.

From his time onwards, for at least fifteen hundred years, he changed the direction of the social currents for the better. I much prefer the religiously indifferent to be lapsing into Christianity than to be lapsing into neo-paganism as 30 percent of the Australian population has done growing from a base of 12.7 percent in 1986. To my mind, Constantine is no saint, although he is canonised by the Eastern Christians and saw himself as the thirteenth apostle, but he did much good.

And now to return to Waugh: I had read all the primary sources on Constantine and felt I had a good grasp of the basic situation, when I decided to read Waugh's historical novel on the life of Helena, Constantine's mother, venerated as the finder of the True Cross. The story was full of the most wonderful and plausible insights into all the major players.

Earlier this year, I was asked to give a paper on Gibbon's *Decline and Fall of the Roman Empire*, describing the triumph of barbarism and religion, and decided to discover what Waugh and Newman had to say on this genius Gibbon, with his unremitting hostility towards Christianity. Waugh did not let me down, writing of "a false historian, with the mind of Cicero or Tacitus and the soul of an animal".[14] For Waugh, Gibbon's style ensured that his version remained in people's minds, like "the Egyptian secret of the embalmers".

Despite my reverence for Waugh's judgement, I was initially sceptical that the word "chaos" best fitted today's neo-paganism. I was well aware of the sophistication of our opponents, and I mentioned my hesitation when I met Eberstadt in Rome one month ago. Mary first replied that the phrase was Waugh's but then went on to explain why the term is accurate. She acknowledged that the chaos Waugh rejected in the 1930s was different from ours, residing in "war, dislocation, and stupendous courage". However, many social pillars were still firm including the battered institution of the family, but outside of Nazism (soon to be defeated at enormous cost) and the longer continuing Communism, she saw that "a Christian understanding of creation and redemption and meaning still prevailed in the West." Under Pius XI in the 1930s and indeed Pius XII, Catholic teachings remained "coherent and consistent", the main reason for Waugh's conversion, although chaos had started its work in the Protestant churches.

Eberstadt adopts the term "chaos" for our situation, recognising that we are "ninety light years" removed from 1930. She gives a checklist of six factors. The first of these is compounding family chaos, dating back decades, which has weakened the family "on a

[14] Evelyn Waugh, *Helena* (1950).

scale never seen before" through low marriage rates, breakups, abortions, and absentee fathers.

There is compounding psychic chaos, exemplified in the extensively documented rise in mental illness, anxiety, depression, disconnection, and loneliness. She might have mentioned the curse of youth suicide, where prosperous, decent Australia has one of the highest rates in the world.

She then mentions political chaos, the dissolution of clan and community, although I see this as a less virulent example than the others. Democracy still prevails in Australia, Britain, and the United States, despite the cancel culture and the removed or damaged statues.

The anthropological and intellectual chaos she describes are obviously related. For her, the thinking about gender is magical and preposterous, whereby "many people no longer even know what little children know—namely, who they are." It is extraordinary that young people, sometimes many years before they are entitled to drive a car or cast a vote, can begin to change their sex without their parents' consent; and in the state of Victoria in Australia, they are denied by law prayers and contrary counselling.

By coincidence, I recently re-read the Russian Alexander Solzhenitsyn's 1983 Templeton Address, where he warned against the atheist teachers in the Western world teaching their people to hate their own society. Eberstadt is particularly scathing about elite education in the United States, which she sees as "hiding in a post-modern cuckoo's nest for decades". Too many who do not believe in truth "now run institutions charged with discerning it", she claims. She particularly objects to the election of an atheist chief chaplain at Harvard, but "if there is no truth, there are no contradictions." She finds her final example of contemporary chaos in the Catholic Church in the Western world, among those who want to transform Catholic teaching and are often hostile towards those who hold and teach the tradition. This is not a completely new situation, but a rerun and development on a wider range of issues than the confusion after the Second Vatican Council, when tens (hundreds?) of thousands of priests left the priesthood. In the term "pro-abortion Catholic", she sees as much sense as in the terms "atheist chaplain" and "former man". Here, for her, we have a "signature irrationalism", a demand that we cancel Aristotle and believe "A and not-A at once".

For a cautious prelate like myself, committed to hoping the glass is half full rather than almost empty, these claims are unpalatable. But while I can point to many places where such extreme alternatives do not flourish, I cannot deny the logic of the claims where such forces are in play. They are illogical; they are examples of a radical chaos.

Eberstadt did not mention in her address to the social scientists another spectacular contribution to the chaos, although Ross Douthat in his 2020 book, *The Decadent Society: How We Became Victims of Our Own Success*, devoted space to the topic. Douthat pointed out that as fertility collapsed because of the 1960s invention of the pill and the consequent renunciation of procreative sex, men and women had more difficulty in "permanently pairing off" (divorces increased) and cultural alternatives to old-fashioned copulation increased. He quoted a recent study from Japan, probably a pathfinder for the West and not a weird exception, which showed that 45 percent of women and a quarter of men ages sixteen to twenty-four were "not interested in or desired sexual contact".

More explicit pornography increased in the 1960s and 1970s. In the 80s some feminists and a number of Christians, like myself, believed that a strong link would be revealed between watching pornography and violent, sadistic crimes. This has not happened. Constant porn has made arousal more challenging and normal sex less immediately attractive. In the U.S.A., surveys show drops in teen sex, teen pregnancy, teen smoking, teen binge drinking, and teen drunk driving. The fantasy world has become a substitute for flesh and blood behaviour. An end result like Japan's represents a special problem and not just for Christians.

Pornography addicts today are like Midas, who was condemned to having everything he touched turned to gold so that he could neither eat nor drink nor copulate. Addiction to porn is essentially narcissistic, creating prisoners paralysed by habit. Already it is wrecking marriages. I repeat that it is a spectacular contribution to the chaos.

What Is to Be Done?

Bob Santamaria was an Australian Catholic writer, political activist, and strategist deeply involved in the fight against Communism and in defending the Judeo-Christian foundations of our society. He is the greatest layman the Catholic Church has produced in Australia, and I was privileged to preside at his state funeral in Melbourne in 1998. He would regularly state, "The important question is What is to be done?", generally leaving unsaid the fact that Lenin is believed to have been the first to publish this line in his pamphlet from Switzerland.

I wish to make two suggestions, and the first is a direct appeal to you to understand and support the importance of preserving Catholic identity, the unity constructed around the apostolic tradition.

We believe that Jesus is the Son of God, that the basic teachings of the Catholic Church are revealed, not the product simply of human intelligence and experience. We certainly believe in fundamentals, but we are not fundamentalists who reject the use of reason and lament the achievement of theology. Neither do we deny that there is a development of doctrine in many areas within the tradition, starting with issues such as the recognition of the New Testament canon (or list of books), then the development of Trinitarian doctrines, and moving to doctrines as disparate as the legitimisation of interest, the rejection of slavery, the Immaculate Conception, and the Assumption. The last word does not come from the world, from contemporary understandings, but from within the tradition as authorised by the successor of Peter and the successors of the apostles.

The second reason for fidelity is found in recent history where the adoption of a radical liberalism in faith, morals, and liturgy provoked the collapse of church life in a generation or two. We have seen examples of this in Catholic Holland, Belgium, and Quebec since the 1960s and in liberal Protestant groups such as the American Episcopalians. Regular prayer, reverent celebrations of traditional liturgy, fidelity to the Ten Commandments do not guarantee religious survival and prosperity, but they are essential prerequisites. A good deal of Catholic decline is self-inflicted.

A few feel that the paedophilia scandal has affected so many countries that a new sort of Catholic Church is required. The figures are scandalous, represent a cancer, and the recent statistics from France were another bitter blow. But sexual abuse comes from sinning, not following the principles of Christian morality, and the historic failures of the Church leadership to deal properly with the problem, especially before the 1990s are also examples of moral failure, even though bishops were usually implementing the practices popular then in the wider society. In Australia, and elsewhere, e.g., the United

States, the Church broke the back of this problem in the 1990s, as the recent royal commission acknowledged the collapse in the crime rate, in sexual abuse violations from that decade in Australia.

The scandal is one expression of weakened faith and reflects the moral confusion that increased with the 1960s as the recent revelations of juvenile abuse among the *soixante-huitards*, the revolutionary left in France, have shown. Some changes are necessary and useful, such as the screening of future seminarians and religious, and more emphasis on psycho-sexual development in seminary formation itself, but the whole grim saga, the massive suffering involved demonstrate that we must practise what we preach, not change our moral teaching. There should not be Australian or German versions of the Ten Commandments.

This crisis has brought consequences for Church membership, but as an example of my claims about the destructive consequences of liberalism, in the years between 2011 and 2016 in Australia, the Anglicans lost 579,000 from a community of 3,680,000; the Uniting Church had 195,000 fewer from a base of 1,065,000, and the Catholic Church diminished by 147,000 from a community of 5,439,000 despite bearing the brunt of most of the hostile publicity. These losses bring no consolation, but the patterns are different.

One might paraphrase my first suggestion by stating that traditional Catholicism, and the Jewish traditions from which it drank, are heading in the right direction. The Catholic story demonstrates that the message is marketable and improves humanity. The mix works.

My second suggestion is that you, my listeners, strive to understand that secular modernity causes multiple forms of suffering that we can often ameliorate when we understand their true origins.

Eberstadt is quite explicit that this truth has gone unsaid for too long. Secularism is an inferior culture, small of heart, which defines suffering down, so that victims are not acknowledged as victims but as justified collateral damage. The secularists are wreckers, and they are busy at work. Chaos is the end result. Chaos is the main characteristic of the way of life the secularist wreckers are imposing upon us. Not health or peace of mind or communities united beneath and beyond their differences, but a tribal, fretful void, anxious, divided, and regularly frightened: now by COVID and the spectre of global warming. The forms of misery today are acute and various.

Is the widespread sexual dysfunction caused by pornography in Japan to become the norm in our society; yet another cross for our beleaguered youth? Language is used cleverly to define suffering down. Homosexuals are gays; when all the evidence shows they are often as miserable and sad as the rest of us. Prostitutes are sex workers sometimes ranked ahead of the churches in the COVID crisis as providing essential social services. Data about the transgender population is often whitewashed such as data about suicide rates, eating disorders, substance abuse, and other forms of mental distress. Similar processes are at work among young people generally, especially those from broken and blended families.

There is a strong correlation between mental distress and the decline of organized religion when social bonds are weakened. Damaged people do not thrive, and Christianity in particular, deepens the sense of community and social belonging. Anxiety and depression are connected with disconnection and loneliness. Drugs, such as marijuana, are long-term depressants; drugs damage perceptions and self-understanding, but it is a reassurance even for fevered minds if they are aware that God is in charge, that God is good, and beyond this vale of tears, all will be well. The damage from drugs now rivals the damage from alcohol.

Children in particular suffer in fractured families, but not just the children; so do the spouses or partners suffer too from nervous distress, hurt, and the subsequent substance abuse from drugs and opioids. In America at least, and I suspect in Australia and the U.K., the no-religioners, the nones, are the most mentally afflicted. And we have the scourge of youth suicide, so terrible and so sad. So often problems in the home don't stay in the home. We must encourage our teachers to continue their valiant work in our schools to bring help and healing to their student victims of the chaos. There are no substitutes for kindness and long-term support.

I believe that today's generation of young Christian intellectuals is presented with an unusual opportunity to speak the truth to the void, to give voice to the voiceless as Eberstadt challenged the social scientists to so act. Change for the better will only come when many voices present the facts, figures, arguments, and evidence about the human causes and costs of the secularization push. The chaos should be named and shamed.

Let me conclude.

Christians are quite rightly warned against rejoicing in the misfortunes of others. The Germans even have a word for this weakness:

Schadenfreude. However, moral culpability is removed when we take consolation from periods of Church history when the situation was quite clearly worse than ours in the Western world today. Neither should we forget the swiftly growing Catholic communities in Africa and the surprising Christian expansion in China. We still have formidable strengths. We take consolation in these lessons from history, not merely because their times were then bad, but because the Church threw up reform movements and leaders to mitigate the worst and promote new growth.

Even with the paedophilia crisis and a widespread decline in numbers, we have nothing like the corruption and disorder in Rome in the ninth and tenth centuries as the Ottonian and Crescentii families struggled for power. The lurid story of Marozia (890–937), the daughter of the Roman consul Theophylact and Theodora, a "shameless whore" according to a contemporary source, exemplifies the worst of it. She became at fifteen the mistress of Pope Sergius III, and Pope John XI was either their son or the son of Marozia and her husband, Alberic I. On Alberic's death, she married Guy of Tuscany. Together they attacked Rome, imprisoned Pope John X in Castel Sant'Angelo, where he died, perhaps smothered by a pillow. She installed her twenty-one-year-old son as Pope John XI. On the death of Guy of Tuscany, she married his half-brother, Hugh of Arles, but then her luck ran out. Alberic II, the son of her first husband, imprisoned his mother for five years before her death in 937.

Her progeny from the marriage with Guy of Tuscany flourished as the Tusculani family and in the next few generations produced three popes and an anti-pope. Alberic II was also father of John XII, who became pope in 955. The later reform movement was vigorously encouraged by Pope Gregory VII (1073–1085) and its best-known leader was Saint Peter Damian (1007–1072). While he rebuked the archbishop of Milan for going hunting on Easter Sunday morning, he certainly struggled against worse abuses. His *Book of Gomorrah* (1049), a colourful denunciation of a wide range of clerical infidelity, which raged "like a cruel beast within the sheepfold of Christ" is a marvellous read; but not for the faint-hearted. He certainly believed in hell.

The fourteenth century saw the coming of the Black Death, killing 50 percent of the people, and the translation of the papacy from Rome to Avignon for seventy years from 1305. Catherine of Siena encouraged a return to Rome, but fifteen cardinals declared the election of Pope Urban VI, a rude and tactless man, to be invalid, launching the Great Western Schism, which lasted forty years, with three rival popes at one stage, and concluded with the election of Pope Martin V in 1417.

This list can be easily extended. The German synodal way is unlikely to result in a new split, a new reformation; as in the early sixteenth century when Luther was able to provoke indignation about the level of corruption, especially in continental Europe, but less so in England, where the split with Henry VIII was originally more dynastic than theological. More and Fisher died for the papacy when there was not one truly worthy pope during their lifetimes. We had some close calls. If Hitler had remained in power, he had decided to set up a pope in every country he had conquered. The point of this tale of woe is to demonstrate the resilience of the Church, provided we remain faithful, still attached to the vine in these new and treacherous times.

Our faith gives us hope, and history justifies our confidence. Napoleon famously claimed to an Italian cleric when Pope Pius VI died in French captivity that the Church was finished. "Sire," replied the Italian, "we clergy have been unable to destroy the Church in 1800 years. The task will also prove to be beyond your powers."

Let me leave the last word to an Englishman, probably the best apologist in the twentieth century, although I find some of his writing irritating, much too clever and paradoxical; but at his best, he is magnificent. I speak, of course, of G. K. Chesterton, who declared he was a pagan at the age of twelve, an agnostic at sixteen, became an Anglican at marriage, and was received into the Church in 1922 at the age of forty-eight. In his best-known book, *Orthodoxy*, he writes of the "thrilling romance of orthodoxy". For him, it is easy to be a heretic, easy to let the age have its head. To "have fallen into any of those open traps of error and exaggeration" would indeed have been simple. "But to have avoided them all has been one whirling adventure; and in my vision the heavenly chariot flies thundering through the ages, the dull heresies sprawling and prostrate, the wild truth reeling but erect."

After eighty years of Catholic living, this is my vision also.

APPENDIX 3

Margaret Pell, R.I.P.

George Pell was back in Rome, twenty months after his release from jail, when he learned of the death of his sister and best friend, Margaret Pell, on December 16, 2021, the fifty-fifth anniversary of his ordination. Returning home to his family, he preached this homily at Margaret's funeral at Saint Kilian's Church, Bendigo, on December 31, 2021. In his voice and style, with a touch of poetry, it shone with love and faith and captured their relationship, which was warmer than it was demonstrative. They enjoyed teasing (on occasions he addressed her as "aunty" and once or twice as "Mrs Bucket", when her hands were full with domestic arrangements, mainly entertaining his friends; on holidays, she set him to work cleaning windows and grocery shopping.) They were each other's strength and stay.

Isaiah 25:6–9, 1 Corinthians 15:35–44, John 11:17–27

We come today to commend the soul of Margaret Anne Pell to our loving God, asking him to receive her into paradise and loose her from her sins.

Death is a great mystery; inescapable, final. In the Christian scheme of things, death is linked with sin and evil, one of the consequences of our fallen nature—a dead end, always confronted with some measure of dread or uncertainty, sometimes profound uncertainty. At other times with the hope that all will be well because the good God is in charge. Some others die without hope or "raging against the dying of the light" or bleakly convinced that this is the last act in a meaningless farce.

Christians, however, are called to believe that death is not the greatest mystery. The gifts of daily life and heaven are much greater, although we regularly take our day-to-day blessings for granted.

513

What have we done to deserve life, happiness, health, family, education, friends? Where do they come from? Why can we enjoy them?

Suffering is a problem for those of us who believe in an all-powerful, good God, but the truth and beauty of life are beyond the explanation of atheists who reduce life to blind chance. As the French writer André Malraux claimed quite correctly over fifty years ago: no atheist can explain the smile of a child.

The Jewish-Christian tradition has used different images to begin to explain the reality of life after death. It speaks of light, peace, knowing the truth, seeing the face of God. It speaks of the descent of the heavenly Jerusalem, resplendent with jewels and illuminated by the light from the sacrificial Lamb of God. It also uses today's image from the Old Testament prophet Isaiah of the heavenly feast, a banquet of rich food on the mountain where tears have been wiped away, eliminated, and the shroud, or mourning veil, has been removed because happiness has triumphed. A banquet for all peoples is one of the best images, or hints, of what being with God in heaven might be like.

Certainly, it is an appropriate image to begin our farewell, our celebration of Margaret's entry into eternal life. I heard the news of her death when I arrived for our weekly priests' dinner at Domus Australia in Rome. We went ahead and toasted her after the meal with a bottle of French champagne, Veuve Clicquot. Margaret was not a wine buff, but she unerringly preferred the more expensive wines and a cold beer.

Margaret was the daughter of George Arthur Pell, born in Perth, who came to Ballarat just before the Second World War to manage the Gordon Gold Mine, and of Margaret Lilian Burke. The Burkes, Irish-Australian Catholics, had been in Ballarat since the second half of the nineteenth century. Margaret's mother, Lil, was one of seven sisters in a family of twelve; all of them capable and strong women, well used to command, decades before any feminist movement.

Margaret was born on April 28, 1944. She was part of a fortunate generation, after the Depression and the War, and didn't like my saying that "there is no point in being poor and looking poor." She rebuked me by explaining that we were never poor.

She grew up in Ballarat, an elegant city by any standard, where the early city fathers used the gold money well to construct fine buildings, the beautiful Botanical Gardens, broad thoroughfares like Stuart Street, good colleges, and the Ballarat School of Mines, the third tertiary institution in Australia after the Universities of Sydney and Melbourne.

She was educated at Sacred Heart College, Ballarat East, conducted by the Mercy Sisters, learning the violin under Sister Mary Catherine of Siena, formerly Gertrude Healy, a renowned violinist, who had studied and played in Europe.

Sixty-five years ago, this small country girls' secondary school had a full student orchestra with student soloists playing the violin concertos of Mendelssohn and Mozart. I think Marg played the Mendelssohn.

She matriculated, following her cousin Mary Burke, to the Conservatorium at the Melbourne University, where she graduated with honours in 1965, then left for Italy, studying in Rome under Angelo Stefanato, leader of the RAI Orchestra, and then Remy Principe, the most renowned violin teacher in Italy.

Earlier, while at the university, she helped out regularly at our hotel, as we all did, working in the bar, an experience which stood her in good stead. She was able to mix with prime ministers and paupers.

She was in Italy for nearly four years, worked hard, and, in 1969, won a place in the first section of the Melbourne Symphony Orchestra, where she worked happily for thirty years. She was troubled by RSI and arthritis and finished up with the orchestra, moving on to the music department at Genazzano College, Kew. She continued to teach privately and was, for many years, a respected examiner with the Australian Music Examination Board.

Margaret was a first-rate musician, who toured with the orchestra on their first overseas tour to the United States and then to Japan. There was much excitement among our younger friends when the orchestra accompanied Elton John's tour of Australia.

However, Marg was more than her music: an educated woman who could take her place anywhere, as much at home in Rome as in Melbourne.

A Catholic by birth, she was also and always a believer. She prayed every day during her three years at Mirridong, where she lived peacefully, stoically coping with her increasing weakness, comforted by her belief in life after death. She received Holy Communion on the day before she died, and the special ministers told us she was at peace. Her faith was typical of the Irish Australians of her generation: loyal, somewhat tribal, real, and undemonstrative. She was never tempted to become a charismatic but admired the Neo-Catechumenal Way. She remarked to friends that she thought my *Prison Journal* was a bit religious!

She was very loyal to family, magnificently helping both our mother and then our father in their last illnesses. So, it was most appropriate that she, in her turn, was so well looked after in her last years by her brother David, his wife, Judy, and family.

Margaret was not only my sister but my best friend, and I owe her an immense debt. One of my deepest regrets is the sorrow and anguish my misadventures caused to my family and friends. Margaret suffered a lot but was always my articulate defender. When she was being harassed in Rome by reporters who asked what I was doing, she replied tersely, "He is praying. And leave me alone."

It can be harder to forgive the hurt done to our loved ones than it is to forgive personal blows. But as Christians, we are called to forgive. Forgive we must, and forgive we do.

Margaret was a good sport, entertaining company, capable of plain speech and of sound but occasionally direct judgements. She was a loyal but discriminating friend of the clergy. We holidayed together for nearly fifty years and had many marvellous times especially over thirty years of Christmas holidays at Torquay, with Archbishop Denis, Sarah and Nick, the Corkills, the Cornwalls, Bloods, Powells, O'Learys, Caseys, Tellefsons, O'Connors, Jack and Dot Crameri, and, of course, Monsignor Portelli and his feasts. For most of that time, where Margaret presided over the household as hostess, we lived in a smallish, squat, flat-roofed building known affectionately as "Hoboth"—hot box on the hill. But we had good times, even though some of the visitors were very aggressive participants in the regular games of Trivial Pursuit.

In her later years, Margaret had also become an active member of the Order of Saint Lazarus and was proud of her promotion to the rank of dame. And now, all this is ended: the good times and the difficult times. Margaret died peacefully and somewhat unexpectedly in the early morning of December 16, which was the fifty-fifth anniversary of my ordination to the priesthood in Rome, which she had attended. It was a providential coincidence, which she would have appreciated.

Many of the ancient Greeks and Romans believed in the immortality of the soul, believed that our life principle continues to exist after it leaves the body. Christians accept the immortality of the soul and also believe in the resurrection of the body on the Last Day, when our all-merciful God will send His Son as Judge to separate the sheep from the goats; those who love truth and regularly helped others, from the self-absorbed, who turn their backs on God and others. The Son of Man then will not be inclusive.

Today's second reading from Paul's First Letter to the Corinthians warns us against being too inquisitive and even denounces as stupid questions about how the resurrection occurs and what the end result will be like.

But Paul is clear that there will be variety among those saved, as humans, animals, and fish are different, as the sun is different from the moon. More importantly, there will be an enormous improvement in the quality of life between now and the hereafter, from the contemptible to the glorious; from the weak to the powerful; from the human soul to the grace-filled spirit. In other words, we cannot begin to imagine the beauty of heaven and the joy of being in God's presence.

Jesus told us all this, and, with Martha, we too believe "He is the Christ, the Son of God, the One who was to come into this world."

Let us conclude by making our own a few lines to our good God from the English poet John Donne:

> All changing unchanged Ancient of Days,
> But do not with a vile crown of frail bays
> Reward [our] Muse's white sincerity;
> But what Thy thorny crown gain'd, that give [us],
> A crown of glory, which doth flower always.
> The ends crown our works, but Thou crown'st our ends,
> For at our ends begins our endless rest.

APPENDIX 4

Summary of the High Court Judgement

The following is the Australian High Court's summary of its April 7, 2020, seven-to-zero judgement that overturned Cardinal George Pell's criminal convictions.

Today, the High Court granted special leave to appeal against a decision of the Court of Appeal of the Supreme Court of Victoria and unanimously allowed the appeal. The High Court found that the jury, acting rationally on the whole of the evidence, ought to have entertained a doubt as to the applicant's guilt with respect to each of the offences for which he was convicted, and ordered that the convictions be quashed and that verdicts of acquittal be entered in their place.

On 11 December 2018, following a trial by jury in the County Court of Victoria, the applicant, who was Archbishop of Melbourne at the time of the alleged offending, was convicted of one charge of sexual penetration of a child under 16 years and four charges of committing an act of indecency with or in the presence of a child under the age of 16 years. This was the second trial of these charges, the jury at the first trial having been unable to agree on its verdicts. The prosecution case, as it was left to the jury, alleged that the offending occurred on two separate occasions, the first on 15 or 22 December 1996 and the second on 23 February 1997. The incidents were alleged to have occurred in and near the priests' sacristy at St Patrick's Cathedral in East Melbourne, following the celebration of Sunday solemn Mass. The victims of the alleged offending were two Cathedral choirboys aged 13 years at the time of the events.

High Court of Australia, "Pell v the Queen [2020] HCA 12" (summary), April 7, 2020, https://www.hcourt.gov.au/assets/publications/judgment-summaries/2020/hca-12-2020-04-07.pdf. Used with permission.

The applicant sought leave to appeal against his convictions before the Court of Appeal. On 21 August 2019 the Court of Appeal granted leave on a single ground, which contended that the verdicts were unreasonable or could not be supported by the evidence, and dismissed the appeal. The Court of Appeal viewed video-recordings of a number of witnesses' testimony, including that of the complainant. The majority, Ferguson CJ and Maxwell P, assessed the complainant to be a compelling witness. Their Honours went on to consider the evidence of a number of "opportunity witnesses", who had described the movements of the applicant and others following the conclusion of Sunday solemn Mass in a way that was inconsistent with the complainant's account. Their Honours found that no witness could say with certainty that these routines and practices were never departed from and concluded that the jury had not been compelled to entertain a reasonable doubt as to the applicant's guilt. Weinberg JA dissented, concluding that, by reason of the unchallenged evidence of the opportunity witnesses, the jury, acting rationally on the whole of the evidence, ought to have had a reasonable doubt.

On 17 September 2019, the applicant applied to the High Court for special leave to appeal from the Court of Appeal's decision on two grounds. On 13 November 2019, Gordon and Edelman JJ referred the application for special leave to a Full Court of the High Court for argument as on an appeal. The application was heard by the High Court on 11 and 12 March 2020.

The High Court considered that, while the Court of Appeal majority assessed the evidence of the opportunity witnesses as leaving open the possibility that the complainant's account was correct, their Honours' analysis failed to engage with the question of whether there remained a reasonable possibility that the offending had not taken place, such that there ought to have been a reasonable doubt as to the applicant's guilt. The unchallenged evidence of the opportunity witnesses was inconsistent with the complainant's account, and described: (i) the applicant's practice of greeting congregants on or near the Cathedral steps after Sunday solemn Mass; (ii) the established and historical Catholic church practice that required that the applicant, as an archbishop, always be accompanied when robed in the Cathedral; and (iii) the continuous traffic in and out of the priests' sacristy for ten to 15 minutes after the conclusion of the procession that ended Sunday solemn Mass.

The Court held that, on the assumption that the jury had assessed the complainant's evidence as thoroughly credible and reliable, the evidence of the opportunity witnesses nonetheless required the jury, acting rationally, to have entertained a reasonable doubt as to the applicant's guilt in relation to the offences involved in both alleged incidents. With respect to each of the applicant's convictions, there was, consistently with the words the Court used in Chidiac v The Queen (1991) 171 CLR 432 at 444 and M v The Queen (1994) 181 CLR 487 at 494, "a significant possibility that an innocent person has been convicted because the evidence did not establish guilt to the requisite standard of proof".

BIBLIOGRAPHY

Brennan, S.J., Frank. *Observations on the Pell Proceedings*. Redland Bay, Australia: Connor Court Publishing, 2021.

Henderson, Gerard. *Cardinal Pell, the Media Pile-on & Collective Guilt*. Redland Bay, Australia: Connor Court Publishing, 2023.

Pell, George Cardinal. *Be Not Afraid*. Edited by Tess Livingstone. Australia: Duffy and Snellgrove, 2004.

Pell. *Prison Journal*, volumes 1, 2, and 3. San Francisco: Ignatius Press, 2021.

Pell. *Test Everything, Hold Fast to What Is Good*. Edited by Tess Livingstone. Connor Court Publishing and Ignatius Press, 2010.

Windschuttle, Keith. *The Persecution of George Pell*. Gloucestershire, United Kingdom: Quadrant Books, 2020.

INDEX

Abbott, Tony, 23, 32, 33–35, 185, 394

Aboriginal communities, 231

abortion, 50, 52, 138, 191–194, 202, 206, 227, 235, 241, 248, 261, 293, 317–319, 329, 331, 345–347, 366, 386, 459, 466, 501, 503

Academy for Life, 50

Acton Institute, 294

Acton Lectures, 251–254

AD2000 (journal), 131, 182, 183–184, 185, 190

Adam and Eve after the Pill (Eberstadt), 502

Administration of the Patrimony of the Holy See (APSA), 57–58, 61, 65, 67, 71, 473, 474

Adoration of the Blessed Sacrament, Santo Spirito, Sassia, 461

Adoukonou, Bartolomeo, 108

Adversus Haereses (Irenaeus), 120

Advocate (newspaper), 172, 173

Agagianian, Cardinal Gregorio Pietro, 105

Agca, Mehmet Ali, 233

The Age (newspaper), 183, 224, 236, 269, 271, 272, 330

Agence France-Presse (AFP), 470–471

AIDS epidemic, 156, 168, 189, 236, 239–242, 331–332

Albanese, Anthony, 38

Alberic II, 510

Alive+ (program for young people), 371–372

Amalgamation Implementation Committee, 187

America (magazine), 391

Anderson, John, 262

Andrews, Daniel, 456, 466

"Anglo-Latin" conflicts, 64–65

Animal Liberation (Singer), 191

Anscombe, Elizabeth, 143–144

anti-American movements, 161, 184

Anzac Cove, Gallipoli, 387–388

Anzac Day, 37n9, 95, 139–140, 376, 387–388

The Apostolic Tradition (Hippolytus), 120

Aquino, Cory, 172

Are Our Secondary Schools Catholic? (Pell), 133–135, 158

Argentina, 64

Arguello, Kiko, 459

Arnold, Matthew, 432, 499

artificial birth control. *See* contraception

Asian Partnership for Human Development, 173

assisted suicide, 50, 55

asylum seekers, 349

Augustine (Brown), 440

Augustine of Hippo, Saint, 112

AUKUS Alliance, 209

Australia

anti-Catholic climate, 413

Anzac Day, 37n9, 139–140, 376, 387–388

Australian Labor Party (ALP), 182–183

Catholic Church in, 257–275

Catholic colleges, 187

child abuse cases, 308

Democratic Labor Party (DLP), 75, 118, 174, 250

Koch, Christopher, 281
Kohlberg, Lawrence, 131–132
Küng, Hans, 198
Kung Pin-mei, Ignatius, 17, 207, 208
Kwiatowski, Andrew, 22

Lahood, Emile, 359
Laudato Si' (Pope Francis), 48,
    381–382
Laumen, Louis, 229
Lawrence, Annie, 219
Lawrence, Georgia, 219
Lawrence, Steve, 219
Lawson, Nigel, 379
Lebanon, 359–360
Le Carré, John, 162, 281
Leder, Richard, 324–325, 339
Lenin, Vladimir, 171
Leo the Great, Pope, 390
Leo XIII, Pope, 199, 200
Letter to the Duke of Norfolk
    (Newman), 345
Lewis, C. S., 501
lex credendi, 180
lex orandi, 180
Life of Moses (Gregory of Nyssa), 162
Light (news journal), 137–140
Little, Frank, Archbishop
    appointment of Pell, 145–146
    as archbishop of Melbourne, 78,
        156, 159, 176, 177–178
    on clergy shortages in Australia,
        185
    on contemporary issues, 183
    criticism of, 33
    resignation of, 211–212
    sex abuse scandals, mismanagement
        of, 406
Liturgiam Authenticam, 300–301
Lomborg, Bjorn, 380
Loquitur (journal), 96–97
Lumen Gentium, 100
Luxian, Aloysius Jin, 207
Lynch, John, 78
Lyons, John, 279

MacKillop, Alexander, 232
MacKillop, Flora, 232
MacKillop, Mary Helen, 137, 219, 232
Mackinlay, Shane, 78
Macmillan, Harold, 114
MacMillan, Sir James, 38
Macquarie, Elizabeth, 287
Macquarie, Lachlan, 287
Magister, Sandro, 48
Maguire, Bob, 325–326, 328–329
Mahony, Michael, 420
Maley, Barry, 286
Mallinson, John, 415–416
Manangatang, Australia, 122
Mannix, Daniel, Archbishop
    as Archbishop, Melbourne, 24
    conscription, opposition to, 140
    death of, 487
    Pell, influence on, 73, 93, 173, 183,
        213
    portrait of, 377
    statue of, 230–231
Mao Tse Tung (Zedong), 171, 205
Marcos, Ferdinand, 171
Marogna, Cecilia, 470
Maronite diocese, 154, 359–360
Marozia of Tusculum, 510
Martin, Louis, 452
Martin, Saint Marie-Azélie Guérin
    "Zélie," 452
Martinez, Victor, 291
Martin V, Pope, 511
Marx, Cardinal Reinhard, 392, 411,
    475
Marx, Karl, 139, 171
Marxist theory, 118, 139, 200
Mary, Mother of God, role of,
    213–214
Mary Magdalene (Boonham sculpture),
    23
Mary of the Cross Centre,
    Melbourne, 232
Masi, Roberto, 100–101
Mason, Michael, 77, 78, 83, 84,
    119–120, 175, 283